GATOR
COUNTRY

GATOR
COUNTRY

DECEPTION, DANGER,
AND ALLIGATORS
IN THE EVERGLADES

REBECCA RENNER

FLATIRON
BOOKS
NEW YORK

GATOR COUNTRY. Copyright © 2023 by Rebecca Renner. All rights reserved. Printed in the United States of America. For information, address Flatiron Books, 120 Broadway, New York, NY 10271.

www.flatironbooks.com

All photographs courtesy of the author unless otherwise noted

Map courtesy of Rhys Davies

Designed by Susan Walsh

The Library of Congress Cataloging-in-Publication Data is available upon request.

ISBN 978-1-250-84257-2 (hardcover)
ISBN 978-1-250-84258-9 (ebook)

Our books may be purchased in bulk for promotional, educational, or business use. Please contact your local bookseller or the Macmillan Corporate and Premium Sales Department at 1-800-221-7945, extension 5442, or by email at MacmillanSpecialMarkets@macmillan.com.

First Edition: 2023

10 9 8 7 6 5 4 3 2 1

For my dad,
who taught me how to tell a story.
Ken Renner
(1958–2014)

CONTENTS

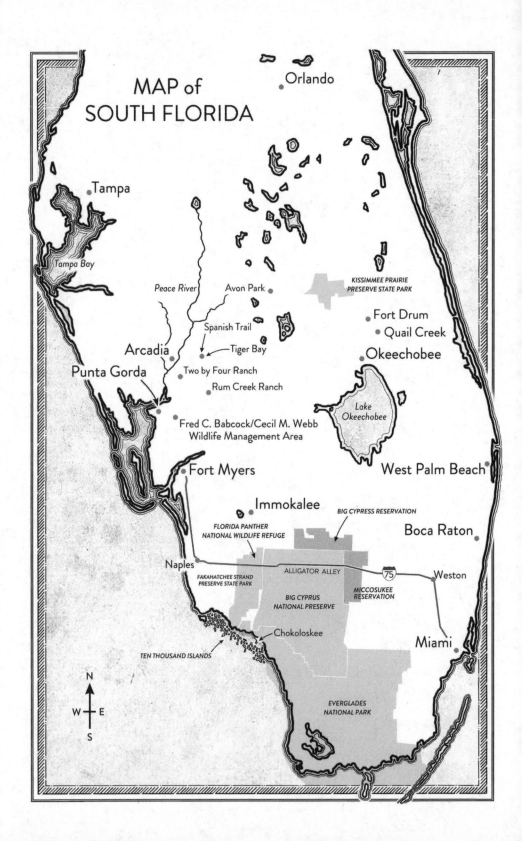

GATOR
COUNTRY

INTRODUCTION

OPERATION ALLIGATOR THIEF

The first time I saw an alligator up close in the wild, I was seven years old. Before I ventured into the swamp by our house, my dad made sure I was prepared.

"The sun rises in the . . . ?" he asked.

"East," I said.

"And it sets in the . . . ?"

"West," I answered.

His call-and-response questioning ran me through the features of the wild country right outside our back door. That area of Central Florida, from the Mosquito Lagoon south by Cape Canaveral, north to the mouth of the St. Johns River in Jacksonville, and west out to Orlando, is one of the most biodiverse places in the country. It's home to temperate forests, savannas, grasslands, marshes and swamps, pineland scrub and hardwood hammocks, estuaries, rivers, beaches, and springs. My home is a place where you're just as likely to see cacti as two-hundred-year-old water oaks dripping with moss, where you're just as likely to get stuck behind a tractor on the back roads as a fanboat towed on a trailer.

"And when it starts getting dark, you . . . ?"

"Come home," I said.

"Atta girl," he said. "Be back in time for dinner."

I set out into the swamp with an empty jam jar, looking to catch something. The twin pair of sinkhole ponds at the edge of the woods teemed with tadpoles. I plunged my jar into the muddy water up to my elbow and brought it up to the light to see two or three tadpoles thrashing among the swirls of duckweed. A pitiful catch. Maybe, I thought, I would do better in the creek.

To get there, I had to hike down through the scrub into a gully where I would find the deepest part of the swamp.

At seven, I was beginning to understand the richness of my world.

I had petted baby alligators on display, their jaws taped shut, at the entrance of the new Walmart that had been built on swampland. I had swum with manatees and dolphins, watched in the tide as skates darted away from my feet in a plume of sand. Still, I hadn't quite grasped the majesty and the danger of the natural world that surrounded me. Down at Spruce Creek, I crossed a muddy stream on a fallen palm log. A foot below me, the water was black, dyed like tea by oak leaves. I was set on reaching a sandy peninsula, half hidden by saw palms, that jutted out into the creek proper. Stepping down at the end of the log, I slipped. When I tried to catch my balance, my other foot landed in the water, and I sank up to my thigh. Was this that ubiquitous childhood danger, quicksand? Would I sink deeper if I struggled?

Then a reflection, like a ray of light on the polished gems I collected, drew my eye to the peninsula. Now in full view, I saw that the small stretch of sandy beach was already occupied by a half-ton alligator. The creature had a hide like an old tire and eyes like fossilized amber. He blinked lazily, sunning himself, and I imagined him sighing at the interruption I had brought. I scrambled up onto the log, mud clinging to my legs. Scared, but also curious and eager for a better look, I scampered up the bank, leaving the jam jar, and when I peered down, I could see a sliver of the gator's glossy snout in the sunlight. Of course, he hadn't moved. He was far less interested in me than I was in him. You don't live to be that big by making unnecessary trouble with humans, even small, loud ones.

This encounter would prove to be the beginning of a lifelong fascination with reptiles, especially alligators. At every chance I got, I would troll the creek for them, hoping to find the same magnificent gator that first lit up my imagination. But gators didn't only pop up in the backyard ponds of my childhood. They took up residence everywhere in popular culture. In cartoons such as *All Dogs Go to Heaven*, fat and zany alligators provided comic relief. Although alligators can be dangerous, there is something in the way they move about the world, and especially in the way we react to them, that is inclined toward the slapstick. Explorers once thought of them as living dragons. They represented the wild, untamable swamps of the so-called New World. Now these extraordinary beasts have been reduced to toothy jesters. Alligators' association with the more recent Florida Man meme takes their inherent humor over the top. It doesn't help that all young Floridians are taught to run in zigzags to escape gators, leading to many a humorous scene where a panicked swamp visitor runs wildly from a stationary and unamused reptile.

But for me, and for many others who grew up in the swampy Deep South, gators are just a part of life, no more extraordinary than a raccoon pilfering seed from your bird feeder. Yet they have appeared in my life when I least expect them. My friend quit the high school swim team to take an after-school job as an alligator wrestler. On visiting my family in New Orleans, Louisiana, I glimpsed alligator heads and claws used as talismans. Sometimes I'll stop at a backwoods outfitter for some boiled peanuts only to be greeted by a head-high specimen, stuffed by a taxidermist to stand like a man and hold a tray of bagged pork rinds. I can't help but think, *You must be so embarrassed, friend.* I wonder what it's like to be such a regal predator, reduced in the afterlife to a junk-food display.

To my northern acquaintances, my relationship to alligators is often unusual. I grew up eating gator meat, a fact that elicits shock and disgust. But gator is fantastic breaded in cornmeal and immersed in peanut oil to fry. (And it's much more sustainable than chicken, even with the alligator industry's minimal regulations.) My family has been eating gator since before much of the South was part of the United States. On the Florida side, I come from a long line of Crackers, the local name for Florida cattlemen, and Floridanos, descendants of the first Spanish colonists to arrive in St. Augustine in 1565. These Floridanos may have been the ones who gave the alligator its name, begat by the term for lizard, *el lagarto*. Later in another southern swamp, my French Acadian forebears took up residence on the vast bayou at the mouth of the Mississippi River. It's been a long time since my family has lived out on that swamp: My great-grandmother, a Gibson Girl, was a famed debutante in the Big Easy. Generations of my family lived in the Garden District. Every once in a while, I visit and confuse my friends by slipping into French conversation with locals in the Quarter. The swamp is in my blood, just as alligators and primordial bayous, hoary with moss and alive with shadows, are a part of the mythos that is America.

So it was no surprise that a line about "Operation Alligator Thief" casually dropped by one of my twelfth-grade students caught my attention. It was 2017, and I was still working as a high school teacher and living in an apartment-size house wedged between the swamp and a railyard. Teaching in the place where I grew up meant that I was privy to my kids' struggles even when they hadn't told me the exact details of their stories. I had lived a version of them, and they knew that. Even as an English teacher, I understood that my students might not be able to afford books, and that the time they might have spent reading was instead focused on more dire needs: helping raise siblings, working after-school jobs to pitch in for rent, sleeping on friends' couches during family quarrels, trying to kick drug habits, or starting families of their own, accidentally or otherwise. These kids—sixteen, seventeen, eighteen years old—already knew that sometimes you have to do questionable things in order to survive. It's easy to speak in terms of black and white, but most of us live in the gray. They knew, too, that like them, I had big dreams for my life even though I was still stuck in that little town. I wanted to be a writer, and I was just getting my first publications. I was surprised that they encouraged me like I encouraged them, but I shouldn't have been, because in viewing my future with hope, they maintained hope for themselves just as I had when I was their age.

The first time I heard one of my students talk about poaching, I was walking by the desk of a young man, eighteen, who came to school clad from head to toe in camouflage in the winter because those were the only warm clothes that he owned. He loved the woods, and all of his writing journal assignments were nature stories. Of course I stopped, because the conversation sounded interesting but also illegal. I was intrigued and concerned. He looked at me sideways and asked straight-out, "Would you narc if I told you somebody who isn't me is picking palmetto berries and selling them to a guy from a drug company for $60 a bag?"

"Well, Somebody-Who-Isn't-You better hope I won't," I said, "with that detailed hypothetical you just gave me." But of course, I reassured him. My dad didn't raise a snitch. "And don't write about that stuff, either," I said, pointing to his paper. "You never know who's going to find something."

He looked down at his paper, which he had already laboriously filled with chicken scratch, and then he looked up at me. "What if I call it fiction?" he said.

"Sure," I said with a laugh. "Looks like a good start to a short story."

Ours was also a storytelling culture down in Florida, and soon I would discover that this was doubly true for the ones among us who were poachers.

For those of you who imagine all poachers to be rich big-game hunters, the idea that high schoolers are out there poaching may come as a surprise. The fact is that the typical poacher has very little to do with glamour or the elephant-gun-toting villains we might imagine. By its simplest definition, poaching is the act of illegally taking flora or fauna from the wild. This is a broad umbrella, meaning the term encompasses everything from criminal syndicates hunting critically endangered rhinos to freegans foraging on public land where taking natural products is against local statutes. The definition gets even muddier from there, particularly when discussing legality, as I would see when I delved further into the tangled and confusing web of wildlife law. Sometimes the laws that govern these practices are difficult to understand, even by some of the people enforcing them. But the truth is that the vast majority of poaching is not perpetrated by high-profile hunters or even by criminal syndicates targeting charismatic megafauna. Those are just the ones you hear about. No, most illegal fishing and illegal wildlife hunting are done for subsistence. These poachers are usually living under the poverty line and hunting, fishing, or foraging to survive. You may not have realized it, but you've talked to poachers before. You may even be one yourself.

But that isn't the narrative the poachers I've known have spun around themselves. According to them, they're taking what should already be theirs. They believe nature is a resource that we all share, and the lawmakers and the officers cordoning off the wild for use by a select few are the ones in the wrong. These poachers see themselves as Robin Hoods. They are protesting the imbalances of power that have left them on the bottom. And interestingly enough, the poachers in my life would balk at the idea that they're hurting nature. They love nature. The wild belongs to all of us, they say. They take no benefit from destroying their world. Instead, they are often the ones with the closest view to witness our wildlands' destruction. All the best poaching stories share an intimate knowledge of nature.

Knowing then that he had an interested listener, my student wove a yarn—a veritable poacher tradition—about the lengths he went to while collecting palmetto berries. He went poking through the scrub with a big stick to whack the berries free inside a trash bag. Oh, the snakes he encountered, the spiders, the hogs, the bears. He even knew where the berries were going: Drug manufacturers turn them into men's health supplements. His berry buyer, according to him, was a researcher investigating the use of palmetto berry extract as a treatment for prostate cancer. To my student, this pricked at the tangled nature of morality. "I'm breaking the law," he mused to me, "but it could end up saving people's lives. How weird is that?"

"Pretty weird," I said, and again trying to redirect him to the assignment at hand: "You should write about it."

"Naw, you should," he responded.

Should I have reported my student? I don't know. There are people who would say yes. But I was far more interested in keeping his ass in class so he could learn to read and write well enough to graduate. My silence over a few palmetto berries seemed an infinitesimally small price to pay for that.

From that day on, anytime he had a good poaching tale, he practiced it on me. There weren't too many. Both of us saw our world as a bit mundane. Then one day, he said, "Miss Renner, you'll never believe what I heard.

"You know how I've told you about the berries and fish and ferns and stuff," he continued, talking animatedly with his hands. "This one is about *alligators*." He had heard from a friend of a friend who had just been arrested that the Florida Fish and Wildlife Conservation Commission, more commonly called FWC, was putting people so deep undercover that they were practically shapeshifters. You'd never know who they were until it was too late.

"There was this FWC guy down south that made this whole big fake alligator farm, but it was a trap. They had the whole place bugged like they were spies, and they arrested a whole bunch of people—like forty people—for catching alligators. My friend's friend was one of them. They hauled him off to county [jail], and he's over here like, 'For what?' He didn't think he was doing anything illegal." He was talking, of course, about Operation Alligator Thief, a multiyear undercover sting that led to the arrests of eleven alleged alligator poachers in one day alone, one of the biggest operations in the agency's history.

"Who knows how many others there are." Fake farms, he meant. Fake businesses. Fake people. Maybe even the researcher buying palmetto berries from him. There could be a face behind that face. Nothing was as it seemed.

"Don't worry, Miss Renner," he reassured me. "I'm not doing that stuff anymore. It's not worth it." He had gotten a job washing dishes at a steak house instead. "It's just—" he said, as I turned to walk away. "What if it was me? It doesn't seem right, what FWC did. Nobody's doing this because they want to. It doesn't seem fair."

As all good stories do, this yarn stuck with me. It stuck with him, too. We both did some research, and we updated each other as we learned more. I told him I would try to write about it, but when I pitched the story to magazines—me with my scant publications and nonexistent reputation as a writer at the time—I didn't get very far. After stories came out about Operation Alligator Thief a few months later, I read them, and in all but one, the writer treated Florida like an exotic backdrop. I couldn't help but feel that something major was missing, but I didn't have the time or the money to figure it out.

Yet the story came back to me again and again. I became obsessed. I needed to dig deeper. I couldn't let it go. So many people had insinuated that FWC broke the law, but details on that were minimal. What had they done? And no one, it seemed, knew anything about the men who ran the operation, not even their real names. Who were these shadowy figures, these puppet masters who had bent reality to work their scheme? I hustled and learned and grew, entering the world of journalism. In a matter of three years, I went from churning out clickbait for content mills to writing for *National Geographic* and *The New York Times*. I wrote about invasive species, pollution, imagination, neuroscience, and dreams. I had all but given up on Operation Alligator Thief, but every so often, it would return to me. I would daydream about it, but then I would refuse its call. Even when I pursued the story, obstacles leapt into my way. Chief among them was having to pay my bills. I was scraping by on tenacity.

When I requested information on Operation Alligator Thief, the state had only a few files to share. Thinking they were holding out on me, I got on the phone with the public information officer and tried to charm more out of her. I wanted recordings, pictures, logs. I knew they must exist. They had to. I wanted to see what happened. I wanted to be there. Had FWC really set up a fake alligator farm? Was it just a trap, an empty set, or was it real? Who was this officer, the main man in the sting, whose fake name had been Curtis Blackledge?

"I'd give it to you if I had it," the PIO said. "The undercover officer with the sting is the only one who has what you're asking for."

I had already looked for the officer. Using the scant information I'd gleaned from asking around—Blackledge, appropriately, had black hair; he had been a canine officer; he was perhaps Asian or a Pacific Islander—I combed through old social media posts by FWC until I found pictures of an officer who matched that description. There was only one. His name was Jeff Babauta. I dug up phone numbers that matched the name. I called each one, becoming more and more sure it was him as every line I reached came up disconnected. But a feeling, no matter how strong, is nothing without solid evidence. I couldn't find an address or any social media profiles. No voter records. Nothing.

Whoever this guy was, he had done his job well. He'd vanished before the sting even started. And he was still gone.

I wanted to talk to him more than ever.

"Can you put me in contact with him?" I asked the PIO.

"Sorry," she said. "He's retired. Even I don't have his contact information."

"Can you tell me his name at least?" I needed her to confirm it. I had to know. If I had gotten that far, maybe I could actually find him.

"Sure," she said. "His name is Jeff Babauta." She said this with a laugh, not so much at my expense as at the futility of this exercise. "Good luck."

In January 2020, I drove down from Orlando to the easternmost edge of the Everglades and booked a room in the neon-dazzled Miccosukee Casino & Resort, a hotel in the no-man's-land between the glitz of Miami and the seemingly endless wilderness of the glades. That night, I looked out of my window on the casino's tenth floor, drinking in the surreal feeling of the trip. I had come there on *Outside* magazine's dime to write a story about python hunters.

Out on the glades with the hunters, I quickly realized they weren't who I expected, some caricature of rugged, bloodthirsty hunters. They were intelligent, compassionate conservationists. They were funny, too, with a humor that was equal parts dark and zany, just like my own. I found kindred spirits in them.

After spending the entire day with the hunters, trawling the levees for invasive snakes, we stopped where the levees forked and took a break as the last breaths of light drained from the expansive sky. Before that day, I had always thought of the Everglades as a massive wilderness, untamed and inhospitable. In my mind, the glades had been home to alligators, pythons, a bounty of mosquitoes, and not much else. Yet as fireflies drifted like motes over the sawgrass, a sense of wonder gripped my heart.

"When you really know the Everglades—and not many people do—that's when you fall in love," one of the hunters said. As we gazed out over the black water, a companionable silence fell between us, and we stood in mutual reverence at the altar of nature's savage beauty.

I've seen so many things and people here maligned and misunderstood. You could explore the Everglades for years and never see it all. To bastardize a Gertrude Stein quote, there is so much *there* there. But if you're looking for something else, you might miss it. Just as many writers miss the majesty of the Everglades while they're determined to find something else, writers miss the people of the Everglades, too. They get one concept in their minds—Florida Man, say—or they're too busy playing adventurer, and they manage to walk by the truly extraordinary without a second glance. They fail to be open to the real adventure, to the truth about the place, and to the real lives of the people who call it home; and they end up writing their stereotypical preconceptions.

This motivates me to be a better writer. Even when I'm not writing about Florida, I know I have to challenge my preconceptions, or I might just miss the truth as it goes flying so close to my face that it almost hits me. People make the story. Understanding them, not just why they do the things they do, but the complex and nuanced heart of who they are, is my writing raison d'être.

Of course, this brought me back to Operation Alligator Thief. It was a story of people like me, like these python hunters I sat with out in the glades—not outlandish characters, but folks who could have been my neighbors. So too did it seem a story in life's gray areas. Was what happened to the poachers caught in Operation Alligator Thief's trap fair? Was it legal? I wanted to understand what it was like to be a poacher in the glades. I wanted to live the lives of rangers and wildlife officers, too. I wanted to tell a story of people. No heroes, no villains, just the desperate choices that make us who we are.

When I reached the end of my clues, I knew that if I wanted to keep going there was only one thing I could do. I had to find Jeff Babauta.

As many a strange experience does, the next phase of my search began on Twitter. Completely by accident—after a misunderstanding turned argument turned thoughtful discussion on the social platform—I befriended Will, a former army intelligence agent, who volunteered to help me track Jeff down. We both hunted for Jeff's information and then compared notes. He found the same disconnected phone numbers that I had, and we used those as a touchstone to find an address. By then, the pandemic had hit, and I was locked down in Orlando. Will said he would check the address out for me. No one was home, so Will left a handwritten note. Jeff didn't respond. Not being one to give up, Will wrote another note with his name and phone number, and he stuck this one in Jeff's door handle. Then we waited.

Just when I had all but given up on this particular strategy, my phone rang. It was Will—with Jeff's phone number.

"He sounded a bit iffy about us, but he said to call him," Will said.

So I did. He answered on the second ring.

"Hi, this is Rebecca Renner," I said as brightly as possible, a smile in my voice.

"How are you?" he said, his voice gruff, wary, and—perhaps—curious.

Unbeknownst to us, Will's note had dislodged from the door handle and fluttered against Jeff's leg as he did yardwork. Reading the sender's name, Jeff had thrown down his rake and scuttled inside, locking the door behind him. He peered out of the blinds, wondering how one of the poachers' relatives had gotten his home address. Will, it turned out, shared a surname with someone nabbed in Operation Alligator Thief. However, they were not in fact related.

Jeff read the note again. It said that Will wanted to talk to him. That sounded ominous to Jeff, he would tell me later. But his curiosity won out, and he called the number nonetheless. Instead of a poacher-turned-stalker, Jeff found himself talking to an army-vet-turned-journalist. Will explained his mission and gave Jeff my phone number.

"Thank you for agreeing to talk to me," I said. His silence scrutinized me. "Um, I've been looking into your case, into Operation Alligator Thief. And I'm hoping to write a book about it."

"Is this a personal book you're writing, or is this for *National Geographic*?" he asked.

I usually wrote for *Nat Geo*, and I assumed that's why Jeff agreed to talk.

Jeff was suspicious of me at first. It wasn't in what he said but how he said it, making me feel I could only venture so far into his world as we chatted.

I knew as well as anyone how writers tend to swoop into Florida, get the titillating details of what they think is the story, and then retreat to New York as fast as they can—missing important facts in the process. But as we spoke, the drawl slowly melted back into my voice, and Jeff knew I was of this place just as much as he was. We talked about our love of nature and of Florida books. When he mentioned *A Land Remembered*, the quintessential Florida pioneer novel, I felt the possibility for a connection deep enough that he might really welcome me into his story.

Later, he invited me into his home and showed me his collections, collages of memorabilia in his sunroom from each of his big cases. He had kept his business card and newspaper clippings from Sunshine Alligator Farm. He had photos of the gators and one of him in his full undercover getup. He had also kept every document and recording, boxes of the stuff, and he said he would go through it and determine what he might let me see.

We sat on the couch for another interview, and his hundred-plus-pound yellow Lab, Ruger, wedged himself between my legs, laid his head on my knee, and insisted on being petted. I obliged enthusiastically. Jeff offered to shoo Ruger away, but I said it was fine. We carried on the interview like that, the dog slobbering on my left leg as I scribbled on the notepad perched on my right.

When Ruger suddenly growled, Jeff said, "I'm sorry. He's never like this."

"No, I'm sorry," I said. "It's because I stopped petting him." I started again, and Ruger recommenced his full-body wag. That made Jeff smile, and we talked about our dogs. I had a black Lab–hound mix named Daisy, then thirteen, the same age as Ruger. "You gotta love old dogs," I said. I had tried so hard to win Jeff over, and I had only gotten so far. When I stopped trying and started being myself, the kind of person who's never met a dog she didn't want to befriend, who thinks all creatures—whether fluffy or scaly, feathered or slimy—are cute, who tends to talk to wild birds and otters the same way she talks to her cat, that is when I felt something click into place. I had to be open first for him to be open.

When he showed me a video of dozens of baby gators in a kiddie pool, my heart melted at the sound of their squeaks. Jeff was more somber. He wished he could have done more for them. He felt like he had failed the gators, because they ended up at the tannery anyway. Part of him was confident that the sting had been the crowning achievement of his career. Another part clearly wondered if his efforts had been in vain. Even some of his fellow officers had said, "Alligators? What's the point?"

"Well, what did you say to them?" I asked. We had been poring over documents on his family computer, tucked into a nook of bookshelves.

"I said, 'What's the point?'"—his tone remembering his anger. "'Sure, they aren't endangered, but they have been before. We don't want them to go back there again. You don't wait around for an emergency before you prepare for it. You try to stop these things before they happen in the first place. *That's* the point. More than just the gators go if gators disappear. Everything falls apart.'"

It's hard to spend time in Florida's wilderness without seeing the environmental impact of humanity. Even in my hometown near Daytona Beach, it's there. Just south, the Indian River Lagoon is embroiled in a decades-long fight to clean up Florida's waterways. Once one of the most biodiverse estuaries in the Northern Hemisphere, boasting as many as forty-three hundred species of plants and animals, the lagoon is now dying. Nutrients from runoff have twisted the water composition. Algae took over, sparking a chain reaction that led to the most brutal manatee mortality event on record. More manatees died in the first three months of 2021 than in any other full year. Our love affair with lawns and golf courses is to blame. I was just as much part of the problem as any of my neighbors. It's so easy to forget that our actions, no matter how small they seem, have environmental consequences. We defy nature, bending it to our will. That impulse is so prevalent in Western civilization that most of us have stopped noticing it at all. Nowhere is that animosity so clear as in the Everglades. For centuries, settlers have ripped up, paved, and drained the glades, and now we wonder why those ecosystems seem so irreparably broken that they're poisoning us as we have done to them. The same is happening in coastal wetlands around the world. Just like in the Indian River Lagoon, many wetlands are dying, falling prey to developers, suffering from pollution, or transforming into ghost forests with the pressure of sea-level rise. With so many enemies threatening them from all fronts, wetlands' days are numbered, as are those of the wildlife that call them home, if humans continue our banal and careless destruction.

Jeff saw something similar in alligators. Their security as a species rises and falls with humanity's view of wetlands. When people pave swamps—and when floods, fires, and hurricanes devastate the Deep South—alligator populations take a downturn; and without alligators, a keystone species and apex predator, a ripple effect sends changes throughout the food web, back to the land, and back to us.

Caught between his love of animals and his care for people, Jeff grappled with difficult decisions throughout the sting. Some meant the difference between life and death. Others came from stickier ethical questions: How far do you go to catch a criminal? Is it right to commit a crime yourself if you're bringing the "bad guys" down? At times, that's what Jeff called them, defending his choices, saying that punishing the poachers to the fullest extent of the law was the only way to protect the wild. Other times, he wondered if he could have done more for the poachers themselves. Surely, there must have been a way to stop them without destroying their lives.

Since Operation Alligator Thief first made headlines, the sting had come under question. The agency's head quit, and a great upheaval followed. Some detractors said that what Jeff and FWC did was illegal, that they should have been the ones punished and not the poachers themselves. What happened that was so terrible?

Months passed, and I interviewed Jeff again and again. Jeff himself got into the habit of calling me to check in. Just when I felt too stuck to write anymore, as if by magic, my phone would ring. The screen would read, JEFF BABAUTA CALLING.

I had known him for about half a year when he trusted me enough to hand his case documents over, all of them, every game cam photo, every recording, everything I could have possibly wanted.

The deeper I went into the investigation, the further I realized there was to go. What I found is that it's easy to cast judgments from the sidelines. No one is the character we think they are. The truth confronts us only after we challenge our expectations.

One truth I came across on the way is this: To be at odds with nature is to be at odds with ourselves. We, as a species, stand at a crossroads. We can choose to live with nature or against it. Our centuries of war with the swamp have shown that when we attack nature, nature will fight back, and both humans and nature will lose. However, powers that serve to lose monetarily have presented us with a false dichotomy: that choosing to save nature is a choice for animals, against people. It's not. The equally false idea that humans are an invasive species is the other side of that coin. We're not. We're animals, too, but unlike other animals, we're greedy, and we know, deep down, that when we take too much, it's wrong. What do these two sides have in common? Storytelling. Stories bind us. Stories tell us who we are. They'll rally us. Then we'll have the power to strive and survive.

My hope is that by the end of this book—the story of Operation Alligator Thief—you will come to understand that a gator is not just a gator, and a poacher is never just a poacher.

While I was researching for this book—after interviewing Seminoles and gladesmen, rangers and poachers, digging through the national park archives, driving to every outpost in the glades big and small, and doing a lot of exploring by car and boat and on foot—I ended up below Everglades City, past the edge of nowhere in Chokoloskee, in pursuit of the legend of a man named Peg Brown. If the stories I had heard were true—and by that point, I'd heard dozens—Peg had been the most deadly and prolific alligator poacher who ever lived. The stories about him seemed impossible. He had killed thousands of gators, they said. He had bamboozled rangers, played tricks on them in the swamps, and he always got away. Peg had been a real person, but he had died in the 1980s, so I went searching for his next of kin in hopes of getting to know the man behind the legend and, through him, understanding the poachers of the Everglades. Their stories brought new depth to Jeff's, and so while I dive into the story of Operation Alligator Thief, I will also detail the days I spent pursuing the truth behind the legend of Peg Brown.

During this quest, I went on an adventure with two old gladesmen to see the former hunting grounds where they once, allegedly, poached alligators. To them, that wide and wild expanse of glades was a part of them as much as it belonged to them. As we ducked under vines in wild sanctuaries made of ruins held together by strangler figs, we talked about birds and how some were disappearing. Zipping on a motorboat among the Ten Thousand Islands, they told me about how trees could migrate, a slow escape along those distant latitudes so that the whole landscape had changed without any intervention. They told me about the hurricane that obliterated the town and caused fish to fall from the sky like manna in the desert. It struck me how down there the tallest tales were the truest ones, because no one has taken the time to sand down their edges and make them abide by the laws of what we're willing to accept as true. I saw so much of myself and my family in them, too. It was clear we shared a culture, one of storytelling and a deep connection to our own fragile estuaries. So as I witnessed the beauty of their world, I realized that I had grown numb to the magic and wonder of my own. After my adventure ended, I would need to return home and see it with new eyes.

That is what this book became—the tale of a wildlife officer who disguised himself as a poacher to protect the swamp and the American alligator, true, but also a study in awe. Writing a book is itself an adventure. No matter how much you plan, you must be open to the unexpected, the outlandish, because that is where the story lives. Along the way, it occurred to me just how many orchids I had stepped over without a second glance. So hell-bent was I on forward motion that I became numb to the quiet splendor of the wild world at my feet.

Without that revelation, I might not have seen these gladesmen or the people in Jeff's story for who and what they really were, people who are greater than the sums of their parts—because everyone is. In that, this book became more than a study of crime and character. The instability following on the heels of climate change has put us all in a crucible. Some of us are already making difficult decisions in order to survive. What we do when we're faced with these impossible choices reveals who we really are. Jeff would come to such a crossroads, a choice between saving alligators and saving poachers. The deeper I went into the story and into the Everglades, the more I realized that this is not such an easy choice at all.

When I was with the gladesmen, we went to a local museum, an old trading post where famed Wild West–style murders had taken place. It all seemed to have a sepia hue to it, but maybe that was because they were saving on lighting and had left the windows open to the breeze and the mangroves and the salty afternoon sky with its forever horizon on the gulf.

While they showed me around the museum, they stumbled upon an artifact it seemed they had forgotten: an alligator scute, one of the bony plates that grow under the skin of an alligator's back, forming an armor-like protection beneath the hide.

It was about the size of a quarter, squarish, and raised in the middle to a ridge. I had seen the things all my life, sitting on my great-grandfather's windowsill down by the canal, heaped like potpourris in a bowl in my grandmother's sunroom, and after I became a journalist, adorning the porch railings of the Old Florida types I went to interview, finding their homes full of cast-off treasures, coral and harpoons and dolphin skulls. One of the gladesmen told me that these scutes were shrinking just like their gladeland home. He put this on my list of things to discover, and placed that small bony plate in my palm. I can't explain why, but it felt imbued with magic. I would learn later that some cultures, including the one I'd left back home, use them in folk magic practices as talismans. Sure, I'm a science journalist, but there will always be a bit of gator country in me.

I carried the scute in the pocket of my jeans for the rest of my interviews and placed it on my desk back home, hoping for good luck. The more I thought about it, the more I realized why it meant so much to me. When the gladesman pressed it into my hand, that porous white bone warmed from his own, he was entrusting me with the unknown, with the fears of that land in transition, with its life, its loss, its hope, its despair. That small gift was a symbol. It said: *This is our story. We give it to you. Our story is your story, too.*

There is powerful magic in that.

1

THE CHASE

t was nighttime in the orange grove, and the sound of helicopter blades beat overhead. Otherwise, it was dark, and the dark was quiet. No frogs chirped. No crickets sang. Not even a mosquito whined through the open windows of Jeff's patrol truck. He blamed the smell for the quiet. The grove exuded the sickly-sweet scent of acetone. Pesticide. Of course it was quiet here. When the *chak-chak-chak* of the helicopter blades faded, it left only the hum of his idling engine and the sigh of his K-9 in the back seat.

Jeff's CB radio crackled. He sat up straight, and so did his dog, a Goldador named Mack, dressed in his working vest and looking very official. They were ready to track down the poachers whose flashlights the chopper spotted from the air. But it was too soon, the crackle just radio chatter. Mack rested his chin on his paws.

This wasn't Jeff's first time on a detail, where a group of Florida Fish and Wildlife officers like himself would spread out on the edge of the Everglades and wait. When the time came, an alert would snap over the airwaves, and the trucks would come to life all over the county and close in around the suspect. Sometimes it was a small-time hunter bagging deer out of season. Other times, they were something more, endangered fern thieves, turtle smugglers. Jeff never knew what they were going to flush out of the swamp until it came.

But first he had to wait.

Jeff was fifty-three years old and coming to the end of his long career as a wildlife protector, so he knew there was no such thing as a usual day on the job. A lifetime ago, his family had moved from Guam to Colorado then down to the Everglades, replacing one kind of big sky for another. There in Homestead, the southernmost town before US-1 hops the southern glades and Blackwater Sound to become the Overseas Highway, he became a short-order cook and fell in love with the waitress who would become his wife. He fell in love, too, with the glades and the swamps, with the untamable backcountry that most people who don't know any better revile, mistaking the grasses and tangles of cypress domes for wastelands when in reality they are the most abundant tracts on Earth, paradise within paradise. It called out to him. Soon he joined the Florida Game and Freshwater Fish Commission as a fisheries technician. His career evolved from there into game warden then patrol officer. For nearly thirty years, Jeff ventured out into that rough land determined to protect every scraggly inch, from the most charismatic flora and fauna—your orchids and your panthers, your sugar gliders and your black bears—to the crawling things and the slithering things, the fearsome, the slippery, the bug-eyed, the things it seemed no one loved except for him. He saw the beauty in them. He often wondered, *Why can't everyone else?*

No matter how much he loved the wild, he was glad that his time as an officer was coming to a close. His black crew cut was beginning to salt. Smile lines touched the corners of his eyes. He had kept in shape, his five-foot-eight frame maintaining a martial boxiness. He ran, lifted weights, practiced tae kwon do and karate. Yet the aches of age had come all the same. He was anxious, too, for a chance to enjoy the wilderness he had fought so long to protect. Still, he knew he might have to move. As the only Pacific Islander on the force, he was recognizable, though no one could ever exactly place him. *Hawaiian?* they would guess. *Māori?* Never Guam, but that was okay by him. The better for his anonymity. Unless they had been in the military, most people whom Jeff talked to had never met anybody from Guam before. He worried that the men he had put in jail would come back to take their revenge. Retirement, and the choice to move or stay, was three years away. There were days when it couldn't come soon enough.

Jeff sat with his thermos full of coffee, windows down, glad for the humid chill in the air and the lack of mosquitoes, even though he found the void of sound and the reason for it unsettling. While he waited, he contemplated the future, perhaps a cabin in the mountains, time to spend with his wife and son and his dogs, a stream where they might fish, the wild duck that would be their dinner, the trails they would

hike, winding up through the oaks and hemlocks to a rocky edge overlooking the misty uplifts of the Blue Ridge and the valley below where
the setting sun hit reservoirs and rivulets, turning them into molten
gold.

But what did leaving mean, really? Sometimes it felt like escape,
other times, like abandonment. The Everglades and the swamps around
them were more than a place to Jeff. They were part of him. Sometimes
it seemed he knew them better than he knew himself. He could identify
every type of grass in a glade, every species of tree, every paw print in
the mud, every plaintive hoot punctuating the usual music of the night.
He saw himself as doing good for the people, too. He was quick to let
folks off with a warning. He preferred educating them to slapping them
with fines or worse. As much as he felt a strong connection to his job at
FWC, Jeff knew not everyone at the agency felt the same way. When he
left, they might replace him with someone who held the law in higher
regard than he held humanity. That kind of thinking didn't help anybody, and it certainly didn't stop wildlife crime.

Could he leave that life? Even if he did, would it ever leave him? For
that matter, did he want it to?

Though outwardly gregarious, Jeff was a big reader and a contemplative man. Waiting for the call from dispatch, he sank into thought,
brooding about the fate of this wilderness, or what remained of it, after
he left. This grove was wild no more. The rows of orange trees, taller than
his truck and heavy with round, ripe fruit, were so long and straight—
controlled—that they shrank into the distance, met the horizon, and
kept going on into the dark. The cities surrounding Tampa Bay gave a
faint, sallow glow to the lower edge of the sky. Jeff listened, hoping to
hear a lonesome croak or yowl.

Nothing.

There had once been a time, twenty years ago when Jeff was a game
warden, when more panthers prowled up to this latitude rather than
remaining in their paltry preserve just north of the Fakahatchee Strand.
While on patrol, he could cruise for miles without seeing any hint of
human presence except the highway, his only company the ephemeral

flash of orbs on the roadside, the spooked eyes of white-tailed deer raising their timid heads before they fled past the tree line, or, if Jeff was lucky, the lumbering boulder of a black bear or a glimpse of a tawny Florida panther tail as it slunk into the scrub. Such sightings were brief and rare, even then, like the glimmer of a comet seen through a telescope, there and gone. When Jeff looked into his rearview mirror, these atavistic figures would invariably have vanished, leaving him to wonder if he had seen the creatures at all or if they had been will-o'-the-wisps, tricks that swamp gas had played on his tired eyes.

Such was the state of this disappearing wilderness, even more so now than it was then: Sightings of some animals were becoming so scant that they had risen to the level of the supernatural, the extraordinary. Jeff knew there was a time before, when the swamps and humanity had lived with each other, before *swamp* had become a cursed word, before developers and vacationers and miners and factory farmers pushed the things that had crawled and dug and swum and flown there since time immemorial to the margins so they could take larger bites of a place they said they loved and would ultimately destroy. But Jeff hadn't seen that time. No one alive had, not really. Only the oaks and cypresses had been there that long, and their numbers had shriveled, too.

Yet still, within his own memory, the night had once writhed with wildness, with songs and chirps and croaks and growls. That was why Jeff could recognize a bull gator's guttural bellow. He knew, too, that a panther's roar sounded almost human, close to a scream but more sharp-toothed and primal. These days, folks thought the woods were haunted if they heard such a fiendish noise out there in the dark. They had all become interlopers there, hiding along the coasts, disconnected from the shrinking wilderness just beyond their backyards, its dwindling night music fading to an echo of a vanishing chthonic past. Jeff admitted he had become one of them, living in a safe world of manicured yards and trappers capturing the wild things to keep them where they supposedly belonged.

The radio squawked once more, rousing Jeff from his ruminations. The chopper had spotted lights in the brush not far away, outside the little town of Wauchula. When the closest officer checked in on the man and his accomplice, they sprinted to their pickup truck, jumped in, and fled. That officer was in pursuit already, but the suspect refused to pull over. They had a car chase on their hands. Dispatch summoned all nearby units to join the pursuit. Sheriff's deputies were on their way as well. So much for that quiet night.

"Let's go to work!" Jeff exclaimed to Mack, and the dog perked up.

Jeff snapped his seat belt and flicked on his lights and sirens. They wailed into the silence of the grove, now lit a swimming blue. He peeled out and sped through the back roads, heading for where he predicted the chase would go. He swerved onto the county road, and there, ahead of him, a single set of blue lights was shrinking rapidly into the distance. Jeff floored it.

Speeding off in pursuit always got Jeff's blood up. He felt alive, excited. He was doing something to protect that wild country instead of just thinking about it. But also, he admitted, he liked to go fast, to get out on a clean stretch of road, so straight that he could see the wink of oncoming headlights from miles away, and really open up his engine. He raced between the pines and cypresses, zipping around a semi-truck like a streak of light beneath the tufts of palm heads standing on their spindly trunks below a limitless sky and its splash of stars.

The blue lights in front of him grew until he was right behind them. He and the first officer had a quick exchange over the radio. The officer was pulling information on the license plate, but Jeff already knew who it was. He recognized the truck, a green Dodge with a topper. It belonged to a man named Clyde, a habitual poacher. The last time Jeff saw Clyde was when he sent the man to prison. That was several years ago. In the intervening time, Jeff had worked in the Florida panhandle. Even while he was away, landowners in Manatee County, his old jurisdiction south of Tampa Bay, called him up to shoot the breeze and tell him about any nefarious goings-on down there in the swampland. One had said Clyde had gotten out of prison and was back at it again, not only poaching but frequenting local bars and hangouts and bragging about how many deer he'd killed. Jeff was nothing if not meticulous. He wrote himself a note—he kept notes for everything—to check in on Clyde and others if he ever worked in Manatee again.

So when Jeff transferred back a few weeks prior, he began to investigate the leads from his notes. He asked around about Clyde but didn't find anything. Now here he was, racing through the swamp with a growing herd of black-and-whites on his tail.

Clyde wouldn't let up. The chase zagged from Hardee County down into DeSoto, deep river country beneath enormous live oak trees heavy with Spanish moss, before swinging into gladeland, back roads, sawgrass, and open sky. By two thirty in the morning, they had careened across three different counties, twenty-one miles. Their attempts to cut Clyde off or reroute him had failed. They reached speeds over a hundred miles per hour, going so fast that Jeff could smell his transmission burning. Now the Dodge veered onto a levee, lit from above by the helicopter's spotlight.

He's going for the canal, Jeff thought. If they got to it, the suspects could steal a boat—or perhaps hop into one that was waiting for them—and abscond into the alligators' kingdom like many a fugitive before them, never to be found.

They had left the domain of so-called civilization behind and had entered the swamp. There, the primordial past still reigned, stubborn and unconquerable, rebuffing all the future's attempts to push its way in. The swamp has swallowed whole planned subdivisions. A Space Race–era rocket facility sits abandoned in the southern glades, its warehouses and missile silos the prey of wet air, graffiti, and nature as the land takes itself back. Shot-up planes downed in cypress domes tell the story of cocaine cowboys and a lawlessness that lives on just out of sight. Skeletons of 1940s automobiles nestle in the saw palm fronds. People have dumped just about everything in the glades: cigarette machines, backhoes, pet snakes, dead bodies. In that country, it is easy to disappear. It's almost hard not to.

Jeff couldn't let them get that far. He sped up. The other officers followed suit.

Clyde's passenger flung something out the window. Possibly a gun. Jeff only had a split second to note the location of where whatever it was flew into the scrub. The chase kept going. By then it had started to rain. They had drifted back into farm country. On a slick stretch of road, Clyde lost control of his vehicle. He hydroplaned, and no sooner had Jeff blinked than the Dodge had run off the side of the road. It hurtled past the ditch and crashed through a fence, sending posts flying into the air like Popsicle sticks. They rained down. Some stuck into the soft ground, standing straight up. The Dodge kept going through barbed wire. It finally stopped in a sod field, wheels spinning, stuck and flinging mud. The rain was really coming down by then. A witching-hour mist hovered over the grassland, and the air seemed colder than it should have been. It was a wet kind of cold that sticks in your bones and makes your jaw ache. In the swamp, the wet had a way of amplifying everything. It sharpened the cold, inflamed the heat, enveloped you, and made you aware of your skin and the heaviness of your body, that you were a corporeal thing, animal and fragile, and at risk in that wild country.

Clyde fumbled out into the slop and tried to run. He bent double, close to the ground, as if he could escape detection in the sawgrass. His passenger ran in the other direction. Like a snap, the officers ran after both. Jeff made for Clyde. He slogged over the wet earth, picking his knees up high with each step, but Clyde was almost to the tree line. Jeff drew his firearm and used the flashlight on its top to cut through the downpour. Seeing a suspect ready to wriggle out of his grasp, another officer might have shot. But Jeff had made it through his entire career without firing his weapon outside of training. He wasn't about to start now. He kept the safety on. This wasn't cops and robbers. Their pistols weren't toys or props, despite how some yahoos treated them. Jeff wasn't the kind to go out and act like a cowboy.

Instead he dug down deep in himself and found a burst of speed. He closed the gap between himself and Clyde, grabbed the man by the arm, and wrestled him to the ground, where they both got a mouthful of mud. Other officers closed in around them. As they read Clyde his rights and cuffed him, he looked over his shoulder and spotted Jeff.

"Buta, you're back!" Clyde exclaimed, using a nickname that only Jeff's intimates knew. After stalking this fellow through the woods for

fifteen-some-odd years, Jeff supposed that made them familiar enough
to be friendly even while on different sides of the law.

"Yep, I'm back," Jeff said. "Now, where's your gun?"

Jeff had first met Clyde some years ago, back when he was a new
game warden in Manatee County. Jeff worked weekends and odd
hours then, but on Sunday mornings, he took his son to catechism and
followed along with Mass. In the pews next to him sat the same landowners who would call in tips about strange lights they saw in their
woods at night. Next to these ranchers, unbeknownst to them, sat some
of the same poachers whose spotlights had glinted among their trees.

On Sunday evenings, Jeff worked through the list of tips he kept
in his black leatherette-bound notebook, some leads from conversations he'd had, others thoughts he'd jotted down. Jeff knew how to work
a source. His greatest asset, he believed, was his mouth. Other bullet
points were from the tip hotline. One tip referred to a man named
Clyde, a convicted felon well known in those parts for getting drunk at
local bars and boasting about his crimes to anyone who would listen,
a veritable poacher tradition. Jeff followed the tip to an approximate
location in the scrub. Soon he spotted lights bobbing among the trees.
He chased the poachers down, but they made it to their truck before
Jeff could nab them. A short chase ensued. While they sped through the
backwoods, Jeff watched Clyde pass his rifle through the truck's back
window and lay it in the bed.

That was what Jeff had been there to arrest him for. Not only for
poaching but for possessing a firearm while on probation for a felony.
Clyde knew it, too. After ridding himself of the offending rifle, he
banged on the roof, clearly telling the driver, his girlfriend, to pull over.

While Jeff was talking to them, the landowner rolled in and listened
for a bit and then said, "Come to think of it, I did give old Clyde permission to hunt back here."

The landowner and Clyde shared a look.

That night would have to be a catch and release.

It would take more work to bring Clyde in that first time, including
some sleuthing to track down how he had come into possession of a

rifle. After finding surveillance footage of Clyde's girlfriend buying the gun for him, Jeff informed Clyde's probation officer, who told him to put a warrant out for Clyde's arrest.

That was how their odd sort of relationship started. They were adversaries. That was true. But they weren't enemies.

By the night that long car chase had ensued, Jeff had already arrested Clyde twice and sent him to prison both times. Each time, on their way to the jail, Clyde sitting cuffed in the patrol truck, Jeff would give him what he called his come-to-Jesus talk.

"Why are you doing this to your mom and dad?" Jeff said the second time. "You need to grow the fuck up."

Clyde nodded his head and said, "Buta, you're right."

Despite this seeming sincerity, Jeff's talks never really stuck. Still, Clyde wasn't a bad fellow, Jeff thought. He clung to the idea that even the worst criminals still had a grain of good in them. Most folks who crossed his path in the woods were one-time offenders. He'd try to educate them, make them understand what they had done, that it was more than breaking the law: Out in nature, even a small crime can affect an entire ecosystem. Jeff had decided long ago that he would rather do this and never see that person again than hike up his arrest numbers. Those didn't matter. The people and the animals did.

When Jeff found a man out poaching to feed his family, he remembered what it was like to be poor. He had grown up on Guam in a large family who struggled to make ends meet. What a lot of people don't realize is that in paradise, everything is expensive. What you had then were beautiful views and hard work. Jeff had never poached himself, but he could imagine the line of thought that brought a man to that place. It was one not of evil but of cold necessity. He felt for the people brought to that kind of need. Fines or court dates would just add more weight to their load.

Instead, he'd tell them to pack up, dump their catch, and go. "Just get out of here, man," he would say. "Don't do this again."

To Jeff, helping his fellow man was the moral thing to do. So what if it let them slip through the cracks of the law. Doing the right thing was far more important, and maybe, he thought, doing that one right thing would make them do the right thing later: They would get the opportunity to poach again, but perhaps they would remember Jeff and how he'd let them go, and they would let their quarry go, too.

Then there were times when they didn't. Like with Clyde. People were still people, imperfect. You could still be friendly with a man even if he remained on the wrong side of the law.

———————

Trying to help, even rehabilitate, people like Clyde complicated Jeff's relationship with poaching even more than that of the typical wildlife officer.

While I was writing this book, an article about a very different kind of wildlife officer appeared in my Reddit feed. Titled "Kaziranga: The Park That Shoots People to Protect Rhinos," the BBC article boasted that park rangers in India shot poachers on sight in the name of conservation. I cycled through a plethora of emotions—joy at the thought of saving rhinos, horror at the denial of human rights like the right to justice in a court of law and the right to life, disgust at the commenters cheering on that violence. The next time Jeff called me out of the blue, I asked him what he'd do.

"I'd probably shoot 'em," he said. "It's easy to say whatever from the sidelines, but when you're right there, in the heat of the moment, and you're the only thing standing between that rhino and extinction, you'd do it, too."

I was shocked. But he was right. I probably would.

"But what about the poachers?" I said.

Half a lifetime of wildlife law enforcement had brought both nuance and conflict to Jeff's view of poachers. He cared about those folks who crossed his path in the woods. They had a lot in common, sometimes histories of poverty, definitely a love of the wild, and a little bit of that hardscrabble cunning that defines those who make their lives on the land.

"In this job, sometimes you have to make tough choices," Jeff said.

At one time, the popular imagination viewed poachers as lovable rogues. One such poacher has come to represent the archetypal heroic rebel, a gentleman thief. He robs from the rich to give to the poor. Sound familiar? The character of Robin Hood, the green-clad archer and trickster who uses his cunning and charisma to best his foes, was already popular in pre-Renaissance Britain before the printing press arrived to spread his tales. Robin Hood represented the class struggle of the late Middle Ages, especially conflicts over landownership and use. But he was also a classic anti-hero, and one of the world's most well-known tricksters.

The trickster has been one of the most popular archetypes to occupy narratives for as long as humans have been telling stories. From the Coyote spirit in Indigenous myths of the American West, to the spider Anansi in West African folktales, to the Norse god Loki (and the continued popularity of his Marvel character), it seems that every corner of the world has their beloved tricksters. Over the centuries, the trickster archetype has remained much the same, with the character playing both hero and villain, but always with a complicated ethos and a great deal of panache. Many modern tricksters are thieves, like Arsène Lupin, the gentleman thief and master of disguise in his eponymous novels by Maurice Leblanc; the crew in the Ocean's movies; and scores of others.

While thieves have seemingly risen in popularity along with culture's ongoing love affair with anti-heroes, poachers have not enjoyed the same forgiveness from the zeitgeist. Poachers were once folk heroes, but they have now become acceptable targets. If a beloved character happens to be a poacher, readers tend to push that fact under the rug rather than explore it.

Poaching is complicated because it's theft of a living thing, a theft that sometimes leads to its death or, using more loaded language, its murder. That is true in the case of alligator poaching, where the point is often to obtain the hide, which eventually becomes leather goods, often soaring in price along the way. That means alligator poaching, in some ways, has multiple victims. Unlicensed alligator hunting doesn't only take a resource from the public, if done on public land such as national parks like the Everglades, but also takes freedom and life away from the alligator itself. The matter becomes even more complicated from there. Unlicensed hunting on the small scale typically has little effect ecologically or monetarily against the greater good. But when unlicensed hunting tips into larger scales, it can do lasting damage to the environment, not just to the species in question but to the landscape, too, and everything and everyone that depends on it.

"You try not to get to that point, where it's life and death," Jeff had said while we were talking about the article. "It's better for everyone, humans and animals included, when things don't get that far." That's what they'd been trying to do with Operation Alligator Thief, to stop us from ever living in a world where alligators became so rare that rangers could shoot alligator poachers on sight. That almost happened once already.

In the early twentieth century, alligator populations began to take a downturn. By the 1950s, biologists estimated that fewer than one hundred thousand gators remained in the swath of land across the southeastern US that I call gator country. Alligator populations are sensitive. Since alligators depend on precise temperatures and water levels to ensure viable clutches of eggs, even small fluctuations in weather can take their toll, leaving them especially sensitive to habitat destruction, flooding from hurricanes, and sea-level rise. Such inhospitable conditions can ruin nesting seasons, killing tens of thousands of eggs and creating a gap that could become the first domino in the row toward steep population decline. Alligators aren't a traditional sentinel species, but perhaps they should be. They would be if we paid close enough attention. It takes more than legislation to save a species. So, what was truly at fault for the species' peril? And how did alligator numbers rise again?

Raising the alarm, environmentalists sought to protect the remaining fragile enclaves of gators from further decline. Those same states listed the alligator as an endangered species in 1967. With Everglades National Park already extant from 1947, the newly minted self-proclaimed environmentalists who had come to live in all that former swampland in the Sunshine State felt they had taken care of the problem of habitat destruction—not that they had anything to do with that in the first place. Whether it was obliviousness or selfishness (or a fun combination of the two), all the people who had suddenly moved down to the coastal redoubts that ate away at the edges of the glades didn't seem to see the toll taken by all their new houses, subdivisions, condominiums, and roads that stanched the Everglades' natural southward flow. Coming to live in the paradise they'd fallen in love with in *River of Grass* and *The*

Yearling may have done more to change it irreparably than any poacher ever could.

Nonetheless, armed with their prejudices, South Florida's newcomers demanded action. They hounded the park service into one escalation after another. Even as alligators were making a comeback—by 1970, their numbers were already double the low they'd hit two decades before—the park service was buying more planes and staying out all night to watch for poachers.

Were the rangers justified in their escalation? I'm not so sure. Going after the latter-day robber barons building condominiums would have done more good. They were the ones who took more than they needed in the first place, who snatched the land and made hunters into poachers. The more they built, and the more people came, the more expensive life became in the Everglades. It was no longer a remote place of quiet wonder, where the immortal flow breathed life into the water that in turn gave life to everything around, man and beast and flower. The glades and the islands and the coastal cities that bound them became a playground for the rich. Movie stars came down to the Rod & Gun Club, a hotel in Everglades City, to live like Hemingway. The newcomers held the keys to the kingdom. They were the law. They pointed metaphoric guns stronger than any real firepower. They said it was the poachers' fault, and so we blamed the poachers. The poachers, in their way, fought back. Not by taking more than they needed, never that, but by telling stories. And so the poacher as folk hero was reborn in the Everglades.

The most legendary among them, the one whom the rangers would never catch, was Peg Brown, whose real story, I would learn, was even more fantastic than his legends.

More land down there would become protected over the years, and alligator populations would skyrocket into the millions. "But the old ways die hard," as John Rothchild wrote in his story "Poacher" for *Tropic*, the now defunct magazine insert in the *Miami Herald*, "and there is probably no such thing as a truly retired poacher."

That sentiment seemed to ring true with Clyde. Jeff, on the other hand, was ready to get going. Just a few more years and he was out. The agency had other plans.

2

THE CALL

Driving up into the panhandle, the landscape on the roadside gradually shifted from prairie and palm scrub to oak hammock and upland hardwood forest. It was spring, so the air was cooler. As Jeff drove, he approached the thriving center of the North American Coastal Plain, an area that incorporates much of the southeastern United States and is one of the planet's most vital biodiversity hot spots. This majestic coastal plain is also home to the American alligator. Though not endangered, *Alligator mississippiensis* is no stranger to threat after the species' brush with extinction in the 1950s.

Recently, alligators in Louisiana had faced another challenge. Storms and floods, along with the already looming threat of sea-level rise, had nearly wiped out an entire bayou nesting season. Alligator farms rely on wild-harvested eggs to replenish their yearly stocks, as alligators almost always refuse to breed in captivity. Faced with a dearth of eggs in their home state, many Louisiana farmers turned to Florida, where the harvest was still plentiful and local farmers with egg-collecting permits were more than happy to sell their bounty for 1,000 percent of its usual price or more. Whenever the price of a wildlife commodity skyrockets like this, poaching skyrockets along with it. Poachers, if nothing else, are opportunists. They go where the money is. So poachers across the state of Florida became alligator thieves, stealing from both farms and the wild, and selling their take for as much as they could get. Unbeknownst to Jeff, FWC took notice, and they started building a sting operation to curtail the onslaught of alligator poaching before Florida lost another nesting season, too. But their sting had already run into trouble, and they needed a new agent to step in. This was a sensitive case. That agent had to be the right person, someone who knew the wilderness like the back of his hand.

With his encyclopedic knowledge of the woods, Jeff could identify every tree and shrub, the poetry of their names as thick as the overstory that shaded the road. There were loblolly pines and laurel oaks, white ash, American sweetgum, hickory, and beech. There was hophornbeam and devil's walkingstick, winged elm, magnolia, gum bully, flowering dogwood, and cherry. Perhaps somewhere among them grew the critically endangered Florida nutmeg, considered by some botanists to be the rarest conifer in North America, or more elusive still the spindly Florida yew, one of the rarest trees in the world.

Tangles of greenbriar and trumpet creeper vines, with their red-orange flowers, a favorite of fast-flitting ruby-throated hummingbirds this time of year, languidly strung themselves among the lower branches. Summersweet flowers and cinnamon ferns, carnivorous pitcher plants and fly-eating sundews, visited the limestone-cragged understory and speckled the swampland below.

Even though he was driving too fast to see all of these things, the delicate birds and their flowers danced in Jeff's imagination. He knew the trees down to the splay of veins on the undersides of their leaves, the birds by their calls and the gloss of their wings. He conjured, too, less charismatic creatures, the things, it seemed, few people loved except for him: Cave walls came alive with the fuzzy chittering of threatened gray Myotis bats; an eastern indigo snake curved like living obsidian through the brush; reticulated flatwoods salamanders wriggled their slick speckled bodies back beneath a hoisted log. Jeff had spent most of his life mentally cataloging the natural world, especially the things that many people would see but never care to know about, as though if he did not hold them in his thoughts at least once they might be forgotten completely.

Among these natural wonders hidden in plain sight seemed to him an apt place for the agency to hold undercover training for wildlife officers, and that was what brought him to the panhandle that spring morning. About ten miles from the Florida-Georgia line, Jeff found the law enforcement academy campus. It was hidden in the forest back from the main road, the same sort of building floor plan used and reused for schools and prisons alike. After signing in, Jeff reported to the barracks that would be his home for the next week. About twenty other wildlife officers, his classmates, trickled in to claim their beds. Some came from as far away as Montana and Alaska. Some still looked turned out and spit-shined, with pristine grooming and crisply ironed clothes that would peg them as cops to anyone with even an ounce of savvy. Jeff and a few others knew better. Their instructions said to show up in plain clothes and pack the kinds of everyday outfits that would allow them to blend in with civilians. The agency would furnish unmarked units. Jeff arrived dressed, in his mind, like a "dirtbag." He tied a bandanna around his head to hide his crew cut. He had cut the sleeves off a T-shirt so the armholes practically hung to his waist. The groomed fellows in the dorm eyed him with suspicion. But that just told him he'd hit the mark.

The officers didn't spend much time in the classroom. Most of their days happened in the field, running through scenarios that mimicked real-life undercover missions, something Jeff never planned to encounter. Even though he did a little bit of his own covert surveillance while running down leads for poachers—chatting folks up in bars, listening in on a conversation serendipitously heard through a display at the hardware store—Jeff saw the training as merely the opportunity to learn something new and have a little fun so close to the end of his career. He had signed up out of curiosity, chose the course from the lineup because it seemed interesting. Even though he never planned on going undercover, he liked a challenge.

The first scenario his group received mirrored a real-life tip-line report. In the parking lot of a local Walmart, a suspect had been seen exchanging money for fish from his coolers' stock.

Jeff and his team set out to investigate. They were dressed down, most of them in flip-flops, unusual footwear for Jeff. He considered that someone used to dressing like that would have a flip-flop tan. His feet, pale compared with the rest of him, would give him away. He chided himself for not thinking about that. He was always so meticulous.

His team drove in separate unmarked cars to the Walmart. They split far apart. They took notes, describing the man, the scene, what he was dealing—it looked like fish. Jeff held his phone up like he was sending a text message and snapped a photo. His team reported in to one another. Some changed positions or went inside to buy something so they could walk past. Jeff was used to this part of the job, the watching and waiting. He settled back into it so quickly that for a while, he forgot that this wasn't reality. Every time a buyer walked up to the poacher and his coolers, Jeff noted his features, his clothes, his approximate height and weight, the time of their exchange, and what it looked like was changing hands—catch for cash. All the while, the officers in charge of the training were watching them, grading. At the times Jeff remembered this was just a training exercise, the whole thing felt surreal: The officers in charge were watching them watch others. He was pretending to pretend to be someone else. The suspect left the parking lot. They tailed him. Jeff kept several car lengths' distance so as not to arouse suspicion.

Jeff followed the suspect for about half an hour, staying just out of his sight in traffic, all the while talking on the radio with his team, trying to determine the suspect's destination. Finally, the suspect stopped at a dollar store.

Jeff didn't turn in to follow him. That could have been too suspicious. Instead, he informed his partner in the car behind him, and she took over the tail. Jeff circled the block while she parked, grabbed a shopping cart, and went inside. By the time she arrived at their meeting place, it was well past dark. Jeff wasn't tired. The electric thrill of excitement was keeping him awake.

"They were buying a bunch of fishing gear," his partner said, informing him of her observations. "I think they're gonna do this thing tonight."

It all felt so real.

Except when it didn't.

When the trainees arrived at a bar the next day, their instructor gave them the scenario: Your partner has been compromised. Create a distraction that allows them to escape the scene and reach safety without being compromised yourself.

Act normal, Jeff told himself. Yet he was all too self-conscious.

The man whose turn it was got down on one knee in front of one of the female officers and proposed. Of course, everyone around them looked and cheered when she said yes. The officer who was supposed to slip away stood up from his table. He walked toward the restroom and disappeared down the hall.

At the next bar, the trainee went up to the house band's microphone and gave his eloquent proposal as the band accompanied him with a love song. Too many of the female trainees suffered these public professions of love. The next morning in the classroom, one of the officers in charge stood in front of them and said, "No more." The sudden rash of amorous proclamations was becoming suspicious.

When Jeff's turn came, he roughed himself up and stuck wads of bags in his pockets. He went into the fried chicken restaurant where his partner was in trouble and proceeded to dig through the trash looking for something to eat. He swallowed his pride and thought only about the task as his character would have, searching in desperation for something to eat while not meeting anyone's eye. He found a bone and started gnawing on it. That was when a man approached him and gently offered to buy him some bread. By then, his partner had vanished.

Jeff had no idea that more people than just the instructors were watching him.

Back down in Manatee County, Jeff settled into his normal life, to early-morning runs and dark evenings of peering into the overgrowth in search of spotlights, of weekends with his family. He tinkered on his truck, grilled, and gardened. He took pride in the look of his yard like he took pride in his grooming. There was seldom a blade of grass out of place. Early one Saturday morning, Jeff pushed his lawn mower along the edge of his driveway, stray shoots of turf snowing the concrete and sticking to his blue jeans and the dew-slick sides of his sneakers. He reveled in the herbaceous smell of the freshly mown grass. It was the smell of youth, of summer, of running through sprinklers in the heat of July. It was aimless and easy, two things his life had never been but would be soon when retirement finally arrived. There awaited ten thousand days like this one.

His cell phone rang. Reaching to answer it, Jeff saw the name on the caller ID and said aloud, "I'm in trouble."

It was Lieutenant George Wilson, someone Jeff had known *of* since the 1980s. He didn't know much about the lieutenant at all actually. He outranked Jeff. He was in a different section of FWC, but Jeff had no idea what the lieutenant did. Maybe in-house investigations or internal affairs, the branch that investigated accusations of misconduct within the agency. Jeff wondered what he could have done.

Then another thing struck Jeff as odd. *How did I get his phone number?*

He answered quickly, worried about letting the call go to voicemail.

The lieutenant wasn't much for pleasantries. After a brief exchange, he launched straight into his business. "Have you thought about doing any undercover work?"

"No," Jeff answered, aware of his lawn mower engine chopping in the background.

The hurricanes. That was how Jeff had this spook's phone number. Back in 2014, they had been assigned to the same recovery area. The lieutenant had been Jeff's supervisor for the deployment. But they hadn't traded more than a few words.

"We've got a crime we're investigating," the lieutenant went on.

When Jeff pressed for details, he wouldn't say. Jeff shook his head. *Why am I even asking? It doesn't matter what this thing is. I'm not doing it.*

"Hell, no," Jeff said, only barely letting the lieutenant finish. "Sir," he added.

Jeff was too close to being retired. In less than five years. If he got hurt—or worse—he could say goodbye to his ten thousand days of summer. No job was worth that. He knew his wife would likely agree.

Now he had to get the lieutenant off the phone before he agreed to anything he didn't want to do.

"Nice to hear from you, Lieutenant," Jeff said. "You take care of yourself."

They hung up, and Jeff hoped that was the end of it. But it wasn't. Of course it wasn't. Investigators are nothing if not persistent. Another officer, Rett Boyd, called Jeff while he was hunting in North Carolina. A third called when he got back home. Wilson called several more times in the following months.

Jeff thought back to the first time they had met. It was 1988. Jeff was working as a lab technician in Osceola County, where he helped manage Three Lakes Wildlife Management Area, a sixty-two-thousand-acre plot of land about seventy miles southeast of Disney World comprising major portions of the Kissimmee Prairie, the second-largest dry prairie in the United States.

Connected by an interlocking chain of lakes with the headwaters of the Everglades, that expanse of grassland transformed with each season of renewing fire and life-giving flood. A stunning multitude of birds abounded there. Red-cockaded woodpeckers tapped out an insistent tempo in the pine savannas' lonely heights. The orange-and-white-beaked crested caracara swooped down through an oak dome, a dense patch of tree cover over a watery gash in the limestone bedrock. Endangered grasshopper sparrows nested hopefully in the wire grass under a seemingly boundless sky.

These quiet ecosystems once covered about ninety million acres of the peninsula, but due to urbanization, farming, settlement, and the disruption of natural fire cycles, longleaf pine forests and savannas now measure less than three million acres, according to the Florida Forest Service. It's the same story for their neighboring grassland prairies. Such habitat loss has played a major role in the endangerment of some species and the extinction of others, such as the dusky seaside sparrow, a small bird with black-and-white mottled feathers that once nested in the salt marshes of nearby Merritt Island. The United States Fish and Wildlife Service declared the sparrow extinct in 1990.

Though they were already exceedingly rare in Jeff's time, he may have been lucky enough to see one. In those days, his management area was largely devoid of human activity, save for the odd hunter or birder. The nearby Kissimmee Prairie Preserve State Park would earn a designation as an International Dark Sky Park in 2016. Before that, darkness was just darkness. Due to the area's isolation, there is no light pollution to dim the brilliance of the stars.

The great splash of the Milky Way enveloped the prairie's tremendous sky the night a hunter went missing inside the wildlife management area. Jeff went to meet with the law enforcement personnel in charge of the search, and he told them about seeing spent shell casings on the ground. Wilson was the canine officer whose dog would nose around the palm hammocks in the hope of turning up a trail.

Each time Wilson called him again, they spoke longer. Jeff remembered the wild country where they first met and his motivation for becoming a wildlife officer in the first place: It was all well and good to catalog nature. But he had wanted to do more, to defend it, to be the champion of the wild things he loved so much instead of just watching as the tamed and greedy part of the world continued to swallow them. Why mourn for something when you can fight to save it instead?

"How would you like to go out with a bang?" Wilson asked.

He liked the idea: one big mission to finish his career. It would be something to look back on and know he'd really done something, that the world had been a better place for his being there. The lack of details about the mission only served to whet his curiosity and his excitement.

"All right," Jeff said. "You've got me. I'm interested to hear more." Jeff agreed to meet with the investigation's leaders.

They told him to come in plain clothes and borrow another officer's unmarked vehicle. His curiosity reaching a crescendo, Jeff drove to Tampa to meet them. He pulled into the restaurant's palm-shaded parking lot and looked around, as if someone might be watching him.

Inside, he found a table with Boyd and Wilson. They both stood to shake his hand. After they sat, Jeff leaned in and whispered, "So what's this all about?"

"The agency needs someone to go undercover to finish a job," said Boyd.

"You already told me that, sir," said Jeff. "What am I going to be doing? What's involved?"

"We can't tell you just yet," said Wilson. "We need a commitment first. The operation's already underway. We can't risk it by giving away details to anyone who isn't involved in an official capacity."

"Well, tell me this, then—" Jeff said, leaning back to scrutinize both of them. "Why me? Why send some old guy into the field when you have so many young bucks who'd jump at a chance like this?"

Wilson stayed stone-faced, but Boyd smiled. "We don't need somebody out here trying to make a name for himself," said Boyd. "We need someone seasoned, someone with experience." They also needed someone smart, someone who could learn.

"It's because of how well you did at undercover training," said Wilson, all business. "You're a natural. Plus you have the background for this."

A spark went off in Jeff's mind. *That was a clue*, he thought. He'd been at this for around thirty years by then, doing everything from counting birds and testing water to chasing down poachers. His career had started in fisheries. Could this job have something to do with aquaculture? Or some fish poachers running amok, maybe?

Jeff looked at Wilson hopefully, as if he would say more, but he didn't. Jeff wanted to say yes. He felt compelled to at this point. They had pursued him.

They told him all the right things. They said he could make a difference. They seemed to need not just someone like him but him in particular. Ridiculous as it sounded, he was the one. Nonetheless, he lived in reality. He needed to know how this would affect his life. "What's the commitment?" Jeff asked. "How long will I be at this? Can you tell me that? I need something to tell my wife."

Sandy, his wife, hadn't wanted him to go into law enforcement. She dreaded "that call," she said, the one that comes in the middle of the night to tell you your loved one will never come home again. She had been against the undercover mission, too. "You're almost done," she'd said. "Why would you take such a big risk?"

"For the challenge," Jeff had answered.

She studied him with both unhappiness and—was that understanding in her eyes? She was a blond woman with a large, opinionated personality that shouldn't have fit into her small frame. They had been married nearly thirty years at that point. No one in the world understood him better than she did.

"You're going to do it, aren't you?" she said.

"Not if it makes you this unhappy."

"I'll manage," she said, her arms crossed, her expression hard.

He shook his head.

"You should," she said. "You'll regret it if you don't."

"At least a year," Wilson said at their meeting, across from him at the table.

"Does that mean you're in?" Boyd asked.

"I suppose it does," Jeff said. "I'm in. I'll do it."

3

SOFT SHELL

The secrecy continued even as Lieutenant Wilson began to outfit him for the job. *A job* was more like it. He still knew nothing when Lieutenant Wilson arrived at his house in plain clothes, driving an unmarked vehicle, and told Jeff to get in. Jeff already knew not to ask where they were going. Lieutenant Wilson demanded absolute trust. He would see Jeff through. From this point forward, secrecy would be a usual part of his life.

They drove to a parking lot near the airport. "I know the guy who owns this place," Lieutenant Wilson said. As the lieutenant in charge of undercover operations, Lieutenant Wilson kept all the gadgets for his officers. Likely not there, Jeff realized. This was a middle ground. He probably kept them somewhere else, a warehouse, maybe a storage unit, some nondescript box secretly full of handguns, Tasers, discreet security cameras and listening devices, and keys to any vehicle they might need—ATVs, trucks, airboats.

They stopped and got out beside a white Ford F-150.

"This is your unmarked," Lieutenant Wilson said.

They started it up to make sure it worked. The needle on the gas gauge dipped down toward empty.

"Damn," Jeff said.

"Could have sworn I just put gas in this thing," Lieutenant Wilson said. "Looks like you'll need to fill the tank. That's your next stop."

Lieutenant Wilson had Jeff's gun, too, a Smith & Wesson .38 revolver. It didn't look like a cop gun. It looked like the kind of gun fellas buy as an accessory to look like a 1930s gangster. *That'll do*, Jeff thought. He didn't have an undercover character in his mind yet. He didn't want to have to improvise. But without knowing the scenario, what could he do? Trust that he'd know when it was time, that's what.

"I'll have more for you later," Lieutenant Wilson said. Jeff hoped he meant information, not gear. Jeff could only have so much faith before he started to get antsy.

A few blocks away, Jeff mused about his daring new undercover life while pumping gas.

"Hey!" someone shouted. "Hey! Hey, buddy!" When the man finally got Jeff's attention, he said, "Something's pouring out from under your car!"

Jeff stopped the pump and contorted to see underneath. Liquid was gushing all over the concrete. It was coming from his—gas tank? Jeff swore under his breath.

He called Lieutenant Wilson and a tow truck. The truck got there first. With an irritated frown, he watched it winch his brand-new unmarked onto its bed.

Off to a great start, he thought.

In his now fully functional truck, Jeff and Lieutenant Wilson drove out to Lake Placid, a small town about thirty miles northwest of Lake Okeechobee. Along the way, Lieutenant Wilson filled Jeff in on the work ahead.

The species at the center of this investigation was *Apalone ferox*, the Florida softshell turtle. Measuring between the size of a dinner plate and that of a hubcap, this dark-brown amphibious reptile resembles a large mud pie with a piglike snout. While not the most fetching creature in the swamp, the Florida softshell turtle has other strong points that make it a target.

Though not a species of concern to the International Union for Conservation of Nature (IUCN), softshell turtles play an important role in their habitats, feeding on snails and fish, which keeps the population of those organisms in check. (Larger softshells, however, have been known to snack on prey as large as ducks and herons.) A sharp dip in their numbers could distort populations in other parts of an ecosystem, and when an ecosystem's balance goes awry, its most vulnerable inhabitants, especially the protected ones, are the first to suffer. So FWC was looking out for the state's less photogenic fauna as well as its charmers.

Because of their lack of protected status, catching softshell turtles wasn't illegal, but smuggling them out of the country was. While the difference between poaching and hunting isn't as clear-cut as it seems, the definition of wildlife trafficking is much more straightforward. At the most basic level, poaching is taking organisms from the wild without appropriate licensure. This "illegal take" comes in many forms, most of which aren't nearly so obvious as the act of a big-game hunter shooting a rhinoceros. Poaching can be as small as catching a fish that isn't the right size and not throwing it back. Hunting certain animals outside their designated season is poaching. Harvesting plants from public land can be poaching. Sometimes, taking anything at all from the wild on public land without the appropriate permits is poaching, too. Laws governing humanity's rights to the natural world get more complicated from there. This poses the question: If the law is incomprehensible—not just to the average person, but even to the educated one—can carrying it out be justice?

Wildlife trafficking, however, is a more obvious crime. If you don't have a permit, you can't take that turtle anywhere.

National and international law enforcement agencies were tracking the trafficked softshell turtles across the world. On the ground in the Sunshine State, FWC had investigations underway to locate the poachers snatching turtles from the wild and selling them to the traffickers.

"There's big demand for them in the Asian markets," Lieutenant Wilson said. Softshell turtles are a favorite addition to traditional Chinese dishes like hot pot and congee. It's so popular, in fact, that in recent years wild populations of Chinese softshell turtles (*Pelodiscus sinensis*) and related species have suffered a decline. The Chinese softshell is now listed as vulnerable by the IUCN.

The agency already had a list of suspects lined up, Lieutenant Wilson explained, and he needed Jeff to go undercover and investigate one of them with him.

Is this the big mission I've been waiting for? Jeff wondered. His gut told him it wasn't. His gut was right. This short operation turned out to be field training for Jeff, and it gave Lieutenant Wilson the opportunity for one last evaluation before the agency took the final risk on Jeff and divulged its secrets.

Lieutenant Wilson's first lesson for Jeff would be on improvisation. They parked at a house near the suspect's that looked run-down and abandoned. Lieutenant Wilson brought out a measuring tape.

"People will get suspicious if they think we're here for no reason," Lieutenant Wilson said, nodding toward the house. "So today we're real estate agents checking out this house while we're really watching them over there."

"It's a real fixer-upper," Jeff said.

This was Jeff's next lesson: Use what you already have to craft a backstory. The fewer lies you have to tell, the better.

They watched the house for several days, noting comings and goings. As the day when they would finally make contact with the suspect loomed closer, they began preparing their backstories and accumulating the props that would set the stage. This would be Jeff's first time playing a character undercover. Lieutenant Wilson scrutinized him as they prepared.

"You backed into that spot," Lieutenant Wilson noted the next morning upon Jeff's arrival. They'd met in a parking lot, as poachers often did. "Why'd you do that?"

"I don't know," Jeff answered. "Force of habit, I guess."

"You see anybody else here who backed in?" Lieutenant Wilson asked. "Not many. It's a law enforcement habit, one you have to break if you don't want to get burned."

Burned, meaning discovered, his cover blown.

"Ten–four," Jeff said, catching himself before the code for *yes* slipped all the way out of his mouth.

Wilson smiled knowingly. "That, too. The cop lingo? You have to break all of those habits."

So much of who he was, Jeff began to realize, came down to muscle memory. He had to practice being a civilian, on a deadline, too. The closer they came to the day, the more pressure piled on his shoulders. But he was also excited. This was new, exhilarating. He hadn't switched up his routines in so long.

Before they set out, they rigged a hidden camera setup, hollowing out the locking mechanism on a toolbox and tucking in a camera smaller than a nickel. Jeff pressed the button to turn the camera on and tucked the box into the front end of his truck bed.

The morning they planned to make contact, Jeff faced off with his mirror again, practicing. He slouched and turned to look at his reflection. *Should I stand like this?* Jeff straightened up, shoulders back, chest out the way he normally stood. He pulsed with nerves and excitement. Even if the suspect didn't know why, the way Jeff held his body might telegraph that something was off. His posture made him look like someone with too much respect for authority. He stood like an officer of the law. *Have to unlearn that*, he thought. He raised and lowered his shoulders, watching them move in the mirror. He shook out his arms. He imagined being the kind of person whom no one had ever called to attention. He had saluted no man. Still, he had respect for himself. Jeff eased into a comfortable stance, straight but loose.

"I'm Jeff," he said, offering the mirror a handshake. They didn't have fake names yet. First names only would have to do for now. *Do normal people stand like this?* Jeff thought, turning to the side.

He started over again, introducing himself to the poacher he imagined standing beyond the mirror. "Who's buying these turtles?" he asked. He made a sweeping gesture. It looked weird, stiff, like he was trying to sell a used car or get a part in a Shakespeare play. He shook out his shoulders again. Besides, that question was too straightforward. *Got to be more subtle.* He glanced at his watch, *shit*, it was time to leave. He pulled on a camouflage shirt, a dirt-cheap one he'd picked up at Walmart. He roughed up his scruff of a goatee, situated a camo baseball cap on his scraggly hair, and slipped on a pair of rounded glasses. He frowned at himself. "Ready or not, it's time to go."

Jeff and Lieutenant Wilson had loaded up his unmarked truck with landscaping supplies. Fake real estate agents no longer, they were partners in a landscaping business. That let them go pretty much anywhere. Few people give lawn guys a second thought. Today these props included a new addition, a hundred-quart cooler with a softshell turtle inside.

Their target lived out in the backwoods, several miles from the main drag of that little town. Lieutenant Wilson had already driven by and had a plan for how to make an introduction without raising suspicion.

He shared that plan with Jeff before they set out. They needed to make a connection with the turtle seller, preferably a business one. The goal was to get him to buy turtles from them. The rest they'd play by ear.

They pulled into a small clearing of mossy oaks and drove down a sandy semblance of a driveway. The house was concrete block, painted an egg-yolk yellow and backed up by a series of sheds. Kids shouted and laughed somewhere in the back, accompanied by the sound of dogs barking.

They parked beside a pickup truck with a dog box, a mobile kennel used to transport hunting dogs, in the bed.

"Follow my lead," Lieutenant Wilson said as they got out. They slammed their doors. Dogs bayed at the sound. Jeff's adrenaline soared.

While they were walking up, a middle-aged man with brown hair and a mustache emerged from the house. He appraised them as he approached. "Can I help you guys?" he drawled.

"We own a nursery up around the Tampa area," Lieutenant Wilson said. "And we noticed your dog box here. You wouldn't happen to be catching hogs, would you?"

"That's all I do," he answered. "I love catching hogs."

"Do you have any hog meat we can buy?" Lieutenant Wilson asked. "Preferably a whole hog. We're feeding a lot of people." He went on to explain that they owned a landscaping company, and they were throwing a barbecue for their employees and their families. It would be a big crowd, so a pig roast would surely take care of them and be something to remember.

"Yeah, let me get your name and number," the hunter answered. "My name is Alonso, by the way."

Jeff felt awkward, like his nerves were getting the best of him. He wanted to be the best, to show Lieutenant Wilson he was ready for the big show, but here he was, not doing anything.

As if on cue, the turtle scrabbled loudly in their truck bed. "What was that?" Alonso asked.

"I'll show you," Lieutenant Wilson said. He lifted the lid of the cooler to reveal the softshell turtle inside.

"Where'd you get this?" Alonso asked.

"I caught this at our nursery," Jeff said.

"There's a canal out back, and we see these things all the time," Lieutenant Wilson said.

Reading the interest on Alonso's face, Jeff added, "You want this thing?"

"Hell, yeah, I want it," Alonso answered.

"What are you gonna do with it?" Jeff asked, playing dumb, a valuable tool in his investigative arsenal, as he would learn. It seemed like a realistic enough question. *What the hell do people want with these things anyway?*

"I've got some Chinese guys who are interested in buying some turtle meat." Alonso pulled out his phone and showed Jeff and Lieutenant Wilson pictures of large softshell turtles and a huge snapping turtle. Men posed around them, showing off their prehistoric size. *These are the buyers!* Jeff realized. Their recognizable blue van was parked in the background.

It can't be this easy, Jeff thought, amazed but wary. *Don't stop now,* he told himself. *Keep going.*

"Man, if you show me how to really catch these things, will you buy them from me?" Jeff asked. "I'm always trying to make extra money myself. I mean, cutting lawns gets old after a while."

"Sure!" Alonso said. "Follow me into my backyard."

While they talked, Jeff glanced around. *This guy wouldn't be keeping turtles back here, would he?* Outside the shed, there were several tubs covered in palm fronds. "What's in here?" he asked.

"Come see," said Alonso. He crossed to the closest tub, lifted up its makeshift lid, and nodded for them to come over.

Jeff and Lieutenant Wilson peered over the edge. And there it was. The guy had shown them right to it. An enormous softshell turtle, so big it took up the whole width of the tub. Its claws scrabbled against the bottom as it tried to get away from the light.

Next, Alonso showed them the large hooks he used to catch them. He went on to explain the types of fishing line they needed.

Jeff already knew how to catch turtles. *Just play the game,* he told himself. *Make him comfortable. Make him like you.*

"For bait, you can use chicken or gizzards or whatever," Alonso continued. As Alonso spoke, his voice tightened. *Why?* Jeff wondered.

Jeff considered himself a perceptive person. He could read people. It seemed to him that Alonso knew what he was doing was illegal. Jeff needed to ease that tension so they could strike up a partnership and he could figure out where all of these turtles were going. Usually, Jeff would cut tense moments by cracking jokes, but this didn't seem like the right time for a zinger.

He nodded along and acted excited, hoping his high spirits would affect Alonso. Gradually, Alonso loosened up and began to smile, too. They agreed on a price for Jeff's future turtles and shook hands. Then Jeff and Lieutenant Wilson got going. They'd hardly made it out of the driveway when a blue van turned the corner and headed toward Alonso's house. *Too easy*, Jeff thought. He whipped out his phone and snapped a picture of the license plate.

N ow how the hell am I going to get all these turtles?" Jeff said as they drove through the woods back toward Tampa.

"I know a guy," Lieutenant Wilson answered.

That guy, a fellow named Mike, was a commercial fisherman who'd found Jesus and turned his life around. Now he was eager to Bible-thump and, luckily for FWC, eager to give back and make amends for his own past transgressions. For three months, Jeff got up before dawn about once a week and drove to Auburndale—a little town between Orlando and Tampa that was made more of lakes than it was dry land. Jeff and Mike baited hooks, sometimes as many as eight hundred, strung their lines clear across lakes, and caught the turtles he would later give to Alonso.

In those quiet hours just this side of daybreak, the morning light seemed awash with memories. As they worked baiting hooks, their hands slick with juices from the gizzards, Mike looked up at the fading sunrise, a somber expression on his face. "In my day, we would be able to catch sixty or seventy turtles with one line like this," he said. "Now I'm lucky if we catch four. Nobody was thinking about the future."

Jeff hadn't expected Mike to say something like that. It floored him. Mike knew that he was a plainclothes officer, vaguely understood his purpose there. Still, he kept up a neutral friendliness toward Jeff that acted like a wall. He hadn't trusted Jeff. Their shared moment over the quiet morning water had broken that. Mike's words had given Jeff a glimpse into the fisherman's hidden depths. Mike regretted so much. Most of all, it seemed, he regretted the greed he'd been caught up in. It had been so ubiquitous, they hadn't recognized it for what it was.

Usually talkative, Jeff just nodded and listened. The truth was that somehow he'd seen this epiphany through Mike's eyes. He already knew humans exploited nature to its breaking point. Understanding that was his job. But to have this fisherman suddenly give voice to his part in the careless destruction of his own livelihood and home opened Jeff's eyes again and reminded him of his purpose, of why he was wading into the unknown, bearing all that secrecy, to go undercover in the first place: to protect the wild from threats most people would never see.

Each morning before he made a delivery, Jeff would go through his routine, practicing what he would say in the mirror. He couldn't seem like he knew too much. In this scenario, he was just some fella who cut grass for a living, but that didn't mean he didn't have an inner life. If Jeff the landscaper didn't know too much, perhaps he wanted to know more. Jeff mused that his character was a curious fellow, asking questions not to lead to any particular place, but because he had recently realized that he had lived too long without a sense of wonder, and now he wanted answers to all of life's small mysteries. He just wanted to know how things ticked. Jeff made the last delivery to Alonso alone. Before he set off, he situated the hidden camera in the back of his truck so it would pick up everything Alonso said as they unloaded. He drove around back, and Alonso sauntered out of his screen door to meet him. The dogs bayed.

The landscapers hadn't seen as many of the turtles this month. That was Jeff's excuse for his delivery being smaller.

"Can you use this?" he said, opening a burlap sack to show Alonso the turtle. It was about the size of a dinner plate, a small one at that.

"I'd have to ask him," Alonso said, meaning his buyer, the one with the blue van from the pictures Jeff had seen before. Other agents could track that van to see where it was going. Jeff needed to gather intel that would keep them on its trail.

Don't be too forward, he thought. You had to meander toward your questioning, just chewing the fat like a regular person. He mentioned the cold front they'd been having. "Maybe that's why there are so few," Jeff said. "I think it's because they like hot weather, right?" It was right. Jeff knew that. But his character shouldn't, he scolded himself, watching nervously for a reaction from Alonso. Knowing too much might arouse suspicion.

"Yeah, they're more active in the sun," said Alonso.

They kept talking casually while they unpacked the turtles, carefully removing them from their sacks. Once they had freed a turtle from its pouch, Alonso placed it in a laundry basket that hung from a nearby tree limb by a spring scale. All the while, his dogs created a ruckus, barking and shouting and whining. Alonso stuck two fingers into his mouth and let out a loud whistle. "Quit!" he yelled at the dogs, and their chaos momentarily dwindled. He called out to his kids in softer-toned Spanish, and Jeff switched the conversation to hog hunting, slowly meandering his way toward the information he wanted to know. He was a hunter himself. He knew how to walk softly in the forest. This was much the same but with words.

While they chatted, Jeff opened a cooler on his truck bed and offered Alonso a beer. He took one himself, popped the cap, and put it to his lips as if taking a swig. The beer only touched his lips and the tip of his tongue. This was another set piece, another layer of disguise to make him seem believable. Even though Alonso seemed like a friendly enough guy, Jeff needed to stay sharp just in case all these layers of cover fell away and he found himself exposed. If he got "burned," as Lieutenant Wilson said, he would blow this case and lose the chance at the bigger one. Getting burned would put his life in danger, too. Alonso *probably* wouldn't pull a gun on him. Probably, not definitely. If he did, he wouldn't be the first.

Alonso called out to his wife inside and asked for a saltshaker. She brought one out to him. "I like salt with my beer," he said.

Weird, Jeff thought. So weird that it signaled Alonso had grown comfortable enough for Jeff to push forward.

"I still have a whole 'nother line of these fellas to take in," Jeff lied, acting like he'd been catching the turtles on his own instead of enlisting help.

Alonso seemed alarmed that Jeff had left turtles out on a line. It had rained earlier that day, and Alonso said hurriedly that they could have drowned. Money down the drain. Then he slowed down. "As long as they can surface for air, they should be fine."

Jeff stopped himself from clarifying the lie. He'd just been making chitchat. No point in digging himself in further. Jeff let the conversation settle, and let his nerves settle, too, and then he asked Alonso how much he was going to pay for this batch of turtles.

"I can't give you nothing right now, 'cause I don't know what he's gonna give me," Alonso said, referring to his buyer again. "Or if he'll take 'em. Some of 'em are real small."

They were edging close to something—information Jeff could use. He couldn't push too hard on this. Alonso was perceptive. But if he knew where the turtles were going—and what the buyers were doing with them—that was the difference between a deliberate crime and an accidental one, *and* he had the information Jeff needed.

"Oh, they like the big ones?" Jeff asked. "I figured they'd clean it and eat it. You know, get the meat off."

"I'll try to get him here so he can look at 'em and tell me." Alonso was starting to sound annoyed, like he didn't give a damn what they did with it as long as they paid him.

"Well, what are they doing with it, just selling it at a market?" Jeff asked. He was pushing it, but they were right there. If only he could push a little harder without getting caught, Alonso might tell him something.

"They pick 'em up and take 'em. I don't know," Alonso said sharply. "I don't know more than I want to know. The less you know, the better."

Jeff felt like he was running up close to the edge. One more push. "What are you sayin'?" Jeff asked, a conspiratorial note to his voice. He leaned in slightly. "I better not get caught with these? This illegal or something?"

Alonso paused for a moment. Sometimes people say more with their silences than they do with their words.

"I don't know," Alonso said. He sounded grim, as if he had once been inquisitive, too, and he had asked too many of the right questions, and they had led him down a rabbit hole to a place that he couldn't unsee.

The other side of the investigation saw that place. At 3 AM, another set of officers placed a tracker in with the turtles. They followed the turtles on their long journey, one set of officers passing the surveillance detail off to the next, out into the Everglades to a farm where the smugglers collected and fattened up their catch. Another tracking device and a fresh set of officers tailed the shipment of turtles up from Florida all the way to New York State, where a crew smuggled them hidden in false bottoms of shipments leaving the port. Eventually, they sold for $65 per pound, up from the $0.75 to $1 per pound that the buyer was paying the poachers.

Other FWC officers made the arrests for that takedown. Alonso only ended up paying fines. His Chinese buyers, on the other hand, had bigger trouble to contend with. By then, Jeff had completely faded out of his uniform, and putting it back on would risk blowing his cover. Nearly three months had passed, and the agency still hadn't told Jeff what the big undercover operation would be. He had put complete faith in Lieutenant Wilson. Yet he still wondered how much the two jobs had in common.

The turtle operation gave him some clues, though. For one, it had much higher stakes than was first apparent, and Jeff guessed that what lay ahead did, too, if not more so. While softshell turtles aren't endangered, their loss would cause a domino effect through the food web, affecting organisms both lower and higher, including plants and their habitat itself. Rather than waiting for such horrific effects to take place, FWC hoped to avert them entirely by rooting out the problem of softshell turtle poaching before it took hold. To Jeff, this was the best way to do conservation: Solve problems before they get out of control. And, you know, solve problems while it's still within the budget to do so. Poaching, and the trafficking of animals, had to be the subject of this upcoming case; he was sure of it. Hopefully, Jeff was getting there before the situation had gotten out of hand.

High-profile poaching cases, of endangered species especially, have come to our attention because they are already out of control. The stakes are dire. The combatants are armed. Violence escalates. Poachers kill game wardens. Game wardens kill poachers. Like cutting the head off the Hydra of Homeric myth, another poacher comes back in his place, this time more heavily armed. The cycle goes on, escalating into the sky, and no one is winning. Taking the long view, in protecting the smallest and most unlikely creatures, FWC was preventing such an eventuality from ever happening. As Jeff has said, if you have to pull your weapon, you've already lost.

The case that awaited Jeff existed a few steps further down the line from the turtles toward that danger. The animal in question was worth more, in the monetary scheme of things, at least. He would find that the animal itself was more dangerous, too. And closer to being in danger. It had once nearly gone extinct, and in the wake of its near disappearance, changes rippled through the swamp. Saving this animal was saving the swamp itself, and with the swamp, that fertile and maligned paradise of nature's wild splendor, humanity's hopes to bring our world back from the brink of disaster. That animal, of course, was the American alligator. The risks Jeff would take to save it would defy his worldview and change his life. He would soon find that even he did not truly know the swamp.

A few days after the takedown of the turtle poachers, Jeff received a set of keys and an address. The agency instructed him to report there immediately. That was where his real undercover mission would begin.

4

THIS IS GATOR COUNTRY

Driving down toward the Everglades, I soon passed from the thick of river country into an unlimited landscape of marsh grass and sabal palms, and when the trees finally parted, glades seemed to stretch on in all directions. My GPS location dot had gotten stuck in place several miles back. Good thing it was a clear day so I could navigate by the angle of the sun. Not that I really needed to in a place where I could see everything for miles and all the roads were straight; but people get lost there nonetheless. The deeper I drove, the more my cell signal dwindled, and soon I was out of contact with the rest of the world, with no one to answer to except the wilderness, no source of help except myself.

I was driving down there to pursue the legend of Peg Brown, the infamous poacher who had become an Everglades folk hero, partially due to the sheer number of gators he'd allegedly killed, which reached into mythic proportions, and partially due to the storytelling itself, which had elevated him from mere mortal into the rarified ranks of legends. I wanted to understand the man behind that legend, who he really was and what that said about the glades. Peg himself had died before I was born, but he'd left behind numerous kin. I was about to meet up with some of them for the first time. First, I had to get there. Not such a daring feat, normally, but my car had one wheel in the junkyard and was quickly becoming what my father would have called a Willit, as in, *Will it start?*

My dad and his jokes and stories were on my mind a lot, so much so that they had become a part of me. He was the one who taught me how to tell a story. That journey started on my grandmother's dock on the St. Johns River, an anomaly itself as, unlike most rivers, it flows north like the Nile. The kids would sit on the planks at the feet of the grown-ups and listen to them tell stories about the way things used to be. They did not see the past through a rosy sheen as it seems many people do. No, these were stories of hard times, always, of felling palm trees down by the bay for swamp cabbage, of my great-grandfather poling down the creek in his skiff on the hunt for whatever might feed them, of wading out into the river to cast a net for shrimp, of baking biscuits and handing them out hot in handkerchiefs to the migrants who rode the rails and hopped off at their little town because that place was as good as any. Each story had a moral. Many of them were the same: You are never too poor to help your fellow man. Keep yourself honest, even when you think no one is watching. Grit and storytelling are the keys to survival, and when those fail, the swamp will provide.

As I got older, I started telling stories myself, and when I was fifteen, I decided I wanted to be a writer, a declaration that many families meet with scorn. I grew up in a house full of books, in a culture immersed in stories. It's no surprise how my family answered.

"You can do anything you set your mind to, kiddo," my dad said.

"If you want to be good, you have to work hard," my grandmother said, her voice the rasp of a lifelong chain-smoker. "You're not good yet."

"Mom," my dad scolded.

"She'll never amount to anything if you coddle her like that," she said.

"No, she's right," I said. "I'm already working. I'll keep working."

"Good," she said, smiling.

She would die four years later of lung cancer, and my dad would die five years after that, colon cancer, leaving me with a house full of books, a head full of stories, and a broken heart. Every story worth telling orbits around a core of grief. Because what are stories if not memories made into myths? This one, I suppose, is no different. My dad and his storytelling shaped how I understand the world. The yarns he spun showed me that every person, from the most educated to the least, holds a story close to their heart that tells them, and others, who they are. Places, especially ones as alive as the Everglades, are the same. If you listen closely, you can hear them.

Above all, that was my mission there: to go into the Everglades and listen.

If there was an untold story at the heart of the Everglades, it was the story of Peg Brown. Nobody from outside seemed to have ever heard of him. Such local fame piqued my interest. There was something mysterious about it. Who was this Peg Brown person, really? And why had his legend lived on for so long unnoticed by the outside world? I believed that if I could find the truth behind the tall tales, it would illuminate the Everglades for me and would help me understand the underworld Jeff took on as he disguised himself as a poacher. So far, I had only gotten small tastes of tales secondhand.

One that stuck with me had a pang of familiarity. It was something I could imagine my family doing. When Everglades National Park came in, the rangers hired locals to help them map and memorize the area. One of these locals was Clarence Brown, a fishing guide whom everyone except the rangers knew as Peg. He arrived on the rangers' dock with the rest of that motley guide crew, including his ever-talkative brother Loren "Totch" Brown. When the ranger made note of their names, he asked, "Y'all related to this Peg Brown I keep hearing about?" Peg had only recently returned from the war, but already his reputation preceded him.

"Peg?" Totch said. "Never heard of him. What kind of name is that?"

"Beats me," said the ranger. "You keep an eye out for him. He's been up to no good."

"Doing what?" Totch said with a straight face.

"We've had reports he's poaching alligators out in the park," the ranger answered.

"Oh no, we can't have that," Totch said. He looked at his brother, whose smile betrayed nothing. "We'll keep our eyes peeled, won't we, Clarence?"

"Of course we will, Loren. Like it's our job."

Still, they set about showing the rangers around. Each took one or two out on his flat-bottomed skiff, a small boat that they called a pitpan in those parts. They wove through cuts between the islands and shady hammocks in the sloughs, telling the names of those places and their stories, too. They made sure that the rangers knew the shallows where their boats might run aground, the places where these outsiders could get stuck or hurt, because they didn't want that. Even if the Browns saw the rangers as their adversaries, they knew full well that if these fellows got lost, they'd be the ones to run in and find them: Nobody gained if these dopes died in the glades. Still, the tales they wove on their way made all those islands and marshes seem properly dangerous. It was best to scare the rangers and keep them in their little huts, safe and out of the way.

If that failed, there was always misdirection. Before they had met on the dock, the guides had convened at a bar and laid out all the places that—as far as the park service was concerned—would not exist. The trees where Peg strung up his hammock at night vanished. The lakes where the most gators gathered were gone. For every main waterway, a separate and invisible cut zagged through the vegetation, a ready getaway for a poacher who needed to disappear.

Only a few nights after the tour of the swamp, the rangers put Peg to the test. They bore down on Peg, the might of their motor against his. When he glanced over his shoulder, he had to squint against their spotlight. He could have shot it out, of course. But what was the point in that? It would scare those goons and leave them stranded in the dark. Or maybe it would make them want to shoot back. Who knew? Not everyone had had their fill of that in the war. No, he left his rifle under the seat and turned his rudder for a bend between the islands. He gunned the motor, the nose of his boat lifting over the water, skipping like a stone the faster he flew. With one hand, he extinguished his lantern. With the other, he cut the power to his engine. Silently, he glided toward the shore and between the trees into a creek, one not on the rangers' maps. He slowed among the cypress knees. Just beyond that stand of trees, the rangers' engine grew louder as they approached. Their spotlight swiveled in Peg's direction. Peg lay down in his boat. The light passed over him. He watched it make the cypress shadows dance.

"Are you sure he came this way?" one ranger called.

"I guess not," said the other. "Maybe he took the other fork. Let's double back."

Peg waited for their engine to leave earshot, and then he waited longer, counting the stars that winked through gaps in the canopy. The rangers might have been making a play to lure him out. They weren't that smart, but he had to be sure. When the only noises came from the mouths of frogs and owls, he rose and poled his boat in silence toward the hunt.

Did it all really happen that way? I don't know. Through my interviews, I heard several variations of the story, each subtly different from the last, except the most harrowing parts. Those always remained the same. The legend of Peg Brown seemed to reside somewhere in that murky space between folktale and history. But where did one end and the other begin? Now I was going to where his stories allegedly took place so I could disentangle the facts from the fantasy, and through both sides, the storytellers and the story, the truth and the myth, come to understand the heart of the Everglades.

Alongside the highway where I drove, a creek writhed, the blue-black reflection of that limitless sky practically tying itself in knots within the canebrake. A little powerboat zipped along with it, to and fro, each angle sending a cascade from its propeller. I passed a tackle shack, a concrete-block building painted a utilitarian white. Its sign touted both lunch plates and live bait, a Florida special. It sounds like a bad idea, buying lunch at the same place where you get bait. But honestly, the best food in Florida is at the dives, your greasy griddles, *lechoneras*, truck stops, and tackle shacks. I smiled as I passed the sign. Even if I was out of cell service, I was very much still connected to the rest of the world, the real world. The deeper I went into the glades, the more the haves and the have-nots stood in contrast. Beefy 4x4 pickups, gleaming with chrome, hauled pricey motorboats. Others carefully dipped theirs into the river down at the ramps. I felt a little jealous of them as I whizzed by in my Honda Civic. But I wasn't venturing down into the glades to vacation.

I was there on a mission. I also wanted to really get to know the Everglades and its people. I already knew quite a bit, but I had to make sure that didn't stifle my curiosity and prevent me from learning. Instead, it had to be a starting point. I was tired of reading stories that treated the glades, and all of Florida, really, as a wild and wacky backdrop where characters and tall tales abounded, where "normal" folks vacationed but where real people didn't live. While some folks treated the glades as their playground, thousands of others made their lives in little hamlets, some the poorest places in the country, inundated with smoke from sugarcane burning or toxins from algal blooms, and try as they might to fight it, they found too frequently that other people's money always shouted louder.

That was the story all across gator country, that large swath of the Deep South stretching from Florida Bay at the outflow of the Everglades, up the entire state of Florida, along the Low Country wetlands of Georgia and the Carolinas to touch Virginia; and to the west, from the Florida panhandle, across Alabama, Mississippi and its river delta, Louisiana, and the Gulf Coast of Texas down toward the Mexican lagoons. It is roughly analogous to the biodiversity hot spot that is the North American Coastal Plain and a nearly perfect overlay of the impoverished Deep South. This is the kingdom of the American alligator, where marshes, swamps, and bayous harbor hundreds of endemic species of flora and fauna, many of which occur nowhere else in the world. Over the centuries, gator country has drawn the roughest of settlers. Before the invention of air-conditioning, only the hardiest survived there, and only the most stubborn bothered.

Before the railroads came, each small town was like an island in a sea of wilderness. Venture past the tree line, and you were—metaphorically, and quite literally—on your own. Since then, more and more people came to live against the land instead of with it, creating an adversary of gator country itself. Destroyed and maligned, the swamp has fought back. This wild country itself is as stubborn as the American alligator.

As I drove, the levees around Lake Okeechobee rose above the grasslands and the narrowing highway in the distance. Up ahead, the Caloosahatchee River met the lake. Folks from outside the state, and even from clear across the world, know about Lake O, because it's the largest landlocked body of water in Florida, so big that it showed up on early satellite photography. These days, satellites are recording something there other than wonder. The green plague on the lake, as it's called, is a toxic algal bloom, thick with cyanobacteria that contain the neurotoxin BMAA. That's beta-Methylamino-L-alanine, exposure to which has been linked to neurodegenerative disorders such as Alzheimer's, Parkinson's, and amyotrophic lateral sclerosis, more commonly known as Lou Gehrig's disease. Research on the link is ongoing but strong.

Bodies of water are never closed systems, even when they're technically landlocked. This is especially true of Lake Okeechobee. When colonists first arrived in South Florida, the flow of the Everglades covered nearly half the state, with the headwaters springing from Shingle Creek, a small waterway about ten miles east of Disney World, and about two hundred miles north of the uppermost boundary of Everglades National Park. Besides the theme parks, in that area, you'll find the sprawl of suburbia, and within every decorative retention pond, as if by law, there is at least one alligator. Leave the Orlando sprawl in any direction and you'll quickly find yourself in river country, the alternating patches of pasture, of cows languidly chomping grass under a hill's sentinel tree, of sandhill cranes; of creeks and pine scrub, of red-bellied woodpeckers ra-ta-tatting out the forest rhythm through the flaking bark of a longleaf pine, of scrub-jays who quirk their heads at the hikers who've ventured onto their dune island that has risen above the savanna—this, too, is gator country.

Going east from the headwaters, you'll find thick oak groves and cypress standing heavy with Spanish moss. A single fanboat might buzz by. Along the banks of the Halifax River, shrimp boats float past paddle wheels and hurricane-weathered docks slump into the sallow estuary over the oyster beds, one flood away from driftwood. Dolphins play in the wake and manatees drift like weightless stones just below the surface, bronzed in rippled light by the brackish water.

South along the coast, the Indian River Lagoon system stretches behind barrier islands. The lagoon once flourished, but now abuse of the state's water—especially the dumping of pollutants, such as phosphate runoff from agriculture—has caused other toxic algal blooms, which in turn spur die-offs in the seagrass beds, leaving gentle manatees with nothing to eat and causing them to die by the hundreds. Across the river, past arching water oaks and a thicket of sea grapes, white sand beaches stretch north and south, so far in each direction that they disappear into the distance.

Inland once again, in a bog, the many-colored heads of rare carnivorous flowers wait arrayed in sticky spindles or heavy cups, shooting up among the reeds and the unctuous muck. Sundews open up like land-bound anemones, each stalk capped with a pearl of mucilage like a dewdrop in the morning, a beautiful and deadly trap to lure its prey. Butterworts hang their hooded purple heads, and bladderworts peek above the water's surface like daffodils with a dark secret. The air hangs heavy with petrichor from the sweet, wet decomposition that keeps the understory alive. Within the bog itself, the muck scarcely remembers that, when dinosaurs walked the Earth, it was once plant matter. Its constituent parts have congealed beyond recognition, becoming something new, a fertile mire that is in turn both disgusting and wonderful. Beneath this muck lies concealed the truth about Florida's history. Researchers at the Windover Archaeological Site near Titusville, Florida, have uncovered the remains of 168 people who lived in the area during the Stone Age. Even though carbon dating estimates indicate the "bog bodies" could be as much as eight thousand years old, the unique composition of the bog's muck has kept them remarkably whole. And who knows what else lurks beneath that primordial ooze.

Death and life are the same in the swamp. After the spark leaves, life goes on, becoming muck that scintillates with microscopic organisms, the muck itself a living thing that continues, not by volition but by perpetual motion, forever keeping itself alive with itself, a snake eating its tail. Outsiders only see the death, the decay, the unruly rawness of this wild country, without seeing the beauty in it, much to our harm and the detriment of this world.

For millennia, the Everglades dominated the Floridian peninsula. Back in the early 1800s, when that wild country only seemed to call out to the most rugged, the most desperate, and those wanting to disappear—and of course, those who were already there—the Everglades began at the headwaters, flowed south through unmarred grassland, and collected in Lake Okeechobee before proceeding down through swamp, then sawgrass prairie, over the porous limestone shelf that encases the Floridan aquifer, through a strip ridged like the whorl of a fingerprint with sloughs of clear, flowing water, ridges of sawgrass, and tree islands of cypress and palm rising above the rest. To the west, pine flatwoods and Big Cypress Swamp guarded the flow's border. The verdant scent of life rested amid the grass. Cypress stands and the Atlantic Coastal Ridge swooped down from the east to guide the flow south into marl marshes, then to squeeze into the Shark River Slough, which released through the Ten Thousand Islands, a variegated scatter of mangrove-clawed cays, of keyholes in that spiny vegetation, and of flows like Lostmans River, so named because it was easy to wind up there and disappear. That was outlaw country then. It may well still be, though to some extent defanged like the rest. Past that still, the Everglades breathed out into the gulf through Florida Bay. Tiny outposts dot the coast, some largely unchanged since settlers got there, others consumed by tourism as a lure is by a hungry goliath grouper. The last sentry between there and the map's edge is a flat bean of grass ringed with mangroves, called Little Rabbit Key. After that, it's open water.

Settlers already had the great body of the glades in their sights by the 1840s. Like much of North America that has been called frontier, no matter what was there before they arrived, settlers saw it as future farmland. They saw swampland as waste in both senses of the word: one as soil not put to the plough and therefore not living up to its full potential; in the other as an uninhabited wasteland, terra incognita. Beyond here be dragons. So, these settlers petitioned the federal government for help laying claim on this land against itself. This is man versus nature, only nature is not the assailant here. It seldom is.

However, the land got a reprieve as the Civil War came, and then it became embattled once more as the United States went to war against the Seminole Tribe for the third time that century. The US fought for this land that they sought to wring out like a sponge. Perhaps it wasn't so much for the land itself as it was to go against the Seminoles, who allied with that impassable landscape. Though the US forced many Seminoles out, several hundred remained in the Everglades, fortified and defended by the depths of Big Cypress Swamp, a land their assailants reviled and feared and did not understand. And so, to this day, some Seminoles call themselves, their tribe, the Unconquered; and others still consider themselves at war with the United States, because they never lost, and they never gave in.

By the time Theodore Roosevelt and his Rough Riders galloped through in 1898 on their way to Cuba to fight the Spanish-American War, those who wanted to carve some civilization into the glades had won out, and the Army Corps of Engineers was already laying out their plans to dynamite and divert the incredible River of Grass into oblivion. Over the next few decades, their canals and dikes manhandled the Everglades' southward flow into submission, diverting it east and west to create hundreds of thousands of acres of farmland, and intractable plots destined for waterlogged homesteads, some sold for as little as five bucks a pop—and worth even less.

The growing wealth of the roaring twenties gave rise to a new middle class to dupe. Con artists and pyramid schemers sold any land they could get their hands on, and some they could not. They peddled plots sight unseen to working-class folks looking for a slice of paradise, and they could have it, they found, if they were willing to suffer the mosquitoes and wade into their new property, which was inaccessible except by flat-bottomed boat. This, the Florida land boom, ushered more than a quarter of a million new residents to the state between 1920 and 1925. It also gave a foothold to Florida's time-honored tradition of the grift and the phrase, "And if you believe that, I've got some swampland in Florida to sell you."

One of the dupes who moved to this fractured paradise was landscape architect Ernest Coe, who witnessed the casual poaching of orchids and wildlife with horror. Even worse was the developers' quest to gobble up the land, regardless of the flora or fauna hidden in its foliage. Intent on saving the glades, Coe spearheaded the move to consolidate Everglades National Park. But by the time his dream came to fruition in 1947, the result paled in comparison with what he had envisioned.

It also gets more complicated than that. When the national park came in, they kicked longtime residents out, people whose families had been living there more than a century—or in the cases of many of the

Seminoles, since time immemorial. The story of the Everglades isn't just one of environmental strife and a need for redemption, it's one of class struggle, too: All environmental stories are if only you dig past the topsoil.

As I drove deep into the Everglades, the roadside came alive with the stories of Florida's past. Just as Jeff could name every creature and sprig that he saw, every part of the landscape launched a story into my head. I saw visions of war with Seminoles crouching in sawgrass, smugglers' planes going down in the mangroves, poachers stalking through the sloughs. The main one who came to mind, of course, was Peg Brown.

He was the logical continuation of the story of the Everglades, which went from paradise to paved, free and unbound to owned, partitioned, captive, and, most importantly, taken away from the people, both Native and settler, who had once called it home.

The federal government said the national park would protect the Everglades, but it did so at the expense of the people who lived there, so has it really protected the Everglades at all? Don't get me wrong. National parks are wonderful. I love visiting them just as much as anybody else. But many of them began as theft. If we want to do better by the wild and by our fellow human beings, we have to learn from these past mistakes, so it's far from environmentally sacrilegious to admit them. It's necessary. The advent of Everglades National Park pushed whole communities into crime. It pitted environmentalists against hunters, against the working-class people who lived there, the people who were already stewards of the environment in the first place. In removing the glades' keepers, and removing their livelihood as well, the park struck a false wedge between the gladesmen, the Natives, and the wild.

Some folks down in Chokoloskee said that the park came in and separated them from what was rightfully theirs and had been theirs for generations. The park represented the government, the powers that be, coming to oppress the little man. Of course, in their minds, anyone who broke the new laws was standing up for the downtrodden. That's where the stories of Peg Brown came in, and that's what I was hoping to understand in going to Chokoloskee, a place whose name had become nearly synonymous with poaching.

I had driven through the entirety of the glades to get there, passing from the marshes and savannas below the headwaters, through wide tracts of open space; past the phosphate mines of Bone Valley; past farms of every variety—orange groves, strawberry fields, cornfields, cow pastures; through little palm-studded towns with only one stoplight, where smoke from sugarcane burns drifted over makeshift migrant trailer-villes and the collective life expectancy had dipped below that of decades before; past rodeo arenas and fishing villages, abandoned gas stations, RV resorts spangled with a battalion of American flags whipping in the wake of passing cars; past Presbyterian churches with steeples reaching into that limitless blue sky; past Native American casinos; past luxury subdivisions with rolling golf course greens; then miles and miles of wide-open country, until the grasslands gave way to hardwood slough. Cypresses towered before me, casting cool shadows over the road. I had entered the Big Cypress Basin, a wetland watershed where the rare Florida panther still prowled, and ghost orchids bloomed in the night.

Past the crossroads at Alligator Alley, a stretch of highway that links Naples on the west coast and Fort Lauderdale in the east, obstructing the flow of the river of grass in the process, another fifteen miles of the most sparsely inhabited swampland put me in Carnestown, a mere intersection punctuated by a gas station and a monolithic radio tower. By then, the vegetation along the roadside had turned to mangroves, the once solid ground beneath to a clear stream, giving the feeling that the road itself was on an island hovering over the water. I rolled down my windows, turned off my air-conditioning. Truth be told, it wasn't working that well anyway. I had driven my little Civic to death, and it was on its last legs. The AC only puffed out hot air. I didn't have money to fix it. The breeze, though, would always be free.

The wind that whipped at my hair was alive with the verdant smell of flowing water. For those who have never been to the Everglades, it may be easy to imagine that wide expanse as a turgid mire of foul water, dangerous creatures, humidity, and mosquitoes. There are definitely mosquitoes, but the real glades are neither turgid nor foul. The Everglades is a living thing. It filters our drinking water. Before it sinks back into the aquifer, the water flows over the lime rock, watering the plants, carrying their pods and polyps; a symphony of microorganisms connects one living thing to another, and the result is what seems to me like the glades exhaling. Anyone who has ever been to the glades and stopped for a moment to just take in their surroundings and *breathe* knows that they are surrounded by a vibrant cosmos of life. The Everglades isn't a foul backwater or a hostile wasteland. Most of it isn't even a swamp. It is part of the lungs of our planet.

Although the Amazon rain forest garners more fanfare as an ecological sentry against climate change, wetlands such as Florida's coastal estuaries and swamps account for a larger percentage of the globe's carbon sink biomass. Wetlands cover nearly four million square miles of the Earth's surface, or about 7 percent of the world. By comparison, even the magnificent Amazon covers about 4 percent. Destruction of the Amazon is met with outrage. Destruction of swamps should be, too. The Everglades are one of the largest wetland ecosystems in the world. Deriding and destroying the glades puts us in a perilous position, one that threatens the water we drink and the air we breathe.

What do the gladesmen think of that? I wondered. As I drove on to Everglades City and then the long bridge over Chokoloskee Bay, I had a feeling I knew the answer.

They saw themselves as part of that maligned swamp, didn't they? Even as the outside world destroyed their home, pushed them out, told them who they were and who they should have been instead, and what they would have to do to save the glades—as if they hadn't been doing those things already—they rebelled against those powers, and they immortalized that rebellion in story.

I parked beside a long, rocky shore, the only car in the lot without a boat trailer. I turned around and took in the bay on every side. Whenever I'm in nature, I find myself consumed with such simple joy that sometimes I have to go where my whims take me. After that long drive down the state, the salt air beckoned me across the road to the sand, where I slipped out of my flip-flops and dipped my feet into the water.

Bright silvery leatherjackets, tiny herring, minnows, and little needle-nosed ballyhoo shimmered along the shoals. I wondered if I might chance a glimpse of an endangered smalltooth sawfish, a sharklike ray with a gnarly chain-saw-shaped snout. As few as two hundred of them may still exist in the wild, and most of those in Florida. If I was going to see one, it would be there. The sadness of that struck me. I hated the idea that I was excited to perhaps see an animal before it disappeared. I don't want to live in a world of disappearances when there is so much beauty to preserve.

I could admire the fish later. Right then, I had work to do. It was time to chase the legend of Peg Brown.

5

BECOMING BLACKLEDGE

We've given you a false identity, the letter said. The envelope, from FWC headquarters, had arrived in Jeff's mailbox like any other. Yet it contained an entire life, an alternate reality where a man who looked remarkably like him had lived out an existence totally unlike his own. The details were few—a name, identifying information, an address. He would have to come up with the rest. It was January already, a new year, and Lieutenant Wilson still hadn't given him the particulars on his undercover assignment. *Secrecy with this kind of thing is normal,* Jeff reassured himself again and again. He hadn't expected both his anxiety and excitement to build so much as the final revelation of those secrets loomed. Now Jeff would have to begin sloughing off all the things that made him who he was, a life and sense of self that he had built up for more than forty years, and transform himself into someone who, as a wildlife officer, would have been his antagonist. What kind of life had he lived? What was his story? What compelled him to get up every morning and do the things that he did? What did he hope for? What did he fear?

His name was Curtis Blackledge, and Jeff would have to search within himself to find him.

The physical transformation into Blackledge began while Jeff was still in uniform. Every morning after washing his face, he would look up into the mirror and see a different person. He found it somewhat unsettling. By January, his once neatly buzzed black hair had grown into a shag, his clean shave replaced by a disreputable-looking goatee. He dyed his salt-and-pepper hair an inky black. He looked fifteen years younger and a quarter as wise.

"I don't recognize you, man," he said to his reflection.

His mother seemed to feel the same way. As his undercover work took on a new life around him, the increasingly few times that he had seen his mother, he had watched a gradual expression of grief sweep across her face. She and Jeff had always been close. He would proudly call himself a mama's boy. Every time he got the chance, he would visit her and help her with anything she needed, building, fixing, you name it, or just spending time with her, soaking up the comfort of her constancy. She was a matriarch, a pillar, her love for Jeff and all of them as steadfast as the sun coaxing flowers into bloom.

Yet now that secrecy had consumed his life, he could no longer come to visit. She missed him when he was away and missed him in person, too. Despite her unchanging love, Jeff himself was changing before her eyes. He imagined the pain that caused her. He wanted to remedy it, to hug her, to reassure her that he was still Jeff inside, that the disrepair he'd fallen into was a costume. Watching the heartbreak in her eyes hurt him all the more, because he couldn't tell her a thing, not even that he was undercover. So every time he saw her, he looked forward to his mission's end. That mission had hardly started. He was still crafting the person who Blackledge would be. As he looked at himself in the mirror, thinking of the life he was leaving behind, he came upon the biggest difference between Blackledge and himself: his mother. Now Jeff had to imagine who he would have been without her.

He liked to think of himself as the kind of person who would always do the right thing, even when it hurt. Jeff worked hard. He came up from nothing, made a life for himself, found a slice of the American dream. Yet he made a conscious effort not to think less of the folks who couldn't do that. It went beyond putting himself into another person's shoes. He wanted to believe that everyone deserved a little grace, a second chance. The world didn't work so well without that.

But the things that had shaped Jeff's life hadn't happened to Blackledge. So it was hard to see Blackledge feeling the same way. Jeff imagined a person who had experienced some of the same hardships, perhaps, but he hadn't made a conscious effort to look beyond himself. He hadn't striven for the life Jeff had, either. He wasn't married, didn't have any kids. Perhaps he liked to party a little too much, Jeff considered. Maybe the pleasures of life had called to him more loudly than family and career. If it ever came up, Jeff decided he would say Blackledge had once been addicted to crack cocaine, but "I'm not about that life any-more." Other undercover officers had found themselves in situations where they'd been offered drugs. Jeff needed a way to turn them down without blowing his cover. Sobriety added a level of believability. The detail from his past made a story people would remember. In their minds, he would become a real person, a flawed one with a history. But maybe when it came down to it, Blackledge wanted to work hard. He'd make that clear, too. He wanted a chance at something bigger than himself. Didn't everyone?

After the first letter, a second letter had come, this one from the Department of Highway Safety and Motor Vehicles. It summoned Blackledge to a secure location to have his photograph taken for a new ID. He stood in front of the white backdrop, trying to think of how he should hold his face for the picture when the camera flashed. The print came back like the typical ID mug shot. The ID looked real. It *was* real. Only the man inside it was not. But back at home, he started receiving credit cards in Blackledge's name. Little by little, all the paper trail of a typical life built up around him.

Soon after that, Jeff received the envelope that contained the address and the keys. From then on, Lieutenant Wilson would start fading back, too. More and more of their contact would come in envelopes.

Following these latest instructions, the ones that appeared along with a key, Jeff drove out to Arcadia, a small frontier town about sixty miles due west of Lake Okeechobee and a little less than a hundred miles north of Everglades City. One hundred years ago, a lawlessness that rivaled the Wild West reigned there. Truly, the place had made the West look tame, because at least in the West, you could see where you were going. In that junglelike growth where river country oak ham-mocks and seedy uplands met the shadowland of the swamp, outlaws could disappear just past the tree line, and only those who knew the way—or those that brave or that foolish—could follow. The fact was that not much had changed since then.

That Arcadia came to be in a time of poets, Romantics and tran-scendentalists, who sought to leave the squalor of city life behind and immerse themselves in nature in search of the sublime. Some centuries before them, the pastoral poets used "Arcadia" to represent utopia, a place in perfect harmony with itself. In Greek mythology, that Arcadia was an untamed wilderness, an idyllic glade where the spirits of nature resided apart from the vulgar realities of civilization. Thus, the poets reimagined it, a world apart from their own, unspoiled by human endeavors. Their Arcadia remained wild and therefore pure, noble.

The original mythic Arcadia was a kind of paradise, and home to Pan, god of the wild. Pan was the archetypal trickster. Often depicted as a satyr playing a syrinx, better known as a pan flute, this Pan became associated with many things, among them mischief and chaos. At times he was playful. At others, frightening. The word *panic* is derived from his name, from the feeling he inspired in the nearby folk when he let out a terrible shout upon an unceremonious arousal from his afternoon nap.

This real place, Arcadia, Florida, had once been on the edge of Jeff's patrol territory. He had spent many days cruising along the Peace River in an airboat, on the lookout for poachers. He knew the place, knew it to be untamable, a last bastion of the ever-shrinking wild, and so, too, a mysterious borderland between the safe, known world and the edge of the map.

The address the agency had given him was no different. Kudzu hung like land-bound clouds over the fences. Grass sprang up like the place itself was a glade, though it seemed to have once been a lawn. A strange concrete dome rose among the blades like an immense tortoise. Farther back in the clearing there was a dilapidated mobile home. Beside it, a new-looking camper gleamed white in the fading daylight.

My God, Jeff thought. *Look at this dump. It's a damn jungle.*

Jeff had talked to other officers who had done short-term undercover work in the past. They told him how the agency had put them up in swanky apartments or rented fully stocked suburban houses with pools. Didn't look like that was going to happen for Jeff.

He entered the combo and unlocked the gate, then drove into the thick of it, following a barely recognizable path, two lines of grass-blades slicked over to form faint tire tracks. Inside, the trailer didn't look much better. The smell of mildew hung heavily on the air. Wallpaper peeled and shed like longleaf pine bark. Trash littered the floor, and craters remained where appliances had been ripped from walls.

Is this where I'm supposed to live? Jeff thought. He enjoyed camping and do-it-yourself projects, but this was ridiculous.

He found the camper in less of a state. It gave off the hopeful smell of new upholstery instead of moldering decrepitation. Still, as he poked around, he held on to a hope that he wouldn't have to live here, even temporarily. He thought of his wife and his dogs, his carefully kept lawn, the bougainvillea dripping from their pergola, hummingbirds dipping their beaks into the spring hibiscus, and he found a pang of regret. He had kept his life meticulously curated. *I'm leaving all of that for this?*

His adult son, Chris, had made a surprise visit before Jeff left. When Jeff told him about going undercover, Chris's face fell. He might as well have said, *I can't believe you're doing this, Dad.* This visit went on longer than he'd planned. Chris had inherited both worry and steadfastness from their family, so he made the decision to move home to be there for his mother while Jeff was not.

Despite the sometimes-treacherous adventures Jeff fought through to track down wildlife crime, his was a safe life, tame. More than that, his family—his wife and son, his mother, his siblings and their big, involved clan—they were everything to him. What did he want with going out with a bang?

You must've lost your damn mind, Jeff, he thought.

But there was no going back now. The reality of it settled heavily over him as he explored deeper into the property. It was more of the same, about nine or ten acres of increasingly dense growth. Jeff had seen enough. He hopped in his truck and headed for home, about an hour's drive north. On the way, he called Lieutenant Wilson.

"Did you go by your place?" Lieutenant Wilson asked.

"Yeah," Jeff said. "It's not exactly what I was expecting. What's this all about?"

"We've been having some issues with alligators," Lieutenant Wilson said. He went on to explain—finally—that reports of some nefarious dealings among alligator farmers had made their way to the agency.

Preliminary evidence pointed to laundering: Farmers were concealing the origin of their eggs, possibly to pass off illegally harvested eggs as ones obtained fairly. Lieutenant Wilson believed that rampant poaching was going on, particularly during nesting season, which was coming up. "We need you to pose as one of them." They wanted him to start an alligator farm, a real one, and stock it with full-size gators. Then he would infiltrate their numbers and find the poachers from the inside.

To make his task even more difficult, it came with a built-in ticking clock. As soon as Jeff witnessed a violation of the law, that clock would start counting down the days until the statute of limitations ran out, and the state could no longer prosecute. For felonies like alligator poaching, the state could take three years to gather a case. Longer than Jeff wanted to be out there, sure, but it gave him plenty of breathing room. Misdemeanors, on the other hand, such as the violation of alligator egg collection permits, had a statute of limitations of one measly year. If the state filed charges while Jeff was in the field, they risked blowing his cover—and the case as a whole. So as soon as Jeff saw an infraction, the case would go into overdrive, and he and his handlers would have to race to gather evidence and make arrests. If they waited too long, crimes against nature could go unpunished. Before they got to that, he had a whole lot to learn.

Up until then, Jeff had never even seen an alligator egg. Birds, deer, fish—those were more his purview. None of those were liable to eat you alive. *What have I done?* he thought. He wouldn't just have to transform himself in this thing. He wasn't just an actor. He would have to be a damn zookeeper. He would be a set designer and choreographer. The fucking sound technician. He was the whole damn cast and crew. He had to become a new person and then remake the world around him, a fiction real enough to pass for fact even under the scrutiny of those who knew better than him, out of thin air. Then, after all that, Jeff would have to track down as much evidence of alligator poaching as possible. Of course, witnessing the crime of poaching itself, especially if he could catch it on camera, was his prize. They needed enough evidence of each count of crime to prove wrongdoing in court. But evidence that pointed to a wider organized poaching network—that was the holy grail. He wasn't just watching and waiting in costume. He had to become a spy, to dig in places where he didn't belong. That was where the real danger waited, not within reptilian jaws, but among the swamp's most dangerous predators: men.

"We can't give you much money to do this, either," said Lieutenant Wilson. "We really can't give you anything at all. No one should be able to track your finances back to us, so you have to make it yourself."

Shit, Jeff thought.

Of course they would pay him. He'd get the same salary as he always did, akin to that of a public school teacher, in other words, a pittance. The agency had a small fund to get the farm started, too—with money from proceeds from the turtle operation and others like it—but after that, he was on his own. Like most state agencies, FWC lacked adequate funds to accomplish everything they needed to do. To bridge that gap, agents either did without necessities or got creative.

To make matters worse, Wilson explained that another agent had tried this scheme before him. He found the alligator underworld to be closed off and impossible to penetrate. Even the most upright farmers considered the intricacies of their practices to be trade secrets. In place of the usual southern hospitality, the farmers had met him with polite exclusion.

Beginning in 2013, FWC started getting intel that state-licensed alligator farms were paying poachers, laundering eggs, and possibly turning poacher themselves. Hundreds, even thousands, of gators were disappearing. A sizable chunk of the year's predicted hatchlings had vanished. If things got much worse, the species would be in jeopardy, and so would gator country. FWC tried to drum up a sting operation, but it quickly ran into a snag: The alligator farming culture in the state was so exclusive, a veritable good ol' boys' club, that the undercover officer couldn't gain entry. The operation's subsequent plans quickly went awry. Their agent came off as too straitlaced, suspiciously stiff. Tension spread among the farmers, who were already mistrustful of outsiders. They knew someone was poking around. Anyone FWC sent now had to be so seamlessly in character, so convincing, so flawless, that the farmers and the poachers working with them would never know they were a wildlife officer in disguise. He should be charismatic, a flexible changeling who could doff his outer officer and become the character. The agency had seen this in Jeff. What he saw in himself was a different matter.

What was more, that previous officer had blown his cover. Sick of camping out in the trailer, he joined a gym under his false identity so he could shower and work off some of the tension. Then he fell in love. And that, predictably, had been his downfall. Since all women need to have a bit of a sleuth in them, she suspected something was up. She dug a little and found out he wasn't who he said he was. Cover blown, the agency reassigned him.

So Jeff was going into this thing with the odds against him.

"This won't be easy," Lieutenant Wilson said. "But we have a good feeling about you. We chose you for a reason. Just don't go falling in love, okay?"

After saying goodbye to his wife for what felt like the last time for a long while, Jeff set out in his unmarked white pickup into the tangled morass of river country. As he drove out of the city, the concrete and the strip malls and the sea breeze and the swirl and glint of traffic in daybreak's farther edge receded into greenery and shadows. Vehicles peeled off as the highway narrowed from course to trickle. Then finally the long, straight track of the country road shrank into the distance to dissolve against some faraway swamp in a mirage of heat and light.

Jeff knew every back road and waterway in the area. But this time, it felt different to leave town and become submerged in the growth of the forest where the trees almost touched one another over the road and pattered the cracked pavement with remnants of sunlight. It felt brand-new because he was new. Jeff had left himself behind, and in his place, and through his eyes, Blackledge was seeing this world for the first time.

Before he donned that final mask and left, Jeff had visited with his family, a get-together, a family barbecue like any other, except at this one Jeff asked his nieces and his nephews to untag him in pictures on Facebook and not put up any more. Everyone asked questions: "What's up with you lately?" "What's going on?"

"It's for work," he would say, leaving them feeling curious or slighted, yet, after a while, they stopped asking questions. Meanwhile, they speculated among themselves. He would catch whispers of it. Was Jeff getting a divorce? Was he dying? What would make their ebullient Jeff become so taciturn and secretive?

Jeff understood what losing him must feel like, because the loss of them was starting to grind him down. Yet, unlike his family, he knew why he was coming apart. He reassured himself by imagining the day when he would tell them all the truth. He might gather them around at a cookout, teasing like he had a tall tale wound up just for them. *Remember when I was looking a little scruffy?* he might say. *Well, there's a story behind that. Let me tell you.*

In the meantime, he was still fading out. He deleted his profiles from everything, scrubbed the internet clean of himself, not leaving so much as a picture of his face in a crowd. Except for his wife's last name and his adult son, it was as though Jeff Babauta had never existed.

Unbeknownst to his family, new evidence of his life had sprouted in its place. Curtis Blackledge seemed to have always existed, at least according to digital evidence. He was now a real person with a family and friends and a life. There were the pictures to prove it. Facebook, an Instagram, a network of people who knew him. He had lived a more or less ordinary if not slightly disreputable life, and there it was on the internet for anyone who was curious to find it. He owned a condo in Ruskin, which he was trying to sell. He liked dogs, because who didn't? And, of course, he liked to have a drink or two down by the water, taking in the sunset, another escapist on permanent vacation in Florida. Now he was putting paradise to work.

Jeff set about creating an alligator farm out of nothing, Blackledge alongside him like Peter Pan's shadow, starting with a deeper inspection of the raw materials he had to work with. He circled the perimeter of the property, wading through the weeds. Beside the barn, the overgrowth hid a few ponds that Jeff suspected had once been used to farm tilapia. The air around them retained the funkiness of cheap aquaculture. On closer inspection, Jeff would find the fish still living there, and with them turtles, including some softshells. Only one of the ponds was fenced in, and near the entrance to the property, a concrete dome like a holey-roofed igloo hunkered, a chelonian boulder among the foxtails and horseweeds. Building and selling domes like that one was a business venture of the guy, an engineer and entrepreneur, who owned the property. He intended them as mini weather bunkers. The domes were so heavy that even a tornado couldn't rip them off the ground. And therein lay the problem. Made almost entirely of superthick concrete, the domes were a pain to move, and short of hiring cranes and backhoes, they were parked permanently wherever you put them. With his business a bust, the engineer rented out his property, but not without trying to sell Jeff on his business venture first.

The officer who had come before him, the one who had fallen in love, had managed to do a few things around the place, like putting up the fence and equipping the camper. It was a thirty-two-footer with a slide-out that made it bigger inside, but cramped and narrow nonetheless. Otherwise, the place was a shell, a canvas for Jeff's imagination to play. It needed a lot of work, and given his lack of a wealthy, deceased family member, that meant applying elbow grease.

He put in air-conditioning and lights. He fixed anything and everything that was broken. He ran all the electrical himself, mowed down the weeds, fenced in a pond, dusted, cleaned, and made the place not just look livable but like an actual business. He enjoyed working with his hands, but those tasks got lonely quickly. He started borrowing his dogs from home one at a time. If anyone asked—not that anyone else was there yet—Jeff would say he was dog-sitting. Sometimes Mack, his Goldador K-9, attended him, solemnly watching Jeff work or sniffing around, his tail up in a pert wag. Other times it was Ruger, his big, dopey yellow Lab, who would fetch anything he could pick up, even if it seemed too heavy. Then there was Jack, the aptly named Jack Russell, bounding around with his limitless energy, chasing dragonflies, all bark and vigor without a care. He never took Bali, his German shepherd. That breed, he thought, looked too much like a K-9.

Each of the dogs was a piece of home. They eased his loneliness somewhat, though the loss of his usual routines, especially having to sit and wait instead of going out and sleuthing for crimes, made him feel restless and edgy.

In those early days, Lieutenant Wilson allowed him to go home once a week. Spending so much time without his wife left Jeff feeling as if a piece of himself were missing. Just seeing her became a necessary respite. Though they helped his sanity, those returns were also necessary because he needed to file reports, and Lieutenant Wilson didn't allow him to keep his state computer or any personal effects that marked him as Jeff Babauta at the farm.

During that time, Jeff put the finishing touches on Blackledge, too.

Blackledge was what in his younger days in Colorado the locals would call a goat-roper, a rural character who held no allegiance with citified society, who took from the land when he could to make a scratch living. He was a redneck, but also something more, because wasn't everyone more than they appeared to be?

After thirty-something years of failing his folks, drinking and partying and getting into trouble—but not so much trouble that he'd ever crossed hairs with the law—and just getting by on the scarce paycheck from week to week, Blackledge had suddenly and unexpectedly come into some money, so much money that his benefactor, though dead, had believed it would do him more ill than good if the sum didn't come with stipulations. Blackledge had been raised by his aunt out west and then in South Florida, just like Jeff. (All good lies, Jeff knew, contained as much truth as possible. The less he had to fake, the better.) That aunt had taken over raising him from his parents in Saipan. They wanted him to grow up on the mainland where opportunities and jobs weren't quite so limited. He loved this aunt, though in his adolescence his youthful puckishness, which lasted well into his thirties, had brought her much disappointment and irritation. Jeff imagined she was the kind of lady, this auntie, who would scold as much as she would coddle, who would love people by cooking rich meals, who would say, "Everything we've done for you, all the sacrifices we've made, and this is what you turn out to be? Some layabout? Some good-for-nothing?" Sometimes *we* meant "your parents and I." Other times it referred to something bigger than them, a family on a grander scale of centuries of ancestors who had scraped and persevered just to amount to him. And yet, even though all he did was let her down, she still loved him with a fervor that was stronger than any disappointment could ever be.

Prior to his entrance onto the alligator farming scene, Blackledge's auntie had died, leaving him as the heir of a small fortune and a condo on the river. He was not the executor of her will. She didn't trust him that much, a reluctance Blackledge knew he'd earned. He didn't have a steady job. He hadn't settled down with a wife. There were no new little Blackledges on the way to disappoint the family. So it was not surprising that the executor merely told him about the money first instead of handing him a check. This inheritance would only be his when he met certain conditions. He had to show the executor what he would do with the money, and it had to be something worthwhile. No buying yachts or blowing it all on a raucous party in Key West so good that no one in attendance would be able to remember. No, no. To get this money, Blackledge had to submit a business plan. And he thought: *Why not start an alligator farm?* It was just outlandish enough to be worth his while— Blackledge balked at the ordinary, despite having lived such an ordinary life of boozing and malaise up until that point—and it fulfilled the will's demands. The executor left the money with a trustee. Blackledge was now a trust-fund brat, receiving a small sum each month. With it, Blackledge got started.

He had imagined farming alligators would make for a humorous backdrop, and it would give him room and funds enough to live it up. Blackledge quickly found he had been wrong in both regards. Farming alligators was more work than he ever imagined, and not knowing the business, he hardly made ends meet.

Did Jeff need such a rich backstory? He certainly thought so. He wanted to be prepared for any question. In his ideal operation, he would never be caught off guard. He wouldn't learn until later that the average undercover officer never went to such lengths. Jeff didn't see himself as average, so he never paid those kinds of people any mind.

However, Jeff's real life quickly overlapped with Blackledge as he ran into the same difficulties: The farm was eating through cash, and fast, and without a dead auntie and a trust fund, he had to create a working alligator farm from essentially nothing. It really had to make money. He thought about how to do that as he continued cobbling the place together.

At the edges of the ponds, he hammered poles into the earth and topped them with yellow caution signs. NOTICE, they said. KEEP YOUR DISTANCE. This was written around the silhouette of an openmouthed gator. This detail seemed right. *What else?* he thought. He practiced thinking like Blackledge with Jeff as his shadow. Jeff knew too much, but Blackledge knew too little. The wrong missing knowledge here could lose you a hand—or worse. Not that there were alligators in the ponds yet, as far as Jeff knew. Not ones he had put there anyway, but you could never be too sure. More often than not, the odds were in your favor to spot an alligator in any Florida watering hole larger than a puddle.

Before he brought in alligators, the place needed a name. After that, everything would come together. The previous undercover agent had dubbed it Joe's Alligator Farm. That sounded fake to Jeff. And certainly not something Blackledge would use.

As Jeff mowed, he played with word associations in his head, all sorts of permutations on alligators and swamps. Then it occurred to him to hide some sort of Easter egg, give the place a name that had an overt meaning then another covert one, a sort of inside joke with himself, a clue in plain sight that the farm wasn't what it seemed. Florida's tourism board used the slogan "Sunshine State" to make it sound inviting, like a land of endless summer. Sunshine Alligator Farm had a ring to it. The name also held a double meaning for Jeff. He would be investigating wrongdoing, finding poachers and bringing their deeds into the sunlight. Sunshine reminded Jeff of his background motivation, one reason among many to remain meticulous and upright: Florida's Sunshine Laws. Like the national Freedom of Information Act, the Sunshine Laws mandate that state agencies provide information, such as the schedules of political officials or emails made from government accounts, to the public on request. More often than not, "the public" here isn't the average state resident. The people who make Sunshine Law requests are typically lawyers, private investigators, and, of course, journalists like me. Jeff knew it was possible that a journalist might snoop through his files someday, picking over his every action and airing them out to be scrutinized by the jury of public opinion. Everything he did had to be clean, his every move logged.

Keeping honest wasn't so hard for Jeff, though. It was already how he tried to live his life. Don't do anything you wouldn't be proud of. It doesn't matter if no one else sees what you've done. You see it. Who you are in the dark is just who you are. Live like everything is out there in the sunshine.

So Sunshine Alligator Farm would be the name. Jeff made a logo to match, a green alligator opening his mouth as if to bite the word SUNSHINE above his head.

Jeff applied for permits and had received a preliminary go-ahead from the state to start his business. He jumped in. This new venture started to feel real and exciting. It *was* real. It had to be, not just because that would be more convincing, but because there would be real animals involved, real people—all with their own lives and needs.

For now, though, he was just making the set. He cleaned out the old barn, removing the fish food from the previous inhabitants, setting up tables and workstations, wiring up the lights. Back when he was first starting his career with FWC, then called the Florida Game and Freshwater Fish Commission, Jeff had been a fisheries technician. That involved a lot of wading in the muck, collecting water samples, and counting fish to understand how their populations were changing over time. It also meant he knew how to set up and run an aquaculture lab, and he assumed that's what this would be—at least a makeshift one. Although Jeff had hog-tied more than a few nuisance alligators, he had never so much as seen an alligator egg. Luckily, it made more sense for Blackledge not to know what he was doing. Still, that grated on Jeff. He knew himself as the type of guy who checked off every box, who liked to do things right, not a perfectionist necessarily, as nothing in life could ever be perfect. At the very least he was a fastidious realist.

With the barn as done as it would be right now—with metal and pegboard walls and a shined concrete floor, another sign on the outside wall, and secret hiding places for his wallet and phone—Jeff drove to the gate to add some final touches. He installed a new mailbox outside on the fence, and he fastened warning signs to the metal gate: POSTED NO TRESPASSING and BEWARE OF THE DOG.

He leaned a ladder against the arch that framed the entrance, two vertical wooden beams like telephone poles holding a third over the road about fifteen feet in the air. Jeff stamped the ladder's feet into the sand and climbed up, acutely aware that he was doing this—not just hanging the sign but the undercover operation itself—alone. If he fell, if he failed, there would be no one to catch him. The agency would help as they could, but another officer had already flunked out of this gig. There would be no second chances.

He lashed two loops of chain to the crossbeam about a yard apart and climbed down. The ladder creaked with each step. In the lonesomeness, Jeff supposed, this job was like any other he'd been assigned. It recalled solitary nights in the deep woods as a game warden, his only company his dog, the intermittent squawk of his CB radio, and the chorus of frogs that filled up the cool emptiness of the night air. Only now that lonesomeness bled over into the next day and the next, and it left him counting down the days until he could steal away home, kiss his wife, and marinate in the simple, domestic pleasure of being in the easy presence of someone he loved.

Jeff threw a cable over the crossbeam, then connected one end to the trailer hitch of his truck. He looped it around a cable already connected at two points of the sign to make a yoke. The sign sat on the ground face down.

Jeff got behind the wheel, turned the ignition, and idled forward. He craned his head back and watched the sign rise, proclaiming the name of the farm to whoever drove by. When it was high enough, he got out, climbed back up, and secured the chains to the sign. He leaned back and watched it shift in the wind. The chains held.

Back on the ground, Jeff stood at his tailgate and surveyed what he'd done. The farm was finished. Now came the hard part.

6

ALLIGATOR MISSISSIPPIENSIS

The agency gave Jeff a few hundred bucks. With that, they expected him to stock the farm with a reasonable number of gators. It wasn't so different from how the school board gave his wife a minuscule yearly stipend and asked her to work miracles. If it weren't for ingenuity—and dipping into personal funds—not much would get done. The scenario wasn't foreign to Jeff. After growing up poor and then working for the state since his early twenties, Jeff knew how to stretch a dollar.

Knowing that the seed money would run out quickly, Jeff had to finagle a way to start producing revenue fast. He started calling local trappers, both with the state and from private enterprises, on the lookout for some big gators, some real showpiece beasts, so big, he imagined, that no one who saw them would ever doubt Sunshine Alligator Farm was anything but legitimate.

"Hey, this is Curtis Blackledge," he said, the name rolling off his tongue in an unhurried drawl with an easy ownership that no one could question. "I'm opening up a farm. Would you be interested in selling me any of the alligators that you catch?"

They would always say yes, almost without question. Such nonchalance pricked Jeff's investigative instinct, and he made a note to himself to follow these guys a little more closely.

The alligators they trapped had been deemed nuisance animals. They had shown up floating in backyard pools or had basked too long on the wrong golf course. Perhaps they had taken too long to stroll across an intersection that had been built on the mudflat where they'd hatched and grown, or maybe one too many toy poodles went missing near a suburban pond and the trappers chose the first alligator they saw as a convenient scapegoat. One fewer lizard in the neighborhood would keep the residents happy and quiet for a while whether or not he was the real culprit.

Jeff found it ironic that alligators of all animals—living dinosaurs that explorers once called dragons—had become labeled with such a prosaic word as *nuisance*. There once was a time when alligators were oneiric creatures, guardians of that chthonic threshold between the land of the living and the land of the dead. To some Indigenous tribes along the North Atlantic Coastal Plain, the alligator acted as a psychopomp, a spirit guide who protected the dead on their journey into the hereafter. They were syncretic cousins to the ferryman Charon on whose boat souls of the departed cross the River Styx. As part of the Green Corn Dance, a spiritual ritual of purification and thanksgiving each spring, Seminoles and Creeks sang the Alligator Song, invoking the power of this great protector. To these tribes and others like them, alligators were all things life and death and in between. In much the way the tribes of the western plains revered and made use of the bison, tribes of the Southeast ate alligator meat, used their bones, claws, teeth, and hides, and regarded them as so much more than beast.

It's no surprise then that European colonizers would come to view the alligator and its home, the swamp, as adversaries. Ever since Europeans ventured into those same swamps, they associated alligators with the untamable wild. This was not the unspoiled wilderness of the pastoral poet's Eden. Nor was it the transcendentalist's escape. This was no Arcadia. It was more akin to the panic of Pan, a miasmic Styx, a wasteland waiting to be drained, with all the chaos that entailed.

Spanish explorers didn't know what to make of alligators at first. As I've mentioned, alligators draw their name from the Spanish *el lagarto*, the lizard. The Spanish had read of—or perhaps even seen in person— the famous crocs of the River Nile, who had their own place in Egyptian history and myth. But despite the resemblance, alligators are not crocodiles. The two can be as different in stature as alligators and iguanas. Alligators differ most from crocodiles in their temperament. Medieval bestiaries described crocs as "a curse on four legs." Crocodiles are more volatile, more aggressive, more likely to attack, whereas the alligators the first Spanish explorers encountered were more likely to blink at them apathetically before slipping below the surface of their murky pool.

In the 1600s, both Spanish and Huguenot colonists, following the

Timucua Tribe's cue, began hunting and eating alligators. It's hard to imagine seeing a creature as both dragon and dinner, but in desperation, one is willing to eat just about anything, even seemingly mythical beasts.

By the 1700s, the alligator's aura had taken on a much more exotic hue. Naturalist William Bartram, in a fanciful depiction, likened them to living dragons, imbuing their descriptions with fury and smoke. Some of his contemporaries back in Europe criticized his travelogues as ridiculous and overwrought. His was no longer the time of dragons, but the age of humanism, the scientific process, investigation, and taxonomy. Alligators were curiosities, novelties unseen in Europe, yet understood enough that they had lost their magic. They were no longer the creatures they had been in medieval bestiaries. They were predator and scourge, then big-game trophies, stuffed and mounted as décor.

For Edwardian tourists, the hunting of these real-life dragons came into vogue as alligator-skin purses popped up in the hands of socialites as far away as New York City, London, and Paris. Alligator fever swept the globe. Seminoles, forced from their lands into the Everglades, set up roadside tourist attractions featuring live alligator wrestling shows, hoping to make a buck on the white man. Hunters came to shoot their dragons. Settlers carved up the swamp, and within half a century, the American alligator's numbers plummeted toward the brink of extinction.

By the 1960s, biologists doubted that the species would survive. It was about to go the way of the Carolina parakeet, a colorful bird that was abundant in the eastern US before hunting and habitat destruction drove it to extinction in 1904. Desperate to stop such a loss, environmentalists persuaded Congress to protect the Everglades with a series of parks and preserves. That alone seemed not to be enough. But after Congress created the Endangered Species Act of 1973, which barred the capture, killing, or trade of any plant or animal it listed as threatened or endangered, *Alligator mississippiensis* bounced back, almost miraculously so. Their numbers boomed, and in 1987, only fourteen years later, the US Fish and Wildlife Service (FWS) removed them from the endangered species list. About five million alligators call the southeastern United States home, according to estimates by the US Geological Survey. They are so plentiful now that the idea of an alligator being a nuisance—like a squirrel chewing through a telephone line—isn't so bizarre.

Even so, viewing a resource as bottomless is one of the easiest ways for it to not be so bottomless anymore. FWC feared that if poaching was left unchecked, alligator populations might decline once more. Though they seemed plentiful, there was no telling where that tipping point was between plenty and the type of sudden decline that happened seventy years ago.

This, the state's mentality of protection, did little good for the so-called nuisance alligators that Jeff was turning up, who found themselves with their mouths duct-taped shut and their feet trussed up against them in the back of a trapper's pickup truck.

Jeff cocked his head to look at the critter, inspecting the gator as if he knew what he was looking for. It stretched nearly the length of the truck bed, likely over seven feet, with scales like the tread of a semi-truck tire, that is, if a tire could gleam. Its eyes shone like dragonflies in amber. Still, it looked pitiful at this peculiar meeting at the back of a Walmart parking lot.

"Hundred bucks," the trapper said.

"I'll give you fifty."

"How about seventy-five?"

Fine, Jeff thought. At least this wasn't coming out of his own pocket. Rather, Lieutenant Wilson had dipped into a state bank account where revenue made by previous undercover operations accumulated, including money from his softshell turtles. The account wasn't bottomless. Jeff couldn't go hog wild. But it at least gave him cash to grease his introductions and let him start meeting folks at the fringes of the alligator industry.

After they shook hands, Jeff paid, and the trapper helped him transfer the gator to his truck, hoisting it between them, the trapper at the head and Jeff at the tail, and plopping it down on some towels. The whole enterprise felt surreal. This was a majestic creature, a dangerous wild predator, and here they were bartering and trading it like the catch of the day.

Despite the dodgy tinge of the whole affair—with the same feel and setting as many an exchange between poacher and buyer that Jeff had witnessed before—this transaction was completely legal. That was because the trapper was licensed and paid by the state. Jeff, too, or really Blackledge, was a legitimate alligator farmer, and had a license to buy and sell live mature alligators, hides and meat, hatchlings and eggs, as long as all those goods came from an aboveboard source. Dealers ran into trouble when they failed to examine the supply chain that carried these denizens of the swamp to their doors. Or perhaps it wasn't so much that they failed to as they casually looked the other way. Buyers couldn't be held liable for what they didn't know.

Jeff had come by this trapper's name the other way around, however. Lieutenant Wilson had given him a list of people—trappers, farmers, and the like—to investigate while sniffing out poachers. And just by this legal exchange, he couldn't be sure if the trapper was up to no good or not. After Jeff signed the check and placed it in the trapper's hand, he tried to dig a bit deeper.

Blackledge was of course new to the business, but he wanted to do right by his gators and learn as much as possible, especially about how they lived in the wild. That would help him build more comfortable habitats around his ponds, and, he hoped, that would make them more likely to breed.

"You're never gonna get them to breed," the trapper said. "It just don't happen. Most folks harvest their eggs."

Jeff nodded as if this was new information. "Still, I'd like to come out with you if that's all right."

The trapper shrugged and agreed.

Back at the farm, Jeff backed his truck up to the edge of his pond. He climbed into the bed and hoisted the gator up on his shoulders. He fireman-carried it down to the water's edge, where he lay it in the grass, cut the bindings around its legs, then quickly used his knife to slash through the tape that kept those powerful jaws closed, ripped it off like a bandage, and leapt out of the way.

After buying a dozen or so hatchlings from a farmer and adding those to the stock of mature gators—ten females and one bull, with keen hopes on them breeding if for no other reason than to prove the trapper wrong—Jeff had a farm that was beginning to look legitimate.

Solving one problem, however, caused another to pop up in its place. Now he had mouths to feed, and on a budget of exactly zero dollars. What Jeff lacked in cash, he made up for in charisma. He soon befriended the owner of a fish house over in Punta Gorda, a town at the inlet of the Peace River from the Gulf of Mexico, and he agreed to save all his scraps for Jeff, who could have them for free as long as he came to collect them.

It took half an hour for Jeff to reach the docks on the southern coast of Charlotte Harbor off the Gasparilla Sound. He parked next to the fish house and went around back, where he was met by the bloody reek of fish guts. It was coming from enormous five-gallon buckets of the stuff, and not a lid among them. A fish head stared at him glassy-eyed from the muck. *The things I do for my job*, Jeff thought. Grimacing, he lugged the buckets into the back of his truck and packed them in as tightly as he could before starting the foul trek back to Arcadia. No matter how gently he took the turns, carapaces and entrails went flying. There was no such thing as a free lunch.

In the summer months, Jeff tried to feed the alligators a few times per week. This started with the fish parts, but as he made more money—mostly from harvesting and selling alligator eggs—he began frequenting a local market in Arcadia to buy chicken quarters by the case. Each piece cost mere spare change. They felt so cheap they were practically free. He would go out with huge sacks of them, making a squeaking noise like an alligator call as he waited on the pond's bank. The gators were wary of him at first. They would float far out in the pond, watching him. It made sense. Most of them were less than six feet long and typically stood a foot or two off the ground at most, and Jeff, despite not being too great in stature, towered over them. All humans did. And if they'd encountered any humans in the wild, they knew that members of our species can be vicious predators. It was best to stay away.

But after a while, their wariness wore down to familiarity. On any given day, he would go down to the pond and begin his ritual of coaxing, calling out to them in what he hoped sounded like their mother tongue. For some, he would lay the chicken quarters out on the grass. For others, he'd gently place them into the beasts' small jaws. Some swam up calmly to grab their dinner. Others raced, jumping over one another, kicking and thrashing to get to the food, eager and hungry. But never quite so eager as Jeff would expect. He kept them well fed.

One by one they would approach. When he made a sudden movement, some would flinch away or drop their food. He would talk to them, but of course they didn't understand. Or did they? He'd pick up that dropped thigh, moving slowly, and hand it to the gator. *This human isn't so bad*, he wanted them to think.

One alligator lingered in the reeds, munching on her meal and watching him before swimming away. He wondered what she was thinking, and if it took the shape of recognizable thoughts at all.

The bull gator would always come last. He was the biggest, twelve feet or thereabouts, and he always came at his leisure, like a king. His subjects would wait for him. He glided up to the surface and toward Jeff. You had to be old to get that big, so it was possible that this bull gator had been around in the days when the species almost went extinct. Big alligators are survivors. Ornery, old, deserving of respect.

When Jeff saw the bull gator coming, he laid down the chicken parts and stepped back. "Here comes big boy," he said to himself, but it was almost like a heralding, as if a creature so immense and majestic needed to be announced when it arrived. It only felt right. Jeff watched from a safe distance, admiring the bull gator as it devoured its dinner.

Despite keeping them well fed, Jeff worried about his gators. It was his worst fear that one would get sick and die. Not only would that reflect poorly on him—always at the back of his mind was the idea that every move he made would leave a paper trail, and with that paper trail, people could criticize the agency—but having sick gators felt antithetical to his mission, namely helping to defend their species. That's why he got into this whole business in the first place, not just this job in particular but the whole shebang of wildlife protection. When it came to these gators on his farm in particular, he'd started growing attached.

He realized after days of feeding them that they were individuals. They had personalities. Some were skittish by default, others easygoing. His bull gator ruled. All of them would come when Jeff drew near even if he didn't have food. He wondered if they recognized him and had forged a bond or if they just saw him as the delivery guy.

As much as some people seemed to like alligators, Jeff found that most imagined them as dumb beasts with no inner lives. Perhaps it was because they cast such forbidding and alien figures, covered in scales instead of fur or feathers.

We grant such rich and intelligent lives to birds, who share a common lineage with alligators. Bowerbirds build complex collections, and Corvidae such as crows and Florida scrub-jays forge relationships with their favorite humans, sometimes bringing them shiny little gifts like thimbles and bottle caps. Birds remember us. Some, such as macaws, even learn and mimic human speech. Jeff's own parrot back home swore a blue streak, having picked up a few too many expletives from sitting next to his wife as she yelled at football games on TV. Other birds have recognized themselves in their reflections, leading scientists to postulate that they may possess self-awareness, consciousness. Why not alligators?

Neurological studies have shown that the brains of many non-human animals release the same neurochemicals as the ones we associate with strikingly human emotions and concepts: fear and sadness, of course, but also kinship, friendship, and love. This isn't just primates, either. Comparative neurological studies have found that even though the brains of animals traditionally associated with intelligence, such as the higher orders of primates and dolphins, are structurally more similar to those of humans, in terms of emotional resemblance it's dogs who are our closest kin. We are not anthropomorphizing our dogs when we say, for example, *He missed me*, as Jeff's did when he had to leave them behind to go undercover. They really did seem joyful when they came to visit the farm. Dogs can grieve. Dogs really do love us. Does your dog experience cognition in the same way you do? Probably not, but it's possible that animals experience emotions and cognitive schemes that *we* can't comprehend. Animals may think in esoteric signs and symbols. They may replay images of the world inside their minds. Hell, they might cogitate in an intricate language based entirely on smells.

To call someone a "birdbrain" is actually a great compliment, as the mass-to-cognitive-power ratio of a bird's brain is one of the highest in the animal world. It's not the size. It's what you do with it, or in this case, your neuronal density. Birds can solve complex problems and have intricate social structures. They have rituals and preoccupations. Alligators are similar problem solvers. They climb fences, break out of cages, sneak into backyard pools like navigating a maze. They have personalities.

People who work with animals can see, have witnessed repeatedly, that animals exhibit behaviors that the pedants of the world seem to only think exist for humans. Jeff had already gotten a taste of this in his short time as an alligator farmer. He looked into their eyes and experienced a connection. He wasn't just the guy who brought their supper. They knew him. They were individuals. Alligators—all animals, really—are so much more than we imagine. Assuming we know everything robs the world of wonder.

Jeff was learning that. He took very good care of his gators, motivated by his natural empathy and his growing relationships with them. That meant he was ready to do whatever was necessary to keep them healthy, even pumping water into the ponds when the weather got dry. It seemed like there was always work to be done, and there was always something new to learn.

In watching his gators and seeing their distinct behaviors, Jeff began to wonder: Why don't we grant the same depth of possibility to birds' scalier cousins, the alligators? He mused that perhaps we fail to allow alligators to have inner lives because we categorize them as frightening, the ancient, the other. We don't see our own faces in the shape of theirs, and this is one of the problems that hinders their conservation.

If I could change people's minds, he thought, *and make them see alligators for what they're really like, they would understand what makes them worth saving.*

Knowing his gators, too, helped him forge ahead through the coming trials. As his mission began to seem more and more impossible, he would look out at the reptilian eyes peeping at him from the surface of the pond, realize that they were watching him, and remember his purpose: to save the forgotten creatures, the ugly things, the scaly things, the things it seemed no one loved except for him.

7

MERMAID IVORY

Chokoloskee, Florida, is a small village on an island within the Ten Thousand Islands chain, a many-faceted archipelago of tangled mangroves, sloughs, and flows with evocative names like Lostmans River, Hell Gate, and Blackwater Bay. Peg Brown reigned as a legendary alligator poacher for decades in the Ten Thousand Islands before hanging up his bang stick in the 1960s or 1970s. Knowing that I liked tales of that sort, an editor at the *Miami Herald* had given me a tip. He had grown up with Peg, knew him a bit but not well, though it seemed everyone down there knew his legend. The editor told me I should look into contacting Peg's family, but first I had to read a particular story in *Tropic*, a defunct magazine insert of the *Herald* that ceased printing decades ago. No physical copies of the story seemed to exist, not even in microfiche. But there was one scanned copy in an archive. I read it, and I wanted more. It was just a taste of the story that was to come.

"Truth to tell, there's nothing much you can do with alligator hides anymore, the future having dropped slap off that particular dodge some few years ago. But the old ways die hard, and there is probably no such thing as a truly retired poacher," John Rothchild wrote in *Tropic*. These two sentences open Rothchild's story "Poacher," published June 18, 1978. I became obsessed with these two lines. Their commanding, eccentric voice smacks with the golden age of gonzo journalism. I'm ready to jump in, and then it just keeps getting better.

"Peg Brown, they say, is the most outrageous alligator poacher who ever lived," Rothchild continued. "And now that the statute of limitations has run out on anything he is alleged to have done in his time, he'll modestly concede that he's sent probably 10,000 gators to the promised land."

Peg snuck around the swamp, bamboozling rangers, barely scraping out of danger, always ready to dupe his pursuers but never firing a single shot their way. Even poachers have standards. Peg seemed larger than life, by degrees a classic rogue and an archetypal trickster. The stories of him had transcended mere rumor and cast him squarely in the level of legend. He was a folk hero. All Peg Brown stories, I began to see, took the same shape as traditional trickster folktales: one wily hero, for better or worse, against the powers that be. Although he could have beaten the rangers with violence, he battled them with cunning and humor instead. He was a stand-in for the little man, giving him hope that one day he, too, could face impossible odds and win.

By the late 1960s, rangers were making regular overnight patrols. They caught some alligator poachers, but others, they knew, were still at large. They chased after them by boat and by chopper. They had even heard the stories of Peg Brown, the same tales in which they played sheriffs of Nottingham to his Robin Hood and Merry Men. I wondered what they thought about being the villains in these powerful tales of an underdog's triumph. No doubt they felt as Jeff did about his job, that they were following a righteous calling to protect the wild. That feeling of righteousness can be dangerous. Though not without difficulty, Jeff was able to hold that calling in his head in harmony with his compassion for those people committing crimes. Countless others in wildlife law enforcement resist such empathy for their fellow man, considering it at odds with their duty. They begin to see the world under a false pall of black and white, full of good guys and bad guys instead of real people making hard decisions to stay alive. When you lose sight of that, righteous thinking can justify the worst kinds of evils.

In that view, the escalation of force against Peg and his compatriots seems unfair. Facing those odds is also what made him an underdog in the first place. Rather than a villain, he was a renegade outlaw sticking up for his community and working to feed his family. By night, he faced down all of the park service's firepower. Yet they never caught him.

Of course, no matter how good "Poacher" was, it wasn't enough to satisfy my obsession. "There are so many Peg Brown stories in currency that at this point they all have names," wrote Rothchild. I wanted to hear every last one of them. Not only would understanding these stories—and the people behind them—give me deeper insight into the culture of the Everglades, but discovering the real history behind the Peg Brown tales would also grant me an unbeatable look into the hearts and minds of the poachers of the past and the ones in the present who had taken up their mantle as latter-day Robin Hoods and tellers of tales. It was hard to tell where Peg Brown's legend stopped and the man began, so I knew the truth had to be one hell of a story.

I started digging. I found almost nothing else about Peg other than a few fishing tournament wins, and a mention or two in his brother's book, *Totch: A Life in the Everglades*. A veteran journalist friend of mine swore up and down that that brother, Loren "Totch" Brown, was the real alligator poacher in the family. As good a journalist as my friend was, I had my doubts. The story was missing something, and now it had conflict. It seemed as though the family had room for only one major alligator poacher. That meant one of them was a legend and the other was a liar. I had to know who. I reached out to the Browns. Over the past few years, rural journalism has gotten all the more difficult as propaganda has surged through the internet and turned mild distrust for journalists into outright hatred. I have been cussed out and threatened and stalked, all for doing little more than introducing myself. I can usually turn people around: In person, I don't exactly look threatening. A smile and a sincere handshake go a long way. But having noticed the distrust for society in general borne by the people of the Everglades, I knew I would need to get down to Chokoloskee and show them I was sincere.

I was surprised that it wasn't too hard to get in touch with Peg's surviving relatives. Nearly one in three people in the town, it seemed, had the surname Brown. Even some of the ones who weren't named Brown were family, too. After a series of calls, everyone referred me to Kent Daniels, whose business card, if he had one, would say RACONTEUR. Kent was the unofficial mayor, press officer, historian, and one-person welcoming committee for Chokoloskee. Kent was half Seminole, but he didn't belong to the tribe. He didn't really take a shine to being told what to do. To him, the tribe was just another form of authority to avoid. Kent offered to introduce me to Chokoloskee and that lower edge of the Everglades, give me a tour and tell me the stories behind everything we saw, including and especially the legends of Peg Brown. He could also give me invaluable insight from the Native perspective without having to pass through the tribal council's filter. I hoped his stories would help me see the other side of Jeff's operation, understand the alleged poachers' motivation beyond just money in a way those particular men themselves could not have put into words. They were too close to what happened. Some of the other men I talked to in Chokoloskee, alleged poachers themselves, had no skin in that game. And contrary to the men Jeff ran into, these guys wore the name *poacher* as a badge of honor and tacked on *alleged* with a wink and a nudge. I would meet up with them later so I could see the wilderness from their viewpoint without getting tangled up in the law.

Kent said when I got down there—essentially a straight shot down the middle of Florida from where I lived in Orlando—I could find him in the lobby of a little waterside motel called Outdoor Resorts of Chokoloskee, an establishment owned by—you guessed it—more Browns. When I walked in, I looked around, confused at how it seemed there was a small, poorly lit convenience store and tackle shop attached to the lobby without a partition. The men sitting around the front table all gave me a look like I didn't belong there. I went up to the desk to introduce myself and ask after Kent.

"I'm Kent," one of the men behind me called. "You must be Rebecca Renner."

"Guilty as charged," I said. The group of chatters' expressions had changed, opened up, welcoming. One gave up his seat, and they invited me to talk with them before Kent and I set out. When they heard why I was there, they took turns exchanging stories. It was like being back home, before so many of my family members had died, in a time when we'd sit on my grandmother's dock and the old folks would tell stories about the river and the ocean, and how the past had played out along the sandy banks. That was perhaps why I became so taken with Chokoloskee, its stories, its people: They reminded me of a home that I thought only existed in my memory, one that I believed I would never see again, because the swamps were razed, developed, and polluted, and as the estuaries faded, the stories faded with them until it seemed the only one who remembered them was me. As I listened to them, I heard the long-lost kin of my own history, a missing part of myself that I hadn't realized was gone.

Each of the men took a turn telling me a related story until they all seemed to coalesce into a single yarn spun with Craig Daniels, Kent's younger relative, at the lead. Craig is the type of character you can't get away with in fiction. He is just too much to be true, and yet there he was, sitting right there before me: a local pastor who was missing a finger, who had been shot and gone to prison, who preached with the same panache he used in telling poaching stories. He said a gator took his finger. He was Peg Brown's grandson. It was Sunday morning, and he was about to leave to lead his congregation, but first he had to regale me with a little violent family history.

When the national park came in, it pushed everyone there off their land, the Brown and Daniels families included. Even if they hadn't lived within that tract, they had all fished or hunted there, and with the nearest dose of civilization apart from the hamlet of Everglades City about forty miles away in Naples, most made their livelihood off the land. The Browns made most of their money fishing and hunting, so they kept on doing just that with the additional obstacle of running from the law while they were at it. They were a hardy and raucous bunch, stubborn the same way that was in my blood. (My own apocryphal family story says that my great-great-uncle disappeared into the swamp in those same days and went south, perhaps to Everglades City. Wherever he went, no one in the family heard from him again, so there's no telling where he turned up, if he turned up at all.)

"Tell her the one with the hammer," Kent said, gesturing at Craig.

"Oh, that one," Craig said. "Are you sure she can handle it?"

I see what you're doing, I thought. They were baiting the story, tag-team style. I knew how this went. I was supposed to say, "I can handle anything." And so I did.

"Are you sure?" Craig said. "This one's not for the faint of heart."

"Good thing there's nobody like that here," I said.

Craig grinned. He seemed tickled that I was in on the show. "All right. Once, maybe thirty years ago, my uncle—his name was Floyd Brown—was out hunting. Killing gators. Where he was, there were so many that they'd been watching him as he did it. Hundreds of eyes watching him from the water. Every time he'd kill one, another would jump out. Bang! He'd have to shoot it. They were nearly on top of him. There were so many he was running out of ammunition."

"How many were there?" I asked, knowing that was my next line, too.

"Oh, hundreds," Craig said.

"At least," Kent said. "Over a thousand."

"He had to keep going, or he was going to get ripped to pieces," Craig said. "Jump, bang, jump, bang!—and then he ran out of bullets."

Had I been anyone else, I would have thought they were lying to me just to yank my chain. But I knew better. In the storytelling tradition that I come from, yarn spinners employ hyperbole to create evocative and memorable images, and to get the visceral feeling of the story across.

"And then he used a hammer?" I asked.

"Yep, it was the only thing he had," Craig said. "If he didn't think of something, they were gonna eat him alive. So he looks around his pitpan and sees the ball-peen hammer, and knows that's what's gonna save his life."

"How's that work?" I asked. "How do you kill a gator with a ball-peen hammer?"

Craig swung his hand, wielding an invisible hammer at Kent's head. "Whack! You put its lights out."

"But that made 'em madder, didn't it?" Kent asked.

"Absolutely," Craig said. "They were mad as hell. They started coming faster. But Floyd was a machine. He just kept going. Jump, whack, jump, whack! Thousands of them."

How many gators did Floyd really kill? The number didn't matter, but Floyd's resourcefulness did, and the hyperbole amplified that. He was overwhelmed. But he made do with what he had. There was a stubbornness in this family. And that wasn't the end of it.

In those days, the men said, taking turns filling in the story, just seeing a man committing a crime wasn't enough to arrest him. Rangers had to physically catch poachers to bring them in. When the rangers spotted him, Floyd had to leave the thousands of alligators he'd just killed with only a ball-peen hammer behind. That happened with many a story, the law always on the tail of the heroes, who made it just in the nick of time. The heroes were nefarious, but they were still good folks, deep down. They had their reasons. They also had their standards. In this family, poaching was fine, but you didn't steal from your neighbor.

All these stories orbited around kernels of truth. The most ridiculous parts of them were liable to be true. Obvious hyperbole aside, spinning yarns takes sanding down the edges of a story to make it easier to swallow, not adding outlandish things that don't belong. Though sometimes you meet someone who abides by a different tradition of backwoods storytelling: When at all possible do as Peg did with his high jinks, and bamboozle the outsider. I knew how to spot it when it came along, of course. I'd done it before, myself.

After their stories petered out, Kent assumed his role as my tour guide. He insisted that we take my Honda Civic and that I drive, something I warned would not make for a comfortable ride, not to mention that I wouldn't be able to take notes, but my complaints went unanswered. He should have known better when we reached my car, and he saw that an empty cylinder remained where the driver's-side lock had once been. But there was no changing his mind. Too stubborn, I guessed. I reassured myself that it would be okay. I would figure it out. I always did. So we boarded my jalopy and set off in search of his tales of the Everglades and other yarn spinners who would pick up the story along the way.

Kent gave me verbal directions and nagged me to follow the speed limit. We cruised back through the mangroves to the mainland, where we pulled into the Rod & Gun Club, a hotel with a bar and restaurant that looked like the kind of place Hemingway would have frequented. A twelve-foot gator skin stretched across the wall over the billiard table. In the gleaming cherrywood of a small back barroom, Kent gestured to the bar and said this was where the storytelling magic happened. All the poachers would come here, drink, and exchange tales of pulling one over on the law. Though Kent was a yarn spinner and perhaps a long-retired smuggler, he had never been a poacher himself. He didn't seem like the type who would have liked killing things, even out of necessity. Later one of the men who had been a poacher back in the day refuted Kent's claim that they frequented the Rod & Gun. That place was for Yankees and tourists, he said. Celebrities went there. The poachers went for something with rougher edges and lower prices. They frequented a pub called the Oyster Bar, which had long since gone belly-up but lived on in the stories of the stories that were spun there.

As Kent shot the breeze with a woman in the kitchen, I listened, just taking everything in. They talked about local businesses on hard times. The woman, Patty, mistook me for the daughter of a local, and I thought about that long-lost great-uncle of mine, and I wondered if when he'd allegedly disappeared into the swamp he'd wound up down in Everglades City. In these parts, it wasn't outside the realm of possibility.

With his social call over, Kent led me back to my car and directed me to drive farther inland. I obeyed, interviewing him along the way with my digital recorder rolling in the cupholder so I could keep my hands on the wheel.

Some interviews, you have to ask a lot of questions. But Kent seemed to need no prompting. He directed me to drive toward the swamp, noting landmarks along the way so I could come back later. As we ventured deeper into Big Cypress Swamp, passing the ranger station into the national preserve, flat marshes of sawgrass, wire grass, bulrushes, and canebrake extended past the road in seemingly endless plains. Far off, a line of slash pines bristled from the saw palm scrub. We passed the "official" skunk ape research headquarters, an exhibit dedicated to Florida's odoriferous answer to Bigfoot. Islands of cabbage palm or larger cypress domes sprang up in the middle of these wetlands where the water belowground gathered in deeper pools in the limestone. Gradually, this more majestic growth overtook us, and we entered the swamp proper. Big Cypress National Preserve is larger than the state of Rhode Island. The entirety of New York City could fit inside it three times over, and there would still be room.

Hardwood hammocks like rain forests cast the rich understory into a tranquil gloom. An exuberance of bromeliads issued from the boughs of trees like fireworks. I would later venture deeper there on my own and sit beside a pool that had collected in the shadows where a dozen or so alligators swam, undulating away out of sight, or drifted, sleeping. Some watched me as if expecting food. Overcome by the peace of the place, I sat and listened as the purple cast of gloaming shifted into the evening dark, and the hot buzz of katydids gave way to the thousand voices of frogs and toads in chorus. It met the shimmer of the crickets' song and the mysterious plink of drops into water. I wanted to be like Jeff, to be able to recognize every voice in the night music. To know each name was to know the swamp itself. I wasn't there yet. But I recorded the enchanting songs so I could figure it out when I once again returned to the electric world of Wi-Fi. There was something extraordinary in the wonder I felt in hearing those enigmatic calls. I wanted to know everything, but I couldn't let answers wash away my sense of wonder.

That trek would all happen much later. Right then, me and my Honda Civic were about to be in trouble.

"Turn here," Kent said, pointing to a dirt road, one that had no sign that I could see.

"Are you sure?" I asked.

"Would I lead you wrong?" Kent said.

I don't know, would you? I thought. "Where are we going?" I asked as I turned.

"Through the swamp," he said. "I want to show you something."

Something about tomatoes. He was talking so fast I could barely register one idea before he jumped to the next. The canal along that trail existed because of the tomato farmers, he said. I was willing to believe him, but I saw no tomato farms there, just pine and palms in scrubland as far as the eye could see—except for the road, if you could call it that. A trail of calcified shells ground into bone-white sand stretched on into the distance until it dissolved at the horizon in a billowing white sandstorm. There was no way to tell where we were going or how far away from there we would reach the end. If there was an end.

The turbulent ground under my tires jarred the car so violently that it threatened to knock something loose. I can drive in just about any conditions, but at a certain point I, too, succumb to the limits of logic and physics. By then, we were several miles outside of cell contact from anyone who might come to the rescue. At every clank, I imagined something important falling from the undercarriage, like a rear axle or my entire engine block, and I knew that if we broke down there, I would be walking back to the ranger station by myself in that vengeful summer heat, regretting every decision I'd ever made that led me up to that moment. Tropical heat has that effect on people.

Unperturbed, Kent kept talking. I never had to ask a question. He never left any dead air. He talked about the effects of farming and the parks on the people. There was oil drilling, too. Every manner of industry was allowed in the glades, as long as you had enough money to do it. Anything was legal if you knew which palms to grease.

But the changes to Florida really started with the Spanish conquest, he said.

I nodded, interested. That was just the kind of thing I wanted to hear about, conquest from the Seminole perspective. I didn't dare look at him, afraid he'd stop talking to scold me about keeping my eyes on the road.

The Spanish even changed the environment, he said. I knew they'd logged to build ships, as did other settlers all along the coasts for centuries. Magnificent bald cypress groves had fallen to become masts and planks, dock pilings, shingles, caskets.

"Here's something you might not know," Kent said. "Manatees are an invasive species! The Spanish brought them along for food, used them like livestock. Tastes like pork."

Huh?

I had to interrupt him there. "I'm sorry, what? Manatees?" The Spanish had released a variety of invasive species upon their so-called New World, among them the mustang horses of the West and the wild boars whose populations have boomed across the southeastern United States and California, plus regions of Chile, Argentina, Uruguay, Paraguay, and Brazil. (Tenacious and destructive boogers. Well traveled, too.) But manatees? *That's not right*, I thought.

"Yeah, manatee steak," Kent said. "Great on the grill." Not that he would shoot one, he said, because the animals were protected, but Kent thought they shouldn't be, and it was a conspiracy that they were.

"But—but manatees are from here," I said. When I'm interviewing, I try not to interrupt. I'd rather be a fly on the wall and listen, getting the unadulterated tale from my subject, whatever that tale may be. That meant learning to let people be wrong. But I have my limits.

"Manatees are from the West Indies," Kent said pointedly. "Their full name is the West Indian manatee. They're from India."

The West Indies is the Caribbean, I thought. I shot him a confused and beseeching look before quickly returning my gaze to the dust-clouded road. Kent was such a knowledgeable fellow. He'd seemed so smart up until then. *He can't actually believe this*, I thought. *Is he trying to screw with me?*

I had read a few other magazine articles reported from Chokoloskee before I'd ventured down there, and in every last one, there had been major gaffes in fact, real howlers clearly gleaned from local sources that any journalist familiar with South Florida would know to be untrue. Although they may not have hoodwinked visitors anymore, as tourism had become Chokoloskee's lifeline and main industry, it seemed that bamboozling writers had remained a time-honored tradition here. The only story I read that passed was from Peter Matthiessen, the author of the award-winning novel *Shadow Country*. Ironically, I would end up working in Matthiessen's shadow, as several of the old-timers whom I interviewed said that I was the second journalist they'd ever talked to, the first being Matthiessen himself nearly half a century ago.

Kent went on, deriding manatees, saying people should be able to hunt them. Hunters would come in droves if they had any idea how much mermaid ivory was worth. According to Kent, mermaid ivory was the name for the ivory derived from manatee bones, which he said was worth hundreds of dollars per piece. A single manatee could bring in thousands.

Mermaid ivory? I thought, incredulous and a bit offended. *Do I look like I just fell off the turnip truck?*

"Yes, there's so much people from outside don't know," Kent said. "Such as, mangroves are invasive, too."

What? I went into this interview knowing Kent had a propensity for embellishment, but at that point I knew I'd have to sit down and comb through his assertions one by one to disentangle the facts from the shenanigans. *Man, you are giving me more work than you realize.*

"The whole Everglades has changed," he said. "People who aren't from here don't realize. The whole place is unrecognizable. Nothing looks like it did fifty years ago. If you showed me a picture of all this back then, I wouldn't know the place." The big trees had disappeared. The mangroves had migrated. I'd never heard anything about that, but just because I hadn't heard of it before didn't mean it wasn't true. I reminded myself to withhold judgment.

A thick cloud of sand descended upon us, completely whiting out my windshield. Wary of continuing forward, I slowed to a crawl and put my wipers on. Their rubber strips proceeded to unravel from the blades, and they screeched back and forth across the glass, smearing the sand, tatters flapping in the wind.

Oh, for fuck's sake, I thought.

I sighed and looked at Kent. "It'll be okay," I said, my tone falsely sunny.

"You need new windshield wipers," he said.

No, really? I thought. I rolled down my window and stuck my head out so I could see, and we set off again. Out of the corner of my eye, I could see him staring at me, judgmental and vaguely horrified.

I had gone down there to get to know the people by seeing past the Florida Man clichés. Now here I was acting like a Florida Woman.

"Turn those things off," Kent said. "You're gonna damage your glass."

He was right. I turned off the wipers, parked the car, and got out to clean the windshield with a rag as best I could. When I got back in, he told me to drive to Naples to get new wipers and to do so before it rained or I was in real trouble. He said he wouldn't take me anywhere else until I did that, which, okay, I admit was reasonable.

Several hours later, we made it out of the glades more or less intact, I treated Kent to dinner, and then, after dark, retired to my dockside motel room, exhausted, where I copied down notes from the day and started fact-checking. Manatees, of course, are endemic to Florida and the Caribbean. As are mangroves, but I had more questions there: Could mangroves have migrated into that portion of the glades? It didn't seem impossible. Kudzu had spread across the Southeast within a generation. But if mangroves were endemic, what could cause such a mass migration? To my surprise, the most outlandish of Kent's claims was true. Mermaid ivory is real.

Although it bears a mythical name, mermaid ivory comes from the bones of real animals in the order Sirenia, a name derived from the Greek Σειρῆνες, the Sirens who transfix sailors with their beguiling songs and lure them to their deaths in the deep. By the time they appeared in medieval bestiaries, these Sirens had become mermaids much as we know them today. According to legend, sailors mistook manatees for mermaids. Anyone who has seen these Rubenesque mammals up close knows those delightful tales are questionable at best. Nonetheless, it follows that their bones would take on a florid name like mermaid ivory. Most of the mermaid ivory on the market comes from fossils of the Steller's sea cow, another member of the Sirenia order that went extinct in 1768. Because the animal is extinct, trade of this mermaid ivory is legal. However, trade of manatee bones is not, as they're protected internationally under the Convention on International Trade in Endangered Species of Wild Fauna and Flora (CITES) and in the US under the Marine Mammal Protection Act, the Endangered Species Act, and others. Some of the first-ever conservation laws were ratified to protect manatees.

Mermaid ivory, who would have thought. I was so excited to learn something new, even if it wasn't the story I was chasing. I went to sleep in that blessèd air-conditioning, imagining what other new discoveries the next day's adventures had in store.

The next morning as storm clouds darkened the skies, I made the hour trek from Chokoloskee to Naples, the closest city and my most realistic hope of resuscitating my car. By the time I made it back to the Ten Thousand Islands, a wet wind told me the storms would blow over. I called Kent. As the sun peeked out from behind the clouds, he insisted it was going to pour. If I was dead set on getting wet, he said, I could talk to someone else. But, he added, "Call me if you run into any trouble, and I'll get you sorted out."

I think he's done with me, I thought.

So I called Jonnie Brown. Jonnie was one of Peg's many sons, and so he had firsthand stories of that legendary poacher. If Kent had been the keeper of the tall tales, Jonnie was my closest hope to seeing past the tales to the real man who had inspired them. Though I'd talked to him several times on the phone, I hadn't met him in person yet. I enjoyed the sound of his voice, a throaty drawl particular to the backwoods of Florida. He sounded like a large, imposing man. He reminded me of my father, especially when he checked in on me and said things like, "Everybody's being nice to you, *right?*"—the implication being that he'd knock their heads together if they weren't.

When the phone rang, he answered fairly quickly, happy to hear from me. I told him what was up, what I'd done the day before, and how Kent had canceled our plans and left me with the day open.

"You know he's a *bullshitter*, right?" Jonnie said.

I had to laugh.

"I'm aware that Kent is an—expert embellisher."

Jonnie laughed, too.

We'd gotten lucky, he said. He happened to be free all day, and we made plans to go out on an adventure. This time, thank God, we'd take his 4x4 truck.

Together we would delve into the Everglades and into the past, and I would come to see Peg as his son saw him, as a man of many opposites: a quiet man and a storyteller, a rough customer and a smooth talker, a moonshiner and a war hero, a poacher and an outdoorsman, an adventurer and a dad. Jonnie would also offer me a glimpse of the wild from the poachers' perspective. Though far from legendary, he had followed in his father's footsteps. Surrounded by the true places from the legends, I would become a part of their story in a way that I could never have predicted.

8

GOLDEN EGGS

Moths and beetles flicked around the yellow-tinged light above the barn door. Despite the season, winter by then, the night was always alive—especially the air, which teemed with every manner of biting and stinging thing. Jeff and Lieutenant Wilson ducked under that winged cloud and into the coolness of the barn. With its concrete-block walls, the air always felt a little wet, but it was welcome nonetheless. They chitchatted back and forth about what Jeff had been doing.

"How far have you gotten on your list?" Lieutenant Wilson asked.

The most crucial, but still frustrating, tool in Jeff's arsenal was his list of names. They were people who'd applied for permits, people who'd once been arrested for alligator and alligator-adjacent crimes, and other folks who handled alligators, like trappers, who may have had ample opportunity to do some illegal sales or smuggling just by the nature of their jobs. Had they already? Who knew. It was Jeff's job to find out.

"I've gone out with a few trappers," Jeff said, "nobody I've seen doing anything illegal."

Lieutenant Wilson nodded, his expression businesslike. "And the farmers?"

"That's where I'm having some trouble," Jeff said. "Lot of doors slammed in my face, both figuratively and actually."

Jeff had started cold-calling the people on the list, working his way down. No one wanted to talk. On some calls, the person on the other end hung up immediately. After going through nearly the whole list like that, Jeff realized he needed a better plan.

"Do they suspect anything?" Lieutenant Wilson asked.

"Not as far as I can tell," Jeff said. The possibility of being found out, the fear even, always lingered at the back of his mind.

"Well, keep trying," Lieutenant Wilson said. "That's not why I'm here tonight. I'm here to discuss a concern with you." *Oh shit*, Jeff thought.

A previous visitor, a higher-up from FWC, had raised a potential issue: If the neighborhood kids climbed Jeff's outer fence, then the fence around the pond, they could be killed by a gator. A death—anyone's death—would put an end to Sunshine Alligator Farm and possibly to the investigation entirely.

As far-fetched as the possibility seemed, it started the gears of worry turning in Jeff's brain. He'd been so focused on the gators that he hadn't considered that anyone might want to break into an alligator farm. But "Florida Man Brandishes Alligator at Walmart Checkout Counter" has to get his gators from somewhere. While it was possible that teenagers might sneak into the farm, as teenagers in the middle of nowhere will be teenagers in the middle of nowhere, Jeff's greater concerns were meth addicts, weirdos, and anyone else who'd wised up to the fact that the price of alligator eggs and skins was skyrocketing.

In the previous year, flooding along the Lower Mississippi Delta caused thousands of alligator nests to become unviable. Just as in Florida, Louisiana alligator farmers relied on permits to harvest wild alligator eggs to maintain their stocks of hatchlings. As the number of eggs and hatchlings coming in dwindled, Louisiana farmers turned to other sources and were ready to pay ten times what they had before for these now golden eggs. The rumor around the industry was that many farmers relied on poachers. But if they could prove they didn't know the origin of the eggs, they could escape prosecution, even if their poacher—or thief—suppliers got caught. So poachers got in the habit of falsifying harvesting or farming documents, or bills of sale, and the most unscrupulous among the farmers stopped asking questions.

It was no surprise then that other farmers across South Florida had seen an influx in alligator thieves. By night, camouflaged shadows would cut fence wires and duck in. Hunters in their normal lives, they would sneak by the light of headlamps to grab eggs by the tray and baby gators by the dozen. They already had all the equipment they needed for backcountry espionage. They had the waders and the guns and the ammunition. They had the boots. They had the false foliage to lay over themselves, becoming part of the brush. More often than not, they were also packing enough desperation to do something stupid in the name of quick cash in their wallets. Learning this, Jeff knew he couldn't be too careful.

On that visit, Lieutenant Wilson helped Jeff devise a series of listening and recording devices to place around the farm.

"You won't be seeing as much of me anymore," Lieutenant Wilson said as he was getting into his own truck to leave. "I'll be dropping information packets in your mailbox. Otherwise, you're on your own."

The next day, Jeff put up game cams, also known as trail cams: small, weatherproof surveillance cameras made to record outdoors. They were especially useful at night, when they were designed to pick up the smallest movements on a dark trail. He stationed them so they observed the exterior doors, and then he put one at the gate so that it might track movements out there, even cars that pulled in to turn around. It all served to keep him wary. He never knew when the short flash of a pickup truck might be thieves casing the place for later. He became vigilant about break-ins and keenly aware, in the quiet of the night, just how alone he really was out there. The cameras could only do so much. The real deterrent was him, his lights on in the camper, his silhouette against the dark, his dog barking from inside, the low growl that warned about its ready jaws.

As the farm grew, his work there became less and less of a charade. He finagled an official permit for his alligator farm, evading the inspector (a man whom he knew from the agency) in the process. Get recognized by just one person from your old life, and the mission would be over. He disguised his voice over the phone like some cartoon villain. He made excuses not to be at the farm while the inspector came around. Now on to the little details. He needed it to look like a real business. He made business cards that said SUNSHINE ALLIGATOR FARM, along with the farm's contact details. He concocted a website. He got into designing the whole thing, exactly, he felt, like a real business owner would.

He wanted T-shirts, mugs! *Calm down, Jeff,* he told himself. *Don't start bleeding money before you've gotten the show on the road.* So instead, he did the sober thing and drove around town, tacking the card to the community boards at the feed stores and the Tractor Supply. He wanted people to know the farm existed. He was open for business, no trap set yet. He needed to get a lay of the land first.

And just like that, Sunshine became a real alligator farm. The perfectionist in Jeff grated at how haphazard the farm looked, but as he invested deeper, he came to understand how the farm's imperfections weren't flaws but, oddly, details that made it look more real. The more perfect it seemed, the less realistic it would be. So finally, flaws and all, his farm, his set, had come to fruition, complete with real bills to pay.

The agency wasn't about to cough up for any of that: They couldn't. It wasn't just that such a paper trail would have blown Jeff's cover, and paying in cash would have raised suspicion; the agency didn't have any money to spare.

What he needed more than anything was help from people who knew better. If he could make a connection with an alligator farmer, just one person who knew how to make this all work, he could overcome all the worries he had about taking care of his gators and really start digging into his investigation in earnest. Such help, however, had not appeared.

As one would expect in a subculture so entrenched in the moneyed Old South, the alligator industry was not exactly welcoming to outsiders. Jeff continued to reach out to farms, cold-calling them or chatting up their managers at meetings the state held to apprise the farmers of the current state of the wild alligator population—and how many eggs the law entitled them to harvest that season. They would smile and shake hands, ever polite and cordial. As my father, in his life an old southern man himself, would say: They had cultivated a talent for so gracefully telling a man to go to hell that he left looking forward to the trip.

Desperate to make connections, Jeff began frequenting local bars. While he wouldn't exactly have called himself a city slicker, these weren't the kinds of establishments he was used to. A man of Jeff's age greatly preferred his own backyard or a family cookout to the watering holes in

Arcadia, with their Western-style saloon signs, polished wood paneling, and colored-glass lamps that hung over the tables. The crack of billiard balls punctuated the laments of country songs on the radio.

Jeff didn't do any drinking. Things got tricky if you let your faculties fog over with even a few beers. Still, he had to make it look real. He'd order a longneck and nurse it, making conversation and taking mental notes for a while. Then he'd head to the bathroom, taking his beer with him. He'd pour it out and replace what he'd spilled out with water. Always a little on edge, he'd look around again then head back to his conversation. If he was there long enough, he'd have to imagine the alcohol he hadn't drunk loosening his tongue. *Talk too much. Make it realistic. But always be ready with an ear for someone to divulge his secrets.*

Still, for all that work, the leads he found this way dwindled into nothing.

It was more than just an unwillingness to reveal trade secrets. It was that Jeff was not one of them. He was an unknown commodity. An outsider. And no matter how kind and hospitable you are to an outsider, wisdom said not to trust him—that is, until he showed you who he was. The more doors shut in his face, the more Jeff began to wonder if they detected, even if they couldn't put it into words, that something was off about him. People were perceptive that way, Jeff had learned after a lifetime of studying them in his encounters with poachers and hunters in the field. It was the same way a doe might scent a threat on the wind, a hunter watching in a blind, still as can be yet human and alive and breathing.

Jeff *wasn't* who he said he was. There *was* something off about him. And when it came down to it, he couldn't go any deeper, couldn't slough off his memories, his duties, his former life—could he?

The next weekend, Jeff went home, and as they always did, he and his wife, Sandy, traded war stories, tales from the trenches of their jobs. She detailed her students' antics. He talked about how he was up against the impossible, and he had even more work now that Lieutenant Wilson wanted him to not only keep a log but file a report on nearly every move he made.

"Wipe your ass?" Jeff joked. "Write a report on it."

Sandy laughed. She was chopping vegetables for their dinner as the dogs ganged around their feet and the parrot squawked in the living room, knowing it was nearly dinnertime.

"What's worse is that he expects me to do it all on this damn thing," Jeff said, gesturing to his state laptop where he sat at their kitchen island. "But I'm not allowed to keep it at the farm. Oh no, they're not allowed to make things that easy on me. Instead I have to waste my precious time with you doing this." He would have preferred to be cooking with her instead of sitting around typing.

"It's all right," Sandy said. "But what if—you did bring it with you?"

"George said I can't," Jeff answered, referring to Lieutenant Wilson by his first name. They had become that familiar by then. "Somebody might find it."

"You've hidden a bunch of other things," she said. "Why not that? It's not like he's there looking over your shoulder."

She was always his voice of reason. He'd already thought of bringing his computer, of course, but had balked at this small act of disobedience. Turned out, all he needed was a little push.

When Jeff returned to the farm, he snooped around for another "hidey-hole," as he called them. He hollowed out a section like a shelf behind a pegboard wall and tucked his laptop inside. Guilt nagged at him about disobeying Lieutenant Wilson like that, but every time he needed to write a report and the computer was right there, pragmatism and relief won out, and he shooed the guilt away.

Over the months, he and Lieutenant Wilson had developed an increasingly complicated relationship. Jeff liked the man and trusted him completely. He could say that in all honesty. When this was over, and the lieutenant was no longer his commanding officer, he could see them being friends. Yet as the operation went on, it became apparent that they didn't see the world the same way. Lieutenant Wilson saw things as black-and-white, the "good guys" versus the "bad guys." Jeff knew reality fell in shades of gray, that the "bad guy" you met in the woods could be a decent fellow having a bad day. Lieutenant Wilson expected unfailing perfection. As perfect as Jeff wanted to be—and he strived to do everything in his job and in his life by the letter—reality often reminded him of his martial arts training: The strongest men are like bamboo. When adversity pushes against them, they bend, because if you don't bend, you break. The agent who had come before him in the operation had broken and then failed. Jeff couldn't be like him. He had to bend. So he hid the computer. Even though he went home less and less as the investigation picked up, the time he spent there was his lifeline. Without having to write reports, he could be fully present. He could remember who he was. Jeff Babauta.

On the other side of that coin, he could be fully present at the farm, too. He could inhabit the essence of Curtis Blackledge. That was increasingly important, as Blackledge really had some work to do. Running a farm was a never-ending cycle. As soon as money came in, it seemed to go out.

If he didn't think of something, he'd have to dip into his own funds to feed his gators. As an alligator farmer, he did have one option. He could legally go out into the swamps and harvest alligator eggs, but that was risky without anyone willing to teach him. His best resource ended up being an episode of *Dirty Jobs*, a show that revealed the greasiest, the muddiest, the filthiest, and the grittiest careers America had to offer. As he hunched in the glow of his laptop screen in the camper, watching the show's host wade through the filth, Jeff looked on the bright side that at least now there wouldn't be any surprises. Or so he hoped. What choice did he have?

When the summer months came, Jeff woke on a misty morning, when sawgrass pierced those earthbound clouds, humidity so thick in the air you could drink it, and condensation beaded on the cold camper panes like the outside of a glass of iced tea. It was finally nesting season. He packed up his truck and headed low into the wetlands, whispers of the night's rhythm parting for the new day's pulse, the nocturnal chorus giving way to solitary singing somewhere high in the loblolly pines from a seven-story vantage over the savanna, a lonesome sentinel to the daybreak.

Permit in hand, Jeff joined two plainclothes officers, and together they worked methodically over the marshy terrain in search of alligator nests. This had to be careful work. Despite all that ambient serenity, danger hovered, too, at ground level with the mist. There were your usual hazards: wild boars, poison ivy, rattlesnakes shivering out a warning from their hideouts in the brush. A checklist of these occupied a space at the back of Jeff's mind, not a worry so much as a readiness. He knew from years of practice that the swamp only posed a threat to the uninformed, the unprepared.

But wasn't he one of the nearly clueless now, out there picking through the weeds? Seeking out the stinking lairs of these armor-clad anachronisms and hoping Mama Gator wasn't there to protect her eggs? It seemed like a bad idea all around, but he had to do it.

Back when he was Jeff Babauta, if someone like a park visitor or a friend from up north had asked him how to stay safe around alligators, he would have said: *You don't* stay *around them at all*. See a gator and get out of its way. It seemed obvious, really, and it was more or less the natural reaction visitors—and most people—had to the reptile. It's no surprise then that alligator attacks account for an average of one death per year in the United States. Just one. Bees—yes, *bees*—are significantly more deadly. That isn't to say that people ought to cozy up to wild alligators—that would probably change those statistics entirely. Sometimes a little bit of healthy fear is a good thing. It stops you from doing something stupid. As he rooted through the weeds on what felt like the riskiest of Easter egg hunts, Jeff had a distinct worry he would be that one person this year.

Alligators rarely attack humans unprovoked. The keyword there is *unprovoked*. Invading one's nest and absconding with her unborn children felt like the very definition of provocation.

Jeff recognized that he was out there both literally and figuratively looking for trouble. As he traipsed along the path—if you could call it that; it was barely more than a line of pine needles, a narrow gully in the rough sawgrass waves that the habits of deer had traced over time—he memorized the sounds of his own footfalls, his ears perked to the wetlands, ready for a new disturbance to cut across the placid whispers of the morning. He was keeping an ear out for the louder and more sudden sound of an object splashing in the river.

Using a snake hook, Jeff combed through the brush, purposeful and methodical, pretending to know exactly what he was doing. The other half of his attention remained in cervine alertness to his surroundings.

Jeff continued along in his search, watching as the new and trepidatious day unfolded along the forest floor with unassuming splendor. The resurrection ferns along the oak boughs began to curl and close, protecting their night-caught moisture, and the creeping things and the slithering things and the clawing things and the flitting things, all of nature's wonderful myriad of ugly and beautiful creatures, began to stir. A Carolina wren trilled an exuberant song, hidden in the architecture of the canopy. A woodpecker tapped a cadence on the spindle of a hollowed pine. Even as the fog rose with the dawn, the dew-cooled morning lingered on that shady trail, a brief reprieve from the dense summer heat. Golden orb spiders poised themselves, anticipating insect rush hour in their droplet-strung hammocks. The night's mosquitoes had retired to their mysterious homes to lie dormant until their next dusk hunt, but the bluebottle flies and the gnats had yet to arrive at their persistent duty of annoyance, giving the air a quality of repose, a transient and peaceful waiting into which the wilderness would pour its full vigor in time. Far below, much nearer, unexpected, palmetto fronds shook as an armadillo hopped and scurried through the scrub, leaving its trail rustling. Once it reached a safe distance, it stood up on its hind legs and observed Jeff for a moment before it turned and bounded away.

It didn't take long for Jeff to find a nest. At first, he thought nests would be hard to find. Then the smell hit him. Alligator feces has a distinct stench, one he had come to recognize after these months of keeping the farm. It was like a chicken farm mixed with a shallow oyster bed that had grown hot in the sun. Earthy and gamey and funky. The stench put him on alert. Not only did it mean a nest was nearby; it was more than likely that the nest's owner was around, too.

Scanning the area, Jeff followed the smell to a low-lying thicket. Behind it was an alligator slide, a strip of mud remembering the repeated impression of an alligator's belly as it slid down into the water. And in the middle of the thicket, there was a dark, wet mound—about a yard in diameter—constructed of pine needles and leaves, twigs and mud, and the ripest dung. Jeff grimaced at the smell, but there was no use in being squeamish about it. He took one more look around to check for Mama Gator. Then he lifted the thatch of mire that roofed in the nest. The inside exuded a fetid heat. Jackpot. The stark white curves of eggs poked out from the rank compost.

The law said he could only open a designated number of nests, only take a certain number of eggs. Open more, and anything you took after that was poaching. This way, a considerable number of nests would remain undisturbed, protecting wild alligators from the threat of population decline. For alligator farmers and anyone else with an egg-collecting permit, such a law meant that if they opened their set number of nests and none of them contained eggs, they would go home empty-handed. The law-abiding among them would, at least.

With another quick look around, Jeff squatted to pick up an egg. It was warm, alive. His first alligator egg. He paused, drinking in that poignant moment. It felt momentous, but he didn't know why.

He marked the egg's upward-facing side with a Sharpie, put it in the box of soil he'd carried with him for this purpose, and then recorded the egg with a tally mark on his sheet. Mama Gator hadn't shown up, but Jeff wasn't going to wait around for her. He packed up those unformed creatures in their dirty little pods, visited other nests to collect more, and then spirited them all back to the farm, reporting his numbers to the state by phone as he went. He was careful to keep them warm and alive, even though he didn't plan to hold on to them for very long. As soon as the new day came, he hustled to turn those eggs into money. A single day's harvest like this could net between $3,000 and $5,000, straight into the farm's account, keeping the rent paid and the lights on and chicken in his alligators' bellies. Or at least, that's what he was doing as Curtis Blackledge.

Under his new farmer guise, Jeff went out to catch an egg launderer. In this context, laundering meant passing off illegally harvested eggs for legal ones—and reaping the profits. It works like this:

The farmer who bought fifty-three eggs from Jeff recorded that he purchased only thirty. That left space in his logs for him to fill with twenty-three eggs he'd gotten from anywhere, including ones poached from the wild. Why would someone do that? Well, if you could buy illegal eggs from poachers for pennies on the dollar, but then turn around and sell those eggs, or the little alligators that hatch from them, for the same price as legal ones, you could make a profit, one that added up quickly in those days when alligator eggs sold for upward of $60 apiece.

That farmer paid Jeff only five bucks an egg. As Blackledge, he felt slighted. As Officer Babauta, on the other hand, the discrepancy between the number of eggs he'd sold and what the farmer reported constituted damning evidence that would land the farmer in court.

FWC saw that kind of thing going on all across the state. Laundering was rampant. The agency suspected a larger organized crime ring waited in the shadows. That's what Jeff was after. Finding the ledgers, false books that kept track of their illicit sales, would be his holy grail.

Still, that could wait. With his current paltry sum, he needed to feed his gators. Somehow, in just a matter of months, Jeff's gators had gone from accessories in his operation to true companions. The protectiveness he felt for his family and faithful dog Mack had found its way to his gators. Was it Blackledge who insisted he did what he could to provide for them? Or was it Jeff? The lines were blurry. The longer he spent in the field under the guise of his character, the more it seemed they were blending together. He was losing his identity so gradually that he didn't realize until a piece of it felt missing.

He was past due for a break.

He drove back to his wife—his real home—in his unmarked unit, the white pickup truck. The closer he got to the realm where his life as Jeff Babauta resided, the more anxious he became that someone was watching him. He caught himself looking over his shoulder constantly. That truck in his rearview mirror—how long had it been following him?

Jeff was no stranger to this well-founded paranoia. In his days as a uniformed officer, he frequently saw folks he'd arrested around town.

Even before this, he used to leave home for days at a time for other work assignments. He always worried about his family's safety, and for good reason. His wife's long days as a third-grade teacher left her preoccupied and vulnerable. One incident in particular stuck with him. There had been a big takedown of a poacher, someone who knew not only Jeff but also his family. The man could have picked Jeff's wife out of a crowd. He had targeted another officer and his family before. This sent Jeff into a panic. His son, in high school at the time, was frantic as well.

If something goes wrong, Jeff thought, *if something happens to them—or God forbid, her students—it'll be my fault.*

Worries like this haunted him. He was meticulous for a reason. When you fucked up, when you forgot something, people could get hurt. Sometimes those people were the ones you loved most.

I'm the one who agreed to do this, he would think. *Not them. This isn't their fault. Don't target them. You know better, don't you?*

Just because someone had committed a crime, or even several, that didn't make them a bad person. It wasn't who they were. This belief never stopped him from worrying. What if people like Lieutenant Wilson were right? What if there really were "bad guys"? Jeff liked to think the best of people. He had to. It was the only way he could get by in a job like his. *But what if?*—the thought always nagged him. What if wanting to believe the best in people was the flaw that would lead him to getting burned? What if he let his guard down for the wrong person?

After the takedown of that poacher, his fears of reprisal climbed. That night, Jeff had sat his son down in the living room of their home, their dogs' paws tapping on the linoleum, the parrot uttering minced oaths like a jambalaya of his wife's favorite curse words. This was their safe space, his little kingdom in the suburbs, but now here he was, saying out loud the worries he turned over in his mind on long drives—and how he dealt with them.

"I just know somebody's going to target me," his son had said.

"They're after me, not you," Jeff had tried to reassure him. But the worry still nagged at Jeff that he might be wrong. "That said, you never know. Be vigilant. When you're out, be aware of your surroundings. Look around and make sure nobody's going to jump out from behind something. Lock your car doors when you get in." Noting the panicked look on his son's face, Jeff had added, "But, you know, the people I deal with, I don't believe that they would do anything like that. But you just don't ever know. So just stay vigilant and keep your eyes open. Be careful what you say on the web."

At his son's high school, everyone knew Jeff was the game warden. His son ran in a crowd of guys who hunted and fished, and they'd razz him sometimes. *Your dad busted my cousin,* a friend might say. If it wasn't a cousin, it was someone else's dad. To that, his son would say matter-of-factly that Jeff must've thought he was doing something illegal. Don't do the crime if you're going to gripe about the consequences. His son was used to being a little extra vigilant. But none of those folks had ever made them feel scared until then.

The poacher-lawman dichotomy was just the way of the world. To step outside of it, to treat either man as an out-and-out villain, was to cross the line of taboo. They played each other's antagonists. Regardless of the archetypes embodied by each group in fiction, the roles they played in reality were something different entirely. In the narratives of their lives, the poacher and the lawman were each other's punch-clock villains: They could face off on the clock, but afterward they could sit side by side at the same dive bar, drink the same shitty beer, and share fish stories.

Not that Jeff did, though. In the past, Jeff and his family would have to leave a bar if they saw someone he'd previously arrested. Still, nobody ever confronted him. People seemed to like him, even the ones he arrested. He once heard someone say, "If you ever get confronted by Jeff, you better go ahead and tell him the truth. He'll know you're lying. Either way, he'll deal with you. So you just tell him the truth and keep it friendly." Those were guys catching the wrong kind of fish or bagging deer out of season. They were poaching by opportunity. But an entire poaching operation, an organized one with money to throw around, as FWC had suspected existed in the shadows—that was a whole different ball game. As the stakes grew higher, so did the danger. The poachers had much more to lose.

Jeff turned all this over in his mind as he drove home. He parked his truck under his utility shed and pulled down the tarpaulin cover. No one, not even his neighbors, would see it.

As he unlocked the door, the dogs barked and howled. They nearly mauled him with kisses once he got inside. Then they cleared the way for Sandy, who got her own kiss, too.

Jeff raises the sign at Sunshine Alligator Farm. *(Courtesy of Jeff Babauta)*

Jeff had business cards printed for Sunshine Alligator Farm, a necessary detail he hoped would bring possible suspects his way. *(Courtesy of Jeff Babauta)*

Picturesque royal palms—a species of tropical palm tree native to South Florida, Mexico, and the Caribbean—mark the trailhead at the Fakahatchee Strand.

A trail of crushed shells leads into the thick of the Fakahatchee's eponymous strand swamp, a type of swamp that grows lush because of the linear stream of water that flows through the limestone beneath it.

A boardwalk winds through head-high ferns and palm trees, part of the Royal Palm Hammock Trail in Collier-Seminole State Park.

An alligator hide hearkens to Everglades City's rugged past in the billiard room of the Everglades Rod & Gun Club.

A small lighthouse lantern, hurricane lamps, and other artifacts of Floridiana decorate the Everglades Rod & Gun Club's quiet back barroom.

The alligators line up for their supper at Sunshine Alligator Farm. Jeff learned how to mimic a hatchling's chirp, and he used the call to beckon his alligators to feeding time. *(Courtesy of Jeff Babauta)*

Fresh tire tracks cut through the mud in Big Cypress National Preserve. Perhaps they belonged to a hunter. Unlike in the national park, hunting is legal (with regulations) in the preserve.

The golden hour illuminates the understory of a cypress dome in Big Cypress National Preserve. Cypress domes are unique habitats where water pools deeper in the limestone bedrock, allowing taller trees such as cypresses to grow and provide shelter for abundant life on the forest floor.

Nicknamed the Fakahatchee Hilton by backpackers, this way-stop on the many miles of the Fakahatchee Strand's backcountry trails acts as a location marker so visitors know they're not totally lost.

Another angle of the Fakahatchee Hilton. Rustic homesteads like this one served as hideouts for alligator poachers in the Everglades' not-too-distant past.

The crew from Sunshine Alligator Farm prepares to hunt for eggs by land, water, and air. *(Courtesy of Jeff Babauta)*

Suspicious of covert work going on at the farm at night, Jeff installed trail cams. Here, one captures a secretive delivery of alligator eggs. *(Courtesy of Jeff Babauta)*

Hatching season has arrived at the farm. Here, a hatchling emerges from its shell. *(Courtesy of Jeff Babauta)*

In the area Jeff called Sunshine Daycare, kiddie pools serve as makeshift nurseries for newly hatched alligators. *(Courtesy of Jeff Babauta)*

Mangroves in Ten Thousand Islands National Wildlife Refuge offer shelter for marine life such as the smalltooth sawfish, a critically endangered ray with a chain-saw-like snout.

The Smallwood Store of Chokoloskee came into existence as a trading post and general store in 1906. Today, the Smallwood Store is a museum, offering visitors a glimpse into Florida's past.

Alligator scutes, or osteoderms, make up a bony layer under the crocodilian's skin that serves as armor.

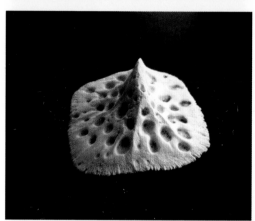

Some gator country cultures use alligator scutes as talismans in folk magic practices. Gladesmen gave this one to me on my journey in the Ten Thousand Islands.

Spanish moss, a type of air plant related to bromeliads, hangs from gnarled oaks in Merritt Island National Wildlife Refuge.

"It's been a while," she said.

"Sorry," Jeff said. "I got a little wrapped up in things."

More like I lost myself there for a second, he thought. On the way there, he had swiped his hand over his face like an actor preparing for a scene. "Jeff Babauta," he had said. "Jeff Babauta. Jeff Babauta. Jeff Babauta."

"I understand," Sandy said. "This is important. Don't worry. I have plenty of work for you to do here, too." She gave him his honey-do list.

Jeff smiled and shook his head. He both loved and hated fixing things and working in the yard. But now these tasks served another purpose. Curtis Blackledge did not have a wife. Curtis Blackledge didn't have a yard to keep up. Curtis Blackledge didn't know the satisfaction of trimmed bushes and cleaned gutters. Curtis Blackledge didn't like firing up the grill with his family. Jeff Babauta did.

Jeff Babauta, he thought as he started the lawn mower. *Jeff Babauta. Jeff Babauta. Jeff Babauta.*

9

THE INNER CIRCLE

All too soon, Jeff was back at the farm again. The bills were paid, but he'd hardly made any headway in the investigation. Jeff kept up the cold-calling. He got more aggressive with his friendliness. The more he did all this, the more Jeff began to realize that acting a fool, even when he didn't know things and needed to learn, was embarrassing. So just as with everything else, he got in front of the mirror and practiced. Like an actor doing rehearsals and loosening up before a scene, the more he practiced, the more he went out into the world as Blackledge, the easier it became to flow into that persona, to settle into the idea of not knowing, to be comfortable enough in his foolishness to ask questions. And that was how you learned, wasn't it? Perhaps Blackledge wasn't such a fool at all.

Swallowing that pride, he pursued his leads with more intention. When calling didn't work, he knocked on doors. He drove out into the country where kudzu made battlements out of fences, and the canopy of wild old oaks concealed farms, some just as old, back in their shade. He began to recognize the fetid smell of an alligator farm. He knew one was there, even when he couldn't see it. People started opening up. Pressed for hospitality, they eventually gave it.

"Hi, I'm Curtis Blackledge," he would say. "Most people call me Jeff. I know it's weird, but that's what my aunt always called me, and she raised me." When undercover, it's best to move toward using your real name as quickly as possible, Lieutenant Wilson had explained. That way, if someone shouts your name in public, they won't compromise your mission. "I started an alligator farm of my own, and I'm hoping to learn more about doing it right. I can already tell you have a top-notch facility here. Mind if I come in and tour the place? Really see how things are done?"

And—it worked. Persistence had been his welcome mat.

Perhaps they thought, *Anyone who cares this much is worthy of the inner circle*. Or maybe it was something else. He had spent so much time setting his own trap that he couldn't help but wonder if he was walking into a trap himself.

These farmers, salt-of-the-earth folks, had him over for lunch. He toured their facilities, cracking jokes and making them smile, humor the most effective tool in his kit. The look in their eyes said he'd made a connection. They were glad they'd let him in.

Then there were the ones with old money who remained stubborn as the swamp.

He would launch into the same introduction. These were the same people who had hung up on him at first. Now he wasn't going to take no for an answer. He decided to use a little psychology on them. He talked to them with familiarity, as if he had already succeeded in winning them over. Perhaps they were confused. Maybe they actually liked him. Either way, they stayed on the line and made excuses.

"Fuck you," he said once. "I'm coming to your place."

He showed up at their farm, jovial and charming. Faced with his disarming grin, they seemed to change their minds.

The more farms he toured, the more Jeff realized how great a spectrum there was from the best to the worst. Even without much money or training, Jeff's own farm sat squarely in the middle. He felt pride that he had done much better than he could really afford. He wanted to do better. He always wanted to do better. But he knew that he needed to find the sweet spot between having what was best for the gators and keeping a place that looked shabby enough to be real. So he kept touring, both to learn and, hopefully, to sniff out poachers.

By midsummer, Jeff's pestering opened the door at Shady Creek, an Arcadia alligator farm under the shade of river country's moss-heavy oaks.

Jeff had already tried to get a tour there. A few weeks before, when he'd first started knocking on doors and cold-calling, Jeff had driven over to the farm, which wasn't too far away from his own, and they had greeted him with the same general indifference as everyone else. The person who met him at the fence said they were about to have a business meeting. "Why don't you come back some other time," he'd said, an amiable way of saying *Get lost*.

After the gatekeeper deserted him, Jeff had craned to see through the foliage to the inner workings of the farm. The place seemed very official, put together. It wasn't just some hole in the ground beside a barn. There were various pools and what looked like the entrance to a clean workroom. Jeff caught the scent of bleach alongside the fishy smell of the tanks and the mossy scent of running water. There were only about five employees, and it looked like they were getting ready to huddle. They really were having a business meeting. They had official T-shirts and everything Jeff had wanted for his own business.

Now he was finally getting in.

A bright-yellow sign with the farm's name encircling a grinning alligator marked the entrance to a long driveway that led Jeff into the swamp. Jeff parked by their barn and greeted the man he'd spoken to on the phone, a square-jawed fellow named Robert.

"Jeff Blackledge," Jeff said, shaking Robert's hand. "Pleasure to meet you."

"Likewise," Robert replied with a curt nod. As they started into the facility, Jeff sized Robert up. He had short light-brown hair, looked like he kept in shape, cared about his appearance, like in another life, he could have been an actor. He spoke, too, with a quiet, nonchalant intelligence. It was clear to Jeff that Robert wasn't like so many of the people he'd met out there in the boondocks. Robert had depth. Yet he had no desire to flaunt it.

When he was making his initial overview of the list, the case agent had said they'd worked him already, meaning Jeff's predecessor had checked in with Robert's operation and found nothing out of the ordinary.

No way this guy's breaking the law, Jeff thought. Still, Robert seemed distracted, irritated even. Something was on his mind, and it had nothing to do with Jeff.

Robert guided Jeff to the facility's back entrance, where he motioned to a shallow pan like a paint tray in the St. Augustine grass beside the walkway. The water in it smelled like bleach. Robert directed Jeff to dip the soles of his shoes and wash them off before they could move on. The formality of this act, and the whiff of science-backed agriculture that attended it, impressed Jeff. *This isn't just some backyard rodeo*, Jeff thought. *This is some agriculture-department-grade rule following.*

While he slipped the soles of his boots through the caustic water, Jeff's admiration gave way to myriad questions. *Is this something I should be doing at Sunshine?* he thought. *How terrible is it not to have one of these?*

"What's this all about?" Jeff asked. "Because, you know, if I need to do this in my facility, then I don't know nothing about it."

"Oh, the Department of Agriculture guy was here last week," Robert said with a tone of complaint.

So that's what's on his mind, Jeff thought. *I knew he was distracted.*

"He told me I need to make some changes," Robert explained. "To keep bacteria from entering the building, you have to be cleansed. Or like how in the butcher shop, you have to wear hairnets for example. Things like that. You already know a lot of it. It's common sense."

"But you weren't doing it," Jeff said with a grin. If Jeff had learned one thing from his career in Florida wildlife law enforcement, it was that *common sense* was an oxymoron.

"Oh, we were." Robert cracked a smile for the first time in their conversation. "We just weren't doing it to the nth degree. They want this place spotless. If that's what they want, that's what we'll do." He said it with a tone of honest piety, like deep down he enjoyed the work it took to follow the rules.

This fellow's got a good aura about him, Jeff mused. To Jeff, Robert seemed upstanding, a man he could trust. He wore a crucifix on a chain around his neck. As a Catholic himself, though not an especially devout one, Jeff saw Robert's faith as another vote in his favor. Jeff believed he could learn a lot just from basking in his farm's proverbial glow. Perhaps Robert could someday count as a friend to lighten the burden of Jeff's loneliness, too.

Even though Jeff's facility, at this point, wasn't putting out any products, and its true mission was to act as a backdrop, he wanted it to be functional. And it wouldn't hurt if he was eventually turning a profit. He wasn't doing any butchering. His gators lived in the fenced-in ponds, not inside any sort of facility, so they were frolicking in whatever bacteria nature had to offer. Jeff didn't need this stuff. And yet—here came his impulse to do everything to the letter barreling in. Here were boxes he hadn't checked off. He made a mental note to tackle them when he got home. *No, not home*, he thought. *The farm. The farm isn't your home.*

After Robert sloshed his feet through the pan as well, he led Jeff inside, where he gestured to long tanks like raised lap pools where baby alligators, dozens of them, most no more than a foot long, swam in the same undulating motion as their much larger elders did: on the pivot of their head where it projected through the surface. Others fought and rolled around with one another. More lounged on Styrofoam islands. They squeaked and peeped at the sight of the men. Robert called these tanks raceways. Each was twenty feet long and five feet across.

"We use them for grading," Robert explained. He indicated the dams that blocked off the ends of the raceways. Each had a hole in it big enough for a baby alligator to squeeze through. The hole in each consecutive dam was of a progressively smaller size, so only the smallest alligators could fit into the last tank. Thus the alligators "graded" themselves by size without the farmers needing a ruler or a scale, or to handle them at all for that matter. This was an aquaculture concept. Not every facility had such a thing. Having visited an increasing number of farms, Jeff was quickly learning that farmers implemented whatever technology, both low and high, they could afford. The ones with shallower pockets made do with more MacGyvered solutions, like the place down in Moore Haven that used shipping crates and pallets for egg candling.

Robert opened the door to their butchering room, and a puff of clean, cool air washed over them. Jeff studied the shine of the concrete floor, the coolness of the concrete-block walls, the stainless-steel tables that looked untouched but weren't. The place was spotless. Alligator meat is relatively cheap, more of a by-product than a main source of profit. (Although when you can find it in the grocery store, the prices vary wildly, ranging from the cost of chicken breast to the wallet load of a decent steak, with most of this price due to the middlemen. Purchase gator meat closer to the source, and it can run as low as a few bucks a pound.) The real profit comes from the skins, which often go for hundreds of dollars for unblemished, high-quality hides.

From the sheen and hygiene of Robert's facility, it was obvious that the owners had money. Had Jeff been back in his real persona as Officer Babauta, he might have assumed that they'd scrubbed the place down before he arrived. But he wasn't. And they hadn't. Jeff was nobody. They didn't care what he saw. Sure, they were making improvements for inspections, but a farm didn't get this good overnight. Their facility was just like this. That's how Jeff wanted his to be.

In terms of the case, not only was Jeff learning, he was also trying to spy clues of wrongdoing. He knew no one would likely keep obvious displays of poaching or laundering out in the open, but if something was going on, there would be hints of it. He looked for something off, like one unlabeled box amid labeled ones, loose CITES tags, mess, or disorganization. Even if nothing overt called his attention, Jeff's gut would tell him something was off. Jeff's gut had a career's worth of practice. By now, he knew he should trust it.

Jeff's gut said that Robert and Shady Creek were aboveboard. More than aboveboard. Shining examples of what he aspired to be. Jeff could have inspected every inch of the place for hours, but the tour came to a close all too quickly. In less than an hour, it seemed like they were shooing him out the door. Jeff understood, though. As someone often preoccupied with perfecting his own work, Jeff saw the same in Robert, and so he could forgive his brusque demeanor and short tour. He wanted to return to Shady Creek. Yet he had a feeling he wouldn't be back again. There were no problems there that he could see, and they had no time for him. You win some. You lose some.

Still, this new window to the inside had whetted Jeff's appetite. He wanted more tours, more calls. He wasn't quite ready to call this one a draw.

A few weeks later, in the midst of summer nesting season, the idea to call Robert sprang into Jeff's head. As a farm manager, Robert would likely be going out to collect eggs, and maybe if Jeff asked, Robert would let him join in.

Standing outside the camper, leaning against the side, watching the sunset turn the treetops into shadows, Jeff called Robert. The line rang itself out then went to voicemail. Jeff left a message. *Oh well*, he thought. He went inside, removed his laptop from its secret compartment in the wall, and got cracking on some paperwork.

About an hour later, his phone rang. It was Robert. A small miracle.

"Hey, how ya doing?" Jeff said, genuine warmth in his voice. "Didn't think you would call me back."

"I would have picked up in the first place, but I'm already in Okeechobee collecting eggs, and you know how it is down here," Robert said.

"That's what I called to talk to you about," Jeff said. "I'd sure like to tag along and learn a thing or two. You don't need to pay me nothing. I'd just like to see how this operation works. Hell, I'll even pay for my own hotel room. I'll meet you down there."

"Sure, sounds great," Robert said. "I'll call you tomorrow and see what we can work out." He hung up before Jeff could say another word.

Jeff finished his work. He read a chapter of a novel and went to bed. The next day, Jeff kept his phone close. As he finished various chores around the farm, he would pull it out and look at the screen, thinking maybe Robert had called, and Jeff just hadn't heard the ring. Nope. Nothing.

He just wanted to get me off the damn phone, Jeff thought, frowning and shaking his head.

On the third day, Jeff called again.

"Hey, man, I thought you were going to call me," Jeff said. "I was all ready to come help you."

"Sorry, I got caught up in the harvest," Robert said.

"I'm all packed," Jeff said. "I can still come."

"Unfortunately, we're done," Robert replied.

"Done for the day?"

"Done for the season. Maybe next year. Keep in touch."

Jeff put his phone down on the counter of the barn workroom and sighed. He wanted to like Robert, but the more he worked, and the more he thought about his brief glimpse inside the upper echelon of alligator farming, the more Robert's cordial dismissiveness hurt. It put a nick in the farm manager's otherwise golden sheen.

No use dwelling, Jeff thought. He told himself to put Robert out of his mind and keep moving forward.

It was time to pick up more fish guts.

Jeff had managed to dodge the agency inspector when he came by the farm. When the man called again, Jeff deepened his voice, hoping the inspector, a man he had known for years, would not recognize it.

"Everything shipshape?" Jeff asked.

"The place is coming along," the inspector said.

The noncommittal answer made Jeff's heart sink.

"I want this place to be perfect," Jeff said. "What am I missing?"

"You need more square footage to bring you up to code," the inspector said. "Meaning, you need more room for the gators, even though you don't have them all yet."

"So the kiddie pools are all right?" Jeff asked. The previous agent took a few steps toward creating the farm before he got burned, buying kiddie pools for the hatchlings, among other things. In lieu of concrete raceway tanks like at Shady Creek, several of the less well-heeled farms Jeff toured used kiddie pools, the cheap and ubiquitous plastic lounges of childhood summer, as nurseries for their tiny gators. Jeff planned to use these, too. Stacks of them sat in the barn, giving off the hot smell of plastic.

"They're fine," the inspector said. "But you're going to need more of them."

More? I already have a bunch.

"How many more, you think?" Jeff asked.

"Oh, a dozen or so ought to do it," the inspector said.

Jeff thanked the inspector, and afterward, he drove into town, hitting every store he could think of that might possibly stock kiddie pools. He was well aware the whole scenario was ridiculous.

You can't make this shit up, he thought, shaking his head and smiling at the absurdity as he stacked kiddie pools onto a cart.

At one checkout counter, the cashier looked at his stack of pools and said, "Damn, you have this many kids?"

"No," Jeff responded, amused with himself. "I'm an alligator farmer."

"Oh," the cashier said, as if enlightened by Jeff's answer. He craned his head over the checkout counter to watch Jeff leave.

At Jeff's next stop, the hardware store, he spied a familiar face at the end of the aisle. "Well, look who it is!" Jeff called out as he approached.

Robert turned from the tools wearing an irritated frown. When his eyes landed on Jeff, he conjured up a closed-lip smile. "Fancy seeing you here," he said, shaking Jeff's hand. "How's the farm coming?"

"It's really coming along," Jeff said. He gestured at the kiddie pools. "I have my own inspector problems." Jeff explained, and Robert's forced expression gradually gave way to one of genuine, albeit light, amusement.

"Whatever works," Robert said. "I'm buying some things for the farm myself. I have to get the place well situated before the family and I go up to the mountains for our annual hunting trip."

"What do you like to hunt?" Jeff asked. *Finally, something we have in common*, he thought.

They chatted about hunting, Robert's family, and their farms; and by the end of the conversation, Jeff had felt Robert warm to him. Or, if he hadn't warmed, he'd at least thawed.

"We should go hunting together sometime," Jeff offered.

"You bet," Robert said as he walked away. "I'll call you."

By the end of the day, Sunshine Alligator Farm sported some forty or fifty pools, all ready for hatchlings. Jeff himself sported a new hope that he had found a way in.

When days and then weeks passed, and Robert hadn't called, Jeff shrugged. He could have called Robert himself, but what was the point? *I can take a hint*, he thought. So he got on with his life.

Jeff's days, like most farmers', started early. Before he ate breakfast, Jeff would get dressed and take a quick turn around his farm, observing every gator, making sure they were all well fed and looked healthy. He would check the temperatures of the ponds as well as the water level. In the summer, alligators would spend a great deal of each day either in or under the water to keep cool. During cooler months, the gators would spend more time basking to bring their temperatures up. Jeff mowed and used the Weedwacker around the ponds to keep their basking space open. Sometimes when he got bored, he'd train them like dogs.

He threw a soft Frisbee toy toward the pond. "Here boy," he called out.

To Jeff's surprise, the Frisbee flew just close enough to the gator that it chomped down and—kind of—caught it.

"Fetch?" Jeff said. *I didn't think this through.* "Or, you know what? Maybe just keep it."

A real alligator farming operation hires people to do all of these things. The more alligators they have, the more people they bring in to maintain them. There's someone for everything: a food specialist, a veterinarian, a butcher, a skinner. When the alligators reach maturity, they'll skin them. While the butcher processes the meat, the skinner will soften the hides enough so they'll roll like vellum. If prices for skins are too low, he might stash this set in the freezer and sell them when the price goes back up again. Butchers at big enough farms have deals with supermarkets and specialty meat distributors. Smaller farms sell straight from their own shops. In the right parts of Florida, it's not unheard of to spot hand-painted signs along the roadside enticing drivers to pull over and partake in some alligator jerky. (Who thought it was a good idea to take an animal whose meat is already tough and stringy and make it even tougher and stringier?) Some facilities make money on the heads and claws, sending them to a taxidermist's shop. They then go on to roadside orange stands and tourist shops in greasy gas stations stocked with useless Florida bric-a-brac. The alligator skulls will persist there, cultivating a layer of grime, languishing under the fluorescent lights and bathed in the unctuous odor of the fossilized taquitos that have been turning on the roller grill since the beginning of time.

In the corners of gator country, folk magic practitioners incorporate alligator claws and teeth into their rituals, which seems a more fitting end for these majestic beasts. At the very least, it's one that does not denude them of their power after death. Though, as the owner of an alligator scute once given to me by a gladesman as a talisman of protection, maybe I'm a little biased.

Jeff wasn't doing any of these things. Knowing he would soon have to part with them, he refrained from naming his gators. Yet he loved them enough to leave them intact. It pained him to think of them as a commodity to be bought and sold.

He watched over them that January as the weather grew cool. In the depths of winter, alligators' metabolisms slow down. If it gets cold enough, they'll go into brumation, the reptilian version of hibernation. They don't eat much during the winter, so Jeff spent less on food. He needed less money to run the farm. Everything seemed to slow down. These doldrums just stretched on and on. Jeff was beginning to feel like a weather-chilled alligator: The world kept moving around him, but here he was, standing still.

Yet, on the other side of every winter, spring arrives to bring the thaw, to awaken life within the swamp, to instill it with the vigorous and undeniable impulse toward creation. With spring would come mating season. The rumbling bellow of bull gators would hum through the cypresses and reeds. When one bull met another, they would fight, open-jawed, tooth and claw, the dragons of Bartram's journals.

"Behold him rushing forth from the flags and reeds. His enormous body swells. His plaited tail brandished high, floats upon the lake. The waters like a cataract descend from his opening jaws. Clouds of smoke issue from his dilated nostrils. The earth trembles with his thunder," Bartram wrote. Although the naturalist's writings are a bit much sometimes, and they're often not factual in the literal sense, like the yarns from the backwoods of Florida, these hyperbolic descriptions capture alligators in their essence, as the majestic, ancient swamp rulers they really are. Such alligator duels and the couplings that come after bring forth a new generation to rule the swamp with no less majesty than their progenitors, even as the cold facts of modernity have diminished their magnificence under many an unimaginative gaze.

And so, in place of winter's quietude, summer would follow spring, and with the rising temperatures, the inevitability of new life. The drama and danger of nesting season would seize the swamp once again. With nesting season, Jeff knew, just as inevitable as all that new life, crime would arise again and slink through the shadows of the swamp's hot night.

10

THE BALLAD OF PEG BROWN

I f the numbers from the Peg Brown tales were true, then Peg killed upward of ten thousand gators over the span of his career as a poacher. Only counting the time after he returned from World War II up until the Endangered Species Act of 1973, when he allegedly stopped hunting alligators entirely, that's twenty-eight years, or about one gator a day. To put those numbers into perspective, now that alligators are numerous, homeowners can call an FWC hotline to report them—think the "nuisance" gators who take up residence in Nana's Boca Raton pool.

Between 1997 and 2021, Florida trappers caught more than 320,000 nuisance alligators, some of which they released, while others were sold. More than half of those alligators, however, were "harvested," the agency's deceptively bland euphemism for "euthanized." In just those twenty-four years, the state of Florida killed about eighteen times more alligators than Peg ever did by his own estimations, yet those losses have shown little impact on alligator populations overall. In other words, even the most notorious and prolific poacher ever to wreak havoc on the glades would have had very little impact on his own. Peg and his kind, however, made for very convenient scapegoats for the sudden and dramatic decline of the American alligator in the 1950s and 1960s when South Florida's newcomers demanded action, hounding the park service for one escalation after another. The rangers obliged. They bought more planes and stayed out all night to watch for poachers. By the thousands of pages I've read of their barely legible logs, these efforts were successful. They caught dozens of poachers. But Peg, it seemed, always remained just out of their reach. Then they beat him, too. Tired of facing down so much firepower every night, Peg gave up their cat-and-mouse games for good. Or did he?

I went over these numbers in my head as I waited for Jonnie, remembering what Rothchild wrote in *Tropic*: "There is probably no such thing as a truly retired poacher."

When Jonnie Brown pulled up—in a white Ford F-150, just like Jeff's—to where I stood in the breezeway of the Outdoor Resorts of Chokoloskee, I recognized him immediately. I'd never seen a picture of him; it was just that his person very much matched the deep drawl I'd heard on the phone. He was an imposing man with ruddy cheeks from work in the sun and short graying hair. I considered for a moment that, had I been someone else, his stature and blue-collar roughness might have put me on the defensive. Instead, it was those same qualities that made me warm to him even more than I had on the phone. He would have fit right in at a Renner family reunion. I knew that he would take great care on the adventure that he had promised.

We shook hands, and I smiled. "You must be Jonnie Brown."

"That's right," he said. "And you must be Rebecca."

"That's me. It's nice to finally meet you, Jonnie."

I found myself slipping into my river country drawl, a leisurely, broad accent that shies away from hard consonants, an accent not unlike the one spoken in the Everglades. For most of my life, my parents tried to correct that speech away. They would make me repeat after them, *But-ton. Cot-ton.* By high school, I could speak with the chipper blandness of a newscaster. By the end of college, I wished I could get it back. I wished I could sound like my great-grandmother, who had lived her entire life on the edge of the swamp. Yet that flavor only crawled back into my words when I least expected. It snuck up on me when I stopped trying.

Often when I'd slip back into it while talking with gladesmen, I could see their shoulders relax, their tension uncoiling, as if I had transformed from predaceous outsider to someone who might understand if they spoke their hearts to me.

I didn't see Jonnie having lots of heartache to spill, but I try not to assume. Of course, being a pragmatic man, he launched into planning the day almost immediately. He asked me what I wanted to do, and I said, "You're the boss. It's up to you. Tell me and show me whatever you think I need to see. I have questions, of course, but I don't know what I don't know, you know?"

He laughed. "Right."

What I really wanted were primary sources, documents and the like. My holy grail would be a diary or a journal, and I told him as much.

As we got into his truck, he said, "Don't have anything like that. Don't have much, in all honesty. We lost a lot of pictures. Somebody threw them out."

"Damn," I said.

"Even his war memorabilia," Jonnie said as he pulled in a circle out of the shell-gravel parking lot. "My dad was a war hero. Did you know that? Had a gold star for valor." Jonnie indicated a photograph print on the console between us. It was Peg in his military regalia, spangled with his gold stars. "He was a rifleman in the First Infantry," Jonnie continued. "That much I know. He hardly ever talked about it. In fact, I only heard him mention it once."

They were drinking together at the Oyster Bar, the now-defunct dive bar that the outlaws frequented, and Peg had gotten drunk enough to start reliving long-buried memories: It was December 16, 1944. The pines reached so high in the forest of the Ardennes in Belgium that the whole landscape would have fallen under a false twilight if the thick crust of snow hadn't blanched it. Peg had never seen snow before the war. He was made in the swamp and built for that climate. The cold might have defeated a weaker Floridian, but Peg was tough. He never complained.

The snow deepened as the days went on. The troops were tired. Earlier that month, they had made a drive through the Hürtgen Forest and had withdrawn to rest before pushing forward against an unexpected German offensive.

As the infantrymen fought, Peg and the other riflemen guarded the line. He had learned to shoot in the Everglades, in cypress domes where the junglelike tangle obstructed the view of even the sharpest-eyed hunters. Despite the bitter cold of that foreign blizzard, the air itself seemed clear. Peg let off shot after shot, one hit after another. It was the same as back home, except here there was a man at the other end of your bullet. That wasn't the same as hitting a gator or even a panther. It was best not to think about it. He had to keep firing.

He fired so much that even in that record cold his gun overheated. When the gun got too hot to keep firing, too hot to touch, his assistant rifleman would fill his helmet with snow and dump it on the gunstock. The snow would melt almost instantly, then freeze, forming a layer of frost so thick and stubborn that Peg couldn't fire the gun again until they'd beaten away the ice. They repeated that unending farce, hardly taking breaks to eat and sleep for weeks on end. They pushed the Nazi offensive back, forcing the enemy troops from the wider roads onto barely passable trails. American tanks trundled over waves of rocks and snow.

This long counteroffensive beneath the Ardennes's venerable spruces, a fight that would become immortalized as the Battle of the Bulge, was not a victory of strength over weakness. It was a battle of grit. Plagued by the forbidding elements in a battle that seemed to never end, only soldiers too stubborn to consider quitting held out. On the American line, no matter how weary they became, stubbornness was never in short supply, especially in the boys from Florida, who knew something about hard times. They knew that storms are temporary and that their hardship was nothing compared with whom they were fighting for.

By January 1945, the 1st Infantry had won out. They returned to Germany and crossed the Rhine. The snows of winter were only a memory by the time they reached Flossenbürg concentration camp, where they broke through its fortifications and released thousands of prisoners, many of whom were too starved to walk.

Peg never talked to Jonnie, or anyone as far as Jonnie knew, about the concentration camps or what he saw there. He had hardly talked about the war at all. The sheer amount of liquor it had taken to pry this one story from the recesses of his mind and the tenor of his voice as he recounted it, how he pantomimed the futile gesture of beating the ice from his rifle over and over again, told of a persistent memory more indelible than a photograph. He would never admit that it haunted him, but it was hard to imagine it hadn't. Perhaps it returned to him during his nights in the swamp, the mosquito-thick air suddenly falling chill as the cypresses morphed into spruces and the water and the weeds and the mangroves became snow in the Ardennes, and a hail of gunfire he tried to forget sang out over his head. Or was that the beat of a helicopter blade? The rangers' spotlights through the trees ratcheted Peg's pulse. It's easy to forget where you are, *when* you are, when the past is so alive within you.

As Jonnie drove toward Everglades City, eager to find us a place for lunch, the tableau of the icy gun repeated in my head. It was such a striking image, visceral just like the stories of Peg's poaching, and yet it showed a completely different person from the one I had assumed Peg to be. In the Ardennes, Peg had not been a valiant folk hero, a John Henry–like figure of impossible feats in the swamp. He was just a mortal man faced with the futility of war. With guts and grit, he kept on going, because that's what you did, but not without a significant loss. Something inside of him had broken. He carried that quietly all his life. And it's in the quiet night of the swamp that he was alone with the darkest thoughts he left unspoken.

That complicated inner world of Peg's changed the stories for me. His cat-and-mouse games with the rangers had subtext. After all of that fighting, Peg had come home to find his world changed. Loggers had stripped the land. The Army Corps of Engineers had diverted the water, causing what foliage remained to shift year by year, almost imperceptibly, until people like Peg no longer recognized the Everglades anymore. Alligators, the species that had been his livelihood, took a downturn. Adding insult to injury, rich developers and newcomers blamed Peg and other hunters for that loss even though their impact was small compared to all that new construction. Tricking the rangers made Peg feel less powerless. Perhaps that's when he became the folk hero in his own eyes. Because no matter what else they took, developers couldn't take away the poachers' stories. The wily trickster and his humorous resistance remind the downtrodden the world over that when you're smart you still have power. Some things never change.

Jonnie took us to a little fish house where we ate lunch and then remained in the oversized, shiny booth for our interview. Jonnie was a fisherman, a legal one. In those days, he mainly caught Florida stone crabs. They're so ungodly expensive—with consumer prices for claws ranging from $35 to $95 per pound in 2023—it's almost a crime anyway.

Jonnie reiterated a lot of the stories I'd already heard, adding that Peg had crafted many of them himself, their origin being at the Oyster Bar where many a poacher had spun his yarn.

"The Rod & Gun was for tourists," Jonnie said.

He told me about Peg killing a gator outside the rangers' station, the same one I'd read about in the ranger's report. This particular gator passed his days floating in the estuary in the shade of the mangroves by the station. After seeing the gator every day, the rangers came to think of him as a pet. They even named him and erected a sign by his wallow with that name and a warning not to mess with him. One night, Peg came by, killed the gator, and changed the sign to say the gator was gone, because that dastardly Peg Brown had sent him to heaven. I found that story both grimly funny and sad. I've become attached to many a gator that has shared a habitat with me. I'd be pretty sore if somebody went and killed one of "my" gators. Jonnie told me about Peg getting lost one time and then ending up drinking coffee with the rangers at their station. When his brother showed up to fetch him, the rangers were asking Peg if he knew any poachers, "like that Peg Brown fellow," whom they just couldn't manage to catch.

"Never heard of him," the Browns said before quickly slipping away.

The rangers had initially met Clarence—Peg under his Christian name—because they'd recruited locals to teach them how to navigate the glades. The rangers had come to work at Everglades National Park from all over the country, from the Rocky Mountains to the Ozarks, places they thought made them rugged. They assumed they could surmount any environment—and then they faced the Everglades. Poachers quipped that the rangers were easy to outsmart because they were afraid of the mosquitoes. On hot nights, they'd hunker in their station, unwilling to venture forth into that inhospitable swamp that was both their charge and their foe. The poachers, however, bore the swamp no such ill will. It was their home, their friend, the primary accomplice to their trickery. The locals certainly taught the rangers the ropes, but they left out important details, fudged here and there to stop rangers from stumbling on the hideouts where they poached. It was in their best interest to make the swamp seem unnavigable. This is not the place for the faint of heart. One of Peg's neighbors nailed a sign to a tree that said it all: WHOA YANKEE TURN AROUND.

I had stumbled upon that picture in an archive, and it made me laugh. I asked Jonnie about it, and he said he knew where it was.

"We can go find it later," he said.

I was happy to hear some confirmation of all these tales from Jonnie, but at the same time, I worried that some of them were just folklore. I wanted more than confirmation. I wanted evidence. I wanted firsthand accounts. It was starting to seem like I was out of luck, though, because Peg had gone out so much on his own, and his brother Totch's versions of the tales that made Totch himself the star were the ones recorded in print. If Totch was the famous one, did that make him right by default? I didn't like that. It seemed antithetical to the stories themselves, erasing their element of tenacity. As captivating a storyteller as he was, Totch was no underdog.

So I asked Jonnie, "Do you happen to know anybody who went hunting with Peg who's still alive?"

Jonnie gave me a slow smile. "Well, there's me," he said.

"Really?" I said, alert, my pen poised and ready. "Can you tell me about any of that?"

"Of course," he said. "What do you want to hear?"

In the year 1960, Jonnie turned eleven. By then, great change had already befallen Chokoloskee. In the very early years of Jonnie's life, neither road nor electricity connected the island to the mainland. Jonnie attended a one-room schoolhouse on the island. Some other kids rode in on a boat that acted as their school bus.

The Browns lived on a "house-lighter," their word for what outsiders might call a houseboat. Rather than floating on the water, it stood on stilts overlooking the tide. It was white with blue trim. Jonnie's father had built it himself when he came back from the war.

They had no electricity. Neither did any of their neighbors. Jonnie did his homework by the light of kerosene lamps. Not that he always did it. Jonnie was what he would later call a "real mean" kid. He would shoot cans from their garbage pile with his BB gun and teach innocent neighbor kids how to cuss. He had plenty to be ornery about, but he didn't fully realize it at the time.

In 1956, the state built a bridge that connected Everglades City on the mainland with Chokoloskee. With the bridge came all sorts of outsiders. According to the adults in Jonnie's life, the two worst types of outsiders were the tourists and the environmentalists. Even a journalist had started poking around. Peter Matthiessen was working on a book about endangered species, he said. Yet he kept asking all kinds of questions to anybody who gave him the time of day. He was in love with the mystique of the Everglades, like most of the outsiders were, but he also seemed transfixed by a murder that had happened at the trading post about half a century before. The Brown clan and the Daniels clan, by then united by marriage, had both been involved. Unlike with their other alleged undertakings, they were more than happy to tell the story of how in 1910 they killed Edgar Watson, a violent sugarcane planter who treated his workers like slaves.

"The bastard deserved it," Jonnie said. "Nobody knows who shot him, because near every man in town was there with his gun, and they all shot at once."

Chokoloskee was proud of the Wild West–style justice they had meted out. Uncle Totch had taken it upon himself to become the island's unofficial historian and storyteller (Kent's spiritual predecessor), and so he befriended Matthiessen and showed him around, hoping to catch a little bit of fame along the way.

All this new attention brought newfound trouble. Peg had always made his living fishing and poaching alligators. In those days, the numbers of alligators had shrunk in some parts, while in others, like around Big Fox Lake, they remained plentiful. The outsiders seemed preoccupied with the alligators, even more so than the people whose livelihoods depended on them. They came in seeking to change everything rather than realizing it was the change they had brought that started the problems in the first place. If everyone had just left the Everglades the hell alone, the adults said, the alligators wouldn't be having so much trouble.

Jonnie frequently went hunting with Peg. They would skin the alligators out in the mangroves then take all the hides down the road to the mainland, where they would meet a fellow named Graham, one of the buyers. He would throw the salted hides into the trunk of his car, really load it up until it barely closed, and then he would count out bills from a roll, $5 per foot for hides five feet and over. That was a lot of money back then and well worth the risk.

Everything got more expensive when increasing crowds of tourists came to the Ten Thousand Islands, so the Browns struggled more than ever to put food on the table. Jonnie had two sisters and six living brothers, and he was the second-oldest boy. He and the six younger kids lived with their parents on the house-lighter. The oldest two lived down the road with their grandparents. It was a good thing that fish were free and plentiful. They ate a lot of ibis, too, usually the brown ones. Even though hunting the white ibis was illegal, so many people on the island did it that even folks outside the Ten Thousand Islands started calling them Chokoloskee Chicken.

Come hurricane season of 1960, the gauges on all their barometers plunged, and even before the radios proclaimed the approach of Hurricane Donna, the residents of Chokoloskee knew a major storm was on its way. The adults in Jonnie's life—his parents, his grandparents, and their neighbors—feared losing their belongings. They battened down the hatches as best they could, then evacuated across the island to the Blue Heron Hotel, where the owner allowed them to stay for free. The tourists fled in a panic. As the adults watched and waited, the kids squirmed with that particular excitement that precedes the coming of a hurricane. Regular storms were awesome and wonderful, but hurricanes were something else, mighty and dangerous. Just living through one was an adventure.

Their excitement reached a fever pitch as the wind howled outside. Periodically, they would peek out of the blinds. The big fig tree out front had bent nearly double. The wind gauge on a nearby roof climbed as high as 185 miles per hour. The glass of a car outside flexed with the record low pressure then exploded the way a bubble pops.

During the eye, everything went still. Jonnie couldn't help himself. He ran outside. He had never seen the island so quiet. There were no cars, no people. Not even the birds sang. For a moment, he gazed around in wonder, awed by the stillness wrought by nature's fury. Peg marched out and dragged his dumb ass back inside. Soon the winds picked up again. Torrents of rain pelted the hotel. All kinds of strange sounds enveloped them: the screech of metal, the crack of splintering wood, a long groan that sounded like the song of a whale.

When the skies had cleared, the Browns ventured out into the daylight. Water had risen up to cover the entire island. Peg waded away to get his pitpan. Jonnie followed him through that foreign landscape. On the shore where their house once stood, they only found debris. Their house-lighter was gone. Luckily, Peg spied his boat, or at least a boat that looked enough like his to pass for it. Who knew in all that mess. He and Jonnie went around picking up serviceable wood scraps and piling them in the pitpan. Thousands of fish littered what was left of the dry land, some too far away to have washed ashore on the tide. There were little minnows, puffer fish inflated from fright, even an immense grouper nearly the size of a cow. They ate the fish that night at the hotel, like a Sunday fish fry that they all had together.

Peg built a new house from reclaimed wood. This one was wired with electricity. That wasn't the only change that settled over them after the hurricane. Peg poached less and less. He focused on his fishing guide business, even had a friend paint a sign on the side of their house. NATIVE GUIDE, it said and touted his wares, adventures for sale. He decided to capitalize on the tourists instead of fighting them. Even celebrities sought out Peg, like Christopher Plummer and Gypsy Rose Lee, who came to film *Wind Across the Everglades*, a 1958 film in which Totch Brown played a bit part. They came to Peg not just for guiding services but also for a taste of the exotic life of the glades. As he steered them through the mangroves, sometimes with Jonnie as his assistant, he spun yarns for them, tales that brought the glades to life. Rip Torn came fishing with them, and Peg didn't know who he was. But Rip had heard of Peg. It was always like that.

On the way back to Chokoloskee, Jonnie drove us by the rangers' old houses, two bungalows raised on stilts over their carports. Back in the day, Jonnie would drive by like this to see if the rangers' cars were in their driveways. Then he'd drive past the station and glance over the docks where the rangers kept their boats. If all the boats and trucks were accounted for, the coast was clear to go out hunting. That day, the docks were full with everything from small motorboats to bigger trawlers.

"Looks like the coast is clear," Jonnie joked.

Back on the far side of the island, Jonnie drove down increasingly narrow dirt roads. Near the pebble-strewn beach, a stand of Australian pines, an introduced species, cast cool shadows over the lot. The house was a regular house, not on stilts, not a lighter.

Jonnie mused aloud that he didn't know who lived there anymore. He had moved up the coast decades ago in search of better opportunities as a fisherman, and so he had become disconnected from Chokoloskee. The distance seemed to sadden him, as if he was separated from his past and the person he used to be, and merely visiting did little to bridge that gulf.

He did know the fellow who lived next door, so he drove around and parked next to where a land-bound catamaran waited in the grass. He got out and walked around, and I followed. At the corner of the two fences, there was a clutch of trees. Jonnie gestured at it. "Sign's gone," he said. He meant the WHOA YANKEE TURN AROUND sign we'd gone looking for. It was a marker of a bygone day. Now Chokoloskee's only industry was tourism. WHOA YANKEE COME BACK (AND SPEND YOUR MONEY) would have been more fitting.

Jonnie walked around the house, remembering stories as he studied the changes. He recounted the one time that the rangers ever came close to catching Peg. Peg had been burning prairie grass so he could get his pitpan through to the next waterhole in the slough. Before he knew it, he heard chopper blades overhead. He threw palm fronds over the boat and lay down underneath them. Thus thatched, he hid. The whirlwind from the helicopter drove downward, pressing in on him until he could have touched the landing gear with his oar. He waited, not moving, his heart hammering as the palm blades fluttered. After a while, the chopper seemed to give up, and Peg returned to the hunt.

Planes and helicopters had chased both of them down more times than Jonnie cared to count. Rangers in a plane once locked onto them with a spotlight. It was hair-raising for Jonnie, but not for Peg. Nothing ever ruffled him. At least, it didn't seem to. Who knew what was really going on in that quiet man's head.

Then why did Peg stop poaching? Perhaps it was no longer worth the risk. Perhaps the rangers had won. Perhaps he never stopped. He just stopped spinning yarns about it. Once a poacher, always a poacher, right?

Once when Jonnie had gone out poaching on his own one night, he inadvertently left behind his gun and the salt he used to cure the hides out in the open. Come daylight, a ranger stumbled upon them. Somehow, he knew who they belonged to, and he tracked Jonnie down.

"I was never as crafty as my dad," Jonnie said with a chuckle. "Nobody was."

When the ranger came to arrest Jonnie, Peg told his son to do as the ranger said. "Don't worry," Peg added. "I'll take care of it." These were just the facts of life when you were an alligator poacher. Unruffled, Peg went out to his boat. He never told Jonnie what he did, but when he arrived later to bail him out, he had money that he didn't have before. There was one thing that Peg knew how to do that made good money.

Jonnie had barely finished this story when a car pulled into the driveway. Earlier, we had asked after a man named Mac at the Smallwood Store, which he owned with his wife, a descendant of the original Smallwood. Mac had tracked us down. He was a light-haired, sturdily built fellow with a disarming smile and a carefree attitude that reminded me of the Keys.

"Who's this?" Mac called out from his truck. "She's way too pretty for you."

"Sorry, I'm a journalist," I said in a deadpan, joking tone. "And I'm too pretty for you, too." For a second, they were silent, and I was afraid my joke hadn't landed. There's always that danger when my mouth gets ahead of me. Then Mac and Jonnie roared with laughter, breaking what could have been a tense moment like the popping windshield in Jonnie's hurricane story.

"You got me," Mac said. "I walked right into that one." If he had been closer, he might have slapped me on the back like I was one of the guys. I had proved I could take it as well as dish it out. Once he'd parked and come over, he gave me a firm handshake and a grin, and we exchanged more proper introductions.

My relief came from more than having avoided a tense moment. I've found that many Floridians employ a genre of sarcasm that seems to go over some people's heads. When we're together, we speak in this often-dark repartee, but when outsiders show up, especially when they're extremely serious journalists, they take our remarks out of context, and we go from figuratively misunderstood to literally misunderstood, which would be funny in itself if it didn't happen so often and in such otherwise reputable periodicals.

Mac had become an insider, but he hadn't always been. He lived across the street and knew Jonnie well, but he wasn't from Chokoloskee. He wasn't even from Florida. He proudly called himself a Michigander, yet no one seemed to treat him with the same hostility toward northerners that had once inspired the sign WHOA YANKEE TURN AROUND. Though some of that sentiment still lingered in the Everglades and back where I came from, Mac seemed to exist in a different category. Without having to erase his roots, he had been accepted as one of them; not just allowed or tolerated, he was a pillar of the community. That made me wonder: Why had Mac been accepted while other outsiders remained, well, outside?

I thought back to the celebrities visiting Peg. They took his fishing tours and listened to his stories, but perhaps they didn't really hear him, and by the end, they only saw him as a character, set dressing, part of their experience of the glades, as I had when I first came to Chokoloskee. Then without knowing it, they and other visitors and newcomers, having fallen in love with the Everglades, or only the caricature of it that they were willing to see, rallied for laws and regulations to protect the place from the people who lived there, the very people who had acted as stewards of that land for generations, or, in the cases of the Seminole and Miccosukee Tribes, since before humanity transcribed history into words.

Peg and other guides like him had welcomed tourists, and then those same visitors turned around and begged violence against them from the park service. It's easy to forget that the American alligator became endangered *after* Everglades National Park came in. So what happened, really? Habitat destruction had been the first to take its toll, but no one could drain or build in the park. So it wasn't that. Poachers like Peg did continue hunting, yet the number of alligators they took was statistically insignificant and could not have resulted in their decline. Yet the tourists blamed the poachers, decried history, and didn't bother to look deeper to see their stewardship of the glades. With fewer locals traipsing through that swamp, no one who knew what they were looking at was there to take the pulse of the species.

Given the stories I'd heard, I had a theory. In the 1950s, the Army Corps of Engineers installed a series of floodgates that allowed the Everglades to flow—or so they said. In true 1950s fashion, the corps put out a promotional movie reel, touting their triumph over nature: The corps controlled the Everglades. They told it where to flow, and flow it did in places where it never had before, creating floods made all the worse by Mother Nature's fury. Jonnie's story about Hurricane Donna gave me an aha moment, and it linked, like many things in their stories did, back to Jeff's investigation.

Just like how flooding from hurricanes had ruined a bayou nesting season and prompted Louisiana farmers to call on Floridian egg hunters to replenish their stocks, kicking off the need for Operation Alligator Thief in the first place, after the corps "triumphed" over nature, rainwater from hurricanes, which had once flowed through the Everglades, now pooled and mired and mucked up the place. Then the situation went from bad to worse. Hurricane Donna washed away over half the mangrove trees in the Everglades. This happened in September 1960, a time of year when nesting season becomes hatching season, and vulnerable hatchlings rely on vegetation like mangroves for shelter.

If flooding really did play such a major part in the alligator's downturn, how did the species bounce back? The Army Corps didn't fix their problem. They've been trying to mend that particular blunder to this day. For this answer, too, I can look back at evidence from Peg Brown stories. Although alligators tend to aim for the same nesting grounds that they have used year after year, they are not as unyielding as sea turtles: The alligators moved, many to the southernmost reaches of the glades where Peg continued to hunt and tend the land, such as by burning off excess brush left after storms to prevent blocked flows and pooling water, the very act that alerted the park service choppers to his whereabouts the one and only time the rangers almost caught him.

"You never take more than you need," Jonnie had said to me when he described their family's way of subsistence living. They cared for the world around them, because if they didn't, there would be nothing to sustain them anymore. When outsiders pushed them out of the Everglades, more was at stake than a sense of ownership. The Everglades was everything to them: their home, their past, their future, their culture, their identity.

Championing environmental causes by ignoring the people who live there, or worse, by working against them—wherever that may be—does not work, because to ignore the people is to ignore the land itself. They are the ones who have been listening to the land, many for a long time.

When tourists come down to the glades, or to any culture that has become a destination, it's all too common to partake of that culture like a commodity to be bought and sold. Tourists are so eager to experience what they think that culture should be that they ignore what it actually is. Journalists are guilty of this, too, when they jump in to take down a story without really paying attention, and it's why making fools of those same journalists remains a beloved Chokoloskee tradition. As much as I want to lay the blame elsewhere, we're all guilty of consuming culture like this in one way or another. It's just more apparent, and more hurtful, when it happens in your own backyard.

Although Mac had come from outside, he had done the very opposite: He arrived, he listened, he absorbed. He made it his life's cause not only to protect the place, but to continue its history and retell its stories. Maybe that was why the old-timers had ultimately accepted Peter Matthiessen, and why their descendants let me in, too: No matter what we *didn't* have in common, storytelling bridged the gulf. Matthiessen knew that the most important part of telling a story is, first, to listen.

Jeff had lived like that, watching people, talking to them, trying to understand them. He wanted to see the best in everyone. He wanted to know their story. He knew that no one breaks the law without a reason. He tried to withhold judgment. Because he was a mere mortal, that didn't always work. The same had happened for me on my journey into the Everglades.

I'll admit I'd held a concept of what poachers are like in my mind, and it was not a kind or understanding one, not one prone to listen. *What kind of person hurts a defenseless animal?* I thought, a hypocritical idea to countenance as a meat-eater. I crafted a caricature of the poachers I would meet in my head: rifle-toting, opinionated, camo-clad roughnecks who would have no respect for me or for the environment, who delighted in the pain of the animals they caught. What's worse is that I knew better. I already knew most poachers weren't like that. Yet the stereotype persisted in my thoughts until I had encountered such a shameful amount of evidence to the contrary that any single-celled organism could have understood that I was wrong.

Peg was a soft-spoken man, a listener. It was the creation of the park borders that had defined him as a poacher. Before it came in, he was only a hunter, and there were no Peg Brown stories.

Jonnie had been a poacher, too. He was soft-spoken at times, commanding in others. His livelihood as a fisherman depended on the balance of nature. He and Mac knew that stretch of glades better than I ever would. And instead of keeping me out, they wanted me to know more, because they knew I was ready to take it all in as it was, not as I thought it should be.

Jonnie explained to Mac what I was doing there, and Mac offered to take us out on his boat through the Ten Thousand Islands.

"You game for that?" Mac asked.

"Absolutely," I said. "Let me grab my notepad first."

11

THE HOOK

A tip came to Jeff from his handlers at the agency. They told him to check out a man named Wayne, who it seemed owned an alligator farm and kept half a dozen backwoods side hustles going, including guiding tourists on harrowing alligator hunts at night. So Jeff cooked up a story that he wanted to go into the pet trade. He called Wayne up and asked him if he had any hatchlings to sell that might make good pets.

The fact is that really no alligator makes a good pet. While federal law governs their private ownership because they are considered exotic pets, individual states dictate which animals are legal to own within their borders. It's legal to own a pet alligator in Alaska, but it's a crime in Georgia. In Florida, you have to have a permit and get it renewed once a year. Still, it's inadvisable. Former pet alligators under the care of specialists at rescues and rehabilitation facilities exhibit strange behaviors that range the gamut from excessive aggression to unnatural docility. Some display disrupted circadian rhythms. Others show up at rescues malnourished and missing limbs. Even private owners who believe they're treating their alligator properly are likely depriving it of the basic needs it would be fulfilling in the wild. And just as with any exotic animal that becomes too much for an owner to handle, if the owner releases it into the wild, it's unlikely to survive, as it has adapted to a bathtub and not to a swamp.

"Alligators don't make good pets," Wayne chided Jeff in a buoyant drawl. "I'm more interested in hunting 'em, myself." Wayne told him about his new alligator farm and the hunts he led. The juxtaposition of those two concepts sparked Jeff's interest.

Wonder if he's doing anything illegal, Jeff thought, *like pulling alligators from his farm and planting them to be hunted.* After their conversation ended, Jeff went back to work, all the while thinking about how to get close enough to Wayne to investigate him. He hadn't been at it for long when a dirty-looking truck pulled up the driveway and parked in front of the barn. Jeff peeked outside to see who it was.

"Hey!" A man in a cowboy hat waved, hailing him. "Are you Jeff?"

"Yeah?" Jeff said apprehensively.

"We were just talking on the phone." The young man, Wayne, strode over and gave Jeff a rowdy handshake. "You must be Jeff Blackledge." He seemed like the kind of fellow whose voice you could hear over everyone else's at a party, and yet you didn't mind.

"Nice to put a face to the name," Jeff said. "Come on in."

Jeff invited him into the camper for some beers, and they got talking about everything alligators. Wayne could sure talk. He was a real yarn spinner. A few beers in, the sun had gone down, and Jeff found himself greedily absorbing all the information Wayne had to offer. The time slipped by, and soon he had to abscond home to the missus. Jeff told him to come around anytime, and he meant it. He really did hope that he'd see Wayne soon.

The next morning, Jeff was cleaning the barn when he stumbled on a pair of sunglasses, camouflage-print, expensive ones, the ones Wayne had been wearing the day before. Remembering that he worked in a sporting goods store on the coast, Jeff called him up and offered to deliver them, saying he needed to pick up some hunting equipment anyway. Wayne agreed, sounding grateful, so Jeff made the trek and nosed around the store for a while so he wouldn't look too eager, and then he approached Wayne. To make it look convincing, Jeff bought a T-shirt, and he handed over the sunglasses.

"Tell me again about this hunter you're going to take," Jeff said, referencing a guided hunt Wayne had mentioned the night before.

"You want to help me with it?" Wayne asked.

"Shit, yeah, if you need help," Jeff answered.

"All right," Wayne said with a grin. "Here's what we're gonna do . . ."

A Swedish big-game hunter had come to Florida with the singular purpose of killing an alligator. He contracted Wayne to make that happen.

"This guy wants a ten-footer," Wayne said, talking about the gators at his farm. "I don't believe I've got a ten-footer, but I might have an eight."

So they planned to catch that gator. Setting the plan into action wasn't quite so easy. Two days later, they floundered around Wayne's alligator pond, trying and failing for nearly three whole hours to wrangle the slippery beast. The four other alligators in that watering hole watched that day's entertainment with bored disinterest. When Jeff and Wayne finally dragged their quarry from the water, they wrestled it quiet enough to tape its mouth closed. Then they loaded the gator into Wayne's truck and brought it to an orange grove, where they hooked its mouth as if it had chomped down on some bait, and they staked the hook line next to a canal. Wayne texted the Swede that they had "bait out." No need to mention it was already inside the alligator. Maybe if they couldn't sneak up on one, they could catch a gator that way, he said.

Stepping back, Jeff appraised the gator. *This ain't no ten-footer*, he thought. The Swede had promised to pay Wayne five grand for a ten-foot gator. Jeff didn't know how Wayne was going to figure his way out of this one.

Then they drove back into town, where they met the Swede and his wife in the Walmart parking lot. By the time they reached the grove, Wayne seemed nervous. Jeff had seen him drinking off and on throughout the day, and by then, he didn't trust him behind the wheel. So Jeff took over. *I'll just act like I'm his partner, and this is all part of the plan*, Jeff thought. But he felt embarrassed driving Wayne's truck. It was filthy. Styrofoam cups and other garbage littered the bed. *Blackledge wouldn't care*, he thought. *Now focus. You've got a job to do.*

Jeff acted like a tour guide, giving his hunting party a taste of real Florida adventure as he drove around the orange grove, hoping for the impossible, for an actual ten-foot alligator to show up in answer to his prayers.

They drove around the orange grove, between the rows of trees, crouching and peering through the leaves like fake safari guides at a theme park. For hours, they came up with nothing. Not a surprise. Almost by design, really. The longer the wait, the higher the anticipation. But as the sun began to set, the grove quieting toward dusk, this anticipation began to morph into impatience and dissatisfaction. Wayne decided it was time to turn toward the canal.

"We set a hook out there," Wayne said, his words slurring a bit as he intimated that, surely, they were about to come upon their elusive prey. That was Jeff's cue.

"Look," he said, pointing toward the canal bank. "There's a gator slide." The tourists craned to see it. And there was their alligator, now a bit worse for wear. By then, he had been out there several hours. He had tried to escape, dragging the hook and line along with him into the water, and he'd become tangled there in the weeds and underwater branches. He was hard to see past the sharp lip of the embankment, but Jeff knew he was there. "I think we got something on that line," he said.

Jeff looked to Wayne, who seemed to be downright drunk at this point. Was he playing a character, too? Was this all a part of the ambience? If Jeff had been in his shoes, he would have been nervous. A big-game hunter seems like one of the last people you'd want to dupe.

Jeff grabbed the thick plastic line and gave it a tug. The Swedes piled out after him, gawking and videotaping. *Time to ham it up*, Jeff thought. He wanted to get them excited, so the dullness of their wait would turn back into excited anticipation. "This feels good," Jeff said, laying it on as thick as possible. "Oh boy, this feels like a *big* one." He kept tugging on the line, feigning intense strain. "Oh my God, this guy's heavy!"

They could see the gator now, practically hog-tied by his tangle. He wasn't moving. *Shit*, Jeff thought. *Did we drown this poor fella? What a sorry way to go that would be.*

As if in answer, the gator gave a violent thrash, pulling Jeff off-balance. He let the line slacken, several feet slipping through his hands. If he hadn't, he would have pitched face-first into the canal. The Swede drew his .44 Magnum and let off a round with a resounding crack. They all peered over the embankment. The gator's thrashing had ceased.

"Good shot," Jeff said, clapping him on the shoulder. "Looks like you got him. I'll bring him on up here."

Jeff clambered down into the canal. He reached for the line. A great crash of water and reeds caused him to leap back. Partially freed, the alligator scrabbled toward him. *This joker came back to life!* Jeff thought. He grabbed for tufts of grass, weed stalks, anything to use as a handhold to pull himself up out of the canal to safety. *This damn thing is gonna bite me!* Those jaws snapped too close to his leg.

As Jeff panicked, Wayne watched from the bank, cocking his head at the commotion.

The gator closed in on Jeff, mouth open. Jeff pressed himself against the embankment. He dug into the root-sinewed dirt, desperate to gain purchase and avert the fate playing through his head, of those jaws coming down on his leg and pulling him beneath the water for a death roll.

"Grab your gun!" Jeff hollered. "Shoot him again! Shoot him again!"

"Gimme that," Wayne said, snatching the enormous gun from the Swede's hand and pointing it at the gator. He closed one eye and steadied himself. Jeff yelped and flattened himself against the canal bank. The bang went off over his head.

The alligator tumbled backward, and the splashing ceased. Jeff breathed a sigh of relief. He pulled himself up by a sapling as Wayne reeled the gator in—now thoroughly dead—by the cord. The Swedes snapped picture after picture, posing with their prey.

"Put it on your shoulder," Jeff suggested. They hoisted it up and took more pictures.

Wayne still seemed nervous. How long could they delay measuring that critter? Once they'd loaded the gator into the truck and returned to the Walmart parking lot, Jeff had his answer. He went around to drop the tailgate, and the Swede followed.

"I want to see that it's a ten-footer," the Swede said. "Let's measure it."

"Sure, let me see if we have some measuring tape," Jeff said. On the other side of the truck, he pulled Wayne aside. He told Wayne what the Swede wanted, and Wayne grimaced. Sweat pilled on his brow. "Don't worry," Jeff said. "I have an idea. Let me keep him up here by the head. I'm gonna teach him some more gator anatomy while you stretch the tape on down, and when he's not looking, you holler it's a ten-footer."

Wayne gulped and nodded. Then they set their plan into action. Jeff held the end of the tape on the tip of the snout. "You see this little hole right here," Jeff said. "This is his ear."

The Swede examined the gator intently and nodded.

"Hey, what do you know, he's ten foot two!" Wayne called out. Jeff let go of the tape, and it slithered back with a snap.

The Swedes whooped and clapped, thrilled with their catch. The husband paid Wayne in cash. Then they started for their car.

"Wait, don't you want your—?" Jeff gestured to the alligator.

"No," the Swede said.

"How would we take him on the plane?" his wife added with a laugh.

"We just came from South Africa where I killed a fourteen-foot crocodile," the Swede said. "We left him there, too."

Such nonchalance at the lives and deaths of majestic alligators did not begin and end with big-game hunters. Even within the alligator farming industry, the relative paucity of regulations spoke of either a widespread assumption of the crocodilian's sturdiness or a general disregard for its well-being. Because who could connect with such alien creatures? Who could tell if they were suffering? Jeff thought he could, but sometimes it seemed he was the only one.

There are no certification meetings, no classes to attend. You do not have to prove you can wrangle an alligator. Just about anybody can open a legal alligator farm as long as they have the money and enough know-how to get by. You do not need a veterinarian on staff. You do not really need a staff at all beyond yourself. Maybe that was why the old-school farmers were so reticent to talk. Not only is their world steeped in secrecy, it is also steeped in the trepidation of knowing that the biggest hoop someone has to jump through to do this is to be brave enough to actually see it through. In other words, if you write a check to the state of Florida and manage to pull together an alligator farm of your very own, all you need to do then is file the paperwork and have an inspection, and voilà: You have a legal alligator farm.

But to become one of the Golden 30 is another thing entirely. The Golden 30 is what FWC calls the group of alligator farms that receive eggs from the state with little to no effort on their part. Because the farms don't have to lift a finger, FWC says they are "golden." Of course, as with anything else wildlife-related in Florida, farms have to follow certain guidelines, pay $250, and get a permit. Only the first thirty farms that are accepted to the program get to participate. Theoretically, the farms can take wild-harvested eggs, incubate them, nurture the hatchlings, then raise them into maturity to cultivate a breeding stock. The initial idea was that farms might do this, then after achieving a high enough number of livestock alligators, they should be able to perpetuate their farm through breeding and never have to dip into wild alligator populations again. In this hypothetical eventuality, these farms would be launching entire bloodlines of alligators—thousands upon thousands of individual creatures—who had never seen a swamp before, and never would. To Jeff, it seemed a great loss, but one he couldn't put into words.

Whenever he pictured an alligator, he also conjured up an image of the swamp. In his mind, that vision of a reptile floated almost totally submersed in glassy, dark water, eyes breaking a surface stained nearly black with the tannins of oak leaves, sending out a ring of ripples that warped the reflection of the white-dappled daylight from the canopy above. The alligator's second eyelid might smooth like a meniscus over his green and piercing reptilian eye, itself shining with a vision of the swamp. The association between alligator and swamp was so strong that it was hard to fathom one that had never been there. What were alligators without the swamp? What would they be if their wildness were ever tamed, their status reduced to livestock, seen more like chickens or pigs than the living dinosaurs that they are? If alligators became just another commodity to be bred and bought and sold, even if they weren't gone entirely, even if there were some left in the wild, their mystique would have washed away, and the "dragon" naturalist William Bartram spoke of in his effusive travelogues would have all but disappeared.

It was a good thing and a bad one that that eventuality wasn't on the horizon, as alligators, like most other animals, seldom breed in captivity.

The best farms and zoos, as Jeff was learning, tried to replicate swamp conditions. At Gatorland in Orlando, for example, most of their resident alligators live in a swampy lake environment so large that it seems like the enclosure's only boundaries are the ones that separate the guests from the alligators. There's no outer fence in sight—though surely there is one, right? Jeff's alligators, too, had their own little slices of swamp in his farm's large ponds. Still, at most of these places, including Jeff's, alligators just didn't get frisky, and even if they did, they didn't build nests. While creating his farm, Jeff had talked to biologists about how to make this work. Being the person he is, a problem solver, he wanted to figure out why exactly alligators didn't breed in captivity and fix the problem. Maybe there wasn't enough foliage for nest building, he thought. Was it a privacy issue? Who knew. Come nesting season, he adorned his enclosures with palm fronds and grasses to no avail. Removing gators from the wild had to some extent taken the wild out of them, and with it went their natural imperatives. No need to hunt, as the food came to them. No need to reproduce, because why bother. It was like being a big fish in a tiny bowl. It had no space to grow—and no reason to do so, either. If Jeff couldn't figure it out, it wasn't so surprising that no one else had, and there seemed little need when all the big guys, the larger farms with enough resources and experience to solve this problem, were in the Golden 30 getting wild-harvested eggs practically for free.

Before nesting season called egg hunters into the swamps, FWC called an open meeting for state alligator farmers, so they could discuss the possibility of expanding the Golden 30 into the Golden 35, and what requirements these extra five might have to achieve to become golden. As with all such wildlife-rule meetings, the people who came had strong opinions and pontificated on them like southern lawyers straight out of a John Grisham novel. Jeff always had strong opinions about wildlife law, too, but he wasn't there to sway any minds. He needed to make the connections that'd break open his case.

Jeff used the meeting as a way to schmooze. He shook hands and grinned and gave out business cards. Most people were cordial. That much he'd expected. They were in the part of the world, after all, where even if someone's skinning your name alive behind closed doors, they'll give you a smile in person. Many alligator farm owners either had money or came from money. Farming alligators isn't a lucrative business, so most farms were pet projects for the rich. Which was why Jeff had imagined his character Blackledge to benefit from a trust fund in order to get into the game. Yet, somehow, he still wasn't ready for how polite-ness greased every conversation, smoothing the way from introduction to goodbye before Jeff knew what happened. After the disorientation of this amiability subsided, he felt like he'd gotten somewhere, even though, deep down, he knew better. These people were playing characters just like he was, their faces veneered with charm. The deeper the pocket, the better the actor, the more entrenched this falsity was within their rung of society. If you went high enough up, people were Russian nesting dolls of façades, motivations inside motivations, deceptions all the way down.

During the meeting, Jeff caught sight of Robert opposite him in the back of the room. He wasn't with his friends from Shady Creek. When the talks ended and the schmoozing began, Shady Creek's main owner, a mega-millionaire whom folks called Brother Parker, made a show of avoiding Robert, and everyone else, it seemed, followed suit. Jeff watched Robert try to network, shake hands, and pass out his business card. Every person he tried to corner managed to slip away.

The last time they'd seen each other, Jeff thought they had a good rapport going. They'd connected over hunting. Robert had promised to call and make plans. That was January. This was May. It was possible Robert had gotten caught up in running his farm. But from the looks of it, more was going on.

As Robert made his exit, he nodded at other folks, but they mostly gave him a wide berth. People treated Robert with even less cordiality than Robert had treated Jeff, and he wondered why. He had a feeling it had something to do with Brother Parker.

I should ask around and find out what happened, Jeff thought.

Y ou dodged a bullet if you ask me," Wayne said. Squinting up his rifle barrel, he swiveled, searching for the doves that had taken flight with the report of his shot. He let off another. *Pop!* "If I were you, I'd stay away from that Robert guy," Wayne went on.

They stood out in front of Jeff's camper, Jeff with a beer in hand and Wayne with his stationed at his feet as he tried to take down the doves. Wayne had gotten into the habit of coming around Sunshine just to hang out with Jeff and drink his beer, libations that Jeff purchased for that specific purpose, but Wayne didn't need to know that. Jeff enjoyed his company. That was what mattered.

"Why?" Jeff asked. "What's wrong with him?"

"Oh, his whole crew is trouble," Wayne said. "I've heard all kinds of stories about him."

"Are we talking about the same Robert?" Jeff said. "He seems so upstanding."

Wayne raised an eyebrow and smiled knowingly. "Really, Jeff," he chided. "You should worry about them the most." He fired a shot into the sky.

Ridiculous, Jeff thought. Wayne's opinion of Robert didn't seem backed up by fact. Sure, Robert may have thought he was too good for Jeff, but Jeff couldn't read the man's mind. He didn't know, and he probably never would. He'd given up on hearing from him ever again. Even if he saw Robert at the hardware store, he probably wouldn't stop to chat. Why bother?

That seemed to be the general consensus others held for Jeff, though: Why bother?

In fact, no one he'd given his card to at the meeting called, and no one called him back, either. But then, on a hot summer afternoon at Sunshine Alligator Farm, Jeff's cell phone started ringing. This was it, finally. The big break he was waiting for, breathing on the other side of the line. He'd known it was coming. He'd put in the work. The only thing that surprised him was the name on his caller ID. It was the last person he would have expected: Robert.

12

THE FIRST EGG HUNT

I want to apologize for missing you at the meeting," Robert said over the phone.

Missing me, huh? Jeff thought. It was the day after the meeting, and Jeff was still smarting from Robert's snub.

"I didn't mean to ignore you," Robert went on. "I had other things on my mind."

Rumor had it that one of those other things was a falling-out with Brother Parker. Left without a job and a steady source of income, Robert had been hustling to get someone else to partner with him—and he had failed.

"Sure, I know how it is," Jeff said, trying to sound magnanimous.

"Hey, what are you doing next week?" Robert asked. "I'd like to come talk to you."

The season was awakening, and the wild things were coming alive from that brief respite that is springtime in Florida. With mating season over, the female gators had already begun to dig their nests and lay their eggs.

Jeff went to Robert's house, where Robert proposed the idea of a business partnership. They would collect alligator eggs from the wild, and Robert would use Jeff's farm facilities for hatching, updating the farm as he saw appropriate. In return, Robert offered to guide and educate Jeff on the alligator industry.

If Jeff had been Jeff Babauta, he might have turned Robert away. As Blackledge, he wanted to chalk their previous missed connections up to misunderstandings. Plus, he needed a way in, desperately—and here it was.

Nonetheless, he sat on it, as if considering the proposal, but really he just didn't want to seem overly eager.

Afterward, Jeff called Lieutenant Wilson at the agency.

"Man, I don't know what this guy's doing," Jeff said, "but I think I just got into an agreement to collect eggs."

"Fantastic," Lieutenant Wilson said. "With who?"

Jeff told him about Robert and the rumors swirling around him. "He seems like a decent enough guy though," Jeff said. "What can it hurt?"

"Let it ride," Lieutenant Wilson said. "See what he offers."

By May 20, Jeff's birthday, Robert had stood Jeff up then called again, and they bartered back and forth for close to a month before it seemed the time had come to lay their deal out on paper. He met with Robert and his wife, Robin, at a gas station on the corner of two desolate country roads.

"So it's all settled," Robert said. "I'll teach you everything you need to know about raising alligators. All you need to do is let us use your facility. We'll even update it for you, make the place state of the art."

"All of that sounds great, but—" Jeff said.

"But?"

"My accountant didn't like what he saw of our agreement," Jeff said. "I am running a business after all. I need to make money. So you can't use the place for free."

"Well, it wouldn't be for free," Robert said. "I would fence in that pond of yours, and I'd transfer in some adult alligators."

"Yeah, that would be great," Jeff said. "You can do that. *And* you also need to pay me." *What I'm asking of you is normal*, Jeff thought. *Don't balk at this*. Jeff was afraid of scaring him away, but at a certain point he risked coming across as a pushover.

"How about $5,000?" Robert asked. "To use your farm for the season."

That's it? Jeff thought. But he nodded. "All right," he said. "That sounds fair." Except it didn't.

"We'll give you half up front and half after the harvest," Robert said.

"It's a deal," Jeff said. They shook hands.

Cars sped by under the live oaks.

Robert took out a set of FWC forms and explained them to Jeff, which made Jeff chuckle in his head. But Robert knew his stuff.

"Can I see your farm license?" Robert asked. "I need to take a picture of it." He did that while Jeff signed the forms. Robert explained how the private lands application would allow him to transfer alligator eggs harvested from the wild to Sunshine Alligator Farm.

"I'll send all this stuff to Florida Fish and Wildlife," Robert said. "Don't you worry. I'll take care of everything."

He further explained that Jeff would only be accepting eggs and not hatchlings or adult alligators. "That's what our permits are for," Robert added. "Eggs only, understand?"

"Eggs only," Jeff said. "I gotcha."

See? Everything to the letter of the law, Jeff thought. *I don't know what the heck Wayne was talking about. These are good people. They got nothing to hide.*

After they both signed the egg-collecting application, with Robin witnessing, they said their farewells and started toward their trucks.

That was when Jeff glanced back and saw Robin had done the same. She was glaring at him.

She's giving me the evil eye, Jeff thought. Once she'd turned around again, Jeff reasoned with himself. *Maybe I'm just imagining things.*

In June, Jeff absconded to the mountains of North Carolina, a brief and much-needed family camping trip that he covered up with the lie of visiting his girlfriend's parents. By the end of the weekend, Jeff knew he had to hurry back to work. Throughout the drive back down to Florida, his phone rang incessantly. The thing gave off every beep and buzz in its arsenal, texts, emails, the whole bit. He glanced at them as he drove. It was Robert sending him paperwork—permits in Curtis Blackledge's name, all ready to go.

I didn't apply for any of this, Jeff thought. *Did Robert just hijack my damn farm?*

It was all happening too fast. That set off an alarm in Jeff's head. Something wasn't right.

Jeff decided to let Robert keep going.

Let's just see how far this gets, Jeff thought.

He hadn't talked to Robert between May and June 7, when Robert asked for his Social Security number to fill out yet another form. After he got back from the mountains, Jeff drove to Robert's house unannounced. Inside, all his planning and paperwork sprawled across the dining room table.

"I've been putting in a lot of work while you've been gone," Robert said.

"I can tell," Jeff said. "I'm impressed.

They discussed when they were going to start collecting eggs, what machines they required, which ones they had that needed to be cleaned or serviced—Robert acting like he wanted Jeff's input when they both knew he was just using Jeff for the farm.

In the coming weeks, Robert threw money around. He bought dozens of large plastic crates for transporting eggs. He purchased equipment large and small, from thermometers and cleaning supplies to an entire airboat.

Where is he getting all of this money? Jeff wondered.

"We got so lucky with this," Lieutenant Wilson said on the phone later. "He took over your farm. He's doing all the work, and now he's buying all this stuff for you? It's a windfall."

Jeff's feelings, however, were more muddled than that. The case finally felt like it was opening up for him. And yet he couldn't help but feel slighted. All the hard work that he'd put into the farm, and here Robert just came in and took over and brushed him aside. It seemed like everything was once again in a whirlwind around him while he was standing still.

Later, Robert and Robin paid a visit to the farm. They pulled up to the barn's back loading door, and, seeing Jeff, Robert announced, "I got some eggs."

"Where'd you get them?" Jeff asked as he helped Robert carry a cooler into the barn.

"We collected them last night from the Seminole Reservation," Robert said.

Jeff lifted the cooler lid to peek inside. Rows of dirty white ovals nestled in a mulch of mud and bark.

"They'll be all right where they are," Robert said, handing him the transfer document. With that, Robin and Robert left, saying they would be back in a few days.

As the investigation progressed, a tragedy was unfolding back at Jeff's home. A few days earlier, Sandy had told Jeff that his K-9, Mack, had been acting lethargic. Sandy had sensed something was wrong. At first, she thought that Mack just had the blues. He missed his patrol partner. Maybe he missed his feeling of purpose, too. He would watch the front door with the other dogs, waiting for Jeff to return. While the others kept up their patient and faithful routine with unflagging earnestness, Mack seemed to fade. Sandy told Jeff she was taking Mack to the vet. Jeff worried, as was his way, but he assumed as Sandy did that the Goldador was only suffering from the kind of homesickness we feel when separated too long from the people we love. Heartache though it was, they believed it one with an easy cure. So with effort, he put the dog out of his mind and continued with his farm work.

Later, under the cover of darkness, Jeff removed his personal phone from its secret compartment. A message from Sandy asked him to call when he got the chance. He did and listened to the ringer with a growing sense of dread.

Sandy told him that she had bad news. Mack had a tumor on his heart, and they had to decide what to do. The vet believed that surgery would do more harm than good. There was only one option, really.

"We have to put him down," Jeff said, a lump forming in his throat. He told Sandy that he wanted to be there. He loved that dog. He didn't want Mack to go through that without him. "I have to get permission to leave, but I'm coming even if they say no."

Sandy agreed that she would wait for him, and after he hung up, Jeff took a moment to breathe. The life he had shared with Mack flashed before his eyes. Their days on patrol stretched out through the pine-woods, hours of quiet punctuated by sudden moments of fear and excitement. "It's time to go to work!" Jeff would say when those moments came. He loved how much Mack would perk up. The eager look in his brown eyes would say, *Yes! I'm ready.* Mack could sniff out anything. Fast on a scent, he would race through the forest, his golden tail alert and rippling like a feather plume. Mack always found his mark. Mack could heel at attention, as poised as a soldier, then at home he would frolic, carefree as any other dog.

The agency had the compassion to let Jeff go. No need to explain to wildlife officers why an animal meant so much to him.

Jeff drove home, tucked his unmarked vehicle away, and went to the vet with Sandy. There, he placed a hand on Mack's soft head. "There's a good boy," Jeff said. "Daddy's here." Mack licked his wrist, but that spark of energy that once propelled him through the woods had faded. Jeff knew that this was the right thing to do. He would save his friend so much pain. That didn't make it hurt any less for him.

Jeff stroked Mack while it happened, reminding him that he was such a very good dog.

He couldn't leave the farm unattended for too long. After it was over, Jeff had to go back. The whole drive, that same lump that caught in his throat remained there, and he tried not to think about how much he was missing by not being at home. The truth was, he'd missed nearly a year in his dog's life. He feared that he was missing more—of his wife, his son, his mother, his siblings, their kids—than he would ever know.

No matter how important this mission was supposed to be, it meant losing time with the people he loved. Jeff could never get this time back. Mack's death reminded him that he had so much more to lose. There was no telling what bad news might come on Sandy's next call, or if someone would call about her. All this worry and heartache had built up over the past year. It made him feel worn thin and old, and so ready for this job to be over. He couldn't wait to go home, his real home.

He pulled into the farm's driveway and shut the gate in the glare of his headlights, those feelings still building up, straining against his will not to let them go. He parked in front of his camper, went inside, and locked the door. He swallowed against the lump in his throat, but it wouldn't give way. This loss of time was so much more of a sacrifice than he ever anticipated making. The heartbreak overtook him.

That was my baby, he thought, and he let the tears flow.

On the last day of June, Jeff and Robert met up with a pilot at the Arcadia Airport, a small municipal airstrip that sat abreast of farm-land and trailer parks on the edge of town. The three of them climbed into a helicopter, donned their headsets, and zipped up into the air.

Jeff was no stranger to helicopters. After the Florida Game and Fresh-water Fish Commission had merged with Florida Marine Patrol, the new superagency owned more aircraft than any other law enforcement agency in the state. They used them for search-and-rescue missions, flora and fauna counts, spotting covert marijuana growers, and, of course, chasing down poachers. To ignite controlled burns, fire technicians would drop Ping-Pong balls of combustion chemicals from the aircraft. When they made contact with the forest floor, they would burst. A thousand acres of brush could go up in less than a day. On the night detail, they would shine spotlights down through the overgrowth, trying to spy hunters, hideouts, a cache of illicit wares.

Jeff had trained his dog Mack to ride in helicopters, for assignments on barrier islands or other places almost no other vehicle could reach. Mack had enjoyed flying about as much as Jeff did—which was not much.

This helicopter was smaller than the ones Jeff was used to. The smaller the aircraft, the more dramatic its movements feel. It had no doors, so the wind whipped at his hair. It felt like being in a tornado. After a couple of hours, Jeff felt nauseous. He toughed it out. They flew over Avon Park bombing range with its enormous bull's-eyes painted like surreal earth-works over the swamp. The helicopter swooped down close enough to spy the dark mounds of alligator nests. They stood out against the lushness of all that green. Later, they would return on foot to make their harvest.

A few days later, back at the farm, the sound of Jeff's cell phone ringing beside his bed startled him awake. He swore under his breath and swiped at it. He grabbed it and read the screen, its glare washing over his squinting face like he was driving into oncoming traffic. It was about 4 AM. The caller ID said ROBERT. Annoyed and weary, and most of all tired as hell, Jeff answered and mumbled a salutation.

"Hey," Robert said. Then, without much preamble, he launched into his business. "We're going to collect tomorrow," he said.

Collect, Jeff thought, his brain still feeling liquid from sleep. *Collect! He means gator eggs!* He'd been waiting more than a year for this. Sure, Jeff had collected eggs on his own already. But now he was finally getting to learn how a real operation was done. The lightning strike of this opportunity woke Jeff up in an awful hurry.

"I'm interested," Jeff said.

"Get something to eat and head over here to the house," Robert said.

Jeff threw some clothes on, stuffed breakfast in his mouth, and was at Robert's homestead within the hour. The place fluttered with activity, every porchlight aglow, dogs barking, the crew Robert had amassed chatting with excitement. Jeff jumped in to help and found himself in the middle of the fray. Everyone was wired with a purposeful energy. Everyone seemed to have something to do, to be bent on a task and hurtling toward it with conviction; but that's all it was, dramatic energy and forward motion. No one seemed to know what was going on except Robert, who attended to his disarray of papers spread from the head of his dining room table all the way down to its foot.

As Jeff tried to help, he wondered if this uninformed chaos was by design. Keeping people on their toes by denying them necessary information was a well-known manipulation tactic. Jeff paused to study Robert for a moment. It was as if the man stood inside a hurricane's eye, untouched by the tension and nervous energy around him. If this was manipulation, it was good. Well, good for Robert. Effective. Bad for Jeff. Not only did it obscure any possible wrongdoing behind a flurry of activity, but it also meant that he was onto something. Had he sensed something was off about Jeff? *Are you cunning or just disorganized?* Jeff wondered. Robert was more of an enigma to him than ever.

Then he remembered Robin's evil eye.

They didn't arrive in Fort Drum until 11 PM that night, nearly nineteen hours after Robert's call plucked Jeff from sleep. What was left outside Fort Drum's highway oasis amounted to a pioneer graveyard and a scattering of houses under the loblolly pines; it was named after a Seminole War–era battlement that had long since receded into the soil. This was the kind of place where the ground was thick with clay-red pine needles, where the quiet made you think of ghosts and a history long forgotten by all but a few. The town boasted that it was the origin of the St. Johns River, one of the most significant rivers in Florida. That made Fort Drum a kind of belowground juncture, too. Within the cavernous aquifer, living water destined for the glades intermingled with contrarian tides bent on flowing north, a little metaphor for the backwoods attitude if ever there was one.

Millions of years ago, Lake Okeechobee stretched far beyond its current boundaries up the Floridian peninsula, covering the tract that would become Fort Drum and the area that surrounds it with a vast inland sea. While traipsing through the woods here, it's not uncommon to find remaining clues to that sea. Some in the form of animals whose species evolved in isolation upon islands in the sea, like the Florida scrub-jay, a threatened species of corvid with Caribbean-blue feathers and a knowing look in its eyes. Back underground, there lies another such uncanny artifact of Florida's bygone past. The limestone deposits that protect the aquifer have also trapped the chalky shells of prehistoric mollusks. It's not uncommon to stumble upon a trail made chalk white by the pulverized calcium of fossil shells, a sight unusual in the understory's fecund decomposition, like folk magic crafted by the soil itself. This is the oldest kind of magic, where the land speaks even when no one is around to listen. The shells beneath Fort Drum became jagged while still submerged within that primordial sea: Calcite crystals swirled new skeletons around them like sculptures of shimmering finger bones. The land tells its unique story.

Jeff had spent plenty of time in that area as a game warden, but he was seeing it through new eyes on his first trip with Robert's crew.

Their pickup truck caravan trundled along the dirt road that led into Fort Drum Wildlife Management Area, headlights throwing a sallow tunnel forward across the grassland. In the clearing before the tree line, they circled their trucks and parked. Beyond the flat patch where they stood, the world opened up into the darkest night. Without intending it, they had ventured into Jeff's old stomping grounds. The capital of dark sky and the fragile nests of endangered birds. He paused for a moment to look out along the prairie where distant marshland pools reflected the enormity of the cosmos. The result was an optical illusion that made the heavens seem to devour the earth, flooding over its curvature like a dam broken after the rain. It was easy to lose yourself in awe. Not just here, but anywhere in nature that lets you take a breath and notice all the small wonders we usually pass by.

This was why he was here, doing this mission. Any day when things got too grungy, when the job got too hard, when it started to feel like just a job, he would have to remember moments like this. He stored it up in his mental file as a reminder: He was looking for poachers. That much was true. But in that, he was looking to prevent a tipping of the delicate balance. Unlike the story of the sparrows there, who were nearly at the brink of extinction, a place where alligators had been half a decade before, the alligators Jeff was trying to save represented a proactive approach to conservation rather than a reactive one.

There were rumors that, during those trying times for alligators, entire species of plants shifted place in the Everglades. Alligators are ecosystem engineers. But we don't know the entire extent of their influence. If alligators ever faced extirpation or, worse, extinction, there was no telling what would happen to their habitats—and our planet—without them. Jeff's grand-scheme purpose there was to make sure that we would never find out. So he carried this thought with him: He was saving the alligators—along with the sparrows, the panthers, the burrowing owls, the bears—and the constellation of this hopeful act stretched out from that little patch of plain and swamp into everywhere the water flowed, all the people who drank it, all the plants that sucked it up through their roots, all the oxygen that they exhaled—a little thing in the grand scheme could mean the entire world. He was saving the darkness, too, the enormity of the sky only possible because people like Jeff guarded the land from destructive human hands, keeping the channels of possibility open for the primordial wonder we feel, our smallness, our place in the universe, when we look into the stars.

He needed that stolen bit of hope sooner than he expected. They slept in their trucks. The heat of the day had hardly dissipated. It was nearly a hundred degrees out, the sleeping arrangements uncomfortable, the bugs out in their vast array, and even though Jeff always brought his Thermacell, he could still hear them out there in the dark, going *hmmmm hmmmmmm*, lusting for his blood. It was a rough night; a perfect way to launch egg-collecting season.

In the morning, they started about their business. By then, Robert had pulled a suspicious 180, suddenly becoming organized. Or perhaps he had been all along.

They ventured along the trails through the hardwood swamp, toting snake hooks and large plastic containers to store the eggs. Jeff had woken up on the wrong side of the driver's seat, and he remained disgruntled and achy the rest of the day. The sheer weight of the heat didn't help. He kept on guard for nefarious happenings, but he already knew, after a lifetime of experience, that poaching and legal hunting (or egg collecting) looked exactly the same save for two things. The first was that poachers typically did not have the correct paperwork or legitimate hunting tags. The second and more obvious difference was that legitimate hunters seldom ran when you came upon them in the woods. There's an old Irish saying that the guilty man flees while no one makes chase.

The one thing that had stood out to him most was Robert's organization. No matter where they went in field or swamp, Robert always carried an aluminum lockbox, the type used to keep important papers safe. The mystery of what might be inside piqued Jeff's interest. Robert was hiding something. And you don't hide things that aren't incriminating. When no one was looking, Jeff made a note of it on the side of his shoe. Just BOX. He would remember.

Some of them paired off to make more efficient work of the egg hunt. Jeff went with a fellow he'd already met named Tommy. Tommy was in his thirties, perhaps. He wore baggy clothes and small oval glasses, the kind that had been in style when Jeff's son was a teen in the early 2000s. Behind those, he wore a disdainful expression.

As they walked along the trail, carrying the plastic egg tub between them, a tense and uncompanionable silence drew taut between them as well. Jeff grew increasingly uncomfortable, so he made a joke to cut the tension. Tommy acknowledged that Jeff had spoken, but he didn't laugh. His expression remained sour. The longer this went on, the more Tommy's unsociable demeanor got underneath Jeff's skin. Jeff kept cracking one-liners. He got a laugh or two out of Tommy, but he still hadn't drawn the fellow all the way out. He told himself this was more than discomfort. He didn't need Tommy to like him. He needed Tommy to trust him enough to divulge information. He kept pressing.

While this was going on, Jeff and Tommy continued from nest to nest. Jeff tried not to take the lead, just let things flow as they were, because if they were doing something illegal, he had to toe the line between leading the crew into crime and leading them away from it.

They located a nest from the makeshift map they'd made during the helicopter ride. It was a mound of mud and reeds nestled in a copse of water oak saplings and the sharp appendages of saw palms.

"I'm that guy who when Robert says, 'Hey, I need that eleven-footer caught,' I'm the one they call in to go catch him," Tommy boasted as he sifted through the brush to reach the thatched mound of a nest.

"So you're the brave one, huh?" Jeff asked, trying not to laugh.

"Oh yeah," Tommy responded.

Oh, so this is who you are, Jeff thought. He was beginning to miss the terse silence. Half an hour later, Jeff had a feeling that if he was going to blow the operation, it would be on account of Tommy's incessant pontificating, especially in contrast with his results, which were nil. They moved on to the next nest, this time with Jeff glowering silently along the trail as Tommy yakked his ear off.

Good Lord, could Tommy brag. It seemed to be his greatest talent. Worse, he was the king of one-upmanship. If you caught a fish, he caught a bigger one. If you felled five deer that season, he bagged thirty.

They eventually reached the nest. As they approached, a loud hissing noise rose above the rhythmic buzz of the katydids. Jeff paused and cocked his head. He put out his arm to block Tommy from venturing onward.

"What the hell is that?" Jeff asked.

They didn't have much time to ponder before the answer lunged at them. An angry mother alligator darted toward Jeff, putting herself between him and her nest. Her mouth was open, emitting a vitriolic hiss. When people associated alligators with the phrase *Fuck around and find out*, this situation wasn't quite what they had in mind, but it should have been. Jeff and Tommy had grown careless. They'd been too preoccupied by their conflicting personalities. It was just another day at the office. How easily they'd forgotten that, no matter the sense of normalcy Jeff's mind painted over his surroundings, no matter how usual, how tame the swamp had grown in his thoughts, it was the wild, stubborn and unconquerable, both as a reality and as a millennia-old symbol for the forbidding nature of these remote parts of the world, despite human endeavors to bring them to hand.

Jeff and Tommy had fucked around. Now they were going to find out.

They backed off, and the alligator followed at a surprisingly quick gait, undulating her rough-hewn body back and forth, dragging a rapid S-curve across the leaf litter. She closed the gap between them. Jeff was close enough to see the flecks of green and gold reflect from within her piercing reptilian eyes. She stopped. So did they. They paused in a standoff.

While alligators don't usually attack humans, like any animal, humans included, they will attack when they feel threatened or cornered, especially when they perceive the lives of their offspring to be in danger. Many are willing to die for their young. *Will this mother alligator go so far?* Jeff wondered. *Is it worth the risk to find out?*

Tommy must have thought so. As soon as the mother gator began her retreat, he followed. "Cover me," he said. He levered the nest's top thatch open with his snake hook.

"She's already coming back!" Jeff warned, raising his voice.

"Well, swat her with something." Finding a trove of eggs within the stinking refuge of the nest, Tommy straddled their egg box and began picking eggs out and drawing a line on each shell with a permanent marker to indicate which side had faced up. Jeff would later learn why this step is important. If you put an egg in upside down, the hatchling inside will crush its umbilical cord, and it will die.

The nest was open. Now there was no turning back. If they did, they'd waste yet another tally.

Jeff stood over Tommy, putting himself between him and that narrow clearing's scrubby edge. Tommy worked quickly. He plucked an egg, rubbed away the caked bark and mulch, wet with hot rainwater and likely piss, and held it up to the sun. Satisfied that it was fertilized and viable, he put the egg into the box. He wasn't at this for long when the hissing filled Jeff's ears again.

The mother gator crashed through the brush. Before she could jump from the thicket of saw palms, Jeff swatted her on the nose with his snake hook with a dull *whack*. She closed her mouth and recoiled. He hadn't hit her very hard, just enough to startle her. Still, he felt bad. She was defending her babies, after all. He certainly would have squared off against some fucker who was messing with his kid. *Sorry, gal,* he thought. *That's the food chain for you.* Him being there would be better for her—and her future hatchlings—in the long run. Or so he hoped.

He hated having to sacrifice a few animals for the benefit of others, but that's often what conservation comes down to these days. Whether you are hunting animals from an invasive species that have cast their adopted environment into disarray—such as the Burmese python in the Everglades or the lionfish that had spread from a likely introduction point in South Florida up and down the Atlantic and Gulf Coasts of the Western Hemisphere—modern conservation is constantly faced with ecological trolley problems: sacrifice the few to save the many. Populations of species that have gotten out of hand, even endemic ones, threaten to destroy their habitats and decimate the other species around them, whether they are predator or prey.

Alligators have proven so resilient since their earlier struggles that their numbers have skyrocketed into the millions. With an excess of predators, prey species decline. It's impossible to pinpoint just one impact from this. But theoretical dominoes line up to tip into vegetation overgrowth that spurs wildfires, invasive species supplanting native ones, or other species further down the food web either booming or withering. As human influence is usually to blame for such ecological disequilibrium, it's up to us to set things right, or as right as we can. Humans are just as much a part of the grand scheme of ecological balance as are the alligators, or the deer, or the snakes or rabbits.

It's tempting to say the best way for humans to save the ecosystems we've mucked up is to leave. Yes, many parts of the wild are better off without us. But to get really unpoetic here, you can't un-lick that ice cream cone. You can rewild the wilderness, but you can't make it untouched. One is conservation. The other is abdication, and it looks a lot more like abandoning a burning mess than it does leave-only-footprints conservation. Since our human species is just as much a part of this biome as everything else, we need to learn to live within it again. As Indigenous peoples all over the world will tell you, from the Sami of Finland to the Dukha of Mongolia and the Māori of New Zealand, we are in and of the Earth, not apart from it. Indigenous farmers don't clear land, for example. They don't graze grassland till it's bare. The wild is not untouched but listened to. *What do you need? What have we done wrong? How can we make things right?*

As much as Jeff sometimes felt at odds with his mission, he knew that he was already in the thick of things—we all are. To really get something done, you have to break a few eggs, so to speak.

The mother alligator lingered, floating half-submerged in a nearby mire, watching Tommy pick through her nest, but she didn't approach again. Jeff wondered what she was thinking, if she felt defeated.

Sorry about this, Jeff thought toward the mother alligator. *It is what it is.*

Meanwhile, indifferent, Tommy sorted through the nest, launching into a long diatribe-slash-explanation about alligator-egg hunting, and alligators, and hunting, and how he knew better than everyone about everything on this green Earth, and—good God. Jeff regretted ever trying to draw the man out of his shell. How could he stuff him back in?

Tommy claimed to have caught two hundred deer, not just an illegal but a horrifying number. He was one of those guys who seemed to live his life to poach and cheat the system, like the world owed him something, like he was being cheated himself, and, in lieu of an easier target, he was taking his due from nature. If he wasn't bragging, maybe he was just lying to make Jeff feel small, lying to assert dominance. There's a big difference between this and the river country storytelling tradition of embellishment. The former can be a bit underhanded. The

latter, when listeners are accustomed to that particular storytelling device, serves for emphasis.

Having ventured too deeply into the weeds of his own lecture,
Tommy paused with an egg in his hand above the tub. He furrowed his
brow and looked at the egg again. He held it up to the light. The mother
alligator continued to hiss but from a safe distance away. With the sun
glowing through the shell like a flashlight through a finger, he ascer-
tained the position of the embryo and marked it with a fat permanent
marker, then set the egg into the tub with the rest.

13

ALONE IN THE SWAMP

They moved on to Cecil M. Webb Wildlife Management Area, inconveniently located clear across the girth of the state inland of where Punta Gorda projects into Gasparilla Sound. Once again, the crew didn't reach the site until well after nightfall. They set up camp in an area of white sand. From there, Jeff could just make out the ghostly spindles of the pines where they shot up above the flatwoods. To the southwest, the purple of the sky faded into a yellow like a half-healed bruise. The cities lay down that way, Fort Myers and Cape Coral straddling the outlet of the Caloosahatchee River. Except for the light pollution, the night whirred with a peaceful buzz dotted with the percussion of ribbits. The distant sea breeze allayed the heat they'd felt in Fort Drum, so as they set up camp, Jeff thought of how much tonight, unlike the night before, felt like a relaxing camping trip.

With his corner of the camp set up, Jeff wandered over to the group where Tommy sat with CW, another member of the crew. They squatted around a pile of sticks and leaves and criticized one another's bushcraft skills as they tried to start a fire. The crew's numbers had swelled beyond ten. Robert said he anticipated that this location would prove fertile ground for alligator eggs, so they brought every soul they could muster. The guys' wives and kids would join them the next day. It made Jeff wish he could bring his family, but he couldn't, for numerous reasons. For one, he couldn't blow his cover, but even if that wasn't a factor, he didn't want to put them in danger, not that he really thought any of these guys—no matter how annoying or rough one or two of them seemed—posed much of a threat. But getting his family tangled up in this version of his life would put them in unnecessary peril, hypothetical or not. The desire to have them there was moot, though. His superiors would certainly veto the idea. And if all that wasn't enough, Jeff had begun to establish more characters in his backstory, including the girlfriend he claimed to be texting whenever he had to answer a message from his handlers at the agency. When the crew asked why she never came around, Jeff answered, "She's not into this wild stuff." Made a good cover, too, for when he needed to quickly tap out a note or snap a picture for evidence.

"Man, that bitch is obsessed with you," CW had said the last time Jeff made an excuse while he took down a note in plain sight.

Jeff had laughed. "Yeah, but I love her." His reaction wouldn't have been quite so affable had CW called Sandy a bitch. For a fictional girlfriend, that was one thing. For a wife, those were fighting words. He would have broken character.

While Jeff watched CW and Tommy bicker like birds squabbling on a nature documentary, another one of their crew dragged a cooler over and offered Jeff a beer. He took it and thanked the guy, not letting him see his internal hesitation. In every other situation before this, Jeff had faked drinking. He'd used beer as a prop. He tried to act progressively more inebriated, his tongue loosening, divulging fictionalized details about Blackledge's life. *Do I really need to be so on guard tonight?* Jeff asked himself now. *One beer isn't gonna hurt.* He took a swig. That really hit the spot. Jeff always thought cold beer went down smoother when you were out camping. It lifted some of that muggy Florida heat. *It's just beer*, he told himself. *Not like it's whiskey. These guys aren't up to no good. They don't know who I am. And I've been working hard. I deserve to relax.*

Once the fire came to life, they all gathered around it. They shook folded camping chairs open, whipped up dinner, and talked while they ate. Another beer in, Jeff told them more about himself as Blackledge, like why he was getting into farming alligators in the first place.

"My family thinks I'm a fuckup," he said. "I got this inheritance but I don't really got it, you see. I have to prove that I'm doing something with it other than having a party. I wanna prove it to myself, too, though, prove I can do something with my life other than being a waste."

His listeners nodded and let out murmurs of understanding, empathy even. They knew what that was like.

"I'm going to help Brother Parker with something," Robert said, getting up. "I shouldn't be too long." More of the crew gradually peeled away, saying they needed to attend to this and that.

As the conversation went on, Jeff let himself fade back into relaxation. He felt one with his purpose out there. With a sense of calm, he took a swig of the second beer he was nursing and studied the fire. The flames had dwindled so they rippled over the shapes of logs they had reduced to cinders, whitening the bark into scales not dissimilar to an alligator's back. A frill of ash still glowing with a red rim of fire lifted from the bark and wafted skyward. Jeff's gaze followed it up while its glow turned to dust until it disappeared into the murky canvas of the night, a tiny speck indistinguishable among the few rare flickers of the stars. As was his custom, he stilled himself and opened his ears to the night music.

That was all he heard. The night music.

He looked back to the seats around the campfire. Each of them was empty. People had been walking off one by one for a while, but Jeff hadn't noticed *everyone* was gone. A chill ran from the backs of his arms up his neck. Heartbeat rising in his throat, Jeff scanned the tree line. *Where is everybody?* he thought. He considered calling out, but then thought better of it. *Why would they leave me behind like this?* His eyes darted from truck to tent. He looked behind him to the dirt road and followed it into the dark where it faded, then to the woods on the other side. He had let his guard down. Maybe they had wanted him to. Had they found out who he really was? What had tipped them off? Must've been the story he told. He knew he was laying it on too thick, knew he shouldn't have had those beers. It was always like this. You follow regulations to the letter or else—this happens. This was his worst-case scenario. A bunch of fellas, armed hunters all, had suddenly discovered he was the law, an interloper among them. He had deceived them, and now he would pay for that mistake.

What if they're hiding in the woods to ambush me?

Slowly, Jeff rose to his feet. He walked back to his truck, head on a swivel. He wondered if they were in the woods, watching him. As he unlocked his passenger-side door, he scanned the trees. Was that a glint? The eye of a deer? Or the brief flash of a cell phone screen, moonlight catching a watch face. If they were out there, they were armed. They knew how to use their weapons.

Jeff opened the glove box and retrieved his revolver. He didn't like keeping it on him. Even when he hunted, he usually did so with a bow. Some officers toted around their gun like it made them powerful. Jeff knew better. The reality was quite the opposite. His power was in his words, in the way he treated people, in his reputation. He believed that once you had to draw your gun, you'd already lost. You'd already fucked up somewhere. As he had here. Big time. If Blackledge had been found out, then it was time for him to leave. *You guys want to play this game?* he thought. *Then let's play.* He tucked the revolver into the back of his waistband. Watchful of the shadows, he changed into a dark shirt so he could blend in with the night. He exchanged his flip-flops for boots.

I'm Jeff now, he said to himself. *Jeff Babauta. You're in my world. Come and get me.*

For half an hour, Jeff sat alone in the dark, revolver in his hand. What remained of the fire smoldered like crevices of lava beneath the dying coals. Tension gripped him by the shoulders. He didn't want to have that gun in his hand. He was worried for his own safety, but he also felt like a failure. He couldn't believe he'd fucked up like that. He was going to fail just like the guy before him, and now the whole operation would be a bust. If this came to violence, he'd feel doubly guilty. He'd gotten into this to protect the wild, to save what was left of it, not to act like a damn cowboy. He was willing to do anything to prevent that. *You have to defuse this situation,* he thought. *Think!*

A female voice called out in the dark.

The hair on Jeff's arms stood on end. None of the wives had stayed with them overnight.

He looked around. Every shadow of every tree teemed with imagined enemies. Yet none stirred. Perhaps, he considered, he hadn't heard a voice after all. The yowl of a Florida panther sounded eerily like a woman's scream. But those sounded more—banshee-like. This sound had been clear and ringing, the voice of a young woman calling out in question.

There it was again. "Is that a campfire?" she called out. "There are lights there. Stop, stop!"

Jeff turned in the direction of her voice, his heart hammering in his throat. Floodlights made silhouettes of the saw palm fronds. What looked like a truck passed through the trees, first coming toward him, then turning away.

Who was that? Jeff thought. *Biologists? It has to be,* he reassured himself. About twenty years prior, that had been his job. Around this time of year, he would go out at night to conduct the deer census. He and the other biologists would shine their lights through the trees, looking for the reflective orbs of eyes hovering in the darkness. It was both mundane, collecting numbers for statistical analysis, and undeniably spooky.

The logical part of him said that voice belonged to a young biologist. The animal part of him remained alert and on edge.

Just when his pulse was starting to ease, another light swiveled in the pines. A will-o'-the-wisp? No. A flashlight. It bobbed through the scrub, growing brighter, drawing closer. Jeff placed his hand on the grip of his revolver.

A figure emerged from the trees. He followed the path, reached the throw of the camp's light. Tommy.

Recognizing him didn't make Jeff feel better. Then he saw Tommy's face. He was grinning from ear to ear and leading a wheeled cooler like a puppy on a leash. He had some sort of long pole tipped back over one shoulder, and he strode with a buoyant gait, looking like Huckleberry Finn. *That sure doesn't look like a guy who's about to jump anybody,* Jeff thought. He took his hand off the gun.

Seeing Jeff, Tommy called out to him. They met back at the camp, where Jeff saw the implement slung over Tommy's shoulder wasn't just a pole: It was a three-pronged spear capped on one end. Such nasty-looking spears are called gigs, and using them, typically to catch bottom-feeder fish or frogs, is called gigging.

"I caught so many damn fish," Tommy said with a smile. The simple glee on his face really made Jeff want to like him.

Tommy loaded the cooler into the back of his own pickup truck and told Jeff to get in. Jeff, ready to be magnanimous with the fellow on account of his good mood, obliged and climbed into the passenger seat.

Still wanting to impress Robert, Tommy suggested they get a head start spotting some alligator nests before bed. They couldn't open them or pick up eggs then. Their permit dictated a specific time when they could begin, and they had to stick to that. Any egg harvesting outside its strictures would be poaching, but that didn't mean they couldn't look. It was late, but Jeff agreed. He didn't want to stay at the campsite alone any longer.

Tommy started the car and turned down the dirt road that ran through the woodland. *Could he be taking me off somewhere to trap me?* Jeff wondered.

When Tommy slowed the truck to a crawl and leaned out his window to search for nests, Jeff did the same. They pointed high-powered flashlights into the weeds and tall grasses along the marshy roadside, trying to spot nests to revisit in the morning.

He's not crafty enough to trick me like this, Jeff thought. *We really are looking for nests.*

Unidentified bugs hurtled through Jeff's beam like meteors. He wasn't seeing anything, and the tension from twenty minutes prior still nagged at him. Even if Tommy had just been out gigging, that didn't mean the others, Robert especially, weren't out there waiting, plotting. Jeff still had the revolver. It pressed up against his back where he sat. Now even more than before he hoped to God he wouldn't have to use it. He couldn't wait to tuck it back in his glove compartment where it belonged.

When they came to a field, Jeff shone his light across it. It sparked on the glare of a reflector. He darted the light away, but he was sure that had been a vehicle. A white truck. *That's got to be the game warden*, he thought. *Hope he doesn't see us.* If the warden pulled them over and opened the coolers, he'd probably find fish illegally caught out of season. He might charge both of them with poaching. That would mean the end of the operation for Jeff. He looked over at Tommy, about to warn him.

"Shine that light back over there again," Tommy said before he could.

Cautiously, Jeff let the beam flick over the field, arcing over the truck just fast enough to catch the glint of the refractors inside its headlights. Then he drew it back to the roadside.

"Damn, I'll bet you that's the game warden," Tommy said, echoing Jeff's thought.

Jeff imagined the biologists leaving him then, just out of earshot, calling up the agency to report their illegal camping. *I'll guarantee that's him,* Jeff thought. Now a new worry ran alongside the others. Jeff had worked in that exact area for more than a decade. More likely than not, the officer in that vehicle would know him on sight. *He's gonna blow this whole thing wide open.* That would be worse than getting arrested. Because then Tommy would know who he really was, and Jeff would be stuck out there in the wilderness with him, his worst fears coming to life.

The training academy taught all wildlife officers that while on uniformed patrol, they might one day encounter officers working undercover, very likely officers they knew and could recognize even with their disguises. Their training said that if you, the uniformed officer, recognized someone, you were supposed to get out of there as soon as possible. Just cut conversations short and get the hell out. That was what they were *supposed* to do. But regulations were one thing. What happened in the field was something else entirely.

Jeff and Tommy didn't get too far down the road before a set of blue lights flared in the rearview mirror. The closer they came, the harder Jeff gritted his teeth. *Oh God. Here it goes.*

Tommy looked at the rearview mirror, then, as if that might have lied to him, he checked the side view. "Yeah, I knew it was the game warden that you hit the lights on back there," Tommy said. "I guess we need to pull over."

The truck eased to a stop on the shoulder. Jeff's thoughts raced faster and faster. He needed this officer to turn and leave sooner rather than later.

The game warden parked behind them and flicked his lights. By then it was about 10 PM, and wispy streaks of rain darted through the headlights. Tommy glanced back, then got out and walked toward the officer's truck. Jeff stayed where he was, simmering in anxiety. He watched Tommy's reflection in the side-view mirror chat with the officer through his window, then hand over his ID.

"Hey, Jeff!" Tommy hollered. "The officer needs to see your ID!"

"What for?" Jeff yelled back.

"To check if you're wanted," Tommy answered with a laugh.

"Okay." Reluctantly, Jeff climbed out and walked back to the patrol truck. As he handed over his ID, he studied the officer's face. *Who the hell are you?* he thought. Somehow, from that tiny local branch of the agency, there was an officer Jeff had never seen before, much to his relief. He was a brand-new hire just out of the academy, Jeff would learn later.

The officer squeezed the button on the radio receiver attached to his shoulder. "29P," he said. Jeff knew that code. It meant to check and see if this guy was wanted.

Until then, Jeff's undercover license had been just another set piece. He'd never had it run before, not even to check it. He had absolutely no idea if it would work.

A few moments later, their dispatcher's familiar voice called back to him. "Ten–fifty-four," she said. "Ten–twenty-nine P." *10–54. Negative.* That meant, *No, your man isn't wanted.* His ID had worked.

All the tension Jeff had been holding unraveled at once. He found himself smiling. But Blackledge wasn't supposed to know 10-codes. He decided to play it off. He stuck his head in the window. "What does that mean?" he said with mock-worry. "I'm wanted by the FBI?"

"Nope, you're good," the officer said. He handed back Jeff's ID. "All right, guys, you know you're not supposed to be camping out here, right? It's late tonight, so I'll let this slide, but you'll need to find a different campsite after that." He wished them a safe night, and they parted ways.

As the officer's taillights faded, Jeff silently rejoiced. *He didn't recognize me. My driver's license worked. He didn't even check the coolers.*

They sure were lucky that it was raining, and, just like the new Everglades park rangers and the fear of mosquitoes that kept them out of Peg Brown's way, this officer hadn't wanted to get wet.

The next morning, the crew met around the campfire. As they gradually came back to life after that rainy and dismal night, Jeff studied the faces of his compatriots out of the corner of his eye. They drank their coffee, ate their breakfast, grumbled to themselves; the more outgoing among them tried to strike up conversations. None so much as cast Jeff a sidelong glance. No matter how much the rational part of his brain said last night's disappearances had been a coincidence, the other part of his brain said there was no such thing. Even if they hadn't been prowling through the darkness, ready to shoot Jeff and give his body to the swamp, they still didn't trust him enough to apprise him of their plans. This told him two things: One, they sensed something was off about him; two, they had something to hide.

He settled into that uneasiness. *Be cool*, he told himself. *They don't know anything. Acting shifty will just tip them off.* He tried to liven up his posture. He smiled. Nothing had happened to Blackledge. Blackledge had to keep on being his goofy self. He cracked a joke to Tommy. He received a strained smile, a combination of elation from his gigging adventure tempered by the irritation of an early morning. At least Tommy was easy to read. Regardless of how at odds their personalities were, Jeff and Tommy had seemed to reach a kind of equilibrium: Each knew that the other didn't like his particular brand of bullshit, and that was all right as long as they got the job done and didn't end up as Mama Gator's dinner.

As the sun rose beyond the pines and the woolly heads of the cypresses, the sky shifted to a soft yellow and then to a brilliant crosshatch of red, heralding coming storms. Cars and trucks began to arrive, bringing not just the wives and kids of the crew members but also more hands to lighten the work. Robert gathered them around and introduced everyone. He wasn't hiring them. It was more like a fishing trip for most of them, a fun family outing in nature. Jeff had already met Robert's wife, Robin, and their kids. But there were new people, too. Lots of them. Folks from out of state who wanted a taste of the swamp life, friends from the city, anybody who was willing to give them free labor and competent enough not to get in the way.

One fellow whom Jeff didn't know very well yet called himself CW. CW was a caricature of himself. The phrase *blinged out* came to mind. Gold bracelets adorned each of his wrists. Gold necklaces—yes, multiple—were slung around his neck. According to Robert, CW worked as a pesticide sprayer at an orange grove. That made Jeff want to cock his head. *Where are you getting the money to dress this foolishly?* This was just the kind of riddle that made Jeff want to investigate someone. Jeff snuck over to his truck to write down the fellow's name.

The final addition to their crew was David, a retired wildlife biologist in his seventies. With white hair and attire befitting a genteel jungle explorer, David seemed more like a David Attenborough knockoff than a potential criminal. He was supervising the egg hunts to supplement his paltry state pension. Jeff greeted David warmly, and David made a face as though he found Jeff slightly distasteful. That made Jeff want to laugh. As Jeff Babauta, he was even more clean-cut than David. As Blackledge, on the other hand—well, his disguise seemed to be working.

After everyone had been properly introduced, Robert issued his instructions, and the small army of alligator egg hunters split up to commence their search. Robert paired Jeff with Tommy again and assigned them a zone to survey. Before they left, Tommy puffed up his chest and told Robert about the nests they'd spotted last night on their impromptu survey. They'd run into Robert not long after the game warden left, and they'd given the boss a rundown of the night's events—save Jeff's justified paranoia and the heat he had been packing. Robert had seemed concerned about the game warden's presence. The slight change in his facial expression dinged the alarm bell in Jeff's head. Something was off. *He doesn't want the game warden poking around,* Jeff had thought. *Why not?* The expression of concern dissipated as quickly as it had appeared, and Robert said he would take care of the camping situation. He told them not to worry.

Small clues were starting to pile up, and Jeff could no longer write them off as mere coincidences. Something was going on. He had to keep his eyes peeled now to figure out what.

Jeff and Tommy parted from the group and cut down a trail to go deeper into the swamp. Wet earth stuck to Jeff's flip-flop soles. The foliage around them shivered with latent raindrops, a peaceful patter, and the land itself exhaled the scent of petrichor. It wasn't quite enough to cover up the smell of piss exuding from the hot, wet flop of an alligator nest. But Jeff had to take it as it was. As they had before, Jeff and

Tommy set to work. They located a nest. Jeff went to mark its location. But Tommy was already kneeling next to it, opening it up.

"What are you doing?" Jeff asked.

"Checking if there are eggs in here," Tommy said. "What's it look like?" Tommy pried up the top, glanced in, and then, noting the eggs, he closed it back up again. *What the hell are you doing?* Jeff thought. As if in answer, Tommy said, "Robert said we should see if they're full, then wait to open them for when the biologist comes around with us. You know, that way we don't waste any nests for ones that are empty."

That ain't legal, Jeff thought. He wanted to say something, but he bit his tongue. His suspicions had been right. Robert's crew was poaching. Now the question was: How much and for how long? To figure that out, Jeff had to stay the course. *Don't break character. Just keep watching.*

Jeff kept a vigilant eye on the trees for angry mother gators. This time, too, he was wary of the presence of men, of the poachers he may have discovered and what they, in turn, had discovered about him.

They returned to the camp for lunch. Jeff dug out a bottle of antibacterial soap and scrubbed himself down like a surgeon prepping for the operating theater. Only then did he join the others around the unlit fire. With the woods as wet as they were, you'd have to import dry wood from elsewhere if you wanted to get a spark. Nonetheless, the fire circle had become the camp's unofficial center.

The food Jeff brought was part of his character: a can of beans and franks and a packet of saltines. In his regular life, he loved to cook; the food he made ranged from homestyle comfort food to game meat prepared in a way some might consider gourmet. Blackledge, on the other hand, was useless in the kitchen. Being the easygoing fellow that he was, he didn't pay much mind to his diet. He just ate whatever. And since he'd been poor for so long, up until his aunt passed away and left him all that money, he had a taste for the refined in the sense of refined carbohydrates, Cheez Whiz, processed crap.

As he sat down to his beanie weenies, he watched Robert break out a can of Spam, and as if some unheard signal like a dog whistle had issued from it, half the crew lined up to get some. Robert sliced off a hunk thick enough for a sandwich, and Tommy held out his hands. *This is like goddamn Oliver Twist,* Jeff thought. Even though the scene seemed mundane enough, the absurdity of it struck Jeff, and he couldn't let it go. Tommy left the line with his Spam slice and went to the next part of the conveyor belt to grab some Wonder Bread to make a sandwich. The line kept going like that, Robert diligently slicing off Spam hunks and gently placing them in the hands of his hunters; complex and quiet Robert as the schoolmaster, his laborers the wee Victorian children asking for more.

"Want some?" Robert called. He'd seen Jeff staring. Maybe he was calling him out on it, or maybe he genuinely wanted to feed everyone.

"Nah, I'm good," Jeff answered. But he was overwhelmed by the strangeness of all of it. He turned to the person next to him as if they might share a look of understanding. It was David. He sat with his hands folded in his lap. "You a Spam guy?" Jeff asked. David responded with a look that said, *Sir, do I look like a Spam fellow?* That made Jeff grin. "You not eating anything?"

"No, I'm fine," David said.

"You should at least drink some water or something," Jeff said. "'Bout to have a long day in the heat."

"I'm used to it," David said. "I used to be the head wildlife biologist for the Virgin Islands, the American ones."

"Must've been mighty interesting," Jeff said.

David perked up a bit. "Oh, it was." Soon, they got to talking, and David told him about how his research specialty had been mongooses. David smiled, happy to expound to an interested listener. It was clear he realized he had misjudged Blackledge. That quick shift, the ease with which David could overcome his preconceived notions, made Jeff like the guy almost immediately.

It was a good thing they bonded, too, because after the lunch hour ended, the old biologist joined him as his airboat passenger, and together they zipped over the marsh. Intrepid and experienced though he was, David hung on tight, one hand gripping the noise-blocking headset to his ears, the other latched to the underside of his seat. They careened through the spartina grass and the rushes. Snowy egrets lifted up in flocks to escape the startling noise of the airboat's massive propeller.

They met Robert, CW, and Tommy out there on the grass island. By then, the storm clouds augured by the morning's bright sky had begun to gather overhead. Thunder rumbled in the distance.

Robert looked up at the sky. "We may need to make this quick," he said.

The hunters went to the egg nests marked on the map. David followed with his clipboard. Robert, too, kept his notes, the enigmatic aluminum box tucked under his arm, always with him. They'd been to these nests before. Did David know? Jeff hoped he didn't. Lo and behold, there were eggs inside, and the hunters set to digging them out, checking their shells against the light, nestling them in their box for the next leg of their journey. A wet wind blew over the marshes. It smelled like ocean. The storm had traveled far to get to them.

Jeff and Tommy finished their nest. Then they hiked over the marsh island to reach the others, who were doing the same as they just had. David stood, observing.

"What kind of bird is that?" Tommy said, pointing to a great blue heron. Jeff knew it. But Blackledge didn't know squat.

He smiled at Tommy. "Gray one? Definitely a gray one."

"Which bird?" David asked, and Tommy pointed it out. David cleaned his glasses, which the dense humidity had fogged up. He squinted through them. "Ah, that is a great blue heron, *Ardea herodias*, I believe."

"You must know everything there is to know about animals," Jeff said.

"Hardly," David answered.

The sky darkened and they retired to the airboat to wait for the others. From there, they spotted more birds, identified and talked about them, and Jeff forgot himself again. He loved the swamp and the things that lived there. For once, he was in the presence of a kindred spirit. He let his knowledge shine through.

"You know quite a bit about animals yourself," David said.

"Me?" Jeff said, grinning. *Shit, what did I say?* "Nah, I don't know anything about anything."

"Certainly you do," said David. "Frankly, I'm surprised you couldn't identify that heron. Perhaps you need to clean your glasses as well."

How can he be onto me already? Jeff thought. *This fella's too smart for his own good.*

"I guess I just watch too many nature documentaries," Jeff said. "Love to have a beer and turn on National Geographic. Who doesn't?"

"Well, perhaps you've missed your calling," David said. "You've surely retained a great deal of that information."

What are you trying to say? Jeff thought. *You know, don't you. Is my cover blown? No, it can't be. Even if you knew, would you tell somebody? Are you on my side or theirs?*

After a while, their conversation fizzled out, and David, unbothered by his surroundings, clasped his hands over his stomach, leaned back, and went to sleep. Watching David sleep made Jeff wonder if he was being paranoid. David clearly meant him no harm. Their conversations, too, had shown Jeff just how jumbled his identities had become. At that moment, he felt like he was losing both of them, Jeff Babauta and Curtis Blackledge. They had tangled into a new person who was both and neither. Although as Jeff Babauta he had never poached before, through the eyes of Curtis Blackledge, he had seen into the other side. He had witnessed the gamut from casual lawbreaking to perhaps what might turn out to be an elaborately contrived scheme. He would never be the same. Now he knew that even the most clean-cut and religious veneers could hide the sordid, the illegal.

As good a judge of character as he thought himself to be, Jeff reminded himself he couldn't read someone's heart or their mind. *You're not being paranoid*, he thought. Lightning jolted overhead, accompanied by a gut-shaking boom of thunder. Jeff swore. He wasn't usually scared on the job, but sitting in a metal boat during a lightning storm would have that effect on anybody. David shot up, wide-eyed and awake. The others came running down to their airboat as the sky opened up and a veritable deluge flowed over the swamp. *Time to haul ass*, Jeff thought. He cranked up the propeller, and they were out of there.

The crew stayed at Cecil Webb for another couple of days. During that time, it became clear to Jeff that David didn't know he was an undercover officer. He found himself regretting that rather than rejoicing in it, because from the evidence he'd gathered in those same days, Jeff believed David was complicit in the poaching as well. He saw what Robert and Tommy were doing, and he looked the other way. Jeff wanted to set David straight before he could dig himself in too deeply. He just had to figure out how.

When their time in that swamp drew to a close, Jeff, Tommy, and the other central spokes of the crew sat up on the levee with flashlights, counting eggs. It was nighttime, totally black out as the clouds had failed to disperse after the storm. A fog of mosquitoes fell down upon them to feast. While the others broke camp, Jeff, Tommy, and their crew candled the eggs, a process that told them if their eggs were viable, if they could one day hatch into baby alligators. A viable egg would have an opaque white ring around its center. Unviable ones, which Tommy had started calling *light bulbs*, would only show as translucent, a view into a simple yolk and nothing more When they noticed one that wasn't viable, its finder would make note of it, then fling the dud over his shoulder, unceremoniously disposing of it in the marsh below.

"Another light bulb," Tommy said and sent his egg sailing into the dark, where it landed to a rustle of spartina.

All told, their army of hunters had collected 488 viable eggs, many from nests Jeff believed twice or thrice opened, a detail the crew, of course, did not put in the official reports they rendered to FWC.

The crew moved on from one slice of wilderness to another, crisscrossing the state according to whatever permit they had in hand. Many collections happened on public land, but others were on privately held tracts. Jeff soon discovered that the woods harbored strange things, separated from the public and the outside world by just a thick stand of trees, things that even he had no idea existed just out of sight.

Come mid-July, their itinerary took them to Rum Creek Ranch, only a hike from Cecil Webb, but it might as well have been in another world. Past unassuming fields where cowbirds by the dozens stalked like miniature raptors, past the sentinel oaks that stood watch over rain-soaked fields, ten-foot-tall fences cut through the shade of the woods. There, a well-guarded gate opened for the crew, and the caretaker led them inside the secret wildlife sanctuary.

When they stopped at a staging area to collect themselves and prepare to venture into the bush, the caretaker issued a warning. "No photography here," he said. "Not even on your cell phones. What we're doing here isn't illegal, but we don't want anyone to know we're here, got it?"

Got it.

"What *are* they doing here?" Jeff asked once the caretaker was out of earshot.

"They're breeding exotic animals, like endangered ones," Robin said. "It's like Africa in here." She held her camera bag awkwardly. Seems she had hoped to take some pictures, and now she was hesitating about whether or not she would comply with the caretaker's order. Robin and Robert already knew him, so it wasn't like they'd face too much trouble if she snuck a picture or two. The caretaker viewed the others, including Jeff, David, and another of Robert's visitors from out of state, with suspicion.

If people are breeding something in captivity, odds are you can find that something in Florida if you know the right unmarked country road down which to venture. In the Everglades alone, you can find monkeys, camels; everyone already knows about our tigers. Florida is fertile ground for fertility. But Rum Creek wasn't one of those exotic dog and endangered pony shows. Nor was it some rich guy's private menagerie. A billionaire indeed funded Rum Creek, but in the name of conservation and achieving the impossible. As of 2016, the ranch's official report to FWC put its exotic animal population at 1,275 individuals across twenty-four species. "It has, for example, 35 white rhinos, 62 impalas, 338 Javan Bantengs (a species of wild cattle) and about 100 Eastern Bongos, a large forest-dwelling antelope facing extinction in the wild," Mike Vogel wrote for *Florida Trend*.

"I'm sorry, we'll be hunting eggs where with *what*?" Jeff said. He was used to standing guard against alligators, but looking out for rampaging rhinos had never come up in all his wildest dreams and nightmares about this investigation.

The caretaker gestured for Robin and Tommy to follow him. They were going to collect eggs in the rhino preserve. That left Jeff with Robert's out-of-state guest and David. Part of the property was marshland and all but underwater. Avoiding that area, they started collecting eggs along the levee. Every so often, a gazelle would bound by. Jeff would see it, return to his work, then immediately look back up, because *Damn, that was a gazelle!* The peculiarity of it all, and the suddenness of the sightings, cast a surreal hue over their work.

But Jeff couldn't let himself get distracted. Without David going into the rhino preserve with Tommy and Robin, none of the nests they opened there were properly supervised, leaving them all kinds of room to sneak eggs out unaccounted for.

David never said anything when they left him behind. Each time it happened, Jeff felt more certain that the venerable biologist was complicit in their scheme. But a feeling was just a feeling. He needed to know for sure.

After that, Robert's crew split up. Their egg collections took place all over the state, as far south as parts of the Everglades proper, and as far north as Paynes Prairie just south of Gainesville. Robert, Robin, Tommy, and CW drove up there to complete that job. Jeff tried to join them, but their car drove past him going south on the highway, the opposite direction. They had left before he could get there, and they hadn't bothered to tell him, either. *Evidently, they didn't want me to be a part of this operation,* Jeff thought. Jeff called Robert, holding his cell with one hand, on speakerphone. The line rang hollowly. Thankfully, Robert picked up.

"Hey, I'm coming to meet you," Jeff said. "I'm on the highway right now, and I swear I just saw you going the other way."

"We're headed to Gainesville," Robert said. "We got David with us. Go ahead and head back to the farm and start with the hatching."

Something about this made Jeff uneasy. They had kept him out of too many conversations. They were doing this on his farm. It wasn't like he was just some farmhand. He was a business partner. He deserved to know what was going on.

Whoa, Jeff thought. He had slipped into Blackledge without thinking. Those were the kinds of things Blackledge would want. Jeff Babauta needed to be in on their conversations, sure, but for a totally different reason.

Unsettled by them and unsettled by losing himself to the character, Jeff pulled a U-turn and headed for home. *Not home*, he thought. *The farm. The farm is not your home.*

14

SUSPENSION OF DISBELIEF

Mac disappeared and a few minutes later, his boat swung around the bend. It was a broad, long split-hulled boat, a powered catamaran with an excess of seats in the bow for tourists. Mac, among other things, was a tour guide. He wore an affable smile and a Columbia shirt, and he seemed to take great joy in showing off the islands and telling their stories. Mac pulled alongside the dock, and Jonnie, helping out, towed the boat forward until it bumped along the wood. I stepped down onto the deck and chose a seat that faced forward. With Mac at the boat's wheel a few seats behind me, and Jonnie leaning beside him, I knew my position would make interviewing them awkward. I told myself I was there to experience, to witness. I could ask them follow-up questions later. The tableau of nature is often fleeting. Who knew what miracle might unfold before us, a brief glimpse, there and gone.

"Ready?" Mac asked.

As a way of saying yes, I brandished my pen—a waterproof Sharpie.

Mac and Jonnie shared a glance as if they thought me trying to write on a moving boat was crazy. They might watch, amused at my failure, but they weren't about to tell me what to do. I saw echoes of my own culture in the gladesmen. They treated me with kindness. Sometimes I caught them looking at me with admiration, like I was one of theirs who had gotten out and made it, like they were proud of me.

That was something I noticed about the two swamp cultures, the one in the glades and the one a little north in river country: a respect and kindness toward women that is difficult to explain to outsiders. Growing up, my family always had a matriarch. It made sense, as men often died younger, in their sixties or seventies, while the women lived into their nineties or even to a hundred. They had as much as forty more years to accumulate wisdom. Everyone, even the men, treated each woman, no matter her age, like she would be that matriarch someday. This didn't look how you might think. It meant that, in addition to cooking, sewing, and what have you, women were expected to be able to do anything a man could do, as a matter of practicality: gut a fish, fix an engine, run a saw, build, mend, make—you name it. Conversely, the same was expected of the men—not being able to cook, sew, or garden was a deficiency to be corrected, not expected of someone else. The result was that everyone was a complete person, independent and able to subsist in that wild country on their own. That also means that the most rugged men I've ever met—the swamp men, the alligator hunters, the mechanics, the war heroes—didn't waste a single moment of their time worrying about being manly; rather, they endeavored to take care of the people around them. My father is the one who taught me how to sew.

After too many nights alone in the swamp, you realize that rugged individualism is bunk; just because you can subsist on your own doesn't mean that you have to or should. Community and family are much stronger than any misplaced ideas of toughness you've heaved upon yourself, and the best thing a person can be—whatever their gender, whatever their responsibilities or needs—is caring. It takes great strength to care. Looking back at my childhood, the most rugged and determined figures I remember were also the gentlest. That is what I recognized most in Mac and Jonnie. They cared, and it was obvious.

As we motored through the dark water, brackish and murky there at the confluence of the glades and the gulf, Mac told me about the area, the Ten Thousand Islands, a submerged coastal plateau speckled with hundreds of islands before the drop-off of the ocean basin. Even the name Ten Thousand Islands showed a bit of storytelling hyperbole.

"There used to be a lot of oysters here," Jonnie said. "The mangroves have edged them out. None of this used to look like it does now."

What did it look like before? I tried to imagine.

In some places, it looked like jungle, he said. In others, like sandy shoals and beaches. Still more, the grasses of the glades had spread marshy fingers out into the water. To my surprise, Jonnie said that the mangroves were invasive just like Kent had. I was beginning to think that there must be a grain of truth to that. Mangroves weren't invasive in the scientific sense, as they're endemic to Florida; but they had *invaded*, the fast-growing plants moving in over time as settlers cut down trees and others fell prey to sea-level rise, the new salinity in the earth beneath their roots a death blow. Elsewhere, that same process created ghost forests, coastal stands of dead trees that had succumbed to the ingress of salt. But here, there were mangroves, and mangroves were opportunists. They glommed onto whatever soil they could and tangled together to create impassable, forbidding, and ever-changing mazes of life.

Although the landscape was different than it had been, with the mangroves, the Ten Thousand Islands had gotten lucky. Mangroves staved off the death that comes with ghost forests. They gave rise to new habitats. Migratory birds nested in their back bays. Fish from tiny minnows to gargantuan goliath groupers made nurseries in the trees' shade.

Flocks began to light on the trees. Some rookeries sported hundreds, pops of white like bolls of cotton. Moody clouds curled overhead, each lined with the gold of rising noon. The sky cast a glaring gray over the mangrove forests. Birds huddled among the leaves as the wind picked up, scratching whitecaps over the estuary's dark water. A cooler gust carried with it the damp of a coming storm. As if summoned, Mac, Jonnie, and I all looked up in unison.

"Might need to hurry this along if we don't want to get wet," Mac said.

"I won't melt," I said. "My paper might, though."

Mac asked me how I felt about going a little faster.

"Go as fast as you want," I said.

Mac grinned at me as if to say, *If you say so*. He pushed the throttle. As the boat picked up speed, the bow lifted higher and higher out of the water, until we were angled toward the sky, skipping over the whitecaps.

They kept talking, and, much to their amusement, I kept writing.

"Let's see if this brings my friends out," Mac said. "There they are. See 'em?" He nodded toward the boat's wake, and I stood, craning for a glimpse of—dolphins. Two Atlantic bottlenose dolphins leapt in the curls of the waves trailing behind us, gaining height as if they knew we could see them. "Show-offs," Mac said. "But the tourists love 'em."

"Who doesn't?" I said.

"Right?" he answered.

They didn't feed them or anything. The dolphins just seemed to like the attention. This made me think of the dolphins that used to swim near me when I did open-water training back home. They would put themselves between me and the open water, following until I exited up the beach. These same dolphins did this day after day, every time I went out to swim. One time, a fisherman on the shore ran over to me when I walked out of the surf and informed me with alarm about the shark that was in the water.

"Oh, those are dolphins," I said.

"No, past them," he had answered. "A big one." He said that he'd watched the whole thing: The dolphins had protected me from the danger that lurked in the deep water. It seemed implausible, and yet—why would this stranger lie to me?

Of all the animals I've interacted with in the wild, it's dolphins who make me wonder the most. They clearly have memories and motivations. Dolphins are powerful predators. They could have hurt me if they wanted to. Instead, they remained at a distance and observed. Perhaps I filled them with the same sense of wonder as they did me. They have complex and curious inner lives that I will never know.

Ultimately, that may be the thing that captivates me most about nature: Just like any story I have investigated, when I immerse myself in the natural world, I realize that the more I learn, the more there is to discover. Right when I think I know everything, nature strikes me with awe, and I am astonished.

"How are you doing?" Mac asked.

"So far, so good," I said.

That was his cue to really gun the engine. We zipped through the keyholes of the islands. I stopped writing for a while so I could take it all in.

The sky was growing dark and moody, the tail end of that storm front that Kent had warned about. I worried that the sky would open up and drench us. I hoped it would wait so that I might see more of that rugged country.

After a while, shallower waters and no-wake zones demanded slower speeds. We were deep in the wilderness of mud and mangroves. We circled back north and threaded through Sandfly Pass. Mac said we were going to Sandfly Island.

Not a very inviting name, I thought.

Before I had much time to think about it, Mac angled the boat into the mangroves. Startled, I braced for impact. We glided untouched under the canopy, and the hull ran up the shell beach until the bow rested before an outcropping of roots and mud.

"We're here," Mac announced.

Jonnie asked me if I needed help out, but I had already jumped ashore before he finished the sentence. Mac led us up the hill to a bedraggled trail. Some distance away, a national park informational sign indicated that this all had once been kept up. A recent hurricane had battered the islands, knocking down Sandfly's pier and whisking away its porta-potty, among other things. It seemed as though we weren't technically supposed to be there. I only saw the sign that said, DANGER, TRAIL CLOSED, as we were leaving. Mac and Jonnie, had they known, didn't pay it any mind. Those sorts of things were for the tourists, not people like us.

"We won't go around the whole island," Mac said. "I believe half of it's underwater. But we'll go where we can reach."

Sandfly Island was partially artificial, according to Mac. In the Paleolithic era, the Calusa tribe had used shells and earthworking to shape the island into a curve with a bay in the middle that drew fish into their nets. Thousands of years later, when the first European settlers arrived, the Calusa were already gone, but their engineering remained. A fifteen-foot shell mound was the remnant of their civilization. Homesteaders took advantage of the edifice the Calusa left behind. They built a big house, two stories with nine rooms, a veritable mansion in those days. The homesteaders built a cistern, too, and an artesian well that issued fresh water from the aquifer.

We climbed toward it, up the hill under red-barked gumbo-limbo trees. The coming storm and the thickness of the canopy cooled our trek into a mysterious gloom. At the top of the hill, a strangler fig wrapped around a mossy buttonwood tree and reached forth to grasp the archaic concrete walls of the cistern's pool. The water inside was dark, steeped with fallen leaves. On the other side of the path, fresh spring water, its smell verdant and full of life—no salt here—rose up from the lime rock.

"Everybody thought that well had dried up," Mac said. "Then the hurricane came, and it must have knocked something loose. Hadn't flowed in years. Suddenly it came back to life."

The idea seemed both mundane and miraculous: a spring coming back from the dead. I didn't know what to make of it. Hurricanes didn't work like that. It didn't make sense, but here sense was just another made-up rule that reality didn't have to follow. I considered that and the idea of renewal, new growth, hope, as I ventured toward a railless boardwalk like a bridge over a dark pool.

Up ahead, the far length of the walkway disappeared under the water. The boards, sodden from the recent storm, sank with my weight. Over the water, the cool, still air dewed against my skin. Mangrove snappers, schoolmasters, and gar angled and darted beneath my feet. Overhead, the mangroves seemed to weave together to create an intricate and endless knot that blocked out all but the sun's most persistent rays. The canopy was alive with the buzz and whisper of insects. Fish plunked at the water's surface when they swam up for a mouthful of mosquitoes.

Mac and Jonnie followed. We started talking about disappearances. Mac was a relative newcomer to the glades, but Jonnie had known them since the days he went out hunting with his father. He had witnessed the shift, a drawing back of the wild things that had once lived in such abundance. Now there were fewer birds, fewer fish.

"My dad shot a panther in Chatham Bend," Jonnie said. "You might be horrified now. Back then, that wasn't such a big deal. There used to be so much more of them. Now how long has it been since I've seen one? Decades?"

He liked to watch the painted buntings peck at his bird feeder back home. Even they seemed scarce, of late.

"It's the pesticides," Mac said. "All the farms trying to kill their bugs, they end up killing everything else, too."

"Whoa now." Jonnie laughed. "If you aren't careful, talk like that makes people think you're an *environmentalist*." He said it like it was a dirty word.

In another circumstance, I might have been tempted to butt in and defend environmentalism, but here there was no need.

Mac laughed. "Maybe I am," he said with mock confrontation in his voice. "The tourists like to hear that stuff, but—it's no sin to give a damn. You do, too, and you know it."

By then, I had walked so far out on the planks over that little lagoon that I had reached the part that dipped under the water. I could see where it carried on, coming up above the surface again to follow a tunnel through the mangroves before turning out of sight. The walkway sank beneath my feet. The algae-flecked water rose above my ankles and threatened to come higher still. I heard the boards shift. Alligators likely lingered in the shadowy water below, but none gave any sign of movement.

Jonnie called out to me, and I turned around. He was halfway to me on the boardwalk. Mac had remained on the shore. They both looked at me like, *Where the hell are you going?*

"Come on back," Jonnie said.

"We're not going over that," Mac said. "I mean, *you're* welcome to. I'm not going to stop you, but we don't have any towels."

"Fine, let's do the reasonable thing," I said sarcastically, coming back toward them.

Back on solid ground, I looked around at that idyllic place once more, breathing in its surreal beauty. The shade from the canopy did make it look like a dream. Or perhaps it looked like a dream to me because so many of the nocturnal adventures of my subconscious happen in swamps.

The first stray drops of an afternoon shower splashed down on the boat as we crossed the broad sweep of the bay, and the most recognizable building on Chokoloskee Island came into view: the Smallwood

Store. From far away, it seemed much smaller than it actually was. The former trading post rose on pilings above the shell-cracked shore. A storm-worn porch on the upper floor hung over a dock that wrapped around the red building. A single cabbage palm leaned over the tin roof as if posed there on purpose to complete the Old Florida ambience.

Mac ran the boat up the rocky shore beside it.

"I'll meet you inside," Mac said as Jonnie and I hopped out. Then he backed the boat out and returned to open water. We took our sweet time, as one does in those latitudes when touched by a breeze that relieves the oppressive heat, even if that breeze is the presage to a thundershower. As Floridians, we were used to rain. Even though we had made quick work of coming ashore, as small boats tend not to make good shelters from lightning and we hadn't wanted to get fried, the afternoon rains of a Florida summer bring a welcome respite.

The Smallwood Store had started its life as a trading post in 1906 when Ted Smallwood moved down to that last frontier and saw that while the families who had set up there were rugged, they were still in need of produce, supplies, and mail. The store remained more or less unchanged until it closed in 1982. The Smallwoods then locked the doors with the goods inside, a time capsule waiting for Ted Smallwood's granddaughter, Mac's now wife. Recognizing what she had as an intact gem of Florida history, she reopened the Smallwood Store as a museum in 1990, and it has continued on like that ever since. It was open right then, too, and about a dozen visitors perused its aisles.

Venturing inside was like stepping through a time warp—or into my great-grandfather's toolshed. The main long aisle of the store ran from the front door straight to the back door, which remained open to the upper porch and the breeze. Cast-iron skillets, pans, and washtubs hung from the ceiling along with the lazily turning fans. On one side of the main aisle, a counter was piled high with new and old books, worn photographs, hats, canned goods, and endless other memorabilia. The counter itself was slanted inward from the top to accommodate the hoop skirts from back in the day. The next aisle seemed to be a gift shop, but items scattered throughout the store had price tags, making it hard to tell where the true store ended and the museum began. This was especially true of the books, which claimed space on every available surface. When Mac joined us, I asked him, and he said, half in jest, "Anything's for sale if you offer the right amount of money."

"I suppose that's true," I said. I wished it wasn't, that money didn't speak quite so loudly as it did, but it did and always had. Those who had the most gold ruled. People willing to take will keep on taking. That, in part, was the story of the Everglades. I could see that on the small scale in just about everything Mac and Jonnie showed me.

Mac gave me a tour around the store. Jonnie pointed out things donated by his family. There was so much there that I was a bit overwhelmed. They pointed at the upper porch, out the back door, and Jonnie said, "That's where they killed old Watson, the cruel sugarcane planter. If you believe the stories, a Brown fired the killing shot. Then Watson tumbled over the railing, and—*splash*. A bunch of people fired at the same time. He was that kind of hated, and everybody says that his was the bullet that did it."

"Seems they all sort of did the job together," I said. "Bullets work together like that."

"Yep," Jonnie said.

We lingered in thought there, studying the planks, the tide whispering in and out some twenty feet below.

"There used to be a gas pump down there," Jonnie said, the twinkle of nostalgia in his eye. "Smallwood would pay us kids to pump the gas, literally pump it by pushing on this lever to get the pneumatics working and pull it up from the tank."

It seemed the past had lingered longer in this part of the glades. Technology had trickled in more slowly, the things that had come at all. Take away the cell phones, and you would have had an impossible time identifying what decade we were in. I think that might have been part of the place's draw: Life moved at its own pace in Chokoloskee. It reminded me of something my dad used to say: *We'll get there when we get there.* That slow pace made the change that surrounded Chokoloskee seem all that much quicker.

Mac went behind the counter and lifted up a conch shell larger than a basketball, the veneer inside its lips quite pink and alive despite its age, perhaps seventy-five to a hundred years old. "Feel that," he said, handing the conch to me. My hands plummeted under the weight. I barely held the shell above the glass counter. The conch felt like it was made of solid concrete. I turned my head to look inside to see if it was filled with something. It was not.

"Heavy, innit?" he said with a pleased smile. "They all used to be like this. The shells of the conches have been getting thinner."

"Why?" I asked. By that point in the day, I had doffed my journalist hat for one of pure curiosity, as if they were estranged uncles I'd just met that morning, eager to show me around the world that I had missed. I asked why because I genuinely wanted to know. Why would that happen? Why would conch shells be getting thinner? Was it something in the water? Ocean acidification? Was there a reason they would have less calcium to use to fortify their shells?

"Don't know," Mac said. "I think it has something to do with water pollution."

"There you go again," Jonnie said, smiling and shaking his head. "You did, you've turned into an environmentalist."

Mac gave him a look. "Everybody cares about clean water," Mac said. "Especially you. You're a damn fisherman. Look me in the eye and tell me this doesn't worry you. You've seen it, how things have changed. You probably know better than I do."

Jonnie looked thoughtful for a moment. "Fine," he said. He'd noticed the change on other shells, too. It had come slowly, like the movement of the mangroves. He mused that perhaps they were connected. "You know I care. But that doesn't make me an *environmentalist*."

"She's laughing at us." Grinning, Mac pointed at me.

"No," I said, laughing. Jonnie was shaking his head at both of us and laughing himself.

"Well, Miss Writer, do you know why this is happening?" Mac gestured at the shell.

"I could hazard a guess," I said. "But I don't rightfully know, no."

So many things in their world were like that, changing around them as the influx of visitors grew, the tourists never wise to the idea that the

Everglades they saw were not the same as they had been just twenty years before.

"Maybe you could figure it out for us," Mac said, and I thought, *What the hell do I know? I'm just as blindsided as you are to see my world so changed.*

They moved on to other knickknacks, pictures, and displays. We passed a shadow box of shells laid out like rings in a jewelry store. Jonnie pointed to something behind the glass. "I recognize that," Jonnie said. "I found it."

I peered down at it. "What in the heck is it? I've seen a million of those, and I don't know what they are."

"It's a scute," Jonnie said.

A scoot? I thought.

Mac unlocked the case, removed the scute, and handed it to me.

"One of the plates on an alligator's back, under the skin," Jonnie said. "I found that one down in the water, on the beach." I wondered how it had gotten there, and as if reading my mind, Jonnie said, "This one's sort of fossilized. So, long time ago, the gator probably died, and the pieces of him went with the tide."

I examined the porous, bony scale. I had seen those things all my life, and yet I had never thought to ask what they were. The more time I spent in the glades, the more I realized that was true of so many things back in that wild place where I was from: The extraordinary had become ordinary. I had listened to people deride my home for so long that I lost my ability to see its wonders. What else had I missed?

"Those bones are shrinking, too," Mac said, nodding at the scute. I held it out to him to give it back, and he shook his head. "Keep it. That way you'll remember to figure out what's going on."

I nodded, solemn, as if he had bestowed a weighty task upon me.

Later, I would learn that the reason the conches and other shells were thinning was twofold. Over the years, as the pH of the ocean has decreased by what would seem the tiniest of measures, shellfish have become increasingly sensitive to the water's acidity. The acid isn't dissolving their shells. Something more complicated is happening here. The rise of carbon dioxide in the ocean has made calcium more soluble, and so the biological mechanisms that shellfish have used to compose their shells for millions of years no longer function as they once did. The process of converting calcium into shell is now slower. Population dynamics are at play, too. Conches with thicker shells are older ones. If we're only turning up young conches, it means something is happening to the others, likely increased predation or predation by another name, overfishing.

I slipped the scute into my pocket and followed them onward to the far aisle. There, we reached the final display.

A shallow, square-cornered skiff bore the tools of a hunting expedition: a rifle, an ax, jugs, a bedroll. My great-grandfather had one of those boats, I realized. It was a pitpan in the Peg stories, but we'd never called it that. This was yet another revelation that my home was worth having a place in stories after all.

An entire Totch Brown exhibit occupied the far end of the museum, and that pitpan was part of it. A video of Totch telling a story played on a boxy television perched in front of mismatched chairs. Memorabilia piled around that. *Why is this all Totch and not Peg?* I wondered. I felt somewhat slighted by this display, as if Totch had not only lied but also succeeded in stealing someone else's glory and had gone down in history as someone he was not, all because he had befriended Peter Matthiessen, while the real legend of Peg Brown was at risk of being forgotten. I wanted to hate him for this. He was a glory hound and a story thief, and that made him exactly what people expect from Florida, a con artist. I had heard all the Peg Brown stories. I had read Totch's book, which contained some tales that were too close to Peg's but told as if they'd happened to Totch. That seemed to me like a dirty betrayal, made all the worse because they were brothers. I needed to know once and for all: Who was the real poacher, and whom should the stories have been about, Totch or Peg?

"Okay, serious question," I said, and Mac and Jonnie both turned to listen. "I don't know how to put this, so I'll just come out and say it: These aren't really Totch's stories, are they? Is Totch a liar?"

I had expected them to meet that question with either confusion or indignation, but both Mac and Jonnie smiled knowingly.

"Every single one of Totch's stories is true," Mac said.

"They just didn't all happen to him," Jonnie said.

"Well, doesn't that make you mad?" I asked, becoming indignant myself.

"Why would it?" Jonnie asked.

"Because he stole your dad's stories," I said.

"And other people's," Mac said.

"Then why are we celebrating him and not, you know, the truth?" I asked.

A tourist who had been sitting at the exhibit watching Totch weave a yarn gave each of us, in turn, a critical look before getting up and walking out the back door without a word.

"Totch was a storyteller," Mac said. "He collected people's stories and spoke with the real voice of Chokoloskee. Peg knew what he was doing, but he wasn't the fame-seeking type. Sure, he was legendary, and he'd tell a story or two to friends, but he wouldn't have wanted all of this."

"He was a quiet man," Jonnie said. "Not a big talker. Hearing his stories told was glory enough for him."

"Then do you want people to keep believing that all of this was Totch?" I said, feeling disappointed and vaguely defeated in a way I couldn't put into words. "Do you not want me to write this story?"

"Oh, no, no, nothing of the sort," Mac said. "We're tickled that you're interested in all of us."

"We don't need to give old Totch the boot," Jonnie said. "But it's been nice to remember my dad, too."

In other words, I had things backward. Centuries of enmity with humanity had taken their toll on the Everglades, and within their life-times, Mac and Jonnie had seen their world diminished in ways they struggled to put into words. The damage was already done, and if no-body cared, it would keep getting worse unseen in those remote reaches of the tropics.

Stories made people care. Stories showed people from outside the Everglades that the place wasn't a wasteland, that there was something down here—myriad things—worth saving. Not just for the animals, not just for the tourists, not just for the people who live here—for all of us.

Curiosity will save the glades. Curiosity will inspire scientists to investigate its mysteries. Curiosity will bring visitors, who themselves will take stories home, igniting more curiosity. My hope is that this curiosity will be the kind that listens. Instead of the destruction we have visited upon the obsessed-over places and cultures of our past, we should come with openness, leave no trace of our presence, imbibe their stories with wonder, and admit when we have been wrong.

I was wrong about Totch.

Perhaps he had been Chokoloskee's original bullshitter. Perhaps also, I could admit, I might not even know about Chokoloskee if it weren't for him. Matthiessen had cared. Totch recognized that. He let Matthiessen in and told him stories. More celebrities took interest, and so on. *River of Grass* had already kicked off Everglades fever, but it was Totch who made sure the stories weren't about an empty place, but one where people already lived. Those people cared before you ever got there.

To Mac and Jonnie, telling stories like this was more important than ever. As the outside world shouted louder and louder, it had become nearly impossible for one voice to rise above the fray—until it did.

To them, the world had room for plenty of stories. Trickster thieves, noble outlaws, curious writers, conflicted lawmen, alligators, and gator poachers—they could all fit. The secret was in the telling. So they had to let the right people in.

15

BACKUP

L ate one night after an egg collection, when the rest of the crew had gone home, Jeff stayed to tidy up the barn. While he swept the workroom's concrete floor, his phone rang. The screen said GEORGE, Lieutenant Wilson's first name.

"Evening, sir," Jeff answered.

"How you holding up?" Lieutenant Wilson asked.

"I'm keeping it together," Jeff said. Egg-collecting season had started a week prior, and the work hadn't stopped since. Even sweeping in the draft of the night breeze through the open door felt like a break.

Over the past year, Jeff's relationship with Lieutenant Wilson had shifted. Maybe it was because some days, especially now that he was too busy to go home, it felt like Lieutenant Wilson was his only link to the person he used to be. The tenor of his periodic calls had shifted, too, from all business, checking in on his "asset," to friendliness, until Jeff could read a tone of genuine care in his voice.

Lieutenant Wilson asked about Jeff's progress, and he answered with a tale of his days in the swamp.

"Wait, wait, wait," Lieutenant Wilson said. "What did you say?" He sounded stunned. But why?

The events of his story had blurred together for Jeff. *What could I have said to make him sound so shocked?*

"How many nests did you open?" Lieutenant Wilson asked.

"All of them," Jeff said.

In the brief pause that followed, Jeff imagined Lieutenant Wilson's expression: wide-eyed and taken aback. Such a reaction made Jeff realize how complacent he'd become. He had grown so used to seeing Robert's crew break the law, he hadn't anticipated that the simple facts of his days could elicit shock.

Nobody else is seeing what I'm seeing, Jeff thought.

"You guys aren't skipping any nests?" Lieutenant Wilson's voice grew. His tone was unreadable. Was that anger? Horror? Excitement? Some mutant combination of the three?

"No, George, listen to me," Jeff said emphatically. "We are taking *every* frickin' egg out of *every* frickin' nest that we find."

"*Every* nest?" Lieutenant Wilson repeated quietly. "Robert and them? What the hell happened? I thought these guys were aboveboard!"

"So did I," Jeff said.

It had been a gradual change, the fudging of a few numbers here, opening and closing nests there, whispering out of earshot. And then it was like something happened, something in the background that Jeff couldn't see, and their infractions went from little mistakes and misdemeanors to a deluge of poaching, plain and simple.

Had there been signs? None that Jeff remembered. Except maybe that one time Robin glared at him outside the gas station. Or when Robert kept lying, telling him again and again that, yes, of course he'd call back; they'd make plans. So determined to see the good in people, Jeff had chalked all of that up to coincidence. He still wanted to. There had to be a reason they were doing all the things they did. If he could figure it out, he thought, maybe he could find a way to show them reason, to navigate his maze of identities without revealing them, and save Robert's crew from themselves.

"And that's not even the half of it," Jeff went on. "I give these guys the combination to my gate. Then I'll come back at nine, ten o'clock at night, and there'll be boxes here. Full of eggs. I don't know where the hell they're coming from. So I need a second guy here."

"You know we're running this operation on a shoestring," Lieutenant Wilson said.

This wasn't the first time Jeff had asked the agency to assign another agent to help him. Every other time, he had taken their negative or noncommittal answers. This time, he insisted. His scare in the swamp had pushed him over the line from want to need. And now all of this.

"There are going to be times," Jeff said, "when I just can't be here. Who knows what'll happen then."

"I'll see what I can do," Lieutenant Wilson said.

"Please," Jeff said, "I need this. And the investigation won't wait on him, whoever he is."

Even in his desperation, Jeff worried another agent would blow his cover. Blackledge had been conceived, been born, and lived an entire life in the matter of a year, coming to a crescendo as a fully-fledged human being whose thoughts, feelings, and desires were unlike Jeff's own—initially—but had become increasingly hard to shake. Jeff was Blackledge even when he was alone. Could another person catch up in time?

Besides, the agency had other problems. In addition to scrounging up the money to pay this new undercover's salary, things were happening so fast with Robert and his crew that FWC needed to find an agent in less than a week without blowing the case. So they started looking outside the agency. They couldn't trust the case's veil of secrecy to remain intact, even among the officers of FWC.

Jeff thought back to when he was ferrying fish guts to feed his new gator stock. It was a lifetime ago, and he had needed that lifetime to become one of them. He remembered the guts spilling everywhere. He had been green. Now after every egg hunt, when the crew loaded the egg crates into Jeff's truck bed, he would drive carefully through the darkness, minding the turns and twisting the wheel with a contemplative gentleness of the sort he should have used from the beginning. If he'd been deeper, like he was now, those kinds of clumsy mistakes could have cost him. He and Blackledge had become one and the same. So he as Blackledge, he as himself, would park and one by one heft the tubs of eggs inside into a barn that had become as pristine and precise as Robert's old place. Now he had the skills to care for the eggs like a true alligator farmer, checking the temperature inside the barn, making sure that every single tiny, nascent life had the optimal conditions in which to be born. Could backup do that?

The next day, Jeff opened the door of the camper to find a truck parked outside the barn. He hadn't heard it drive up. It looked familiar, but still—when the hell did it get there? Apprehensive, Jeff crept inside the barn.

"Hey, Jeff!" Tommy called from the end of the barn where the egg tubs were stacked.

"Hey, yourself," Jeff said. "Whatcha doing here so early?"

Tommy gestured to the tubs at his feet. "Got some more," he said.

"Spent all night out there hunting, and I got a big haul. Where should I put 'em?"

"Man, is that even legal?" Jeff said, finally unable to contain the words that had been playing through his thoughts like ticker tape since egg-harvesting season began.

"You worry too much, Jeff," Tommy said.

Jeff glanced at the table beside him. The boom box with the covert recording device sat in the middle, facing Tommy. Jeff couldn't have set it up better if he tried. With one surreptitious move, Jeff turned it on. *Good gracious, Tommy*, he thought. Even though he sometimes found Tommy grating, Jeff felt both victorious and guilty about catching his illicit delivery on video. It seemed too easy, un-sportsmanlike. Yet the voice of Jeff Babauta that remained in his head said, *How you act when you think no one is watching—who you are in the dark—reveals your truest self. I shouldn't feel guilty for turning on the lights.*

"The guys'll get it all taken care of," Tommy went on.

In all the days of this investigation, after having it drag on with nothing for more than a year, Jeff never would have imagined that receiving such blatant evidence as a confession of intent on video would have him reacting this way: irritated, frustrated, conflicted, and wanting to parent this guy, because somebody needed to. He sighed and shook his head. "You can leave 'em here, but don't do any more of that, all right? You're gonna get me in trouble."

"Don't worry so much," Tommy said. He clapped Jeff on the shoulder. "Like I said, nobody's gonna know."

Over the next few nights, Jeff's wariness spiked. Tommy slipping in during the misty hours of morning spooked him. If he had done that so easily, there wasn't much to stop others who might wish him harm.

He texted Lieutenant Wilson and asked him again about backup.

Wilson: I'll tell you when I have something for you.

In the meantime, Jeff beefed up his security, added more cameras, now up to four, one out by the trees near the gator pen, another at the entrance gate, and one outside his camper to protect himself, too. Robert's crew commented on them.

"Watching for coyotes or something?" Tommy said.

"Gator could take a coyote," CW asserted.

"Bet," Tommy said.

"I think they're a good idea," Robert said, joining them around the camera. "We don't want anybody coming in and making off with our hard work."

Rumors of alligator thieves had spread across the state. Because breeders were willing to pay an all-time high for the eggs, they'd become a hot commodity, worth risking life and limb to steal. More willing to face the dangers of the state's most lethal biped than to cross the seldom-armed fury of the prehistoric lizards themselves, alligator thieves had started breaking into alligator farms and egg-napping. Cameras and motion detectors were a decent defense, so even Jeff's slapdash security system had an alibi.

He made use of his false walls, hiding anything at all that might seem incriminating. He had to manually turn the cameras on and download the footage. He downloaded from the game cams every other week and stored the Jumpdrives in hideouts like the one he'd built for his laptop before he could pass them off to Lieutenant Wilson.

One night while Jeff sat at the table in his camper, completing his logs for the day, a noise flicked at his ears. He stopped typing and listened. The low hum of an engine running outside wafted around him. His heart leapt into his throat, and he swore under his breath. He slammed the laptop closed, pried open the secret compartment in the wall, and stuffed his computer inside along with a flurry of papers. Then he peered through the window. His breath fogged up the glass. He could barely make out anything in the dark, just the low glow of idling headlights creating a slim outline of the hood. He couldn't even make out what kind of truck it was.

Somebody rose from the driver's seat and slammed the door. Whoever he was, he was tall, wearing a cowboy hat. The cowboy started toward him. The automatic lights came on, and the cowboy lifted his face to squint through them. *Goddamn it, Wayne.* Jeff opened the door.

"What the hell are you doing here in the middle of the damn night?" Jeff called from the top of his steps. "You scared me half to death."

Wayne guffawed, grinning. He seemed tipsy. The version of Blackledge that Jeff had created in the beginning had spent most of his adult life as a dirtbag partier, the kind of guy who would always have beer, among other things, with his friends. So Jeff kept his fridge stocked. Something that became increasingly difficult as he befriended Wayne, and Wayne helped himself.

"Aw, I scared you," Wayne drawled, his voice sticky with sarcastic glee. "Poor little Jeff. How you feel about really getting scared tonight?"

Turned out, Wayne was on the job as a trapper and wanted a second set of hands to make the work a little more entertaining. Tonight his mission was to catch some delinquent alligators at a camping resort.

"Sure, I'm up for an adventure," Jeff agreed.

Jeff got in the truck cab. Wayne's teenage nephew rode in the bed, whipped by the wind.

Wayne was an entertaining fellow, a real character. Never a dull moment with him. That's why Jeff kept agreeing to tag along, not because he especially thought Wayne would be up to no good. He just enjoyed his company, and living life as Blackledge without a friend ground him down after a while.

When they arrived at the RV resort, Wayne's nephew jumped down.

"We got a nine-footer here two weeks ago," he informed Jeff.

"Did you now?" Jeff said as they trooped toward the camper-surrounded pond. The listening device he kept tucked under his hat picked up their conversation. "What'd you do with it?"

"Put it in my uncle's pond," the kid answered.

Jeff gestured to get Wayne's attention. "Was that the same alligator we used for the hunt?"

A memory of the escapade that had first united them seemed to put a grin on Wayne's face, and he laughed. "Yeah! Sure was."

It struck a different memory into Jeff's head. On the same day all that happened, Wayne had told him he'd gone to this very RV resort with a biologist to conduct the survey he needed for an alligator-harvesting application. Those applications could take a while to process.

For God's sake, Wayne, you don't really have a permit for this, do you? Jeff thought. He wanted to tell Wayne he needed to do better. *Quit breaking the law so much. I don't want to arrest you.* But that would entail divulging his dangerous secret. Spending time with Wayne was like gaining a friend and losing one at the same time. He enjoyed Wayne's company. Yet he knew that the time would soon come that he would have to turn evidence of the growing list of Wayne's crimes over to the uniformed officers who would bang on his door with a warrant.

No more of that sentimental stuff right now, Jeff thought. He breathed out and settled himself back into the persona of Blackledge. And for that rascal, it was time to nab a gator.

They stalked through the camping resort, shining spotlights on the water and in the reeds. Wayne would try to be quiet at first—he didn't want to scare the gators away, because whatever he caught he could sell—but after a while, he just got too giddy to handle the silence, and he'd launch into a story. Wayne was the yin to Tommy's yang. Both bragged and boasted, but where Tommy was trying to be better than others, Wayne was trying to entertain and astound. His stories were half true, half full of shit, and damn, they were good. Adding a little flavor never hurt anybody, he would have said, especially not anybody who was smart enough to tell a storytelling device from a malicious deception.

Unable to sneak up on any gators, Wayne and Jeff strung baited lines across the marshy patches. They waited for a gator to bite before they pounced. They caught one, then another. After a while, they saw a hulking form lift from the water. They shushed each other and craned through the parted weeds to watch.

The venerable alligator closed its great jaws with a chomp. As he pulled away, he dragged the line with him. They scrambled after him, snatching at the rope, but this was a game of tug-of-war they couldn't win. The line whistled through their grips, the friction heating Jeff's palms. He let go, and so did Wayne.

"Did you get a look at the size of that monster?" Wayne crowed. "Must've been fifteen, twenty feet long."

"Twenty feet, my ass," Jeff said. "This ain't Jurassic Park."

That made Wayne bust out laughing.

I like you, man, Jeff thought. *I wish you wouldn't do all the things you do.*

Their night of adventure wound to an end, and they returned with their catch to Wayne's farm.

Wayne threw an alligator carcass into a big utility box right outside his barn. Up close, Jeff couldn't believe the size of the thing. It was evidence of what they'd done that night. The dark around them sang with crickets and frogs. Hardly any of the light from inside reached far enough to illuminate the gator. Jeff had to try to take a picture anyway. While Wayne's back was turned, Jeff held up his phone and took a snapshot. The flash went off, a sudden sharp light that threw stark shadows over the clearing, before they fell into darkness. Wayne turned on him. Jeff could only see his outline.

"What the fuck are you doing?" Wayne yelled. "Are you a fucking undercover?"

"Undercover what?" Jeff said, taken aback by Wayne's anger. "I was trying to find the flashlight on my phone, just so I can see how big this thing is."

Wayne eyed him.

Was this it? Was Jeff done for? They remained in this standoff for a beat. It was a tense moment of reflection for Jeff. *What would I do if I was in Wayne's shoes?* he wondered. *Would I kick the undercover's ass or just kick him out?*

Then Wayne broke his glare and returned to the barn to clean his alligator.

Or, if he was my friend, Jeff thought, *would I pretend nothing had happened?*

He watched Wayne, framed by the harsh light from inside, take off his hat and wipe the sweat from his brow.

Think ahead next time, Jeff told himself. *You've got to be more careful.*

The more days that passed without backup from the agency, the more time Jeff marinated in his anxiety. He began second-guessing himself. He would lie awake, turning through the events of the day, wondering about all the things he might have missed—and all the things he might have seen if he'd been two people.

The next night, convinced something important had happened under his nose, he rewatched the recordings of secret footage taken from the barn.

The egg room appeared on the screen. Towers of egg tubs stacked in the background beside the white of the pegboard made a theatrical tableau into which the voices entered before the characters themselves had shown. Jeff remembered where he was in that situation. He had just turned on the hidden camera, something that had to be done manually before it could record a thing, and he had sat on a cooler, leaning against the wall outside the camera's view, and listened to Robert like he was keen on learning.

"You offered the landowner a certain amount?" Jeff asked.

"I pay the landowner per egg, between $40 and $50 per egg," Robert explained as he and Tommy entered the shot carrying boxes. They set them down and lingered to chat. "Tommy, what are you doing tomorrow?" Robert asked. "Are you taking off, or are you going with me and Chris?"

Chris was a certified biologist who worked for them.

"I'm going—what are you talking about?" Tommy said.

"I kind of do need you there," said Robert. "Now, Chris's going to be a little bit different than what's his name? He's actually going to be a little stiffer than, uh—"

"David?" Tommy offered.

"Than David, believe it or not," Robert said. "Chris will have to visually see every single nest. His interpretation of the laws is a little different than David's. Chris will have to see every nest. He won't have to see it opened. You'll let somebody come behind me and him, and open them."

"So that's what you're gonna do?" Tommy asked.

"What I'll do is I'll bring you all, show you one or two, tell you how to collect it," Robert explained. "And then we will go on to the next. You know what I mean? You all collect it while I'm gone. You'll have to open one, get the eggs, go to the next one. Open it, keep the eggs, but say it was one nest."

Holy shit, Jeff thought, watching. *They're laying out exactly how they're laundering the eggs, their whole poaching plan.*

"Right," Tommy said on the screen.

"See what I mean?" Robert said. "Cover it back like it was never touched, and there's bad eggs in it."

"Leave the bad eggs?" Tommy asked.

"Leave the bad ones, and say it was never opened," Robert said. "The good ones, you can say they went with another clutch. See what I mean?"

"Where y'all going?" Tommy asked.

"We're going to Spanish Trail."

Jeff stopped the video. He unplugged the Jumpdrive and held it in his hand while he paced and called his case agent, his main contact at the agency other than Lieutenant Wilson. When he picked up, Jeff said, "I have something you need to see."

Backup finally arrived. The minute he saw Jeremy Munkelt, Jeff was filled with both relief and worry. Jeremy pulled up to the barn in a black Dodge pickup. Sunglasses on, he swaggered inside. Jeremy had sunburned cheekbones and a scruffy sailboat trash look about him that seemed too real to Jeff to be a costume; that his previous position had been in the Keys didn't help.

Jeff showed Jeremy around, got him acquainted with the farm's setup. As he was going over the minutiae of egg incubation, Jeremy cut him short. "Yeah, I got it." Jeff bristled. Their characters may have been easygoing layabouts, but Jeff and Jeremy were anything but. When Jeff had asked the agency to find the right person, he hadn't considered they would find someone just as stubborn and sharply organized as he was.

"This is a complicated operation," Jeff said. "I've been working it for more than a year. The guy here before me blew his cover and got yanked. This isn't gonna be easy."

"Right. I never said it would be."

Jeff asked him if he had any questions.

"I'll ask 'em when I have 'em," said Jeremy. "We'll tie this operation up soon so we can both go home. Don't you worry."

Jeff pointed a chastising finger at Jeremy's chest. The man was nearly half a foot taller than Jeff, so he felt a little silly looking up at him to make a threat. "I put a lot of work into this operation," he said. "Don't blow it for me." Truthfully, though, Jeff was more worried about blowing it himself.

16

HATCHING SEASON

t was July 23, already time to go out for another egg collection. Jeff set out, leaving all the work he'd put into the farm in Jeremy's care with a great deal of trepidation. The drive wasn't long.

Not far away in Arcadia, rows of orange groves stretched on as far as the eye could see. This was a private collection, the place called Two by Four Ranch. They raised cattle. Within the pastures, small ponds like watering holes attracted every river country denizen that could reach them—egrets, storks, turtles, and alligators, because what was a pond in Florida without the requisite alligator. They stopped at the farmhouse and parked beside Robert's truck.

Robert stood on the porch talking to the caretaker, the owner's daughter. Jeff was about twenty feet away, but he could read lips passably enough to estimate their conversation. Understanding a conversation you couldn't hear was more about body language than the words themselves. The caretaker looked at Robert sternly. She asked for something and held out her hand.

"Let me see your paperwork," she seemed to say.

Robert opened his aluminum lockbox and shuffled through its contents before picking out the right page. He presented it to her, and she looked it over.

"All right," she might have said, reluctantly handing them back. "Just make sure you guys have your shit together. I don't want any problems."

Once Jeff huddled with Robin, Robert, Tommy, and the crew, it became clear what had caused her concern. The permits said they were only allowed to collect 560 eggs. Anything over that would be poaching. Poaching could get the caretaker in trouble, too, as the landowners could be held liable for any known crimes happening on their property. The crew had to be strict today.

Jeff knew almost immediately that this wasn't going to happen. The

crew split up, scattered all over the property. Robert's strategy had them
all starting on the periphery then closing in on one spot like they were
circling prey. They had surveyed the property in a helicopter a while
back, and Robert sent Jeff and Tommy in search of a particular nest
they'd seen from the air. Robert and Robin split off on their own. Jeff
and Tommy climbed into the side-by-side utility terrain vehicle (UTV),
which looked like a swamp buggy the size of a go-kart, and got going.

The UTV slogged through nearly two feet of water, a trench of
mud that separated grove from pastureland. The black water gurgled
under their wheels and threatened to brim over the wheel housings
and soak their legs. The UTV rocked and hobbled over the unseen soft
bottom of the muck. Out across the wide-open green of the field, cypress
domes cropped up like islands of swamp forest in a sea of grass. Jeff
looked around, trying to get his bearings. Familiar landmarks began
to arrive: a weeded pond area, a stand of pine trees.

"It's gotta be here," Tommy said. He kept one hand on the wheel
and held a ruggedized GPS in the other. He looked down at it then
scanned the surroundings, down, scan, down, scan. "Gotta be around
here somewhere."

"You know what, let's take a right here and go up on the hill," Jeff
said—meaning, *Let's stop playing in the mud and get up on dry land*—
"and go around the big cypress head. There should be a stand of trees
up there."

"How do you know that?" Tommy asked.

"Well, I remember it from the helicopter."

Tommy frowned. He never got invited on any helicopter adventures.
Jeff wondered if he resented that, and thinking about the favoritism that
showed from Robert, Jeff's chest involuntarily puffed up with pride.

The cypress dome, a wetland characterized by tall trees that grew like
an island in a sea of marsh grasses, hid a fantasy world set apart from
the mundane by the trees' peculiar protection. Smaller plants grew in
the dome's shallow waters. The farther you ventured into the concentric
circles of trees that created the dome, the taller the plants grew, because
the water flowing through the lime rock below was deepest at a cypress
dome's center.

Jeff cut through this wild botanical garden. In the deep swamp, the coolest strata of shade came from pond cypress and swamp tupelo. Deeper still, a subcanopy of sheltered trees with poetic names—sweetbay, slash pine, loblolly bay, coco plum, and dahoon—enveloped Jeff and Tommy. Here within the fold of the cypress shade, fetterbush, wax myrtle, Saint-John's-wort, and willow hung over a grotto of chain ferns and royal ferns, cinnamon ferns and moss. Beneath this smallest canopy, nesting inside all the others up above, cryptic orchids opening their arms to the heavens cascaded in ecstatic shocks of purple, pink, and red. Was it this place that had inspired settlers to dub their wild outpost with such a bucolic name as Arcadia?

Jeff and Tommy traipsed through the fairyland, unaware of the rare and endangered things shrouded in the understory just out of sight. In a narrow shaft of light, Jeff spotted the nest he'd seen from above. They collected thirty eggs from it and found no others. It was the only nest in the entire area.

They went back to the farmhouse, where they met up with CW and his wife.

Tommy and Jeff sat in the UTV, and Tommy leaned over the ledger where he kept track of the eggs, scribbling things down. Jeff glanced at the page. He saw a number 7. Then two other numbers. *We are way over 560*, Jeff thought.

"So," Jeff said, "are we on point?"

Tommy slammed the book shut, like he didn't want Jeff seeing any more of what was inside. Then Tommy looked at him and CW. "No," Tommy said sharply. "We're over."

"Don't tell Mike about this," CW said.

Mike was the landowner, someone Jeff now realized he had met before. The caretaker was his daughter.

Of course we're not going to report it to Mike's daughter, Jeff thought. He felt a tug of guilt at cheating someone he knew, even an acquaintance.

Robin and Robert went to a spot they called the dam area, which everyone had joked about, saying things like, "Which damn area? That damn area." "Well, damn." "I'll be dammed." That is, before the mood of the expedition had turned so sour. The whole crew met up in the dam area later. Robert, Tommy, and CW went off to the side by themselves. Jeff could tell they didn't want him to be a part of that conversation. *They don't want me to hear they've screwed up*, Jeff thought.

Their previous egg collections had been supervised—a biologist (like David) accompanied the egg harvesters and made the call when he thought the crew had taken enough. The collection that day had been unsupervised, which per regulations meant that only a specific maximum number of eggs could be gathered.

"Let's all go back to our staging station," Robert said in a panic, "and try to figure this out."

They hurried back to the property entrance. They hustled, sorting through the boxes of eggs, checking their viability, transferring them from one container to another. Robert stood back with the calculator on his phone, a strained and frantic expression on his face.

"How many eggs you guys have?" Robert hollered at Jeff and Tommy. They answered, and Robert jabbed the numbers into his phone. He asked the same of his wife and punched in her numbers, too. Then he ordered them to load all the boxes into Jeff's truck.

It was then that the caretaker pulled up. She got out of her car. "How'd you guys do?" she asked Robert.

"We collected five hundred fifty-nine eggs," Robert answered, "one shy of the permit."

Jeff watched this conversation from where he stood leaning against his tailgate. He laughed to himself about Robert's howler of a lie. The evidence was right there next to Jeff, nestled in crates in his truck bed.

Back at the farm, he examined it himself.

"Help me unload these eggs," he said to Jeremy.

They brought them inside and counted them together. Altogether, the eggs tallied up to a little more than 700. They were 151 eggs over the mark, and they'd shorted Two by Four Ranch a significant amount of money. Jeff whistled at the magnitude. If he hadn't been sure Robert's crew was poaching before, he was now. And cheating people, to boot. They paid landowners for every egg they harvested. Years before, the sum had been as low as $5 a pop. But after the floods had ruined Louisiana's wild alligator stock, prices were reaching as high as $60 per egg, and that was just what Robert had paid to harvest them. They had just robbed that ranch of thousands of dollars.

Was this the Robin Hood mentality at work or something else?

Jeff felt like the case was cracking open, but he worried his cover was, too. The crew was candling harvested eggs in the barn one day when Robin all of a sudden looked at Jeff and asked him where he was from. Jeff had gotten used to that question, because people of his ethnicity—a Pacific Islander from Guam—are uncommon in Florida. He was also likely the only Guamanian person employed by FWC, so knowing his ethnicity would be a dead giveaway. When he was making up his backstory, he decided to tweak his origins just slightly, but not so much that it was implausible. His story went that his aunt raised him in Florida, and that he was from Saipan, where he'd never been. Saipan is next to Guam.

"My aunt tells me I'm originally from—"

"Guam?" Robin blurted out.

His heart dropped. He collected himself as fast as he could. "Guam?" he said. "I have no clue where that is. I'm from Saipan, but I've never really been there. They tell me it's an island out in the Pacific." He needed to shove the conversation onto a different subject. This was inching precariously close to fearful territory. Did she know he wasn't who he said he was? "So how many eggs are we at now?"

The conversation moved on easily. Still, his racing heart would not subside.

Later, Jeff watched the undercover video of that conversation, studying it to see if he'd missed a tell in her body language that indicated her intent. *I can't believe she said Guam*, he thought. When he told people where he was from, the typical response was, *Where's that?* Robin's assumption had caught him off guard. Yet her body language on the footage didn't suggest much of anything. His own, however, would have been a dead giveaway if Robin had known what she was looking for. He flinched when she said it. His eyes went wide for half a second before he composed himself again.

Had she seen that? Did she know he was lying?

After all these years protecting the wilderness, Jeff had learned to trust his gut. Now, it seemed he was taking any reason he could to doubt it. His gut said that someone had figured him out, that the trap he had set was fixing to turn against him. He had grown to like all of these people. He wanted to be wrong. He had let such softness turn him into a naive optimist, and yet, he wasn't willing to let it go. There had to be a way to keep that empathy without risking his mission. If he couldn't, then Jeff really would lose himself to Blackledge for good.

It was now August, and hatching season was just starting. Jeff had to admit that he was excited, but it meant that Robert and Robin were hanging around the farm far more often, a secretly tense situation after Robin's question had set him on edge. They also brought their daughters to see the baby gators. The little girls marveled at the glossy-eyed hatchlings and asked Jeff questions, and while he answered them, his stomach started to sink. If these girls' parents got arrested, what would happen to them? Where would they go if both parents went to jail? Even temporarily losing two parents seemed like a punishment they didn't deserve. They hadn't done anything wrong.

He had already met many of the others' families out on egg collections. Some had invited him over to their houses. Once, a while back, Wayne brought his wife and daughter to Sunshine Alligator Farm to meet Jeff, and another time, he invited Jeff over for a lobster dinner, a catch he'd brought back fresh from the Keys. Jeff missed his family, and the companionship made some difference, but if anything, spending more time with them made Jeff feel uncomfortable. The state would come arrest them soon on his account. It was becoming increasingly hard to draw the line: He couldn't get too involved in their social lives. That wasn't fair to them. In the evenings, they needed to part ways.

He thought about his own family then, first of his mother, who had feared the worst since his transformation into Curtis Blackledge. She had taught him the Golden Rule: Treat others how you would like to be treated. It went beyond simple reciprocity. It had instilled in Jeff a loud conscience. Some people, it seemed, could ignore the little voice in their head that said, *Thou shalt not.* Jeff's was anything but little. And it was beginning to speak up.

To do what was right, he would have to enforce the law. But his conscience knew that sometimes enforcing the law hurts more than it helps. Arresting these families would tear them apart. Without thinking, he put himself in their shoes. He imagined that he really was a poacher, that his wife and son had come out to help him in the swamp. He imagined his son, Chris, was still a child, and a wildlife officer came to arrest him and Sandy. He imagined the look on his little boy's face as the officer put them in cuffs, on the verge of tears but too shocked to shed them.

There had to be another way. Jeff would have to come up with something fast. He wasn't willing to uphold the law at the expense of his conscience.

For every time that Robert's crew showed up at Sunshine Alligator Farm unannounced, there was another that they should have showed up and didn't. When this happened one day during hatching season, it left Jeff—and luckily now Jeremy, too—running here and there across the barn, helping babies out of their shells and transferring them to their new tanks, the plastic kiddie pools. They set these in an open area on the side of the barn, where all the hatchlings would peep when they walked past. Jeff started calling the pool area Sunshine Daycare.

It was a wonder to see all the tiny alligators climbing over one another. They were anything but calm. They would pick fights for no reason, it seemed, but their inborn feistiness. Once latched onto a brother or sister's tail, the hatchling might commence a death roll, a terrible fate in the jaws of a full-grown alligator made endearing and comical by their minute size and the ferocity of their angry squeaking.

"Quit that," Jeff said, tapping a scaly baby on the head so she would relinquish her enemy's tail. "Break it up." Careful not to hurt them, he pried another pair apart only for them to bite each other's tails again, forming a furious and ridiculous hoop. They would only settle down when he lowered the lid, an inverted kiddy pool cut with air vents, over them and put them to naptime in the cool darkness.

Jeff reached into one of the tubs toward an alligator egg. Bits of mud and bark sullied its white shell, a skin that bulged outward around the hatchling inside eager to break free. Jeff pressed his thumb through the skin at the same time the hatchling tore through it with his egg tooth. The little alligator, wet with amniotic fluid, wrestled himself free.

"Look at him," Jeff said. "Isn't he cute?" Jeff tickled the little alligator's head, and it turned around and chomped down on his finger. Tiny teeth pierced his skin like needles. "Ouch, shit." He gently shook the hatchling off.

The little gator squeaked angrily, and a chorus of hatchlings, newly emerged into the world, joined in.

Cute *and* born mad. Jeff could appreciate the fight in them. Once a swamp creature, always a swamp creature. They were stubborn through and through.

Late one night as Jeff and Jeremy scrubbed out pools, cutting at the scum of alligator poop with bleach, they looked at each other, as if the sheer depth of the drudgery demanded they share a moment. Nothing bonds you to another fellow quite like shared misery. And despite all the times Jeff rallied, telling himself he had a grander mission, that he was there for a reason, to protect the wild, they had plenty of misery, and much of it stank.

"This is something only you and I will ever know," Jeremy said. "How tough this operation was, you know, when it's all over."

Jeff thought back to everything the farm had put him through before Jeremy showed up. The long days that turned into nights. Sometimes a drizzle turned the air to mist, humidity so dense that it collected on glass and pilled into droplets even when it wasn't raining. Those days, it was hard to tell if your shirt was wet from perspiration or ambient dankness, though likely it was both. He'd stand in front of the enormous fan in the barn, its breath turning the sweat to salt crystals across his skin, unmoving enough to practically fall asleep. Having lived in Florida so many years, Jeff was used to the weather, but not doing hard labor in it with no real avenue of escape. He spent those days wet to the bone, wet to the core, wet to his very soul. Other times, he'd dug through nests made of gator feces and leaf litter infested with fire ants, longing for the days when the air felt like bathwater, because at least then he wouldn't feel quite so rank. He cringed just to think about it.

"Yeah, man," Jeff said. "This shit is hard."

Truth was, Jeremy had taken on more than just half of Jeff's burden with the farm. He had alleviated the burden of his loneliness. Jeff came from a big family. Before the investigation, they always got together, had cookouts, and played major parts in one another's lives. They spent hours on the phone, checking in, gossiping. Coming from that to spending most days holed up on the farm like a hermit came as more of a shock than he liked to admit. By the second year of the investigation, Jeff was stir-crazy. He needed to talk to someone about everything that was going on. He needed to talk to someone he wasn't also lying to. Despite their differences, Jeremy's addition to the team came with an immense sense of relief. Finally, Jeff didn't feel quite so alone. And yet it had been a tough adjustment.

Jeremy had arrived thinking he knew everything. He started in with the bad habit of disregarding Jeff's advice, and that always made Jeff bristle.

"You've been an officer for what, five years?" Jeff said one time, confronting him. "We're not gonna do this." He meant their disagreements, going toe to toe. They were allies, and they had to act like it. That didn't change the fact that they were two stubborn people, separated by generation and experience, and so both seemed to know that one would never concede to the other.

Jeremy had his idiosyncrasies, too, ones that didn't quite fit with his character. And ones that Jeff didn't quite agree with. For one, he brought his own refrigerator to the farm and kept it stocked with foods Jeff thought of as fussy.

One morning, Jeff sat down to breakfast with a plate of eggs and bacon, and he looked across the table to Jeremy. He studied the spread the junior officer had laid out before him: six strawberries on a paper towel, a cup of yogurt, and a spoon.

"What the hell are you eating?" Jeff said.

"What's it look like?" Jeremy said.

"You can't be eating like that in front of the guys."

"Why the hell not?" Jeremy bit into a strawberry.

"It doesn't fit with your character," Jeff said.

"Maybe *my character* wants to take care of himself," Jeremy said pointedly. "Maybe *his* body is *his* temple."

"Maybe he oughtta watch what the other guys do and try not to stand out so damn much."

"Nobody's paying that much attention to what I'm eating," Jeremy said.

"You don't know that. Even something little can tip somebody off."

That didn't stop Jeremy. When they went to lunch another day with Wayne, Jeff ordered a hamburger and fries. Whatever Wayne ordered, Jeff tended to copy.

The waitress asked Jeremy what he wanted, and he asked her about the bread. Was it stone-ground rye or pumpernickel?

Jeff shot him a look like, *What the hell are you doing? You might do this in your real life, but you're not playing that life.*

Then Jeremy asked her what type of mustard they had.

"This guy thinks we're at a fancy restaurant," Jeff said to Wayne to cover, but Wayne just grunted. He didn't seem to suspect anything was amiss.

But after a while, Jeremy got the hang of it. He started dressing sloppier, wearing flip-flops, T-shirt untucked. Jeff and Jeremy came to respect each other. Jeff wanted to help him have a good career by sharing his experience. Sometimes, they would drive into town for a bite to eat and have a talk. They would work out together at the bench press they had in the yard, and Jeff even convinced Robert to take Jeremy along for some of his expeditions.

There was always more to someone, Jeff knew, than his first impressions.

Although Robert's crew not showing up left Jeff and Jeremy with more work, their absence also had its advantages.

Early on, when Jeff learned that CW had been poaching an excess of nests and bringing the eggs to the farm, and Tommy had been, too, Jeff knew that simply setting the eggs aside wouldn't be enough to maintain them as evidence, especially as multiple poachers were involved. So he devised a scheme: When the eggs hatched, he needed a way to mark the baby gators that would set them apart from the others. His handlers at the agency gave him an idea.

He mixed glow-in-the-dark paint with waterproof superglue, and on the days when CW's hatchlings finally came out of their shells, Jeff and Jeremy would mark them. They had to do it fast, before the superglue could harden. If the hatchling belonged to CW, Jeff swiped a line of paint along the tail. If it had come from Tommy, Jeremy marked down its leg. If the crew was there, they had to hustle, flicking the paint over the scales before anyone could see. But when no one else was there, they could be more methodical. The little gators squirmed as if the swabs tickled.

Afterward, Jeff hit the lights to see if their sticky scheme had worked.

In the shadows, Jeremy and Jeff stood over the hatchling pools, watching tiny glowing tails and feet flicker and slide among the rest of that black mass like glowworms. Jeff looked down then and found the outline of his hands glowing in the dark.

Despite his initial evasiveness, Robert was also starting to open up to Jeff. Jeff had spent hours at his and Robin's house, getting to know them, building trust—like a real business partner would. He learned that Robert grew up nearby in a fairly prominent family—not that they were rich, but that everybody knew them. In college, he had a scholarship playing golf. He had wanted to work as a medevac transporter. He was smart, learned from everything he did, and advanced, but he remained quiet about it. As a quiet man in a sea of loudmouths and braggarts, his sober reticence came off as lofty and enigmatic. He was organized but didn't want to trouble others with the minutiae of his spreadsheets. He'd even bought a mobile home for his mother when she was about to be evicted.

One afternoon as they sat on the floor of the barn candling alligator eggs, Robert let a name slip that he'd never mentioned before. Benny.

"Who's that?" Jeff asked.

"Oh, Benny Cenac," Robert said. "He's the guy who owns Golden Ranch Farms."

"Who and the what now?"

Robert explained that Golden Ranch Farms, an alligator farm in Louisiana, was where they'd be taking the hatchlings. They'd been paying Robert to find the eggs, hatch them, and get them ready. Cenac also wanted to start an offshoot of Golden Ranch in Florida, and Robert wanted the job of farm manager, an extra motivation to do well besides the money.

Jeff sat thunderstruck, reeling from all this new information. This changed everything. They were poaching, then transporting the ill-gotten goods across state lines. *I might have to get the feds involved*, he thought.

Throughout the operation, Jeff had noted the way Robert threw money around, like when he leased the helicopter to spot the nests from the air. Initially, he thought the money had come from the dissolution of his business with Brother Parker. Then as the legality of their affairs became murky, he'd thought, *Maybe this dude's cleaning all his money*. But now Jeff understood—it wasn't Robert's money. Cenac had employed him to legally harvest Florida alligator eggs, hatch them, and transport the hatchlings to Golden Ranch in Louisiana. Just like all the paperwork he sent to FWC, everything Robert was sending to Golden Ranch made his operation seem aboveboard.

In the past few weeks, Robert had risen in Jeff's estimation from a vague outline of a man to a quiet mastermind. If something truly underhanded was going on, Robert had been covering his tracks so well that Jeff would have to see details—logbooks, ledgers, something concrete, anything—to know on which side of the law he stood. If Jeff had to hazard a guess, Robert was straddling it.

He wasn't going to find out staying in Florida, though. The truth, he knew, would follow Robert to Louisiana, so Jeff had to follow Robert, too.

17

ON THE ROAD

I n 1885, when the Everglades was still an untouched wilderness, plume hunter Guy Bradley and his brother ducked among the blooms of muhly grass, searching for the white speck of an egret. Marl prairie spread around the Bradley boys as far as they could see. It took their set of binoculars to glimpse the shifting purple mirage of the pine flat-woods on the horizon. They were scouting the land for French plume hunter Jean Chevalier, who would go on to sell the feathers they'd collected in Key West each for more than the average person could earn in a week.

During that time, a fashion craze was sweeping the globe. Glamorous society ladies wore wide-brimmed hats dolloped with the immense plumes of wild bird feathers. The more fashionable the lady, the larger the plume. Poachers ravaged rookeries from the Everglades to the Carolinas, targeting flamingos, roseate spoonbills, egrets, and other birds with prized "snowy" white feathers.

By 1900, hunters had killed 95 percent of all Florida shorebirds, driving the snowy egret close to extinction and completely wiping out the Carolina parakeet. That wild frontier era had taken its toll on nature. Environmentalists spoke out against plume hunting, and so, the very same year, Congress adopted the Lacey Act, the first wildlife protection law in US history. The original intent of the act was to criminalize poaching, specifically the sale of illegally captured animals and animal products across state lines. The Lacey Act, in other words, essentially outlawed plume hunting in the US, putting Bradley out of a job. Rather than continue poaching, Bradley became one of the country's first game wardens, a short-lived career that would ultimately end in a shootout on a boat and Bradley's untimely demise.

When Jeff heard that Robert was planning to transport the hatchlings to Louisiana, he knew the Lacey Act was about to come into play. As Jeff finagled his way onto Robert's upcoming trip, Lieutenant Wilson got in contact with the US Fish and Wildlife Service (FWS). While FWS runs a variety of programs, including the National Wildlife Refuge System, the US's own endangered species list, and the Migratory Bird Program, the service's law enforcement division investigates wildlife crimes that reach the national and international scale. By crossing state lines with illegally harvested hatchlings, Robert's crew, Jeff and Lieutenant Wilson believed, was in violation of the Lacey Act, and so their actions came under the jurisdiction of FWS. The service frequently partners with other law enforcement agencies, including state agencies like FWC, providing not only the support of additional officers but also the equipment and infrastructure needed to beat the biggest wildlife-trafficking cases. Their arsenal includes the only wildlife-crime-specialized forensics laboratory in the world. Their aid would be invaluable in bringing down this egg-laundering scheme.

Too bad they declined. Lieutenant Wilson's contact at FWS said they couldn't help out, because the federal agency believed they had seen evidence that FWC's operation at Sunshine Alligator Farm was breaking the law by wiretapping.

"Wiretapping?" Jeff shouted. The accusation had brought him from calm to raging in an instant. He thought of himself as mild and even-keeled, so this sudden outburst was uncharacteristic. The feds' denial had come as that much of a blow.

Knowing he was about to undertake a dangerous trip, Jeff had stolen away for a night at home. So what if Jeremy was green. His presence at the farm offered Jeff that small window to take a break. He hadn't been expecting Lieutenant Wilson's dramatic interruption by phone. He paced his sunroom—past his martial arts awards and his trinkets collected from the outdoors, like the rearticulated skeleton of a snake that he had placed on an ant pile for them to clean with their formic acid—trying to expel the anger that had filled him up like a steam valve. He stopped, turned. Terra-cotta tiles paved the floor. He counted them, with each one wishing away the rage. *I've been working so hard*, he thought. *I've been doing things perfectly. Everything to the letter. Always.*

"You still there, Jeff?" Lieutenant Wilson asked.

"Wiretapping?" Jeff asked. "I haven't done any such thing. You know I wouldn't. Where the fuck did they get that?"

"It's that video of Tommy and Robert."

"What?"

"The one in your hatching room."

Jeff thought back. The tableau of Tommy and Robert in front of the pegboard. Robert's detailed instructions.

Leave the bad eggs? Tommy had asked.

Leave the bad ones, and say it was never opened, Robert had answered. *The good ones, you can say they went with another clutch. See what I mean?*

"What do you mean?" Jeff said. "What's that got to do with wire-tapping?"

"The feds think that you got spy equipment rigged up to catch them saying something they wouldn't say in front of you."

"Well, didn't you tell them I was right there? You told them that's not possible, right? That I have to turn the damn camera on manually, and—"

"I did, Jeff," Lieutenant Wilson said. "Of course I did."

"Let me talk to them," Jeff said. "I'll tell them what *really* happened. I'll talk some sense into them."

"I can't let you do that. There's no point. They have their minds made up."

Jeff had thought being discovered by the guys was his worst nightmare. No, his worst nightmare was this.

"That mean we're through?" Jeff asked, feeling stunned. "Just like that? All our work down the drain? This whole thing is over?"

"Hell no," Lieutenant Wilson answered. "We keep going without them."

"What about Lacey?" Jeff asked. They couldn't prosecute for Lacey Act violations without the feds.

"Kelly's smart," Lieutenant Wilson said, speaking then of the district attorney assigned to their case. "She'll think of something."

Night had fallen over the swamp, and Jeff had eased into watching TV, a nature documentary. He was just getting comfortable when his phone rang. Wayne's name appeared across the phone's screen. Jeff listened to it jangle for a moment, contemplating whether he should answer it or not. The last time he had seen Wayne, the hunter had given him a scare. Jeff's heart beat faster just thinking about it.

You a fucking undercover? Wayne had shouted. The light of Jeff's flash had just gone out, leaving behind it a more intense darkness than had been there before, and for a moment Jeff had wondered if he was going to make it out of there alive. Then Jeff played it off. He joked, and Wayne's apprehension seemed to fade. Was Wayne cunning enough to invite him into a trap?

You're being paranoid, Jeff, he told himself.

Jeff answered the phone. "Hey, Wayne, how are ya?"

"Peachy. What are you doing right now?" Wayne asked.

"Watching TV," Jeff said apprehensively. "Why?"

"Well, we just killed a hog and an alligator, and we thought we'd come by and, you know, you can help us out with cleaning them."

Jeff had never skinned an alligator before. This would be the way to catch an undercover who didn't know his way around a hunt. But Jeff had butchered other game animals. Even if this was a trap, it wouldn't catch him, he thought. Plus it would get Wayne off his scent long enough for them to wrap up the operation.

"All right," Jeff said, doing his best to hide the apprehension in his voice. "Head on over."

Wayne and the tourist from that day's hunting crew heaved the gator down on a table in Jeff's barn. As Jeff surveyed it, his confidence fell. *I don't even know where to start,* he thought. A sudden fear rose within him. They were about to realize he wasn't who he said he was. *I can't screw this up,* Jeff thought. By then, he knew a few things about alligator skinning—certain parts of the hide had to stay intact to make boots and wallets, say—but those details fled his mind now. He pictured himself filleting a fish. He cut off the tail. The tourists from Wayne's guided hunt watched, nodding, looking impressed. Confidence renewed, Jeff dove into butchering.

"What the fuck are you doing?" Wayne said.

Jeff's heart leapt in his throat. He froze.

"You're doing it all wrong," Wayne said, marching over.

There was something about the look in Wayne's eyes that said he had caught a glimpse behind Blackledge's mask.

"What? What are you talking about?" Jeff said with a nervous laugh. "This is the way my buddy taught me down in the Everglades."

Wayne studied him warily. "All right," he said. He didn't sound convinced. He took up his knife again and returned to butchering the hog.

He knows, Jeff thought. *Then why isn't he doing anything about it?*

Jeff told himself that this was his paranoia again, that if Wayne knew, he'd at least cuss him out and leave. But perhaps he had misjudged Wayne. It was possible that Wayne was going through the same turmoil as him, the struggle of knowing that he had made a friend on the other side of the law, and of trying to find a way to end all this so neither one of them would get hurt.

Remember, even Peg Brown had coffee with the rangers.

In the middle of August, two weeks before Jeff thought they were set to leave for Louisiana, Robert called. It was early in the morning, so early that the dew mists still hovered over the fields, unfazed by the dawn. Robert's voice sounded breathy, drawn, as if he was in a panic.

"There's been a change of plans," he said. "We've got to leave as soon as possible. I'm on my way right now."

"Why? What happened?" Jeff asked.

"Nothing to be overly concerned about," Robert said. "Just start getting the hatchlings ready, and when they're all packed in the crates, we'll load them up and get going."

Shit, what's going on? Jeff wondered. Robert sounded like a man being chased. Had he, like Wayne, sensed that the law was on his tail? Worse yet, had Wayne said something? *Naw, Wayne doesn't care for Robert. No way he'd stick his neck out for him like that.*

Jeff hurried to get dressed. He woke Jeremy and informed him of the sudden change in plans. Together they removed the hatchlings from the kiddie pools they'd been calling Sunshine Daycare and organized them in plastic crates they stacked in rows inside the barn.

It was August, the hottest month of Florida's summer, so they would keep the little gators in the barn until right before it was time to go so they didn't overheat. In the darkness of their confines, they quieted down, but whenever Jeff lifted the lid to a pool, they would become alert, squirm over one another, chirp and peep. He wished these little gators could live in the wild, that their fate could be different. He wished that the few didn't have to be sacrificed to save the many. In a perfect world, he could save them all. Hell, in a perfect world, they wouldn't need saving in the first place. No use in that line of thinking now, though. There was nothing he could do for them except keep them safe while they were under his charge.

Robert and the others gradually arrived to help out. Then another pickup pulled into the driveway.

"Wayne, what are you doing here so early?" Jeff asked, wiping his hands on a towel as he strode out to greet him.

"Oh, just dropping by to shoot the shit," Wayne said. "By the looks of it, you're pretty busy."

"We're leaving for Louisiana sooner than we planned," Jeff said.

"Need some help?" Wayne asked.

"I'd be grateful for it, actually," Jeff said. Then he explained what Wayne could do.

At noon, they broke for lunch.

"How 'bout some burgers?" Jeff said to Jeremy and Wayne. Jeff and Jeremy returned to the camper to grab supplies, and Jeff went outside and popped open the grill.

"How do you feel about some Chokoloskee Chicken?" Wayne said.

Jeff knew that meant curlew, the common name for *Eudocimus albus*, the endangered white ibis.

Wayne had grabbed the rifle from his truck and headed toward where rainwater had pooled in a nearby field. Jeff followed Wayne's line of sight. Then he saw them—a trio of white birds wading on the other side of his fence.

"I don't think you're allowed to—" Jeff started.

"Watch this," Wayne said.

Wayne sank to the ground and army-crawled through the grass. The door to the camper opened, and Jeremy came down the steps. As Wayne peered through his scope like a big-game hunter, Jeremy pulled out his phone and started filming. He snuck forward and hid behind Jeff's truck to get a better angle on the birds. Jeff started recording, too. Wayne crawled closer. He waited. And waited. Then he popped off a shot, and one of the curlews fell. The other two took wing, circled overhead, and flew away.

Wayne took another shot, but missed. "I didn't have a good angle," he said to Jeremy as they convened on the fallen bird. Jeff watched from a distance as they walked back toward him with the carcass. When it came down to it, Jeff liked Wayne, and watching this left a pang of disappointment in his chest. *Why does he have to go and be so dumb?* Jeff thought. Wayne borrowed Jeff's knife and used it to cut out the breast, which he seasoned and threw on the grill. *No use wasting it,* Jeff thought.

"We need to get rid of this." Wayne indicated the curlew's remains. "I'll drive you out to the gator pen," he added to Jeremy, "and we can dump it there."

They threw the evidence in the pen and waited until turtles and birds, the gators' wild freeloader neighbors, started pulling the carcass away from one another before finally dragging it beneath the water.

Jeremy would later inform Jeff that on the way Wayne's mouth got the best of him. He flat-out confirmed he knew what he'd done was a crime, that shooting curlews was "highly illegal" and punishable by a hefty $3,000 fine per bird. Why had he done it if he'd known? Jeff would never understand the thought process in that. Maybe he was showing off. Maybe drinking had gotten the better of him. Or maybe he was testing them, and he thought $3,000 was a small price to pay to flush the undercover officers out of hiding.

After they all sat down to a less-than-legal lunch, Jeremy surreptitiously slipped his hand over and flicked the power on a camera hidden in the camper wall beside the table. Wayne kept talking and talking, as was his way, his mouth always the thing to get him in trouble.

"I think I know why old Robert's in such a hurry," Wayne said.

By then, they were sitting in the back of Jeff's pickup truck, taking a break for a beer to cut the heat. Jeff cocked his head at Wayne. At the same time, he clicked the button on his key-fob camera and shifted his leg so it was angled in Wayne's direction.

"There's a traitor in our midst," Wayne said.

Jeff's heart skipped a beat. *This is it.*

"I got a call the other day from FWC," Wayne went on, "asking about Sunshine and Robert."

This isn't it! Jeff rejoiced in his head.

"Wow, so you think they're watching Robert?" Jeff said.

"I don't think, I know!" Wayne exclaimed.

"You mean the local game wardens?"

"They ain't local," Wayne said. "Think bigger." He laughed.

"They think Robert's up to no good, and I'm involved?" Jeff asked, keeping his voice even and calm. In actuality, the situation was verging on being too ludicrous to keep a straight face. Good thing Wayne usually made him laugh anyway.

"No, they don't see you as being involved," Wayne said. "They think you're a pawn."

"They must be watching you," Jeff said.

"They weren't watching *me.*" Was that a note of smugness in his voice?

"Maybe they got their drones out," Jeff joked.

"Maybe he was sitting in a fucking bush over there," Wayne said. Often, their conversations went like improv sets. One joke spun off into another. *Yes, and?* They laughed. Wayne went on, explaining how the agency had wised up to thousands of eggs disappearing from the swamps. "By the time they get this figured out—and oh, they'll figure it out—it'll be too fucking late, because y'all are fixing to leave. Which may be why Robert called you out of the blue and said, 'We need to leave tonight.' Y'all better go soon and pray you get across the state line."

He doesn't know it's me! Jeff could have laughed out of happiness. But that joy faded nearly as soon as it struck. *Wayne doesn't know, but does Robert?*

Jeff thought ahead to their long drive to Louisiana with a growing sense of dread.

The crew worked all night and into the morning getting ready. In the evening of the next day, with the sunset falling behind the western trees, the crew stacked the crates of hatchlings in Jeff's trailer, about 40 to each crate, making 2,434 little gators in all. Unbeknownst to the rest of the crew, the undercover officers had painted 153 of them with fluorescent forensic dye in the hope that those markings would help them discern the illegally gotten gators from the rest. On top of this, they added three coolers of alligator hides, salted and frozen and ready for sale.

Jeff took his place in the passenger seat, and Robert climbed in the driver's side, where he pulled up map directions on his phone.

"It'll probably take us about eleven-and-a-half hours," Robert said, indicating the line on the screen that led from southwestern Florida, up through the panhandle, and across the Gulf Coast to the bayou of Louisiana. "Stops and fuel will probably make it more like fourteen."

It was about eight thirty in the evening when they set out, crossing through empty flatland pastures, strands of gnarled live oaks with dangling Spanish moss, farms in the scrubland, small bridges over creeks, then back into the coastal sprawl of cloned homes built on swampland, golf courses and advertisements and a thousand indistinguishable street corners of the same gas stations and restaurant chains that now populated the gators' domain.

The modern world had triumphed over the wilderness. The suburb had drained the swamp, bringing with it purgatorial big-box stores and tasteless fast food, country clubs and lawns and grid-drawn streets more deceptive than a swamp maze. They called it "civilization," like it was a good thing that the organized had won out against the untamed.

You, too, can have your own little slice of paradise; all you have to do is destroy that paradise in the process. This kind of banal desire, and the greed that sold it, has been Florida's true destruction. Developers pitted man versus nature, not as it had been before as a struggle for survival out in a harsh and remote wilderness, but as a struggle to uphold a false hierarchy of creation. Humans are more important than animals, they said. The soil is ours to scourge and conquer. Marketing has convinced us that trivial luxuries are more important than the natural world, as if we are not part of the natural world ourselves, as if our consumption is not a bid against our own interests, one in favor of concrete and routine against the unwieldy and awe-inspiring, monotony against biodiversity, pesticides against night music, the greed of a few against life itself on our planet.

Dozens of species go extinct every day, with perhaps a million more under threat of extinction within our lifetime. Corporate greed tells us this doesn't merit our attention. If you feel bad, cut back on your own, because it's certainly not *their* fault. Such PR sleight of hand shifts the blame, feeds our guilt, inflames our anxiety, convinces us to consume more and more, until we give up caring, if we ever cared at all. Without thinking, we have become numb to the quiet collapse going on around us.

Everything is connected. A species dying is a piece of our world dying. If the world dies, we die, too.

After about forty-five minutes, Robert pulled into a parking lot at a massive planned community southeast of Bradenton. It seemed he had just remembered necessary transport paperwork required by FWC, so he filled that out, and they got going again. They followed the curve of Tampa Bay north, past towns with names as varied as Progress Village, Mango, and Thonotosassa. Once they had left the Tampa area behind, Robert said he was exhausted. They stopped to switch places.

You're exhausted? Jeff wanted to say. *You had me running around all night, and now you get to sleep?* At that point, he hadn't slept in about thirty-six hours. He resented Robert for passing the responsibility off on him, but he told himself that, despite the strain, it was for the better. An unconscious Robert would be a Robert he didn't have to worry about. As long as he was asleep, he wasn't going to catch Jeff at anything. That could buy Jeff an opportunity to snoop.

"Drive toward I-10 West until you're exhausted," Robert said. "Then we can switch out." He reclined in his seat, and by the time Jeff was cruising northward on the interstate again, Robert had fallen asleep.

Jeff tried to shake the sleep from his eyes. He was too old to pull an all-nighter, let alone two in a row. *The things I do for my job*, he thought.

As Jeff drove through the dark, the night sky blending with the tree line, a text message illuminated his phone, casting a sudden light through the truck cab. Jeff's pulse quickened. He glanced down and saw that the text was from Lieutenant Wilson. His eyes flicked to Robert. He hadn't stirred. He turned the phone face down so that wouldn't happen again.

The longer time stretched on, the more difficult the drive became. Trees on the roadside loomed to impossible proportions. The ground ahead seemed to well up like a tsunami about to swallow them. The woods writhed with visions, and the oncoming headlights melted and smeared. *You're seeing things, Jeff*, he said to himself. *Just a trick of the eyes. Not enough sleep.* By that point, an insomniac delirium had overtaken him. *I can keep driving*, he thought. He was almost giddy.

He drove up through the land of springs and rivers, of old, untouched pine forests and massive swamps that divided farmland from farmland. They drove through prairies where, unseen in the dark, wild horses and bison slept upright under gray-bearded cypresses that stretched toward the stars, all sharing the world with sawgrass and alligators as the plains flowed into the marsh.

By the time Jeff reached Pensacola, enough of his senses had returned that he had the wherewithal to pull over, cut the engine, and shut his eyes for a moment. In a blink, Robert roused him and asked how he was doing. Jeff held back an exasperated groan.

It was still dark out when they got breakfast, around 5 AM, and Robert took the wheel. Only half an hour down the road, much to Jeff's beleaguered frustration, Robert asked him to take over once again. *He couldn't be fucking with me more if he was doing this on purpose*, Jeff thought. Again, he considered that perhaps Robert was onto him. Maybe Wayne had been, too, even if he hadn't informed Robert. He had gotten too close to these men already. His job was hard enough without letting himself succumb to an overactive sense of guilt. All that aside, Jeff questioned whether Robert would have taken him along if he knew his true identity.

Still, Jeff worried. In the worst-case scenario, a sinister end awaited in Louisiana.

Come daybreak, Robert woke. He sat up and looked around. "Where are we?" he asked.

"Crossing into Alabama," Jeff said. He hoped Robert would tell him to pull over and offer to take the wheel.

"All right," Robert said. "Stay on I-10 West into New Orleans," he instructed. He closed his eyes, leaned back again, and slept.

The bleary, rising light cast a strange pall over the empty roadway. All around them, eerily straight rows of southern yellow pines, tree farms, stretched on without end. A sulfurous stench followed. Paper mills. The interstate narrowed onto a small concrete bridge to cross over the winding Styx River. If Jeff noticed the name, he thought nothing of it. He was too preoccupied with staying alert and on the road.

They crossed over Mobile Bay, a grassy marsh that deepened and widened into a windswept pane nearly the same blue as the sky out into the ocean. The road dipped under the muddy Mobile River and spat them out in a tangle of overpasses, ramps, and causeways, under a scant few skyscrapers, then out among the kudzu.

Robert slept all through Mississippi, then into Louisiana. Through the clatter of the Twin Span Bridge over Lake Pontchartrain. They sliced through the bayou. Then chain restaurants and apartment complexes sprang up around the road again. A high bridge lifted them over a canal, between Gentilly and Desire, and on into that storied city on the Mississippi they call the Big Easy, New Orleans.

Jeff gave Robert a nudge, and he roused. "We're here," Jeff said.

Robert nodded and pulled out his phone. He programmed in their destination out on the bayou, a place called Gheens, and set the GPS to talk Jeff through the directions. At a gas station, they finally switched places. While Robert filled their tank, Jeff reached in to grab his overnight bag, hoping to make himself look more presentable than he felt. Something on the floor caught his eye. It was the transfer document that Robert had filled out at the beginning of their trip, clamped to a silver clipboard. Jeff looked around. Robert wasn't paying him any mind. Jeff slipped his phone out of his pocket, took a covert picture of the document, and sent that to Lieutenant Wilson. He didn't know if there'd be anything on it, but every new piece of evidence was one more than he had before.

On the other side of the Mississippi, suburb once again gave way to swamp. Everything was a lush shade of green. You could almost taste the moisture in the air. The farther out they went, the more the trees dwindled. Claws of dead cypresses withered toward a glaring sky. These were ghost forests. Battered by hurricanes, tarred with oil spills, and inundated with salt water rising through the soil, they made this side of Louisiana teeter on the narrow cusp of a death-haunted future.

In the community of Gheens, too small to be labeled a proper town, stubborn live oaks resisted the salt water's call. They reached out, wide and twisted, some so old and gnarled that their many branches resembled chthonic tentacles. Nonetheless, it was a peaceful-seeming place of farms, houses, and churches. On the other side of that little hamlet, an industrial gate blocked the road. They entered, following the road through fields to the set of industrial buildings that was Golden Ranch Farms. It was a place, like the rest of Louisiana, built on a deep history. If the stories were true, the plot had been the Cenac family homestead some centuries ago. The ancestors of billionaire owner Benny Cenac remained buried beneath its soil.

At the main office, ranch manager Andrew, a young man in his thirties, met them and showed them to the factory-chicken-house-like barn they called the grow-out facility. The entire building was roughly the size of a football field and crisscrossed by echoing, steel-walled corridors and holding tanks. It was darker than Jeff expected. Alligators remained so much more docile in the dark.

Andrew directed his employees to follow them back to Jeff's truck, where he, Robert, Andrew, and four ranch hands began to unload. Before he started, Jeff fumbled at the keys clipped to his belt. With a furtive gesture, he clicked the button on his key-fob camera to turn it on. He had to remember he was two people here: Blackledge delivering the alligators and Officer Babauta, collecting as much information as he could. He needed to know if Golden Ranch realized they were bringing in illegally harvested wildlife. If they did, that would change everything. The case would go from a few small arrests to a high-profile sting, bringing down an interstate wildlife-smuggling operation.

They carried the crates of hatchlings one by one into an industrial tunnel, where they deposited the newborns into tanks through holes cut in the metal wall. Jeff felt a pang of regret as he watched them wiggle around the shallow water inside. He hadn't been foolish enough to name them. But they were still cute little animals. He'd helped them out of their shells the day they were born. Sure, several of them bit him, and who knew if any of them remembered him or not. That didn't matter. He'd always done his job to protect wildlife. Now what he was doing felt like a betrayal not just of his cause but of them as individuals. On an intellectual level, he could reason that it was the sacrifice of the few to protect the many. That didn't turn off the feeling part of him that despised the fate he'd given them—they would live the rest of their lives in a dark metal box, so far removed from the wildness of the swamp that, day by day, the stubborn fury that had lived inside of them from the moment they were born would fade away, until one day in the not-too-distant future, they would docilely go to the slaughtering room, and their hides would become purses, wallets, boots.

They were his babies. He wanted to protect them. But he couldn't. It was so hard to let go.

He pushed the thought out of his mind and turned to walk out into the daylight.

Once they'd deposited the last of the hatchlings, Robert asked Andrew if he was interested in buying the alligator hides they'd brought in the coolers.

"Sure," Andrew said.

They drove to another building, where a short tour showed hatching alligator eggs and farmworkers grading hatchlings by size. Jeff and Robert measured the hides, each with its appropriate CITES tag, and Andrew showed them out to a huge walk-in cooler full of alligator skins to finish their delivery.

They lingered in the other building, talking with Andrew, who would reveal later when questioned that he did not like or trust Robert. Andrew told them a little about the facility: The building where they stood could support forty-five thousand hatchlings. As for the rest of the farm, it covered around fifty thousand acres. It was likely the biggest alligator farm in the US.

He'd first talked to Andrew on the phone—when they'd had questions or problems back at Sunshine, Robert would call Andrew, put him on speaker, and he'd get them sorted out. Andrew had taken over his dad's position. His dad had worked for Cenac for most of his adult life, almost forty years. Then he died suddenly in a helicopter crash out on the bayou. He and Cenac had planned to go out together—some said to look for alligator nests, others to appraise land that Cenac was thinking about buying—but Cenac called to cancel last minute, claiming he felt under the weather. A while into the flight, the helicopter fell from the sky. The NTSB investigated and ruled it an accident. Still, some people thought there were just too many coincidences involved.

Golden Ranch did have a certain moody ambience—it was the old plantation where the Cenacs were buried, steeped in history, sinking into the gulf with the rest of the bayou, isolated from the outside world— like the setting of a southern gothic novel. That didn't mean anything sordid had happened there. Then again, it didn't mean it hadn't. Like an old alligator who had survived so long by not making any trouble, Jeff could recognize when he shouldn't go poking his nose where it didn't belong.

18

THE GOLDEN EGG SHEET

Time was closing in on them. The statute of limitations for any misdemeanors Jeff had witnessed in the early days of the case was fast approaching. Yet he still hadn't gotten what he needed to bring the biggest scheme down. Jeff had to work quickly. If he couldn't find Robert's "dirty" books, the agency would be forced to choose between charging the early misdemeanors or these more substantial crimes.

Of all the possible poachers in their net, Robert's crew represented the biggest catch. Losing them would mean losing the sting. Jeff had considerable evidence against CW and Tommy, both of whom had flagrantly brought in extra eggs beyond their allotted counts. The hatchlings painted with forensic glow would vouch for their crimes. With Robert himself and his wife, Robin, proving their crimes would be much harder. They had also collected beyond their legal counts, but since their hauls had been mixed in with the legal eggs from the beginning, there was no way for Jeff to tally exactly how many eggs the duo had stolen from the wild.

"What you need is documentation," Lieutenant Wilson advised Jeff one night after Jeff had returned from Louisiana. Lieutenant Wilson had come to the farm to retrieve video and audio recordings so his team could comb through them for evidence such as covert discussions of illicit activities. After he'd taken what he needed on a Jumpdrive, he stayed to debrief Jeff and Jeremy in the now much less crowded barn. "You say Robert's fairly organized?"

"Yes, sir," Jeff said. "At least with the paperwork, that is."

Some instances of Robert's disorganization—like the sudden trip to Louisiana nearly two weeks ahead of schedule—might not have been disorganization at all but a clue. Perhaps Robert had hurried them off early for a reason; maybe he had scented FWC on his trail, as Wayne had suggested. Or maybe something else had set off Robert's panic. Jeff tucked this back in his mind to ruminate on later.

"Then he's bound to keep a record of what he's doing," Lieutenant Wilson said. "Look for a ledger or a list of numbers. It might be labeled in a code, but there will be something to differentiate some numbers from the rest."

"Would he really keep something so incriminating?" Jeremy asked.

"You'd be surprised," Lieutenant Wilson said. "You see this with organized crime investigations all the time. There will be a clean book—a ledger that looks aboveboard—and then they'll keep a dirty book that tallies every little detail of what they've done."

Organized crime. *Is that what this is?* Jeff thought. None of the folks he'd tracked in the investigation seemed like hardened mafiosos. But perhaps he should have known by then that people were always more than what they seemed.

"I bet you if Robert's keeping something, it will be in that silver box of his," Jeff said. "Sometimes he leaves it around. I haven't seen inside it yet. But I'll try to take a peek next time his back is turned."

Jeremy agreed to do the same.

The tangible, obvious proof such a ledger would provide was the only thing that stood between Jeff and the Sunshine crew's arrests. It's also what stood between him and the end of the sting. He was ready to go home. He missed his wife. He missed his son. Heck, he even missed the chores his wife would give him on his infrequent visits. What he really missed, though, was being Jeff Babauta.

Robin joined them on their next trip to Louisiana. They set off at night like they did before, this time much more prepared and better rested, and with a third person, the drive was less strained. They traveled up the state at a leisurely pace. Robin kept the conversation flowing, and Jeff welcomed the chatter.

"Look, a Bass Pro Shop," she said, pointing to a billboard. She suggested they stop to shop for a little bit. She and Robert wanted to stock up on gear for hunting season, and since the most Arcadia had was a Tractor Supply, a chance to peruse a Bass Pro Shop was a real treat.

They pulled in and looked around. Jeff ambled by displays of recurve bows. Taxidermied wildlife stared blankly from their perches atop the aisles.

A text message chimed at Jeff's phone. He flinched and looked around to make sure no one was about to sneak up behind him and read his phone. Then he opened the text. It was from Lieutenant Wilson.

> Wilson: Your tail has lost visual on you. What is your status?
> Jeff: My tail?

Jeff sent a picture of a hatchling coming out of its egg, its comparatively large tail sticking out below a snout that seemed to smile.

> Wilson: There is a team tailing you for backup. What is your location?

Jeff could almost sense Lieutenant Wilson's irritation coming through the phone.

> Jeff: I'm fine. I didn't realize I had a tail. Everything is still going according to plan. We stopped at Bass Pro Shop.
> Wilson: 10–4. Keep us apprised of your movements.

This stop was not a one-time affair. It seemed that every time Robin spotted a billboard for a Bass Pro Shop, they pulled off the highway to go shopping, and every time, Jeff became a little more annoyed.

> Wilson: Where the hell are you? Are you at Bass Pro again?
> Jeff: Yes.

He confirmed their approximate location.

If we stop at Bass Pro one more time, so help me, Jeff thought. *And I thought I was losing my mind on the first trip.* Somehow this seemed worse.

Wilson: Next time they stop, hang back and look for that silver box.

Jeff: 10–4.

"Oh, Boot Barn," Robin said the next time they were on the road, indicating a sign for a western outfitter. "I need some new boots. Let's see what they have."

Once again, they left the highway. Jeff could feel his anger welling up. Perhaps Robin could sense it.

"Want to come shopping with us?" she asked.

"Do I look like a damn cowboy to you?" Jeff snapped.

She gave him an amused smile. "Or stay out here. We won't be too long."

His irritation smoldered as they walked off, leaving him in the truck. He got out, stretched his legs, and then remembered himself. This wasn't just an annoyance. It was an opportunity. He peered under Robert's seat, and there it was, the silver box. He looked back at the store entrance. No sign of Robin or Robert.

Better make it quick, he thought.

He lifted the box's latch. It wasn't even locked. This was too easy. Maybe there wasn't anything important inside. He riffled through the papers. They didn't look like much, just forms and ledgers. But Jeff took pictures of them anyway. He sent the photos to Lieutenant Wilson. He closed the box just in time to hear someone call his name. He stashed the box under the seat then turned around to greet Robert and Robin, a shopping bag dangling from her arm.

Do you realize what you've found?" Lieutenant Wilson said over the phone.

Jeff had completed the delivery trip with Robin and Robert, once again returning to life on the farm.

"You've hit the jackpot," Lieutenant Wilson continued. "This is the golden egg sheet."

He meant that Jeff had found Robert's dirty books. They had appeared like a revelation in one of the many nondescript snapshots of papers he'd sent to Wilson. The team back at the agency had deciphered Robert's code and realized that he had indeed kept track of every egg his crew had poached.

Jeremy had snapped pictures of his own evidence as well, including forms Robert seemed to have forged in the name of a man who worked for the Seminole Tribe.

They had what they needed to prosecute Robert. Now all that was left was to bring him in.

While Jeff carried on his duties at the farm, his team behind the scenes at the agency started pulling all the clues together.

Cenac flew in himself to collect the last set of hatchlings. Despite Robert's eagerness to impress the billionaire, Cenac seemed keen on avoiding him.

To Jeff, Cenac was an enigma at first. When Jeff looked into him, he turned up mixed results. On the one hand, in 2013, Cenac seemed to have violated campaign finance laws and had pleaded guilty to making false statements to the FEC. On the other hand, he threw his money around for good, too, making donations to things as varied as college culinary programs, the Audubon Nature Institute, and the IUCN Species Survival Commission's Crocodile Specialist Group. Although Jeff planned to check out Cenac and his operation at Golden Ranch more thoroughly, unwilling to leave any stone unturned, the idea that Cenac might be involved in Robert's schemes seemed increasingly unlikely. Not because of his philanthropy, but because of the wealth that allowed it. Cenac was a billionaire. The amount of money to be made poaching alligator eggs was so insignificant in comparison that allowing it was not only pointless, it would threaten the farm's reputation and the conservation initiatives he had funded.

Instead, as the agency deciphered the documents, clues began to surface that Robert was stealing from Cenac as well.

On their first trip to Louisiana, Robert had driven out to Houma in the hope of visiting Cenac. The billionaire shipping magnate kept his offices on a hulking barge on the Mississippi River like a floating fortress.

"It's designed that way so when hurricanes come, instead of his business getting destroyed, tugboats can come drag the entire ship out into the gulf," Robert said. "They anchor out there and let it ride the waves."

They parked and went to the ramp. Security stopped them and asked for their credentials.

Robert explained who he was. "I'd like to see Mr. Cenac if I can," he said. "He knows who I am." The security guard looked skeptical, but he radioed in their presence anyway. After a while, the response came. Cenac didn't want to see them. No further explanation or invitation to come back another time.

It turned out that Robert wasn't just poaching—he was hoodwinking everyone, including Cenac. Cenac had given him an open checkbook, and Robert was using it to buy parts for fanboats to build them for himself, marking those funds as spent on eggs and farm supplies.

He was on salary, so he wasn't even getting paid by the egg. Despite this realization of embezzlement, it didn't make sense that he was poaching so many alligator eggs from the wild. The risk of getting caught didn't seem worth the reward of impressing Cenac, especially while stealing from the man at the same time. In a way, Robert was like Robin Hood after all, poaching and stealing from the rich. He just wasn't giving to the poor, unless he counted himself. The trickster who robs the rich to give to the poor gets called a hero. The trickster who robs the less fortunate, man or beast, to give to himself tends not to win many hearts.

So does the end justify the means like the trickster-hero archetype seems to suggest? As makers and consumers of culture, we're interested in underdogs, Horatio Algers, Davids triumphing over Goliaths, the righteous and deserving getting their rewards. But this coin has another side: The triumph isn't so sweet if those we perceive as undeserving don't lose in the process. As a culture, we're into punishment as much as we are into redemption. The second doesn't taste nearly so sweet without the first.

19

THE MONGOOSE

As counts added up against Robert's crew, Jeff started to let himself speak up more when they were crossing the line of legality. The more frequently he pushed, the more they admitted to their wrongdoing, wearing it like a badge of honor, all except for Robert himself, whose reticence, most times, maintained his plausible deniability.

Of all the people who came on the egg hunts, Jeff had gotten the closest to David. Jeff enjoyed talking to him about wildlife, and in these times, when they were alone, perhaps Jeff would spot a bird and identify it, forgetting who he was supposed to be. It was that easy to exist alongside David, so easy that he found himself slipping back into being Jeff Babauta in a way he thought he couldn't anymore. Such ease, Jeff worried, could be both a relief and a danger, not just of blowing his cover, but of not being able to do his job. With David, he *had* crossed the line. He *had* gotten too close. He didn't want to arrest David. He wanted to protect him.

Lieutenant Wilson and Jeff's agency handlers believed that David was working in collusion with Robert and his gang. Even Robert's own words—especially the ones Jeff had recorded in the hatching room—seem to imply that David was flouting the law, as if closing his eyes to every instance of poaching that he was supposed to be watching out for.

"He could just be making mistakes," Jeff said, advocating for David over the phone to Lieutenant Wilson.

With all the evidence they had amassed over the months, the agency decided it was time for their trap to snap shut, for Jeff to close up the farm, and, as soon as Blackledge had vanished, for teams of uniformed officers to show up at the alligator thieves' homes, arrest warrants in hand, and bring them in.

"I know you like the guy, Jeff," Lieutenant Wilson said. "But that doesn't mean he's innocent."

"Give me one last chance," Jeff pleaded, "to prove he doesn't know what he's doing."

Lieutenant Wilson breathed out. "All right," he said. "One last chance."

So Jeff convinced David to invite him over, a conversational sleight of hand pulled when the subject drifted toward gardening, and David started in on all the fruit trees he kept. Citruses, mangoes—just about any plant that loves the tropics will bear fruit in South Florida.

On October 5, Jeff drove to David's Punta Gorda home, an old-fashioned bungalow with a porch to let in the breeze. Before he set out, Jeff had concealed a Bluetooth recording device under the brim of his baseball cap, and as he drove, he rehearsed the questions he would ask. He needed to unravel David's involvement in the poaching scheme. Was he just making innocent mistakes? Was Robert using him? Or was he the mastermind behind his own actions?

Rain clouds had started to gather by the time Jeff pulled up to David's house, and after they had strolled through David's lush garden, Jeff eagerly listening to a veritable biology lecture on the exotic trees and fruit that David grew, that whisper of an afternoon shower turned into a downpour. Jeff and David ducked into the closest shelter, Jeff's truck. In the sudden cold of his air-conditioning, Jeff remembered why he was there. Now he had to play verbal chess with this smart man, probing to find out how much he knew. If he was guilty of aiding Robert in his scheme to poach and launder alligator eggs, then maybe Jeff could get him to come clean and set him on the path toward redemption, too, all without divulging his own identity behind this mask in the process. Jeff would have to be careful. David was an expert in one of nature's craftiest animals, the mongoose.

The biologist had spent the better part of a lifetime researching mongooses in the Virgin Islands, where farmers had released dozens of the small mammals in an effort to combat pests. The mongooses, however, tenacious and wily—and prone not to listen to instructions, it seems—multiplied and began preying on native species, leading many people to change their minds about the formerly beloved animal: Authorities called the mongooses invasive and crafted plans for their eradication. Quite a long way to fall for an animal that ancient Mesopotamians associated with magic. Stories in classical Sanskrit, though, portray the mongoose as loyal above all, a plucky little hero eager to defy odds and defend its human friends from the mighty cobra. Modern trappers know that mongooses are just as crafty as millennia of stories have portrayed them: Like the tricksters of myth and legend, mongooses have been known to outsmart their ostensibly more intelligent foes, us humans, by unlocking traps and setting themselves free. Perhaps David had learned a thing or two from watching them all those years, whether that be loyalty or—well, Jeff would see.

He chatted with David for a bit until it seemed the rain would not relent, and they would be trapped in the truck together indefinitely unless they wanted to get soaked to the bone. *Now or never*, Jeff thought. *Time to jump in.*

"The reason I was asking you about yesterday," Jeff said. "I don't know what we ended up with." He was referring to the number of eggs they had harvested. Even as hatching season progressed, the crew had continued their hunts whenever they could.

"That's why I didn't want to get in the mix," David said. "Because I actually never counted the eggs."

For real? Jeff thought. *Trying to make it seem like you saw nothing, is that it?*

"You were around in times I wasn't even present," David went on.

"I wasn't sure you were required by the state to keep track of that," Jeff said. "So I don't know what all Robert brought in." Jeff laid on the acting, tweaking his tone into one of anxiousness. After their initial differences, Jeff had tried to give David the impression that he was rough around the edges, but he meant well. By then, he believed that David thought of him as generally good, not a lawbreaker, a fellow looking to start his business up right—one who had stumbled into company who wanted to fool him and use him against his will. That was what was happening to Blackledge, after all. No need to cook up a scheme or backstory here.

"I think there were some other sources," David said, meaning that other eggs were coming in from who knew where. "I'm kind of suspicious of that. You and I both know that CW has brought in lots of additional eggs."

Jeff nodded. He furrowed his brow and tried to look upset. "So my biggest fear was getting—" He took a tense breath. "Robert keeps talking about FWC raiding my place. He has me worried."

"They can't," David said, consoling. "While the number of eggs and the number of hatchlings are justified"—the tallies matched up in Robert's books—"nobody can possibly sort out how many eggs were collected. Now that there's been hatchling gators, and export of gators, there's no way that anybody can verify anything right now."

Jeff tried to seem confused. He needed David to say something, anything, to prove his involvement one way or another. "So I guess what you're saying is if I had those eggs, what's showing up on my clipboard"—where Jeff kept tallies of his own—"does not add up to what we have?"

"I've been aware without actually counting a single egg—I've been aware that's going on," said David. "He knows what he's doing." He meant Robert. "Think if you were a prosecuting attorney. I mean, we both will totally agree that Robert is a sharp number. I've seen him manipulate people. I go along with it, and he tries to manipulate *me*. I think he recognizes he can only manipulate me a little way." He paused and looked out through the cascade of rain over the windshield as if seeing back in time to an instance when Robert tested his wits against him and lost. "Having sat through a lot of law school classes, if I was a prosecuting attorney and wanted to bring a case against Robert, I would look at available evidence and the way we could present things—and I'd never bring a case. It's obvious to me that there were shenanigans done, but that they were done with such finesse that I'm not going to prevail in court. Any defense attorney that's worth his salt is going to be able to get this case thrown out for lack of evidence."

That is where I draw the distinction between Robert and his crew and Peg Brown. Peg wore the title *poacher* like a badge of honor. These wily egg hunters did not. Above all else, it's not how they saw themselves but how they saw other people that separates the Peg Browns of the world from all the others: Peg tricked the rangers so he could get away with poaching, sure. But even as he duped them, he thought of them as men with families, with responsibilities and flaws and consciences, with needs sometimes as desperate as his own. In his empathy, he could read them, and he could give them mercy, and the rangers could do the same. They could chase him down and make his life difficult, build up their firepower until his nightly adventures seemed impossible, but in the end, they had a decision to make. Perhaps that is the real reason why they never caught Peg Brown: They didn't want to. It was better for everyone—for his family, for the island, for an Everglades in need of a hero, and for their consciences—if they let him go.

In many ways, Peg is more like Jeff than he is like Robert and his crew. The "shenanigans" David described at Sunshine seemed to use people, moving them around the swamp like pawns with no regard to their well-being; like the eggs they plucked from the wild, like the hatchlings they passed on to Louisiana, their pawns were a means to meet an end. Such disregard, and the hubris that empowered it, would ultimately prove their downfall, a trap they set for themselves. They thought too little of Curtis Blackledge. Their assumptions took away his depth, and so they didn't see, behind that mask, there was Jeff Babauta, whose unassuming cleverness had been honed not through manipulation but empathy.

As David spoke, Jeff nodded and let his expression soften just a bit, as if relieved by the knowledge of Robert's cunning. David smiled. He hadn't said enough to clear his name or condemn it. Jeff needed to push harder. This was just like the end of the softshell case, when he was questioning Alonso in his backyard as they weighed the turtles. He'd toed right up to the line then, the one that separated curiosity from a suspicious need to know too much. That's how this worked, he realized. When you let yourself go just a little too far, when you risked everything—that's when the most harrowing truths came into the light.

"Let me ask you this, because it's another concern of mine," Jeff said. "Because if I do this next year, I want to make sure I'm following the rules. Robert was supposed to be holding my hand and guiding me." This painful betrayal came bubbling up in his words. It really did hurt that Robert went back on his word. He held Blackledge in such little regard that he'd been willing to use Blackledge's farm to commit crimes for which Blackledge could have taken the blame. He was willing to ruin Blackledge's life, and for what? To impress a billionaire? Laundering eggs didn't earn Robert any more money than he would have gotten if he'd followed the law. So try as he might, Jeff couldn't wrap his mind around why he did it. What was the point?

"You don't necessarily want to do it the way Robert did," David said.

Ah, now we're getting somewhere, Jeff thought.

"Going back to that 50 percent," Jeff said. "Especially like at Webb—we're supposed to go harvest a nest then skip one, technically, under that 50 percent rule, right?"

David nodded. "Yep."

"Then go on to the next one."

"Yep."

I need you to say it! Jeff shouted in his head.

"Harvest that one and skip that one," Jeff said. "We didn't do that."

"We did *not* do that," David said emphatically.

That was it. That was enough. David had confirmed Jeff's suspicions. He hadn't only been supervising the egg collections when he said he wasn't paying attention; he also knew that the crew had been breaking the law, and had just stood by and let them. His job had been to speak up for the state of Florida, for the alligators, and he hadn't. It wasn't a slip. It wasn't a little mistake. He let all of this happen. The revelation came as a blow to Jeff's heart. *Oh, Dave,* he thought. He tried not to let the disappointment play across his face.

"Did we not do 100 percent?" Jeff laughed, hoping that the bittersweetness of that victory did not carry over into his voice. "How is Robert going to justify that?"

"You look at Robert's records, and you'll see." Now David laughed, too. "Robert's records say we only harvested *half* of what we did."

For his whole career, being friendly with the folks who sometimes snatched things from the woods was part of his job, a necessary one. It was part of who he was, too. Jeff Babauta was the kind of person who cared. Try as he might to separate himself, or who he had always believed himself to be, from the man he had to become for his job—he couldn't do it. To defy this part of himself by calling them criminals or bad guys was one part of his identity he couldn't shake when he stepped into Blackledge's skin. He had all but lost himself to the character—except for this. He was told that this was necessary, this loss. He had to forget. He had to be neutral to do this job. But he was starting to embrace that without this compassion he would be missing why he was here in the first place, why he'd become a game warden and dedicated his life to protecting the wild. It was the central tenet of his being. It was the thing holding him up inside on those long nights he spent alone looking after the farm, nights that could have cracked him open and left him in the dark valley of his soul. Without compassion, there was no point to him being here, doing this, not any of it. Without compassion, he would lose Jeff Babauta for good.

Even though he was about to bring charges against so many people he had gotten to know, Jeff still saw room in there for a little much-needed compassion.

"I don't think we should arrest Robin, or any of the wives, for that matter," he told Lieutenant Wilson over the phone.

The agency was working with the DA to put together charges, and while that was building up, Jeff's time as Blackledge was winding down. It was December, with Christmas around the corner, and Jeff was eager to get back to being himself again, whoever that was now.

"Why not?" Lieutenant Wilson asked. "Robin was as involved as anyone else there, maybe even more so."

"If we arrest both of them, who's going to take care of their kids?" Jeff asked. "They have three kids, George. Do you want to leave them without a dad *and* a mom? I don't."

If they had to choose one of them to prosecute, Jeff said, it should be Robert, whom several of their crew had called the mastermind behind their schemes, on camera no less. Though Robin was no less intelligent—and perhaps even more perceptive—than her husband, she had not orchestrated any plans to defraud the wild. She had only been accessory to them.

Most of the poachers had brought their families along for egg harvesting. Husbands and wives had worked as poaching teams. Most of the wives knew what was going on. But if both husband and wife were arrested, what would happen to the kids? Jeff thought about his own family. He imagined a world where both he and Sandy were suddenly taken away, leaving their son when he was young. That's a loss he never would have recovered from. Hurting those kids would have been wrong. All of Jeff's career, he had tried to treat poachers as he would want to be treated. Now this was his final test. If he wanted his career to go out with a bang, he'd have rounded them all up and brought them all in, and the number of arrests would be glorious. But if he wanted the operation to reflect his career, to reflect who he was as an officer and an environmental protector, he would have to trade glory for redemption.

Jeff thought of himself as the kind of person who always did the right thing, even when it hurt. This hurt now, for sure. But he would be able to sleep at night knowing that he'd done his best for both the animals and the people. He had vowed to protect the wild. That meant protecting the people who lived there, too.

Lieutenant Wilson breathed out, and Jeff was afraid he'd veto that plan for compassion before they could discuss it. Maybe Lieutenant Wilson would say Jeff had gotten attached to the poachers and their families, and if he was being honest with himself, Jeff would agree. Maybe Lieutenant Wilson would argue that this sting was the crowning achievement of both of their careers; lowering their arrest numbers would be selling themselves short of their full glory. Things like that didn't matter to Jeff. He didn't need glory. He just needed to do the right thing.

"Just the men?" Lieutenant Wilson said. "I'll run it up the chain, but—I think we can do that."

"Yeah?"

"Yeah. I'll see what I can do."

As Blackledge, he made excuses to all the new people in his life, both Robert and Robin, Tommy and CW, and the harder goodbyes to Wayne and David. Lieutenant Wilson and Jeff's team at the agency had decided that it would be too dangerous to leave Jeff in place at the alligator farm while the arrest warrants went out. So Jeff had to disappear as cleanly as he'd arrived. He needed to dismantle the farm, spirit away the spy equipment in the dead of night, sell all the alligators, and take his personal effects home, always keeping watch in his rearview mirror as he drove for cars that seemed to follow just a little too long.

"What, you dying?" Wayne had asked. He had showed up once again to drink Jeff's beer, and they stood, looking out over the alligator pond.

"No, no, nothing like that," Jeff answered. "I'm just—I'm done with this game."

"I hear ya," Wayne said knowingly.

How much does he really know? Jeff wondered. *If he knows, wouldn't he have said something by now? Then again, wouldn't I?*

With Wayne, Jeff felt caught between loyalty to his mission and loyalty to their—was this friendship? On the surface, it felt like friendship, but below that, Jeff knew you couldn't really be friends with someone who didn't know who you were. He liked Wayne. In another life, he and Blackledge could have continued their harebrained adventures. But this was reality. In this life, Jeff reminded himself, he had come here with a mission to protect the wild. Wayne had violated that wild, even though Jeff knew he loved it. He'd flouted the laws put in place to protect nature. Why? Some could have been simple mistakes. Others seemed to hover close to the same mentality of the gladesmen that had begotten Peg Brown, a dogged defiance spun from injustice and woven into myth. Problem was these were no longer the days of Peg Brown, nor was it the age of Robin Hood. Since then, the way we see animals has changed.

In the poacher-as-hero narrative, animals often amount to little more than props. That's largely because this narrative hails from a time and a place, medieval Britain, when the common sentiment toward animals denied them agency. Some writers have blamed the prevalence and dominance of Christianity in that time; however, it more likely came about as a part of rejecting pagan beliefs in their entirety instead of as a wholly formed belief itself. Either way, medieval stories mark animals as beasts of burden, food, foe, or ready symbolism—though sometimes they're pleasant scenery if they're lucky enough. However, the further away we've gotten from those so-called Dark Ages, the more the general attitude toward animals has returned a selfhood to them, especially when we tell stories about them.

That is why the poacher-as-hero has seen his downfall. When his adversary is an animal, we no longer see him as David: He's Goliath, so we want him to lose. And with loss, in this narrative scheme, comes punishment. Because that's what we want as consumers of story. Loss isn't enough unless we get revenge; we want that fulfillment, because revenge isn't something most of us get (or thankfully even strive for) in our lives off the page. So poacher-as-hero narratives have gone the way of the dodo, and, unless the writer and readers gloss over his poaching acts, he is replaced generally by the poacher-as-villain.

Perhaps, in this way, the most satisfying end to a poacher-versus-billionaire story would be one in which everyone loses. But reality is never so simple and clean as it appears in stories, and the machinations of time certainly aren't looking to create the most satisfying narrative end. People aren't archetypes. Poachers, like the rest of us, contain multitudes, like how Peg Brown was a dedicated war hero, a good dad, a pillar of his community, and a damn good storyteller. It's easy to forget that everyone is the hero of their own story. Most of us are just doing our best to get by however we can. Sometimes that means making difficult choices in order to survive.

The people who insist that every act is morally unambiguous are the ones who are suspect, because they fail to see the conflicts others face: A poacher may hunt to feed his family. A thief may steal because he feels powerless—from not being able to make ends meet, from the grind and hustle modern life has forced upon us—so he's stepping out of bounds, transgressing, freeing himself for at least one act, but everything we do has a consequence. The people who think they've never hurt anyone or anything in their lives are the ones most oblivious to the trail of pain they've left behind. If you're living—really living—there will be consequences. Even if you're always following the law, the law isn't always right.

Jeff, a wildlife officer, seems an unlikely person to have this realization. He spent his whole career upholding the law. Yet, through all those years, he saw that even laws that protect the innocent, the wild creatures who depend on us to be stewards of this planet, can have profound consequences for the people who break them. Jeff had watched all his career. He'd listened. By then he knew that guilt did not mean someone was beyond redemption. No one is. They were all just real people trying to survive, forced to make some of life's most difficult choices. The small act of trying to feed your family can shatter your life. Jeff didn't want that to happen with the poachers caught in Operation Alligator Thief. If he could, he wanted to do his job by causing the least damage. And if he admitted it, he'd come to really like the people. They had trusted him, brought him into their homes. He felt guilty, too, because of this. He was the traitor in their midst. He'd betrayed all of their trust.

"So what are you going to do with the gators?" Wayne asked.

"Sell 'em, I guess," Jeff said. He took a swig of beer, a real one this time. "Why, you want 'em?"

"Hell yeah," Wayne said.

They bartered a dirt-cheap price, and later, they set out on their last escapade, to wrangle the remaining alligators and put an end to Sunshine Alligator Farm.

S o, this is it," Robert said.

"This is it," said Jeff. They stood outside what had been Sunshine but was now a shell, their decals peeled off the walls, the alligators gone. Jeff was more than ready to be gone, too, and he was definitely done with Robert. As he gave Robert a stiff handshake, he looked him in the eyes for a brief moment. *You think you're such a mastermind, like you're so much smarter than everyone else*, Jeff thought. *You think you've played all of us, don't you?* Jeff wondered how Robert would feel when he realized he was the one being duped all along.

Robert signed the check for $2,500, the remaining fee for using the farm. "Sure I can't interest you in another season?" Robert asked. "Next year? We could really use you."

I bet you'd like to, Jeff thought.

"No, I think I've had my fill of alligators," Jeff said. "This is it for me. I'm moving on to something else. But I have to thank you. I really learned a lot."

After Robert left, Jeff took out his phone. He opened David's contact page. His finger hovered over the call symbol. *No.* Jeff shut the app and put the phone in his pocket. He couldn't face the man knowing what he was about to do.

December came and went, and in the new year, the state built a case against the alligator thieves. Without the possibility of bringing Lacey Act violation charges, the DA had to come up with something else. In a twist, she decided on racketeering charges, ironic because big corporations often wield the RICO (Racketeer Influenced and Corrupt Organizations) statute against environmental activists, journalists, and public figures who have gotten in their way or otherwise spoken out against them. (This practice is so common that activists and journalists have a name for it: SLAPP, or strategic lawsuits against public participation.)

The warrant for Robert's arrest charged him with racketeering, conspiracy to commit racketeering, scheming to defraud, and fourteen counts of unlawful possession of alligator eggs, a number of eggs that reached into the thousands. Tommy's list of charges was a little bit thinner, with conspiracy to commit racketeering and six counts of unlawful possession of alligator eggs. Although CW had harvested over a thousand illicit eggs himself—earning $58,000 in only three months—his charges included only four counts of unlawful possession, and also, of course, conspiracy to commit racketeering. The charges against David said he was in on their scheme. His arrest warrant accused him of conspiracy to commit racketeering, one count of unlawful possession of alligator eggs, and uttering a forged instrument, a special law in Florida that criminalizes lies and counterfeited or forged records made with an attempt to defraud. Last, there was Wayne, who received the least of the charges. The accusations against him included three counts of unlawful possession of alligators, take (poaching) of white ibis, and attempted take of white ibis. In all, the state of Florida brought charges against eleven people in Operation Alligator Thief, including six suspects not mentioned in this book.

Before long, May arrived, and it was time for the trap to snap shut.

The day before the arrests were scheduled to take place, the agency along with the DA held a meeting to brief all the officers. Jeff sat at the side of the room, taking it all in. He was so moved that he had to record. He took out his phone and scanned it slowly over the crowd as the DA presented the case. Over sixty officers from five counties were listening to her speak. They were there because of the work Jeff had done, all of them, uniformed officers, plainclothesmen, protecting these prehistoric beasts that Jeff had come to love.

He could barely sleep that night. That morning, he told his wife that if anything happened, if anyone came after her or Chris, she should call him immediately. They reassured each other that everything would be fine. He left the house while it was still dark and drove to the command center, the secret location from which he, Lieutenant Wilson, and their team would direct the arrests. He met Lieutenant Wilson inside.

Lieutenant Wilson clapped him on the shoulder the way a coach might rouse his star player before the big game. "How you feeling?"

Nervous. Excited. Worried. "Feeling good, George," Jeff said.

"Good," Lieutenant Wilson said. "It's showtime."

The takedown clock began ticking at 6 AM. The longer it took for the field officers to make the arrests, the more likely it became that the suspects would catch wind of the sting and flee. The electric pulse of worry thrummed inside Jeff. He was safe there, surrounded by his fellow officers, but what about his wife and son? What if that car he'd seen had been following him? What if the poachers knew where he lived? What if they heard about the sting? What if they slipped away before the officers arrived? What if—

All across the state, the officers banged on doors. They shouted the suspects' names. "Open up," they demanded. "We have a warrant."

One by one, the doors opened.

One by one, the suspects presented themselves to the officers.

One by one, the officers read them their rights and cuffed their wrists.

The only one who protested was David. He insisted then and kept insisting he didn't know what he'd done.

EPILOGUE

As I explored the stories of *Gator Country*, a phrase in Latin kept returning to my mind: *Et in Arcadia ego*, roughly translated as, "And I am in Paradise." The most famous use of the phrase appears as the title of a painting by French baroque artist Nicolas Poussin in which toga-clad shepherds and a woman examine an epitaph inscribed on a tomb, possibly *Et in Arcadia ego*. This instance isn't the first use of the phrase, and it's far from the last, with others ranging from mentions in novels such as *The Sound and the Fury* and *Brideshead Revisited* to more recent appearances such as the title of two episodes of *Star Trek: Picard*. With much of this book occurring in a town called Arcadia, every time I heard the name, I thought, *Et in Arcadia ego*, turning the phrase over like a stone worn smooth by the current of a river.

Beyond its literal translation, *Et in Arcadia ego* has come to mean that even in paradise, death awaits us all. Memento mori and all that. That phrase and *Et in Arcadia ego* were, excuse the pun, done to death by the invention of the movable-type printing press. And like every popular trope, they deserve to be subverted. Death waits for us. Sure, okay. But so does new life.

Nature's most deathly places are where it's most full of life, not despite that death but because of it. Dead things decay and enrich the soil. Endangered salamanders in electric hues scamper under fallen pine trunks half consumed by time and worms. Bogs mix life with life, congealing it together into its most fertile essence. Rare orchids unfurl over the mire. Death comes for all things, but so does a kind of resurrection. Death is inevitable, as those phrases remind us, but as millions of years on this planet have shown, so is the triumph of life. Life blooms from death. Life is not the victor. Death is not the enemy. Life and death are not at odds but in inseparable agreement.

Even people who don't believe in a literal afterlife can still look forward to a reincarnation back into soil, back into life, because the elements that make up our bones and flesh also make mother-of-pearl, birds' wings, lilies, and stardust. We are a part of everything, quite literally. To make an enemy of swamps is to make an enemy of yourself. On the grand scale, swamps are massive carbon sinks, swallowing up the gasses that endanger our planet. On the smaller scale—an infinitesimally smaller one—microorganisms in healthy soil may boost the human body's microbiome, one possible reason why people who spend time outdoors live longer. Our bodies benefit from nature, likely in more ways than we can even imagine or have yet discovered. Our relationship with nature is symbiotic. When nature thrives, our bodies thrive, our species thrives. The antithesis is also true: When the wild faces ruin, so do we. We don't just lose a metaphor. We don't just lose a playground. We lose ourselves.

Just as we are connected with nature, so is every other animal. The loss of a single species poses a threat to all the rest, including us. That is why Jeff and FWC put such an effort toward protecting alligators.

All told, the crew from Sunshine Alligator Farm took more than thirteen thousand eggs from the swamp in a single year, far more than the numbers allowed on their permits, far more than even Peg Brown, whom Chokoloskee storytellers called the most "notorious" alligator poacher to ever live, took from the Everglades over the span of three decades. It's true that alligators are far more plentiful now than they were then. That is, at least in part, because of regulations that limit egg harvests. As Jeff told me during one interview at his house, the population of any species will have a tipping point, and if we're not careful, it can go from plentiful to in decline before we know what's happening. Harvesting all the eggs in an area, for example, puts alligators there in danger of extirpation, the word for a localized extinction. If alligators disappear, their prey animals get out of control, and the domino effect goes on to other species, to vegetation, to the earth itself, and it could ripple outward from that spot to others. When nature tips out of balance, it's impossible to know just how far the damage will spread. That is why FWC and the state of Florida wanted to punish the poachers to the fullest extent of the law.

They hoped to protect more species than alligators by showing that the risks of poaching far outweigh its rewards.

But did it work? Well, yes and also no. Operation Alligator Thief sparked a conversation about alligator conservation—and about preventative instead of reactive conservation in general—which eventually reached me. Before I listened to the yarns of my student, though, the operation had already borne fruit, as evidenced by the way I heard about it in the first place.

A good yarn well spun takes on a life of its own. Just like how the Peg Brown stories became Everglades legends, the strongest yarns keep traveling until everyone knows a version of the tale. The wild story of Sunshine Alligator Farm and the chameleon wildlife officer who had brought it to life had spread through what seems like every backwoods outpost in the state before any writer even dreamed of putting it to paper. That did something more than entertain: The young man who told me the story swore off poaching. Likely, others did, too. To Jeff, that is a success. Though he never met my student and probably never will, Jeff's efforts set him straight. As my student retold the story, perhaps it had the same effect on others. Some of his listeners likely retold it as I am now. You never know who's watching, was the moral of his tale. Don't do anything you aren't willing to defend later. Ultimately, I realized the story of Operation Alligator Thief came full circle back to the reason I started telling stories in the first place. It had the same moral as the stories my family told on our dock all those years ago: Who you are in the dark is your truest self.

The guys accused in Operation Alligator Thief would agree, as most of them fought their charges. At the time of their arrests, however, they didn't know what was happening. After the officers served their warrants and booked each one of them into a holding cell, they had time to wonder. Wayne, in a bittersweet way, must've felt affirmed: *I was right, I can imagine him thinking. There was a traitor in our midst.* But who was that traitor? The crew wouldn't know for sure until he appeared in his uniform in court.

When they saw him, they kept their irritation, anger, and feelings of betrayal to themselves. They couldn't do anything that would jeopardize the arguments against their charges. As Jeff took the stand, he looked out at their faces. Sometimes, they avoided looking him in the eye. Most of the time, when their glances landed on him, their expressions read of cold indifference as if they were looking at a stranger. And he was one, wasn't he? They didn't know him, not really, he would tell himself. Likewise, he didn't really know them. Yet the times he had spent with some of them—like joking with Wayne and chatting with Robin—had been genuine. Maybe in another life, they would have been friends. They weren't so different from the people he knew already.

The wives whom Jeff opted not to prosecute, however, showed less stoicism than their husbands. When Jeff walked by Wayne's wife, where she sat next to the courtroom aisle, she hissed a single word at him. "Asshole."

It could have been worse, and Jeff didn't begrudge her the anger. There were so many things he could have said in return. What good would that have done either of them? Were the tables turned, maybe his wife would have said the same thing. No, he kept on walking. It was best for everyone if he pretended he hadn't heard.

As the trials rolled on, the tension increased. The crew really seemed to believe they hadn't done anything wrong. Yet, one by one, their arguments failed, and the court found each one of them guilty of their crimes. The judge slapped Wayne and David with fines and probation. Tommy and CW, tried in tandem, received sentences of almost a year of jail time each. The crew that had convened at Sunshine was also sentenced to pay restitution to the State of Florida to the tune of more than $80,000. Adding insult to injury, the state tacked on reimbursement costs for the investigation as well.

In 2019, while the trials were still going on, Jeff, Lieutenant Wilson, and the DA left the courtroom. They waited together in the hall for the elevator. They were done for the day, on the way out, and they chatted about their plans. When the elevator opened, they turned toward it. Then they stopped. The three people already in the elevator likewise stood frozen: Robert, Robin, and their lawyer. Robert was on his way to plead out in hopes of a lesser sentence, Jeff would learn later. The judge would sentence him to three years in prison, a small fraction of the maximum possible penalty, an egregious 160 years. Right then, Robin pulled Jeff's attention. The anger, no, fury, in her eyes stabbed at him. None of them moved. Then the elevator dinged, and the doors slid shut, gradually eclipsing the burning hatred on Robin's face until all Jeff could see was his own blurry reflection.

Over the course of my writing this book, Wayne, Tommy, and CW all appealed their sentences.

After he was arrested, Wayne would swear up and down to anyone who would listen that he suspected Jeff was an undercover officer from the beginning. When I first started looking into the story, I thought that didn't sound right, but the further I dug, the more my previously held belief came into question. I realized that the stereotype I had believed about poachers had informed my doubt. *If Wayne had known*, I thought initially, *then he would have jumped Jeff out in the woods.* He had ample opportunity. Yet he didn't. As the months went by and I got to know more poachers—and their legends—I began to consider that Wayne could have been going through similar inner turmoil to Jeff.

Should I tell him that I know? Wayne might have thought. *Naw, I'll just play it as it goes.*

If that's true, then the betrayal of his arrest would have stung all the deeper.

After he learned I was writing this story, David sent me frantic emails affirming his innocence in the hope that I could help, but what could I do? He was afraid that this black mark on his record would overwrite his lifetime of research and conservation work, and I don't think it should. My hope is that it's clear no one is a villain, that we are all flawed. Personally, I don't trust stories about perfect people. Perfection means that something's missing.

In the absence of perfection, though, sometimes we have peculiarity.

In their appeals, Tommy and CW argued that the RICO statute did not apply to their case, and so their sentences should be overturned. Their harvest of eggs, they claimed, was a victimless crime. CW's lawyer argued that poaching alligator eggs was not theft in a legal sense, because the Florida statute states that theft is taking "property of another," and therefore their acts did not fall under the umbrella of the RICO law.

At CW's new hearing, his lawyer took that argument a step further. "The only entity that owns wildlife is a higher power," he stated, "not the State of Florida." In other words, theirs was a crime against God.

"While remaining duly agnostic on the counsel's theological premise," Judge J. Andrew Atkinson of the Florida Second District Court of Appeal wrote in his November 2021 mandate, "this court finds the gist of the argument persuasive and dispositive." No one owned the eggs the crew had allegedly stolen, he said. "Perhaps more importantly," Atkinson wrote, "the State's attempt to shoehorn the violation of a regulatory statute into the enumerated RICO offense of 'theft' illuminates a damning deficiency in its case: the legislature did not include violation of alligator egg harvesting regulations among its list of predicate acts that can form the basis for a racketeering conviction." In other words, whether or not it was a crime against God, conspiring to take alligator eggs could not be a violation of RICO. Although taking eggs without a valid permit was a crime, the judge wrote, "it did not constitute theft sufficient to support conspiracy to commit racketeering," because no individual person owned the alligator eggs while they were in the nests—neither the private landowners nor the state.

The Florida legislature added wildlife crimes to its definition of racketeering activity in 2021, about five years after the commission of the acts in this book. Therefore, the court mandate states, the trial should have acquitted CW. His original sentence was upheld in part and reversed in part.

"We vacate the conviction for conspiracy to commit racketeering but affirm the remaining convictions and sentences," Judge Atkinson wrote.

Tommy, however, didn't get so lucky. The same court of appeals upheld the original decision in his case. Both Tommy and CW received downward departure sentences, punishments below the typical minimum sentence for such crimes.

As for Wayne, he pleaded guilty to the counts of poaching and attempted poaching of a protected species (the white ibis), but he appealed the charges of alligator poaching. Since Florida law bars people found guilty of alligator poaching from making money through the alligator industry for a set number of years after their sentencing, a guilty verdict on these counts put Wayne's livelihood on the line. Initially, it seemed like luck was on his side. In early 2021, the court reversed its decisions on Wayne's three counts of alligator poaching and remanded the case for a new trial. That trial took place only a few months later, and Wayne's luck finally ran out. The court once again rendered a guilty verdict on all three counts and sentenced Wayne to pay fines and complete four years of probation.

Neither David nor Robert have appealed their sentences.

While Robert was still serving his sentence in prison, he passed a message to me through his correctional officer. "I just want to put all of this behind me," he said.

Who owns the wilderness? The true answer is both an existential one and a legal one, and according to the law, who owns the wilderness depends on where the wilderness is. In American courts, most of the time, animals, especially wild ones, do not have legal agency. An alligator, obviously, cannot sue on its own behalf. Although I believe that wildlife crimes, first and foremost, are crimes committed against wildlife itself, such crimes committed on public land like Everglades National Park are crimes against the nation and anyone else who would come to enjoy nature's majesty.

Still, there are places in the world where nature itself has more rights than simply to be owned. The Everglades Headwaters is one of them.

In the 2020 election, the majority of residents in Orange County, Florida, "voted yes on the Right to Clean Water Charter Amendment," as I wrote for *Sierra* magazine in 2021, "making this seemingly esoteric legislation, which passed by a landslide margin of 89 to 11 percent, the most popular item on the ballot." According to the charter amendment, the county's rivers and lakes, including Shingle Creek, from which the Everglades springs, have the "right to exist, flow, to be protected against Pollution, and to maintain a healthy ecosystem."

Inspired by the *Citizens United* verdict of 2010, which said more or less that corporations can be legal persons, the Florida lawyer who spearheaded the charter amendment thought that rivers could be people, too. They already are considered as such in many parts of the world. Judges in India and New Zealand, among other places, have granted the rights of personhood to natural features in their countries. Now Florida has joined their ranks.

It doesn't seem like such a stretch to say that a crime against nature is still a crime. And when nature loses, we all lose. Orange County citizens can sue on their rivers' behalf. What does this mean, if anything, for poachers? Only time will tell. However, the charter amendment's landslide passage does make one thing clear: Most people, regardless of their political leaning, do care about the welfare of nature as an end in itself. That gives me hope.

Jonnie Brown, the most infamous alligator poacher's son, cares. It seems his father did, too. They had intimate knowledge of the Everglades, that wild place they called home. If the newcomers had respected that and listened, and if developers and the Army Corps of Engineers had never carved up the glades' flow, maybe alligators as a species never would have gotten in trouble in the first place.

In fact, conservationists have already been on the long road toward learning how to listen for decades now. Down in the Everglades, one result was Big Cypress National Preserve, the creation of which took in the voices of native tribes and other long-time residents, making a protected area where it is legal to hunt (with restrictions, of course) and play while still respecting the splendid gifts of the many-faceted wild that is gator country.

After finishing my trip to Chokoloskee, I reversed course and returned north, back through the Everglades, going opposite to their flow, through sawgrass plains and wild strands of jungle, through dry savanna to the land of lakes and rivers where those same glades spring forth—that is to say, I went home to Orlando, the state's epicenter of tourism and perpetual road construction.

Back home, having spent so much time out in the wilderness, I couldn't seem to stay inside. On a whim, I drove east to the coast, where Merritt Island National Wildlife Refuge sits under the rocket launches of Cape Kennedy. To the uninitiated, the sprawling barrier island and the lagoon it protects look like the Everglades. The two places are indistinguishable in pictures unless you really know what you're looking for. The refuge is a place of wild boars and endangered birds, carnivorous flowers, orchids, turtles, and, of course, alligators.

Armed with my camera and a thorough coating of bug spray, I ventured off the boardwalk and into the thick of the hardwood forest. As I walked, I listened to the birdcalls, the rustling in the brush, the shift as shadows fell over the narrow path from the whirring insects of the day to the croaking, chirping chorus of the night. The air smelled verdant and damp, rich with petrichor and sweet with woody decomposition. I squinted to see. I hadn't brought a flashlight. I hadn't planned to stay so long, really, but the farther I followed the path, the more I felt compelled to continue forward. I didn't know what waited in front of me. It was the excitement of venturing into the unknown that had captured my attention.

The same sensation had hit me when I was in Chokoloskee. After Mac had dropped us off below the trading post, I had looked out over the water, thinking it was like something in a movie. It also reminded me of my home. *If this place is paradise*, I thought, *how much of my own world have I missed?*

I had grown up about thirty miles north of the wildlife refuge in land that looked much the same, a woven backcountry of swamp and marsh. For years, I had seen my home as little more than a backwater. I had let people convince me that the clichés about Florida were true. I found myself wishing that I was from someplace interesting, someplace that mattered. Then, as I researched Jeff's story, I started learning to see the world as he saw it. I learned the names of birds and flowers, of trees and fish, and it shocked me how I'd failed to notice the many extraordinary and wonderful things that had made the backdrop of my young life. I was struck to discover that the little purple flowers that peek their heads over the mud, making the swamp a riot of color in the right season, were orchids. They were rare and beautiful, yet I had let them grow mundane to me. *How many orchids have I stepped over without a second look?* I wondered. Hundreds.

Venturing into that darkening wild, I was stunned to see it new. In the process of discovering gator country, I had rediscovered the majesty of my home. I sloughed off the opinions that had been cast upon it. I learned to see again.

Wonder, I believe, is a necessary component of hope. Without hope, even our greatest efforts will fail. Writing this in the darkest of times, I have been reminded to see the world like Jeff, not only with a sense of wonder but with a sense of compassion as well. If the past few years have taught me anything, it's that finding a scapegoat is easy. Working to fix problems, like the economic issues that push most people into poaching in the first place, is hard. With hope, we can do the hard thing.

The first hard thing is challenging our own expectations. I did. I got to know some poachers. And you know what? I liked them. I didn't agree with them or what they'd done, but I understood why they did it. I cared about them. I realized I could care about both humanity and the wild. It isn't cowardly to stop seeing the world as black-and-white. It doesn't make you complicit. The gray is where compassion lives. You can care about people who are doing things you think are wrong. Jeff did, too.

I got to know Jeff pretty well in the course of writing this story, to the point where, when a hurricane smashed through Central Florida, I predicted exactly what he would do after the fact: load up his truck with tools and see who needed help. Still, sometimes he would surprise me.

Midway through my research, I drove down toward the Everglades, this time stopping in Arcadia. Jeff had asked me to meet him in the parking lot of the Walmart where he had once bought alligators to stock his farm. He gave me an external hard drive of photos and files, and he drove me around town, showing me the farm and other locations he had mentioned in his stories. Back in the parking lot again, I went into the store to grab a snack, and when I got back outside, I couldn't find Jeff. I hesitated to open the door to his truck while he wasn't there. Then I saw movement inside. I squinted through the window. Jeff had bent double to hide under the steering wheel.

What the hell is he doing? I thought. I opened the door. "What's going on?"

"Shh," he hissed. "Get in and shut the door."

Confused and a little bit paranoid, I glanced around then did as he said. He put a mask over his mouth and nose and, thus disguised, rose to peek out of his window.

Are we being watched? I thought. I sank down in my seat.

Jeff examined a truck and trailer that had parked next to us, watching its driver as he got out. The closer the driver came into view, the more Jeff sat up. I scooted up to do the same.

"I thought that was Wayne," he explained, taking off the mask.

"If it had been, would there have been a problem?" I asked.

Jeff studied the look on my face—perhaps one of concern and confusion, likely one eyebrow raised. Then he looked down at where he'd been hiding. He sat up tall and laughed at himself. "No," he said, "probably not."

It was clear to me, though, that while I had been inside, he'd thought danger had come to call. Though Operation Alligator Thief had ended about five years prior, the anxiety that it carried had lingered with him. On paper, the sting was over. But for Jeff, it would always be there.

Ever the journalist and not one for small talk, I swooped in with a pointed question. "Do you think the operation changed you?" I asked.

"No," he said. Then he thought about it. "Well—"

When he returned to being Jeff Babauta, the first thing he did was cut his hair. After spending a little time with his wife and son, he drove to his mother's house. Over the course of the operation, she had watched him change, her once polished and together son seeming to fall apart. He couldn't tell her anything, and when she called, asking where he was, his wife would have to lie. Her heartbreak at the unexplained change in him made him feel so guilty. It was one of the worst losses that had come with the sting.

When she opened the door and saw her son polished and together once again, hair buzzed short, shirt tucked in, a grin spread across her face.

"There's my boy," she said, immense relief apparent in her voice.

They embraced, and then he said, "Have I got a story to tell you."

And yet, Blackledge came back when Jeff least expected him.

He would jump whenever he heard the ringtone he had assigned Robert on his undercover phone. He no longer had that phone. So it would happen in public. He'd flinch, his heart racing, as if expecting new orders from the man who had planned it all. He would remember himself bit by bit and then go about his business, but in the back of his mind, Operation Alligator Thief would always be there.

Some days he would forget to be himself. He might catch a glimpse of his reflection while running errands and realize he'd left the house in flip-flops and a paint-flecked shirt. He'd quickly tuck that shirt in and shake his head.

You're not Blackledge anymore, he would think, scolding himself for the uncharacteristic sloppiness. *You're Jeff Babauta.* That thought would cause another memory of the sting to spring forth: Driving home from the farm, he had waved his hand over his face like an actor collecting himself for a scene, saying, *Jeff Babauta. Jeff Babauta. Jeff Babauta.*

In that parking lot, Jeff admitted to me again that the alligators never really scared him, but the fear of reprisal refused to fade. So, too, it seemed that Blackledge would always be with him.

After our final interview of the day, I had stepped out of his truck and was heading toward my new Jeep when he stopped me. I was afraid he'd ask me not to write about something he'd said.

"A little bit ago you asked me if I was afraid of anything during the operation," he said, leaning through the truck cab from the driver's seat.

I held the door open, wary. "Yeah," I said.

"I don't think this is what you were looking for," he said. "It's silly, but it is what it is. My biggest fear in the whole operation wasn't about getting hurt or anything like that. It was that nobody would care."

He recalled hatching time, helping the baby alligators out of their shells. For many of them, he was the first thing they would ever see. The hatchlings' feisty personalities endeared them to him. Even though their fate ended at a factory farm, thousands more of their brothers and sisters remained in the wild, where Jeff hoped they would survive and flourish.

I remembered how he told me about the other wildlife officer who had dismissed the sting as unnecessary. *Alligators?* the officer had said. *Why bother?*

By then, I had already ventured through the Ten Thousand Islands. I had become immersed in the legend of Peg Brown. I had learned how sometimes the most outlandish and impossible things are true; I had befriended poachers who had become environmentalists; I had heard stories about fish falling from the sky, of nature defying man, of man defying expectations. I understood now how stories tell us who we are and who we're supposed to be. The best stories do more than show us that underdogs can triumph: they ignite hope within us and inspire us to do the same.

Before I started writing this book, I might have agreed with that officer. But then all of these people came into my life. Jeff, Jonnie, Kent, Mac—and voices from the past, Peg and Totch Brown, too—challenged my expectations about the Everglades, its people, and the alligators that call it home.

"I care," I reassured Jeff. "And a lot of other people will, too. I promise."

ACKNOWLEDGMENTS

So many people helped get this story onto these pages and onto the shelves that I could write an entire book just to thank them. Instead, I have to squeeze it all into just a few pages, so here it goes, in no particular order:

I would like to thank my dad, Ken Renner, who raised me in a house full of books with a head full of stories. While the parents of other would-be writers tried to dissuade them from pursuing their dreams, my dad always believed in me and encouraged me, even when I had all but lost hope myself.

Then I need to thank my high school English teacher Mrs. Mularkey (great name, right?) for developing my love of stories into a love of literature. She read the terrible fantasy pirate novel that I wrote at fifteen, and she encouraged me to keep writing even though it was objectively not very good. She deserves a gold star for that.

Later, in college, my professor Mark Powell helped me find my voice. As he guided me through southern literature and fiction writing, he became the first person outside my family to treat the stories I told about the place I'm from as if they mattered. When he reads this book—and I know he will—I'm sure he'll recognize the parts of it that grew from ideas I had just started to contemplate while in his class. Thanks, Mark. You helped me become the best version of me.

There were so many other professors who inspired and helped me along the way: Dr. Farrell, Dr. Davis, Lori Snook, Dr. Terri Witek, Juan Carlos Reyes, Veronica Gonzales, Laurie Foos, Chantel Acevedo, and many others.

I also need to thank the many magazine editors who kept me afloat after I quit my day job—Corinne, Libby, Marcy, Nsikan, and too many more to list, thank you all for taking a chance on me. I couldn't have gotten this far without you. At the same time, I found a community of journalists who welcomed me into their fold. Their camaraderie and commiseration helped me remember that I am not alone. I am especially indebted to my adamantly encouraging peers like Wudan Yan and the mentorship of veteran journalists, including Murray Carpenter and Craig Pittman, who answered even my stupidest questions with a magnanimity I hope to pass on one day.

Thank you to my friend Molly Beckwith, who introduced me to my agent and who has been there for me through all the trials and tribulations of finishing this book. And thank you to my agent, Julia Eagleton, for seeing something in me even before I had anything major published. When lecturers at writing conferences describe the perfect agent, they must have no idea that Julia exists, because she is so much better than that. Julia, I am grateful for everything you do.

Then there is Bryn, who edited this book. She is the most tireless, patient, and compassionate editor I've ever worked with, and that is really saying something, because I've worked with so many wonderful people. This book isn't exactly what I pitched her. It is so much better. Like I did while investigating the story, she put aside her expectations and let herself see the astonishing, even when I didn't. That takes a lot of talent and a lot of hard work. Thanks, Bryn.

Circling back to my family, I have to thank them for their excitement and encouragement. Most of all, I have to thank my aunt Kate, who nagged me absolutely to death, making sure that I wrote this book. Even after losing so many people, I'm grateful to know there is still somebody who loves me so fiercely. Love you back, Aunt Kate.

Next, I have to thank Alex and Melissa, my first beta readers when we were in high school. Now you finally get to read something of mine that's good. Thanks for reading all the crap along the way.

Thank you to everyone I talked to in Chokoloskee. You made me feel welcome. It was like being back home, and I won't forget it.

And finally, I have to thank Jeff Babauta for his lifetime of protecting nature and the people who live there, too. Thanks for trusting me with your story, Jeff. I hope I did it justice.

ABOUT THE AUTHOR

Rebecca Renner is a contributor to *National Geographic*, and her writing has appeared in *The New York Times*, *Outside*, *Tin House*, *The Paris Review*, *The Guardian*, *The Washington Post*, *The Atlantic*, and other publications. She holds an MFA from Stetson University. *Gator Country* is her first book.

THE
RIDE

THE
RIDE

A Shocking Murder
and a Bereaved Father's Journey
from Rage to Redemption

BRIAN MACQUARRIE

DA CAPO PRESS
A Member of the Perseus Books Group

Designed by Pauline Brown
Set in 11.5 point Fairfield Light by the Perseus Books Group

Library of Congress Cataloging-in-Publication Data

MacQuarrie, Brian.
   The ride : a shocking murder and a bereaved father's journey from rage to redemption / Brian MacQuarrie.
      p. cm.
   Includes index.
   ISBN 978-0-306-81626-0 (alk. paper)
   1. Curley, Bob. 2. Fathers of murder victims—Massachusetts—Boston—Biography. 3. Curley, Jeffrey, d. 1997. 4. Murder victims—Massachusetts—Boston—Case studies. I. Title.
   HV6533.M4M32 2009
   364.152'3092—dc22
   [B]
                                                                    2008055397

Published by Da Capo Press
A Member of the Perseus Books Group
www.dacapopress.com

Da Capo Press books are available at special discounts for bulk purchases in the U.S. by corporations, institutions, and other organizations. For more information, please contact the Special Markets Department at the Perseus Books Group, 2300 Chestnut Street, Suite 200, Philadelphia, PA 19103, or call (800) 810-4145, ext. 5000, or e-mail special.markets@perseusbooks.com.

10 9 8 7 6 5 4 3 2 1

*To the Curley family
and to all missing children.*

CONTENTS

Prologue

HUNDREDS OF PEOPLE huddled in the autumn air, waiting for the words of a grieving, shattered family. Parents held their children, mouthed a prayer, or simply hugged their numbed neighbors in a communal search for solace. Bob Curley, a Fire Department mechanic, approached a bank of microphones and looked into the stunned and disbelieving faces of East Cambridge, a community shaken to its core by his son's horrific death.

The unthinkable had happened here.

Bob had never spoken to a large group before. But today, with a compelling natural eloquence, he issued a chilling warning, coupled with a loud call for action.

"My Jeffrey's not going to feel no more pain," Bob said, his voice clear, angry, and commanding. "But my Jeffrey died with the heart of a lion. I know that. And that's why God put this on us. Because we're gonna take it, and we're gonna go forward, and all you people remember this!"

Bob's neighbors nodded, many of their faces lined with tears. Children who could not understand this agitated man, but were frightened by his rage, tugged their mothers a little closer.

"Remember Jeffrey!" Bob said. "Remember the pain you feel now! Remember how scared you are now! We'll all stand tall as a community, and we'll work to change the laws. We'll work to keep maggots like this away from our children."

The time had come to bring the death penalty back to Massachusetts, Bob ranted, in the opening salvo of a bitter, personal crusade that would radically transform his life.

"God love you all," Bob concluded, his voice cracking with emotion. "Thank you so much. It's been so hard."

———

— 1 —

Inman Square

BOB CURLEY rolled out of bed, tossed a glance toward the Boston skyline three miles away, and dressed for another day's work at the Cambridge Fire Department. There would be no dawdling for Bob, a broad-shouldered, good-looking man with thick brown hair, glinting blue eyes, and the no-nonsense look of this edgy neighborhood, where grit was as embedded in its men as in its cracked and crumbling sidewalks.

Bob hustled out the door at 6:45 A.M., only a quarter hour after waking up and less than two miles from the firehouse, where he and another mechanic repaired and prepped the ladder, hose, and pumper trucks that raced through one of the most densely populated cities in the country.

The morning was October 1, 1997, a warm, Indian summer Wednesday when New England was awash in a season-bridging spectacle of color.

Bob, at forty-two, commuted to work on a battered bicycle, coasting down a steep hill from his new home in East Somerville, a curmudgeonly cousin to the Inman Square streets where he was raised and now worked. At the bottom of the descent, Bob blocked out the jarring sound of heavy trucks bouncing in and out of gaping potholes and banked hard into a right-hand turn.

There, Bob entered what he called "the ghetto," an unsightly stretch of ungroomed growth pocked by jagged, uneven pavement; honking, impatient traffic; and a hilly warren of narrow, one-way streets. Focusing on the pedals, not the panorama,

3

Bob passed a grimy repair shop, a Brazilian church, the tired facade of Buddy's Diner, and half-organized graveyards for used auto parts, where old mufflers and piles of rusting radiators lay stacked against the neglected sides of sagging buildings.

Just after a confusing slalom of twists and turns through Union Square, Bob rose from his bicycle seat, legs pumping like pistons, to scale a short, tough incline beside the commuter-rail tracks. Atop the crest, breathing hard, Bob cruised through a cheek-by-jowl neighborhood of modest, two-story, wooden homes, a well-tended place of front-yard Madonnas and corner stores that had yet to fall victim to the gentrification creeping through Greater Boston's blue-collar core.

Finally, after catching his breath, Bob veered left on Springfield Street several blocks away, where he could see the Renaissance design, graceful bay doors, and soaring bell tower of the century-old Inman Square firehouse. And near the square, where scraps of early-morning litter blew across a junction of six chaotic city streets, a small sidewalk sign marked the indistinguishable boundary between Cambridge and Somerville.

Here, in Inman Square, Bob had matured from boy to man, fathered three children, and found a steady job among the people, sights, and sounds that had anchored him in good times and bad. The neighborhood was his turf and always had been, a cocky, changing crossroads of Irish pubs, upscale coffee shops, gay bookstores, and Portuguese social clubs that had managed to retain a spit-on-the-sidewalk chippiness from its immigrant past.

Whether it was the sports talk that attracted Bob to the bare-bones Abbey Lounge or the politically incorrect banter from third-generation firefighters, Bob loved this place as much as ever, even as the hard-drinking men's bars and bottom-dollar barber shops that had long ruled its unpretentious social life had all but disappeared.

The place remained a comfort zone that kept Bob grounded, even if trauma had distorted his childhood there. His father, John, a transplant from St. Joseph, Missouri, had been a gambler and serial womanizer who left the family when Bob was twelve. Money was scarce, clothing could be shoddy, and do-

mestic tranquility was seen only on television. To escape, the boy sometimes retreated to an attic room he called "the Tomb," where he could lock out, if not forget, the dysfunction that roiled his family.

For family outings, Bob's father would cart some or all of his six children across the city to Suffolk Downs, a scruffy, third-rate, thoroughbred racetrack in East Boston, where the desperate could bet on a miracle from an overused nag. And while John Curley tried his luck, something he did nearly every day of the racing season, the children amused themselves in the racetrack parking lot. If John won, the clouds lifted, and the family would stop for ice cream on the ride home or venture to Revere Beach for a roast beef sandwich at Kelly's. But if he lost, which was often, there were neither treats nor conversation. Bob, a quiet kid not quite seven years old, thought this was how most people spent their summers.

On October 1, 1997, those days had long been consigned to the past. And at 7:00 A.M., Bob wheeled his bicycle into the landmark brick firehouse, home to Engine 5, where a hose-carrying truck and bright red pumper screamed through Inman Square more than two thousand times a year. The men of Engine 5 called the company "The Nickel." And like firefighters everywhere, their camaraderie was a palpable, living thing that bound them with an intimate communal history, where shared worries and hopes, success and failures, were often felt more intensely than within their own families. "If you get in a pickle, call The Nickel," boasted the company's informal motto. And Curley, who had worked at Inman Square for three years, was an integral, upbeat, dependable part of that fraternity. Nearly everyone liked Bob, whose quick humor, passion for Boston sports, and stoic work ethic fit neatly into the fabric of Engine 5.

A man of routine, Bob walked to the rear of the firehouse to a cramped repair area he called his "office," a place where a box of corn flakes and a container of milk always lay stashed in a small refrigerator. After breakfast, Bob strolled past the dispatcher's desk and climbed the stairs to the second-floor kitchen for coffee, gossip, and head-shaking regrets that the Boston Red

Sox, a fourth-place team in the death throes of a dreadful season, would not be World Series champions for the seventy-ninth consecutive year.

From this men's club perched in the heart of the square, Bob and the firefighters could watch the ever-changing urban drama unfold on the star-shaped intersection below. They watched the fistfights, judged the women, and sneered at their left-leaning neighbors as they ambled across the street.

Bob didn't participate in, or even talk much about, politics. Like most of his coworkers, Bob thought "liberal" was pretty much a four-letter word, even though he rarely voted Republican and joked that the working class should be registered Democratic at birth. But for political radicals in a city only half-jokingly nicknamed the "People's Republic of Cambridge," the firefighters reserved a special, vitriolic scorn. To Bob, they were "phonies," which to him was just about the worst label he could pin on anybody. To the firefighters, the world of Engine 5 was different, a place where grown men referred to each other as brothers and where risking one's life was a given, not a choice. They cooked for each other, pulled pranks on each other, and went drinking together at the Abbey and the Druid. And to ensure that their mission never lost focus, the yellowing photographs of Inman Square firefighters from the past, some of them killed on the job and some dating back a century, hung on the wall as a constant, silent, inspiring reminder.

Life had taken an upward trajectory for Bob. He loved the firehouse and now had a spacious Somerville home bought four months before, thanks to the financial resources of a petite, attractive, and effervescent psychologist named Mimi, a native of Colombia with whom he had been living since late 1995.

Bob was separated from his wife, Barbara, who lived five blocks from the firehouse in a small condominium that Bob had helped buy before he left. His two oldest boys, Bobby Jr., nineteen, and Shaun, seventeen, were in good health. And his youngest son, Jeffrey, a precocious ten-year-old, was a constant, frenetic presence in the neighborhood, a boy who often whiled away his time at the firehouse, bantering with the men, riding to fires in

the trucks, and peppering everyone within sight with a never-ending barrage of questions.

Bob had seen Jeffrey the previous day at Barbara's condo, where Shaun had badgered his father into helping him repair his Oldsmobile Regal, an abused, decade-old dinosaur that Shaun had bought for $400 a few weeks before. The car, Shaun's first, wouldn't start. So, Bob drove his mechanic's truck to the house, charged the battery, figured that a little gasoline would prime the carburetor, and sent Jeffrey scurrying into the house to find a small plastic cup to pour the fuel.

Jeffrey did as he was told, always eager to help his brothers and father negotiate this fascinating men's world of tools, lawn mowers, weed whackers, and snowblowers. Despite his age, Jeffrey—a four-foot, six-inch, seventy-seven-pound tornado—had a fearlessness and urban street smarts that made him seem much older.

Bob used the occasion to lecture his youngest boy about the dangers of gasoline.

"This is dangerous stuff. Be very careful how you use it," Bob said, cleaning his hands before hopping back in the truck to continue his rounds of the city's firehouses.

"Okay, I will," said Jeffrey, a broad smile exposing his crooked front teeth. "Nice going on the car, Dad."

Jeffrey, a blue-eyed boy with close-cropped brown hair, had left his fifth-grade class at the Charles G. Harrington School earlier that day. A school nurse had called Barbara, a slow-to-smile woman with auburn hair and a weary gaze, to tell her the boy felt nauseous. Barbara, who worked nearby, left early from her cashier's job at Bradlees, a discount department store, to retrieve her youngest son.

After walking the zigzagging half mile together from school to home, Barbara gave Jeffrey some medicine and looked ahead. Though not scheduled to work the next day, she could not afford to stay away for an extended illness.

"Jeffrey, why don't you stay home tomorrow," Barbara said. "If you get yourself run down, then Mommy's going to have to miss work Thursday."

Jeffrey nodded, turned, and trudged upstairs to bed.

The relationship between mother and son was a rare and close one, bound even tighter since Bob had left the spare, three-bedroom condo. While the older boys inhabited a world of girls, beer, sports, and mischief—living at home but not entirely of it—Jeffrey remained Barbara's link to a world of maternal nurture and family norms that had all but shattered for her.

When the separation began and the pressures of parenting increased, Barbara switched from part-time night work at Bradlees to a forty-hour week of day shifts. Any extra income, she knew, was needed to support the family and pay the mortgage.

Bob continued to contribute the bulk of the money for the household. Often, when no one was home, he would stop at the olive-green building, walk up a short flight of stairs, and leave most of his paycheck in a cabinet over the stove.

Times, admittedly, had been hard when Bob and Barbara lived together. "We were struggling with the kids, and there wasn't enough money," Bob said. "Her working nights all the time, me working days—it was tough."

In those days, Bob seemed focused on three priorities: food, clothing, and a roof for his family. In return, he asked Barbara simply to have dinner on the table at 5:00 P.M. before she went to work. The family never went out to eat, and Bob's after-work routine, usually conducted from the couch, revolved around Budweiser and the television remote control.

Despite the domestic tension, Bob's decision to break up nineteen years of marriage devastated Barbara. "She just became more miserable every day," recalled Bobby Jr., who suddenly found himself the man of a cramped house from which much of the joy had been sucked away.

As much as Bob claimed these streets, the neighborhood's familiar blocks were Barbara's, too. Her late father, a Cambridge firefighter for thirty years, worked two jobs and brought home just enough money to raise five children across from the Harrington School. There, in a small apartment, Barbara and her four siblings were taught to respect their country and the Roman Catholic Church—and to take no lip from anyone.

Like Jeffrey, Barbara had attended the Harrington School, and the adjoining ball field where he became a Little League all-star was the same green oasis where Barbara had scampered as a child. The games there of jump rope and hide-and-seek, which Barbara played until the 8:00 P.M. horn sounded at the Woven Hose Company, were replayed in 1997 by a new generation that was more Hispanic and African American than the Irish and Portuguese who had dominated the neighborhood in the 1960s. But as the twentieth century drew to a close, most of the ethnic wariness in and around Donnelly Field remained the province of the parents.

Barbara had met Bob in early 1977, at a time when guys and girls from the neighborhood would gravitate to the street corners to conduct the generations-old mating ritual of one-liners, easy laughter, and flirtatious one-upmanship. Barbara knew of Bob as a popular, funny, tough guy from the heart of the square. And after they met, she learned that "everything I had heard about him was basically true." Bob had a truck mechanic's job during the day; a night job tending bar at the Mad Hatter, one of Boston's most popular discos; and a joke for nearly every waking minute.

Less than a year after the pair met, they were married in a small civil ceremony at the Middlesex County Courthouse, just up the street from Inman Square. The no-frills reception was held at the house of Bob's sister Francine, a rambunctious affair for which Bob supplied the alcohol and Francine supplied the food.

After a brief stint in Somerville, the couple rented an East Cambridge apartment around the corner from Barbara's parents. And into this cocoonlike world of grandparents, aunts, uncles, and cousins, Bob and Barbara brought three boys, who renewed and embraced a clanlike attachment to family.

More so than his brothers, Jeffrey was an ever-visible, peripatetic presence in the neighborhood, one of the poorest and most crowded in a city better known for Harvard University, the Massachusetts Institute of Technology, and activist, brainy intellectuals. A confident imp who thought nothing of bicycling

alone in city traffic, Jeffrey knew all the shortcuts in this working-class enclave, all the side streets, and nearly all the neighbors, both the upright and the shady.

To Bill McGovern, one of those neighbors and a longtime Engine 5 firefighter, Jeffrey embodied this insular universe. "I'd be working around the house, fixing the front stairs, and he'd yell, 'Hey, Magoo,'" said McGovern, whose thick glasses had spawned his cartoon-character nickname. "He was always with the questions. They were rebuilding the park across the street one summer, and the guys had laid new granite slabs. And the whole time the guys are working there, he's over there, talking to them, asking questions. He was pretty much a hands-on individual."

Jeffrey thrived on a whirlwind of activity. He'd hitch a ride on city garbage trucks and pocket a couple of dollars for his trash-collecting efforts. He'd help a Cambodian bicycle mechanic on the next street; shovel ice shavings from the local rink during hockey games; make flavored ice at Sarchioni's, the corner grocer, in exchange for a sandwich and a soda; and even rush to blazing fires, either on his bicycle or in the trucks that screamed from Inman Square. "Give him twenty-five cents or a pat on the back, and he was the happiest guy in the world," said Shaun, who marveled at his little brother's energy.

The day before he became ill, Jeffrey and his class of city kids had traveled to a country orchard. On their return, Jeffrey stopped at Sarchioni's store, holding his apple-picking haul proudly in hand. At first, he gave away a few to the corner regulars. But keen beyond his years, he soon realized there was money to be made and began selling apples for fifty cents apiece.

To Barbara, Jeffrey was a shining light in a world turned upside down since Bob had left to live with Mimi. Barbara initially thought Bob had decided to bunk at the firehouse. And in October 1997, although Barbara knew of Mimi, she still did not know exactly where they lived. "I kept hoping he'd come home," Barbara said of Bob. "It was like losing someone that you loved dearly, like them dying and passing away. I was crying; I was scared; I was all those things. I had been with Bob since I

was twenty years old, and then, just like that, I'm thinking, How am I going to pay a mortgage and raise three boys? Who's going to watch the kids if I work nights? It was hard for me because I had always been home with my children."

Jeffrey saw many of her tears. And when she lashed out at his father, Jeffrey would try to console her. "Mommy, don't worry," he'd say. "I'll always take care of you. I love you, Mommy."

At age ten, Jeffrey continued to sleep in the same bed as his mother. He roller-bladed to Bradlees in the summer to join her for pizza. And he often greeted Barbara at the end of their thirty-yard driveway, astride his beloved bicycle, when she walked into view at 5:20 P.M. after yet another shift.

The boy's cockiness defined him, but Jeffrey had a soft side that returned and redoubled his mother's love. He would sit by her side on the living room couch, watch the television series *Home Improvement*, and match her critiques with knowing nods and giggling wisecracks. And in a summer outing to Canobie Lake Park in New Hampshire, he once persuaded his mother to join him on a thrill ride, where he held her hand to calm her fears.

In return, he always received the most fuss and the best Christmas gifts. "My mother would have new roller blades for him, new outfits, new schoolbags, new books," Shaun said. "Jeffrey got everything from her, and he couldn't be away from her." If the household's division of affection seemed skewed, the older boys rarely mentioned it, except as a joke. They recognized the strain on their mother, who saw in Jeffrey, her "little pooh," something innocent and vulnerable in a life of hard, unanticipated edges.

Jeffrey also enjoyed the company of Barbara's mother, Muriel Francis, who lived a block away and was a near-daily source of after-school soft drinks and companionship. For Barbara, her mother was another layer of supervision for the ten-year-old son of a working woman. The older boys helped fill that role, too, and Barbara would call them frequently to check on Jeffrey. But being teenagers, the boys were not natural babysitters. "It would be like, 'Ma, will you stop it? He's in the

neighborhood. Don't worry about it,'" Barbara recalled. "And I would say, 'That's my job, to worry about it.'"

Bob was also a familiar presence in the neighborhood, driving past the condo on congested Hampshire Street nearly every day to check on the boys and catch up on their activities. In this close-knit world, Bob's biggest worry was that Jeffrey would be hit by a car.

When Bobby Jr. and Shaun were younger, the Curley sports world revolved around hockey practice at the nearby Gore Street rink, where Bob would change Jeffrey's diaper while sitting on unheated stands in subfreezing temperatures. Although Jeffrey began skating at age four, money had become tight in the Curley household, and the cost of organized hockey meant the boy was destined for less-expensive sports. For Jeffrey, that meant baseball, baseball, and still more baseball. In 1997, Bob umpired in the Cambridge Little League—it was more of a hobby than a job at $20 a game—and watched Jeffrey play for the Marlins. Bob loved baseball as much as Jeffrey did. And that September, as the days grew short, Bob would take Jeffrey to a ball field on the Boston side of the Charles River, where he tossed sky-high pop-ups to his wide-eyed son.

Jeffrey had been to his father's new home only once, but he became immediately fascinated by Bob and Mimi's top-to-bottom renovation of a bland, funereal place into a bright and vibrant home. There were walls to strip and floors to refinish, and Jeffrey congratulated his father and his girlfriend on doing the work themselves. Captivated by "this beautiful little boy," Mimi, who had no children of her own, hoped to know Jeffrey better in the months ahead.

By the morning of October 1, Barbara remained adamant that Jeffrey stay home and rest. This way, she could help him recuperate, as well as enjoy the uninterrupted pleasure of his company. While Barbara woke to see a pleasant autumn day on Hampshire Street, Jeffrey slept late into the morning.

Sixty miles to the north, in Manchester, New Hampshire, Charles Jaynes awoke at 9:00 A.M. in a tawdry, one-room apartment he rented for $105 a week under the name of Anthony Scaccia. Jaynes had used the alias, lifted from a Massachusetts man killed by a hit-and-run driver in 1987, to elude seventy-five arrest warrants for a notoriously impressive string of bad checks and ATM theft. In August, the newspaper in Jaynes's hometown of Brockton, Massachusetts, had published his photograph in a "Most Wanted" feature. By then, Jaynes had moved out of state, first to Maine and then to Manchester, where he wrote in his rental application that he wanted "a change of scenery."

The scenery in his three-story downtown building, which housed twenty-four apartments and an Army Navy surplus store, was unrelentingly drab. Many of the tenants had no family, no contacts, and no cars to ferry them from a bare-bones, pay-as-you-go pit stop where a fugitive could feel relatively safe.

Unlike many of the building's tenants, Jaynes could boast a semblance of a social life. By October 1, he had lived there only two months but already had an unsavory reputation for loud, obnoxious parties. One neighbor was struck by the party-goers, mostly teenagers, whose tastes tilted toward nose rings, tongue piercings, and messy, multicolored hair. Jaynes also enjoyed a few other amenities. His doting mother paid the rent and even hauled his laundry back and forth to Brockton. The phone was listed in the name of Laurie Pistorino, his out-of-town girlfriend.

Living off others was not unusual for Jaynes. By his mid-teens, he had learned that scamming and scheming were much more lucrative than minimum-wage work. In one brazen example, Jaynes obtained a driver's license after persuading his best friend to let him use his Social Security number. Once he had the license, Jaynes opened several checking accounts in the friend's name, diverted the bills to a third-party address, and ran up thousands of dollars in bad checks and bad charges. A year later, the unsuspecting friend, a high school senior, was blind-sided when he learned that seven arrest warrants had been filed against him.

When Jaynes did work for his money, he cleaned new cars for his father in the Boston suburb of Newton, Massachusetts. He also had experience pouring coffee behind a Dunkin' Donuts counter.

Wherever he went, Jaynes cut a distinctive figure. The caramel-colored son of a black father and white mother, Jaynes carried three hundred sagging pounds on a five-foot, nine-inch frame. The sight could be startling, at least according to one Manchester neighbor, who once stumbled on Jaynes standing in the hallway wearing only his underwear, talking on a cell phone in the middle of the night. He had a squeaky voice, and a pizza-parlor cashier in Kittery, Maine, was struck by his "weird eyes." His seventh-grade reading teacher, Rebecca Moffitt, found his presence more unnerving—glowering, know-it-all, and menacing—than that of any other pupil she had taught in thirty years.

If Jaynes's appearance and manner repulsed people, he seemed oblivious or uninterested. Growing up in Brockton, he always held a high opinion of his worth. He even styled himself a savant and an artist, once winning a regional art award as a twelve-year-old. A decade later, the award from the *Boston Globe* still hung in a place of honor in his parents' home. However, the ten years that elapsed between award winner and car cleaner had shown that Jaynes would not pursue much of anything creative besides finding new ways to steal money.

To outsiders, Jaynes seemed just another rootless, overage adolescent in search of the next party. But inside his Manchester apartment, in places only his closest friends saw, the décor, possessions, and paraphernalia offered a raft of ominous clues that Jaynes had other, twisted predilections.

Born in 1975 under the Zodiac sign of Leo, Jaynes found meaning in the astrological symbol of the lion and became obsessed with the movie *The Lion King*. Posters of the film were tacked on the cheap walls of the apartment. *Lion King* figurines and knickknacks lay clustered on small tables. A *Lion King* towel even hung on the bathroom rack. One friend said she had seen the movie with him at least a dozen times.

The walls were also papered with posters of child actor Jonathan Taylor Thomas, a star of the series *Home Improvement*, who had supplied the voice of Simba, the cub son of the Lion King. The images showed Thomas in languid poses designed to stir the hearts of preadolescent girls. But to Jaynes, the pictures spoke to unnatural desires he had harbored for a decade.

Those thoughts took disturbing expression in his senior year at Brockton High School. After being lectured for disrupting a study hall, Jaynes left an unsigned note in the teacher's office. In the letter, described by Rebecca Moffitt as the vilest she had ever read, Jaynes wrote in shocking, deviant detail of an imagined sexual attack on the study-hall supervisor. The letter contained the teacher's home address, the names of her children, and where they boarded the school bus. The handwriting was eventually traced to Jaynes, who was expelled. The terrified teacher moved to a new home far from Brockton.

About this time, Jaynes began to tell friends he was sexually attracted to boys as young as six years old. He kept a pair of binoculars in his car and barked and whistled out the window when he passed a teenager or someone younger whom he found attractive. "I'd like to do that boy," he'd shout. On one trip to New York City, friends recalled, Jaynes repeatedly stopped the car outside arcades near Times Square. As his annoyed companions stewed in the automobile, Jaynes strolled inside to ogle his imagined prey. "He discussed it very freely," said William Pelligrini, a friend whom Jaynes had met at meetings of the Boston Alliance for Gay and Lesbian Youth. Drawings of nude boys could be found strewn about his Cadillac.

Jaynes seemed constantly on the prowl for new targets, acquaintances said, and his appetite seemed insatiable. To pique those desires, Jaynes kept pornographic material in his apartment. He stored gay porn magazines in a duffel bag as well as below a shelf near the head of his king-size waterbed. He corresponded with the North American Man/Boy Love Association (NAMBLA), an organization that advocates legalized sex between men and boys. A NAMBLA membership card, made out

to Anthony Scaccia, lay in his kitchen closet. A half dozen NAMBLA bulletins had been placed by his bed.

Writings about pedophilia also were scattered throughout the apartment. One book was titled *Loving Boys*. Another, his hard-cover diary, contained a meticulously written record of Jaynes's sexual experiences and fantasies, including memories of his first intimate encounter with another boy, when both were eleven years old. He also recorded that he once paid a boy $120 for sexual favors.

In the diary, Jaynes wrote that he did not begin to understand his desires until 1996, when he read a NAMBLA bulletin. The organization, Jaynes said, "helped me to become aware of my own sexuality and acceptance of it." Founded in Boston in 1978, NAMBLA two decades later had grown into a loosely knit group of a few hundred people across the country. Its Web-based manifesto proclaimed support for "the rights of youth as well as adults to choose the partners with whom they wish to share and enjoy their bodies." The group aimed, in its words, "to end the oppression of men and boys who have mutually consensual relationships."

For Jaynes, the vision of a mentoring, nurturing, sexual bond between an adult and a child struck a soul-altering chord. He rhapsodized about the possibilities. "Warm breezes, green grass, the air is fresh and crisp," he wrote in his diary. "Spring will soon roll into summer. Beautiful boys in shorts and T-shirts play basketball at the park.

"Boys in shorts with smooth, tender, muscular legs and arms, not yet ruined by adulthood.

"Ruff [*sic*] boys with their arousing arrogance.

"Impoverished boys, with their discerning attractiveness, that I wish to hold and caress in my arms."

NAMBLA, Jaynes wrote, helped him realize he was more than merely bisexual. Now, he also understood that he had the sexual desires of a pedophile and that others accepted that urge in themselves without shame.

Meanwhile, Jaynes continued to pursue relationships with adults of both sexes. Laurie Pistorino, who met Jaynes through

a gay and bisexual social group, considered herself his fiancée. Pistorino had spent the night of September 30 in the Manchester apartment, where Jaynes cooked before they watched *The Tonight Show*. On the morning of October 1, stumbling over and through unsorted heaps of dirty clothes, some of them stacked knee-high beside the couch and waterbed, the two prepared to drive to Boston.

As they traveled south on I-93, Jaynes stopped briefly at the Massachusetts border for coffee. Less than an hour later, he dropped Laurie off at the Boston Public Library in tony Copley Square, where she stocked shelves until 9:00 P.M. Jaynes planned to report to work at 4:00 P.M. at his father's car-cleaning business eight miles away. But before then, he had time for a quick trip across the Charles River to East Cambridge to meet his new best friend, Salvatore Sicari.

Sicari, an unemployed twenty-one-year-old misfit, had met Jaynes in 1996 when they both lived in Brockton. The introduction came courtesy of Sicari's girlfriend, Charlene Letourneau, who had just left an abusive relationship with Jaynes's brother. At first, Letourneau believed she had found a soul mate in Sicari, an unloved outcast whose experience as an abused child, like her own, might foster a bond between them. She even found Sicari a job by persuading Jaynes's father to hire him. But that good deed was punished when Sicari, who had bragged of his mechanic skills, proved he could barely change the oil.

Edward Jaynes Sr., a bald, muscled man nicknamed Kojak, found he had no use for Sicari shortly after he hired him. "He was nothing but a thief and selling drugs when I met him. Ask him to put a water pump on. Ask him where to put the antifreeze," Jaynes said, scoffing at the notion. "He looked at my son and said, 'I got something here.' And my son said, 'Hey, I got a friend.'"

Edward Jaynes eventually fired Sicari, and Letourneau broke up with him, worn out and frustrated by his chronic dishonesty, philandering, and unwillingness to find a job. Sicari moved back to his mother's apartment in East Cambridge, but he maintained a close friendship with Jaynes. And the pair,

cruising around in Jaynes's hulking gray Cadillac, quickly established themselves as neighborhood fixtures.

To Sicari, who rode a bicycle to get around, Jaynes was a winning lottery ticket with a big payoff. Suddenly, Sicari had access to transportation, and his new friend was generous with other people's credit cards. This was a good thing for Sicari, a high school dropout who had quit the twelfth grade at a Boston-area school for struggling adolescents when he could not find the energy or the muscle to pass gym class. He had never held a steady job, already had two children by two women, and was wandering through life with the snarling, defensive front of a hopeless sociopath. But now Sicari had Jaynes. And even after he was fired, Sicari would help his friend at Kojak's, for free, as the world passed him by in the early fall of 1997.

For Sicari, the high-energy atmosphere of a busy car dealership was a refreshing change from his second-floor apartment, where the blinds were nearly always drawn, the thwack of slaps was common, and the family was considered the strangest in the neighborhood. "He was a loose cannon," said Kris McGovern, who hung out with Sicari and a half dozen other friends nearly every night on the street corner below Sicari's apartment. "He didn't seem like he had any kind of stability at home or any kind of support, morally or physically. He just—I don't know—his life was just weird." Indeed, one of Sicari's elementary school teachers said he might have been the most neglected child she had ever taught, a sad little boy nicknamed "Pigpen" who seemed on the fast track to a sorry, stormy life.

If Sicari felt neglected at home, he never seemed self-pitying to his small circle of nightly acquaintances. It was always Sicari the tough guy, even if he stood only five feet, seven inches and weighed 160 pounds. He'd break into cars with them, smoke pot on the corner, and steal from friends and strangers alike. "He would act out a little bit more than the rest of us," McGovern said. "Exaggerate his hand gestures, maybe, or the look on his face. But you could see right through it."

According to McGovern, Sicari's ambitions fell far beneath the very low bar set by most teenagers and young adults

on the corner, where most of the guys thought only about the next day. "Salvi never worked. He just ripped people off," Mc-Govern said, using Sicari's nickname. "Riding around and smoking weed, that was pretty much his thing."

Sicari already had an extensive criminal record by October 1997. He had been arrested five times, convicted of seven offenses, and given a six-month suspended sentence for assaulting the mother of his twenty-one-month-old daughter at a Brockton doughnut shop. Letourneau witnessed that beating, in which Sicari stomped the woman after she and Letourneau confronted Sicari in a stinglike ruse. They both suspected him, correctly, of cheating on them with the other woman. "I had to pull him off of her," Letourneau said of the May 1997 assault. "He took off running."

Sicari's other child, a boy from a different mother, had been born within six days of his daughter.

Worse trouble arrived at the Sicari household in September, when Sal's sixteen-year-old brother, Robert, was indicted and later convicted on charges of raping a young Cambridge boy from the neighborhood. To ingratiate himself with the youngster, Robert Sicari had dangled the promise of a new bicycle.

Both Sal and Robert Sicari were well known to Jeffrey Curley, who often rode his bicycle past the Sicari apartment on Market Street that summer. He would stop at the curb to listen to the spicy conversation on the stoop, offer smart-ass comments, and often return any of the obligatory ribbing with an extended middle finger. Jeffrey knew the Sicaris were different and dangerous, particularly after Sal body-slammed him on the hood of a car in late July. The contact was hard enough to leave a dent, but Jeffrey shrugged off the incident, even laughed, as he rolled off the hood and rode off on his bike. Jeffrey could dish out the insults, but he made a point of showing the older crowd that he could take them, too.

Barbara did not know Sal Sicari well, but she had heard about Robert, and she repeatedly warned Jeffrey to stay away from him. Any infraction of that rule, Jeffrey knew, would mean automatic grounding.

As the summer of 1997 crept into August, Jeffrey began seeing a new visitor to the neighborhood. And that visitor, Charles Jaynes, soon made Jeffrey feel like he had a new buddy—one with a big car, surprise gifts, and hours of available attention. The attention was inviting because Jeffrey's best friend, an inseparable cousin, had moved forty miles away that year. And Jaynes's Cadillac, with its plush seats and preening self-importance, was a vast, exciting world of its own. Jeffrey and Jaynes, surveying the world from the front seat of the oversize car, cruised the familiar streets of East Cambridge several times that summer. Occasionally, they roamed farther afield.

One such trip, on September 11, took them to Assonet, a village thirty miles to the south, where Jaynes picked up Robyn Neil, a nineteen-year-old friend who had asked to spend the weekend with him in New Hampshire. When the Cadillac pulled into the driveway, Robyn did a double take at the sight of a young boy in the passenger seat. Robyn had never seen or heard of Jeffrey Curley, but she did know that Jaynes had prurient interests in boys. The previous year, she discovered a book in Jaynes's bedroom that showed photos of boys engaged in sex. Also, Robyn knew that Jaynes kept gay pornographic books and letters in that room, locked tight in a purple-and-aqua Rubbermaid container.

If she had any concerns, Robyn concealed them. She readily climbed into the backseat, and the trio headed north on busy Route 24 toward Cambridge. Once on the highway, cruising at sixty-five miles per hour, Jaynes asked Jeffrey if he would like to steer the car. The boy jumped at the invitation, shifted to the middle of the front seat, and placed his left hand on the wheel. For fifteen minutes, tucked against Jaynes's side, Jeffrey lived a boy's dream as he "drove" the mammoth Cadillac.

Once in Cambridge, Jaynes dropped Jeffrey near his home. The ride, and its unexpected thrill, would not be mentioned to mother or brothers. Other outings with Jaynes would not be mentioned either, such as the trip to a shopping mall where Jaynes posed in a photo booth with the boy on his lap.

The picture, framed with an Old West motif, read "Wanted" on the bottom.

The details of the night of September 16, when Jeffrey dined at Vinny Testa's, a popular Italian restaurant in the heart of Boston's fashionable Back Bay, would also remain a secret. Laurie Pistorino had expected to be dining alone with Jaynes that evening. But when the Cadillac pulled up outside the Boston Public Library at 9:00 P.M., a boy she had never seen was sitting in the car.

"Who's this?" Pistorino asked.

"J. C.," Jaynes said, using the nickname he had given Jeffrey.

Laurie remembered now that he had mentioned the boy before. During the short ride to the restaurant, Pistorino asked Jeffrey a few questions: How many brothers and sisters do you have? Why are you out so late?

Jeffrey ordered spaghetti and meatballs; Laurie, the chicken *picante*; and Jaynes, the baked chicken. As Jeffrey dug into his meal, Jaynes and Pistorino bantered about her day at work. Jaynes also asked if she could pick up two complimentary passes at the library so that Jeffrey and he could visit the Museum of Science.

The dinner ended at 10:30 P.M., when Jeffrey was finally driven the few miles to his neighborhood. "Have a good night. See you tomorrow," Jaynes called out as the boy scampered toward his house. Inside the condo, Barbara was angry. Jeffrey, in need of a quick explanation, cobbled together an alibi that he had gone to the movies with a friend and her mother.

During that summer, Jeffrey had also become a familiar face at Honda Village in Newton, where Kojak's Reconditioning occupied a cramped and gloomy space in the basement. Jaynes brought the ten-year-old to work at least a half dozen times, sometimes in the company of Sicari. There, in this little boy's heaven of gleaming new cars, Jeffrey would roam the shop at will, peeling white plastic coverings off the automobiles and chasing his older friend with the water hose.

To many employees, Jeffrey seemed to crave Jaynes's company. One worker recalled seeing Jeffrey leap into Jaynes's arms, screeching with delight. Another saw Jaynes give him piggyback rides. For some at Honda Village, their camaraderie raised a host of troubling questions. When one worker asked about the child, Jaynes answered simply that he was babysitting. "No," Jeffrey shot back with a grin, "I'm babysitting *him!*"

But for other workers, their childlike friendship seemed natural. Jeffrey might have been the son of an old family friend. The two might have known each other for years. How else to explain the boy's big smile or the way he would run to Charlie, yell his name, and give him a hug?

Henock Desir, a lot manager at Honda Village, spotted Jeffrey riding on Jaynes's shoulders one day. Jaynes was spinning Jeffrey around and around in the basement, teasing the boy, and playfully threatening to toss him in the air.

"I'm going to drop you. I'm going to throw you away," Jaynes said.

"No, no, don't do it! Don't do it!" Jeffrey protested with a laugh. "You can't do that!"

Another time, receptionist Sharon Snow looked up to see Jeffrey in the middle of a school day, standing in front of her desk with Jaynes and Sicari.

"What are you doing out of school?" Snow asked.

"I'm going to get a bike today," Jeffrey answered eagerly.

Later, Jeffrey was saddened to learn there would be no new bike that afternoon.

Jeffrey and bicycles had been a sore point in the Curley household that summer. Jeffrey had lost three, the latest one only recently, and his mother now refused to buy another until Christmas. This way, maybe, Jeffrey would learn responsibility. "Jeffrey, I've told you, and your brothers have told you," Barbara lectured him. "You need to bring the bike in the house. Now, you're going to have to wait until Christmas. I'm sorry, but I can't afford it. You've had three strikes, and now you're out."

Jeffrey had another option, however, which he shared obliquely with his mother. A friend of Sicari's, whom he did not

name, had promised to give him a bicycle, Jeffrey said. Barbara immediately tried to douse that idea. "Nobody gives you anything and doesn't expect something in return," she said in their living room. Case closed, or so she thought.

Teenagers in the neighborhood knew that friend to be Jaynes. Tashika Ellis, who lived beside Sicari, had heard Jeffrey say several times that Jaynes was planning to buy him a bike. In exchange, Jeffrey said, he would have to do something for Jaynes. But what that was remained a mystery.

Barbara did not worry about Jeff's pronouncement, delivered almost as an aside. After all, for someone who had lived her entire life within shouting distance of family and friends, neighborhood security was almost a given. The dangers of the age, trumpeted endlessly in the media, hardly seemed real in the short walk from the Harrington School to Hampshire Street. Despite the petty crime, the fistfights, and the adolescent roughhousing that permeated this crosshatch of crowded blocks, the streets of East Cambridge seemed safe enough.

Even Jeffrey adopted that sensibility. When Sicari had slammed him on the hood of the car, Jeffrey reacted with laughter instead of tears. But ten-year-old bravado did not come so easily in mid-September, when Sicari locked Jeffrey in the trunk of Jaynes's car, revved the engine, and kept the boy captive for five terrifying minutes. Rochelle Cruz, who lived nearby, heard banging from inside the trunk as Jaynes casually watched the scene from beside the driver's door.

"What are you doing? Let him out of there!" several neighbors screamed.

Jaynes and Sicari downplayed the fuss. "It's just a little joke," Sicari said. "We're just playing around. Don't worry about it."

Jeffrey emerged red-faced and sweating. But almost immediately, like a child trying to be a man, he burst into laughter.

Despite Sicari's occasional bullying, Jeffrey prowled the neighborhood throughout the summer, as feisty, undeterred, and unbowed as ever. But his growing familiarity with Jaynes, the newcomer, prompted some of Sicari's friends to urge Jeffrey

to be cautious. Tashika Ellis saw Jeffrey alone with Jaynes in the Cadillac many times.

"Why are you hanging with him?" she asked Jeffrey. "You don't need to be with him. He's too old to be around."

In his inimitable way, Jeffrey fired back, "Mind your own business."

But as he roamed his turf, forever in search of adventure, the boy remained blissfully ignorant of Charles Jaynes's predatory intentions.

William Pelligrini, Jaynes's friend, first heard of those intentions during a September drive to the Manchester apartment. His excitement palpable, Jaynes confided that he had found a darling boy in Cambridge with chubby cheeks, a batch of freckles, blue eyes, and crooked teeth. With help from the Sicaris, Jaynes said, he would steal the boy's bike, buy him a new one, and demand sex in return. And if the boy refused, Jaynes continued, one of the Sicaris would "take care" of him.

In his apartment, on a piece of lined notepaper, Jaynes rendered his evil more lyrically. "I was out visiting friends in the fair city of Cambridge. While on the excursion that should never have started, I glanced a glimmer of a beautiful boy about 11 or 12 years at most," he wrote. "Beauty, beauty. Lord, why have you forsaken me to carry this burden? He had a lovely tan and crystal-blue eyes."

2

A Ride to Hell

JEFFREY WOKE at midmorning on October 1, a rare late start to the day for him. He walked slowly downstairs to the kitchen, where Barbara, already up and about, was looking ahead to a few hours of quiet time with her youngest son. Pale and without an appetite, he clearly had not recovered from the bug that sent him home from classes the day before. Still, pushing the envelope as much as ever, he began to badger Barbara about whether he could go to school, even if only for half a day.

"I'm fine, Ma," Jeffrey said, fidgeting on the couch as he watched the Nickelodeon channel.

"Jeff," she answered wearily, "stay home with me today."

The boy reluctantly surrendered, and at 11:00 A.M. he began to feel well enough to ask for a bowl of his favorite soup, Oodles of Noodles. After eating, Jeffrey left the table to peer out the window for any hints of adventure on Hampshire Street. The neighborhood was quiet, at least for a ten-year-old boy. "Mom, I'm gonna take a shower," he announced.

As Jeffrey clambered up the stairs, Barbara turned on the television to watch live coverage of a sensational murder trial, in which a fifteen-year-old Somerville boy had been charged in the brutal stabbing death of his best friend's mother. The family of the victim, Janet Downing, was friendly with Bob Curley's niece, so Barbara had a tangential connection to the

25

case. Like most of Greater Boston, she had been both horrified and captivated by the crime. Today, a verdict was expected against the defendant, a pudgy former altar boy named Eddie O'Brien, who allegedly stabbed his neighbor ninety-eight times in what prosecutors called an uncontrollable frenzy of frustrated sexual obsession. The murder of Downing, a divorced forty-two-year-old mother of four, had been so alarming that Middlesex district attorney Thomas Reilly had decided to prosecute O'Brien himself.

As Barbara watched the proceedings at Middlesex Superior Court, less than a mile away, Jeffrey reappeared about noon and asked his mother if he could walk to Sarchioni's. He was feeling better and had a craving for another of his favorite foods, a large Italian submarine sandwich, loaded with all the fixings, including hot peppers, which made Jeffrey unique among the neighborhood kids.

Barbara shook her head in disbelief. "Momma just made you some soup," she protested. "I think you need time for that to digest." But Jeffrey was persistent, as always, and Barbara allowed him to head to the corner store, where soda, candy, and a few staples had been squeezed into every available inch of the cramped shelf space.

In fifteen minutes, Jeffrey was back, just in time to see Shaun return from a half day at trade school, where he had shown a knack for carpentry and hockey. Shaun had recently returned from a "boot camp" on Cape Cod for juvenile criminal offenders, and the mixture of tough love and no-compromise discipline he received there had tilted his choices toward the straight and narrow. A few days before, Shaun had tackled the popular Doc Linskey road race in Cambridge. He ran beside his father, finished the five-mile course, and felt good about the result. Suddenly, life was looking up for an often reckless kid who had earned the nickname "Crazy Curley."

Shaun's car now started at the turn of the key, thanks to his father's hands-on attention the previous day. With a short day of school behind him, Shaun planned to drive the Oldsmobile to an out-of-town junkyard to find a replacement for

the rusted front fender. Jeffrey loved junkyards—particularly ones with old cars, where he could climb in the seats, pretend to drive, and fiddle with the knobs, dials, and moving parts—and pleaded to tag along.

"You can't go," Shaun shot back. "We have to go all the way to Billerica. We don't have a car seat, and this car's not safe, anyway."

Jeffrey, crushed and crying, ran into the house to complain to his unsympathetic mother. Shaun had gone, his friends were in school, and he suddenly felt much better. For a hyperactive ten-year-old, confinement to the condo was not a pleasant option.

Unfortunately for Barbara, her plans for a quiet day at home had been upended. Jeffrey was badgering her, and the patience of both mother and son began to wear thin. Finally, about 2:00 P.M., with the O'Brien verdict expected any minute, Barbara relented and gave Jeffrey permission to return to Sarchioni's.

Jeffrey seemed agitated on this visit, enough that the help took notice of his hyperactive behavior. His restlessness didn't end after the short walk home, where Jeffrey spotted his oldest brother, Bobby, standing at the end of the driveway with the family dog, a Rottweiler named Tyson.

Bobby also seemed agitated, but for complicated reasons of late-teen romance. A girlfriend had stopped outside the condo to confront him, angrily asking why he hadn't called her all day or the night before. And Jeffrey, unaware, walked straight into the middle of a roiling tempest.

"Can you take me to do something?" Jeffrey asked Bobby, a tough, husky kid who had graduated from high school the previous year.

Bobby had no inclination to do any such thing. His girlfriend was giving him a hard time, and Bobby was too busy navigating the fine line of laying down the law without damaging the relationship. As Bobby attempted that delicate maneuver, Jeffrey continued to nag him. The strategy backfired. With more than a little attitude, Bobby barked at his brother.

"Go wash the dog, okay? I'll take you later," he said. The message: Get lost and don't bother me. He sweetened the deal by throwing in $10.

A small victory in hand, Jeffrey ran inside the condo, where Barbara agreed to let him walk the dog to his grandmother's house, two streets away. There, under her eye, he could shampoo Tyson just like he had done so many times before.

"Throw a warmer coat on you," Barbara said.

"Ma, I'm fine, I'm fine. Stop worrying. I don't need a jacket," answered Jeffrey, who wore only a Boston College football jersey and a pair of denim shorts.

"Okay, but try not to get yourself wet, because then you're going to get sick all over again," Barbara pleaded.

Jeffrey lifted his head, gave his mother a kiss, and dashed outside.

"I love you," Barbara said.

"I love you, too, Ma."

"Remember, Jeff, I don't want you taking off from Nana's," Barbara added, well aware of the boy's wanderlust. "After you wash the dog, bring him back, and we'll chain him in the kennel so he can dry."

The walk was second nature to Jeffrey, who regarded Muriel Francis as a second mother and her two-story wooden house as a second home. A seventy-year-old widow with a hard, chiseled face, Francis was accustomed to seeing Jeffrey at least twice a day.

On this afternoon, Jeffrey decided on a whim to bypass the house for a few minutes and walk Tyson down the block to Market Park. There, a small patch of street-corner greenery and playground equipment offered children and young adults a neighborhood alternative to the dusty sidewalks and sagging stoops where they usually congregated.

As he neared the park, Jeffrey spied Sicari and Tashika Ellis walking toward him from Sicari's apartment a block away. Ever the scamp, Jeffrey sensed a delicious opportunity to turn the tables on a tormentor who had teased and bullied him

throughout the summer. Jeffrey tightened the leash and prodded the Rottweiler to exact his revenge.

"Get him! Get him!" Jeffrey urged the dog. Tyson, straining at the leash, began to snarl. And Sicari, only yards away,
began to panic.

"You little punk!" Sicari screamed at Jeffrey. He grabbed
a brick, hopped a small metal fence, and yelled again. "Get that
dog out of here before I fuck up both you and the dog!"

Jeffrey, smirking, called Tyson off and continued toward
the park. Sicari, fuming, headed toward Izzy's, a small Spanish
shop where Ellis, a twenty-year-old single mother, planned to
buy a takeout lunch. Only a block away, after turning a corner,
they spotted Charles Jaynes, leaning against his Cadillac on
the side of a busy street.

"I'll wait here for you," Sicari told Ellis, who suddenly
sensed that he had expected to see Jaynes there. "I'm going to
talk to him."

Ellis shrugged and strolled to Izzy's, where, after a few
minutes, she retraced her steps and found Jaynes and Sicari,
side by side, immersed in deep conversation near the Cadillac.

Jaynes, as usual, was annoying.

"How's the food? I've never eaten there before," Jaynes
chortled in his high-pitched voice. He helped himself to some
of her order and then offered Ellis a ride home, an unusual bit
of chivalry considering that she lived only two blocks away.

Why not? Ellis thought. She slid into the back of the
Cadillac, while Sicari claimed his accustomed place of honor
in the front passenger seat. Two minutes later, after several
sharp turns on a few, short, narrow streets, Ellis stood outside
her door. And as she did, she saw Jeffrey walk his dog away
from the park and disappear from sight.

Only fifty familiar yards separated the park from Jeffrey's
grandmother's house. He opened a chain-link fence, climbed a
short flight of concrete stairs, and heard his grandmother and
his uncle Arthur talking in the kitchen. The sounds of their
voices, floating out the door, were yet another comforting
thread in the tapestry of this boy's circumscribed world.

Arthur Francis visited the home at least one afternoon a week so he could linger with his mother over a cup of tea after his shift as a maintenance foreman for the Boston subway system.

Jeffrey greeted his grandmother and uncle and promptly set about a well-worn routine: tethering Tyson to a post beneath the stairway and unraveling a green garden hose to wash the dog. Mother and son could hear water pulsing through the hose as they chatted, warm and reassuring, until they were interrupted by the crash of an opening door. Jeffrey burst into the kitchen, no time to spare, in a whirling rush of sound and movement.

"Nana, I have to go. I have to go somewhere. I'll be back in a little while," Jeffrey said.

"But the dog?" she asked.

"Don't worry, Nana. I'll be back in ten minutes!"

Jeffrey placed the shampoo on the floor and darted out the door. As he left, his maroon football jersey disappearing from the kitchen, Muriel Francis paused and smiled. Her irrepressible grandson, she mused, seemed happy today. At that time, 3:15 P.M., Muriel Francis didn't give another thought to this abrupt change in plans. After all, this was quintessential Jeffrey: a nonstop, upbeat, unpredictable tornado. And, despite all the motion, he almost always was dependable. She couldn't have known what lay beyond the door.

Outside, a lumbering gray Cadillac idled at the curb. Charles Jaynes sat nervously expectant behind the wheel. Salvatore Sicari slumped low in the passenger seat to avoid being seen. And Jeffrey, smiling and ecstatic, bounded into the backseat. A months-long promise was about to come true. Charles Jaynes, his bearlike friend, had declared he would buy Jeffrey a brand-new bicycle today.

Jeffrey leaned forward, as he often did, extending his arms sideways on the upholstery, his crew-cut head jutting forward between Jaynes and Sicari. Jaynes told Jeffrey they would pick up the long-anticipated gift in Newton. The eight-mile trip would be quick and easy, only one exit west on the

Massachusetts Turnpike and not far from the car dealership that Jeffrey knew so well.

On this trip, however, Jaynes did not stop at Honda Village. Instead, he cruised through other parts of the affluent, leafy suburb until he reached a Mobil gas station in the busy Four Corners neighborhood near Boston College. There, pulling his Cadillac close to a self-service bay, Jaynes pumped eighteen gallons into the car.

But as he did, Jaynes interrupted the job to place a rag over the flipped-down license plate and douse the cloth with fuel. Jaynes used an American Express card in his father's name to pay the $27.76 tab, then tossed the rag on the rear floor.

The Mobil station was close to International Bicycle Centers, where Jaynes and Sicari had shopped in September. During their first visit, on September 8, the pair ordered an adult-size, metallic-red Trek 850, a mountain bike for which Jaynes gave $60 as a down payment on the $330 bill. On September 26, Jaynes and Sicari visited again to say they had changed their minds and now wanted a bike for a ten-year-old.

Fabio Selvig, the assistant store manager, showed them the children's bicycles. The pair chose a red model already on the display floor, a Trek Mountain Cub 97. Because the bike was dented, Selvig suggested a blue version, a ready-to-roll model that they could take immediately rather than wait a week for another red one. Jaynes, who used the name of Anthony Scaccia for the purchase, liked the suggestion. "He won't care about the color," Jaynes said.

To Selvig, the comment seemed odd. From experience, he knew that a child who is set on a color wants only that color. Plus, Selvig thought, these men did not seem like the usual customers for children's bicycles.

If Jaynes planned to give Jeffrey the Trek 97, he didn't bring the bicycle on the trip to Newton. Instead, after he left the Mobil station, Jaynes drove the car toward the rear of a small shopping center across the intersection.

Jaynes, who needed to urinate, was joined by Sicari and Jeffrey as they relieved themselves near a brown Dumpster

and a stack of empty milk crates. Here, Jeffrey was just one of the guys, reveling in a midday adventure, his mind far away from a Rottweiler that by now had begun to bark for lack of attention.

Jaynes and Jeffrey finished their business first, returning to the car in a misty rain as Sicari lingered in the alley. In Jeffrey's mind, a good day was about to get better. In addition to the bicycle, Jaynes had said Jeffrey now stood to make the astronomical sum of $50.

Finally, Jeffrey would hear what Jaynes expected in return. The price of his generosity, Jaynes explained, was a sexual favor. The boy, horrified, refused a demand he could barely understand.

Jaynes reacted with a burst of volcanic fury, grabbing Jeffrey with single-minded force and dragging him to the backseat of the car. Sicari turned just in time to see Jeffrey disappear into the Cadillac. Stunned, he bolted toward the car, racing around the vehicle and slamming all the doors. He threw himself into the driver's seat, looked around, punched the gas, and sped out of the parking lot.

Behind him, a violent battle had begun. Jeffrey was fighting for his life, flailing against a three-hundred-pound predator who had sat on him to pin him to the cushion. Still struggling to subdue the boy, Jaynes reached for the rag and held the fuel-drenched cloth to Jeffrey's face, pressing harder and harder, smothering the boy's nose and mouth and forcing him to inhale the toxic vapors.

"Don't fight it!" Jaynes yelled. "Don't fight it."

Instead, Jeffrey lashed out with his arms and legs, again and again, in a furious effort to fight off the killer he had thought was his friend. Unable to see, he strained to find and release the door handle, his short, groping fingers jabbing for the lever under Jaynes's crushing weight. Despite his size, Jeffrey refused to succumb. By now, the gasoline had reached his brain, his blood, and his lungs, searing Jeffrey's respiratory tract and raising raw, painful blisters on his face and neck. Amazingly, Jeffrey continued to battle as the Cadillac mingled

with afternoon traffic. At one point, in a final, futile signal for help, the boy's arm shot straight up. Frightened and angered by Jeffrey's resistance, Jaynes grabbed the arm and slammed it down.

The struggle continued for twenty interminable minutes, as Sicari, his eyes darting between the rearview mirror and the rush-hour congestion, nervously steered the Cadillac on an aimless path to no set destination. At one point, a Newton police cruiser pulled up behind the Cadillac, its blue lights flashing, as Jeffrey continued to fight.

Sicari stiffened. He hit the gas again and lost sight of the officer, unaware that the police had been dispatched on an unrelated call. Now, seemingly safe for a moment, Sicari screamed at Jaynes, "What the fuck did you do?"

By now, Jeffrey's long, desperate struggle had ended, and he lay dead, the frantic fight for life too great for his seventy-seven pounds. His blue eyes stared blankly toward the roof as his small body lay prone on the backseat of a car that reeked of gasoline. Bruises marred his gums, arms, knees, and buttocks. And on Jeffrey's upper left shoulder and arm, the diamond-shaped weave of his football jersey lay imprinted on his skin like a cattle brand.

Jaynes panted while lines of sweat poured down his face. He gasped for breath but seemed oblivious to his deed. Instead of horror, he showed scorn. Instead of fear, he spewed derision. Instead of guilt, he blamed Jeffrey.

"The kid is not going to con a conner," Jaynes snapped. "He thought he was going to get a bike and the money for nothing."

Sicari pulled the Cadillac off the street and into a parking lot, out of sight of traffic and pedestrians. There, Jaynes gagged Jeffrey with the rag and duct tape.

"Ride in back with the kid," Jaynes said.

Sickened by the sight of the corpse, slack on the seat with wide, open eyes, Sicari refused. Jaynes, however, had no such qualms. He used his fingers to lower Jeffrey's eyelids, placed the body on the floor, and rolled the front seat back to hide as much of Jeffrey as possible.

The time was 4:15 P.M., only one hour since Jeffrey had bounded away, smiling and excited, from his grandmother's house. In Cambridge, the boy's restless Rottweiler remained tied to the pole outside Muriel Francis's home. Although Jeffrey had not returned, his grandmother credited the tardiness to a longer-than-usual case of Jeffrey being Jeffrey.

At 4:30 P.M., however, she had heard enough of Tyson's barking and called Barbara. Jeffrey had wandered off with friends, she told Barbara, and not come back. Could someone stop by the house and take the dog? Barbara agreed to retrieve Tyson. On the walk home, she speculated that Jeffrey must have stopped by Donnelly Field. Par for the course for that little rascal, she mused.

In any event, Barbara was preoccupied with other thoughts. Close to the time that Jeffrey hopped into Jaynes's car, the jury had returned with a verdict in the Eddie O'Brien case. First-degree murder with extreme atrocity, the foreman proclaimed on live television. The sentence: a mandatory term of life without parole for the cherub-faced seventeen-year-old. A chill coursed through Barbara as she, and most of her neighbors, watched the verdict. How could such a horrific crime happen to such a woman, Barbara wondered. How could it happen in this community?

Those questions also tugged at Bob Curley, who watched the verdict with several firefighters who had clustered around the upstairs television at Engine 6, an old firehouse near the Charles River. Bob had not known the victim, but his sister Francine and her daughter had been traumatized by the murder of a friend found butchered on the kitchen floor. Like Barbara, Bob felt insulated from such savagery, even though petty crime was a frustrating fact of life in the working-class neighborhoods where they had spent their entire lives. Murder had never visited his family, and, like many of the firefighters around him who shook their heads, its impact was incomprehensible.

Unknown to them, another horror had just hit the community.

A few miles away, Jaynes and Sicari cobbled together a cover-up. The first step led them to a bustling shopping plaza in a crowded, commercial bend of the Charles River near Honda Village. Jaynes, who worked less than a mile away, knew the place well and directed Sicari to park the Cadillac in a side lot, close to an NHD Hardware store where Jaynes would shop for supplies.

As Sicari fidgeted in the driver's seat, fingering the thin growth of beard that lined the edge of his jaw, Jaynes entered the store. His nervousness made an instant impression on Roque Alfaro, a Newton high school student who worked one of the cash registers. Jaynes hurriedly asked Alfaro to point him toward the duct tape. In response, Alfaro summoned Dale Bisson, an assistant store manager, who started to back away when Jaynes began moving toward her, agitated and aggressive. Jaynes was perspiring heavily, and Bisson thought she detected a faint odor of gasoline as she led him to the duct tape. As they moved through the aisles, Bisson made sure she kept fifteen feet away from Jaynes and turned her head repeatedly to track his location.

Once they reached the tape, Jaynes asked Bisson where the tarps were stored. "Just show me where they are," he snapped. "I don't need you to come with me." Bisson, however, escorted Jaynes to the tarps, although she left as soon as she pointed them out. "He frightened me," Bisson said later. "I'll never forget his face." Jaynes chose a nine-by-twelve-foot tarp to go with four rolls of duct tape, all of which he billed to his father's American Express card.

Sicari started the car as soon as he saw Jaynes turn the corner from the store. But before they could leave, Sicari was forced to wait while a medical-office worker, on her way home, walked directly in front of the Cadillac. The worker, Jacquelyn Avant, took a good look at the two men. She noted Sicari's "scrubby beard" and the way he cut his hair: close on the sides, but thick and curly on the top, just like hers. Sicari, sweeping a hand over the top of the driving wheel, politely waved Avant past the car.

From the plaza, the pair drove less than a mile to Honda Village, where Sicari backed the rear of the Cadillac against a wall of the dealership. Jaynes was expected at work that afternoon, and he was determined to stick to his routine, even though his car still carried the warm body of Jeffrey Curley.

As Jaynes walked down a ramp to his job in the basement, Sicari rearranged the Cadillac. He laid out the tarp in the trunk, lifted Jeffrey's body from the rear passenger floor, and carefully placed the corpse in the plastic wrapping. Then, he removed the duct tape from the boy's face, which had been badly bruised. Ugly black-and-blue welts, almost like the remnants of a beating, disfigured his face and eyes. Sicari then moved the Cadillac to a narrow, lightly traveled street beside the dealership. A Honda salesman, Jason Drew, saw the car there about 5:00 P.M. and thought it odd because Jaynes regularly parked in the basement.

To other employees, the day seemed to be business as usual for Jaynes, who prepped new cars as always. Jaynes even joked with some of the workers, including mechanic James Gavell, who sat in the customer lounge about 5:45 P.M., reading a newspaper before the end of his shift. "You aren't really too busy, huh?" Jaynes said, chuckling. "Or busy doing nothing."

While Jaynes was typically wisecracking, upbeat, and obnoxious, his friend Sicari seemed the emotional opposite. While Jaynes placed calls on a dealership phone, Sicari took a seat near Gavell, hung his head, and stared at the floor.

Jaynes phoned Charlene Letourneau, Sicari's former girlfriend, to insist she tell his mother not to drive to his New Hampshire apartment that night. Letourneau and her two-year-old child, the son of Edward Jaynes Jr., had been living at the Jaynes home in Brockton since the beginning of the year. Jaynes also placed a call to Laurie Pistorino at the Boston Public Library. She, too, had plans to stay overnight in Manchester, but Jaynes said he suddenly felt ill.

Two loose ends had been tied, so Jaynes returned to work for two more hours on a slow night. About 8:30 P.M., he ambled back to the customer lounge, where Drew and his

sales manager were watching a baseball game on television. Jaynes asked for permission to leave early, and the manager gave him the go-ahead.

Meanwhile, in East Cambridge, Barbara was becoming concerned. Her first reaction to Jeffrey's decision to leave the dog alone had been mild annoyance. After all, he had stayed home sick from school, pestered her to go outside, and then abandoned Tyson. The time had come for Jeffrey to be held accountable.

Barbara walked into the condo shortly before 5:00 P.M., looked at the clock, and frowned. Dinner would be on the table at 5:30 P.M., although no one else was home yet. At 6:00 P.M., she would attend a condominium meeting at one of four other units in the complex. Jeffrey was playing somewhere close, she was sure, and this meeting was important. So, after cooking three meals for her boys and placing them on the kitchen table under plastic, Barbara fumed and headed out the door of an empty house.

Shaun arrived home minutes later, following a successful scavenger hunt to replace his car's rusted bumper. Missing the 5:30 P.M. dinner was routine for him, so the sight of his supper under wraps was expected rather than extraordinary. Shaun also knew what lay on the table: one of four meals that Barbara rotated for the boys. His favorites in the culinary batting order were chicken cutlets and meatloaf, but Barbara cooked a New England boiled dinner on special occasions— corned beef, cabbage, potatoes, and carrots—that topped all the others in Shaun's mind.

True to form, Shaun didn't linger long. His cousin's parents were vacationing in Aruba, and dozens of neighborhood teenagers had been descending on the house since midafternoon. The prospects of beer, unattached girls, and friends from the hockey rink were plenty of motivation to get out of the condo as quickly as possible.

Bobby already was at the party when Shaun arrived. After dispatching Jeffrey to wash the dog, Bobby had walked the few blocks to the G&J Variety Store near Donnelly Field to

rendezvous with his friends on the corner. The group headed to the party, where about twenty people had gathered by the time Bobby arrived, cooking hamburgers outside, drinking beer, and swapping jokes. When a light rain began, the crowd migrated to the porch and then the attic, a single open room that had been converted into a party-perfect apartment.

The beer came from one of two sources, neither of them legal. Shaun and his crew had mastered the art of breaking into trains in the Cambridge rail yards near Boston's North Station, loading up shopping carts with cases of beer, and stashing the booty in someone's basement. The stakes were impressive: a single heist could yield the group enough free beer for two to three weeks. Another option was the beer truck that stocked the Windsor Tap, a tired gin mill only a short stone's throw from Bobby and Shaun's condo. When the driver wheeled a delivery inside, usually once a week, Shaun and his buddies would climb into the rear of the truck and scamper away with a few cases.

Not surprisingly, the party's agenda included drinking games. In one favorite, a two-liter plastic Pepsi bottle was turned upside down, the bottom cut off, and three or four beers poured into the container. A hose attached to the bottle delivered as much beer as the wide-eyed person on the receiving end could handle—and usually more. The games were intoxicatingly effective, and the party picked up momentum. Raucous, rowdy laughter mixed with loud, thumping music. Life was good, at least for the moment, in a neighborhood where life's options were often limited.

A few blocks away on Hampshire Street, Barbara returned home at 7:30 P.M. to find no sign of Jeffrey.

"He's going to be in big trouble," she muttered, then did an abrupt about-face, pulled her jacket tight, and left the building for a brisk walk to Donnelly Field. All the sunlight had left the evening sky by the time she scoured the edges of a park she had known for forty years, searching all the places she knew Jeffrey liked to sit, play ball, or perform stunts on his bike.

"Okay, no Jeff here," she said aloud. Pivoting for home, Barbara made a mental list of all the parents she would call to track him down. "Does Jeffrey happen to be there with Brian?" she asked one mother on the phone. "Have you seen Jeffrey?" she asked another. Over and over, for forty-five minutes, Barbara dialed two-dozen homes where Jeffrey might have been that day, or where he might be playing still. And over and over, the drumbeat of disappointing answers perplexed and worried her.

At 8:30 P.M., she paged Bobby, who left his cousin's attic to phone his mother. "Your brother's not home," she said. "You boys need to start riding around looking for him. I don't know what's going on." The good times ended with a thunderclap. Bobby and Shaun Curley left immediately to prowl the neighborhood, and with them went much of the party. "Everyone split out of the house after my mother's call—on feet, in cars, whatever," Shaun recalled. Everyone there knew Jeffrey, so Bobby and Shaun's problem suddenly became their problem, too.

Bobby started his search on foot, first to a house a few steps from the party, then to a home two doors from the Curley condo. When those door-knocks turned up nothing, Bobby drove to playgrounds and parks in the immediate area. He scoured the neighborhood until 10:15 P.M., when he broke off the hunt and left for his first night of work at a printing company fifteen miles away. "He'll come home," Bobby said to himself, more miffed than mystified by Jeffrey's disappearance. "He's out there causing mischief."

Shaun also took to the streets, hopping into his beat-up car and crisscrossing East Cambridge in the dark—up by the rusting Lechmere stop on the subway line, down by the posh Galleria shopping mall, and over by the courthouse. "I know Jeffrey," Shaun said to the friend riding with him. "He's street-smart. He's a strong kid. Nothing's gonna happen to him."

As the Curley boys began their search, Jaynes and Sicari left Honda Village and headed to the Bradlees department store in nearby Watertown, purposely avoiding the branch in

Somerville where Barbara Curley worked. The pair arrived just before 9:00 P.M., and Jaynes found his quarry in short order: a green-and-gray Rubbermaid Rough Tote container just big enough to hold the body of a ten-year-old child. The price: $39.99. "I guess I'll spend forty dollars on the kid," Jaynes said.

Sicari lugged the container to the cash register, where he leaned the forty-two-inch bin against the counter and rubbed his eyes, while Jaynes used his father's credit card again to pay the bill. The transaction complete, Sicari awkwardly stretched two arms around the container and followed Jaynes dutifully out the door.

The shopping expedition then shifted a few miles to Somerville, where Jaynes bought a fifty-pound bag of cement and some granulated lime at The Home Depot. By the time of that purchase, at 10:21 P.M., Jaynes had solidified his plan: weigh down the container with cement, cover Jeffrey's face with lime to speed decomposition, and dispose of the body in a watery grave somewhere north of Boston. The scheme resembled a hypothetical scenario that Jaynes had posited to friends two years earlier in a casual, but macabre, conversation. "If I killed someone," he had said, "I would put them in something, put cement on them, and throw them into the ocean."

Jaynes now had what he needed, but he remained worried that his mother would drive to Manchester that night. To ensure that she stayed in Brockton, he phoned her home a dozen times. Letourneau answered most of the calls while Jaynes's mother made her long, obsessive rounds of the Brockton grocery stores, hunting for the absolute best bargains on every item she purchased.

As the night wore on, Jaynes became more anxious with every call. "Tell her she *cannot* come to my house tonight! She *cannot* come!" Jaynes ordered Letourneau, who promised she would relay the message. Jaynes, however, remained unconvinced and continued to phone the house. "Is Ma there yet? I really need to talk to her," he said in one call. "Look, I'm not going to be home, okay? I'm busy. My room is messy." Letourneau, who kept house for Virginia Jaynes in return for

lodging, shook her head. Your room is messy? she thought. Your life is messy. I don't get this.

At one point, Jaynes accused Letourneau of lying to him because he knew she despised his interest in pedophilia. That animosity was well founded. Letourneau had found child pornography in his room in Brockton. She had witnessed his vulgar come-ons to young boys. And she had sorted the mail that came to the house from NAMBLA. Letourneau had also discovered four pairs of boys' underpants in his room, underwear that had been worn, folded up, and neatly packaged in ziplock plastic baggies. Jaynes, to her, was evil incarnate, and she never left him alone with her son.

By midevening, Jaynes was frantic and snarling.

"You're just not telling her," Jaynes snapped into the phone. "I'm sure she's called to check in by now, and you're just not telling her!"

"Charlie, I don't know what to tell you," Letourneau said, tired of this strange and maddening back-and-forth.

But Jaynes was only half the problem. Letourneau also had been fielding a fusillade of calls from Sicari. One after another, like a coordinated relay, Jaynes and Sicari had been alternating their calls to Brockton. Letourneau did not realize the two were together. If she had known, she would have been incensed. Letourneau had forbidden Sicari to fraternize with Jaynes if he wished to communicate with her.

If Jaynes sounded panicked, Sicari seemed his usual, emotionless, unrattled self. Although his complicity in Jeffrey's murder grew deeper by the minute, much of his talk with Letourneau revolved around run-of-the-mill arguments between fractious ex-lovers. Letourneau had considered getting back together with Sicari, but she was furious because he had lied about having a job. Back and forth the chatter went: Letourneau's anger at his deception and Sicari's meek attempts to defend himself.

Occasionally, Sicari would digress into a vague, baffling, unrelated riff concerning a search for cement. At one point, Sicari told Letourneau he might be in a fix.

"What are you doing with cement?" Letourneau asked.

Sicari replied that he and two friends were buying concrete to put up a basketball hoop that night. An hour later, he said they were hunting for even more cement.

"How much cement do you actually need, and why couldn't you buy it at one store?" Letourneau asked. "What the hell is going on?"

Sicari's answer jolted Letourneau from suspicion to alarm.

"I really can't talk about this on the phone, and I really have to get this finished up," he said. "If I don't get this finished up, I'm going to be in a lot of trouble."

Letourneau demanded an explanation.

"I've hurt somebody really bad," he said.

"Tell me what you're talking about!" Letourneau shot back, her anxiety rising and her patience exhausted.

"Remember what we talked about yesterday?" Sicari asked in his characteristic monotone, referencing a fatal car accident that they had discussed.

Letourneau, no longer merely confused, suddenly became hysterical. Had Sal hit someone with his car? Had somebody died? That seemed to be the implication, and Letourneau began screaming. "You're on the phone telling me you just killed somebody?" she asked incredulously. "And you have no remorse?"

Sicari answered with a callous disdain that was chilling for its nonchalance. "I could give two fucks," he said. "It's like a bowl of cereal to me. I could either eat it or walk away."

The phone call ended. This could not be true, Letourneau told herself. Sal had told her too many lies, too many tales of fights and beatings that had never happened, too many inventions of street-punk machismo to make himself bigger in her eyes.

Letourneau had put her closest friend on hold to take Sicari's latest call. Now, she clicked back and bombarded Michelle Ward, a taxi dispatcher, with a frenzied, rapid-fire summary of their talk.

"What do I do?" she pleaded. "Should I call the police? I don't know what to do!"

Ward, at work, paused for a second, then whispered, "Holy shit." To her, this development seemed darkly ominous. She had always disliked Sicari and had long worried that he might harm Letourneau. But these cryptic clues, in some indefinable yet undeniable way, seemed dangerously different.

Unsure of Sicari's meaning or Letourneau's legal liability, the pair decided not to notify police before consulting their relatives the next day. Meanwhile, Ward ordered a taxi to the Jaynes home. Letourneau woke up her son, retrieved a few belongings, and was whisked back to the cab company. There, she huddled with Ward until daylight before moving to her friend's apartment.

By this time, Jaynes and Sicari had begun their fifty-mile drive to Manchester. But before they merged onto I-93 for the quick trip to New Hampshire, the pair made their final purchases of the night. At an Osco Drug store in the Twin City Plaza in Somerville, Jaynes brandished his father's credit card once again, this time to buy a box of Garcia y Vega panatela cigars and three packages of NoDoz caplets. The time was 10:33 P.M. The NoDoz would be needed to keep them awake. The Dominican cigars were valuable for their leaf wrappers, which could be unrolled and reused to hold the marijuana that Jaynes had recently begun to enjoy. For Sicari, pot was almost a dietary staple.

Before leaving the plaza, Jaynes placed the car's trunk key in the ashtray. If a police officer wanted to inspect the trunk, Jaynes figured, he'd simply shrug his shoulders and say he couldn't find the key.

Their shopping complete, the two merged onto the highway at a nearby entrance ramp and hurtled north in light, comfortable traffic. As they did, Bobby Curley might have sped past as he hurried to his new job in suburban Lynnfield.

As usual, Jaynes drove. He prided himself on his sense of geography, and he had become well acquainted with southern New Hampshire and southern Maine since he moved from Brockton to escape arrest. Jaynes's mother had paid for months of accommodation in that swath of semirural New

England to shield her son from prosecution, Letourneau recalled. Nothing was too good for Virginia Jaynes's favorite son. But when resort-style lodging on the Maine coast became too costly, Letourneau said, Jaynes packed his clothes in trash bags and moved to less-expensive digs in Manchester.

Jaynes knew the interstates, the back roads, and the rest stops where gay men and others would meet for furtive trysts under the cover of night. A favorite for Jaynes was on I-93 in New Hampshire just across the Massachusetts border. In his experience, the police rarely checked there. He also frequented venues closer to Boston, particularly garages at mass-transit stations and dimly lit, after-hours corners in fast-food parking lots.

By October 1, according to Jaynes, he and Sicari had been sexual partners for six months. He had been interested in Sicari, however, for twice that long, dating to the day in 1996 when Letourneau introduced them and Jaynes made a brazen offer. "I'll give you fifty dollars if you let me suck your man off," Jaynes told Letourneau, who recoiled at another disgusting, predictable remark from a man she loathed.

Later that day, Sicari became enraged when Letourneau told him of the request. If he later entered a physical relationship with Jaynes, he never spoke of it. Indeed, Sicari routinely bashed gay men in conversation, Letourneau said, and "acted like the most homophobic person you'd ever met in your life." But, like much of Sicari's life, that front might well have been a lie.

On this night, Jaynes and Sicari had work to do. They arrived in Manchester shortly after midnight and parked in the rear of Jaynes's apartment building, several dozen yards from busy Elm Street and the late-night commotion at the popular Black Brimmer bar. Near the back entrance that led to his second-floor unit, Jaynes unlocked the Cadillac's trunk, looked around, and carefully picked up the tarp that held Jeffrey's body. Sicari carried everything else: the Rubbermaid container, the duct tape, the lime, and the cement.

The wooden stairs creaked as they climbed, turned left, and paced halfway down the empty hall before opening a set of louvered doors at Apartment 206. The place, as always, was a shambles. Piles of dirty clothes lay jumbled just inside the entrance, spilling out of cardboard boxes or tossed haphazardly on the cheap blue carpet.

Jaynes crossed the boxlike space that served as living room and bedroom, passed under a Honda Village dealer plate, and lowered the tarp to the kitchen floor. Methodically, meticulously, he slowly took the clothing from Jeffrey's stiffening body: the Boston College football jersey, the denim shorts, the socks, the Reebok sneakers, and the underwear. Then, using a single-edge razor blade, Jaynes sliced a waist button and a label from the shorts that Jeffrey's mother had bought at Bradlees for an employee discount. These were Jaynes's souvenirs, he told Sicari, two small trophies from his first murder victim, which he would carefully preserve as lifelong keepsakes.

Jaynes placed the items on the kitchen table. Then, with Jeffrey's naked body before him, he prepared to plumb the depths of his criminal fetishes. Across the kitchen, he spotted a long-neck bottle of Coors Light beer. As Sicari looked on, he later told police, Jaynes lubricated the top of the empty bottle with petroleum jelly, bent to the floor, and inserted it into Jeffrey's rectum.

Sicari, sickened, retreated to the bathroom.

"Stop being a baby," Jaynes barked. "Come out here and help me hold his legs. He's getting stiff."

When Sicari returned, he witnessed more of the unthinkable. Jaynes rolled Jeffrey over and placed his penis between the boy's buttocks. Later, with Jeffrey on his back, Jaynes used his mouth, hands, and feet to manipulate the boy's penis.

Jaynes encouraged Sicari to sodomize Jeffrey's body, but his friend refused. No matter. Jaynes had added the ultimate horror to his growing inventory of pedophile experiences. And he seemed satisfied, if somewhat surprised. "I didn't know I

was a necrophiliac," he told Sicari. "I didn't know I would like having sex with a dead body."

Nearby, a poster of child actor Jonathan Taylor Thomas added color to the drab walls. A few feet from Thomas, a *Lion King* ad read, "Hakuna Matata," a Swahili phrase for "no worries," in bold, childlike lettering. And on an end table near the couch, carefully folded, lay a child's mesh maroon football jersey, smelling of gasoline and bearing the number worn by Heisman Trophy winner Doug Flutie, a Boston hero. Jaynes wanted to keep the jersey, he told Sicari, because "it smelled like Jeffrey."

His perversions completed for the night, Jaynes prepared to dispose of the body. He and Sicari stirred the cement, used the pasty mix to line the bottom of the Rubbermaid container, and then inserted Jeffrey's corpse. Sicari heard something snap, probably a joint, as they sharply flexed Jeffrey's neck, arms, hips, and knees to fit inside. The boy's bruised and blistered face tilted up toward the opening. To speed decomposition, Jaynes and Sicari spread lime on Jeffrey's mouth and eyes. They snapped the green lid down and secured it with a crosshatch of duct tape.

Two hours after they arrived in Manchester, the pair had nearly completed their gruesome work. Jaynes and Sicari retraced their steps down the stairs, placed the container in the car's trunk, and parked the Cadillac two streets away. Now, all that remained was to choose a place to dump the body.

As they walked back to the apartment, the Black Brimmer's patrons began spilling onto Elm Street. Despite everything that had happened, only minutes after placing Jeffrey's body in the trunk, Sicari suggested they try their luck with the women. Never one to skip a party, Jaynes went along.

The pair approached two girls, struck up a conversation, and persuaded them to visit the apartment. Sicari made progress with one of them, a girl whose blood-alcohol level might have masked the apartment's mess and locker-room smell. Jaynes, however, was a different animal. Rudely arrogant and grossly overweight, he quickly offended the other

girl, who made for the door after only a few minutes. Sicari's would-be companion jumped up. "Let me see if I can talk to her," she said. The woman followed her friend into the hall, but Jaynes had gone too far.

The liaison had been only a diversion, and Jaynes knew he could not afford a distraction. After the girls left, he immediately redirected his attention to something more important: disposing of the container. Jaynes opened an atlas and studied the area near the border of southern Maine and New Hampshire. Tracing his finger along the map, he stopped suddenly at the junction of a small river and rural highway. "That's where we'll dump Jeffrey Curley's body," he said.

The tired streets of downtown Manchester were deserted as they returned to the Cadillac. The sidewalk outside the Black Brimmer was empty, a chill laced the early October night, and the only sounds on Elm Street were the rustle of leaves and two pairs of footsteps. Jaynes steered the car back onto I-93, this time heading north toward the state capital, Concord, before meandering east on a secondary highway to Portsmouth, a historic seaport on the southern bank of the Piscataqua River.

The pair reached Portsmouth just over an hour later, at 4:30 A.M., and stopped at a Bickford's restaurant at the main highway circle outside the city. There, Sicari and Jaynes found a Dumpster, where they tossed the empty lime and concrete bags and some of Jeffrey's clothing.

So far, the cover-up was problem free. But, like the bumbling amateurs they were, the pair returned to the car to discover they had locked themselves out. The trunk key, which also opened the doors, lay stashed in the ashtray.

Jaynes, panicking, scurried into Bickford's for a wire coat hanger. As a few customers watched, the waitress told him to try the front desk of the adjacent Howard Johnson's Motor Lodge. There, a sleepy receptionist found one, and Jaynes and Sicari were on their way.

Less than a mile north on Route 1, Jaynes pulled into a twenty-four-hour Exxon station just as a driver for Poland

Springs water stopped on the opposite side of the highway. The driver, William Merrill, had coffee on his mind when he heard someone yell at him from the Cadillac.

"Do you know any cheap motels in the area?" Jaynes asked.

Merrill leaned down to the passenger-side window and told Jaynes of a few motels just south of the gas station. As he did, he spoke across Sicari, who seemed nervous and kept his head turned from Merrill for the entire conversation.

The roads around Portsmouth had become busier, daylight and the morning commute were approaching, and Jaynes decided that the time had come to dump the container. After a short drive across the Piscataqua River into Maine, Jaynes left Route 1 and headed north on a winding, two-lane road that roughly paralleled the New Hampshire border. After twelve miles and twenty minutes, Jaynes found his spot: a short bridge in the small town of South Berwick that spanned the meandering Great Works River.

Even here, the predawn traffic had picked up, carrying workers to the navy yard in Kittery, Maine, and the Seabrook nuclear power plant in New Hampshire. Afraid of being seen, Jaynes made several trips back and forth across the bridge. He turned around on dirt roads lined with pumpkins and rusted cars and even used the driveways of the few, scattered homes. "No, no, don't put the coffee on," he joked at one house. "We're not staying."

Eventually, they stopped about fifty yards north of the river, popped open the trunk from inside the car, and carried the container to the bridge. From the guardrail, where they rested the box, Sicari could make out the slow-moving current. In the darkness, he noted lily pads, trees on the banks, and bending grasses. Jaynes dropped his end of the container over the side, and Sicari followed suit. When the bin hit the water with a loud, jarring splash, Sicari's throat tightened. A motion sensor suddenly brightened at a nearby ranch house.

While Jaynes and Sicari scurried back to the car, William Smith drove past the Cadillac on his way to the nuclear plant. The car and its location struck Smith as very odd. Here

was a car with Massachusetts plates, heading away from Seabrook and the navy yard, parked on a sand embankment with no visible occupants. Smith checked the side of the road as he drove past, looking for a driver who needed help. He saw no one and proceeded to his job.

Jaynes and Sicari, their deed unseen, reentered the car at 5:22 A.M., according to the dashboard clock. Ten minutes later, they stopped at the Dover Point Variety Store in New Hampshire, where Tracy Carr had just opened up. Sicari, her first customer of the day, walked in and ordered two coffees, a pack of cigarettes, and a Danish. Greg Garvin, a regular customer, was about to enter the store when he saw Sicari exit. Garvin stopped, waited for Sicari to pass, and greeted him with a cheery "Good morning!" Sicari, startled, never uttered a word.

The killers returned briefly to Manchester before driving back to Cambridge. When they reached Sicari's apartment at 9:00 A.M., Jaynes took a moment to consider the anguish that was building, minute by minute, at the Curley household a block away.

"You should go over and knock on Barbara Curley's door, and ask her where Jeffrey is," Jaynes said, savoring the cruelty. "We'll torture her. Next weekend, we'll kill Shaun Curley. The weekend after that, we'll kill Bobby Curley. And then we'll keep calling the mother, asking for her kids."

His goal, Jaynes told Sicari, was to be a famous killer. Just like Jeffrey Dahmer.

3

The Face
of Evil

IN CAMBRIDGE, the evening of October 1 crept toward midnight as Barbara Curley sat anchored to a window seat facing the driveway. Shaun continued to drive the streets and back alleys of East Cambridge, and Bobby reported to work. Finally, at 11:30 P.M., Barbara confronted the inevitable and filed a missing-persons report with the Cambridge police. The officer who reported to the condominium told Barbara that police would be alerted immediately about Jeffrey but that the child would not be considered missing until twenty-four hours had passed.

Barbara was incredulous. "You've got to be kidding me," she said.

"If he's not home by morning, call us back," the officer replied. "He could be sleeping at a friend's house. Call us in the morning."

For Barbara, there would be no sleep. Instead, she began to feel the pangs of panic, even as she clung to the hope that Jeffrey would come bounding toward the house at any second. "He's just at a friend's. He's going to come home," she told herself over and over again. "I'm going to be so upset with him. And then we're going to laugh afterward, and I'm going to hold him and kiss him and never let him out of my arms again." But as the hours marched past midnight, instead of Jeffrey's smile,

Barbara saw only the harsh glare of lonely streetlights on nearly empty Hampshire Street.

Across the city line in Somerville, Bob Curley and Mimi were asleep when Barbara contacted the police. Bob had worked in the garden after an uneventful day at work, watched a television special on Cuban baseball, and greeted Mimi when she walked in the door at 7:30 P.M. after another exhausting, ten-hour day of counseling.

Barbara, who deeply resented Mimi, did not have their telephone number. Instead, when the phone rang at 1:30 A.M., Bob woke to hear his sister Francine's voice.

"Bob, it's about Jeff," said Francine, who had heard the news only minutes earlier and was now at Hampshire Street. "He hasn't come home. The boys are trying to find him. Barbara's hysterical."

"Okay, okay, I'll be right over," Bob said, still groggy. "He's all right, Francine. Don't worry."

"I don't know, Bob," Francine said, her voice trembling slightly.

Bob hurriedly threw on some clothes, leaned over the bed, and murmured to Mimi, "I have to go. I have to go."

"What happened?" she asked.

"Jeff hasn't come to the house."

On the short ride to Hampshire Street, Bob tried to digest what he'd just been told. He was concerned but not fearful. Everyone knew Jeff could be a handful. That little son of a gun, he thought, pulling something like this. But at the condo, as he walked down the driveway to the door, Bob could see the play of shadows in the home. Suddenly, he felt a knot of worry. This can't be, Bob assured himself.

When Bob entered the living room, Barbara turned from her window seat. "The baby's missing," she said quietly.

Her brother Charlie and three friends had joined Francine at the house, phoning hospitals and dissecting the situation. Bobby Jr. called regularly for updates, but he couldn't concentrate and returned home at 3:30 A.M. to join the vigil. Shaun had parked his car near the courthouse on Cambridge Street,

fallen asleep, and then woken with a start. Was this all a dream? he asked himself. By 4:00 A.M., when he arrived home, more relatives and friends had congregated there.

In the predawn darkness, the brothers resumed their search, by the subway tracks, by the Charlestown bridge, and by the idle freight trains where Shaun would steal his beer and Jeffrey would light railroad flares and shake them in the air. At the condo, Bob and Barbara believed daylight would bring a good conclusion. Hope, as yet, had not given way to despair. Someone made coffee, others cobbled together information for a flier, and another person checked the hospitals one more time.

When dawn broke, Francine encouraged Barbara to call the police again, but Barbara, reluctant to cause a fuss, wanted to wait until 10:00 A.M. Unable to hold out, Francine took matters into her own hands and called Officer Frank Pasquarello, who handled the department's public relations.

"What are you doing about my nephew?" asked Francine, who was Pasquarello's insurance agent.

Pasquarello assured Francine that a search had begun. Almost immediately, three officers arrived at the Curley home, including Detective Sergeant Lester Sullivan, a seventeen-year veteran of the department, who investigated domestic violence and sexual assault.

As the police began their work, using standard procedures for missing-persons cases, the Curleys were flummoxed and unprepared. As police are fond of saying, everyone is a suspect, and no one is a suspect. So, when one officer stopped Francine to ask if Bob might have taken Jeffrey to punish Barbara, Francine fired back with an indignant, emphatic, "No!"

The boys also began to wonder if they had become suspects. Shaun became irate when police said his account of the previous day didn't match the versions provided by other members of his family. "You know something, buddy," Shaun snapped. "My point of view might have been different from my mother's. It might have been different from my father's. It might have been different from my brother's. But you just

asked me the last time I remember seeing my little brother, and this is what I'm telling you!"

The officer, sensing an altercation in the making, abruptly ended the interview. "All right, all right, we're going to get this stuff together."

Bobby became offended when he saw police sifting through his belongings. "What the hell's going on?" he barked. "This is my personal stuff!"

By late morning, word of Jeffrey's disappearance had begun to spread throughout the community, and clusters of neighbors walked to the condo to offer help. By early afternoon, their numbers had swelled to the hundreds.

Sullivan now had a full-bore community crisis to manage. To better coordinate the investigation, he asked for the department's mobile command vehicle, a van equipped with phones, tables, maps, and computers, which he stationed near the house. Police began a door-to-door canvass of the entire neighborhood, encompassing hundreds of homes and businesses stacked side by side in an urban jumble. Jeffrey's teachers also had been contacted and asked to compile a list of his friends and classmates. Police knocked at the homes of each of these children, and teams of volunteers scoured streets, alleys, backyards, playgrounds, sheds, garages, and everything in between.

Thousands of fliers, printed and copied that morning by Francine and others, carried a treasured family snapshot of Jeffrey, a bright-eyed ten-year-old with a Little League cap on his head, a bat on his shoulder, and an open, gap-toothed smile. The fliers were tacked on hundreds of telephone poles, showered on commuters at subway stops, and handed to motorists who slowed to a crawl as they passed by the throngs gathered outside the condo.

Bobby Curley continued his painstaking search, both on foot and by car, as the day progressed. The work helped distract him from the dark possibilities lurking behind Jeffrey's disappearance. Bobby knew more about the neighborhood's

criminal underbelly than many of the police, but he chose not to dwell on that scenario. In any event, he ceded the early investigative work to the professionals.

That strategy began to change in late morning when a friend, Elvis Gonzalez, told Bobby that his nephew had just mentioned something interesting. A guy named Charles Jaynes supposedly had offered Jeffrey a bicycle the previous week. And Jaynes, the nephew said, was a friend of Salvatore Sicari's.

Bobby's antennae shot up, and he and Gonzalez began the short walk to Sicari's apartment. On the way, they spoke to a neighbor who knew Sicari and said she had seen Jaynes in the area. "Yeah, friggin' Jeff's been over here," the neighbor said. "They horse around with him. They even threw him in the trunk of a car."

Bobby and Gonzalez rang Sicari's ground-floor doorbell. The sound woke Sicari, who, rubbing his eyes, answered the door dressed only in boxer shorts.

"Where were you last night?" Gonzalez asked.

"I was out drinking with a couple of girls. I just got in," Sicari answered.

"Where's Jeffrey? You seen Jeff?" Gonzalez said.

Sicari paused for a few seconds, stunned by the question and wondering what Gonzalez knew and how anyone could have connected him to Jeffrey's disappearance. He answered that he had seen Jeffrey walking the Rottweiler the previous afternoon.

"Okay, who's this Charles Jaynes character?" Bobby asked. "What's he look like? How do we get a hold of him?"

Sicari mumbled that he had seen Jaynes around the neighborhood but did not know how to reach him.

"All right, put your shit on," Bobby snarled. "Let's go."

Sicari dressed quickly, pulling his Georgetown Hoyas sweatshirt over his head as he stumbled back downstairs, where Bobby and Gonzalez walked him to the front of the Curley condominium. As Bobby pondered his next move, Sicari immersed himself in the volunteer effort. He grabbed

dozens of fliers, handed twenty to a Cambridge police detective, and stood in the middle of Hampshire Street to flag down passing cars.

Gonzalez, meanwhile, entered the house, where he told Francine that he and Bobby had spoken with someone who saw Jeffrey the day before.

"Ask him to come inside," Francine said.

Clutching a fistful of fliers, Sicari joined Francine at the Curleys' kitchen table, where he told her about the altercation with Jeffrey and the dog. Unprompted, he also told Francine that he had met a friend, Charles Jaynes, after the confrontation. He and Jaynes then drove to the Boston Public Library, Sicari said, before stopping at Honda Village in Newton and Jaynes's apartment in Manchester, New Hampshire. There, they met two girls and drank until the early morning.

Why is he telling me this? Francine wondered. Still, she was grateful for the information and asked Sicari if he would speak to the police. Sicari agreed. Across the room, Barbara sat dazed and drained, fighting a losing battle to maintain hope. Shaun Curley spotted Sicari and introduced him to his mother.

"Ma, this is Salvi," Shaun said. "You know Salvi. He's been passing out fliers for Jeff."

"Oh, thank you," Barbara said softly, just as she had thanked dozens of people that morning. As she turned back toward the window, Barbara noticed a fresh cut on Sicari's left palm.

In the meantime, Sergeant Sullivan entered the home, where he saw Sicari standing with a cluster of Curley family members.

"I have some information," Sicari told Sullivan.

The detective suggested they talk in the privacy of his police cruiser, where Sicari, speaking quickly and seeming eager to help the authorities, elaborated on the story he had told Francine.

"You know, I've seen this guy Jeffrey's befriended lately," Sicari said.

"How old is he?"

"About twenty-five, about three hundred pounds, drives around in a gray Cadillac," Sicari answered.

"And he befriended a ten-year-old?" Sullivan asked.

"Yeah, he's been with him. He gives him rides in his car. He offered him a bike," Sicari continued.

To Sullivan, a veteran investigator, something seemed wrong. "I'm taking it all in," the detective recalled later, "and I'm thinking, How does he know all this stuff?" Sullivan handed Sicari a cell phone and asked him to page Jaynes. After fifteen minutes and no reply, the two walked to Sicari's apartment, where they tried again on a home phone, whose number Jaynes would recognize. Again, no return call.

The sergeant thanked Sicari and said police might contact him later. When he returned to the command post, Sullivan called headquarters for background checks on Jaynes and Sicari. What he heard—seventy-five outstanding arrest warrants for Jaynes—amplified his steadily increasing alarm.

Sullivan next called Detective Sergeant Patrick Nagle, a Vietnam-era navy veteran who handled Cambridge homicide investigations.

"Pat, I think you want to come down here," Sullivan said. "We have a missing child, but it might end up being much more. There's media here. They're giving out fliers. It's kind of wild."

"I'll be right down," Nagle replied.

Sullivan added a kicker. "I was just approached by this guy," the detective said. "We got to talk to him a little more. There's something here."

Nagle needed only a few minutes to reach the command van. Sullivan briefed him on his talk with Sicari, whom they could see passing out fliers only a few feet away.

Nagle approached Sicari and introduced himself. Sicari once again related his story as they walked through the neighborhood—past Jeffrey's grandmother's house, past Market Park, past Sicari's apartment, and back to the command post. He had last seen Jeffrey near Market Park about 3:00 P.M. the previous day, Nagle was told, when Jeffrey whipped his "hundred-forty-pound, big-ass Rottweiler" into a frenzy. The

dog tried to attack him, Sicari said, before Jeffrey left for his grandmother's house. After the confrontation, Sicari continued, he met his friend Charles Jaynes, and the two spent the night at Jaynes's apartment in Mansfield, New Hampshire.

"There is no Mansfield, New Hampshire," Nagle said.

"Well, something like that," Sicari replied with a shrug.

Before they separated at 12:45 P.M., Sicari gave Nagle a beeper number for Jaynes and agreed to speak to the detective later.

As Nagle returned to police headquarters, Sicari returned to the Curley driveway, where family members, volunteers, news media, police officers, and the merely curious mixed in a crush of concerned and angry people. Bob Curley stood with Francine on the single concrete step that served as the household "porch," watching the surreal scene swirl around them. Up to this point, Bob had been reluctant to concede the worst. But now, exhausted and disheartened, he confided his fears to his closest sibling.

"I know Jeff. He'd be home now," he said to her. "I know Jeff is dead."

Francine placed her hand on Bob's shoulder, rubbed the back of his suede leather jacket, and offered a few words of comforting encouragement. Unknown to him, she shared his conclusion but had not yet found the ability, or the willingness, to verbalize the unspeakable. Bob had designated himself the on-scene coordinator for the family's search efforts, but Francine remained the unflappable, emotional rock. She kept her distress to herself, smiled at her brother, and wandered over to the police van for another status report.

As she did, Sicari approached Bob.

"I'm sorry what happened. I hope Jeffrey comes home," Sicari said, leaning forward to hug Bob. "Whatever I can do, just let me know."

Bob nodded, accepting this unexpected empathy from a neighborhood oddball and petty thief. In Bob's world, even thieves had shown small decencies in trying times, and he was

willing to concede this generosity of spirit to Sicari. "He was always doing something wrong," Curley said later of Sicari. "But that was nothing that I was unaccustomed to, growing up around here. I knew guys who would steal cars, guys who would do bad things. I didn't hang around with them, but I got along with them, you know? That was kind of the way I viewed him, too."

Then, in a reprise of his conversation with Francine, Sicari began blurting out a riff of unsought information. Not content with a few simple words of consolation, Sicari launched into a bizarre, run-on diatribe about Charles Jaynes, someone Bob had never seen or heard about.

"You know, a lot of people have talked about Jaynes and me being queers," Sicari began. "But there's no way that Jaynes could be fucking queer. Because when we're driving down the street and he sees a girl that he likes, he says, 'I'd like to fuck her,' you know?"

Bob was dumbfounded and unnerved. Sicari's statement about Jaynes, following his awkward embrace, had been so bizarre that Bob immediately became suspicious.

Sicari turned toward the street to hand out fliers, passing Shaun Curley on the way. Shaun was exhausted, and he approached his father for reassurance.

"Dad, Jeff's coming home, isn't he?" Shaun asked. "He's gonna be all right, isn't he?"

Bob hesitated. "No, Shaun, Jeff ain't coming home," he answered, his eyes narrowing. "Something's wrong here, and I don't know, but I think Salvi's got something to do with it."

Sicari stood one hundred feet away, half-hidden by the crowd. But Shaun could see him watching their conversation with what seemed to be a smirk.

"Dad, listen, I've known that kid my whole life," Shaun said, perplexed. "The kid sold drugs, he did whatever, but there's no way, Dad."

"I'm telling you, I think he had something to do with your brother's murder," Bob said. With that, he dropped his head on Shaun's shoulder, chest heaving, and began sobbing

for the first time since he heard of Jeffrey's disappearance. "Listen, this fucking piece of shit right here had something to do with your brother," Bob whispered into Shaun's ear, his voice low, insistent, and desperate.

"Listen, Dad," Shaun pleaded. "I'm telling *you*, there's no way."

To Shaun, the idea that Sicari had murdered his brother was preposterous. Sicari was a nobody, a skittish recluse from the shadows of the neighborhood who had always lived in fear of the Curleys. But Shaun had never seen his father cry before. And he respected his father's gut instincts, honed by a lifetime on these gritty streets. Maybe, Shaun thought, his father knew something.

Now, their arms around each other, Shaun cried, too.

"We've got to pull ourselves together," Bob said, struggling to regain control. "Talk to your brother Bobby, okay? But don't say nothin' to anybody else about what I've told you."

"Okay, Dad," Shaun replied. "Okay, okay."

Bobby, however, had already relayed his suspicions about Sicari to police, who assured him they would take care of the police work. The message, as Bobby recalled, was to take a seat on the sideline. Bobby wasn't interested in that option. This was his brother, and no one was going to tell him what to do.

Bobby consulted with Gonzalez. "Okay, forget the police, forget everything," Bobby said. "We're gonna figure this out." The friends became their own street detectives, circulating through the neighborhood, asking questions, and digging deeper into this murky figure named Charles Jaynes.

Sicari took a break from passing out fliers and returned home. Wayne Garber, who lived above him, was heading out the door as Sicari approached the building.

"Garber, what's up?" Sicari said.

"What's going on?" Garber answered.

"Did you hear little Jeffrey's gone?"

"No, what are you talking about?" Garber asked.

"Little Jeffrey's missing," Sicari repeated. "I'll be going back down to the mother's house and help them put up fliers and stuff."

A few minutes later, Sicari felt his beeper vibrate with an urgent page from Detective Nagle.

"Sal, can I speak with you at the station?" Nagle asked when Sicari returned the call. Sicari agreed, and Nagle dispatched two detectives to pick him up. Like Sullivan, Nagle sensed Sicari might have valuable information he hadn't offered. And he was bothered by an evasive phone conversation he had just finished with Charles Jaynes.

The exchange began when Jaynes returned a page from an unfamiliar number. When Nagle answered and identified himself as a police officer, Jaynes apologized for dialing the wrong person.

"No, you didn't," Nagle answered. "Could you come to the Cambridge police station to answer a few questions?"

"Why do you want to speak to me?" Jaynes asked.

"It's regarding a ten-year-old boy named Jeff Curley."

"I don't know any Jeff Curley."

"Where are you?" Nagle pressed.

"I'm working in Dunkin' Donuts."

"Okay, which Dunkin' Donuts?"

"In Brockton," Jaynes replied. "I can't come to Cambridge. I'm working a double shift."

Back and forth the pair went. Jaynes tried to assure Nagle he would call the next day, but the detective relayed his concerns to his supervisor, Deputy Superintendent Thomas O'Connor.

"I don't know where this kid Jeffrey is, but we have to make it top priority," Nagle said. "Right now it has Lester Sullivan's interest, and it has mine, too."

Top city management agreed to ask for outside help. Within hours, the Massachusetts State Police, Federal Bureau of Investigation, and National Guard committed personnel and resources, including uniformed officers, detectives, helicopters,

and dogs. The news media's interest also grew exponentially. Dozens of reporters had begun gathering outside the house, and by midafternoon, local television trucks had secured the few remaining parking spaces near the home. Microphones and notebooks seemed to be everywhere, and Jeffrey Curley's name, as well as his Little League picture, began appearing regularly on TV throughout Greater Boston. By now, the hunt for a missing ten-year-old, unseen for only twenty-four hours, had become the most intensive investigation in the city's history.

Bob Curley continued to circulate outside the condo, doling out encouragement despite his certainty that Jeffrey was gone. After another obligatory hug, he stopped himself, shaken by the encounter with Sicari and by his own bleak acknowledgment of the worst. This is not fucking happening, he told himself. I can't think here. I don't know who to listen to. The best thing right now is to try to do something normal. With that, Bob trudged to Inman Square, where he sat alone on a stool at a coffee shop, a broken, disbelieving father in a world where every street corner was familiar but every painful emotion was now devastatingly new.

Barbara felt overwhelmed by similar emotions as she sat by the window, surrounded by well-meaning family and friends but unreachable in the depth of her suffering. She had left the seat only briefly during the day, afraid she might miss Jeffrey's return. Her thoughts had not yet turned to murder, but she seriously considered the likelihood that her child had been kidnapped. And in her heart, Barbara also considered the terrifying possibility that Jeffrey had been raped. I wonder if he's calling for me, Barbara thought. He must be cold. He must be hungry. Oh my God, he only had shorts and a shirt on.

As she agonized, an unending stream of food and drink arrived at the house, as did a steady flow of guests—some known, many not—whom Barbara's sisters screened before admitting them. The phone rang constantly. Reporters from all of the Boston media outlets asked for interviews, and Francine's work supervisor even called to report that his psychic believed Jeffrey was alive. Next door, a fight broke out at the

Windsor Tap, where an innocent patron was assaulted because he seemed suspicious. The wife of the beaten man tried to broker a truce, only to be dispatched to a hospital emergency room with injuries of her own.

Inside the condo, the Curley family had reached a lull, their energies sapped by the long search, the lack of leads, and the relentless, circuslike frenzy. For a few moments, they savored a weary, needed, midafternoon silence.

Suddenly, the front door burst open, the quiet shattered by a shrill, shrieking cry. "Barbara! Barbara!" a woman screamed. The family bolted upright from the couch and the chairs, startled but hopeful that this could be a thunderclap of happy news. The woman's next words, however, served only to crush the family with their bland and unintentional cruelty. "Barbara, I just heard," the woman said. "I'm so sorry." Deflated and despondent, the family sank back in their seats.

As they did, Sicari climbed into the back of a Cambridge police cruiser for the short ride to headquarters, where Nagle asked him to settle into a chair in the Grainger Room, an interrogation and meeting area furnished with a long oval table, a television and videocassette player, and a blackboard. The third-floor corner room, named for a former police chief, was fitted with three large windows whose architectural grace had been compromised long ago by iron grates. The bars were installed in the late 1960s after Cambridge activists targeted the police station in a protest against the Vietnam War.

Nagle now felt in his gut that something criminal had happened to Jeffrey Curley. "I was willing to be wrong, I would love to be wrong, but I was suspicious," he said later. Nagle sat opposite Sicari, who seemed as eager as ever to cooperate. This time, for the record, Nagle told one of his detectives to take notes as he asked Sicari to recount his last encounter with Jeffrey.

Sicari revisited familiar ground: He had seen Jeffrey about 3:00 P.M. the day before; the boy had threatened him with a Rottweiler; he had seen Jeffrey enter his grandmother's house. Then, Sicari added even more about Jaynes, whom he said had

been sitting with Jeffrey in his Cadillac two weeks before. Sicari confided that he had taken Jeffrey aside afterward. "I told him he should go home and shouldn't be hanging with older people," Sicari said. He also told Jaynes "it didn't look right" to be in the company of young boys.

Nagle nodded, invited Sicari to continue, and then listened as Sicari spoke at unsolicited length about Jaynes's supposed female interests. "He made sure that I knew that Jaynes has this girlfriend and that girlfriend," Nagle recalled. "I mean, he's pounding away at these girlfriends. And I'm starting to go, The guy's three hundred pounds, and he's telling me how many girlfriends he has? Are these two gay? Is there something else going on here?"

Despite his unease, Nagle could not hold Sicari. No evidence had surfaced to connect him with Jeffrey's disappearance. And besides, Sicari had provided police with what little information they had about Jeffrey's activities the previous afternoon. Nagle thanked Sicari for his cooperation.

"If you need any more help or questions," Sicari said, "you can reach me on my beeper. I'll call you back."

Sicari was back at the Curley condo in fifteen minutes. And as he picked up a stack of fliers, Sicari heard his name at the head of the driveway. Bobby Curley, Gonzalez, and another friend beckoned to him from Curley's car, a year-old Toyota Camry.

"Hey, Salvi," Bobby yelled. "We're going over to Somerville. We're gonna hang up some of these fliers. Come on!"

Eager to appear helpful, Sicari quickly worked his way through the crowd and took a seat in the rear. To Sicari's left sat Gonzalez. In the front passenger seat, staring straight ahead, loomed Manny, an older friend of Barbara's whom everyone called "the Portugee." No one spoke until the police and volunteers had vanished into the background. In the meantime, another car with Bobby's friends had pulled in behind them.

Bobby, cocking his head toward the rearview mirror, locked eyes on Sicari and asked, "Who's this Charles Jaynes? Where is he? Do you have his phone number?"

"I only got a pager number," Sicari answered. "That's all I got."

Bobby, Manny, and Gonzalez looked at each other, then at Sicari, unconvinced that he had told the truth. Bobby stared again at the mirror. By now, he had shed any pretense of calm, considered restraint. The time had come to find Jeffrey as quickly as possible—and by whatever means necessary.

"Salvi, listen," Bobby said with a short sigh, the menace in his streetwise voice as clear as the anger in his eyes. "You're gonna take us to Charles Jaynes, or we're gonna beat the fucking shit out of you, motherfucker, until you wish you were dead."

"Look, no problem," Sicari said. "All I want is to find Jeff. But all I got is a pager number."

Bobby maneuvered the Camry through heavy afternoon traffic toward the Cambridge courthouse, where he knew of a sidewalk pay phone that accepted incoming calls. Sicari was told to page Jaynes and wait for a reply. He was also given strict instructions not to mention Jeffrey during the conversation.

Bobby parked the car beside the phone, where Gonzalez stood close to Sicari as he dialed Jaynes three times.

"Something's not right with this fucking kid," Bobby said to Manny, shaking his head. The wait continued for several minutes.

Finally, the phone rang. It was Jaynes.

"Hello, who's this?" Jaynes asked.

Sicari, in a nervous staccato, blurted out a warning. "They think we had something to do with Jeff," he said, his rushed words cascading into each other. "I don't know what's going on."

Gonzalez lunged, but Sicari slammed down the phone before he could grab the receiver. Gonzalez, livid, slapped Sicari hard across an ear. "Salvi, what the fuck are you doing?" he screamed. "What is going on? We told you not to say nothing about Jeff."

Gonzalez pushed Sicari back into the car.

"What was that?" Bobby yelled at Sicari. "Some kind of code for him to get his shit together?"

Sicari stammered again that he only wanted to help, but Bobby and the others had turned a corner. They were

now convinced that Sicari knew something about Jeffrey's disappearance.

"Listen, motherfucker, you better bring us to this kid Jaynes right now, or you're gonna be one dead piece of meat," Bobby muttered. "I want to know where he's at."

"Sure, sure," Sicari said, shaking. "We can find him at this car dealership in Newton."

In Bobby's mind, Jeffrey was not dead. He pictured Jeffrey sitting alone in a locked apartment, possibly sexually molested, passing time in captivity with a PlayStation computer game. During the twenty-minute drive to Newton, he planned his next move. Jaynes would be forced to lead them to Jeffrey. But Jaynes and Sicari would not outlive the day. For that purpose, concealed inside his leather jacket, Bobby had placed a loaded .38-caliber snub-nosed revolver.

Bobby reached Honda Village by 5:00 P.M., just in time for late-afternoon, rush-hour madness. Heavy traffic streamed in both directions as hundreds of bumper-to-bumper commuters merged on and off the nearby turnpike. With Sicari in tow, Bobby and his friends walked to the rear of the dealership, where a short, steep ramp descended into the gloomy basement and Kojak's reconditioning business.

"Okay, Salvi, where's this fucking kid?" Bobby asked, squinting as he scanned from wall to concrete wall.

Sicari pointed to Jaynes, who was busy cleaning a car. "That's him, right there."

Bobby moved toward Jaynes, who looked up just as Bobby locked his right arm around Jaynes's shoulders. "Come on, you're coming with me," Bobby said. "We're going for a walk."

"What's this about?" Jaynes sputtered.

"Don't worry about it," Bobby answered. "We're just gonna talk to you."

As they walked, Jaynes's confusion changed to fear. Bobby pressed the barrel of the gun into Jaynes's side, where a thick, limp roll of fat helped hide the weapon.

As Bobby half led, half pushed Jaynes up the ramp, Gonzalez thrust one of the fliers in Jaynes's startled face.

"You seen this little kid, motherfucker?" Bobby snarled quietly.

"I don't know. I haven't seen him. I don't know," Jaynes said.

"We're gonna find out about that," Bobby said, steering Jaynes around the back of the dealership and toward the Camry parked out front.

By now, Jaynes had begun crying loudly enough to attract attention from both the people inside Honda Village and the pedestrians on the street. An employee, watching the commotion, placed a 911 call to Newton police.

Sicari started to speak, but Gonzalez quickly cut him off.

"Salvi, shut the fuck up!" he snapped. "You don't say nothing! You're done! Just shut your mouth and let's go."

When they reached the car, Gonzalez opened the rear passenger door. "Get in!" he barked to Jaynes.

Jaynes bellowed for help, pushing back as Bobby and Gonzalez struggled to force him into the Camry.

"They've got a gun!" Jaynes wailed. "They're going to kill me!"

By now, the crowd had grown to forty people, who stood dumbstruck and frozen as they witnessed an attempted kidnapping in broad daylight on a busy street.

"This fucking kid had something to do with my brother not being around," Bobby shouted. "Anybody that comes near me, I'm gonna hurt you. Stay away!"

No one dared help Jaynes.

Gonzalez and Bobby pushed and pulled, screaming at their quarry and tugging furiously on his arms. Just then, a Newton police cruiser, speeding the wrong way and blaring its siren, braked to a squealing stop. Officer John Geary, a twenty-year veteran of the force, had been on routine patrol when he was dispatched to Honda Village. As Geary stepped out of his cruiser, he found himself outnumbered by a cluster of angry, violent, determined men.

"Freeze! Stay where you are!" ordered Geary, who immediately called for backup.

"Help me! Help me!" Jaynes pleaded. "They're trying to grab me! I didn't do anything! I haven't seen him for weeks!"

Geary had no idea what Jaynes meant.

"He did it!" someone yelled. "He kidnapped the Curley kid!"

Geary had not heard of Jeffrey's disappearance, but he saw that Jaynes was in trouble and pulled him away from his attackers. As he did, Bobby and the others pressed menacingly toward Geary, reaching for Jaynes and forcing the officer to back up toward a wall.

"We're gonna get you, you son of a bitch!" one of them thundered at Jaynes.

"We want him!" another yelled. "We're gonna get him! We're gonna take him!"

Within minutes, four more Newton cruisers arrived, and Geary had the reinforcements he needed. But during the confusion, before the police could restore order, Gonzalez hid Bobby's gun in the Camry and reparked the car down the street.

Geary isolated Jaynes, who told the officer he had no idea why he had been targeted. Minutes later, when Geary spoke to Bobby, he learned that they suspected Jaynes of kidnapping Jeffrey. Geary called Cambridge detectives, who asked that Jaynes be held for questioning. Geary ran a criminal check, saw the outstanding warrants, and handcuffed Jaynes on the spot. Bobby, his friends, and Sicari were told to follow police to headquarters, where investigators would begin to sort out the mess. "If you don't cooperate," Geary told Bobby, "we could possibly take out charges and arrest you for attempted kidnapping."

On the two-mile ride to the station, Jaynes continued to plead ignorance. "I don't know what they're talking about," he told Geary, shaking with anxiety. "I haven't seen that kid in weeks." At headquarters, Newton police placed Jaynes in a holding cell and waited for Cambridge detectives to arrive for a joint interview. Meanwhile, in the second-floor detectives' office, Sicari began to edge away from Bobby and the others.

"You know, you should be happy," Geary said to Sicari. "We've got this guy Jaynes. You guys—"

"I'm not with them!" Sicari shot back, referring to the Curley group. "They forced me to come over here and look for Jaynes. I'm Jaynes's friend."

Geary was surprised but didn't betray his confusion. "Well, you should feel lucky you're not Mr. Jaynes then," he said. "It looks like there's some serious charges. Good thing you're not involved in that."

Sicari turned white. "What do you think's gonna happen?" he asked.

"There's a missing person," Geary replied. "If there's evidence to hold Jaynes on kidnapping, we'll do an investigation. We'll get a statement from him, if possible, and see if he implicates anyone else."

"What's gonna happen if he says something?" Sicari added.

"If the evidence proves it, they'll be arrested," Geary said.

Sicari abruptly stopped talking.

Jaynes, in the meantime, sat alone in a cell, where he awaited a visit from Cambridge detectives John Fulkerson and Brian Branley and State Trooper Alan Hunte. Fulkerson, who lived two blocks from the Curleys, had just begun his night shift when he was briefed about Jeffrey's disappearance. He had suspected something was afoot when he awoke early that afternoon and saw helicopters circling the neighborhood. Still, when he arrived in Newton, Fulkerson's only information about Jaynes was that he had allegedly taken Jeffrey for rides in his Cadillac. "What happened, who did it, we weren't even close at the time, and we didn't have any ideas," recalled Fulkerson, thirty-four, a seven-year veteran of the force. "We figured he might know something, but we didn't know what he knew."

Jaynes was removed from the cell and brought to a conference room, where Fulkerson read him his Miranda rights and, wasting no time, asked whether he knew Jeffrey Curley. Jaynes said he had met Jeffrey in July in front of Sicari's apartment and that he had last seen the boy on Monday, three days

before, about 2:30 P.M. outside the Harrington School. "I picked him up and gave him a short ride to near his house," Jaynes elaborated. "I saw Sal, so Jeffrey got out, and Sicari got into my car. That's the last time I saw Jeffrey." When asked about his relationship with Jeffrey, Jaynes told police, "Just friends."

His story began to unravel when Fulkerson asked for an outline of the previous day. Jaynes said he had stopped at Sicari's apartment in the early afternoon, driven to the Boston Public Library to visit Laurie Pistorino, and then taken Sicari to Honda Village, where they worked for a few hours.

So far, his story matched Sicari's.

After leaving Honda Village at 8:30 P.M., Jaynes continued, he and Sicari drove to New Hampshire and stopped at the first rest area across the border from Massachusetts. There, they parked in a dark, rear corner of the lot, near a Dumpster and far away from the "Welcome to New Hampshire" sign. Jaynes said they drank a few beers, moved to the backseat, "cuddled," and had sex before falling asleep until 7:30 A.M. At that time, Jaynes added, he took Sicari back to Cambridge.

Fulkerson was convinced that Jaynes was lying. At one point, Fulkerson noted, Jaynes denied renting an apartment in New Hampshire. The detective now began asking questions about Jeffrey, whom Jaynes dismissed as "a tagalong little kid" who "loved to run around the lot" at Honda Village. Jaynes admitted that Jeffrey visited the dealership often and that he had treated the boy to dinner at Vinny Testa's, bought him a bike, and even given him $10.

"How can you afford to be so generous to a 'tagalong little kid'?" Jaynes was asked.

"I don't know. I just can," he replied.

Jaynes stressed that he always brought Jeffrey home before 9:00 P.M. "so there wouldn't be any problem with Jeffrey's mother." Barbara did not know of their friendship, Jaynes said, and he had "never thought of asking permission."

"Even though Jeffrey was only ten years old?" the detectives asked.

"No," Jaynes replied tersely.

Ninety minutes after the interview began, Jaynes stopped answering questions. "I think I should now have my attorney here," he said.

The detectives gathered their notes and materials. As Jaynes rose to return to the holding cell, he left police with a startling and mysterious statement: "I want to tell you something about Sal, but I want my attorney present. I could help you guys find Jeffrey." That cryptic comment would be the last communication between the police and Jaynes, whose attorney arrived shortly to introduce himself to a polite but depressed client.

"I don't think he grasped the significance of what was going on around him," said Robert Jubinville, his lawyer and a dapper former State Police detective. "I think it's the first time he had ever been in a jail cell." Jubinville huddled with Jaynes, who asked simple questions about the process and what to expect next. At this point, Jaynes had only been charged with warrant violations.

By now, John McEvoy, the district attorney's first deputy, had traveled to Newton for an update on the high-profile, fast-moving investigation. If any deal were to be made in exchange for information, McEvoy was in position to make that happen. After conferring with his client, Jubinville approached McEvoy with a proposition: "John, give him a second. He'll tell you that Sicari did it, and he'll show you where the body is." Suddenly, authorities had crossed a grim threshold. What began as a routine search for a missing boy had now vaulted into a murder investigation. But whether Jaynes could be trusted, and whether Sicari had played a role in Jeffrey's disappearance, remained gaping, unanswered questions.

McEvoy, a tough, career prosecutor, began to consider Jubinville's offer, the defense attorney recalled. However, McEvoy had no need to be hasty. Jaynes was behind bars for the night, and Sicari was undergoing yet another round of questioning in Cambridge. Sicari had been whisked back to the Grainger

Room about 7:00 P.M., after Cambridge police, concerned for his safety and eager for another interview, dispatched a cruiser to Newton to retrieve their prize witness.

Sicari, who also wished to distance himself from Bobby Curley, agreed to reacquaint himself with Detective Sergeant Nagle. A former boxer and East Cambridge native, Nagle was nothing if not direct. And during this session with Sicari, his third of the day, he intended to determine conclusively if Sicari had been lying. Nagle read him his Miranda rights with another Cambridge officer and an FBI agent present, then opened with a series of simple questions: What's your name? Your date of birth? Your home address? How far did you go in school?

The sergeant then asked Sicari, again, to begin at the beginning: When did you last see Jeffrey? What happened next? What did you and Jaynes do in New Hampshire? When did you come back? This time, Nagle also asked Sicari to work backward from his visit to Manchester. At another point, he asked Sicari to talk about the middle of the evening. "If you're lying, you're going to be off," Nagle said later.

Nagle had never met Sicari before this day, but the detective felt he knew him. Nagle also had grown up and been battle-tested in the neighborhood. Although East Cambridge was within easy reach of the city's "lace-curtain" Irish, the cultural separation sometimes seemed enormous. "You fought every day going to school. You fought every day coming home," Nagle said. "So, you sort of know people. And I thought Sicari was a liar."

Despite that judgment, Nagle interviewed Sicari calmly. After all, Sicari was the best witness he had, and there was no sense in antagonizing him at this stage of the investigation. Indeed, Sicari was free to leave at any time, although it is unclear if he realized his options.

After a long round of questioning, Nagle ordered sodas for everyone in the room, and Sicari asked permission to phone his mother.

"I'm helping the police," Sicari told her at 8:50 P.M. "I'm fine, Ma. I'll be home in a while. I don't need you to come down."

Afterward, Sicari was asked if he would submit to a polygraph test by FBI Special Agent Thomas Donlan III.

"It's up to you, Sal," Nagle said. "It's your call."

"Oh, yeah, I'll do it. I'll do it," Sicari answered nonchalantly.

His willingness hurt him. When Sicari denied causing Jeff's disappearance or knowing where Jeffrey was located at that moment, the polygraph indicated he was lying. Sicari was unaware of the results.

Immediately after the exam, he told Donlan that Jaynes was a pedophile and had wanted to give Jeffrey $50 in exchange for sex. On the previous day, Sicari continued, Jaynes had disappeared several times into an upstairs area at Honda Village. Sicari did not see Jeffrey, he said ominously, but he knew something had happened to him.

By this time, Nagle had received critical, new evidence against Sicari. During a search of Jaynes's car at Newton police headquarters, officers discovered a receipt for concrete and lime, complete with time of purchase, from The Home Depot in Somerville. They also found a second timed receipt, from Bradlees in Watertown, for a Rubbermaid container. Nagle ordered detectives to view the corresponding store-surveillance tapes, which showed Sicari and Jaynes together at the registers. Now, conclusively, Nagle knew that Sicari had lied to him.

The time had come to confront Sicari. But when Nagle reentered the room, he saw Sicari standing, crying uncontrollably, and gasping for air. Donlan asked Sicari to tell Nagle what he had just said.

"I feel something may have happened to Jeffrey," repeated Sicari, who was hyperventilating.

"Whoa, what's the matter, Sal?" Nagle said. "What do you mean something happened to Jeff?"

"Charles Jaynes kept leaving when we were cleaning cars and going upstairs," Sicari said. "Charlie must have done something."

Nagle cut through the smokescreen.

"Sal, have I been with you three or four times during the course of the day?"

"Yeah."

"Have I treated you right?"

"Yeah."

Nagle walked toward Sicari. Pausing for effect, he raised his voice for the first time.

"Then why," he yelled, "are you jerking me around!"

"I'm not! I'm not!" Sicari answered.

"Yes, you are! Tell me about the bag of lime that you bought at Home Depot in Somerville at 10:21 P.M.!"

Immediately, Sicari stopped crying. An emotional wreck only seconds before, Sicari suddenly turned cold and controlled.

"Fuck it!" he said. "Lock me up!"

Nagle, too, reversed roles. "Sal," he asked solicitously, "what would I be locking you up for?"

Sicari did not answer. Instead, he retreated to one of the windows. Nagle, likewise, remained quiet as Sicari thought through his options: Do I save myself? Do I give up Jaynes? Do I have my lies together? What do I do? "The worst thing I could have done was get up and put the cuffs on him," Nagle recalled. "I knew there was more to this investigation."

After fifteen minutes of silence, Nagle emerged from the Grainger Room to find Fulkerson, who had just arrived from Newton. Following a quick briefing, Fulkerson asked permission to question Sicari with State Trooper Hunte.

"Yeah, go ahead," Nagle said.

Fulkerson walked into the room at 12:45 A.M. to find Sicari staring toward Central Square from one of the windows, his body obscured by a set of old, vertical window blinds draped over his back. Fulkerson, relaxed and empathetic, put a hand on Sicari's shoulder.

"Sal, my name's John Fulkerson. I'm a detective here in Cambridge. Would you mind sitting down and talking?"

Sicari wheeled toward Fulkerson.

"Just lock me up! I'm guilty," Sicari snapped. "Get my room ready. I'm guilty."

Then, just as quickly, Sicari reverted to silence.

"I'd just like to ask you a couple of questions," Fulkerson said quietly.

Several minutes later, Sicari walked slowly to the table and sat to Fulkerson's right. He pushed back, slouched in his chair, folded his hands, and buried his head in the hood of his sweatshirt. Fulkerson waited patiently for Sicari to speak, and he was prepared to wait all night. He knew the investigation had turned toward murder, and he sensed that Sicari was the weaker, more vulnerable link.

"I know what's going on. You could help us out with this," the detective told Sicari. "Just relax. Tell us what happened. Let's get this off your chest."

Fulkerson put his arm around Sicari, a gesture from someone who felt instinctively that Sicari wanted to talk. "That hard-guy stuff you see on TV—the good-cop, bad-cop stuff—that really doesn't work," Fulkerson said later. "I tried to be as compassionate as possible. The longer that he thinks he's your friend, and the longer that you can relate to him, the more information you're going to get. I knew it was too late for Jeffrey Curley, but now I was focused on getting these guys to justice."

Fulkerson told Sicari he had just come from Newton and had spoken with Jaynes. He did not disclose what Jaynes had said, but Fulkerson had caught Sicari's attention. "He knew it was bad for him," Fulkerson said. Finally, Fulkerson's strategy paid dividends. After twenty minutes of silence, after the detective's muted questions and gentle persuasion, Sicari began to cry. He lifted his chin, sat bolt upright, and looked Fulkerson directly in the eye.

"Okay, I'll tell you," he said. "I'm guilty, but I didn't kill Jeff Curley. Charlie did."

"Okay, start at the beginning, Sal," Fulkerson said.

Sicari outlined the previous thirty-six hours in microscopic detail. He walked police through the stop at Jeffrey's

grandmother's house, the struggle in the car, the Rubbermaid purchase, the sickening scenes of molestation in Manchester, and the disposal of Jeffrey's body. As Sicari spoke, Fulkerson asked very few questions. He interrupted, gently, only when he or Trooper Hunte were confused or needed further explanation. Otherwise, the officers listened with a cool, professional detachment that masked an inner horror. "He just went on and on," Fulkerson said.

Sicari told the detectives what they could find in the Manchester apartment. The Boston College jersey would be next to the couch, he said. The Coors bottle would be in the kitchen, along with the waist button and the clothing label that Jaynes had kept as trophies. *Lion King* toys and paraphernalia would be everywhere.

This time, Fulkerson believed Sicari. "There was some discussion among us afterward whether he was more involved in the murder or not," Fulkerson recalled. "But it was just the way he was telling us. He was looking me in the eye; there was no hesitation. I believed him all the way."

The time was 3:00 A.M., and Fulkerson asked Sicari if he would ride with him to New Hampshire and Maine, where police would begin their search immediately.

"Are you willing to show us where you dumped him into the water?" Fulkerson asked.

"I'll go with you guys," Sicari replied. "But I won't go with anybody else."

With that, Fulkerson placed Sicari in handcuffs, charged him with the murder of Jeffrey Curley, and escorted him downstairs to the booking room, a small rectangular space tucked behind the first-floor reception area. As Sicari was channeled through a routine checklist of fingerprints, photographs, and standard questions, he seemed only marginally aware of his situation.

"How much time do you get for a murder charge?" Sicari asked George Sabbey, the booking officer.

"I don't know," Sabbey replied matter-of-factly, his eyes focused on the arrest report.

"I should get a few years knocked off for telling you guys I know where the body's at," Sicari said.

No response.

Standing before the Plexiglas divider that separated him from Sabbey, Sicari appeared completely at ease. He grinned, he joked, he answered questions quietly and politely, and he watched Sabbey work with almost childlike interest. He also handed over an earring, belt, pager, set of keys, and seventy-one cents in cash.

After Lieutenant Garfield Morrison, the overnight supervisor, read Sicari his rights, the suspect posed a stunning question. Would the charge, he asked, mean he no longer would be required to attend meetings for alcohol and abuse therapy? Sicari looked quizzically at Morrison, who kept his gaze trained downward. "Sal," Morrison said slowly, "I don't think you have to worry about that. I don't think you have to worry about that at all."

Fulkerson entered the room at 4:15 A.M. and let Sicari make one final call to his mother. Incredibly, he included a joke in the message. His booking number, he told her with a smile—his "lucky number"—was 37735.

"Come on, Sal. Let's go," Fulkerson said.

As Sicari hurtled north in an unmarked State Police car, Nagle drove home on deserted city streets. He had been up for nearly twenty-four hours, during which he had watched a missing-child report turn into the biggest murder investigation the city had ever conducted. Nagle's father also had been a homicide detective, one whose resume included the infamous Boston Strangler case. So, for Nagle, the gruesome particulars of such a job had long been familiar. Even as a kid, he recalled, police talk would dominate discussion around the Thanksgiving table. But something about the Curley case had touched him more than others. When he arrived home, his wife could sense something was wrong as she prepared to leave for work.

Nagle went straight to bed. When he awoke a few hours later, he noticed the strangest thing. One of his Rottweilers, a 150-pounder named Nitro, was curled near him on the bed. The sight confused Nagle because his dogs were banned from

the bedroom. But then, lying alone in the morning, Nagle recalled the events of the previous day. And the dog's presence, a
protective one, suddenly made sense. "I must have been crying," he said.

———

4

The Long
Journey Home

WHILE DETECTIVES interviewed Sicari, much of the Curley family searched for Jeffrey deep into the night. Barbara clung desperately to a fading belief that her son was alive. Most of the siblings, in-laws, and friends who ventured in and out of the tense, edgy condo that evening shared her stubborn faith.

When he returned home from Newton, Bobby updated his father that Jaynes had been arrested, but they both continued to believe that Sicari was complicit. Little information had come from Cambridge police headquarters during the lengthy and complicated interrogation. Until authorities knew exactly where they stood, they were reluctant to share any news that might raise or dash the family's hopes.

Part of the family fanned out toward the Museum of Science in Cambridge, near the Charles River, where they used flashlights to peer into abandoned buildings and patrol a confusing maze of new, nearby construction. Francine joined that group, despite a sore ankle. Overhead, the whir of police helicopters equipped with high-intensity lights and infrared heat sensors heightened the sense of emergency.

Bob, his brother John, and Bobby Jr. headed in another direction, toward Union Square in Somerville, to explore a ramshackle building filled with old radiators, where teenagers and young men from the neighborhood were known to drink

and take drugs. Bob sat in John's truck while his brother and son scoured the lot. The scattershot nature of the search, particularly here in Somerville, seemed to Bob nothing more than the futile, desperate act of a family holding out for a million-to-one strike. We're just fucking wasting our time, he said to himself, staring at an endless stream of taillights in Union Square. We're just shoveling shit against the tide. Elsewhere, Shaun busily canvassed Broadway and other major streets in East Cambridge, tacking fliers on the few poles without them and distributing others to late-night pedestrians, the sober and the not-so-sober.

By midnight, most of the family had returned to the condo, where they tried to buoy each other's spirits before leaving for their separate homes until morning. Bob remained at the house with a few others. Barbara, as always, kept vigil at the driveway window. "I just couldn't leave," Barbara recalled. "I was just kind of frozen there for the longest time, until Bob couldn't take it anymore."

Bob pleaded with Barbara to sleep, concerned that she might collapse, physically and mentally, if she did not rest for a few hours. "Barbara, you haven't slept in a couple of days," he said. "You have to go upstairs and try to lay down. When Jeff comes home, you're not going to want him to see you like this." Barbara agreed and pulled herself slowly upstairs, where she lay down for the first time since Jeffrey had disappeared, in the same bed where Jeffrey had slept beside her.

Bob did not believe his words of hope, and he did not sleep, although a deep stillness had descended over the house. His thoughts, undistracted in the dead of night, revolved endlessly around the what-ifs and the might-have-beens for a father confronted with the unimaginable. Fear and self-reproach had been clamoring for Bob's attention when the phone rang at 3:00 A.M. On the other end was a Cambridge police officer. There was bad news, he said, and he wanted to send a priest. The details would wait.

When the knock came fifteen minutes later, four sets of hands reached to open the door from inside. Then, in a soft,

somber tone, the devastating words were spoken: Jeffrey had been murdered. Bedlam erupted. Shouts mingled with sobs, rage with grief, anger with loss. Shaun screeched in agony, and Bobby ran screaming from the house to Sicari's apartment building, where he howled in anguish on the sidewalk below.

Bob lowered his head and cried, his instincts confirmed and his little son gone. But while pain racked Bob and all those around him, he realized he still had work to do. Barbara lay sleeping upstairs, and Bob knew he must be the one to deliver the news. He walked quietly into the darkened room, sat gently on the edge of the bed, and held the woman who had been his wife for nineteen years. Barbara stirred, her brief slumber broken by the embrace.

"Barbara, Barbara," Bob said in a whisper. "Salvi's confessed. They murdered our baby."

The words cut through the fog of Barbara's drowsiness. Her eyes widened in shock, then horror, and she flailed at Bob with her fists.

"You're lying!" she cried. "You're lying!"

"No, Barbara, I'm not. I'm not," Bob answered, cradling her in his arms. "Our baby's dead."

Barbara sobbed uncontrollably, her soul ravaged by the searing realization that her child had been snatched away, never to return, in an act that was at once unbelievable and irreversible. Her face, transformed and terrified, became a mirror of the depths of human suffering.

Bob let her cry, uninterrupted, until the spasms began to subside.

"What can I do?" he asked quietly. "What can I do?"

Through her grief, Barbara suddenly feared that her sons might hurt others or themselves, tragically compounding the murder's nightmare.

"Make sure that Bobby and Shaun are okay, that they don't go crazy. Right now, I can't deal with anybody," Barbara said. "And, Bob, please, whatever you do, don't let anybody ever forget who Jeffrey John Curley was."

Bob nodded and returned to the living room, where more of the family had gathered and where the sounds of mourning would last long past the dawn.

Francine was among the new arrivals, still recovering from the shock of a 3:30 A.M. phone call in which a woman's unrecognizable voice had screamed that Jeffrey was dead. Through the crying, she eventually identified the caller as her sister Margaret, who had relayed the terrible news while attached to a dialysis machine. Francine drove Margaret's husband, Charlie Francis, to Barbara's condo. His household had been hit particularly hard by the news. Charlie was Barbara's brother, and his wife was Bob and Francine's sister.

As the Curleys gathered to grieve, Sicari sat beside Fulkerson in the rear of a moving State Police car, his hands cuffed and attached to waist chains. The search had now officially shifted to the many, meandering waterways of southern New Hampshire and Maine, and its object from a missing child to a ten-year-old's body. Sicari appeared eager to cooperate and chatted nearly nonstop with Fulkerson. "Sal was talking with me just like a normal conversation, or as normal a conversation as it could be with someone who was just involved in killing a little boy," Fulkerson recalled.

The objective was to retrace the route that Jaynes and Sicari had taken from Manchester to the river where Jeffrey's body was dumped. The police realized the task was daunting, if not impossible: Sicari had little geographic knowledge of New Hampshire and Maine, and his journey with Jaynes had been done at night on unfamiliar roads.

Fulkerson played on the reservoir of trust he had developed during questioning. The pair talked easily all the way to Manchester, touching on family history and likes and dislikes; they even shared jokes. When they stopped at a Dunkin' Donuts at 5:00 A.M., Sicari kidded about how cops treat the place like a second home. Fulkerson returned the banter. When Sicari told him he never graduated from high school because he had

failed gym class, Fulkerson broke into a laugh, asking, "How can that happen?"

"We talked about sports, football, and the fact that he liked dogs," Fulkerson said. "It seemed like he had been an abused kid, that he just wanted to be normal and do normal kid things, and that he didn't have the means to do it." Sicari spoke of his brother, who had been arrested for raping a ten-year-old and of the physical and emotional pain he had suffered at the hands of his mother and her boyfriends. "He made it seem, too, that Jaynes was the real bad guy," Fulkerson said. The detective kept his judgments to himself. "As much as I wanted to hate the guy, my goal was to get Jeffrey Curley's body back to his family. I knew it would torture the family if we didn't."

The police passed through Manchester and continued to Concord. Sicari was unsure where he and Jaynes had left the interstate to head toward Portsmouth, but he had an idea. "I remember four and sixteen," he said. "There was a state seal on a sign that looks like a badge." The police exited when they spotted a highway sign for Route 4. By 6:00 A.M., they had arrived in Epping, New Hampshire, about forty miles away, where Sicari was escorted to a bathroom at another Dunkin' Donuts. Then, on to Dover, twenty miles to the north. Back again to Epping. And, finally, on to Portsmouth.

All along the circuitous route, Sicari tried in vain to remember the bridge and the road where he and Jaynes had stopped. They scouted more than a dozen locations. "We drove along the water, along rivers, and notified different police departments up there," Fulkerson said. "We just kept riding around, and he kept describing the site to us: a white house on the right-hand side of the river, a bridge, a certain type of railing that they rested the Rubbermaid container on, and a light going on at the house." In Portsmouth, Sicari finally recognized his surroundings and directed police to the Dumpsters where Jeffrey's clothing had been discarded. Before leaving the city, they inspected more bridges, but Sicari was unable to identify any of them.

At 11:15 A.M., seven hours after they left Cambridge, Sicari returned to Massachusetts. He led police to the gas station where Jaynes had doused the rag, to the bicycle shop, and to the shops where Jeffrey had been forced into the Cadillac. "Charley killed him in the backseat," Sicari, exhausted, told the officers. "It took a long time for him to die." Police quickly examined the scene, took notes, and drove Sicari to Newton police headquarters, where he would be held until arraignment later in the day.

By now, the news of Jeffrey's killing dominated Boston's newspapers, television, and radio, and his Little League picture became an iconic image of the unimaginable. Reporters from around the country and Canada began making their way to Hampshire Street, where an impromptu shrine of flowers, candles, prayers, and stuffed animals, grew to shoulder height and stretched for nearly a city block.

Inside the condo, Bob struggled with emotions that tugged him in jarringly different directions. As a man, he needed to grieve. But for his shattered family, he felt compelled to be a rock of stability. "Bobby and Shaun were hurt, Barbara was hurt, everybody was hurt," Bob said. "I wasn't really concerned with myself. I was worried about everyone else. But what could I do? Jeff was gone, and he wasn't coming back." Despite the pain, Bob began to look ahead. Okay, we'll deal with this, he told himself. What are we going to do next? What's the next step? We've got to bring Jeff home.

But bringing Jeffrey home was becoming extraordinarily difficult—far more so than Bob had imagined. When he heard from police that Jeffrey's body had been ditched in New Hampshire or Maine, he assumed the container had been left somewhere off I-93. The startling truth came via a television news report, in which Bob saw police divers searching the churning tidal rivers near Portsmouth. The revelation hit Bob like a body blow. "This is fucking going from bad to worse," he said. "This can't be happening."

From exhaustion, despair, and a sudden, strangling fear, Bob's legs buckled, and he slumped unconscious to the floor. Nothing that preceded that moment had terrified him as much as the thought of never seeing Jeffrey again. And nothing would hurt him as much afterward.

Bob revived several seconds later, his siblings gathered around him, and struggled unsteadily to his feet. But when he sat down, his head in his hands, he did so as a broken, beaten, empty man. He figured the odds of retrieving Jeffrey's body were very long, if not impossible. By then, however, police from three states—Massachusetts, Maine, and New Hampshire— had already begun to mobilize and analyze the scraps of information provided by Sicari.

While the search intensified, Arthur Kelly, a Massachusetts attorney, received a phone call at his home forty miles north of Boston. An abduction and murder had occurred in Newton, he was told, and an arraignment would be held that afternoon. The son of a former Newton police officer, Kelly knew nothing about the case, but he was one of a few dozen lawyers statewide on the so-called murder list, from which he could be appointed to supplement work from his private practice. For representing Sicari, he would be paid about $54 an hour. "I don't even believe I paid attention to any news about a missing child," said Kelly, a stocky forty-two-year-old father of two small boys, five and three. "But when I drove up to the courthouse, and I saw a number of TV trucks, I knew this was something more significant than a typical murder case."

Kelly proceeded to a holding cell, where he introduced himself to a murder suspect who appeared calm, polite, and cooperative. Sicari felt that he had done the right thing by assisting police and trying to locate Jeffrey's body. "I think he was made to feel, from the officers involved, that he was a hero, that the family would be at rest, that they would know what happened to Jeffrey, and that, more importantly, he had nothing to do with the death of the child," Kelly said.

Sicari's new attorney delivered the news that, no, he was not considered a hero. Instead, the state's charge of first-degree murder showed he was considered nothing but a cold-blooded killer. "I think, to some extent, he felt betrayed," Kelly said.

But if Sicari felt duped by police, a small army of them now assembled in Newton to protect him. An angry, vocal, and dangerous crowd, including the Curley brothers, had gathered behind the courthouse to await Sicari's short walk from the police station. Jeffrey's family had yet to hear the full depravity of the crime. And although Bob tried to prepare his boys for the worst, he feared they might disrupt the courtroom or try to attack Sicari. "I don't want any outbursts, or any crying, or any wailing, or anything like that," Bob lectured his sons.

When Sicari emerged from the police station, a bullet-proof vest cinched tightly around his chest, the crowd surged toward him. Fearing a confrontation, a half dozen wide-eyed police surrounded, pushed, and hustled Sicari across the parking lot that separated the station from the court. "Why are you protecting him?" someone shouted. "Let us do our own punishment!"

Sicari avoided vigilante justice, but he was unable to es-cape a cluster of reporters who frantically elbowed their way through the crowd to confront him. "Why did you do it? Why?" one television reporter yelled, her microphone thrust toward the suspect. Sicari looked straight ahead and shuffled into the courthouse, where Assistant District Attorney David Yannetti waited to summarize the grisly evidence against him for the first time in public.

Yannetti had been summoned to the Cambridge police station the previous night by John McEvoy while Sicari was be-ing questioned. When he received the call, Yannetti was only slightly familiar with the case.

"Have you heard about the little boy?" McEvoy asked.

"Yeah, I remember seeing something about that on the news," said Yannetti, who lived in a tiny, third-floor apartment in Boston's North End. "What's up?"

"Why don't you come down to the Cambridge police station," McEvoy continued. "We've got two guys we're interested in, and one of them is on his way to Cambridge now."

The news had been merely "background noise" on television, Yannetti said, and he took notice only because the report concerned a possible crime in his jurisdiction. As he drove to Cambridge, Yannetti was not even sure he would be assigned the case.

Yannetti recognized many familiar faces when he walked into the detectives' bureau. He had worked with these officers before and chatted easily with them as they briefed him. Soon, Sicari had made his statement, and Yannetti began mental preparations for the arraignment.

After heading home for a few short hours of sleep, he put on a suit and traveled to Newton, where he saw a scene unlike any he had ever encountered. The buzzing, hostile crowd at Newton District Court stunned Yannetti—as did the throng of reporters. Only then did he grasp the magnitude of the case. "It was at that time I realized that this is going to be major news, and it's not going to be the type of case where the press shows up for the arraignment just because they have to," he recalled. "This was really over the top." For the only time in his career, Yannetti was escorted into the building by a protective ring of burly state troopers.

Inside, the small court was packed with the Curleys, their friends, and reporters jostling for the best seats. Sicari, handcuffed and expressionless, exuded an air of tough, untouchable composure as he faced the judge. Yannetti had never prosecuted a case in a courtroom atmosphere as intense as this one. Spectators dabbed tears from their eyes. Mothers held their children. And Yannetti, knowing what was to come, studied his notes and rehearsed his arguments as he prepared to sketch the full, undisclosed horror of the crime.

As the proceedings began, the spectators sat hushed and morbidly expectant. But within minutes, gasps and sickened moans greeted Yannetti's description of sexual abuse, murder by suffocation, and necrophilia. "I wanted to kill him," Bob

said of Sicari. "But I didn't want to give him the satisfaction that we were hurt as bad as we were."

Two hours later, Jaynes was arraigned separately on seventy-five outstanding warrants from eighteen courts. Charging him with murder was not yet feasible. Prosecutors did not have Jeffrey's body, they did not have a statement from Jaynes, and they did not wish to offer Sicari a deal to testify against his friend. "Things were very much up in the air with regards to Jaynes at that point," Yannetti recalled.

Jaynes's bail was set at $100,000 cash, and reporters peppered Yannetti with questions as he left the courthouse. "Why haven't you charged him with murder?" one asked. "What if he gets out?" another shouted. Yannetti realized that charging Jaynes based on Sicari's statement and convicting him were two different animals. The district attorney's office, he knew, needed a breather to weigh the evidence and build its case carefully. "I think that with one hundred thousand dollars cash bail," Yannetti told reporters, "he's going to have a difficult time coming up with that type of money right away. We're satisfied that he'll be held."

The Curleys were not as confident, and their anxiety about Jaynes's possible release only compounded the depression that filled the house. Barbara began to take heavy doses of medication, but she could not shake the nagging, haunting questions she asked herself, again and again, about Jeffrey's dying minutes. Her great, unanswered concern was that Jeffrey had been tortured, that he had called for her as he died, and that she had been unable to respond.

Barbara did not attend the arraignments, but she later agreed to accompany Bob to the front of the house, where the family made its first public statement about the murder. "If you people only knew," Bob said, scanning a crowd that stood eight to ten deep in a semicircle before him. "Sal was in my house, and he was telling me how sorry he felt. If you only knew how close he came to walking out of the Cambridge police station, you would be on your knees. You'd be throwing up."

The scene was carried on the evening news, and Bob's anguish immediately struck a chord. To many people who saw him on television, he represented the bedrock face of average, overlooked Massachusetts. Here was a simple man, scarred by tragedy, who spoke to the fears and frustrations of everyday families from struggling neighborhoods far removed from Harvard, MIT, and the polished lobbies of Boston's Financial District. He spoke to places where both parents worked and where the daily grind to earn a living and keep children safe seemed ignored by the media, the politicians, and the power brokers.

Ripples from the murder even reached Washington, D.C., where Senator Edward Kennedy of Massachusetts composed a letter of condolence to the Curleys. "Your Jeffrey left this life defending the values you instilled in him as parents," Kennedy wrote. "He was a young man whose inordinate courage brings inspiration into all of our lives. Mrs. Kennedy and I share your grief."

As the Curley household crumpled with tragedy, the neighborhood seemed to die a little, too. The old, comforting beliefs in family and community had been fractured, and East Cambridge no longer carried a gut-level conviction that its streets were somehow any safer or better protected than anywhere else.

State Representative Tim Toomey, a friend of the family who lived near the neighborhood, had never seen anything like the impact of Jeffrey's murder. "It was devastating. It was surreal. It was something that people just couldn't fathom," Toomey said. "We just didn't know how to grasp it, or even understand how something like that could happen to a young kid like him. It really shook the community to its core."

At the Harrington School, fewer pupils lined up after school for the bus. Instead, anxious mothers waited in idling cars to drive them home. Grief-counseling sessions were scheduled for students who previously had thought murder was fantastical, make-believe fare for television—if they thought about it at all. Now, they were asking questions.

Parents demanded answers, too, but answers were not easy to find. A meeting at the Harrington School, packed with five hundred outraged residents, turned ugly with anger. "It's beyond our comprehension, and we're up against it as a group," said Timothy Dugan, a child psychiatrist at Cambridge Hospital, who moderated the tense and fractious gathering. Drucilla Whiting, a seventeen-year-old, spoke for many when she admitted to an unfamiliar fear of random danger and a suspicion of neighbors who had lived among them for years. "I think what kills us the most was that Salvi was one of us," she said.

A virulently antigay streak also infected the mood. Many news reports had described Jaynes and Sicari as homosexual lovers, and a long-simmering, blue-collar resentment toward Cambridge's sizable gay population stoked some of the rage over Jeffrey's death. Bob, however, tried to tamp down those flames from the beginning. In public comments and private conversations, he urged the community not to channel its grief into a homophobic witch hunt.

He had no such qualms, however, about the death penalty. Before Jeffrey's murder, Bob had rarely thought about the morality or application of capital punishment. But in an off-the-cuff statement on Hampshire Street, while mingling with friends and neighbors, he set in motion a roiling tornado that would soon race across Massachusetts from Beacon Hill to the Berkshires.

When details of the crime circulated after Sicari's arraignment, public reaction was quick, loud, and vengeful. Almost immediately, calls to restore capital punishment bubbled to the surface from state politicians, talk show hosts, and the man in the street. If ever a case demanded the ultimate penalty, even in the country's most liberal state, the Curley murder was exhibit A for many citizens.

Nowhere was that sentiment more prevalent than among the throng outside Barbara's home. There, neighbors began to clamor for the death penalty in interviews with reporters who, searching for new angles to the ongoing drama, were eager to listen. One reporter asked Bob whether he wanted Jeffrey's

killers executed. Bob's reply was typically direct: "For anybody who's opposed to the death penalty, you should have been sitting in our house, feeling what we're feeling."

Bob had not realized he was speaking to a journalist. But he meant what he said, and the effect was electric. Bob's call for the death penalty became an instantly irresistible story, highlighted in print, repeated on radio, and trumpeted on the television news. "Once I said that, it was off and running," Bob recalled. "I just blurted it out. I hadn't spoken with the family beforehand, and I wasn't really thinking too much about anything before I said it." For Bob, careful deliberation was not yet possible. As fear subsided, anger took its place. And Bob had found his target. "Being in the spot that I was in, I just couldn't see how anybody could be opposed to the death penalty," Bob said.

No one had been put to death in Massachusetts since 1947, and the state's highest court had ruled a death-penalty statute unconstitutional as recently as 1984. Despite Bob's feelings about the death penalty or how much support he generated, Jaynes and Sicari would not be executed in Massachusetts. No such law existed. But Bob began to look ahead, transitioning from grief to anger to activism against predators. Soon, like a river that gathers speed before a waterfall, the effort became an all-consuming crusade.

One of the first people to encourage Bob was Marilyn Abramofsky, a firebrand who fought relentlessly for tougher prosecution of juveniles after Kenny Claudio, a five-year-old boy who lived with her, had been raped and murdered by a fourteen-year-old neighbor in 1983. Certain elements of the case foreshadowed Jeffrey Curley's murder. Matthew Rosenberg abducted Claudio, a kindergarten pupil, as he played outside Abramofsky's home in the Roslindale section of Boston. Rosenberg beat and molested Claudio, drowned the child, and stored his body in a plastic trash bag in his closet.

Rosenberg, by statute, was tried as a juvenile and remanded to the custody of the state's Department of Youth Services, which was scheduled to release him at age eighteen.

The prospect horrified Abramofsky, who took her outrage to the State House, *The Oprah Winfrey Show*, *Geraldo*, and scores of other venues, in an effort to overhaul the Massachusetts juvenile judicial system. Along the way, Abramofsky founded a group called Parents of Murdered Children. But she also alienated many potential supporters with a brash, confrontational style that included threats of vigilante violence if Rosenberg were freed. "There will be a smile on this face when they lead me off to prison after he's dead," Abramofsky said.

Each time Rosenberg was scheduled for release, Abramofsky unleashed a new offensive to keep him in custody. The case resonated with court-affiliated psychiatrists, who repeatedly judged Rosenberg a danger to society. He was not freed until age twenty-three. In 1996, Abramofsky finally won what she had long sought when state lawmakers mandated that murder defendants fourteen and older must stand trial as adults.

One year later, when Jeffrey Curley was killed, Abramofsky remained an influential voice for the families of Massachusetts murder victims. She knew her way around the corridors of power in the State House, as well as where individual legislators stood on issues of crime and punishment, and she still burned with a passion that bordered on fury. So, when she heard the news about Jeffrey, she headed directly to the Curley home to offer condolences, lend support, and dispense advice.

Bob had never met Abramofsky before, but he knew her case. And when she hugged him at the door, Bob returned the embrace and listened. "I know how you're feeling," Abramofsky said. "But there's a lot harder to come. It really hasn't hit you yet that he's gone. Wait till a week from now, when you see people, and they're shopping, they're buying clothes, they're laughing. And you're thinking to yourself, My kid is dead. Why is everything just going on like nothing ever happened?" She encouraged Bob to be vocal and to ignore advice from the police to avoid the news media. "Murder is not a private thing," she told him. "Murder is public." She pledged that she would return to the house every day until Jeffrey's body was recovered.

Meanwhile, the drumbeat for capital punishment intensified, and Bob Curley became its undisputed champion. In interview after interview, he pressed his case to an audience that soon needed no introduction to this enraged Everyman. "I feel that it's God's way of ridding society of vermin like this that roam our streets," Bob told reporters.

To Bob, capital punishment was one more layer of protection for struggling blue-collar communities, where the need for two incomes inevitably and unfortunately produced latchkey children. "Families have to have two working parents now to survive the way society is," he said in a television interview. "And it's a breeding ground for these people to come in here and prey on the working-class people. They're just sitting back, licking their chops, waiting to get in here and abuse your child. Let's go get them and put the hurt on them. Until people are willing to make a stand, it's just gonna keep going on and on. They hurt me now. They hurt me as much as they can hurt me. And the next person who's gonna be hurt is God knows who."

On Sunday, two days after Sicari's arraignment, Bob and a half dozen members of the family met with District Attorney Thomas Reilly, First Assistant John McEvoy, Prosecutor David Yannetti, and a few State Police detectives to discuss the case. The meeting, in a second-floor conference room at the district attorney's office in East Cambridge, had not lasted long before Bob cut to the point that most concerned him. What chance was there to execute Sicari and Jaynes?

The anger from the Curley side of the conference table was palpable. They knew the death penalty was impossible in a state trial, so they asked Reilly if the case could be transferred to federal court, where capital punishment remained an option. "The main message from them was they didn't want us to stand in the way," Yannetti said. "He came in there wanting the death penalty and made that very clear to us. That was more important of a focus to him than the actual nuts and bolts of the evidence that we had at the time."

Reilly told the Curleys he would explore such a transfer but cautioned that the murder might not meet federal criteria

because Jeffrey had allegedly been killed before he was taken out of Massachusetts. "Our function was to reassure them that we would do everything possible to get the harshest possible penalty on these two," Yannetti said.

Bob realized that the odds, even at the federal level, did not favor a death-penalty trial. As a fallback, he turned his eyes toward the State House. Former governor William Weld and Paul Cellucci, his lieutenant governor, had filed a death-penalty bill in each legislative session since 1991. And during each session, the bill would wither or fail.

After Weld resigned in July 1997 to stand unsuccessfully for confirmation as U.S. ambassador to Mexico, Cellucci assumed the title of acting governor. Less than three months later, the Curley murder occurred, and Cellucci was outraged like everyone else. Bob's calls for capital punishment struck a chord with this new, tough-on-crime governor.

Abramofsky, a well-known figure at the State House, arranged a meeting between the pair only days after Jeffrey's disappearance.

"Governor Cellucci, I'm with Jeffrey Curley's father," Abramofsky said by phone from the Curley home. "I was wondering if you could sit down and talk to him. He's devastated."

"Marilyn, when do you want it?" Cellucci quickly answered.

"Now," she replied.

"Now?" Cellucci asked incredulously. "Where are you?"

"Listen, I'll be right over," Abramofsky said in her trademark, rapid-fire delivery.

Bob took a seat in Abramofsky's car, accompanied by his brother Jim and two mothers from Parents of Murdered Children. Within fifteen minutes, they had negotiated the three congested miles to the State House, where Bob was escorted past the state trooper standing guard and into a private meeting with the governor. It was Bob's first visit to the historic State House, where the golden dome of Charles Bulfinch's architectural masterpiece had dominated the heights over Boston Common for two hundred years.

Inside the governor's third-floor suite, Bob suddenly found himself talking father to father with Cellucci about his loss. The discussion did not focus on the death penalty. Instead, Cellucci offered words of comfort interspersed with a parent's anger. "He really was caring," Bob recalled. "But he was also pissed off, and he wanted to do something about it."

For Cellucci, a small-town governor with two daughters, the case hit close to home. "Like everyone else in the state, I was just horrified by this crime," Cellucci recalled. "The security of living in a neighborhood was shattered for the Curley family and for a lot of people in Massachusetts. People were worried that you couldn't even go outside in the streets around your house."

Cellucci had voted against the death penalty as a young state representative from the semirural town of Hudson, forty miles west of Boston, where apple orchards and a cozy 1950s sensibility helped define a community where not much ever happened and where the residents liked it that way. His father owned a car dealership there, and Cellucci, a horse-racing fan and Robert De Niro look-alike, had risen through the ranks of local politics before his election to the state legislature in 1976. Like many Massachusetts Republicans in those early post-Watergate years, he did not ascribe to a rigid right-wing ideology.

Cellucci's thinking on the death penalty changed in 1988, when he managed George H. W. Bush's presidential campaign in Massachusetts and worked closely with the Boston patrolmen and the state trooper unions, who had endorsed the Republican. The police believed a death penalty would protect them if criminals knew they would be executed for murdering a law-enforcement officer. As a result, Cellucci said, "I wanted to say to the men and women who we ask to protect us that we're going to do everything under our power to protect you."

When Curley and the governor emerged from their meeting, reporters were waiting as the death penalty and Jeffrey's murder became linked at the highest level of state government.

"We want to deter this from happening again," Cellucci said grimly. "No one is saying the death penalty is a panacea, but I believe the two individuals in this case should not see the light again." Bob challenged state lawmakers to take a stand against "lowlifes" and predators. And Abramofsky, who had arranged the meeting, issued the same kind of unapologetic warning she had used in her long campaign to change the sentencing laws. "If they don't do something about this murder," she warned under the Bulfinch dome, "this house is going to be torn down."

For nearly a week, Bob Curley's private grief had morphed into a very public drama played out every day to a rapt audience of millions throughout New England. In the process, he had become the most recognizable "average" citizen in the state. He also had become increasingly comfortable with a limelight he had never sought but now would not avoid.

The world, however, looked much different to Mimi, who had entered an anonymous, private purgatory since the murder.

Since Bob awoke to the news of Jeffrey's disappearance, Mimi had seen him only five to ten minutes a day. He would stop by the house, brief her on the day's events, pick up a fresh set of clothes, and hurriedly return to Cambridge. Most of her news came from the television, where Mimi would watch her lover expose a pain that she could neither share nor ease. Mimi would watch Bob place his arm around Barbara or watch Barbara cry, embrace her husband, and lean on his shoulder for physical and emotional support. "I was part of it, but not really part of it," Mimi recalled. "I was seeing at a distance what was going on. He was married to Barbara at the time, it was his son, and I was just in the house on my own."

Mimi could not escape the case. She worked as a staff psychologist at a Cambridge Hospital clinic only two blocks from Barbara's home. On her commute to the office, Mimi would pass the TV trucks, the memorial shrine, and the throngs of mourning neighbors. "I was trying to be there for him, trying to be there for my patients, trying to be there for me, and I'd

be losing my sanity," Mimi said. "I didn't have anyone to turn to. It was really tough."

At the clinic, terrified patients would talk about Jeffrey's killing. And as they talked, Mimi listened in torturous silence, unable and unwilling to speak of her relationship with Bob. One patient who lost a child to murder was retraumatized by Jeffrey's death. The daughter of another patient had been a classmate of Jeffrey's. And the son of yet another was hospitalized after he tried to commit suicide.

Mimi was reminded of her distant, yet intimate, relationship to the murder nearly everywhere she went. Even while shopping, Mimi saw a flier with Jeffrey's photograph. "It hit me then," Mimi said. "For the next week, I couldn't go to work. I was just glued to the television, waiting to hear if they had found the body. I just wanted to know, and I didn't have anyone to call."

That wait, for Mimi and the Curleys, seemed interminable. Divers from three states had converged on the Portsmouth police headquarters only hours after Sicari was whisked back to Massachusetts. "We are looking at this as a long-haul thing," said Massachusetts State Police Sergeant Greg Foley, who supervised the recovery effort. "If it takes me to Butte, Montana, that's where I'll go."

Massachusetts dispatched twenty divers from the eastern half of the state. Maine committed its entire dive team. And New Hampshire sent a full contingent from the state Fish and Game Division. In addition, State Police aircraft from all three states scanned the many rivers, coves, bays, and tidal shores near Portsmouth. As they did, police pilots soon found themselves jockeying for airspace with a swarm of news helicopters. "It was a circus atmosphere," said Sergeant Bill Freeman, who headed the Massachusetts dive team.

The search first focused on the dangerous, swift-moving Piscataqua River, which divides Portsmouth from Kittery, a seacoast community in Maine. "A lot of times we had to wait for slack tide, when the tide had stopped running," Freeman

said. "That means we only had a twenty-minute window to actually do the dive and search around the bridges."

The effort expanded to Maine and the nearby York River, where police tried to simulate the movement of the Rubbermaid container that held Jeffrey's body. When police dropped a similar container off a bridge, the box sank almost immediately after the lid separated on impact. As a result, police targeted areas near or directly underneath the dozens of bridges they had selected. Later, they would discover that the container used in the crime, its lid sealed tight through impact, had drifted downstream.

John Fulkerson traveled to southern Maine the day after his ride with Sicari. In his travels, he crossed a two-lane bridge over the Great Works River in South Berwick. Everything about the location matched Sicari's description. "I'll never forget it," Fulkerson recalled. "I said, This is it. There's the house. There's the railing. There's the light. And there's a car like the one they saw when they turned around. Jeffrey Curley's right here someplace." Using the impact test as a guide, divers searched only the base of the bridge and found nothing. The search moved elsewhere, but Fulkerson, still drawn to the site, pressed for another dive at a later date.

Exhaustion and frustration, meanwhile, had begun to take a toll on the divers. The work was intense, the stakes were high, and each unsuccessful day brought increasing concern that Jeffrey's body had been carried out to sea. The strain was painfully evident in Cambridge, where a State Police forensic team arrived at the Hampshire Street condo on October 6, the fourth day of the search, to ask for DNA swabs from Barbara, Bob, and Bobby Jr. The request, which could help identify Jeffrey, sent Bob into a frenzy. "What the fuck is this?" he yelled at police. "You already got a confession. What the fuck are you doing here? Why are you wasting our time? Go fucking do some work!"

The next day, a glorious, sunny, autumn spectacular, proved worth the wait. Yannetti and McEvoy had decided after a days-long discussion to charge Jaynes with murder and kidnapping. Even though Jeffrey's body had not been discovered,

prosecutors decided to press ahead with their circumstantial evidence. They could not compel Sicari to testify against Jaynes or even use his confession as evidence against a code-fendant. But they had the store surveillance tapes, testimony of repeated contact between Jaynes and Jeffrey, and articles of Jeffrey's clothing from Manchester. "We'd been working on it night and day for five days," Yannetti said. "On that fifth day, we said, What do we do? We have to charge him. When we did, we thought we'd have a very different case than what we ultimately wound up with." What they wound up with was a "miracle," Yannetti said. Fulkerson's hunch had paid off.

The miracle happened seventy-five miles to the north, at a sharp bend in the Great Works River, where a Maine State Police diver discovered the container holding Jeffrey Curley's body at nearly the same time that Jaynes was arraigned for murder. Working four abreast, a Maine dive team searched downstream from the bridge for fifteen minutes before they made the find in six feet of water. The sealed container was sitting upright on the river bottom, having traveled fifty yards before lodging in the trunk of a fallen tree. The code word for success, "lobster," was relayed to all police involved in the search.

Soon, the area around the bridge became jammed with police, reporters, onlookers, and several of Jeffrey's aunts, uncles, and cousins. After taking photographs to document the crime scene, police inserted the box into a body bag for overland transport to the state capital of Augusta. As they did, one Massachusetts State Police diver, Arthur Huntley, was struck by the scent of roses. "I had never smelled anything like that in my fifteen years of diving," Huntley said. "I was flabbergasted. Why would you have that smell, like perfume, like roses, you know?"

In Augusta, the state's chief medical examiner, Dr. Henry Ryan, cut the duct tape with a scalpel and slowly removed the lid. There, enshrouded in a plastic tarp, lay the body of Jeffrey Curley, entombed in a container filled almost to the brim with cool, cloudy water. Only a small portion of his face and feet were visible.

Jeffrey's body was removed from the box. A crooked front tooth was matched against a photograph of the boy. Fingerprints were taken. But there was no doubt who had been placed naked on the examining table. A detailed autopsy would wait for the next day, when a Massachusetts pathologist could arrive to observe. In the interim, Jeffrey's corpse was placed in cold storage overnight.

Word of the discovery was phoned instantly to the Cambridge command post outside Barbara's condo, where Detective Sergeant Lester Sullivan had continued to work during the long search. Now, he and District Attorney Tom Reilly faced the grim task of informing the family. Stepping just inside the door, Sullivan asked Bob and Barbara to speak with him privately in a semisecluded staircase. "I have some very bad news for you," Sullivan said. "They've located the body."

Bob and Barbara broke down. The sergeant relayed what specifics he knew, and Bob's mood pivoted instantly to anger bordering on violence. "I'll kill them!" he yelled. "I'll kill them!" Sullivan pleaded quietly, but insistently, for calm. The boys and other relatives remained in the living room, and Sullivan was aware of the powder keg of emotion that lay waiting there. "I know it's very painful, but I need you and Barbara to be the strength of this family and present the bad news," Sullivan said. "I will be with you, or I can present it for you, but I need you to maintain control for the rest of the family." And so they did, Sullivan said, despite as wrenching a display of grief as he had ever witnessed. Screams and sobs mixed yet again with cries for vengeance in the shattered household.

The autopsy was completed the next day. Yannetti, who flew to Maine in a State Police helicopter, steeled himself for the scene as he passed over beautiful countryside under clear, sunny skies. He had witnessed adult autopsies before—never one for someone as young as Jeffrey. As Ryan examined the body, Yannetti reached deep to summon all the professional cool he could muster. "It's something that will stay with me forever," he said. "There's something so unnatural about a ten-

year-old boy on an autopsy table, being killed before he had a chance to live his life."

That evening, Jeffrey was returned to Cambridge, where a police escort led the grim procession to the Long Funeral Home. Bob also returned home, to Somerville, where he reunited with Mimi for the first time in a week. Psychically spent and physically exhausted, hollowed by the killing and unsure what the future held, each of them realized that nothing could ever be the same. "I had this sense that I had no right to feel anything because he was not my son, that this tragedy was Bob's," Mimi recalled.

Bob wanted to visit the funeral home with Mimi, before the rest of the family, to see Jeffrey for the first time since his murder. Reluctantly, Mimi agreed to go in the morning. What she witnessed has remained an indelibly harrowing memory. "They had the place locked up, but I knew he was in there," Bob recalled. "I don't think they knew I was coming, but it really wouldn't have mattered what they said, because I was going to go see him." There, in a small, open coffin, Jeffrey lay in a blue suit, white shirt, and blue tie. Rosary beads had been placed between his hands, and a single pink rose lay across his body.

Bob reacted with a visceral rage that alarmed Mimi, even though she had prepared herself for such an outburst. "I'm going to kill those motherfuckers!" Bob shouted, moving suddenly toward the coffin. "Look what they did!" Several of the staff rushed toward Bob, held him, and tried to calm him down. "It's okay, it's okay," they said. The dam burst, and Bob's rage dissolved in tears. Slumped and shuddering with pain, he gathered himself and approached the coffin. Bob placed a hand on Jeffrey's body, studied his placid face, and shared a final, lingering moment between an innocent child and his heartbroken father.

Several hours later, the doors opened to the public, and Cambridge firefighters monitored a steady stream of thousands who came to pay their respects over two days. Their number included the elderly and children, professionals and

blue-collar workers, politicians and parents. And on Saturday, ten days after his disappearance, twelve hundred mourners filled Sacred Heart Church, spilling onto the sidewalk in a funeral that seemed suited more for a dignitary than a precocious ten-year-old. Bagpipes played the familiar strains of "Amazing Grace," 150 uniformed Cambridge firefighters formed an honor guard, police watched from horseback, and Bob and his sons helped carry Jeffrey's silver coffin on a striking, cloudless day. The Reverend Kevin Toomey, the brother of the neighborhood's state legislator, officiated at a Mass attended by Governor Cellucci, Cardinal Bernard Law, and District Attorney Reilly.

In the rear of the church, far from the seats where Bob, Barbara, and the boys embraced throughout the service, Mimi sat quietly amid a shell of protective supporters, her hands held tightly by two close friends. "I tried to stay out of the way. I felt like a stranger," recalled Mimi, who had taken a sedative before the service. "Many times I would think, Would this have happened if he hadn't been with me?"

Mimi had not wanted to attend, but Bob insisted her presence was important. That presence, however, remained a silent, anonymous, and anxious one. "There was this moment when he was carrying the coffin with the boys," Mimi said. "He looked at me, and I looked at him, but I didn't talk to him that day. After the Mass, I just left."

5

Storm at the State House

B Y THE TIME Jeffrey's body was buried in a simple plot at Cambridge Cemetery, outrage over his murder had become incendiary, stoked by a frightening series of gruesome killings that incensed the public and battered the facade of public safety throughout Greater Boston. Echoing the pleas of Bob and his family, a growing chorus of voices, whipped into a frenzy by talk show hosts and opinion shapers, clamored for the reinstatement of capital punishment.

Don Feder, a columnist for the *Boston Herald*, spoke for many when he wrote, "When the brutal killers of ten-year-olds are allowed to live, what does that say about our concern for innocent human life?" He derided Massachusetts as "the last bastion of delirious liberalism" and scoffed at the idea that life in prison without parole was adequate punishment. "Given their sexual proclivities, confining Jaynes and Sicari with men is like locking a chocoholic in a Godiva factory," Feder wrote two days after Jeffrey's funeral. "And if, in a decade or two, some sentimental governor comes along who decides that the duo has suffered enough—'model prisoners,' 'inspirations to others,' 'found Jesus'—these diseased animals could again feel the warmth of the sun on their backs and the grass beneath their feet."

Polling in Massachusetts had long shown deep support for the death penalty. And now, galvanized by Jeffrey's murder,

proponents and sympathetic politicians sprang into action in the volatile weeks that followed. Public support might never be greater, they realized, and a better opportunity might never arise.

That support was fueled by anger over a two-year spate of murders, all highly publicized and all remarkable for their brutality, that had horrified Massachusetts since the 1995 slaying of Janet Downing by Eddie O'Brien, her fifteen-year-old neighbor in Somerville. In June 1996, the region was stunned again by the murder of Kristen Crowley, a twenty-seven-year-old woman from Peabody who had been abducted by two men outside a late-night convenience store and hauled into the brush. There the men, who had just left a nearby strip club, used a forty-five-pound rock to crush her skull. Three months later, a six-year-old boy was abducted in Lynn after a man reportedly offered him a bicycle. A massive search ensued, but Jesus de la Cruz was never found.

In September 1997, the public reeled once more when Catherine Rice and two small sons, ages four years and two months, were strangled in their Lowell home by Rice's former boyfriend, Peter Contos, a respected Air National Guard sergeant who was the boys' father. Contos disposed of the bodies, still clothed in pajamas, in his locker at the Air National Guard base on Cape Cod. Police discovered them there, blood-stained towels wrapped around their necks, stuffed in plastic bags and a backpack.

Two days later, Jeffrey Curley disappeared, and Eddie O'Brien was convicted on live television of the Downing murder. By then, the drumbeat of unconscionable violence had reached a crescendo, only to be reamplified two weeks later when Elaine Donahue of Reading, an obstetrics nurse and mother of four, was discovered battered and dead in a rented storage space. Donahue, who had been missing for nearly a month, was bludgeoned while she slept. The murderer was her husband, an impulsive gambler and self-employed accountant who had become angered by his wife's control of the family finances.

When his wife first failed to report for work, Edward Donahue expressed bewilderment to her coworkers and friends. He scoured the area with neighbors and joined mass vigils in which three hundred people prayed for Elaine's discovery. All the while, her body lay stashed in the basement of their home, where Edward continued to care for his three sons and one daughter. He was arrested after police, during a search of his home, discovered a receipt for a storage locker in nearby Lynnfield, where her body had been moved.

On October 21, four days after Donahue's stunning arrest, tragedy struck again. Annie Glenn was shot dead by an estranged boyfriend as she waited with her three children at a school bus stop in Lowell. Richard Kenney shot Glenn once, then leaned over her prone body to fire twice more as she struggled to protect herself. Kenney, the father of two of the children, was identified by one of them, a four-year-old boy. "Daddy shot Mommy," the boy told police who had rushed to the scene.

The surge of violence, exhausting and relentless, reinforced Governor Cellucci's determination to push through a death-penalty bill. The issue also gave Cellucci a striking opportunity to escape the outsized shadow of his predecessor, William Weld, and put a forceful, can-do stamp on his new administration. Cellucci and other Republicans in Massachusetts, vastly outnumbered in state politics, saw capital punishment as a platinum wedge issue, one that could attract the support of Democrats and independents who had tired of the barrage of violent crime. The Curley murder and others, Cellucci and his aides knew, could help push the death penalty through.

The Republicans also knew the polling numbers, which showed that the public supported capital punishment by a far greater percentage than did their elected representatives on Beacon Hill. In 1994, a Northeastern University survey found that 74 percent of Massachusetts residents favored the death penalty for first-degree murder. In 1995, a follow-up study showed only 45 percent support for the death penalty among

Massachusetts legislators. Nationally, public backing for the
death penalty appeared similarly strong. In 1995, a Gallup survey found 77 percent in favor.

The Massachusetts numbers, in a state renowned for
left-of-center politics, might have startled outsiders. In 1997,
no one had been executed in Massachusetts for fifty years, a
legacy perhaps of Puritan founders who had drastically pruned
the number of capital offenses when they settled the colony.
In seventeenth-century England, one could still be put to death
for one hundred crimes, even for upending a drying rack for
cloth. But in the Massachusetts Bay Colony, its ten capital offenses were limited to murder and a laundry list of religious
affronts such as blasphemy, idolatry, and witchcraft. In 1692,
Salem proved how deadly serious those transgressions were
considered. The Puritan founders also insisted on the right of
capital defendants to an attorney, the first right of its kind in
North America and one not granted in England until the mid-
nineteenth century.

Reluctance to impose the death penalty in Massachusetts waned in the early twentieth century, when violent crime
spiked during a time of dramatic social change. Rapid immigra-
tion, spreading industrialization, and the economic troubles
of the Great Depression had combined to alter the landscape
of American life. Many Americans felt threatened by the upheaval. The notorious case of Nicola Sacco and Bartolomeo
Vanzetti, widely considered to have been wrongly executed in
Boston in 1927, is a prime example of the public's sense that
capital punishment was appropriate in a society that seemed
to be whirling out of control.

After 1947, when Massachusetts conducted its last execution, governors from both parties refused to sign death warrants for twenty-five years. That informal moratorium was
reinforced by the tireless efforts of Sara Ehrmann, a longtime
activist and organizer from Brookline. Ehrmann, whose husband had been a lawyer for Sacco and Vanzetti, helped persuade
the legislature in 1951 to give juries the option of ordering life
in prison instead of death for first-degree murder. By the dawn

of the 1960s, amid postwar prosperity and relatively low crime, enthusiasm for the death penalty had declined across the country. The Gallup poll showed only 42 percent support in 1966, the lowest mark since the organization began asking a death-penalty question in 1936.

In the late 1960s, however, an alarming rise in crime sparked a steady, nationwide rise in support for capital punishment. The Gallup poll showed 66 percent support in 1976, then 75 percent in 1985, before the numbers crested at 80 percent in 1994. That surge met resistance from the U.S. Supreme Court, which ruled against the death penalty in 1972 in *Furman v. Georgia.* By a 5–4 decision, the majority objected to what justices called an arbitrary system with no clear guidelines for jurors. Justice Thurgood Marshall described the death penalty as "excessive, unnecessary, and offensive to contemporary values."

In 1976, however, the Supreme Court revisited the issue after Georgia and several states revised their laws. This time, the High Court upheld the death-penalty statutes, whose changes included greater discretion for judges and separate juries for trials and sentencing. In short order, dozens of states reinstituted the death penalty. By 1995, when New York joined the list, a total of thirty-eight states allowed capital punishment.

Massachusetts did not join the rush, although the legislature tried. The Massachusetts high court rebuffed two attempts by lawmakers to reinstate capital punishment in 1980 and 1984. The fight was not renewed until 1991. Over the next seven years, like legislative clockwork, Governor William Weld and Lieutenant Governor Paul Cellucci filed bills in every session to give Massachusetts a death penalty that would pass constitutional muster. The measures did not reach the House floor until 1994, when the chamber voted on the death penalty for the first time in nearly a decade. Speaker Charles Flaherty of Cambridge, who worked hard to defeat the bill, saw his lobbying efforts pay dividends in an 86–70 vote against the measure.

The debate resurfaced in the following year after the roadside slaying of a state trooper. The death of Mark Charbonnier,

gunned down by a paroled killer during a routine traffic stop, infused death-penalty proponents with new urgency. With Charbonnier's murder fresh in the public mind, the state senate approved capital punishment for the murder of a police officer. The matter moved to the House once again, where the bill lost, 83–73, despite a small gain in support.

One notable opponent was Donna Fournier Cuomo, a Republican state representative from North Andover, who had won her first race for political office in 1993 as a tireless advocate for tough sentencing laws and the rights of crime victims. Cuomo was well known as the sister of Joey Fournier, a seventeen-year-old high school student who was murdered in 1974 in a gas-station robbery north of Boston. The killer was the infamous Willie Horton, whose later prison furlough became the subject of a controversial 1988 presidential campaign ad that portrayed Massachusetts governor Michael Dukakis as dangerously soft on crime and helped propel George H. W. Bush to the White House.

Fournier, a part-time attendant at the station, was stabbed nineteen times after emptying the cash register and handing the money to Horton and two accomplices. His body was stuffed in a trash can, where he bled to death. At the time of the killing, Horton was on parole after serving only three years of a nine-year sentence for attempted murder. He was captured after Fournier's death and sentenced to life in prison. This time, the sentence carried no parole. But in Massachusetts, life without parole did not exclude Horton from a program of unescorted weekend furloughs, even for inmates convicted of first-degree murder.

In June 1986, Horton left prison on his tenth such furlough and never returned. Nine months later, he terrorized a couple in their Maryland home, where over twelve hours he raped the woman twice, stabbed and pistol-whipped her fiancé, and then fled in the man's car. Horton was arrested after a police chase and ordered to serve two consecutive life terms plus eighty-five years. The sentencing judge, cuffing the Massachusetts correction system, declared, "I'm not prepared to take the chance that Mr. Horton might again be furloughed

or otherwise released." Incensed by Horton's escape, Cuomo launched a crusade to end furloughs for first-degree murderers, holding rallies on the State House steps and organizing an ambitious petition drive that garnered seventy thousand signatures. Under angry, growing pressure, the legislature voted to abolish the program.

Despite her brother's death and his killer's weekend privileges, Cuomo did not vote for the death penalty in 1995. She had been a longtime opponent of capital punishment, and not even murder had influenced her to change that view. Two years later, in August 1997, Cuomo voted against the death penalty again when the Joint Criminal Justice Committee issued an unfavorable report on the latest Weld-Cellucci bill.

Although Cuomo opposed capital punishment, she remained adamant that violent criminals should face tough, sure punishment. At the beginning of the 1997 session, she filed a bill to extend the sentences for second-degree murderers. Under her proposal, such inmates would not be eligible for parole for twenty-five years instead of fifteen. Nor would the prisoners be eligible for "furlough, temporary release, or education, training or employment programs established outside a correctional facility" until they had served at least twenty-two years behind bars.

The bill was recommended by the Criminal Justice Committee, which sent the proposal to the Senate, where approval was all but certain before the bill was shipped to the House for enactment. Once in the Senate, however, the bill gained a certain political appeal. Here, in a noncontroversial measure about second-degree murder, death-penalty proponents believed they might have a vehicle for their long-elusive victory. So, with an eye toward winning bipartisan support in the House, Republican Minority Leader Brian Lees and Democratic Senator James Jajuga filed a narrow amendment to execute the killers of law-enforcement officers. Jajuga had been a State Police officer for twenty-one years and was the first recipient of the Hanna Medal of Honor, an award for bravery in the line of duty. The medal was named for another state

trooper, George Hanna, who had been fatally shot during a traffic stop in 1983. The amended bill passed easily, 23–14, in a preliminary vote on September 17. Final approval in the Senate was expected the following month.

The bill received little attention outside the Senate, which had voted for capital punishment in 1994 and 1995. The House, where death-penalty bills routinely went to their legislative grave, would be another animal altogether. The murder of Jeffrey Curley, however, upended and changed that calculus. Legislators who had consistently rejected capital punishment suddenly were inundated with telephone calls from angry constituents demanding that they reverse their position.

One of those calls came from John Curley, Bob's older brother, who awoke early on October 5, four days after Jeffrey's murder, to read a brief newspaper article about Jajuga's death-penalty amendment. Jesus, I hate to see a police officer die, Curley said to himself. I agree with him on that—or any judicial officer, actually—but in my opinion a kid is just as important. A former military air-traffic controller in Vietnam, Curley was accustomed to decisive action. He picked up the phone at 8:00 A.M. and dialed Jajuga at home.

The senator's wife answered, and Curley began to explain why he believed that murders involving children should be added to the death-penalty bill. "Hang on a second," she said. "Jim, get over here and talk to this guy." Jajuga listened politely to Curley and invited him to meet at his State House office. At first, the senator was reluctant to expand the bill, convinced that a limited focus was best and wishing to avoid any perception of exploiting Jeffrey's death. By the end of the phone call, however, he had been persuaded. And on Tuesday, the senator and Lees filed a death-penalty amendment for the rape and murder of a child under fourteen. "They said it was important for them to do something meaningful," Jajuga said of the Curleys. "They said, 'Use us.'"

The Senate wasn't scheduled to consider the amendments for two weeks, a brief window during which activists on both sides mobilized for a short, intense fight. Lawmakers had

never seen such outcry on any single issue, and many of them struggled with a wrenching decision that pitted the dictates of conscience against the realities of politics. For one legislator in particular, the question was excruciatingly personal.

State Representative Tim Toomey, whose district included Jeffrey's home, had voted against the death penalty twice before. Those decisions had been reflexive for Toomey, a product of a religious, Irish-Catholic upbringing that taught no one has the power to determine who lives or dies. But now, Toomey was torn. He knew Jeffrey from the neighborhood and had last seen him handing out water during a road race that passed Toomey's campaign headquarters. "When Jeffrey left the race," Toomey said, "he even took a couple of bumper stickers to give to people." Three days later, Jeffrey was dead.

The lawmaker was also a longtime friend of Jeffrey's uncle, Barbara's brother Arthur, who had worked in all of Toomey's campaigns from School Committee to City Council to state representative. The son of a Cambridge police lieutenant and the brother of a priest, Toomey had been one of the first people whom Arthur Francis called when Jeffrey disappeared. Toomey visited the Curley home during the maddening search, kept in close contact with police, and struggled to comprehend what had happened to his tight-knit community.

Soon, he would be struggling with a very different dilemma. Arthur Francis, the bosom friend who had campaigned tirelessly for him, made a request. He asked Toomey to change his vote on the death penalty. "I really, really wrestled with that," Toomey said. "I probably wouldn't be as successful in politics if I didn't have Arthur helping me all those years. He had never asked me for anything, but he asked me to consider doing that."

Something else helped Toomey rethink his position. The faces of the neighborhood children, he said, convinced him that some crimes are so heinous that society must respond with the ultimate penalty. "A lot of the young kids came up to me. They were very, very fearful," Toomey said. "They felt that having the death penalty was going to protect them."

Wrestling with his conscience, Toomey spoke at length with his brother, the Reverend Kevin Toomey, who officiated at Jeffrey's funeral. The priest, in keeping with church teachings, said he opposed any decision to support the death penalty. "He was somewhat disappointed," Tim Toomey recalled. "He would prefer that I not vote for it, but he knew what I was going through."

A war of opposing emotions raged back and forth in Toomey's mind. "There were the pros and cons, justice or revenge, the whole range of issues," Toomey said. "I mean, it was a massive conflict. But there was also the fact that I was angry, and that I thought these people just shouldn't live, to prevent them from ever getting out and doing something else to someone."

In the end, one week after Jeffrey's murder, Toomey became the first legislator to announce publicly that he would change his stance and back capital punishment. "This whole thing has completely stunned me, and the city is devastated," Toomey told reporters. "This crime is so horrific, I think we have to step back and say something is really wrong. These people aren't even human."

After Toomey's switch, speculation ran rampant at the State House as to who would follow and whether public pressure and private anger could erase the ten-vote margin that had squelched the death penalty two years before. Massachusetts had been jarred by all of the recent murders, but the Curley killing seemed to stand alone as a grim, new standard of depravity. And Cellucci, more attuned than Weld to street-level sentiment, did not need his advisers to tell him that the case, almost single-handedly, could alter the political landscape. To the governor, the case packed a visceral punch that would reach every lawmaker on Beacon Hill. "Any parent has got to feel that," Cellucci said of Jeffrey's death. "They've got to feel it in their heart."

For the Curley family, Jajuga's office soon became a State House headquarters where phone calls were made to legislators, strategy was mapped, and a sense of mission gained mo-

mentum by the day. Bob, at times, felt overwhelmed by the workings of a place so different from the firehouse. "There was so much activity. I really didn't know what the hell was going on," he said. "Here I am, Joe Schmo, working down in Inman Square fixing fire engines, and then two weeks later I'm involved in all this stuff."

Bob, John, and their brother Jim quickly became familiar with the corridors and crannies of the State House, where they would walk into legislators' offices for some old-fashioned, East Cambridge, one-on-one lobbying. Bob's approach, though respectful, was blunt. He would explain his stance and ask for support. If the lawmaker still opposed the bill, Bob would follow up: "How would you feel if you were in my shoes? How could you be against the death penalty then?"

John, the de facto family leader, had a more pugnacious style. "I used to walk into people's offices all day long," he said. "I aggravated the hell out of people." Often roaming the building alone, he prowled the State House with a list of state representatives and a notebook in hand, knocking on doors with no appointment and no advance warning. "They had no clue I was coming," said John, the lone Republican in the family. "I'd go in, tell them who I was, and ask whether they were voting for or against the death penalty. When they said they were against it, I'd want to know why."

Unlike Bob, John would grow heated if he did not hear the answer he wanted.

"Can you guarantee me these people will never kill another child?" John asked one legislator.

"Well, they'll be put away for life," the lawmaker answered.

"Oh, yeah? Well, what happens when we get another Mike Dukakis in office?" John shot back, referring to the infamous furlough program.

"Well, yes, you're right, there are no guarantees," the representative replied.

"Well, I can give you a guarantee," John said, his voice rising. "You put them to death, and they'll never hurt anybody again!"

If he offended some people with his brusque style, John knew that Fran Marini, a Republican who served as House minority whip, would welcome him. According to John, the pair became fast allies on the day he introduced himself with a stack of petitions collected by the family outside Jeffrey's home. Sitting in Marini's office, cradling the petitions in his lap, John made his pitch.

"I need someone to show everybody how many people are actually interested in the death penalty," John said.

"Well, how many petitions do you have?" Marini asked.

John lifted the stack, piled six inches high with thousands of names, and dropped the pile on Marini's desk with an authoritative thump. Marini stared at the stack for a few seconds, then stared at John, and finally looked back at the gift of political gold before him.

"Goddammit!" Marini said. "I'll bring up the son-of-a-bitch myself!"

As Marini went to work, he expected fierce resistance from House Speaker Tom Finneran, a fast-talking, iron-fisted politician from the Mattapan neighborhood of Boston, who knew almost immediately after the news of Jeffrey's killing that a hurricane was headed straight for the State House. Finneran, a Democrat who opposed the death penalty, favored postponing the vote for a year to give passions a chance to subside. Critics howled that Finneran, afraid he might lose, was simply stalling for time. "In my mind, I was thinking that the cumulative political effect of these murders would create a stampede in the legislature and that the effect would be something, in the end, that you just couldn't stop, Finneran recalled. "The public was demanding reciprocal justice. And given the hideous nature of some of these crimes, reciprocal justice for many in the public was, Light up the electric chair! Light it up, baby! I thought, Mother of God, this is going to be brutal." The day after Finneran publicly suggested a postponement, the hurricane blew that plan to pieces. On October 21, in the space of one eventful day, Annie Glenn was gunned down in Lowell, the minority leader vowed to stop House busi-

ness unless Finneran set a vote, and the Senate convened to give all-but-certain approval to the death penalty.

Sitting in the ornate Senate gallery, the Curley family wore yellow ribbons bearing Jeffrey's name as they watched the debate. Below, they saw Jajuga, lashing the air with his arms, arguing vehemently that the death penalty is justified for anyone who would rape and murder a child. "The children of the commonwealth are crying out for someone to protect them, to say this egregious and outrageous behavior will not be tolerated," Jajuga said. "When we have one of our children savaged and ravaged," he added, pausing between the verbs for frightening emphasis, "we can ask the appropriate level of justice."

The amendment, prompted by Jeffrey's murder, spurred opponents to question whether politics was driving the debate. "What about the killers of Janet Downing, Elaine Donahue, and the two young boys whose bodies were stuffed in an equipment locker at Otis Air Force Base?" asked Robert Antonioni, a Democrat from Leominster, who led the Senate fight against capital punishment. He argued in vain. The amendment passed easily, 22–14, and the Senate had only gotten started.

Steven Panagiotakos, a Lowell Democrat, immediately requested the death penalty for murder by torture or extreme cruelty. Eleven minutes after the Jajuga vote, the measure passed, 20–16. Then, in a breathtaking expansion of the bill, Senator Richard Moore, a small-town Democrat from central Massachusetts, asked that twelve types of murder be punished by death. The motion included the previous amendments and added other categories, such as bombings or contract killings, which Weld and Cellucci had requested in the past. Moore's amendment was approved, 20–17, and the bill was dispatched to the House. The transformation had been stunning for its breadth and speed. A simple proposal to toughen restrictions on second-degree murderers, in a startling, rumbling burst of momentum, instead became the vehicle to express the frustrated rage of millions in the state.

Senator Marian Walsh, a Democrat from the middle-class West Roxbury neighborhood of Boston, watched the debate

unfold with the unhappy assurance that passage was inevitable. Walsh opposed the death penalty, even though her district strongly supported capital punishment. Before the vote, she had received two thousand calls from constituents who urged her to change her position. She held fast, however, despite the 1995 murder of a close friend, Assistant District Attorney Paul McLaughlin, who was gunned down at a commuter-rail stop by a gang leader he was about to prosecute. "He ran all my literature drops. We were very, very close friends," Walsh said of McLaughlin. "I can't say that revenge has not visited my heart, but I just didn't let it stay. The reason we created a judicial system was because we wanted justice, not revenge."

As the focus shifted to the House, where three more categories of murder were added to the list, the pundits automatically assumed that Finneran, a master manipulator, would use a toolbox full of artifice and fear to orchestrate the outcome. So, when Finneran declared that Democratic lawmakers should vote their "conscience" on the issue, the pronouncement was greeted with snickers and head-shaking skepticism. "To say Tom Finneran isn't marshaling votes against the death penalty," recalled Rob Gray, the governor's press secretary, "is to say Bill Belichick isn't involved with the Patriots game plan." As a result, Cellucci prepared for the vote as if Finneran would be pulling the strings on the opposite sideline. The governor opened his legislative directory, sat for hours at his desk, and placed dozens of calls to freshman representatives, old friends, and legislators rumored to be wavering.

One of his targets was Anthony Scibelli, a Democrat who had represented the city of Springfield for forty-seven years and voted against the death penalty in 1995. In his mideighties, Scibelli had a reputation for turning the Massachusetts Turnpike into a state-run racetrack for his ninety-mile commute to Beacon Hill. Cellucci tossed his pitch: "Lookit, Tony," the governor said with a mischievous smile, "if you vote for the death penalty, we'll raise the speed limit on the turnpike."

Unlike his predecessor, Cellucci had no qualms about tackling this tedious, time-consuming work. As a former state

representative and senator, Cellucci was well schooled in Massachusetts politics, in shoe-leather ways that Weld had never used, and he was confident of his ability to read and communicate with people. After all, this governor still mowed his own lawn and shopped for the groceries. He was the son of a car salesman who, through charm and persuasion, once sold a dozen burnt-orange Oldsmobiles that his father thought would never move. Twenty years later, Cellucci beamed whenever he saw one of those garish cars still driving the streets of Hudson. Cellucci knew people, and he knew that winning votes on the death penalty meant being polite, but being direct. "The people of Massachusetts are crying out for justice," Cellucci would say to wavering legislators. "The vast majority of people in Massachusetts and your district want a death penalty. And I do believe it is a deterrent."

As the governor worked the phones, his staff scurried behind the scenes to push an issue that had rocketed to the top of their agenda. "It was an all-hands-on-deck situation," Gray said. "We knew the public wanted the death penalty, and we made the public aware there was an opportunity to get it done." News conferences were held to trumpet support from crime victims and their families. Editorial boards were contacted. Op-ed pieces were submitted. Key government officials were made available for interviews. And district attorneys who backed the death penalty were urged to join the fray. "We in the governor's office," Gray said, "applied every tool we could to try to get the death penalty through, because the Curley murder gave it a chance to get over the top."

All the momentum had shifted to Cellucci, as reports circulated almost daily of another state representative who had decided to switch. At the beginning of the session, death-penalty foes had counted an eight-vote cushion in their favor. But the intense, relentless public pressure after Jeffrey's murder had shredded that safety net.

Finneran ceded day-to-day management of the fight to William Nagle, the House majority leader, who represented the liberal mecca of Northampton in western Massachusetts.

Nagle's opposition had its roots in the tainted 1806 murder convictions of two Irish immigrants, Dominic Daley and James Halligan, who were hanged in Northampton at a time of nasty prejudice against foreigners in general and Catholics in particular. Defense counsel was not appointed until two days before their trial, the charge was based on one boy's suspect testimony, and neither Daley nor Halligan was allowed by law to testify in his own behalf. "My father was a rabid, first-generation Irishman," Nagle said. "When we'd drive by Hospital Hill where they were executed, he'd say to me, 'Those guys were hung because they spoke Gaelic, they were Catholic, and they were foreigners.'" The hangings, in a town of twenty-five hundred people, attracted an overflow crowd of fifteen thousand from throughout the Connecticut River Valley and beyond.

The legacy of the case, fraught with bias and mistakes, made a lifelong impression on Nagle, who was determined never to allow Massachusetts the chance to execute an innocent person again. As a result, Nagle approached the death-penalty vote, scheduled for a week after the Senate decision, with a tenacious single-mindedness. His office became the opposition headquarters.

Nagle was allied with a coalition of advocacy groups led by the American Civil Liberties Union (ACLU), which admittedly had grown complacent during the Dukakis administration, when a death penalty seemed out of the question. Now, Nagle and his friends knew they had a desperate battle on their hands and little time to prepare. "It was like watching two trains coming down the track toward each other," Nagle said. "And every day that went by, it got worse." To survive the collision, Nagle met daily with his team to pore over lists of lawmakers to call, schedule meetings with activists across the state, and plead with constituents to lobby their legislators.

Norma Shapiro, legislative director of the Massachusetts branch of the ACLU, and Ann Lambert, a private attorney who sat on the chapter's board of directors, emerged as Nagle's key lieutenants. They approached the challenge with an enthusiastic, full-throttle commitment that matched his. "We

had assignments every single day on this," Nagle said. "If I said to Ann or Norma, go talk to ten people in this district, they would do it. And the next day we would meet regardless if it was eight in the morning or eight at night. Sometimes, we met two or three times a day." To Shapiro and Lambert, the effort was equal parts energizing and nerve-racking. "We had legislators who were helping us count noses, making sure that people were still with us," Shapiro said. "And we'd get messages from their staffs, saying, 'You have a problem with *x*, *y*, or *z*.' We'd go running right out to try to stop the problem, and we were not always necessarily successful."

Besides the ACLU, other groups joined the fight, including Massachusetts Citizens Against the Death Penalty, Amnesty International, the state's public defenders, the American Friends Service Committee, the Boston and Massachusetts bar associations, religious groups, and college organizations. "It took seven years," since Weld's gubernatorial election in 1990, "for all of us to really focus on a single mission, in a single way, in a concerted effort," Shapiro said. As a result, lobbying became disciplined. Visiting a legislator in his office was fine; picketing his house and following the family to soccer games was not. Shapiro, however, knew her side could not win the day on efficiency alone. "The noise out there was against us, and legislators are very sensitive to the noise," she said. "When you have people in church saying we need the death penalty, you know you've got a problem on your hands."

Shapiro and Lambert also felt they were constantly battling a shortsighted news media, which repeated, over and over, that polls showed three-quarters of the state supported capital punishment. A better indicator, Shapiro stressed, would be the Northeastern University poll from 1994, which also found only 38 percent support for the death penalty when respondents were given an option of life without parole. "It was very hard to convince legislators what the real polling looked like," Shapiro said. "The press was particularly bad for us."

As the climactic vote neared, the outcome remained too close to call, even for a head counter like Nagle, who prided

himself on up-to-the-minute numbers. "It was a jump ball," he said. With each passing day, the pressure intensified from Boston talk show hosts who urged listeners to flood the State House switchboard with a deluge of outrage. According to Nagle, the strategy was chillingly effective. "Some of these people who called had never voted, and never would vote," he said. "But if you get a call from Johnny Jones down the street, and he tells you to vote a certain way, you say, 'Oh my God, what's that mean?'"

Finneran continued to insist that he would not pressure any lawmakers, but he did meet with several representatives. Some he invited to his office for a conversation. Others were conflicted and wanted to know why Finneran, who once supported the death penalty, had changed his position. One of those members was Nancy Flavin, a Democrat from the western Massachusetts city of Easthampton, who had voted against capital punishment in 1995 but now was torn and undecided.

Finneran explained to Flavin, as he explained to others, that his epiphany came through Bobby Joe Leaster, a twenty-one-year-old black man wrongly convicted of the 1971 murder of a variety store owner in the Dorchester neighborhood of Boston. Leaster served fifteen years in prison while Robert and Christopher Muse, father-and-son attorneys from Boston, championed his case with appeal after appeal. Finally, Leaster was freed after a schoolteacher, jarred by a *Boston Globe* story on the case, told authorities that Leaster had not been one of the two men he saw fleeing the store.

"What struck me about Bobby Joe Leaster were the parallels in our lives on some very basic things," said Finneran, who had met with Leaster. "We're roughly the same age. When he got into his situation, I was coming out of college, going to law school, falling in love, starting my family. And he's put away for fifteen years for a crime he didn't commit. I'm thinking to myself, God, if we had a death penalty, he would have been gone. So, while I'm marching the fifteen years from here to there, building a law practice and getting elected, he's sitting in a cell for something he didn't do. But there was no

anger, no bitterness, no 'You motherfuckers ruined my life!' There was none of that stuff."

Flavin listened, Finneran recalled, but she remained in a quandary. On the morning of the debate, a day Cellucci proclaimed "Jeffrey Curley and Victims of Murder Memorial Day," the governor believed he was three or four votes short of victory. In the other camp, an anxious Democratic leadership was certain only that the decision would be razor-thin for either side.

For Bob and Barbara Curley, the day held the promise of delayed but righteous justice—if not for Jeffrey, then for future children preyed upon by predators. Barbara shivered in the morning chill as she joined more than a dozen relatives and supporters at an entry arch to the State House. She brightened when a television reporter asked her thoughts. "My son would want me to do this for other children, so it doesn't ever happen to any other victims," Barbara said, her eyes bright and a smile crossing her face.

Bob did not share Barbara's enthusiasm. Pensive and edgy, he approached the day troubled by turbulent, barely contained emotions, which burst from their floodgates when he saw an elderly man, standing alone, protesting the death penalty with a handheld sign. His rage boiling and building, Bob eyed the man for several minutes. Finally, having seen enough, Bob stalked toward the man and began screaming uncontrollably. "You fucking left-wing burnout!" Bob yelled, his eyes bulging. "You've got nothing better to do than to come up here and take sides with Jaynes and Sicari? I should stick that sign up your fucking ass!"

Francine tried to pry Bob away. He turned, glaring at a sister he considered a saint. Today, none of that mattered. "Mind your own business!" Bob screamed at Francine before flinging a few, final words of abuse at the protester. Francine apologized to the man, who was flustered but forgiving. "I understand," he said calmly. Then, he quickly left.

The family regrouped inside the State House, where Donna Cuomo spotted them and offered her condolences. Asked how she intended to vote, Cuomo demurred and said

she did not want to tip her hand. Francine, however, thought she saw an indication that the family would be pleased.

Bob seemed anything but pleased, however, as the long day progressed. And his mood grew even darker when Jim Braude, a liberal activist and media pundit, spotted Bob outside the House gallery and walked over to introduce himself. Bob, bracing for a conversation he didn't want, knew Braude by sight and reputation. "You took one look at him, you knew he was a leftie," Bob said. The firefighters at Engine 5 often saw Braude in the morning, crossing Inman Square on his way to the tidy, trendy confines of the 1369 Coffee House. Bob usually would be sitting on the second-floor couch, reading the sports pages, when an old-time firefighter from the neighborhood announced Braude's appearance with muttering disdain.

"There he is," the firefighter would say slowly, inflicting a wound with every word. "There's that fuckin', left-wing, liberal, fuckin' Braude."

Braude, a former public defender in the South Bronx who opposed the death penalty, had traveled to the State House as an interested observer. He approached Bob to say hello but received a double-barreled blast of vitriol instead. Bob lashed out at Braude with an expletive-laden rant that targeted his two small daughters. The underlying message, Braude said, was unmistakably clear: "If something were to happen to your kids, Mr. Liberal Asshole, let's see what your position would be."

Around the corner, at the small State House coffee shop, Marilyn Abramofsky awaited the vote. Scot Lehigh, a *Boston Globe* reporter, spotted her discussing strategy and asked why she supported capital punishment. "They had no problem killing our children. Why should the state have any problem killing them?" Abramofsky scoffed. "I want stoning, hanging, blowing their brains out."

Lobbying by both sides continued through twelve intense hours of debate. Cellucci invited a parade of twenty lawmakers to his office. Clergy buttonholed legislators in the hallways. And Nagle, scanning the chamber, occasionally left

the podium to sit with individual members for a casual, collegial dose of deadly serious persuasion.

Above them, the large Curley entourage huddled in the gallery, holding photographs of Jeffrey as organized confusion unfolded below. Members wandered in and out. Chatter competed with oratory. And clerks and aides scurried to and from the podium where President-elect John F. Kennedy delivered his final speech before his 1961 inauguration.

For Bob, who had never been in the House of Representatives, the scene seemed clipped from an old movie. "Are these people for real, making these big speeches and all this?" Bob asked the person beside him. "I really didn't think they did this stuff." What Bob saw, in a mixture of bemusement and awe, was a history-steeped room where dark wood and plush blue carpeting lay underneath five heroic paintings of important scenes from Massachusetts history. One of the paintings, titled *Dawn of Tolerance in Massachusetts*, depicted Judge Samuel Sewall's public repentance in 1697 for his role in the Salem witchcraft trials. The irony of the image, overlooking a debate on state executions precisely three centuries later, appeared to pass unnoticed.

As promised, Fran Marini, the minority whip, carried John Curley's stack of death-penalty petitions to the lectern, where he held them aloft with his right hand and passionately urged his colleagues to do the voters' bidding. "Jeff died on October 1," Marini barked in a loud, clipped voice. "This hasn't taken a year to collect. This hasn't taken a month to collect. This is simply a few weeks of our citizens asking us to vote for this bill." Mary Jane Simmons, a Democrat from Leominster, appealed more to the gut. "Don't let these people go on the street," she pleaded, "and do what they did to that beautiful child, with the baseball cap and the blond hair, that will live in my mind forever."

Other lawmakers delivered equally charged speeches of resistance. One opponent, William McManus, a Democrat from Worcester, railed against the political threats he had received from constituents and others. "Shame on you people!"

he said angrily. "This isn't the type of vote that is for sale. . . . I think it's disgusting, and I am not going to cower to it. And if it costs me an election, God bless it. I couldn't care less."

The depth of emotion and public pressure startled many freshman representatives, including Eugene O'Flaherty, a former public defender from Boston's tough Charlestown neighborhood. O'Flaherty, who received hundreds of calls from his district, had generally opposed the death penalty in his campaign but said he would consider capital punishment for the murders of police officers and acts of terrorism. Shortly before the debate, however, O'Flaherty's stance turned to complete opposition when he met Paul Hill, a native of Northern Ireland, who had been wrongfully convicted in 1975 of an Irish Republican Army pub bombing in England. Hill served fifteen years of a life sentence before being exonerated. "By that point," O'Flaherty said, "I was feeling personally comfortable, still politically worried, but personally comfortable with the decision I was making."

A few, such as Flavin, were tormented until the second they cast their votes. Questions of justice, morality, life, death, and unspeakable crime swirled in the heads of the undecided. Flavin, in tears, reluctant but resolved, finally pressed the yea button. "I saw that child's face," she later told Norma Shapiro of the ACLU. "I just kept thinking of that little boy."

After a seemingly interminable wait, the green lights for yea votes and red ones for nays flashed on a board in the front of the chamber. Spectators, reporters, and hushed politicians, eyes darting over the roster, strained to find the answer in the lights. "Holy Jesus," Finneran said, stunned, to a Republican on the rostrum. "You know you guys won?" The unthinkable had happened. By the slimmest of margins, 81–79, the motion had passed.

Joyous bedlam erupted in the gallery. As clergy and other opponents looked on in disbelief, John Curley bellowed, "Thank you for saving our children! We appreciate it!" He was summarily ejected.

To Bob, the scene mirrored a hockey game at the Gore Street rink. "Arms up, high fives, the whole bit," Bob said.

"Just like somebody had scored a game-winning goal." Demonstrations also broke out on the floor, where several members greeted their victory with cheering and hand slaps.

Nagle, devastated by the decision, was disgusted. "That was the mood, you know?" he said. "That was the lynch mob." The displays also saddened Tom McGee, a two-term representative from Lynn, who had made his maiden House speech against the death penalty. "It was a moment I'll never forget," McGee said. "In the pit of my stomach, I had this feeling when you know something isn't right."

After the vote, many legislators adjourned to a Beacon Hill watering hole called The 21st Amendment, named for the act that repealed Prohibition. Some crossed the street to celebrate; others, like McGee, came to commiserate. "It was one of the lowest times I've ever had in the legislature," McGee said. "It hit home that the death penalty was going to return to Massachusetts." Cellucci, who had just scored a major political coup, was ecstatic. "This is a victory for justice and for the people of Massachusetts," he told reporters. Finneran, by contrast, was pessimistically philosophical. "We live in a time in society when our culture is coarse, it is violent, and it has unacceptable, unspeakable levels of conduct that are not always condemned and almost condoned," he said. "In that type of situation, when society becomes unhinged from its traditional mooring, virtually anything goes. People react." Cuomo, who cried as she voted, joined seven other representatives who had changed their positions from 1995 to tip the balance. "I really did not want to disappoint the Curleys," she said, "and I believe the public believes the death penalty is going to make a difference."

Bob, leaving the gallery, was mentally exhausted. "I guess it's a step in the right direction," he said wearily to reporters. "But we have a lot of hard work ahead of us." The Curleys headed back to the Hampshire Street condo, upbeat and energized by what they believed was the climactic conclusion of their monthlong crusade. The family had no idea that the House bill, which differed from the Senate version, was

headed to a conference committee for negotiations before a final vote. In their mind, the death penalty already was a locked-down reality. And for the first time since Jeffrey disappeared, the Curleys enjoyed a few hours of restrained celebration in the very rooms where they had kept an agonizing vigil. "Everybody was pretty pleased at what had happened, yet there was kind of a letdown for me," Bob recalled. "All the stuff leading up to that point had been a distraction. And now, that night, being a little happy on one hand, I was also asking myself, How do we move on here?"

The next day, at the State House, Nagle was asking himself the same question. Once again, time was not a friend. The bill would return shortly from conference committee, and the House would be asked to enact the legislation. To reporters who covered the initial vote and to nearly every other political observer on Beacon Hill, that bit of business seemed a formality. "There seems little doubt that capital punishment will be legalized," Doris Sue Wong and Adrian Walker wrote in the *Boston Globe*.

Undeterred but under no illusions, Nagle went to work to alter the outcome. His primary targets would be the eight legislators who had switched their 1995 votes, figuring that they now might regret the real-life effects of their change. The results, however, were not encouraging. "I spoke to a lot of people," Nagle said, "trying to convince them that this was a historic moment, not only in Massachusetts but in the nation." His pleas, heartfelt and urgent, were not successful.

Instead, Nagle shifted his attention. In poring over the legislative roster, he spotted one possibility, an obscure second-term representative from the blue-collar city of Peabody, a gritty enclave of fading tanneries and crowded, conservative neighborhoods. John Slattery, a thirty-nine-year-old lawyer, had already shown an independent streak by bucking Finneran on several issues. He also seemed ambitious, was well spoken, and had an innate scrappiness molded perhaps by several childhood years spent in a tough Lynn housing project.

Slattery had backed the death penalty in 1995 and again in the first 1997 House vote. But Nagle and others, particularly Majority Whip Sal DiMasi of Boston, thought Slattery would listen, at least, to their arguments about the fatal potential of human error. Because Slattery had performed criminal defense work, DiMasi said, he "understood that potential more than any other person who had voted for the death penalty." Nagle and DiMasi liked their chances for an intellectual connection with Slattery. They also liked his fearlessness. "We wanted to switch somebody, but it couldn't be like throwing a Christian into the lion's den," Nagle said. "We needed someone who was articulate, who could debate, and who could stand his ground as the tank was coming at him. John Slattery was that kid."

Earlier in the year, Slattery had sat on the Joint Criminal Justice Committee during its preliminary deliberations on the death penalty. He had heard testimony about wrongful convictions, about doubts regarding deterrence, and about the high costs of capital punishment. Although he voted in favor at that time, Senator Marian Walsh, who cochaired the panel, said Slattery showed an earnest curiosity.

In the following months, Slattery continued to explore the subject with Walsh and close friends in the House, particularly McGee and Paul Demakis, both of whom opposed capital punishment. Again, he listened. But again, despite emerging questions, he joined the majority in the full House's 81–79 vote. "I was torn, but I thought my constituents generally favored the death penalty," Slattery said. "That first vote was a matter of saying, 'You know what? I'll just be consistent.' And that's what I did."

As the days between votes dwindled from nine to a few, Slattery spoke to lawyers he respected. Over and over, Slattery heard that juries make mistakes, that innocent people are executed, and that minorities are far more likely to be sent to death row. He was still processing this information late on November 5, the day before the final vote, when he received a visitor in his fourth-floor office. DiMasi had walked down the

hall to speak with Slattery, a colleague with whom he often chatted during workouts at a nearby health club.

"John, I know this is a political decision," DiMasi said. "But, as a professional and as a human being, you know that mistakes are made in trials, and that mistakes that are made when there's a death penalty involved can be irreparable."

Slattery said that a switch might spell political suicide in his conservative district. But mostly, he sat silently, listening while DiMasi prodded him to consider the broader implications.

"Five or ten years from now, when you're not here, will you look back and say you made the right decision?" DiMasi asked. "That's the test you have to decide in what you're going to do, because I think you're going to have to live with that decision."

Slattery did not commit either way. But in his eyes, DiMasi recalled, Slattery appeared to be struggling.

Later that night, moved by the weight of argument, Slattery resolved to act. "If we can't be sure we're executing the right person, we shouldn't be executing anybody," Slattery said. "I just felt, at that point, that this was something I didn't want in Massachusetts."

Slattery at first confided his decision only to his wife, a nonpracticing lawyer who helped him weigh the repercussions.

"Are you prepared to leave the political arena?" she asked. "Because I'm not sure what will happen after you change your vote."

"Yeah, I'm prepared," Slattery said. "I think it's the right thing to do."

The following day reenergized the State House with a buzz of fresh anticipation. For proponents of the death penalty, this would be the day, finally, when Massachusetts became the thirty-ninth state to reinstate capital punishment. That afternoon, the Senate stayed true to form by approving the death-penalty bill reported out of conference committee, one that added the three new categories of murder endorsed by the House. The decision by the House, however, was not expected for several hours, which gave lobbyists on both sides time to

work the hallways and offices of the crowded Capitol in a last, feverish attempt to upend or uphold the status quo.

Bob Curley, who thought victory had already been won, learned only that day that the bill would resurface. He alerted friends and relatives and hustled to the State House, where he saw Sister Helen Prejean, the author of *Dead Man Walking* and a fervent death-penalty opponent, plying her brand of gentle Louisiana persuasion. A friend stopped to introduce Bob, but the encounter quickly turned nasty.

"Bob, this is Sister Helen."

"I understand you are in great pain," Sister Helen said, her voice calm and empathetic. "Your son has been taken from you."

Bob responded angrily. Instead of kindness and condolences, he saw an enemy meddling in a stranger's tragic business.

"You don't know me. You don't know Jeff. Why the fuck are you doing this?" Bob snapped, his voice rising. "Who the hell are you to be against the death penalty, when nothing like this has ever happened to any of your loved ones?"

Bob stalked away, unmoved by her compassion.

The confrontation would not be the last for the Curleys. Bob's brother Jim spotted Eugene O'Flaherty and approached the legislator with an aggressiveness that bordered on intimidation.

"Stand up there and say, 'You know what? I believe in this. We have to take a stand. We have to save our children. We have to put an end to this whole thing right here!'" Jim Curley said. "I'm begging you, please do the right thing."

O'Flaherty, facing a press of TV cameras and reporters who had rushed to the altercation, would not agree. Curley, incensed, flew into a rage.

"So Jeff died for no reason!" he shouted.

"I'm not saying that," O'Flaherty answered calmly. "I believe this bill is not constitutionally sound."

With tensions rising dangerously, two fellow freshmen gently pulled O'Flaherty away from a velvet rope that separated him from Curley and the media.

Cellucci, who predicted that the winning vote would hold, delayed a trip to Canada with a Massachusetts trade mission. Instead, he stayed in Boston to monitor developments from the spacious confines of his corner office. With Finneran as speaker, Cellucci knew the unexpected was not only possible, but probable. Unknown to the governor, the machinery of the unexpected had already begun to move. When Slattery arrived at the State House, his mind made up, he called DiMasi and asked him to stop by his office. There, he delivered the thunderbolt.

"I'm going to change my vote, and I want to make a speech," Slattery said. "I may never get elected again in my district, but I'm going to do it because I think it's the right thing to do."

"I don't think you'll ever regret it," DiMasi said.

Slattery also informed Nagle, who warned him of an "acid bath of publicity" to follow. "You can expect to be vilified," he said. "Just be prepared for it." Nagle was elated, knowing he now had the votes to kill the death penalty with an 80–80 tie.

Before long, rumors of Slattery's defection had spread like wildfire throughout the building. Paul Haley, who pushed for the bill as chairman of the Ways and Means Committee, invited Slattery to his office for what became a frustrating, unpersuasive conversation. "It was obvious that there was going to be no reasoning with him," Haley said. Still, Haley delivered an impassioned speech on the House floor, defending capital punishment as a justifiable, necessary message from law-abiding society. "We are not choosing death here today," he said. "Those that have perpetrated the most heinous acts have decided that life should hang in the balance. We are stating unequivocally that, you rob someone else's life for your own twisted end, you put your own life in jeopardy."

Cellucci also summoned Slattery, who remained unmoved by the governor's arguments. Shortly afterward, sensing defeat, Cellucci held a news conference in which he divulged

Slattery's intentions. That announcement opened the flood-gates of recrimination, and Slattery's office was immediately swamped with outraged calls. Radio hosts had begun airing his telephone number and whipping listeners into a frenzy with allegations that Slattery had struck a backdoor deal to boost his political fortunes.

Later, when Slattery took his seat in the House chamber, three rows from the rear, his friend Paul Demakis saw some-one who was extremely agitated. "I think the message to all of us was, leave him alone," said Demakis, who had just been given a glimpse of John Slattery's new life. "I went outside the chamber before the vote, and this guy, with just a crazed look on his face, says to me, 'Are you John Slattery?' Thank God I wasn't, because he would have assaulted me."

As Slattery rose to address the chamber, now hushed for the day's key speech, he ripped into the rumors that he had sold his vote for Finneran's favor. "Let me start off by grabbing by the lapels the argument that I had any connection to the speaker of the House in arriving at a decision here tonight. First of all, I take responsibility for my own acts," he said an-grily, glaring at individual members throughout the room. "And I don't need any one of you to tell me who's responsible for my acts."

Slattery repeated his belief, stated the week before, that some criminals deserve the death penalty. But since that first vote, Slattery told the House, his discussions with lawyers and constituents had "left me with an abiding conviction that we can't be certain in the criminal-justice system that we always get the right guy. And if I can't be certain that I'm getting the right guy, then I have a very big problem with the death penalty," Slattery said. "I don't want to be lying in my bed, at 12:01 A.M., fifteen years from now, knowing that somebody's being put to death, that I helped to create the mechanism for putting that person to death, and not being sure that that per-son being put to death deserves what he got." In conclusion, Slattery said, "I need to be able to look myself in the mirror

the next day and like the person I see. And I can't do that if I
feel that someone innocent might die because of me."

Soon, the bill awaited only the roll call that House members knew would doom the death penalty. Many in the gallery,
however, did not know that the outcome had been determined.
Finneran, subdued, addressed the chamber with the results.
"Eighty having voted in the affirmative, eighty in the negative,
the bill is not passed," he said.

The effect was either devastating or exhilarating. From
the Curleys, a wave of cries and curses rolled toward the rostrum. Once again, John Curley was the loudest. "Are you out
of your mind?" he screamed as Finneran pounded the gavel for
order. At the opposite end of the gallery, lobbyists who had
worked against the bill shed tears for their improbable victory.
And on the floor, where drained members digested the outcome, two security officers told Slattery they would escort him
from the chamber.

"You don't have to do that," Slattery said.

"No, we're walking you out," one of the officers answered
firmly. "We don't want any issues in here. People are pretty upset, and we're going to get you out of the building. Do you
have someone who can pick you up?"

"My brother," Slattery replied.

Upstairs, Bob left the gallery in a daze, unsure how the
bill had failed but certain that the villain was Slattery. As he
emerged, a pushing, jostling throng of reporters surrounded
him, asking for his reaction. "It's disgusting, okay? They probably dug up some dirt on Slattery, and they threw it at him,"
Bob said. "It's up to the people out there to make a stand and
get after these politicians. They just can't have their way and do
what they want. It's an insult." Nearby, Finneran also spoke
with the media. And as he did, the trembling brother of a murder victim shouted, "Coward!"

One floor below, Cellucci strode from his office, nearly
red with rage, to rail at the bitter outcome. "We saw a phony
vote, we saw a deal, we saw chicanery, and the will of the
people was defeated tonight!" Cellucci said, seething. "Have

you ever seen a phony vote like that?" Rob Gray, the governor's press secretary, went further. "He's a profile in cowardice," Gray said of Slattery. "The words 'spineless' and 'hypocrite' also come to mind."

The torrent of withering criticism had only begun for Slattery, who returned home to see a Peabody police cruiser parked outside for protection. Angry calls, some of them death threats, crackled over his telephone for days. "How would you like it if you were murdered?" one caller asked. "How would you like it if your kids were murdered?" another screamed. "Maybe they should put you and all the murderers on an island together," yet another suggested. "One guy threatened to come over to my house. I didn't know what he wanted to do, but I said, 'Hey, come on over,'" Slattery recalled. "He never did." For safety, Slattery moved his wife and three children, ages seven, five, and three, to his mother-in-law's home.

Despite the uproar, Slattery let much of the abuse pass without comment. "Once I've made a decision, I'm done. I felt I reached my decision based on the evidence and in an intellectually honest fashion," he said. "People can scream at me, and it's water off a duck's back. It doesn't faze me one way or another."

One attack, however, infuriated Slattery and his wife. The assault came from *Boston Herald* columnist Howie Carr, who wrote the day after the decision that "Judas Slattery" had sold his vote for "blood money." In Carr's view, Slattery had just endeared himself to a new bloc of friends, the murderers imprisoned throughout Massachusetts who certainly were rejoicing at the demise of capital punishment. "The only shocker," Carr wrote, "is that the Judas hails from the city of Peabody," where Kristen Crowley had been murdered by two men who "decided they wanted a 'piece of that'" before crushing her skull. Carr continued the offensive with a bit of Irish slang. "Rep. Judas Slattery has three children," Carr wrote. "One can only pray that none of his new-found friends ever decide they 'want a piece' of a Slattery spalpeen."

To Bill Nagle, however, Slattery's actions were nothing short of heroic. "No individual I served with compares to the courage he exhibited that day," Nagle said. "Over the years, I served with a lot of people, some very qualified people, and some very, very bright human beings. But for that particular day, he'll always be the one, my personal hero. He was willing to stand up, and it was amazing."

———

—— 6 ——

Uncharted
Ground

IN THE WEEKS following the State House dramatics, the ba-
nalities of everyday life slowly replaced the distractions that
had helped shield the Curleys from the horror of Jeffrey's murder. The television lights had been carted away, the memorial
shrine had long since been dismantled, and family members
had withdrawn to confront, finally, the magnitude of a tragedy
that had made their private loss a very public spectacle.

Bob, like Barbara and the boys, still warmed to the condolences of friends and strangers whenever he ventured outside. And at the condo, hundreds of letters from across the
country arrived in a steady, comforting stream. But despite
this support, Bob and his family found themselves ever more
isolated in their pain. "I can talk to people on the street, and
they tell me they know how I feel," Bob said at the time. "But
they don't. They can't know how I feel."

The tough-minded, almost defiant, stoicism that had been
a hallmark of both his neighborhood and culture became a defense mechanism that helped Bob get on with his life. But the
struggle, a constant and wearing one, was unlike anything he
had ever experienced. "I'm forty-two years old, and I try to
contain my emotions," Bob said then. "But you're just so hurt,
and you feel so violated, and you've got to try to have a disciplined attitude. If I start to fall apart, it won't serve anything."

One path in which Bob channeled his emotions was a dogged continuation of the death-penalty fight, which Governor Paul Cellucci pledged to wage in the next election against every legislator who voted against capital punishment. Indeed, Cellucci offered to campaign for any death-penalty supporter who would run against any of the eighty offending lawmakers. "This battle is not over," Cellucci said. "I intend to go to every part of this state, and I intend to let the people of Massachusetts know what happened, and I intend to support people for the House next year who are going to vote to bring the death penalty back."

Although those elections were a year away, the first test of the political appeal of capital punishment surfaced almost immediately in a special race to replace state Senator Paul White, a death-penalty advocate from Dorchester who had resigned midterm. Three of the four Democratic candidates, whose December 9 primary would essentially decide the race, opposed capital punishment. But the fourth hopeful, longtime Boston City Councilor Maura Hennigan, made its restoration an outsized, controversial cornerstone of her campaign.

Hennigan's staff enlisted Bob Curley's endorsement. The candidate held a news conference at the State House with members of the Curley family. She issued a flurry of press releases that trumpeted her support for capital punishment. And her campaign—without Hennigan's prior authorization, she said—even used the now-famous Little League photograph of Jeffrey Curley on its fliers.

The effect was electric. In a city with a storied history of bare-knuckled politics, even jaded, seen-it-all observers were horrified. One candidate, Eleanor LeCain, derisively commented that Hennigan seemed to be "running for state executioner instead of state senator." The Democratic campaign committee from Hennigan's own ward, in a stinging rebuke, declined to endorse a candidate. And State Representative Brian Joyce, the eventual winner, expressed disgust. "On such a personal matter of conscience, I understand and respect that reasonable people disagree," said Joyce, who had resisted enormous pressure during the State House debate to support

the death penalty. "What I question is Maura's motive. By all accounts, it appears to be shameless political grandstanding." Hennigan made no apologies for her support of the issue, which she said resonated in the district's pivotal conservative suburbs. And besides, Hennigan added, she had been a long-time supporter of capital punishment.

At first, Bob backed Hennigan enthusiastically. He knocked on doors of homes and businesses. He stood in shopping centers. He shook hands in suburbs he had never visited before. And he recited his mantra that the death penalty could prevent the murder of another Jeffrey Curley. "It was all death-penalty stuff, just urging them to vote for her because she was for the death penalty and Joyce wasn't," Bob recalled.

Hennigan asked if Bob knew John Walsh, the anticrime activist and TV host of *America's Most Wanted*, whose son had been abducted and killed in Florida in 1981. Hennigan wanted Walsh to speak on her behalf, Bob said, but he never placed the call. "I was doing all this, but I had an uneasy feeling," he said. "I thought it was for the right reasons, but I just didn't know. Really, I didn't understand what the hell was going on. I was very naive in regard to politics."

Clarity came when Bob first saw the Hennigan flier with Jeffrey's picture. The message stunned him: Jeffrey had become a political poster boy for the death penalty. "Nobody asked me how I felt about it. It was just done," said Bob, who saw the flier by chance on the campaign trail. "What the fuck? They're gonna do this, and nobody's gonna ask me how I feel?" Without fanfare or an announcement, Bob walked away from the campaign. "I just said to myself, I'm out of here. That's it for me."

The issue failed to push Hennigan over the top. Instead of victory, she finished a distant third. Exit polls indicated that the rhetoric about capital punishment had motivated its opponents to vote. The same polling also indicated that voters, particularly the supporters of executions, were startlingly unaware of the state's penalty for murder. Only 11 percent of respondents knew that first-degree murder in Massachusetts carried a sentence of

life without parole. Among capital-punishment supporters, nearly half believed that murderers usually served less than ten years in prison.

Angered by the flier, Bob wanted to shrink from the public eye. But he soon found himself pulled back into the full, harsh glare of the media spotlight.

Only eight days after the special election, Sicari and Jaynes's long-awaited superior court arraignment on murder and kidnapping charges was held in Cambridge. Unlike the separate arraignments two months earlier in Newton District Court, this proceeding brought the two defendants together before a judge for the first time. Courthouse security was bolstered in numbers and intensity, complete with bulletproof vests for the defendants and a ring of police escorts for Sicari and Jaynes, who were hustled past a hostile, jeering crowd less than a mile from the Curley home.

Inside, prosecutor David Yannetti once again detailed the grisly allegations against the pair, this time for Judge Judith Cowin. While he did, Sicari glanced toward the gallery packed with Curley family members. Bobby Curley was certain that Sicari pursed his lips and winked at him, a flippant gesture of nonchalant defiance toward a neighborhood tough guy he despised. "You fucking faggot!" Bobby yelled, lurching toward the railing that separated defendants from the public. "You're lucky you're behind there, or I'd kill you myself!" Cowin quickly ordered court officers to escort Bobby from the room. Later, after Sicari and Jaynes had been led away, most of the Curley family avoided a legion of reporters by leaving through a back entrance obscured from public view.

By this time, Bob had returned to the Fire Department, but his colleagues did not recognize the man who had left work on the afternoon of October 1. "When Bob came back, he was a basket case. He was frigging gone. I mean, he was like an empty skeleton walking around," recalled Bill McGovern, the longtime firefighter and neighborhood friend. "Bob was not a happy guy anymore. Now, he was sullen and very, very

quiet. Everybody was afraid to talk to him because they figured he'd snap."

Despite appearances, Bob considered the firefighters a lifeline to sanity. One of them, whose brother had committed suicide, gave Bob a book on grieving. Others encouraged him to attend "Sparks" meetings on the Boston waterfront, where off-duty firefighters and fire buffs gathered, pagers on their belts, to chase the next blaze. During one meeting, Bob recalled, "Cambridge had a four-bagger—a four-alarm fire—and the place emptied out like somebody threw a hand grenade in the room."

To firefighter Fran Judd, an East Cambridge native raised in the housing projects near the Curley condo, Bob seemed burdened by questions about Jeffrey's supervision. In private conversations and public forums, Bob and Barbara heard murmurs and innuendos that their ten-year-old had been given too much freedom. "I think he probably felt there was a lot of negativity. You know, Why wasn't he there?" Judd recalled. "I never got into that. I thought he was a good father."

Others were not so sure. Some talk show hosts bluntly asked where Jeffrey's parents had been. The implication of gross neglect, delivered to a mass audience, was a stinging and embarrassing reprimand. Who the hell do they think they are to be telling me how to conduct myself? Bob thought at the time. They're not in my shoes. Who's supposed to be in jail? Me and Barbara, or Jaynes and Sicari?

The criticism also came through the mail. One letter, from a Brockton priest, warned Bob that he would go directly to hell, and never see Jeffrey, if he persisted in his campaign for the death penalty. For Bob, the landscape had shifted dramatically and unexpectedly. Once a tragic but empathetic figure, he now reminded many people of a horror they would rather forget.

But Bob could not escape his demons. The regular guy who would toss back a beer at the Druid, who would gab about sports after work, had all but disappeared. Fran Judd,

for one, became concerned about Bob's mental health and would check on him almost surreptitiously at the firehouse. "When I'd leave, I'd go downstairs and shoot the crap with him, you know?" Judd said. "I suppose he wouldn't do anything foolish, but he didn't seem like the same guy. He was bitter, and you couldn't blame him." Certain topics of conversation became off-limits. "You didn't want to talk about your own kids. You kind of laid back from that," McGovern said. "We didn't shun him, but we said, Give him some space, let him heal, and when he's ready, we'll be there for him."

One conversation could not wait. McGovern became ill with stress when Jeffrey disappeared, and the condition worsened as the days passed without any sign of the boy's body. "I could not even go to the funeral, and it bothered me terrible," McGovern said. "My stomach just blew right out, and the more it went on, the sicker I got." Then, two months after Jeffrey's death, just as Bob returned to work, McGovern had a dream. "Jeffrey just came to me and said, 'Hey, Magoo, how're you doing? Everything's fine up here. Don't worry. I'm with God,'" McGovern recalled, his eyes welling with tears. "It was just his face, and he was smiling. I told Bob in the back room downstairs, and we had a good cry. I felt better after that."

While Bob struggled to adjust, Barbara and the boys endured a similar but less-visible version of hell. Barbara could not summon the strength to return to work, Shaun had dropped out of his senior year at high school, and Bobby, a tinderbox of volatility, refused to discuss his feelings during therapy sessions.

Barbara often was unable to dress herself. Instead, she relied on the help of Bobby and two sisters who had moved into the condo temporarily, one of whom even slept in the same bed with her. Jeffrey's grandmother, ill and frail, also came to live with her heavily medicated daughter. "I'd be curled up in a ball in the bathroom, crying my eyes out," Barbara recalled. "Everywhere I'd look, there would be Jeffrey. I'd hear his voice calling, 'Mommy, Mommy, Mommy.'"

Bobby now considered himself the man of the house, but one with frightening responsibilities. At nineteen years old, he

often was the person to lift his mother off the bathroom floor, console her, and try to convince her of the improbability that better days lay ahead. "Every time she cried herself to sleep, I'd be the one there holding her," Bobby said. "I had to step up. I had to talk to her, because she wouldn't be all there. She was just crying, and she was not herself. She said things that really hurt me in the process, but I know she never meant it. I tried to let it go in one ear and out the other, but it's not easy, you know?"

Barbara had become a helpless, broken woman. But Bobby's life changed forever, too, the day Jeffrey disappeared. "Something in your heart's not there anymore," he said. "They could hang me by my feet for months on end, and it wouldn't bother me as much as that pain. They could take every penny I have, they could take everything from me, and it wouldn't bother me." Bobby withdrew from his social circle, distrustful and angry, winnowing his friends to only a select few and casting a wary eye on anyone who tried to draw close. "I didn't talk to nobody, not about what's bothering me. That stuff I keep to myself," he said. "Somehow, some way, I deal with it. It feels lonely sometimes, to tell you the truth, and I'm not really a lonely person."

Although Bobby tried to stay focused and positive, a mere sighting of the Sicaris could shatter his fragile self-discipline. Once, Bobby and Shaun threatened the Sicaris as they passed the family's apartment building. "We seen them on the corner, giving us dirty looks like we did something fucking wrong to *them*!" Bobby recalled. In an instant, Bobby's rage found voice in a vile, threatening broadside that led to the brothers' arrest. Bobby spent a week in the Billerica House of Correction before the charges were dropped.

Shaun, however, was jailed for more than a month in Boston on a variety of charges. In one incident, he chased the Sicaris into their building with a hammer that he fully intended to use. "I came out of my driveway, and I see these people sitting outside in beach chairs, laughing and joking around like it's a celebration," Shaun said. "I pulled my truck

over right in the middle of the street, got out, and chased them inside, pounding on the door. I was going to hurt them." Like his older brother, Shaun had been ripped apart emotionally. "Some days it made me angry, some days it made me sad, you know?" he said. "And being a teenager, you kind of don't want to be sad. You'd rather be angry and take it out on other people. And I took it out on Salvatore Sicari's family."

Shaun responded to therapy much better than his brother, but he also looked to friends and drugs to ease the pain. His mood-altering favorite was Ecstasy, which Shaun favored for the upbeat, "happy" high that provided an escape for several hours. "We'd head into Boston on Friday night," Shaun recalled, "and the clubs there would close at two in the morning. Everybody would still be riled up, you know? We'd be having a good time, so it's like, Why don't we go to New York?" Nearly a dozen times in the first months after Jeffrey's death, Shaun sought release in the New York rave scene, where clubs would open on Friday night and not close until Sunday morning and where patrons could gorge themselves on a mind-numbing orgy of music, sound, and nonstop dancing. "It was, like, take a hit of Ecstasy, go to the rave, dance with a bunch of girls, and, you know, kind of keep everything else outside the club and have a good time," he said. "I didn't get addicted to Ecstasy or nothing like that, but those were, like, really the only good times that I got to really have. It's sad to say that."

As Christmas drew near, the family thought not of the holiday but only of surviving yet another interminable day. There would be no Christmas tree in the condo and none of the presents that Jeffrey had wanted since the summer. No battery-powered car, no new skates, no bicycle. If anything, Barbara felt worse as the holidays approached than she had in those first horrific days after the murder. Disbelief had morphed into reality, and shock had taken new shape as painful, palpable grief.

Jeffrey's room had not been touched since his death, and Barbara could not bring herself to cross its threshold. Still, every so often, she caught herself expecting to hear Jeffrey's

laugh or to see him running down the driveway. "Sometimes," she said, "I thought I'd wake up, and it'd all be a nightmare."

Jeffrey's younger relatives and friends continued to reel from the loss as well. Mary Downey, Francine's ten-year-old daughter, wrote touchingly of her heartache. "At least I have a memory to hold on to 'cause I had to let you go," Mary wrote in large block letters. "Sometimes when I'm in the dark, I feel scared, but you're the light at the end of the dark tunnel that I follow, and you lead me out of the dark and into the light. As tightly as I held, you broke away, and now you're gone. But I have your memory, and that won't get away."

Across the city from Jeffrey's home, in crowded Cambridge Cemetery, a small decorated pine tree and hundreds of flowers brightened a snow-covered plot on the fringes of the graveyard, where a stone bore Jeffrey's Little League image and a chiseled inscription to "Our Little Man." By Christmas, Barbara had traveled to the site only once, Bob twice. Nearly three months after the murder, Jeffrey's grave held no peace for the Curleys, no closure, no comfort. Instead, the family saw only a cold, black marker and a perpetual, engraved smile that reminded them of all they had lost.

After the holidays, the new year introduced the Curleys to the methodical pace of the state's judicial bureaucracy. The tornado of action that had defined the search for Jeffrey had been slowed and channeled into a flurry of motions and hearings preceding the trials. Lawyers questioned whether Sicari had been denied his right to remain silent, whether to hold two trials instead of one, and whether to empanel a jury far from the Boston media market that had made Jeffrey Curley a household name.

Arthur Kelly and Robert Jubinville, the defense attorneys for Sicari and Jaynes, argued before Judge Cowin in a pretrial hearing that Sicari had thrown up his hands at Cambridge police headquarters and indicated he did not wish to answer any more questions. As a result, the attorneys said, his confession should be suppressed. Yannetti argued that Sicari, instead of invoking his constitutional right to silence, was scheming to

evade arrest when he refused to answer investigators for more than thirty minutes during the six-hour session. The prosecutor also noted that Sicari, on two occasions, had signed forms stating that he understood his rights to an attorney and to remain silent. In the end, Cowin sided with the prosecution and allowed the confession to be admitted at trial. She agreed, however, to hold two trials instead of one after Kelly expressed concern that Jaynes would testify against Sicari if they were tried together. She rejected a defense request for a change of venue to western Massachusetts.

Media interest in the trial, scheduled to begin October 26, more than a year after the crime, was predictably intense, and the New England all-news cable channel planned gavel-to-gavel coverage. Cowin, a former prosecutor with a reputation as a smart, tough jurist, clearly realized the extent of public scrutiny about to descend on Courtroom 12B, even if she wrote in one ruling that "there is nothing unique to this case that requires a change in venue." To limit what Kelly called the media's potentially "chilling effect" on jury selection, Cowin allowed only a single reporter to witness the process. She also barred reporters from conducting interviews inside the courthouse and on the sidewalks surrounding the building. The Boston news media were outraged by the ban, which attorneys for three television stations challenged as "unprecedented and unconstitutional." A single justice of the state's highest court quickly overturned the order, which he said infringed on "news gathering in its quintessential form."

Interest in the trial also ran high on Beacon Hill, where Cellucci was involved in the final days of a hard-fought campaign to determine whether he, an acting governor, would be voted into office in his own right. Help came from Bob Curley, who endorsed Cellucci during a State House news conference to promote the first Jeffrey Curley road race, designed to raise money for child-safety programs. Before a cluster of television cameras, Cellucci reiterated his support for the death penalty on the first anniversary of Jeffrey's murder. "We need to do everything we can to make sure that law enforcement and our

criminal justice system have the resources to prevent these horrible crimes," Cellucci said. The campaign staff of his Democratic rival, death-penalty opponent Scott Harshbarger, lambasted the governor. "I think it's clear that Paul Cellucci stands for his own political convenience," said Ed Cafasso, a Harshbarger spokesman. "And he'll use anyone or anything he needs to position himself politically to further his own political interests."

Politics were not on David Yannetti's mind as he prepared for the biggest trial of his career. Much, but not all, of the tedious grunt work of lining up witnesses, conducting depositions, poring over evidence, and plotting strategy was now behind him as he went to battle backed by the formidable human and financial resources of the largest district attorney's office in Massachusetts. Although the public expected a conviction and the evidence seemed overwhelming, Yannetti faced enormous pressure to bring home the first-degree murder verdict that Middlesex District Attorney Tom Reilly, who was running for state attorney general, so desperately wanted.

Yannetti relished the fight. Reilly had hand-picked him, a bright, jockish star in the Middlesex office, as one of his premier homicide attorneys. And by the time McEvoy assigned him to the Curley case, Yannetti had already tried ten murders. A former long-distance runner at Bowdoin College in Maine, he loved both the law and the all-consuming intensity of high-profile cases. Quiet and self-effacing outside the courtroom, Yannetti seemed transformed before a jury, where he would pound home a point with impromptu theatrics, rhetorical flourishes, and long, dramatic pauses.

For six years, Yannetti had been living alone in a barely furnished apartment on a narrow street in Boston's heavily Italian North End. There, in the seven hundred square feet he called home for a sweetheart deal of $400 a month, he buried himself in the minutiae of the Curley case when he wasn't ensconced in the second-floor offices of the district attorney's homicide team. "You're getting up before dawn. You're cramming work into every nook and cranny of the day that you can,

and still trying to get enough sleep so you're not bleary-eyed the next day," Yannetti recalled of his long, grueling hours on the case. "Maybe you'd go out to get something to eat on a Saturday night, but you're basically in the office," he said. "It's almost a twenty-four/seven deal."

Yannetti's strategy would be to portray Sicari as a full-fledged coconspirator in Jeffrey's death, which, if proved, would be enough to win the case. Under the legal theory of joint venture, which Yannetti pursued, Sicari would be as culpable as the actual killer if he shared the murderer's intent and was prepared to help during or after the crime.

Kelly, on the other hand, would seek to deflect blame from Sicari by putting Jaynes on trial in the minds of the jury. In his opening statement, Kelly conceded that his client, appallingly, did nothing to prevent Jeffrey's death. But, he argued, Sicari's actions did not rise to first-degree murder. Instead, Kelly said, the evidence pointed overwhelmingly to Jaynes, an admitted pedophile, as the mastermind of Jeffrey's seduction and the boy's remorseless executioner.

The Curley family filled the first row of the public gallery for all nine days of testimony, some of it mundane, much of it excruciating. Autopsy photos were displayed on a screen for the jury to examine, the Maine state medical examiner described Jeffrey's painful death in exacting detail, and acquaintances of Jaynes testified again and again about his unnatural attraction to young boys. Yannetti called fifty-five witnesses, including forensic experts from the Washington office of the FBI, in a meticulously prepared case that underscored the depth and breadth of the state's commitment to the trial. The defense called five.

Kelly delivered his closing arguments first, pacing like a boxer and jabbing the air. "Charles Jaynes, he killed that young boy. He seduced him and he killed him," Kelly said, his voice alternating between a whisper and a shout. "Salvatore Sicari did nothing to stop it. As reprehensible, despicable, and disgusting as that is, he did nothing. But he did not commit murder in the first degree."

Kelly led the jury through the testimony of witnesses who had connected Jaynes to his perversions and the crime. "Did we see any evidence whatsoever of Sal Sicari with such desires, intentions, or motives?" he asked. "We did not. It was Jaynes, and Jaynes alone, who had the motive, desire, and intent."

Kelly pleaded with the jury to put aside its revulsion and consider the evidence dispassionately. "You stood up and raised your right hand," he said, raising his own for emphasis, and swore "that you would look at this evidence with your mind and not your heart. I'm asking you to do that now. Because if you do that, you will find that the commonwealth has not proven this case beyond a reasonable doubt."

Yannetti immediately went on the offensive. "Mr. Kelly calls Salvatore Sicari's actions on October 1 and 2 unconscionable, despicable, reprehensible, wrong. I suggest to you that there's a more appropriate name for Salvatore Sicari's actions on October 1. That name is murder in the first degree," Yannetti said, his voice rising steadily. "When you boil it all down, this is a very simple case. Jeffrey Curley left Cambridge with two men, the two men who'd been spending time with him, the two men who'd been seducing him, and Jeffrey Curley never came home."

Yannetti became more animated as he continued. He beseeched the jury, he pointed directly at Sicari, and he grimaced at the horror of the crime. Jeffrey, he said, "was a ten-year-old boy who was made to feel like he was a big man. Me and Charlie and Sal. The three of us. The three musketeers. That respect turned to horror and disgust and terror when he realized why they were really treating him like they treated him." Yannetti mimicked Jeffrey's desperate attempts to ward off the gasoline-soaked rag and Jaynes's suffocating weight, flailing his arms in a wild-eyed reenactment of what Jeffrey experienced. "He struggled, he scratched, he clawed, with every ounce of might that his ten-year-old body could muster. You saw the autopsy photos. You saw all the red marks on Jeffrey Curley's face. You saw it on his chest, and his arm, and his eye." As he finished, Yannetti walked slowly before the jurors and showed

them Sicari's booking photo. "I ask you, ladies and gentlemen, to find Salvatore Sicari guilty of murder in the first degree. And nothing less."

The jury deliberated for twenty-two hours over four agonizing days before they finally convicted Sicari of first-degree murder. As the verdict was delivered, Sicari stared ahead blankly, without emotion, just as he had for the entire trial and just as he did when Cowin ordered a mandatory sentence of life without parole.

The Curley family, however, erupted in an outburst of shouts, relief, and rapturous embraces before being muffled by a sharp order for silence. Then, Barbara and Bob Curley—one, tearful, the other defiant—delivered powerful victim-impact statements from the witness stand as Sicari, handcuffed and flanked by two court officers, watched impassively from the back of the jury box. "No justice can ever be served, because nothing can ever bring Jeff back," Barbara said, biting her lip and fighting back tears as she read from a piece of crumpled paper. "Part of each one of us is in the grave with Jeff forever."

If Barbara represented heartbreak, Bob embodied unquenchable anger. Seconds after he began to speak, Cowin admonished him not to look at Sicari. "What we've witnessed here the last two weeks, the people that come through here, is just a small glimpse of the dark side of society that's out there," Bob said, shaking his head and snarling in disgust. "We have to make a statement as a society that we won't allow crime like this. Crimes like this will go punished with the worst punishment we as a society can impose."

Bob did not mention the death penalty specifically. But Cellucci, who won election during the trial, wasted no time invoking what he pledged to make a priority of his first full term. "I have said for a long time that the two individuals involved in the Jeff Curley case are walking advertisements for the death penalty," he stated. "I am glad justice was done today." Capital punishment might not prevent all such crimes, Cellucci said, but the death penalty would give society the means to "express its outrage about some of this horrific violence."

Following the verdict, at a crowded news conference, Bob deflected questions about the death penalty. Such matters, he said, belonged to "the heavyweights" at the State House. He bristled when asked whether the conviction had brought closure to the family. "I hear this word 'closure' all the time, and I don't think I know quite what closure means," he said. "It'll be closure when you guys go home. But when the cameras go off, and six months from now when everybody forgets it, we're gonna have to live with it for the rest of our lives. I don't know if there can ever be closure for us."

Indeed, closure would be impossible for the near future. In less than three weeks, the Jaynes trial was scheduled to begin. One reporter asked Bob, as he moved toward the door, how the Curleys would prepare themselves for testimony that might surpass the gruesome ugliness that they had just heard. "We'll just try to get some rest today," Bob said wearily, "and worry about that tomorrow."

Inside, Bob realized he could not escape the trauma of Jeffrey's death. The tragedy had made him perhaps the most recognizable private citizen in the state, and his son's name had been indelibly attached to one of the most heinous crimes in Massachusetts history. Reminders of the murder could appear anytime, anywhere, and in the most innocuous of circumstances. Acquaintances and strangers often seemed uncomfortable around him, searching for words to express their sorrow or offer support. Ultimately, many of them were unable to say anything.

One such encounter occurred in a supermarket in Chelsea, a rough, working-class city across the harbor from downtown Boston. There, a woman bagging Bob's groceries began crying as she recognized the man who had come to embody every parent's worst nightmare. Bob returned her fixed, sorrowful gaze for an instant, but he could not utter a word. Nothing he could say, Bob felt, would make either of them feel better. Bob picked up his groceries, averted his eyes, and quickly left the store.

At home, Mimi noticed a dramatic change. The fun-loving, carefree Bob she met three years earlier had been replaced by

an angry, driven man who immersed himself in causes that had never interested him before. He advocated for a tough sex-offender registry in the state, railed against NAMBLA, raised money for child-safety programs, received stacks of letters, and spoke with death-penalty supporters from across the country. David Brudnoy, a radio personality in Boston who backed the death penalty, invited Bob onto his talk show. And George Hanna, the father of a slain Massachusetts state trooper, called Bob often to share like-minded thoughts on the need for capital punishment. "I had a full plate. There was no time to sit around and feel sorry for myself," Bob said. "There was a lot of stuff to do, and I wasn't gonna let Jeff go for nothing."

Although she opposed the death penalty, Mimi understood Bob's motivation. She also knew that the work would help channel his anger. "It was a way to make meaning out of the meaningless," she said. "He found that it was important, because he could speak for other people who had similar things happen." But as Bob's media exposure increased, Mimi became worried that he would be manipulated and exploited by death-penalty advocates, many of whom struck her as fanatical and obsessive. "It just seemed like a circus that was getting out of hand. People were coming out of the woodwork," she said. "You know, this man was grieving. This man was a mess. He had no business being a champion of the death penalty."

Mimi did not try to dissuade Bob from his crusade, but its highly publicized intensity added another strain to a relationship whose rhythms and routines already had been twisted and rearranged. For Mimi, the murder resurrected a pernicious personal connection with child sexual abuse, whose victims she had counseled for years. That work had proved unbearable and eventually compelled Mimi to move to other forms of trauma therapy. Now, suddenly, Mimi found herself surrounded by the aftereffects of a similar horror. "Bob was finding out the realities of child sexual abuse and how pervasive it was," she said. "He was a new convert to the cause. But, for me, I had been there and done that. And now it was brought into my home."

Bob was right; closure was not possible. And neither would it be for Mimi, who soon found herself ensnared in a maelstrom of capricious, psychological demons that were holding her partner hostage. The emotional peace that Mimi had long sought and believed she had found began to crumble. And in the process, the crumbling of this rare relationship, one that had blossomed by chance and by courage, accelerated into a devastating implosion.

———

— 7 —

Collateral Damage

THE BEGINNINGS of that romance more than a decade earlier had the flavor of teenage flirtation, although the fire
mechanic and the psychologist had seen plenty of life and
shed their rose-colored glasses long before Bob began noticing
Mimi walking to work at Cambridge Hospital. Mimi had moved
into a modest, first-floor apartment on Inman Street, directly
across from the firehouse, after her second marriage ended in
divorce. The apartment happened to be visible from a small
window in Bob's firehouse workshop, and the movements of
this attractive newcomer immediately caught his attention.

Mimi, however, did not notice Bob. A small private practice plus two part-time counseling jobs at Cambridge Hospital
and Wellesley College monopolized her time and thoughts,
filling up her days and leaving her drained at night. Despite the
demands and distractions of her work, a plaguing loneliness
prompted Mimi, living alone, to consider returning to Colombia.

That thinking began to change in May 1995 as another
semester was winding down at Wellesley College. Mimi had
pulled up to the apartment with a car full of plants from her
office when she saw Bob jogging through the square. Oh my
God, who is that guy? she thought. But just as quickly, Mimi
upbraided herself for giving him more than a passing glance.
Why do you even bother? You may never see him again.

A few minutes later, Mimi heard a booming, friendly voice behind her. "Oooh, plants? I have a bunch of plants in the firehouse if you want some," Bob said with a grin. Mimi turned and saw the jogger. Startled for a moment, she quickly regained her composure, murmured a few words, and scurried into the apartment with her greenery. "Stay away from him," she muttered to herself. "This guy's a wolf. He probably talks to all the women around here."

Staying away proved to be no easy matter. On the three mornings a week she worked at Cambridge Hospital, Mimi invariably would fumble for her keys, leave the apartment late, and rush toward her office only a few blocks away. And just as invariably, Bob would be standing outside the firehouse as she passed.

"Where do you work?" he asked the first time.

Mimi did not break stride. Keep walking, she told herself.

The next time, Bob asked the question again.

"Oh, I work in the hospital," she answered.

About a week later, Bob tossed a follow-up.

"Are you a nurse?" he asked.

"No, I'm not," Mimi answered, smiling. "I'm a psychologist, and I know what you're thinking."

After that exchange, Mimi did not see Bob for several months, and she gradually relegated him to memory as she coped with a more pressing concern. A former student of hers, someone who had harassed and stalked her, had moved into an apartment across Inman Street. Mimi filed a restraining order, but the potential for unpleasant confrontations, even violence, frightened her as autumn turned to winter in late 1995.

Once, after a heavy snowstorm, she trudged to her car while nervously eyeing her surroundings. A man with a mustache stopped his truck.

"Hey, you don't say hello anymore?" he asked.

Mimi glanced warily at the man and recognized, to her relief, that this stranger was her unnamed admirer, who had been clean-shaven the last time she saw him. "Something lit up in my heart," Mimi recalled. "I thought I'd never see him again."

For the first time, Mimi spoke at length with Bob and told him of her worries about the neighbor. And when she did, she saw a dramatic shift in his demeanor, a change from light-hearted flirtation to genuine concern. "Keep an eye out for me, would you?" Mimi asked.

Afterward, they began talking more frequently, and Bob always asked if she felt safe. His interest and sincerity resonated with Mimi, who, in a moment of impulse, scribbled a note on a Christmas card that she placed on the windshield of his mechanic's truck. "I don't even know your name," she wrote, "but maybe some day we should have a cup of coffee!" As soon as she returned to her apartment, panic replaced giddiness. Oh no, what did I do? Mimi asked herself. She rushed outside, ridden with second-guessing, only to see Bob holding the card.

"Don't read it! Don't read it!" Mimi pleaded.

Bob smiled and said he thought the invitation was a good idea. Instead of coffee, he suggested they talk over drinks at the nearby Druid, where Irish accents and dark corners cloaked the place with a casual, Bohemian intimacy.

By this time, Bob had moved out of his house and begun to bunk at the fire station. His relationship with Barbara had broken down, but Mimi knew none of this. So, when he knocked on her door just before Christmas, Mimi was pleasantly surprised. She invited Bob into the apartment for cookies and sherry and almost immediately presented him with a question.

"Are you married?" asked Mimi, who had once seen a child's beach toy in his car.

"No, I'm divorced. I'm living with my mother on Gore Street with my two sons," Bob replied.

"Well, because if you're married," Mimi continued, "I don't want anything to do with you."

"No, no, I'm divorced," Bob said.

Mimi chose to believe him, this fire mechanic with a soothing, caring something that she found attractive. She had a doctorate, and Bob had struggled to finish high school. But there seemed to be a chemistry, and Mimi allowed the flame to flicker.

Soon afterward, Mimi invited Bob to a New Year's party that she energized with the Latin music and salsa dancing she craved. At one point, as Mimi danced intensely and alone to the rhythms of Colombia, Bob sat by himself on the couch, lost and transfixed, an outsider in an exotic culture he had never experienced. A friend of Mimi's noted Bob's predicament. "You're quite the bitch," she chided Mimi. "Look what you're doing to the poor man."

The relationship continued and deepened, but any hopes that Mimi entertained of a normal, grounded romance were jolted into another reality when her phone rang in late January. Bob was on the line, calling from Cambridge Hospital, where he had been admitted for an emergency colostomy. Mimi checked her schedule, saw that she had a cancellation, and made plans to visit him that night.

Again, Mimi knew only a fraction of the story. When Bob began feeling excruciating pain in his abdomen, he turned first to Barbara, not Mimi, and returned to his former home for advice and assistance. "I hadn't known Mimi very long, and I didn't know what the hell was going on with me," he said. "I didn't want to be a burden on her, and I didn't want to go to her house all sick, and in pain, and in agony." Instead, he found a ride to Hampshire Street, where Shaun was stunned to see his father, doubled over on the sidewalk, struggling in a snowstorm to find his footing. "Shaun, I think I'm dying," Bob said.

The boy had never seen his father helpless like this, pants hanging below his hips, hands clutching his stomach, his moaning constant and uncontrollable. Shaun helped carry him upstairs, where Bob asked Barbara to find a primary-care physician. Thinking the pain might be from kidney stones, Bob drank quart after quart of water and cranberry juice to flush away the hurt. When that failed to work, he took a taxi to the hospital's emergency room but was sent home when the medical staff could not pinpoint the problem.

The next morning, still in agony, Bob returned to Cambridge Hospital, where he was rushed into surgery. The last thing he heard before losing consciousness was an emergency

room nurse who shouted, "We've got one going gray." A commotion followed, then Bob woke to find himself being placed in a hospital bed with a colostomy bag attached to his stomach. His colon had burst. "They told me what was going on and that I had almost died," Bob said. "I'm just looking at the bag, saying, What the hell is this?"

Bob phoned Mimi soon afterward. When she rushed into his hospital room, she was surprised to see a woman standing by the bed. Mimi looked at Bob, who rolled his eyes, and the woman turned to greet Mimi.

"Hi, I'm Bobby's wife," Barbara Curley said cheerily.

Inwardly, Mimi was furious and devasted. Outwardly, she was controlled and left quickly. Barbara assumed that Mimi was a hospital employee, and Bob reinforced that assumption.

"She's just some psychiatrist," he told Barbara. "She's crazy, and I told her I don't want to talk to her."

Mimi returned to her office in a blind, seething rage. At the end of her workday, she visited Bob again. This time, Barbara was not present, only a patient from India on the other side of a flimsy curtain.

"How dare you!" she demanded. "How dare you lie to me!"

Mimi snatched a pocket knife that lay near the bed and pointed the blade at Bob.

"I'm going to rip you where they cut you," Mimi said, spitting the words at Bob, prone and wide-eyed on the bed. "I'm going to kill you!"

With that, the Indian patient began wheezing in fright, stunned that a murder might be imminent in the adjacent bed. Mimi lowered her voice.

"You're lucky," she said to Bob. "Give thanks to your roommate that I'm not going to kill you. I don't want you ever to call me again—ever!"

Bob, however, did call Mimi a week later. About to be released from the hospital, Bob needed somewhere to recuperate.

"What do you want?" Mimi barked when she heard Bob's voice on the telephone.

"I'm being discharged, and I'm on my way there," he answered.

Mimi was flabbergasted. A man she hardly knew, someone who had deceived her, had just announced he would be at her doorstep in a few minutes in need of a bed and attached to a colostomy bag.

"Why don't you go to your house?" Mimi asked.

"Because, I told you, I don't live there anymore," Bob replied. Despite her help, Bob had told Barbara he would continue to live at the firehouse. The situation at Hampshire Street was too stressful, he said.

Mimi took pity on Bob, despite the mountain of negatives that had suddenly accumulated. Mimi knew he would have surgery in a few months to reverse the colostomy and that his survival was not guaranteed. In gauging the situation, she stretched the bounds of rationalization. Maybe this means something, she thought. Maybe God is putting him here so I can take care of him for three months, and that's the end of the story. So, let him recover.

Mimi had no expectations for the relationship beyond the second surgery. She spent full days at work, nurses tended to Bob's needs at the apartment, and, as a bonus, Mimi's long-time pet, Picasso, had a new companion. "The cat seemed to get along with him, so to me that was a sign that maybe he was okay," Mimi said, chuckling. "The surgery came, he didn't die, and then I went, Damn, now I'm stuck with this man."

As 1996 progressed, Mimi began to warm to the concept of a long-term commitment. "He was vulnerable, and I said, Well, he's not really married," Mimi recalled. "There had been the Bob before, the one who looked at me on the street. And then there was the guy who was very warm, and giving, and a great friend, someone who seemed innocent in some ways. I knew he wasn't completely innocent, but in his soul he was. There was something about him that seemed kind of soothing, caring, and concerned."

Bob eventually told Barbara that he had moved in with another woman, but he did not elaborate. He did not make the

connection for Barbara between the woman she had met in the hospital and the new woman in his life. As a result, Barbara did not know Mimi's name, what she looked like, or where they lived, even though their apartment was only a few blocks away. What Barbara did know was that her life had changed for the worse.

For Bob, life had taken the opposite tack. He had a vivacious companion, an outlet into a new, wider world, and a future of exciting possibilities. In 1997, Bob and Mimi began hunting for a house when the landlord, displeased by this unattached male occupant, decided to raise the rent. After a few months of frustrated searching, Bob and Mimi found their prize: a two-family home in East Somerville owned by an elderly Italian widow. "They had an open house, and we come in, and there's an old lady sitting in the corner, Mrs. Roselli," Bob recalled. "It looked like a funeral parlor with early-nineteen-sixties decor." When Bob pulled up a corner of the rug, he saw a beautiful hardwood floor. "It wasn't a cheery place, but we could see it had potential." Smitten, Bob and Mimi made an on-the-spot offer of $190,000. The bid was accepted, they moved in June, quickly rented out the first-floor apartment, and set about renovating the second floor and roomy attic for themselves.

For Bob, the location was a wondrous revelation: large, roomy spaces and views of the Boston skyline. And less than two miles from Inman Square. Working on the house—stripping the walls, refinishing the floor, decorating the interior in a colorful, artsy, Latin style—helped bring Mimi and Bob closer. For this seemingly mismatched couple, the tumultuous childhoods they had both endured helped to deepen and strengthen their bond. "I think we gave to each other the missing part we always had," Mimi said. "I felt at home, with him, for the first time in my life, and he said he did, too."

Mimi was also struck by what she called Bob's "emotional language," an instinctive ability to recognize fear and sadness in others and react with understanding and comfort. For Mimi, she had never experienced such empathy in an intimate

relationship. And its resonance proved thrilling. "On the surface, we had these huge differences, we had nothing in common," she said. "But under the surface, there was something very similar and very profound where we connected."

To Mimi's thinking, they both had been "orphaned" as children. In Bob's case, the dysfunctional marriage of his parents had isolated him emotionally. For Mimi, whose father never married her mother and maintained a separate family, she felt shamed and abandoned during her formative years. That fear of abandonment resurfaced when Jeffrey died. "It stirred up all the stuff with my father," she said. "Here's a man who's married with kids; my father was married with kids. I just became so scared."

But in the midst of his own pain, Mimi found reassurance from Bob. "I would say, 'Just take your things. You're just here because it's comfortable. You're along for the ride,'" Mimi recalled. "But he had a way of containing me. He was very, very loving and very patient." That assurance, often wordless, seemed to spring from a deep and hidden place of understanding how sadness felt. That warmth engendered trust, Mimi said, and trust engendered love.

Bob's trauma, however, would batter that love. The initial shock of the killing had strained their relationship, but the trials would prove devastating. The grisly public testimony, the intense media interest, and the actual presence of the killers in court propelled Bob up to, and often over, the border between rage and derangement.

The public rarely saw this side of Bob, who sat grim faced but stoic in the courtroom—first in Cambridge for Sicari, and then in the central Massachusetts village of East Brookfield, where Jaynes had been granted a belated change of venue. In their home in East Somerville, however, away from the public, Mimi saw a man transformed, mentally and physically, by his reacquaintance with the murder. Although Mimi avoided nearly all of the trials, she was forced to live them through the searing wounds they reopened in Bob. "After my day at work, I would come home to find a different person," Mimi said. "I didn't know

Jeffrey Curley in his Cambridge Little League uniform. This photo, published in newspapers and carried on television, became the indelible image of the murder victim. *Curley family photo*

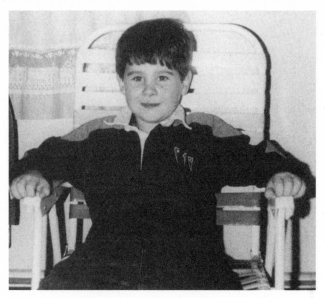

Jeffrey Curley, fearless and precocious, was a constant, energetic presence in his East Cambridge neighborhood. *Curley family photo*

The home of Muriel Francis, Jeffrey Curley's grandmother. The boy left through this door to accept his fateful ride with Charles Jaynes and Salvatore Sicari. *Police photo courtesy of Lawrence Frisoli*

Charles Jaynes used this Cadillac, shown in police custody, to ferry Jeffrey Curley around Greater Boston. He later killed the boy in the car's backseat. *Police photo courtesy of Lawrence Frisoli*

Charles Jaynes used an alias to obtain this New Hampshire driver's license. *Police photo courtesy of Lawrence Frisoli*

The Manchester, New Hampshire, apartment where Charles Jaynes lived, shown in the condition the killer left it the morning after the murder. *Police photo courtesy of Lawrence Frisoli*

Jeffrey Curley's football jersey, folded carefully by Charles Jaynes and left on an end table in his apartment. The No. 8 was used by detectives to mark evidence. *Police photo courtesy of Lawrence Frisoli*

The clothing label and waist button, removed with a razor by Charles Jaynes, from the shorts worn by Jeffrey Curley on the day of his murder. *Police photo courtesy of Lawrence Frisoli*

Posters of child star Jonathan Taylor Thomas that Charles Jaynes placed on the walls of his apartment. *Police photo courtesy of Lawrence Frisoli*

While neighbors strain to hear, Bob Curley addresses a throng of news media near Barbara's condo on October 3, 1997. The search for Jeffrey's body has just begun in Maine and New Hampshire. *Boston Globe Photo/ George Rizer*

John Walsh, 12, joins a candlelight vigil in Cambridge for his slain friend Jeffrey. *Boston Globe Photo/Evan Richman*

A police diver searches murky waters in Portsmouth, New Hampshire, on October 3, 1997. *Boston Globe Photo/Thomas Hurst*

While divers continue to hunt for Jeffrey's body, friends and family members console each other on a Hampshire Street sidewalk. *Boston Globe Photo/Evan Richman*

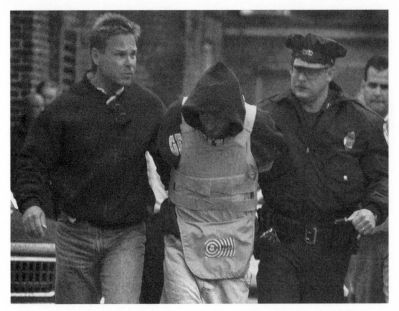

Salvatore Sicari, still wearing the hooded sweatshirt in which he confessed, is rushed into court the following day by police. *Boston Globe Photo/Barry Chin*

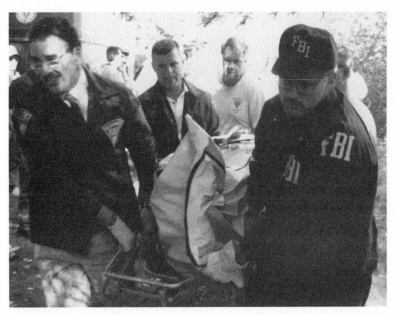

Authorities carry a protective bag holding the Rubbermaid container with Jeffrey Curley's body, shortly after its discovery in the Great Works River. *Police photo courtesy of Lawrence Frisoli*

An impromptu memorial tops a bridge railing in South Berwick, Maine, where the container holding Jeffrey Curley's body was dropped into the Great Works River. *Boston Globe Photo/Bill Greene*

Charles Jaynes, trailed by defense attorney Robert Jubinville at left, is led to his arraignment at Newton District Court on October 10, 1997. Jaynes's face had been scalded while in custody. *Boston Globe Photo/ David Ryan*

Jeffrey's wake at the Long Funeral Home in Cambridge attracted thousands of mourners over two days. *Boston Globe Photo/David Ryan*

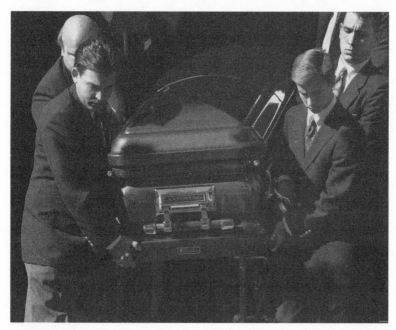

Jeffrey's casket is carried from Sacred Heart Church in Cambridge. *Boston Globe Photo/Wendy Maeda*

The Curley family departs Sacred Heart Church following Jeffrey's funeral on October 11, 1997. From left, Bobby Jr., Barbara, Bob, and Shaun exit the services. *Boston Globe Photo/Wendy Maeda*

Bob Curley, holding Jeffrey's skates, sits on his son's bed on October 16, 1997, in only his second visit to the room since the murder. *Boston Globe Photo/Thomas Hurst*

Bob and Barbara Curley, at the Massachusetts State House, present petitions with thousands of signatures in support of the death penalty. *AP Photo/Gretchen Ertl*

Bob Curley, flanked by Barbara and Bobby Jr., react to the House of Representatives vote on October 28, 1997, to reinstate capital punishment. *Boston Globe Photo/Jim Davis*

Salvatore Sicari, in a typically unflustered expression, listens to testimony on November 3, 1998, in Middlesex Superior Court in Cambridge. *AP Photo/Patricia McDonnell*

Charlene Letourneau, a former girlfriend of Salvatore Sicari's who also knew Charles Jaynes, testifies at Sicari's trial. *Boston Globe Photo/John Blanding*

Prosecutor David Yannetti, during his arguments in Salvatore Sicari's murder trial, carries the Rubbermaid container used to dispose of Jeffrey Curley's body. *Boston Globe Photo/John Blanding*

Barbara Curley breaks down after the guilty verdict is announced against Salvatore Sicari on November 12, 1998. With her, from left, are Shaun, Bobby Jr., and Bob Curley. *Boston Globe Photo/Barry Chin*

The race begins in September 2000. The third annual Jeffrey's Run, held near the murder victim's home, raised money for child-safety programs. *Boston Globe Photo/Tom Herde*

Bob Curley, right, attends Missing Children's Day at the Massachusetts State House on May 28, 2003. Also in attendance, from right to left, are Magi Bish, who lost her daughter Molly to murder; John Bish, her husband; Heather Bish, Molly's sister; and Matt Guertin, Heather's fiance. *Boston Globe Photo/David Ryan*

Bob, Mimi, and Picasso the cat, shortly after the couple had met in the Inman Square neighborhood. *Bob Curley photo*

Five years after Jeffrey's death and a long journey down a tortuous road, Bob and Mimi were married in their home on February 22, 2003. *Bob Curley photo*

Bob and Mimi dance to the sounds of a Venezuelan trio at their wedding reception. *Bob Curley photo*

Jeffrey Curley's grave in Cambridge Cemetery is softened by snow in December 1997. *Boston Globe Photo/Bill Brett*

if he was psychotic. I didn't know if he was homicidal. I didn't know if he was suicidal because he would just go off about what he was going to do to them."

Bob's outbursts were horrifying, and they occurred often. The seams had begun to burst, and even Bob realized he had become unhinged. "I was going crazy," he said. Bob's face would become disfigured, his eyes would bulge, and he would scheme aloud about how to kill the murderers. Mimi would be cooking as Bob concocted his latest recipe for revenge. One monstrous rant involved hiding a knife inside his shoe, leaping over the courtroom railing, cutting Jaynes's throat, slicing open his chest, and throwing Jaynes's liver at his mother's feet. "If I'd been given the opportunity, I would have," Bob said later. "If I thought I could have gotten away with it, I probably would have done it."

Mimi could listen to only so much of the venom. "After a while, I'd say, 'Enough! Shut up! We have to eat!'" Mimi recalled. "And then, he would snap out of it, and we would eat. Later, I would ask him, 'Are you really going to do that?' And he would say, 'No, no, no, no.'" But even Mimi, a trained psychologist, did not know if Bob was being truthful. "I would think, maybe this guy needs to be hospitalized. Maybe the people in court need to be warned that something is happening. Maybe he's just venting," Mimi said. "But I never knew."

As a result, the quality of Mimi's life deteriorated as she engaged in a debilitating, daily struggle to maintain a professional focus at work and gauge whether Bob would harm himself or others. "It was a very fine line," Mimi said. "There were times when he would be in such despair that he would say, 'You know, I just want to hang myself.'" That possibility became one more wrenching piece of the harrowing obstacle course that Mimi was forced to negotiate each day. At work or while commuting, she often stiffened with fear at what the evening might bring. "I had these images," Mimi recalled. "I would say, What if I get home and find him dead?"

Mimi had expected Bob to crash emotionally after the first, consuming blitz of media coverage had dissipated. But

when he did plummet, the foresight did not make the experience any easier. "He was here, but he was not here," Mimi said. "He was sad and sullen and absent. He was just broken. Totally." Normal conversations between them became impossible. And the tensions that pervaded every corner of their home exploded into fits of frustrated anger. "I would fight with him. I would punch him. I would scream at him. I would listen to him. I would cry," Mimi said. "I didn't know what I was doing, but I was losing the man I knew."

Mimi encouraged Bob to go to therapy, but he scoffed at the idea that anyone could understand the journey he had taken or somehow find a way to make his life easier. "You're my therapist," he told Mimi. But Mimi could not reach the caring friend and tender lover she had known before. "It was like we were in an ocean, and I was trying to throw him a life preserver," she said. "I just couldn't reach him, and that was very, very hard for me."

Now, in addition to counseling trauma victims, the Wellesley students, and her private patients, Mimi faced a monumental challenge in her domestic life. The resulting emotional overload, an incessant and uninterrupted burden that affected each and every day, nearly became too much to bear. "I was living it at home, I was living it at work, I was living it everywhere," Mimi recalled. For months, while she commuted to Wellesley College, Mimi would burst into tears, inexplicably, while traveling through Newton on the Massachusetts Turnpike. Only later did she realize that she had cried as she passed Honda Village, the place where Jaynes and Sicari had taken Jeffrey's body almost immediately after the murder.

Eventually, Bob relented and visited a Cambridge psychologist who ran a program for victims of violence. The sessions were excruciating for Bob, who regarded therapy as an admission of weakness by people not tough enough to figure out and endure their problems. Often, he sat fidgeting for almost the entire fifty-five minutes, waiting for questions that never got asked and unwilling to yield any insight into the demons prowling through his psyche.

"How are you doing today?" the therapist typically asked.

"Well, how do I look today?" he answered.

"You look good."

"Well, you look good yourself," Bob offered. "You look like Carly Simon. I'm not shittin' you."

Bob lasted only a few sessions. "I ain't got time for this. I ain't got a lot to say," he told Mimi. "I don't know what the hell to talk to her about. The Red Sox? The weather? What are these people going to say to me? What are they going to do to help me?" Mimi realized further persuasion was futile. In the end, she did not share her concerns with anyone about Bob's potential for violence. Instead, the perpetual turmoil that had become her life was relegated to a private hell endured by two tormented people trying to find their way through the darkness.

Mimi gained a reprieve when the Jaynes trial began in December, sixty-five miles west of Boston in a tiny, small-town courtroom. Judge Cowin granted the change of venue after the Sicari trial had produced incalculably adverse publicity about Jaynes's role in the murder. Bob did not wish to commute, so he stayed in a small motel in East Brookfield, where not much had happened since the 1862 birth of Cornelius McGillicuddy, the famous Connie Mack of misty baseball lore. There, among the rolling hills and sleepy roads, Bob found an outlet for his rage in the long, draining runs he took every morning. And at night, after the day's testimony, Bob made his way to a barstool at a local tavern, where he enjoyed a beer, a hamburger, and Boston sports on the television.

The locals soon recognized him as Jeffrey Curley's father from the TV coverage. "We'd be talking about sports or whatever, but not about the trial," Bob said. "They were just regular, working guys stopping off on the way home for a beer, just trying to be decent people." The interaction helped Bob escape, for a moment, the painful particulars of Jeffrey's story. Occasionally, he even managed a laugh, most memorably when he asked the regulars about the peculiar animals he had seen on his runs.

"What kind of horses are those?" Bob asked one night. "You know, the ones with the long necks?" The locals looked at each other, amazed, and burst into uncontrollable laughter.

"Those aren't horses!" one man snorted. "Those are llamas!"

Bob lowered his head and grinned. "Hey, what do you want from me? I'm from Somerville." For the rest of the trial, Bob smiled every morning when he jogged past the llamas in East Brookfield.

Although Mimi remained in Somerville, Bob often was joined by several members of his family. The trial lacked the wall-to-wall publicity that had surrounded Sicari's case, but the proceedings were no less intense for the Curleys.

And for Yannetti, the task had become even more difficult. Sicari had not agreed to testify against Jaynes, so his admissions to police could not be introduced as evidence. "We knew what Sicari alleged Jaynes did, but we couldn't use any of it, and a jury wouldn't be able to hear any of it," Yannetti said. "So, somebody could sign a statement, but you might as well have taken that paper and just thrown it away." Instead, Yannetti was left with circumstantial indicators—the store surveillance tapes, items of Jeffrey's clothing, and witnesses who placed the pair near the Great Works River—to convince the jury that Jaynes had killed the boy. "It became a mental exercise," Yannetti said, "because you have to subtract Sicari's statement and then make sense of them going to a Home Depot and getting a Rubbermaid container and concrete." The district attorney's office, however, never considered offering Sicari a deal to testify.

Robert Jubinville, who had defended dozens of alleged murderers, was unsure whether Jaynes grasped the case's life-altering potential. "He knew it was a trial, and he knew it was serious, I suppose, because I kept telling him that," Jubinville said. "He's grasping what's going on, but because of his immaturity, he's like, 'It's okay.'" Jaynes had lost more than fifty pounds in the fourteen months since his arrest. He now looked less like a sex-addicted monster and more like a chubby, baby-faced pushover.

Bob continued to fantasize about ways to kill Jaynes, but he and the boys, for the most part, managed to control themselves. Outside the courtroom, however, decorum sometimes broke down. Virginia Jaynes, the defendant's mother, was harassed. Sitting alone in the hallway, a friend of the Curley brothers approached to tell her he had just left state prison and that her son would be raped there and killed. Another time, at the diner where she ate, the owners were warned that the place would burn to the ground if they continued to serve her. Police were informed, and the threat was never carried out.

As the trial progressed, Charles Jaynes maintained a calm, unobtrusive, almost invisible demeanor—at least until Yannetti reprised the dramatic, theatrical closing argument he had used so effectively against Sicari. Vividly describing how the gas burned Jeffrey's lungs, pointing with an outstretched arm, Yannetti directed all eyes in the courtroom toward the defendant. Jaynes, broken by the attention, interrupted Yannetti with a loud, piercing whine.

"I didn't hurt him!" Jaynes cried. "I didn't hurt J.C.!"

Bob bolted from his seat. "You fat motherfucker!" he screamed. "I'll fucking carve you up like a turkey, you fat piece of shit. You're dead! Dead!"

Cowin pounded her gavel, demanding silence, and Jaynes was quickly led away.

After the outburst, Jubinville used his closing argument to place all blame on Sicari. It was Sicari, he argued, who murdered Jeffrey while using Jaynes's car, hid him in the trunk, and then talked Jaynes into paying by credit card for the lime, the concrete, and the Rubbermaid container. Jaynes was unaware of Jeffrey's murder, Jubinville said, until he and Sicari had reached the Great Works River. Only then, the lawyer added, did Sicari reveal that the boy had been killed and that his body lay in the trunk of the Cadillac.

The jurors, who deliberated nearly ten hours over two days, stunned the courtroom when they returned with a verdict of second-degree murder, which showed some uncertainty about Jaynes's intent. Bob shook his head in amazement, but

the family remained composed despite the decision. In the end, one juror said later, the panel did not have enough evidence that Jaynes had planned and committed a first-degree murder. Cowin sentenced Jaynes to the maximum term of life in prison, but the conviction carried a possibility of parole after more than two decades behind bars.

Tom Reilly, the district attorney, approached Bob to express his disappointment. Bob listened politely as Reilly said the prosecution had done its best and that law enforcement would vigorously pursue the fight against organizations like NAMBLA. But no words could erase Bob's feeling that justice had short-changed him. The unsatisfying verdict, against a man Bob considered the epitome of evil, had been a crushing coda to more than a year of ever-present grief.

Bob rushed from the courtroom, grabbed the wheel of a borrowed car, and sped out of the small parking lot with tires squealing. As he headed toward the Massachusetts Turnpike for the solitary journey home, he turned on the radio. An announcer teased listeners about an upcoming news report with the words, "Drama in an East Brookfield courthouse." Bob knew the outcome of that drama, but he was unprepared for the script. When he heard Jaynes protest, yet again, that he did not harm Jeffrey, Bob jabbed violently at the radio. "I don't have to hear no more!" Bob wailed. Frantic and alone, Bob finally punched the button that silenced Jeffrey's killer.

———

—— 8 ——

Questions
and Beginnings

WITH THE END of the trials, Bob retreated from the spotlight once again, drained and disappointed. Although
David Yannetti had presented a painstaking case in the first
murder trials that Bob ever witnessed, Charles Jaynes still
managed to escape a first-degree murder conviction. For Bob,
the option of capital punishment now seemed even more
necessary.

But the battle had exhausted him, and the rage that had
upended his home life with nightly tirades had all but consumed itself. The fire could not burn without new fuel, and
Bob was spent. The killers had been convicted, the death-
penalty debate had been put on hold, and Bob had filed a civil
suit against NAMBLA. The time had come to heal, and Bob
realized he could not survive mentally, and perhaps physically,
if he continued in the role of embittered, howling Everyman
that he had played for more than a year.

Bob received some helpful advice in those early days after stepping down from the media stage—a stage he believed
he had left behind permanently. "I don't know who said it, and
I don't know where I heard it, but someone told me, 'They
killed Jeff. That's bad enough. Don't let it destroy you, and
don't let it destroy anyone else,'" Bob recalled. "That's the best
advice I ever heard: Jeff's dead, and let it end there."

Bob found a beginning in the garden that he and Mimi had created around their house. Mimi had never planted much before, and Bob had been a city kid who grew up thinking that a junkyard was a playground. Their yard in Somerville had limited physical options. A few feet were available on the south side, facing the Boston skyline, where a jungle of untended growth had filled the narrow space between the home and a chain-link fence. In the front, a tangle of weeds, bushes, and brush formed a similar dense patch on a short, slippery slope from the foundation to the sidewalk. The north side had barely enough room for a steep, narrow driveway, and the western edge of the lot, behind the home, had been given over to a parking area. Any evidence of horticulture, if it ever existed, had long since been obliterated. "The only thing I knew about gardening was how to ruin my grandfather's tomato plants," Bob said. "He had a big, beautiful garden—all the fruit, a big grapevine, and he even made wine in the cellar. Until I came along anyway, and that was the end of that."

Mimi studied gardening books, and Bob was relegated to much of the heavy weekend labor: hacking at brush, pulling up stumps, digging out rocks, and laying new stones for a border. The couple spent hours on their creation. Perennials were planted, as well as hydrangeas, rhododendron, roses, and lilies. Kitschy artwork also found a home in the form of small ceramic rabbits, frogs, elephants, and turtles nestled among the flowers. "I kept him busy. It was, Do a hole here, let's get this trunk out, clear that over there," Mimi said. "For rookies, we did pretty good." The work became cathartic in its productive tedium, a purifying freshener for two souls polluted by sadness and a chance to build something new, simple, and honest in a private, outdoor sanctuary.

The same could be said for changes under way inside the house. The second floor and attic sprang into new, colorful life with a lush patina of South American and global influences. The effect was both soothing and eclectic. Mimi added centuries-old Colombian pottery in rooms decorated with dark, intricately carved wood, exotic plants in suspended pots,

and African and pre-Columbian ceremonial masks. The walls were stripped and glazed with swirling patterns of orange and red in one area, grass green in another. Hand-painted tiles adorned a winding, wooden staircase to a small bedroom that they fashioned from the once-forgotten attic. Tables and chairs in rich, muted shades of brown and couches covered in vibrant throws infused the home with a hint of Spanish colonial gentility. The sensation was one of walking in a foreign land, a soulful, breathing paean to Colombia's domestic rhythms and Mimi's worldly tastes.

Little of the place bore a hint of Bob's past, style, or preferences. It seemed almost as if Bob had arrived as a blank slate, a man without a history, someone whose social exposure had been so limited that his tastes were still unknown. Bob did bring an ability to learn and to suspend prejudgment. His openness had impressed Mimi since the beginning, and his willingness, even eagerness, to accept and absorb new ideas increased. The result deepened their friendship as well as their love. "I had been very lonely all my life, even when I was married, but he became my best friend ever," Mimi said. "We became complicit in lots of things. 'Oh, Bob, let's paint this wall,' I'd say. 'Let's work on the garden. Let's buy some paint.' And he'd say, 'Oh, sure. Okay.' We found things that we enjoyed doing together, cooking, little things. And that was our salvation, that we had this place to come back to. This house saved us. For a while."

While Bob recovered in the shadows, the drumbeat to reinstate the death penalty began to reverberate once again at the State House. Twenty-one new legislators had been elected in 1998 to serve in the House of Representatives, and Governor Paul Cellucci was determined to apply pressure, swiftly and firmly, while the memory of Jeffrey Curley's death remained fresh in voters' minds. He unveiled his new bill in February 1999 amid a friendly sea of police officers at a union hall in Dorchester. As the parents of three murder victims stood in support, the governor denounced those "monsters who do not

deserve hope" and liberal legislators whom he ridiculed as being out of step with their constituents. Massachusetts residents, he urged, should "turn the heat up" on a legislature that had yet to warm, as most of the nation had, to the common-sense justice of eye-for-an-eye capital punishment. "I am more determined than ever to wage this fight for justice," Cellucci said, kick-starting another political donnybrook that was expected to match the intensity of the tumultuous debate of only sixteen months before.

Neither the Democratic leadership inside the House nor the death-penalty foes outside the building could predict the outcome. None of the supporters of capital punishment who remained in the House had changed their position. Indeed, several tallies suggested that only one vote separated the two sides. And Cellucci, undaunted by his previous defeat, broadened the bill to cover sixteen categories of murder that could be punished by death. "It will be right down to the wire," warned Bill Nagle, the House majority leader, who foresaw a reprise of the draining 1997 battle.

Unlike 1997, however, Nagle and his allies had been preparing for this war. Caught flat-footed by the dramatic swing in momentum after Jeffrey's murder, opponents of the death penalty began reorganizing immediately after the climactic tie vote that year. This time there would be no surprises, they vowed. And once again, Nagle was backed by a highly motivated coalition of interest groups and lobbyists, who looked to him for direction. They targeted new legislators who had never voted on capital punishment, as well as incumbent lawmakers who had reversed their positions in 1997 and opted to support the death penalty. Their arsenal included reams of statistical data, moral argument, and even some old-fashioned political calculation.

The activists saw two signs that the landscape had begun to shift. John Slattery, whose reversal in 1997 blocked the resentment of capital punishment, easily won reelection in 1998 despite an opponent who hammered Slattery about the vote in a district dominated by lunch pail conservatives. Even

Cellucci, who traveled to Peabody to campaign against Slattery, could not sway the election.

The second sign came from North Andover, where Donna Cuomo, a key supporter of capital punishment in 1997, lost her bid for a third term in a year when no incumbent opponents of the death penalty were defeated. "It helped legislators recognize that they could stand up and say, 'I have a moral objection,'" said Norma Shapiro of the ACLU. "People in the State House took notice of that."

People also noticed when Cardinal Bernard Law, the most influential Catholic in a predominantly Catholic state, declared in a 1999 news conference that support for the death penalty would be a sin. "The teachings of the church are very clear," Law said after Cellucci, a Catholic, reintroduced the death-penalty bill. "For a well-informed Catholic to support capital punishment, it would be morally wrong. And if one knowingly rejects the teachings of the church, it is wrong, morally evil, and a sin," he continued. "It's very difficult for me to understand how Catholics can come to that position." The implications were obvious for Cellucci, who attended Catholic high school and had earned two degrees at Boston College, a Jesuit institution. But the governor, undeterred, dismissed the cardinal's grave declaration as merely a difference of opinion.

Cellucci and Law would soon have an opportunity to pit the secular against the sacred. A marathon hearing on the bill was scheduled for March 21 in an ornate, old auditorium at the State House, where the governor and the cardinal would join dozens of others in arguing for or against the legislation. Cellucci planned to buttress his argument with testimony from the relatives of murder victims, who would sit beside him at the witness table, lock eyes with House members, and plead for the ultimate penalty. In the public's mind, one name belonged at the top of such a roster. So, three months after Bob Curley raced angrily from the East Brookfield courthouse, the governor's staff asked Jeffrey's father to take the microphone again, face the television lights, and demand that Massachusetts execute its killers.

Bob acquiesced, but only reluctantly. Since the Jaynes trial, he had begun to wrestle with nagging questions about a judicial system he had now come to know a little better. The discrepancies in the verdicts did not make sense to him. Sicari, the accomplice, would never walk free. But Jaynes, who was convicted of second-degree murder, could cling to the hope of parole. Bob also began to question why Jaynes, and not Sicari, had received a change of venue. "As bad as Sicari is, we would never have found Jeff if it had been up to Jaynes. He would have never talked," Bob said. "Charles Jaynes is as bad as they come, and Sicari was just an idiot tagging along." In Bob's view, justice seemed to have been skewed unfairly in favor of the worse defendant. "Let's face it, any time you're involved in the court system on any level, it doesn't take long to figure out there's a big difference between what's right, what's wrong, the law, justice, who can afford the best lawyer, and who can't," he said.

So, despite a creeping disillusionment with the system and his concerns about new media exposure, Bob agreed to appear at the hearing. "Yeah, I'll do it," Bob said halfheartedly. Cellucci had been a high-profile friend when Bob needed one in 1997. And now, Bob felt obligated to return the favor, particularly when the request came from the governor.

As Bob resigned himself to testify, the foes of capital punishment mobilized with a zealot's motivation. Families of murder victims who opposed the death penalty were invited. Like-minded congressmen and prosecutors joined the list. And Cardinal Law prepared to bring the full influence of the church to Gardner Auditorium.

To build momentum, Murder Victims' Families for Reconciliation (MVFR), an activist group that rejected capital punishment, organized a speaking tour. One stop included historic Faneuil Hall, the Cradle of Liberty in Revolutionary Boston, where an overflow audience listened to the soft Western twang of Bud Welch, a gas station owner from Oklahoma City, whose daughter had been killed in the truck-bomb explosion

outside the Murrah Federal Building on April 19, 1995. That bombing, the worst act of domestic terrorism in United States history, took 168 lives. The victims included Julie Welch, a twenty-three-year-old Spanish translator for the Social Security Administration, who died instantly at 9:02 A.M., seconds after she met two clients in the building's front lobby. In an instant, in an explosion that shook his house eight miles away, Welch lost an only daughter whom he also considered his best friend. Julie's body was not recovered for three days, and Welch's initial shock and sorrow changed into blind and raging hate.

Like Bob, Welch wanted the killers put to death—without trials and without regrets. "Just fry the bastards," he said of Timothy McVeigh and his accomplice, Terry Nichols. So, when President Bill Clinton and Attorney General Janet Reno announced the day after the bombing that they would seek the death penalty, Welch embraced the news despite his previous lifelong opposition to capital punishment. Now, Welch longed for what he called a "quick fix" to deliver final, merciless justice.

In the months after Julie's death, Welch traveled daily to the smoldering ruins of the Murrah Federal Building. There, he mourned his daughter and railed against McVeigh and Nichols, antigovernment militants whose attack was payback for the deadly blaze two years earlier at the Branch Davidian religious compound in Waco, Texas. On that day, seventy-six church members, including twenty-one children, died in the bloody culmination of a fifty-one-day siege by federal agents. Fires killed many of the victims after tear gas had been released into the compound. Autopsies showed that some of the dead, including sect leader David Koresh, had died of gunshot wounds, possibly the result of murder-suicides.

Following Julie's death, Welch blamed himself for encouraging her to study foreign languages. And he blamed Julie, too, for not accepting an offer from Marquette University, where she had received a degree ten months earlier, to return for graduate studies. If different paths had been chosen, Welch

told himself, Julie would not have been in the Murrah building when McVeigh drove up with a rental truck packed with five thousand pounds of fertilizer and race-car fuel.

For Julie, a woman who loved languages and sought to help others, the lure of home had been too strong. But there was more. For seven months before the blast, Julie had been dating an air force lieutenant whom she met through a young Catholics group at nearby Tinker Air Force Base. The couple were nearly ready to announce their engagement.

On the day she died, Welch had planned to meet Julie for lunch in a cherished weekly ritual at a Greek restaurant beside her office. He awoke just before 9:00 A.M. and had not yet left his bedroom when he felt the rumble that unhinged his life. Welch's son Chris stood in the kitchen, talking on a cell phone when the explosion occurred.

"Dad, what was that?" Chris asked.

"I don't have any idea," Welch said.

Within fifteen minutes, the television carried the stunning answer. And when Welch saw the rubble of the Murrah building, any hope he held for Julie was extinguished.

Welch's life soon careered into a self-destructive, alcoholic dead end. For ten months, each night after he closed his Texaco station, Welch would head home to pour himself a tall glass of rum. "The first thing I'd do when I'd come in that door would be to make a drink," said Welch, an earnest, avuncular man who looks people in the eye. "And if I drank enough by the time I went to bed, I could go to sleep. It was only the next day that I would pay for it." The hangovers first lasted a few hours in the morning, then past noon, and finally throughout the day. The drinking became worse, and Welch also started smoking more, ratcheting up his intake to four distracting packs a day.

Customers noticed the steady deterioration in their friend, who everybody knew had lost his daughter in the bombing. Some patrons even stopped using the gas station, unsure how to behave around a man who had suffered the insufferable.

"They could see clearly what was going on," Welch recalled. "They'd say, 'Bud, you're killing yourself.' And you know what? I'd say, 'I don't give a damn.' My thought was that the sooner I died, the sooner I would see Julie again."

The downward spiral continued through Christmas and into January. Each day, Welch would drive to the bomb site, and each night he would drink himself into a pain-numbing haze. The pattern continued until one cold afternoon when, his head throbbing and muscles aching from alcohol abuse, Welch stood beside the crater that had been the Murrah building and pondered what he needed to move forward. Obviously, the route he had chosen was not working. So, Welch asked himself three questions: Did he need the start of the trials, which were not scheduled for two years, to finally find peace? Did he need convictions? Did he need executions?

The answers did not arrive immediately. But after three weeks of anguished soul-searching, Welch found a path out of the maze of his misery. "I came to the conclusion that, when they take them from their cage to kill them, it simply wouldn't be part of my healing process," Welch said. "I wasn't going to gain anything from an act of hate and revenge. And hate and revenge, I realized, were the very reasons that Julie and 167 others were dead. I finally was able to clearly see what the Oklahoma City bombing was all about: It was about retribution."

Welch reached that conclusion privately, but the repercussions of the choice became national. A reporter, interviewing Welch on the first anniversary of the bombing, continued chatting with him after turning off his tape recorder.

"I bet you'll be glad when this is all over and McVeigh is executed," the reporter said.

Welch paused. "Actually, I'm kind of opposed to the death penalty," he said matter-of-factly.

Later, the reporter called Welch from the newsroom and asked if he could print the comment. Welch agreed, and his change of heart became public. The result was electric. Welch, a third-generation Okie who had been raised on a dairy

farm, began traveling the globe to tell his story, and Julie's, to American university audiences, foreign lawmakers, and anyone else who would listen.

Welch's opposition to the death penalty had been foreshadowed by his Irish immigrant ancestors, who joined the Oklahoma land rush in the nineteenth century after trying their hands as Pennsylvania miners. In their eyes, the frontier punishment they observed was too arbitrary, and too prey to human biases, to qualify as justice. Welch inherited that point of view, almost as one inherits a religion, but he never thought deeply about the issue. After Julie's murder, however, he thought often about her conviction that the death penalty teaches hate and that hate begets hate. Finally, on that cold January day, he began to leave hate behind.

Three years later, Welch made what he considered his most important journey. During a speaking tour near Buffalo, Welch made time to visit Timothy McVeigh's father and sister, Bill and Jennifer, in a meeting arranged by a local Catholic nun. Welch felt compelled to make the trip after watching, by chance, a snippet of a television interview with Bill McVeigh. In three seconds, during which McVeigh stopped gardening to answer a reporter's question, Welch recognized the incredible pain that tormented this grieving father.

Welch sat with the McVeighs at their kitchen table in Lockport, New York, for ninety minutes, talking about their lives but never directly mentioning the crime that had shattered them all. Instead, Welch tried only to connect with two fellow human beings who also had suffered a horrific loss through the same terrible act. At one point, Welch nodded toward a photograph of Timothy McVeigh that hung near the table.

"What a good-looking kid," Welch said.

"That's Tim's high school graduation picture," Bill McVeigh said. Seconds later, a large, single tear rolled down the man's cheek.

Welch wanted the McVeighs to understand that he did not blame them for Julie's death and that he cared deeply about their anguish. That simple gesture of extraordinary compassion was

Welch's gift to Bill McVeigh and Jennifer, a twenty-four-year-old who, like Julie, had been attracted to teaching. In the process, Welch gave himself a life-altering gift as well. As he left, Welch shook hands with Timothy's father, sobbed with Jennifer, and then left them with this thought. "The three of us are in this for the rest of our lives. We can make the most of it we choose," Welch said, cradling Jennifer's face in his hands. "I don't want your brother to die, and I will do everything in my power to prevent it."

When Welch returned to Buffalo, he began crying without shame in his hotel room. The tears continued, uncontrolled, until the long day had reached an emotional, cathartic conclusion. When the sobbing ended, something else began. "All of a sudden, I had never felt closer to God than I did at that moment. After all the crying, this load was taken completely off my shoulders," Welch said. "I wish I could explain it to you." Reenergized and unburdened, Welch continued his evangelism for the abolition of the death penalty. By 1999, he had forged a reputation as one of the issue's busiest and best-known advocates.

That reputation brought him to the attention of Renny Cushing, the executive director of Murder Victims' Families for Reconciliation, who placed Welch high on a list of fourteen speakers he had compiled in advance of the State House hearing. Welch accepted Cushing's invitation to speak at Faneuil Hall and nineteen other venues and also agreed to appear on *Talk of New England*, a public-affairs television show. The program on New England Cable News, scheduled for the week before the hearing, would consider the death penalty from the starkly opposed perspectives of two men who had lost children to murder. Margery Eagan, cohost of the Emmy-winning show and columnist for the *Boston Herald*, invited Welch. Her partner, Jim Braude, placed a call to Bob Curley, his expletive-spewing antagonist during the State House debate in 1997.

Bob balked at the invitation. He had never met Bud Welch, but he assumed that Welch had been plucked from the ranks of "left-wing burnouts" whom Bob had long despised.

Bob was also concerned that Welch, a practiced speaker, would trap him, twist his words, and ridicule Bob's position as something straight from the talking points of a right-wing fanatic. After seventeen months of hell, Bob was tired of the controversy. Besides, Bob told Braude, he did not have a way to reach the station. When Braude offered to send a limousine, Bob said he would not ride in the same car as Welch. He answered every inducement with an obstacle and seemed beyond persuasion.

Disappointed, Eagan phoned Welch with the message that Bob did not wish to participate.

"He doesn't want to be at the same table with you," Eagan said. "He's afraid you're good at debating the death penalty."

"Margery, I would never attempt to back Bob Curley in a corner in any way or fashion," Welch said. "I don't do that. That's not my style. You call him back and tell him I'd be delighted to appear with him on or off television because I want to meet him."

After yet another phone conversation, Bob relented. He would appear on the program, he told the station, but he still insisted on a separate car.

Although the men sat less than a foot apart on the television set, the gulf between them seemed cavernous. Bob avoided eye contact with Welch for the first fifteen minutes of the half-hour segment, in part by twisting himself toward Braude and Eagan in an awkward body dynamic that kept Welch behind his left shoulder and out of sight. Both men sat with their hands clasped before them. Bob leaned back in a stiff gray jacket and tie, his narrow eyes rimmed by dark circles and his forehead creased by long, deep lines. Welch, more casual in a tweed jacket and white turtleneck, hunched forward toward the hosts, his demeanor as humble and homespun as Bob's seemed uncomfortable and defiant.

Welch had never been to Boston before the trip, but he quickly learned of Jeffrey Curley. In every speaking engagement, Welch faced questions about whether Jeffrey's murderers deserved the death penalty. As Welch had done hundreds

of times before, he told his questioners the story of his rage, depression, recovery, and journey from revenge. On television, he did the same.

Bob listened intently, but he refused to look at Welch. Instead, when his turn arrived, Bob spoke of how the death penalty had been a therapeutic outlet, how he had refused to cower silently inside his house, and how he had chosen instead to fight against the monsters who had killed his son and would kill others. His path, Bob said, had been an instinctive reaction to an unspeakable loss, a road to sanity hacked out of a frightening wilderness of unimaginable sorrow. "They don't give you a handbook on how to grieve the loss of a loved one," Bob said.

Welch nodded, recalling the hopelessness that he also had experienced. But his road out of the dark days had taken a different direction, Welch said, toward a sense that hate and revenge would not help him heal. Welch validated Bob's pain, but he could not validate Bob's demands for eye-for-an-eye justice. Although Welch empathized with Bob's suffering, he would not soften his arguments for *Talk of New England*. The brutal, clinical consequences of capital punishment, he said, should not be confined to a few, silent witnesses, corralled out of public view in a small, secure room at 12:01 A.M.

When the camera turned to Bob, his cadence turned forceful and animated. Hate and anger *are* self-destructive, Bob agreed. But society has an obligation, he continued, to use the ultimate punishment against the most heinous criminals. "Some people view it as letting go and forgiveness. But then again, you have to draw the line somewhere," Bob said, his jaw tightening. "God's job is to forgive them. Our job is to keep people safe."

When Braude asked Bob if he could accept an iron-clad guarantee of life without parole, the harshest sentence allowed under Massachusetts law, Bob answered, "My position on the death penalty hasn't changed." Eagan then asked, "How would you feel if Jaynes and Sicari were killed by lethal injection?"

Before Bob could answer, Welch interrupted. The questions were unfair, he said. Jeffrey's death was still fresh, the

pain too near, to consider any option other than revenge. Bob would never get over Jeffrey, Welch continued, and he would miss him every day. But with time, Welch suggested, maybe "he'll learn each day how to live that day a little bit better."

Bob glanced quickly in Welch's direction, again avoiding direct eye contact. But his demeanor had softened. To Bob's surprise, his supposed sparring partner had not come to castigate or diminish him. Instead, this folksy, gray-haired man had accepted his grief and understood his rage. The exchange touched Bob, who also connected with Welch when the Oklahoman spoke of his swift, unsettling transition from anonymous citizen to high-profile spokesman for a controversial cause.

"All I can say is pull me off the front page," Welch told Braude and Eagan. "Send me home to Oklahoma City right now and I'll pump gasoline. Just give my Julie Marie back."

Bob nodded knowingly. "I'm with you," he said.

The program ended with a summary of Welch's rationale for ending capital punishment. "I cannot see how in the world we can cage up a human being, and kill him, and teach our children that it's wrong to kill by killing," Welch said. Bob did not offer a rebuttal or even a last word. Instead, in an almost imperceptibly low voice, he thanked Braude and Eagan for the opportunity to appear on the program. For Braude, the program had been the most intense and moving he had experienced on a television set. That sense also resonated with the public, Braude said, which reacted with phone calls and on-the-street feedback that dwarfed any previous response that *Talk of New England* had received.

After the television camera had been turned off, Bob and Welch moved quietly toward the front of the studio, where two limousines were scheduled to return them separately to Somerville and Cambridge. When only one car arrived, Bob unexpectedly found himself in the awkward position of sharing a ride with Welch and Renny Cushing, who were bound for Harvard University and a speaking engagement at the John F. Kennedy School of Government. During the twenty-five-minute drive to Harvard Square—with Bob in

front and Cushing and Welch in the rear—the three men spoke about their backgrounds, their families, and their tragedies.

Cushing, a former state legislator in New Hampshire, lost his father in 1988 when a neighbor knocked on Robert Cushing's door and greeted him with two fatal shotgun blasts. A retired elementary school teacher, the elder Cushing died on the living room floor in front of his wife, who had been watching a Boston Celtics playoff game on television.

Renny Cushing had always opposed the death penalty, and the murder of his father did not change his stance. But the killing did change his life. "For relatives of the murdered, part of you takes some responsibility for it. You failed your loved one because you couldn't protect them, and you'd do anything you could to change the history," Cushing said. "Part of what is hard about being a survivor is coming to grips with the fact that, try as you want to, you can't change the past. The best you can do is try to control the future."

To do that, Cushing channeled his energies into working against the death penalty and bringing together the relatives of murder victims who shared that goal. "There's this belief that all families of murder victims want the death penalty for closure," Cushing said. "And that, as a consequence, our political leaders are under this moral obligation to provide the execution solution for the victims' pain. We tried to shift that paradigm a little."

During the ride to Cambridge, Cushing spoke about his father. Welch spoke about his daughter, Marquette University, and her love of the Spanish language. And Bob, who mentioned the death penalty only briefly, spoke about the details of Jeffrey's death, as well as his ongoing efforts to bolster child-safety programs. But for most of the ride, the three men shared their stories, forged through pain and perseverance, about the task of coping with extraordinary evil.

Bob had never participated in such a discussion. In previous encounters, the relatives of murder victims had always supported the death penalty. This was new, unexpected, and confounding. Welch and Cushing both seemed like regular

guys, men who spoke straight from the heart and who both knew firsthand the horrible pain of murder. How can they be against the death penalty? Bob asked himself.

Welch had struggled with this question himself and seen the struggle in others. He noted that Bob did not dwell on the death penalty, either on the television set or in the limousine. And Bob's repeated references to the work of child safety showed Welch something else: that Bob had begun to bury his hate in a constructive way.

In Harvard Square, they parted company as new friends. As Welch and Cushing walked away from the limousine, Welch gestured over his shoulder. "He's gonna turn around on this thing," Welch said. "This is really a decent person, someone who has suffered an unbelievable loss, but he's gonna change."

Ten minutes later, the limousine driver pulled up to Bob's house, looked in the rearview mirror, and smiled at his passenger. Before he overheard the conversation in the car, the chauffeur said, he had planned to ask Bob for an autograph.

"I thought you were doing the sports show," the driver said. "I thought you were a baseball player."

"If I was a baseball player," Bob said with a chuckle, "I wouldn't be living here in East Somerville, you knucklehead."

Unsettled by the encounter with Welch and Cushing, Bob grabbed his bicycle and headed toward the Charles River, where a loop from Cambridge to Boston and back again would combine a workout with some serious thinking. As he pedaled, Bob was consumed by jarring questions: How could Welch and Cushing oppose the execution of murderers who had shattered their families and lives? How could they reach that point? What did this say about him? Was it unmanly even to think this way? These questions were more than a mental exercise. The State House hearing, a full-blown media spectacle where Bob once again would be asked to trumpet his support for capital punishment, would be held in less than a week.

Suddenly, Bob was plagued by second thoughts. The reflexive justification he had used since Jeffrey's death now

seemed less certain. In Bud Welch and Renny Cushing, he had seen that opposition to the death penalty did not always signal weakness. "I always kind of viewed myself in a certain way," Bob said later. "You know what I mean? A certain class, a certain attitude, a certain edge, coming from where I came from. I always thought that if you were against the death penalty, you were a wimp." He had never met anyone like Welch and Cushing. Down-to-earth and unpretentious, these men were a different breed from the placard-carrying protesters he had encountered during the 1997 debate. And Bob had witnessed firsthand that punishment did not always fit the crime. Maybe, Bob thought, opposition to the death penalty was not necessarily abnormal.

Head down and legs churning, Bob tried to make sense of his hesitancy. But the questions were too big and the answers too obscure for him to reach any conclusions during a sixty-minute bike ride. He was, however, certain of one thing: He had made a commitment to Governor Cellucci to testify. And because of that agreement, he would not back out. "I was worried about how I'd be perceived if I didn't go and how I'd be portrayed in the media," Bob recalled. "I didn't want to look like a fucking dope, like a nutcase or something." Bob genuinely liked Cellucci, but he also feared the governor's clout. Nurtured in a neighborhood where broken loyalties brought repercussions, Bob worried that reneging on his commitment might invite payback. "That's a high level of politics, and I didn't know if there would be any kind of retribution," Bob recalled. "I was a little concerned, to be honest with you."

On the morning of the hearing, Bob reported to work as usual, dressed in his blue uniform and thinking ahead to his return to the spotlight. A packed auditorium, the cameras, a bank of reporters, and the rapt attention of a dais full of legislators awaited the words of the man who had come to symbolize the public's righteous vengeance. That man did not arrive in a limousine, as he had the previous week at New England Cable News. Instead, Bob rode his bicycle to the State

House, dressed in a suit he had quickly donned to replace the standard-issue clothing of the Cambridge Fire Department. A member of the governor's staff saw Bob pushing his bicycle through Doric Hall, a gilded remnant of the original building, and was startled by his appearance. Bob looked devastated, his pain raw and visible as he made his way to the governor's legal office. "It was a sad thing to see," the aide said.

Bob's voice would join a chorus of supporters of capital punishment, advocates who included high-ranking police officials, district attorneys, and other parents wounded for life by murder. The other side had also amassed a formidable array of speakers. Welch would be among them, as would Cardinal Law, Cushing, and a dozen other relatives of murder victims. The group included Andrew Pryor, the father of a slain nine-year-old girl from suburban Wayland, who once supported capital punishment but later changed his stance.

The hearing was convened by the Criminal Justice Committee, a seventeen-member joint panel from the House and Senate that was believed to be tilted toward the death penalty by a 9–8 margin. Cellucci knew that the committee's recommendation to the full legislature could push the issue either way, in what might be his last, best chance to enact the measure.

Outside the building, the event had taken on all the trappings and buzz of Opening Day at Fenway Park. Satellite trucks from every Boston television station squeezed into the cramped real estate beneath the golden dome. Inside, reporters staked claim to prize vantage points.

As the hearing neared, Maureen Hogan, a legal aide to the governor, escorted Bob to an elevator and the short walk to Gardner Auditorium. Bob was in turmoil. After speaking with Bud Welch and Renny Cushing, the prospect of ranting again for capital punishment gnawed at his conscience. His mind racing and palms sweating, Bob glanced nervously at Hogan. "I really don't want to get into this. You know, stepping into the spotlight again with this death-penalty stuff," Bob said in the elevator. "I don't feel comfortable doing it." With that, the door opened. Bob abruptly thanked Hogan, retrieved

his bicycle, and left the State House. There had been no further explanations, no pleas for understanding from one of Cellucci's top legal assistants. He simply walked away.

As he coasted down Beacon Hill, the chill of March in his face, Bob did not yet know that a new ride had just begun. He smiled, pedaled briskly over the Longfellow Bridge into Cambridge, and returned to work a happy man from whom a tremendous burden had been lifted. Although he did not yet fully grasp what he had done, Bob knew this: He would no longer be Cellucci's angry front man. "I thought there was going to be a death penalty, at least it looked that way to me," Bob said. "And I didn't want Jeff to be remembered for the death penalty every time somebody was going to be up for an execution, or put on trial where capital punishment was involved. I just knew that Jeff's name would be dragged into it."

Inside the building, as Bob sped away, Cellucci pounded the drum again. "I believe we will save many lives," the grim-faced governor told the committee. "But if we can save even one life, it is worth it." Cellucci entered the chamber hoping to sway a legislator or two with his tough talk. Instead, he found himself on the receiving end of some unexpectedly pointed questions from a supposedly friendly committee member. Harold Naughton Jr., a Democratic state representative from Clinton who voted twice for the death penalty in 1997, prodded the governor for estimates about the imposing legal costs associated with capital murder cases. Cellucci could not provide an answer to the former prosecutor.

John Slattery, the governor's nemesis in 1997, asked Cellucci for any credible evidence that the death penalty is a deterrent. Again, Cellucci could not offer any statistics.

"I feel, with the death penalty, that you will execute an innocent person," Slattery said, staring down at the governor who had campaigned hard to unseat him.

"You're trying to protect a very narrow group of people," Cellucci shot back. "I'm trying to protect the six million people of Massachusetts."

To Martina Jackson, executive director of Massachusetts Citizens Against the Death Penalty, the governor's refusal or inability to provide any firm data to the committee had transformed him into an unwitting ally of the opposition. Jackson, whose grandmother was killed at Auschwitz the summer she was born, took pride in the fact that her grandmother's four daughters, including her mother, had opposed the death penalty.

Cardinal Law, who had reached out personally to lobby Cellucci on the issue, reiterated the Catholic Church's unequivocal stance on the death penalty. "The dignity of human life must never be taken away, even in the case of someone who has done great evil," Law said before an audience that included dozens of nuns and priests. "We do not help those whose lives have been shattered by the murder of a loved one. . . . We must not be motivated by vengeance."

Although the governor's supporters were outnumbered, their voices were no less anguished than they had been two years earlier. Susan Gove, the mother of Kristen Crowley, who had been bludgeoned to death in Peabody in 1996, testified for the bill and chided the cardinal for injecting himself into state politics. "What the cardinal must understand is that the cardinal has only one vote in this state," Gove told legislators. After the hearing, she rushed after Law and upbraided him in a crowded hallway before a cluster of reporters and television cameras.

"My daughter had a life, sir!" Gove said. "Don't you feel that the people who destroyed my daughter should deserve a punishment equal to the crime?"

"I believe that the crime against your daughter, the crime against her life, is not going to be taken care of by the killing of another person," Law replied. "It's the killing that has to stop."

Following the exchange, the pair embraced in a gesture of respect if not agreement. The same could not be said of lawmakers on opposite sides of the issue. Frustrated by the governor's resistance to his questions, Naughton told reporters as he left the auditorium that he would rethink his support for the death penalty, a stance cemented at a meeting the follow-

ing morning when Cellucci still could not provide the requested figures. Later that day, Naughton cast the critical vote when the committee decided, 9–8, to send a negative recommendation to the House. After the vote, Naughton said that he continued to support the death penalty but that the state must first identify the funding to pay for legal fees and other expenses that could reach $7 million a case. Naughton said he also had been influenced by the recent exoneration of Anthony Porter, a death row inmate in Illinois who had come within two days of execution. Porter's double-homicide conviction had been dismissed two weeks before the Massachusetts hearing, aided by Northwestern University journalism students who found evidence that helped prove his innocence. Including Porter's release, thirteen inmates on the Illinois death row had been exonerated and twelve had been executed since the state reinstated capital punishment in 1977. To opponents of the death penalty, those life-and-death statistics delivered a jolting message about the fallibility of the justice system.

Naughton's decision all but ensured that the bill would not survive a vote in the full House. And Cellucci, painfully aware of the numbers, appeared to concede defeat. "Everyone I've talked to so far seems to have made up their mind," the governor said. In a reprise of 1997, Cellucci found a villain once again in House Speaker Tom Finneran, whom he lambasted for scheduling the vote before six vacancies could be filled in special elections. The empty House seats, Cellucci argued, meant two hundred thousand residents would be disenfranchised. "Why don't we just dismiss all of the legislators and let the speaker make the decision?" Cellucci said. "That apparently is what he wants."

Finneran defended his scheduling but did agree with the governor that the legislature seemed out of step with the state. In 1999, polls continued to indicate that most Massachusetts residents supported the death penalty. "This is one instance where representative form of government has given us a result that differs from a pure, undistilled democracy," Finneran said.

In the week between the hearing and the House vote, Bob began to question longtime friends about their feelings on the death penalty. "I started bumping into more and more people who I viewed the same way that I viewed myself—same place, same attitude, guys from Somerville, guys from South Boston, guys from East Cambridge," Bob said. And to his surprise, more of them opposed the death penalty than he had expected. The deck was stacked against the little guy, some said. Others rejected capital punishment for moral reasons. And some believed that fatal mistakes were inevitable.

Like most of his friends, Bob had never given much thought to the death penalty before Jeffrey's death. After any heinous murder, the notion of summary execution seemed reasonable to Bob and his peers. But when someone, particularly a middling mobster or ordinary workingman, was found to have been wrongfully convicted, Bob and his circle paid attention. In one high-profile case, Pete Limone and Joe Salvati, two fall guys from the Massachusetts underworld, were released from prison in the mid-1990s after serving more than thirty years for a murder they did not commit. That news, together with the long-suspected revelation that the pair had been framed by the FBI, provided reams of front-page fodder guaranteed to jump-start conversation in the firehouse. The news also planted seeds of doubt. "You hear about a terrible case and you think, Yeah, this guy deserves to die. You know, in a perfect world for me, Jaynes and Sicari should be executed every day from now till the end of time," Bob said. "But then, you start looking at the justice system, and there's always room for error."

The realization that mistakes are made—not only in evidence but in human judgment—struck Bob like a hammer the weekend after the hearing. Leaning back in a stiff, metal chair at the firehouse, savoring the slow progression of a quiet Sunday morning, the questions that had been circulating in Bob's mind suddenly began to crystallize into a startling conclusion.

A once-struggling student who had to be prodded, even threatened, by his sister to finish high school, Bob regularly scoured the two Boston papers, the *Globe* and the *Herald*, for

tidbits about city crime and politics and whatever Boston sports team happened to be in season. On this March morning, the *Herald*'s front page devoted itself to the eye-catching story of a Massachusetts man, a two-tour marine veteran of Vietnam, who was nearing an execution date at San Quentin prison in California. Bob was drawn to the story instantly. Although he had not served in Vietnam, he knew many men from the neighborhood who had, and he knew that the domestic damage from Vietnam, more often than not, was felt in low-ceiling, blue-collar places like Inman Square.

"With every midnight hour, Manuel 'Manny' Babbitt's last days peel away and the Wareham native, who has spent nearly two decades on California's death row, moves closer to the mouth of the animal he calls the 'gray wolf,'" began the story by Ed Hayward. "On May 4, the day after his 50th birthday, Babbitt is slated to be strapped to a gurney; an intravenous brew will put him to sleep and then paralyze his heart and lungs. This is the punishment a jury meted out for the 1980 murder of Leah Schendel."

Schendel, a petite, seventy-eight-year-old grandmother, died of a heart attack after Babbitt savagely beat her during a botched robbery in a Sacramento housing complex for the elderly. Curley grasped the tabloid tighter and leaned forward to read more.

Babbitt, a black man raised in a cold-water shack on the overlooked fringes of Cape Cod, came from a large Cape Verdean family in which sixteen relatives had required psychiatric treatment or committed suicide. At the age of twelve, he survived a serious automobile accident but suffered a head injury that appeared to leave severe psychological and cognitive scars. Afterward, Babbitt trudged through school, aimless and impaired, repeating grades until he dropped out of junior high school at the age of seventeen.

Unable to read or write but inspired by a brother's military service, Babbitt walked into a marine recruiting station in Providence, Rhode Island, and asked to enlist during the height of the Vietnam War. With the help of the recruiter, he filled

out an application his family does not believe he could understand. Within six months, Babbitt found himself at the bloody outpost of Khe Sanh, where isolated marines held out for seventy-seven days against overwhelming enemy numbers near the North Vietnam border. Although Babbitt survived the battlefield, he found himself besieged anew by posttraumatic stress disorder.

Troubled and unruly, Babbitt was discharged in 1970 and soon descended into a life of homelessness and crime. Convicted of robbery in Massachusetts, Babbitt was diagnosed in 1973 as suicidal and schizophrenic while in custody at the Bridgewater State Hospital for the Criminally Insane. He left the institution after three years, but his bizarre behavior did not end. He returned to his family in Wareham but often slept in the woods in a lonely search for solace. Family members finally encouraged him to live with his brother Bill in Sacramento. There, they hoped, Manny would benefit from the love and guidance of a married, responsible, older sibling.

Within months of Manny's arrival in California, Schendel was murdered. And only a few days after her highly publicized killing, while rummaging through a closet at his home, Bill Babbitt discovered a cigarette lighter that had been monogrammed with the initials "L.S." He also found hundreds of nickels stuffed into a piggy bank.

Puzzled about the nickels, Bill Babbitt recalled reading that Leah Schendel had recently returned from a trip to Las Vegas, where she amused herself at the casinos by pumping fistfuls of coins into the cheapest one-arm bandits. The stunning connection brought Bill Babbitt to his knees. Heartbroken but determined to do right, Bill discussed his options with his wife. Should he help his brother escape? Should he put him on a bus bound far from Sacramento? Could he live with himself if Manny killed again? In the end, disconsolate but determined, Bill approached the Sacramento police. "It was a difficult situation to turn your brother in, but I had to do the right thing because I love this country," Bill said later. "That could have been my mother who died."

The police assured Bill that his brother would not be subject to the death penalty because of his apparent mental illness. Instead, they said, Manny would be confined in a locked psychiatric facility, presumably for the rest of his life, where he would receive the help he so desperately needed. Satisfied, Bill told police he would lead them to Manny, who had been staying temporarily at their sister's house. Bill entered alone, greeted his brother matter-of-factly, and enticed Manny to join him for an afternoon of pool. Instead of a pool hall, however, Bill Babbitt led his brother to a waiting police cruiser. And as the police handcuffed Manny, Bill pleaded with his brother for understanding.

"Please forgive me," Bill said. "They're going to take care of you, Brother. You're going to be okay. Please forgive me."

Manny looked up, his hands shackled, about to begin another journey in dangerous, uncharted country.

"Brother Billy," he said, "I've already forgiven you."

Manny's journey, however, would not lead to a no-parole lifetime of incarceration and therapy. Instead, Babbitt's journey led straight to the "gray wolf" at San Quentin. The story horrified Bob, who felt he had much in common with Manny Babbitt's disadvantaged, bare-bones upbringing. Both men had been poor and marginally educated, and both had enlisted in the marines in an effort to escape troubled home lives.

Bob contrasted Manny Babbitt's fate with that of Ted Kaczynski, the infamous Unabomber, who had killed three people and injured twenty-three with mailbombs and other explosives over seventeen years. Kaczynski was arrested in 1996 after his brother, David, approached the FBI with suspicions that the Unabomber's antitechnology manifesto resembled his brother's writings. Although Attorney General Janet Reno sought the death penalty, prosecutors eventually offered Kaczynski a plea agreement that resulted in life without parole. Death for the poor black man, Bob thought. Life in prison for the Harvard-educated white man.

Suddenly, the thinking that Bob had done in the past week, as well as the doubts that had gained traction since the

trials, began to fall into place like the tumblers in a combination lock. Now, the death penalty seemed less defensible. Once considered a hammer of justice, the punishment now seemed to Bob an emblem of inequity. A switch had been pulled in his mind, and its impact was immediate and profound. "It made me realize—being a poor guy, not educated, and from my background—that I'm closer to the guy who's going to be executed," Bob said.

Bob was unaware that Manny Babbitt's case had long been a cause célèbre for many Vietnam veterans and opponents of capital punishment. Both factions had argued passionately for years that Babbitt, irreparably scarred by mental illness, should be imprisoned for life instead of executed. That fight attracted Bud Welch, who lobbied Governor Gray Davis in California to spare Babbitt's life. And it attracted David Kaczynski, too. "Ted escaped by the skin of his teeth. And it was luck, it wasn't merits, it wasn't justice," said Kaczynski, who felt betrayed when Reno announced that prosecutors would seek the death penalty against his brother.

Later, after the plea agreement took execution off the table, Kaczynski received a phone call from Bill Babbitt in mid-1998. "This guy whose name I had never heard, from Sacramento, says, 'David, you don't know me, but I know you. I've read about you, and I think you might be the only person in the world who can understand what I'm going through right now,'" Kaczynski recalled. Because both men had turned in their brothers, and because both men knew the anguish of having exposed them to the death penalty, Kaczynski realized that Babbitt might be right. Who else could understand his emotional turmoil?

Bill Babbitt had become alienated from several of his siblings, who regarded him as a traitor. He endured cruel, racist comments about his brother by coworkers at the Sacramento transportation department, where Bill worked as a mechanic. And he despaired about the fate he unwittingly had sealed for Manny. "When Manny got arrested, I went back to my Bible,"

Bill recalled. "But besides my Bible, I had my marijuana, I had my booze, and I had my Derringer."

After outlining Manny's case for Kaczynski, Babbitt did not hear back immediately. Kaczynski was concerned that joining Bill's cause would reopen fresh wounds by resurrecting his family's story in the national news media. But after lengthy discussions with his wife, Linda, who first suspected the identity of the Unabomber, the Kaczynskis decided to help. When David Kaczynski finally called back in the spring of 1999, about the time that Bob Curley read the *Herald* story, Bill Babbitt was sitting on the edge of his bed, contemplating suicide.

"It's for you," Babbitt's wife said, handing him the phone.

Babbitt assumed the call was from a reporter, seeking yet another comment about the approaching execution. But instead of a reporter, Babbitt heard the calm, measured voice of a new, unexpected friend.

"Bill Babbitt, this is David Kaczynski," the caller said. "Bill, I'm coming to stand with you."

Instead of replying, Babbitt bolted from the bed. "Praise, Jesus! Praise, Jesus!" he shouted, while Kaczynski listened patiently. When Babbitt finally realized he had a phone conversation to finish, Kaczynski agreed to travel to Sacramento to attend Manny Babbitt's last-chance clemency hearing in April.

Three thousand miles to the east, Bob Curley also decided to become involved. He did not know how—he had no friends among the death-penalty opposition—but a doorway into the fight would open.

———

9

Resurrection

WHEN THE Massachusetts House of Representatives convened for six hours of debate, followed by a climactic
vote on capital punishment in 1999, the Curleys were nowhere
to be seen. No last-minute changes were expected this year,
no shouting in the hallways, no high fives on the chamber
floor. All the energy, so different from 1997, had shifted to the
better-organized opposition.

Still, the prospects for defeat did not deter Governor
Paul Cellucci from staging one, last, bitter rally on the broad
sidewalk in front of the State House. Flanked by the families
of murder victims and standing in front of a phalanx of police
officers, Cellucci pointed behind him, toward the Capitol's
gleaming golden dome, and railed against the lawmakers assembled there. "We have a House of Representatives that is
out of touch with the people they represent," Cellucci said,
his voice rising.

The governor was followed by a parade of somber supporters who, angry and embittered, recounted in graphic detail
the gruesome deaths of those they had lost. When the rally
ended, the governor conceded defeat in remarks to reporters.
He listed a variety of reasons: The economy is good. Momentum had waned. The other side is too formidable.

Inside the building, the process crept through a marathon session of theatrical debate to its predictable conclusion. In
desperation, Republicans offered a lengthy string of amendments

195

in a final, unsuccessful bid to make the bill palatable. Postpone the vote until the House vacancies were filled, they asked. Limit capital punishment to killers of law-enforcement officers. Target only those who murder again in prison. The list went on and on, to no avail.

John Slattery took the floor, and this time his fiery denunciations of the death penalty took no one by surprise. "Why is a cop's life more important than my mother's?" he bristled, surveying the chamber with defiance. At the end of the day, exhausted and resigned, the House voted, 80–73, to reject the bill.

On cue, Cellucci once again launched broadside after outraged broadside against Tom Finneran, the House speaker, whom he lampooned as a strong-armed con man bent on perverting the people's will. But, in defeat, even the governor and his supporters seemed to realize that a watershed moment had come and gone. The measure was dead, clinically and emotionally, and not even the resurrected memory of Jeffrey Curley's murder could revive its flagging chances. Opponents celebrated their hard work and brightening prospects for future success. Certainly, the activists believed, their efforts had made a difference in a legislature suddenly less enamored of state-sponsored lethal injection.

Another factor, too, might have played a role. Where was Bob Curley? He had neither testified at the hearing nor attended the debate. His voice also had been missing from the media run-up to the vote. Bob's absence throughout had been glaringly conspicuous. The activists could only speculate because Bob had not confided his concerns to anyone except Mimi. He had been content to sit out the latest skirmish and keep his new opinions to himself.

But Bob could not shake the image of Manny Babbitt, a mentally handicapped veteran, waiting in San Quentin for his date with death. Shortly after the vote, Bob was driving his mechanic's truck through Cambridge when he spotted Jarrett Barrios, a young, liberal state legislator, walking near Inman Square.

Bob stopped the truck, leaned out the window, and asked Barrios for a contact at Massachusetts Citizens Against the Death Penalty, a group that Bob had despised during the acrimonious debate in 1997. Barrios, who had noted Bob's absence at Gardner Auditorium, said he would put him in touch with someone. The conversation ended there, but Barrios's curiosity had been piqued.

He called Martina Jackson, the group's executive director, and relayed Bob's unexpected request. Jackson, as surprised as Barrios, eagerly agreed to phone Bob. When Jackson called, any trepidation she might have felt turned quickly to amazement. The person who answered was startlingly unlike the man who once cursed her during a death-penalty protest. This time, Bob was calm, solicitous, and anxious for a connection to the opposition. He hadn't made a decision, but he wanted to learn.

"There's a group that might be helpful to reach a conclusion," Jackson said. "It's called Murder Victims' Families for Reconciliation. Why don't you talk to Renny Cushing there?"

"Sounds like a plan," Bob replied.

That call led to a follow-up from Bob, which Cushing had been told would occur during a dinner meeting of his group. When he shared the news with other members, the gathering was stunned. Who? Bob Curley? *The* Bob Curley? It was true, Cushing assured them. Bob Curley wanted to contact California governor Gray Davis about the Manny Babbitt case.

Cushing was at the dining room table when Bob called. So was Andrew Pryor, the father of the murdered girl from Wayland. Also in attendance was Tom Lowenstein, political director for Massachusetts Citizens Against the Death Penalty, who was handed the phone shortly after Bob rang. Lowenstein had thrown himself into the Massachusetts death-penalty fray specifically because of Jeffrey Curley's murder. The son of former congressman Allard Lowenstein, a New York civil rights activist gunned down in 1980, Tom left behind a bartending job in

Northampton, Massachusetts, after reading a pro-death-penalty opinion piece by Jeff Jacoby, a conservative columnist at the *Boston Globe*. Jacoby had written with mock sarcasm about the potential reaction to Bob's push to prosecute Jaynes and Sicari in federal court, where a death sentence could be imposed. "Let's hope those Massachusetts authorities tell Curley where to get off," Jacoby said. "Let's hope they remind him in no uncertain terms that the death penalty is barbaric and medieval. . . . Let's hope they point out to him that the death penalty won't bring his butchered little boy back."

Lowenstein, seething, e-mailed every death-penalty opposition group he could find on the Internet to offer his services. "It was one of those rare moments where you get upset about something in the paper and get off your butt and do something about it," Lowenstein said. In short order, Lowenstein, an energetic idealist who favored black leather jackets and semiregular shaves, joined Cushing, Jackson, and other opponents who converged on the State House in the weeks preceding the 1997 vote.

While sitting in the State House coffee shop during that tumultuous period, Lowenstein saw Bob Curley for the first time. Escorted by a half dozen state troopers, Bob was rushing to yet another round of lobbying. Lowenstein was struck by the pain etched on Bob's face, a pain that he, himself, had felt after a mentally ill man shot his father in his Manhattan law office. Lowenstein was startled by the size of the State Police escort and by how the powers of the state had been mobilized for the governor's agonized new ally. "I'm sitting there with the antideath-penalty group, thinking, So, this is the way the government works this. I mean, who are they protecting him from? What's the worry up here?"

Lowenstein had never met Bob when he picked up the phone at that dinner gathering. As far as Lowenstein knew, Bob's concerns about Manny Babbitt might be a onetime exception for the no-compromise zealot he had seen marching through the State House. So, with a little anxiety but a little hope, Lowenstein put the receiver to his ear.

"Hello, this is Tom Lowenstein."

"Hi, this is Bob Curley," he heard. "Listen, there's this guy in California who's gonna be executed. He's a former marine, and this guy's got PTSD."

Lowenstein answered that he knew of Manny Babbitt.

"Look, I'd like to get in touch with Gray Davis. This guy shouldn't be executed," Bob continued. "I'd like some help in putting together a letter."

"Of course," Lowenstein said. "We'll help you write the letter. We'll do anything we can to help you."

Bob thanked Lowenstein but added an adamant, no-misunderstandings kicker. "I'm still for the death penalty," Bob said in a clipped, curt, businesslike tone. "I want to make that clear, okay? I still support the death penalty."

"Sure, I understand, Mr. Curley," Lowenstein said. "I understand exactly where you're coming from. I wouldn't try to convert you."

Lowenstein handed the phone to Cushing, who spoke briefly with Bob and encouraged him to call Davis. When the conversation ended, the ten people gathered at the table were teeming with questions. What did he say? How did he sound to you? What does this mean?

Bob's eagerness to join the fight for Manny Babbitt certainly was a cause for celebration. But perhaps more important, the group agreed, was Bob's need to underscore his continued support for the death penalty. That declaration was a telltale sign that a wall had been breached and that Bob was questioning his once-impervious beliefs. Anyone who opposed a single execution that strongly, the group believed, would eventually oppose them all. On this night and in this place, the leap was far from theoretical. Around the table, among friends bound by individual loss, others had also taken a similar, remarkable, and unexpected journey.

Bob followed up by writing to Gray Davis in Sacramento. He also placed a phone call to California in which he told a governor's aide about Jeffrey's story and why he opposed Babbitt's execution. If Davis was told of the call, Bob never heard.

Manny Babbitt's clemency hearing before the California Board of Prison Terms was held April 26, 1999. Bob did not attend, but Bud Welch was there, as were David Kaczynski, members of Babbitt's family, Vietnam veterans, and even Babbitt's fifth-grade teacher. The family of Leah Schendel also attended, as did prosecutors who scoffed at the notion that Babbitt's behavior could be linked to the siege of Khe Sanh, twelve years before the murder, or anything else he experienced in Vietnam. The facts and factors of the case are simple, the state said: A pathological criminal sought to rob an old woman, and then killed her when she became an obstacle.

Two days after the hearing, Bud Welch received a surprise phone call as he prepared to address a national convention of priests in San Antonio. The voice on the line belonged to Bob Curley, whom Welch had not seen since the Boston television show a month earlier.

"Bud, what are we going to do to save this guy out in California, this Vietnam vet?" Bob asked.

"You're talking about Manny Babbitt?" Welch said.

"Yes, him," Bob answered.

"Bob, I don't know what else we can do," Welch replied. "I just testified before the pardons board the day before yesterday."

The news startled Bob, who had been unaware of the hearing. He had no tool set for this situation, no options for fighting the machinery of a state determined to put a man to death. All his experience had been on the other side, and Bob, upset and deflated, felt helpless to alter a case that had changed his thinking so dramatically.

Davis ended any hope four days after that phone conversation, when he dismissed Babbitt's plea for mercy. "Countless people have suffered the ravages of war, persecution, starvation, natural disasters, personal calamities, and the like," the governor wrote. "But such experiences cannot justify or mitigate the savage beating and killing of defenseless, law-abiding citizens." The Schendel family praised Davis's "commitment to justice," but critics argued that the Democratic governor,

eager to appear tough on crime, had approved the execution to further his national political ambitions.

On May 4, 1999, Babbitt became the seventh person executed in California since the state's reinstatement of capital punishment in 1992. Bill Babbitt stood on a riser as the lethal cocktail began its work, looking not at his brother but at the victim's family, whom Manny had asked him to forgive. The body was brought home to Wareham, Massachusetts, clothed in marine dress blues that fellow Vietnam veterans had purchased. There, in a cemetery plot donated by his former schoolteacher, Manny Babbitt was bid farewell in a flag-draped coffin as brother Bill struggled to hold up their grief-racked mother.

David Kaczynski watched from the fringes on a lush spring day, thinking how his brother had received a first-rate defense team, a plea bargain, and scrupulous attention from the national news media. Manny Babbitt, he knew, had benefited from none of those things. Kaczynski began to cry and could not stop, dissolving on the periphery of the burial in a rolling succession of heaving sobs. "Maybe I'd withheld a lot of tears because I felt I had to be strong, but the tragedy of the Babbitt family was just like a dam had burst," Kaczynski recalled. "I suppose I was crying for lots of folks. For Bill and his family, for my brother's victims, and for the grandmother's family, too."

Afterward, on the three-hour drive home to upstate New York, Kaczynski felt he had turned a corner. "I was coming to terms with the realization that the life I once had, the life I wanted back, was truly gone," Kaczynski said. "I now had seen things and experienced things that had changed me, and I wanted other people to know about them. I wanted somehow to put a face on the death penalty and let people see, in human terms, that it was cruel and unjust." Motivated by Manny Babbitt's execution, Kaczynski sought and was given the job of executive director of New Yorkers Against the Death Penalty.

The execution also impacted Bob Curley, who returned to a cocoon of routine, where he filled the empty spaces with the rhythms of the firehouse and the satisfactions of home improvements. He also watched the slow progression of his civil lawsuits against Jeffrey's killers and NAMBLA. One of them, a $200 million wrongful-death claim, was filed against Jaynes and Sicari in Middlesex Superior Court in a move that even Bob recognized as purely symbolic. "What am I going to get from these two stooges?" Bob asked at the time. "They're going to have a hard time coming up with that making license plates."

Once again, the Curleys became objects of public interest. They were asked in court to recount the lingering effect of Jeffrey's murder on their lives. Tears fell. The news media carried their familiar images. And the fifty-gallon Rubbermaid container, in which Jeffrey's body had been placed, was removed from storage and displayed again to grim-faced jurors.

Neither Jaynes nor Sicari appeared in court. Indeed, Jaynes instructed his lawyer not to present any meaningful evidence in his defense. Jaynes, his attorney said, wanted "to make it easier" on the Curleys. "I will trust in the jury to give a fair and reasonable award," Jaynes said through counsel.

That award was for a staggering $328 million, one of the largest ever granted in the United States for a child's murder. The family's attorney, Lawrence Frisoli, hailed the decision as a landmark deterrent. "This is a measuring stick by which to judge people who rape kids and get caught," Frisoli said. "We can't stop pedophiles from raping children, but we can make it harder on them."

Frisoli also hoped the huge award would help a second wrongful-death suit, against NAMBLA, in U.S. District Court in Boston. In that claim, the Curleys sought $200 million for what the family alleged were Web-based writings that incited Jaynes to murder Jeffrey. The family aimed, Frisoli said, to bankrupt the organization through unaffordable penalties and to send an unambiguous warning to any group that would use the Internet to promote pedophilia or other child abuse.

The lawsuit's connection with the Curley murder was guaranteed to generate publicity. But the case received an added jolt of controversy when the American Civil Liberties Union agreed to represent NAMBLA. "For us, it's a fundamental First Amendment case," said John Roberts, executive director of the ACLU's Massachusetts chapter. ACLU officials acknowledged the public's disgust with NAMBLA's goal of changing age-of-consent laws and allowing consensual sex between men and boys. But political advocacy, the ACLU said, is free speech regardless of the message, no matter how abhorrent. The ACLU compared NAMBLA with the Nazis who marched in Skokie, Illinois, in the late 1970s. "It is easy to defend freedom of speech when the message is something many people find at least reasonable," the ACLU said. "But the defense of freedom of speech is most critical when the message is one most people find repulsive. This was true when the Nazis marched in Skokie. It remains true today."

For all its initial controversy, however, the lawsuit figured to drag on for years with only minimal prospects for success. Outside state and federal court, Bob had other demons to confront. He lashed out at the city of Cambridge, faulting its efforts to protect children and lambasting a mandatory course in diversity training for all city employees. Bob derided the four-hour program, which one city official said would "develop an understanding of how we benefit from being part of a diverse workforce," as "feel-good crap." Derision led to disgust at the first session, where Bob exploded as the facilitator began extolling the advantages of cultural cross-pollination. "You fucking phony!" Bob yelled before storming out of the meeting. He refused to return.

In a twist of irony, Bob secured the services of Harvey Silverglate, a member of the ACLU board of directors and one of Boston's preeminent civil rights lawyers. Silverglate wrote to Cambridge officials, arguing that Bob was within his constitutional rights to refuse to attend. Afterward, the city allowed him to "opt out" of the program because of a "personal tragedy."

The waiver made Bob the only one of two thousand city employees who did not participate.

His distaste for diversity training did not necessarily mean Bob was any more conservative than the men he worked beside. Even if there were liberals in the firehouse, Bob was fond of saying, they wouldn't admit to it. As a result, Bob did not discuss the Manny Babbitt case with his coworkers. As far as Bob knew, everybody in the Fire Department was in favor of the death penalty. And among the public, Bob was regarded as the leader of the pack.

To Mimi, the only person in whom he confided his change of opinion, the shift was a sign of healing, an indicator that he had finally moved beyond the rage and grief that had consumed him for so long. "He told me what had happened with the man in California, and that he'd been thinking that the death penalty isn't only about race, it's also about class," Mimi recalled. "He would say, 'I'm a poor man, and this could have happened to me. This could have happened to people I know.'" Maybe, Mimi thought, Bob was connecting with the person he had always been.

Although Bob confined those feelings to the home, he immersed himself in a wide, public array of programs for child safety and the prevention of sexual abuse, and he soon became a well-traveled and hardworking spokesman for those issues. Through it all, Bob did not disavow the death penalty in conversations with other outreach workers, even though most of them were loud, liberal opponents of capital punishment. They had a natural empathy for Bob's ordeal, but they hadn't forgotten his merciless message from 1997. "At hearings or meetings," Bob said, "you could always feel the tension because of how they viewed me, as a big death-penalty supporter."

As best he could, Bob ignored the sideways glances and the unspoken questions. He'd chosen his path, he had important work to do, and his list of accomplishments grew quickly. Bob helped create the Jeffrey Curley Foundation, which raised money for programs to increase awareness about child safety.

He lobbied hard for a law, backed by Governor Cellucci, that made Massachusetts the last state in the nation to criminalize possession of child pornography. Previously, only producers and distributors of child pornography could be prosecuted in Massachusetts.

Bob and Barbara organized an annual road race, held near the date of Jeffrey's abduction, that provided scholarships for Cambridge students to pursue degrees in child psychology, social work, or similar fields to benefit children. Bob also touched the families of children who had been murdered or abducted. Parents such as Magi and John Bish, whose teenage daughter Molly vanished in 2000 from her lifeguard post, heard unexpectedly from Bob, a stranger, when he called to offer condolences and emotional support. Bob wrote letters to the opinion pages of New England newspapers, urged tougher registration laws for sexual offenders in the state, and worked with Jane Doe Inc., a nonprofit organization that focused on the issue of domestic violence.

Bob's signature campaign led to the Jeffrey Curley Bill, enacted after a barnstorming effort to persuade the legislature to post a list of safety dos and don'ts at all public schools and on state-owned property. The "Eight Rules of Safety," developed by the National Center for Missing and Exploited Children, uses simple phrasing to deliver commonsense instructions, such as asking permission from a parent or supervisor before getting into a car with someone else or accepting gifts. They also are designed to empower children if they become victims of inappropriate contact. "I say 'no' if someone tries to touch me in ways that make me feel frightened, uncomfortable, or confused," one of the rules states. "Then I go and tell a grown-up I trust what happened."

Bob embarked on the crusade with a missionary's zeal, encouraged by Dan Moniz, a phone technician, who reached out to the Curleys in the first dark days after Jeffrey's disappearance. Moniz, who had been circulating the Eight Rules to town halls and police departments for several years before Jeffrey's murder, first saw coverage of the killing on a bank of

televisions in an electronics store. Horrified by the news and thinking of his daughters, ages nine and ten, Moniz began crying as he watched.

Almost immediately, Moniz hatched an ambitious plan to recruit Bob and spread the Eight Rules statewide. First, he needed the courage to pick up the phone, call a grieving father he did not know, and make his pitch. After staring at the receiver for twenty minutes, Moniz finally placed the phone to his ear. On the other end, Moniz found an enthusiastic ally, and the two set right to work.

Bob and Moniz formed a persuasive and effective pair, addressing municipal officials in Cambridge, Somerville, Malden, Danvers, Lowell, and a dozen other communities. They appeared on any local cable outlet that would have them. The road show reaped big dividends in its three-year run. Cities and towns, touched by Bob's story and Dan's moral salesmanship, ordered thousands of posters with the Eight Rules of Safety. Each success gave the lawmakers on Beacon Hill one more reason to pass the Jeffrey Curley Bill. Finally, in February 2001, Governor Cellucci signed the bill into law at a bittersweet State House ceremony.

As the governor spoke, smiles creased many faces among the Curley family, their friends, and state officials gathered at the wide base of the Grand Staircase. But for Bob, the occasion resurrected reminders of why this moment had been necessary. Slouched in a gray suit, the corners of his mouth turned downward, Bob stepped forward to address the news media. Rubbing his chin and trembling with emotion, Bob spoke of his son. "I just hope that Jeff is looking down on this day now, just knowing how much I love him, and saying, 'Way to go, Dad. I knew you wouldn't let my fight be for nothing.'" Bob's words trailed off amid a swell of sustained, respectful applause that echoed off the marble floors and portrait-lined walls.

Despite the accolades, Bob remained as grim as the day he had stood on Hampshire Street and thundered for the death penalty. This time, however, Bob's turmoil was partly a product of the chasm between his public reputation on capital punishment and the private stance he refused to divulge. "I'd

be sitting around the firehouse, and somebody would be reading the paper about some awful crime and say, 'Geez, if they only had a death penalty,'" Bob recalled. "And it always seemed to be when I was there. I'd say, 'Yeah, you're right.' Other than that, I'd basically keep my mouth shut, go about my business, and try to make an exit out the door." Outside work, as well, the death penalty managed to creep into conversation. "I wouldn't be introduced to somebody for ten seconds," Bob said, "and the first thing they'd say would be, 'That fuckin' Slattery,' or 'That fuckin' Finneran. They ought to put in an execution fast lane, the way Texas does it.'"

In Bob's mind, many people brought up the subject simply to make him feel better, to show some blue-collar solidarity with the icon of the state's death-penalty movement. Instead, the topic made him cringe. "After a while, it started to wear on me," Bob said. "I felt like a whore in church, like a fucking coward." But for someone from old-school Inman Square, the prospect of being labeled weak, or a "wimp," or an out-of-touch bleeding heart was simply not acceptable.

In the late spring of 2001, Bob decided he was done agonizing. Jeff's fourteenth birthday would be in a few days, on June 9, and Bob had been playing and replaying the surreal events of that horrible October nearly four years earlier. Finally, tormented enough, Bob resolved to remove the inner tensions that only he could feel. The time had come to make a public statement, lift the burden from his chest, and put the entire death-penalty issue in the rearview mirror.

Bob thumbed through his address book for the telephone number of a reporter for New England Cable News (NECN), a woman who called every several months to renew a standing invitation to talk on-air about the death penalty. Bob phoned to say he had changed his mind and that he wanted to talk publicly. The reporter, suddenly handed a good news story, drove to Bob's home and conducted an interview in the living room. Speaking calmly but earnestly, sitting in his favorite chair, Bob spoke of capital punishment as an attack on the working class, as the ultimate penalty inflicted unfairly on the poor. "You can't have it both ways," Bob said later. "You can't go back

and forth and say this guy goes, and this guy doesn't because he has a better lawyer."

The interview was carried that night as part of NECN's twenty-four-hour cycle, but the news would take time to disseminate. The station's viewership at the time lagged behind that of the three network affiliates in Boston. But as far as Bob was concerned, a minimal amount of media attention would be fine. "For a long time, I'd struggled with what people would think," Bob said. "But when I made that call, I said to myself, Hey, I don't owe anybody anything. I said, I'm gonna tell it from my view. People can agree with me or they can disagree with me, but I do expect people to respect my view. If people don't like it, even if people from my own family don't like it, fuck 'em. After everything that had happened up to that point, I just felt I had an obligation to do this."

The next morning, relieved and refocused, Bob ambled downstairs to scan the morning newspapers. There, tucked inside the *Globe*, was a brief story about a conference at Boston College, scheduled to begin that day, for death-penalty opponents who had lost relatives to murder. Bob nearly fainted. Only a few miles away, only hours after he had announced his switch, hundreds of like-minded people would be sharing their tragic stories, offering mutual support, and validating a common conviction that no one should be killed in their name. "I couldn't believe it. I was stunned," Bob recalled. "I'm saying, there's some other, higher power operating here."

The conference, which had been planned for a year by Murder Victims' Families for Reconciliation, would be the first large gathering of survivors of murder victims in U.S. history. More than one hundred families converged on the college, as did dozens of academics, lawyers, activists, and clergy. The grandson of Mahatma Gandhi participated, as did Renny Cushing, Bud Welch, Sister Helen Prejean, and Cardinal Law.

As the conference opened that morning, word of Bob's change of heart had begun to ripple through Greater Boston. Newspapers carried stories of his switch. Puzzled neighbors asked each other if it were true. And Cardinal Law, welcoming

home the prodigal son, left a long, sermonlike message on Bob's phone machine. "Robert, I'm very, very proud of you," he said.

The news also made its way to Boston College.

"I heard a rumor that Bob Curley was on TV yesterday and that he'd changed his mind about the death penalty," Cushing told Welch.

"You're kidding me. I had a feeling he was going to do that," Welch said. "I'm going to call him right now."

When no one answered, Welch began to leave a message: "Bobby, it's Bud Welch. I just wanted to give you a call. I'm in town—"

Before he could complete his thought, Welch heard a familiar, booming Boston accent.

"Hey, Bud, how you doing!" Bob said.

"Well, I'm with Renny Cushing, and we're sitting in the car on the campus of Boston College, and we've got this conference going on," Welch said. "Renny says you've changed your mind about the death penalty."

"Yeah, I have," Bob replied. "I've given a lot of thought to a lot of things you've said."

"Bob, I'm going to be addressing the full conference Saturday afternoon at one o'clock," Welch said. "I have an hour. Will you come and speak with me?"

Once again, as he had done before their joint television appearance, Bob said he didn't have a car. Then, he said his house would be difficult for a taxi to find. But this time, to squelch the exit strategy, Welch said he'd drive Bob himself. To avoid the maze of East Somerville, they agreed to meet at the firehouse.

On the ride to Boston College, Bob was unable to stifle his fears. He couldn't speak, he said. He didn't have a speech prepared. It wasn't possible.

"Bob, you don't want a speech written out," Welch said, falling back on the lessons he had learned. "You know Jeffrey. You know how Jeffrey was killed. You know the emotions you went through. You don't need that on paper."

As Welch drove to the college, the conference began to buzz with news of Bob's imminent arrival. A little while later,

Susannah Sheffer, a staff member for Murder Victims' Families for Reconciliation, spotted Bob in a hallway, huddling with Welch and Andy Pryor outside a panel discussion on the death penalty's potential to divide families already scarred by murder. Sheffer quietly left the classroom and introduced herself.

"Do you want to speak now," she asked Bob, "or would you like to wait?"

"Whatever you'd like me to do," Bob answered.

Sheffer slipped a note to Jennifer Bishop, chairwoman of the MVFR board, who was moderating the panel. "Bob Curley's here. He'd like to speak," the note read.

Bishop nodded as Bob sat in the front row to hear the horrific story of the murder of Bishop's pregnant sister and brother-in-law. In April 1990, the couple had returned from a family birthday party to find a sixteen-year-old stranger in their suburban Chicago home. The teenager shot Richard Langert, killing him instantly. He then fired at Nancy Langert's abdomen, which she shielded while pleading for mercy. Nancy bled to death, but not before crawling to her husband, dipping her fingers in his blood, and tracing a heart and a U on the wall.

Jennifer Bishop opposed the death penalty, even after the murders, and pledged to work against a political candidate who had sought to make sixteen-year-olds eligible for execution as a way to "honor" Nancy Langert. Bob listened intently to Bishop, who restated her opposition, and also to her father, who supported the death penalty. Soon, Bob knew, his own family would split starkly on the issue.

After the discussion, Welch strode to the podium and introduced Bob to the twenty-five people in the room. Bob needed no introduction. He thanked Welch, wrung his hands, and searched for the words to describe the events that had changed his life. "You got to bear with me, folks," Bob began, his face a wrenching reflection of his metamorphosis. "Prior to losing my Jeff, my only public speaking experience was with my baseball team in East Cambridge, so I'll do the best I can."

The audience laughed softly, and Bob managed a slight smile. Then, in simple language, Bob outlined the grisly de-

tails of Jeffrey's death, how Jaynes had been a member of NAMBLA, how Jeffrey had been "groomed" for abduction, and how Bob's rage had grown limitless and grotesque. Driven by hate, Bob said, "I led the fight in the state of Massachusetts to reinstate the death penalty."

Bob then told the group how he had changed and how Bud Welch, Bill Babbitt, and David Kaczynski had opened his eyes to another, more therapeutic possibility. The effect was immediate and transforming. The audience stood as one, crying and clapping, aware that this short speech had been an unscripted adventure into uncharted territory for a suddenly remade man. "It was one of those standing ovations where you feel like you're levitating," Sheffer said. "You don't even think you're standing. You're just standing because it's beyond words."

Bob was swarmed afterward, but he had other business directly ahead of him. Welch, who was scheduled to deliver the conference's keynote address, asked Bob to repeat his remarks for three hundred listeners. The speeches were nearly identical, as were Bob's pain, nervousness, and struggle to hold himself together. "You can imagine the anger, unbelievable anger," Bob told the larger audience of his reaction to Jeffrey's murder. "But time passes, and you get a chance to take a step back and look at things, and the way things are, and I started to take a look at the death penalty, and the way it's applied."

Bob paused, exhaling deeply as his shoulders began to relax. "It's been a long journey for me. It's something that I've kept inside of me from not long after I met with Bud two years ago," he said. "I don't know what effect it's gonna have on my relationships with people who look to me, or even my own family members," he added. "I don't think they know, but they know now." Soft, empathetic laughter pulsed through the auditorium. "It's ironic, because I'm gonna find out, because today is my Jeff's birthday. He would have been fourteen years old."

Gasps escaped from the audience, who knew the pain of birthdays for any family member who had outlived a child cut

down by murder. And Bob, clearly, was in agony. He paused as the gasps subsided. But when he resumed, glancing at his watch, his tight control began to fray.

"I'm gonna be going to the cemetery at three o'clock, and we'll see what happens," Bob said, his voice breaking. "It's been a long, difficult journey for me, and I feel relieved that I'm here and am able to talk about it. I don't know what's gonna happen on the Fourth of July. Maybe I'll be rolling around the backyard, duking it out with my brothers or whoever, but that's all right. I choose my own path."

Bob, gaining confidence as he spoke, finished with an emphatic declaration of individual determination. "I want Jaynes and Sicari to stay in jail and to see me every day—to think of me, think of my Jeff, the strong, little boy that Jeff was," Bob said, his forehead knit in defiance. "I'm going to try to follow in Jeffrey's footsteps and be as strong as he was," Bob pledged, "and stand and be my own man."

Renny Cushing had tears in his eyes. "Everyone thought of their own pain and their own journey," he said later. "But they also recognized that this was Bob Curley. And for Bob to stand up and say, 'I've thought this over, and I don't support the death penalty anymore,' was incredibly powerful."

Bill Babbitt and David Kaczynski also wept. They had never met Bob, had not known Jeffrey's story, and were stunned and touched as Bob mentioned their profound impact on his decision. "From one human being to another human being who had lost a loved one, my heart went out to this man," Babbitt said. "They must have promised him a nice, cool drink out of this cup called closure. He probably entertained that and said, I know it's gonna taste good when I drink out of that cup. But then he saw David and I, saw how we were carrying on and not hating anybody, and asked, What are those guys having? I want what those guys got."

As Bob spoke, Babbitt noted the familiar "mask of pain"; Kaczynski heard the "conviction" in his speech. Both men recognized an irreversible conversion. "I could imagine the strug-

gle, but I could see a sense of resolution," Kaczynski said. "It was amazing, because it was there. You knew this guy was not going back, no matter what happened from that point on."

After Bob's speech, Welch took the podium and looked down at the man he had met only once before, on the NECN set where Bob began his improbable journey. Welch clasped his hands together, his face riveted on Bob, the admiration evident in his gentle eyes and soft smile. "And I have to speak?" Welch said to the audience with a chuckle. "I'm not real sure I can do this."

Welch, however, talked for forty-five minutes about his relationship with his daughter Julie, his outreach to the McVeighs, his torturous battles with alcohol, and his unflagging commitment to fight the death penalty. Welch also told his listeners that, when he left Boston College, he would fly directly to Indiana to join a vigil protesting Timothy McVeigh's execution in two days. At 1:50 P.M., he ended his soft-spoken call to arms, mindful that he needed to help Bob make his appointment at Cambridge Cemetery, where the Curley family would be gathering for Jeffrey's birthday. Welch leaned down and whispered in Bob's ear, "Let's get out of Dodge."

The pair hustled out the door before they could be enveloped by embraces and congratulations. The Chevy Blazer that had brought Bob to Boston College was parked nearby, ready to ferry the men to East Somerville, where Bob would pick up Mimi's car and drive alone to the cemetery. But after they took their seats, Welch did not turn the ignition key. Instead, he began to cry, overcome by the events of the day and by the startling transformation of the plain, powerful man beside him.

Welch, who cries easily, was not surprised by his reaction. He did not expect, however, what happened next, when Bob Curley, relieved but exhausted, added tears of his own. The men sat for several minutes, sobbing on a college campus in the middle of the day, reflecting on their individual and mutual losses and on a journey that neither man had thought he could endure.

"It was very emotional for me inside that car," Welch recalled. "I'd had the privilege of introducing Bob, who had gone through so much of a change. And to think I had influenced that in some manner. I was having a good feeling about that because I know what it is to live with retribution," Welch continued. "When you're living with revenge, you can't go through the healing process. You just can't do it; it's impossible." Welch saw a different man. In his mind, Bob had stopped blaming himself for Jeffrey's death. This Bob Curley seemed more at peace, had pushed revenge aside, and had reached the place that Welch predicted he would find.

Welch wished Bob good luck as he dropped him off in Somerville. Bob, however, was worried and anxious as he drove the four congested miles to Cambridge Cemetery, located near a sharp, marshy bend in the Charles River. But he reminded himself that his decision was his own and that his choice deserved respect, particularly from family members who had wept and fought beside him in the death-penalty struggle. "I'd finally gotten to a point where I wasn't going to be influenced by anybody else's view on anything," Bob said. "I was going to live and die with the consequences of what I thought."

Since the murder, the Curley family had gathered at Jeffrey's grave every year at 3:15 P.M. on his birthday, exactly the time that Jeffrey had rushed from his grandmother's kitchen and into the Cadillac. Barbara would be there, as would Bobby, Shaun, Barbara's mother, Barbara's sisters, and Bob's sisters Francine and Margaret. Francine would say a few words of remembrance, prayers would be recited, and fourteen balloons would be released into the late-spring sky, one for each year since Jeffrey had been born.

Bob had not spoken with any of his family since the television interview or newspaper reports about his change. But they had all seen or heard the news, as Bob expected they would. Barbara and the boys were furious, as were Barbara's siblings, all of whom had no knowledge of Bob's long struggle

with the death-penalty issue and no warning that he would go public with his decision.

When Bob arrived at the cemetery, ten minutes late, the family had already assembled by the headstone. Their sorrow over Jeffrey's death, muted only slightly since the murder, now competed with the anger they felt at Bob's shocking reversal. As Bob walked the twenty-five yards from Mimi's car to the grave, all eyes turned toward him. Despite the silence, the tension was oppressive.

Finally, Barbara spoke for everyone. "How can you forgive the guys who killed the baby?" she asked, glaring, in stinging disbelief.

"It's got nothing to do with that," Bob replied.

"Yeah, what's up with this, Dad?" Shaun said, agitated. "You're being like a politician. You're flip-flopping. Come on. I mean, what's changed in the last four years?"

Bob tried to head off a confrontation, which could escalate rapidly among a family known for hot tempers and strong opinions. "Look, I just don't want Jeff to be known as a poster child for the death penalty," Bob said.

To Barbara, using Jeffrey to reinstate the death penalty would have been a tribute, a tangible sign that he had not died in vain, and a personal point of pride that his murder might prevent the deaths of other children. Bob's argument persuaded no one. And their body language, particularly among the boys, had become edgy, frustrated, and aggressive.

"Look, we're here for Jeff's birthday," Bob said calmly. "It's for Jeff, okay? I've got my view, and you've got your view."

Bobby, his eyes narrowed, looked at his father with bewildered disgust. "What the fuck is the matter with you?" he barked.

Before Bob could answer, Bobby thrust himself within inches of his father's face, a man he outweighed by thirty pounds, demanding an answer from someone he no longer understood. "I don't want to fucking find out what my father's thinking through the fucking media!" Bobby said.

"Hey, calm down, calm down," Bob answered. "Now's not the time or the place to be talking about this."

The anxious, agonized looks on the others showed that Bob was right. On an already difficult day, a shouting match or worse would be catastrophic for this crippled family. Bobby stepped back, Bob quieted down, and heads soon were bowed as murmured prayers and colorful balloons relieved some of the tension and replaced some of the ugliness.

Too much had been said, however, and reconciliation would have to wait. Bob left quickly when the memorial ended. Any solace it could give had been tainted by anger on top of anguish and by the sense that Jeffrey's legacy had been betrayed. "I just felt, That was my baby. How could you not want a death penalty?" Barbara recalled. "These guys planned this, you know what I mean? Bob was just so far away from what I thought his beliefs were that I couldn't even fathom it." As Bob walked away, an awkward, dejected guest at the grave of his murdered son, he tried not to blame Barbara or the family for their anger. "I fully understood the way they felt, because I felt the same way at the start," he said later.

But understanding did not make the confrontation easier to absorb. Although he had survived the first difficult test of his convictions, the repercussions would linger. Barbara and Bobby would not speak to him. "What my father did with his life at that point in time was his own fucking business," said Bobby, who was staggering under crushing burdens of his own. At twenty-one, he had been guardian of the home for nearly four years, caring for his mother when she cried herself to sleep, keeping Shaun away from drugs and out of trouble—a draining, demanding job that had been unwanted and unforgiving.

Now, after the graveside argument, the divide between Bob and his family had widened even further. On a day he renounced the death penalty, on the day he pledged to be his own man, Bob was mourning the loss of one beloved son and then seemed to lose the other two.

—— 10 ——

The Road Home

BOB HAD CHANGED, and so had the circumscribed world in which he lived. People who had known him as a relentless champion of the death penalty began to look at him differently. Invitations for television and radio appearances dried up. And even a few firefighters, stunned by his renunciation of capital punishment, joked with him in ways that sometimes hurt.

"You sucking up to Tom Finneran now, you fucking bum?" one firefighter asked after the news broke.

"What are you, fucking soft?" Bob said.

Bob realized most of his coworkers were teasing him with a firefighter's brand of merciless humor. But he didn't take all the remarks as a joke.

"How much did they pay you?" another firefighter asked.

"What the fuck are you talking about?" Bob shot back. "Who? Who's gonna pay me?"

Fran Judd, one of Bob's best friends at Engine 5, recalled that he was "horrified" by Bob's new views on the death penalty and that most of the men at the firehouse felt the same. "I believe in an eye for an eye, a tooth for a tooth, I really do," Judd said. "I mean, of all the people in the world who would have a reason to want the death penalty, you know?" For the most part, however, the firefighters left their friend alone to process his feelings in his own way. They might

not agree with Bob on the merits of capital punishment, but his loss and courage demanded their respect, and they gave him that.

"This was a cause that I thought was the right thing to do," Bob said. "I could have gone and sat in a corner, and I think a lot of people would rather that I had done that, you know? If I've got a voice, I'm going to use it. But if you use your voice, the bottom line is that you're going to be criticized by people who oppose that cause. That's the way it is. People don't like it? Too bad."

Bob began lending his voice to groups that opposed the death penalty and to others that promoted child safety. He traveled to Washington, D.C., several times, even attending an October 2002 reception where he spoke with President George W. Bush during the White House Conference on Missing, Exploited, and Runaway Children. In December, Bob flew to Chicago, where Murder Victims' Families for Reconciliation had scheduled a public forum to persuade Governor George Ryan to commute all death sentences in Illinois. Ryan previously had declared a moratorium on executions in the state and was weighing whether to issue a blanket commutation before he left office in January 2003.

The principal speaker at the Chicago conference was Mamie Till Mobley, a black woman whose fourteen-year-old son, Emmett Till, had been kidnapped and murdered in Mississippi in 1955. Two white men accused in the gruesome killing, in which Till was brutally beaten before being shot in the head, were acquitted after only sixty-seven minutes of deliberation, although they later admitted their involvement. The murder drew global attention and helped spark the American civil rights movement.

Other speakers at the Chicago forum included Ross Byrd, whose father, James Byrd Jr., was murdered in 1988 when three white men beat him behind an East Texas convenience store, stripped him, chained his ankles to a pickup truck, and dragged him for three miles. James Byrd Jr., age forty-nine, was decapitated when his body struck a sewage drain.

Pieces of his remains were found at seventy-five places along the route. Despite his father's heinous murder, Ross Byrd opposed the death sentence imposed on two of the defendants.

Bud Welch, Jennifer Bishop, and Bob Curley joined Mobley and Byrd in what Renny Cushing hoped would be a compelling statement that not all victims' families supported the death penalty. Illinois prosecutors at the time had been mobilizing other families to oppose any commutation. "We are an integral part of the victims' rights movement, and we will not be silenced," Bishop said at the time. "Our voices deserve and need to be heard, too." Those voices were featured in *Deadline*, an acclaimed documentary about the reexamination of capital punishment in Illinois, which included part of Bob's speech in Chicago in opposition to the death penalty.

For Bob, the event was an eye-opening, ground-level introduction to important national opponents of capital punishment. Before the conference, he had never heard of Mamie Till Mobley, who made her last public appearance there before dying a month later. "I didn't know who the hell she was. I'd never heard of Emmett Till or anything," Bob recalled. "The Somerville public school system, you know?" He also became friendly with Ross Byrd, with whom he spent a memorable Saturday night on the town in Chicago, watching a college football game and hoisting a few beers.

The following month, Governor Ryan, a Republican who had decided not to seek reelection, made the controversial decision to commute the sentences of all 156 inmates on death row. Nearly all of the sentences were reduced to life without parole. Many prosecutors and victims' relatives were outraged, and Governor-elect Rod Blagojevich disagreed with Ryan. "I think a blanket anything is usually wrong," said Blagojevich, a Democrat. "We're talking about convicted murderers, and I think that is a mistake."

Ryan was adamant and unapologetic as he made the announcement at Northwestern University, where journalism students had uncovered evidence that exonerated death row inmate Anthony Porter nearly four years earlier. "Our capital

system is haunted by the demon of error: error in determining guilt, and error in determining who among the guilty deserves to die. What effect was race having? What effect was poverty having?" Ryan asked. "Because of all these reasons, today I am commuting the sentences of all death row inmates."

Though energized by the decision, Bob was also happy to resume a predictable life bounded by the small triangle from East Somerville to Inman Square to his beloved cycling and running route along the Charles River. He was also ready to marry Mimi. And Mimi, who had watched Bob's mental and emotional health improve, thought the idea had merit, although she had no burning desire to marry for a third time. The decision, instead, was a leap of faith in a man who had shown he could be frighteningly erratic but who had touched her soul in a way that neither of her previous husbands had done. There was no simmering rage in Bob at this time, only small ups and downs, even little tantrums, but all of them manageable. Mimi and Bob had come through so much, endured so much pain, and better times seemed uncertain to lie ahead.

The wedding was set for February 22, 2003, one day after Mimi's forty-ninth birthday. Superior Court Justice Isaac Borenstein, a friend of Mimi's and one of the most liberal judges in the state, agreed to perform the civil ceremony in their home before a small group of guests. Bob dressed formally in a black tuxedo; Mimi wore a black dress draped with a shawl hand-painted with whirling symbols of life that she had bought at an artists' co-op in Harvard Square. As Borenstein presided, Mimi's family and friends, as well as many of Bob's siblings and in-laws, encircled the pair.

Even Bobby had decided to attend, incurring the ire of his mother, who felt betrayed that he would give even tacit approval to Bob's union with another woman. However, the two years since their confrontation at Jeffrey's grave had softened Bobby's attitude toward his father. Part of the shift was maturity; part of it a greater appreciation for what his father had suffered. And if old wounds hadn't completely healed, Bobby had chosen, at least, to try to move past them.

With his brother John behind his left shoulder and a lit candelabra above, Bob carefully repeated his simple vows. As Mimi listened for her cue, the golden ring between her right thumb and forefinger, she gently held Bob's hand and turned beaming toward the judge. Bob, his eyes closed, awaited the ring with a solemn, almost reverential expression. After Borenstein's declaration of marriage, the gathering erupted in a riot of Latin sounds, smells, and salsa. A Venezuelan trio, playing Colombian and classical Spanish music, provided a lush, soothing backdrop to the reception. Bob had learned some dance steps by then, and between fluted glasses of Champagne, he moved well enough to earn the compliments of Mimi's passionately expert relatives.

When the music slowed, guided by the sounds of the classical guitar, Bob held Mimi's hand, shifted gently from side to side, and looked deeply into the eyes of a woman who had remained his partner, improbably, through all the soul-testing darkness. Mimi returned the love with a soft, thankful gaze. For her, after all that had happened, the ceremony meant so much more than the formalities of mature, middle-age marriage. To Mimi, it represented a celebration of renewed and hopeful life.

The celebration continued in Cuba, where Mimi had engineered a honeymoon through a Cambridge travel agent who booked educational trips to the communist island. Neither Mimi nor Bob fit the typical categories of acceptable visitors to Cuba, such as journalists, athletes, or teachers. But the travel agent, accustomed to the ambiguities in the system, decreed that Mimi's reason for visiting would be to study mental-health issues and that Bob would analyze Cuban firefighting. Two days after their wedding, the couple left for Miami, where they boarded a flight to Cuba and a blissful vacation in Havana and its surrounding beaches and countryside.

Bob fell in love with the city, relaxing at harborside cafes with Mimi, walking along the white-sand beaches, and listening to street-corner musicians who played plaintively beneath the worn but haunting architecture of the old colonial capital.

The music would last for hours, some nights until dawn, as the sounds of the island danced from window to window to the open doors on their tiled terrace.

Bob also indulged his passions for cigars and baseball, chatting with old men who told wide-eyed tales of long-ago barnstorming visits by Babe Ruth and other American stars. One new friend, excited by Bob's deep knowledge of the game, invited him to his creaky Havana attic, where he let Bob gaze in awe at a collection of vintage baseball cards dating to the 1920s. There, the images of Lou Gehrig and other Yankees greats peered back from the depths of a worn and treasured shoebox. Bob found his way to Latin American Stadium, too, where he had been steered to watch the Cuban national baseball championship. A fat cigar in hand and a glass of beer at the ready, he passed a long, blissful afternoon in a raucous, dusty ballpark packed with rabid, roaring fans.

For Bob, the torment of the recent past seemed to have been consigned to memory. His partnership with Mimi had not only survived but been cemented. He had cleared his conscience on the death penalty. And his relationship with Bobby was improving. Perhaps most importantly, his thoughts of Jeffrey were not all painful ones. At last, life seemed good again. The man who had rarely ventured out of his neighborhood was flashing a wide, infectious smile at Latin American Stadium, blowing smoke rings in the air, and clapping with his new Havana friends for every stellar play. And, throughout the honeymoon, Bob never forgot the reason he had come to Cuba. "I'm pretty sure," he recalled with a grin, "I saw a fire engine go by on the second-to-last day."

After the vacation, back in Somerville, Bob and Mimi settled into a routine where work, home renovations, and a modest but satisfying social life had erected a tidy framework around them. In this world, normalcy equaled nirvana. But the extended honeymoon would soon be ended by the successive deaths, in April and December, of Bob's mother and his sister Francine. The losses hit Bob hard, especially that of Francine, who had been a surrogate mother to him when he was a rebel-

lious teenager and who had held the family together during the dark, chaotic days after Jeffrey's disappearance. Throughout Bob's life, when trouble seemed everywhere, Francine had been the rock to whom he turned for moral and emotional support. And now, unexpectedly, she had died at the age of fifty-six. "I could never imagine Fran dying, you know?" Bob said later. "Here's someone who never drank, never smoked, and was as close to a saint in my eyes as you could get. She loved me, and I loved her."

For Bob, the deaths replaced a well of unfamiliar good feeling with one of foreboding. Always an intuitive man, Bob now saw signs of gloom in the everyday and the ordinary. He realized many of these fears were irrational, but he felt powerless to control them. "I used to say to Mimi that I feel there's this big, fucking wave that I'm running away from, a wave that's just waiting to overtake me, you know?" Bob recalled. "There was Jeffrey dying, and then my mother, and then Francine, and it was just a lot of stuff building, building, and building. I felt that the wave was just gonna wash over me, and take me out, and that was gonna be it." Bob became almost paralyzed with paranoia, worrying after he left the house that he had forgotten to turn off the oven. He agonized over his work at the firehouse, haunted that he had neglected some chore that would cause a mechanical breakdown and result in a preventable death. "It got to the point where it was crazy," Bob said later. "I used to think, what if I screw something up, and somebody's grandmother has a heart attack around the corner, and Engine 5 can't get there, and she dies because of that? I used to worry about one of my kids getting killed, or Mimi getting killed, and it used to really scare the shit out of me."

Bob's superiors in the Fire Department seemed to recognize that he had suffered a relapse. Although all three mechanics had been transferred on paper to headquarters near Harvard Square, Bob was allowed to spend much of his day at Inman Square. The duties there were nearly nonexistent; the responsibilities, negligible. "It kind of got to the point where they were like, you know, just go down to Inman Square and don't

get in any trouble," Bob said. "They didn't want me doing any-thing on the fire engines. I'd basically go around to the fire-houses and check the lights, change the oil, that kind of thing. They probably kept me on light work because they saw I wasn't doing too good," Bob said. "They probably knew it better than I did."

One day in August 2004, Bob was told to replace a tire on one of the big trucks at another station. It was a routine job, one that he had done hundreds of times—and one that would get him out of the cramped back shop at Inman Square. Bob rolled a tire across a wet, puddled floor, and put his shoulder to the tread as he walked up a wooden ramp to his mechanic's truck. Bob didn't notice that oil had spilled on the wood. And after a few steps, sliding on a slick mixture of oil and water, Bob lost control and tumbled off. Both man and tire bounced on the cement floor, where Bob lay crumpled in excruciating pain. He had wrenched his back and pinched a nerve, and the injury led to an indefinite disability leave.

Bob would recover at home, where Mimi was busy plan-ning for a four-year course in psychoanalytic training that would start the next month. Combined with her private prac-tice, whose income she now needed more than ever, Mimi ex-pected to be out of the house at least twelve hours a day. Almost immediately, Bob began to withdraw, and Mimi did not need much analysis to figure out a reason. Once again, Bob had been disconnected from his lifeline at the firehouse. But un-like the months following Jeffrey's death, this time he did not have an all-consuming crusade to distract him. Bob spoke oc-casionally with acquaintances from the child-safety and aboli-tionist groups with whom he had worked, but even there, his links steadily weakened.

Soon, Bob began each day without a plan, with nowhere to go, and with no other friends who were out of work or had time on their hands. Instead, Bob found, he began to think about Jeffrey every day and in ways that he had not experi-enced since the murder. "I didn't try to avoid places that Jef-

frey had been, but different things would pop up," Bob recalled. "I'd see kids, Jeffrey's friends, and they'd have to introduce themselves to me because they were seventeen years old, and I didn't even recognize them. You lose track of time. It doesn't really hit you until you see these kids, and Jeff's not there."

Mimi noticed that Bob became moodier when certain dates approached—holidays, birthdays, the day Jeffrey disappeared. "Bob, what's the matter?" Mimi would ask.

"I don't know."

"What happened last year around this time?"

"I really don't know," Bob would answer.

Then, Mimi would remind him that his mother, or Francine, or Jeffrey had died.

"You're right. I hadn't thought about it."

Mimi recognized in Bob the "unthought known," a condition in which a person experiences extreme sadness without knowing why, but the timing of which can often be linked to traumatic, tragic events from the past.

Mimi also believed that Bob might be suffering from guilt, although he never acknowledged having any regrets about their relationship and the changes it had caused in his parenting. "Do you feel guilty that you were with me?" Mimi asked. "Do you feel that if you hadn't been here, this wouldn't have happened?" Bob consistently and adamantly denied any such feelings, but Mimi could not push them out of her own head. "Well, I feel guilty," Mimi told him. "Maybe this is irrational, but sometimes in the back of my mind I think this wouldn't have happened if you had been there." Mimi realized that Jaynes and Sicari could have abducted Jeffrey, whom they had carefully targeted, whatever the domestic situation had been on Hampshire Street. Still, the haunting questions about any tangential role she might have played never disappeared.

Bob kept his innermost feelings to himself, or, more likely, never probed deeply enough to understand what he truly felt or why he was prone to such mood swings. And he rarely spoke

about the murder. "He didn't talk about Jeff. He just didn't talk about it," Mimi said. "But I sensed it was always there. I don't think he ever put that behind him."

For a month after his injury, Bob could turn to Mimi to keep his own overwhelming thoughts at bay. But when Mimi began her analytic coursework in September, an already small world began to feel more claustrophobic. Everyone who had clamored for his attention was gone. The cameras had long ago moved on to other stories. And all the energy that Bob once directed outward began to reverse direction. Bob was a time bomb, and the fuse had been lit. "I couldn't run, my back was in pain, and I didn't have the structure of work," Bob said. "I started feeling like a useless piece of shit. I mean, how many times are you going to drive around Inman Square?"

During the interminable winter, Bob looked forward to the arrival of spring and a daily release at the beach, where he planned to listen to sports talk radio, read the newspapers, and kibitz with his sun-worshipping buddies at the L Street Bathhouse in South Boston. At a minimum, he believed, the beach would give him a destination and a place to while away the day. And at first, it did provide a taste of freedom, made more enjoyable by the case of beer that Bob would haul to the beach every day in an ice-filled cooler. To buy the beer, Bob would drive each morning to Rockingham, New Hampshire, just across the Massachusetts border, where he could pick up a case of "the good stuff," usually discounted Samuel Adams or Bass, in a state with no sales tax. Besides, the round-trip up and down I-93 helped shorten each wide-open day by two hours of easy driving.

The weekday routine developed a clockwork precision: Out of the house by ten-thirty, at the beach by one o'clock, and home by five-thirty. Then, Bob would lay on the sofa, watch whatever he could find on television, and wait for Mimi to return by seven-thirty. Mimi did not know of Bob's excursions to New Hampshire, and he felt no obligation to tell her. "I needed an escape, and that's what I was trying to find in the drinking," Bob said. "I thought it was helping."

At the beginning, Bob worked out in the bathhouse gym, took a swim, and talked with the many characters who made L Street a quirky, near-legendary world unto itself. Before long, however, the routine turned disastrous as Bob began drinking heavily every day on a nearly empty beach. What once seemed an escape became an addiction, and Bob's sense of alienation only deepened. "The more I sat there, the more isolated I became, and it just kind of snowballed," Bob said. "I just got to that place where you shut it down."

Now, instead of mingling with the bathhouse crowd, Bob was sitting by himself in a fold-up beach chair, listening to sports chatter through his headphones, and drinking beer after beer until the cooler held only stacked-up empties in a tepid pool of melted ice water. Not even a change of scenery, even a summer at the beach, could help Bob avoid the inevitable confrontation with his sublimated emotions. "I was just getting more depressed. There was nothing to do, same old thing. And at the end of the day, you're fucking drunk on top of it," Bob said. "I didn't want to talk to anybody. I had no outlet, no escape, no nothing." The daily reminders of Jeffrey's death, the estrangement from some of his family, and his own relentless questions about whether he could have prevented the murder added ever more weight to the burden. "All this stuff catches up to you, but I tried to put it aside," Bob said. "I didn't really have any respect for the magnitude of what had happened to me, and I never dealt with it the way I should have. I was just dead inside."

The dead zone expanded to Bob's house, where Mimi would return from work to find a distant, disengaged husband with a TV remote in one hand and a glazed look in his eyes. Mimi tried to speak to Bob, but he wouldn't respond. Instead, he usually stared glumly at the television while Mimi sought other ways to reconnect with the man she had known and nurtured. After a while, saddened and exhausted, Mimi realized the effort was fruitless. "It was his body, his shell, but it was not him," she said.

The relationship also became complicated by a worsening financial strain. Much of Bob's disability income was needed to pay alimony, leaving little for him to contribute to maintaining the household and forcing Mimi to pay almost all of the couple's bills. "I was getting very, very resentful," she said. "I had to get up, run to work, come home at night, and this guy is sitting there after I don't know what he's been doing during the day."

Mimi suspected he was drinking, but Bob never admitted his habits or divulged his routine. Instead, Mimi found herself smelling him for telltale hints of alcohol or searching in hard-to-find places where he might be hiding a bottle. "I felt like a fool, because I think I'm pretty smart," Mimi said. "But I also drew the line that I was not going to be his babysitter." She tried confronting Bob. "What have you had?" Mimi asked many times. "Are you taking something? Are you smoking something? Are you drinking?"

Bob denied everything, but the undeniable result was that, only two years after their marriage, Mimi had been dragged into a corrosive partnership that began to destroy her. "I was just fed up dealing with this life," she said. "It was stalled, it was dead, and I had seen all this stuff." Ordinary, mundane tasks became difficult, draining obstacles. "I couldn't focus. I couldn't concentrate. I couldn't even read a magazine," she recalled. "I had secluded myself from my friends, and I was worried that I was getting very, very far away from the things that were important to me."

Mimi started to fight back with a rescue strategy of passive, gradual disengagement. "I could sustain being different from him in so many ways, but we always had that emotional connection," Mimi said. "Without that, though, there really was nothing. I thought, I have to regain my soul. I have to regain who I am. I have to remember where I come from. This is not my life." Even Bob's work against the death penalty, which Mimi had once considered a sign of healing, became an irritant. "I wasn't interested in hearing that stuff," she said. "I was fed up, burned out, and I didn't give a shit. I just felt that too

much had been brought into my life that I didn't have control over. I didn't care."

As the gulf between them widened, Bob drifted even more to alcohol to escape the numbed, meaningless repetition that had become his life. The relationship reached an ugly nadir one summer night in August 2005. That evening, Bob agreed to cook steaks while Mimi relaxed in the living room. The time passed without conversation, another strained chapter in a badly damaged marriage, as Mimi read and Bob remained in the kitchen. After thirty minutes, with neither the smell of steak nor any sound from the cook, Mimi broke the silence.

"Bob, what's happening?" she asked sharply.

"It's coming, it's coming," Bob answered with annoyance.

Ten minutes later, Mimi pressed again. "Bob, what is going on?" she asked, insistent and frustrated.

Bob took a few steps toward the living room and mumbled almost incoherently. "I just threw them out," he muttered.

"You threw them out?" Mimi asked incredulously.

"Yeah, they got burned."

"Bob, they didn't get burned!" Mimi answered. "I haven't smelled anything getting burned!"

Bob's face began to twist into the crazed, contorted shape that Mimi had not seen since the trials. His eyes bulged, his mouth tightened, and the rage that had been absent for seven years found renewed expression in him. This time, however, the fury was not directed against Jeffrey's killers. The object, instead, was Mimi. He lunged toward her, grabbed her by the wrist, and began to drag her down a long, wooden staircase to the trash barrels outside. "Nothing's burned?" Bob snarled. "Come with me! Come, and I'll show you!"

Mimi was terrified and screaming. Bob's grip had broken her wrist, but he continued to pull her maniacally toward the trash. At the bottom of the stairs, Mimi broke free and ran frantically upstairs to call the police. Bob stayed behind. "I don't get scared that easily, but in that moment I was horrified," Mimi recalled. "Those were the eyes I had seen when Bob talked about slashing Jaynes. He looked like a madman."

When the police arrived, Bob was sitting calmly in a lawn chair, oblivious or unaware of Mimi's shaken state and his own legal predicament. "I don't know what she's talking about," he told the officers. Mimi declined to press charges and have Bob arrested. What he needed, she told police, was a hospital more than a jail cell. She did ask the officers to escort Bob into the house to retrieve some clothes. Later that night, she changed the locks while Bob headed to the Somerville home of Arthur Downey, Francine's widower, who had taken care of him so often during his unpredictable, unfocused teenage years.

For Mimi, the end had arrived. "That was it," she said. "I can't be with someone who is going to be violent with me. I said, I'm divorcing this guy. I don't want to be married to this man. Here's where I draw the line." Her attorney advised Mimi to obtain a restraining order. "If you were my daughter," the lawyer said, "that's what I would tell you to do." Mimi, however, was wary. Bob had never been violent before, and she did not expect him to return to the house. A friend of Mimi's asked her to consider the context of Bob's actions, inexcusable as they were, and the consequences of legal action. "He's dealing with his grief; he's dealing with his trauma," the friend said. "Keep him out. But if you file a restraining order, the media are going to be here. You don't want to do that to him, and you don't want to do that to yourself." Upon reflection, Mimi agreed. She had the power to shatter whatever remained of Bob's disintegrating world. Out of pity or exhaustion, she chose to spare him that blow, however deserved that option seemed.

For Bob, life had rewound nearly forty years. Once again, he was living with his brother-in-law Arthur, sleeping in the attic, with little money, in a world defined by turmoil. Arthur, a former marine drill instructor whom Bob idolized, never passed judgment on him. But Bob, ashamed and despondent, could sense the disappointment as he continued to drink away his days on a South Boston beach.

Bob had cut himself off from friends, although coworkers would call occasionally to ask if he'd recovered from his back

injury, which he hadn't. In those conversations, Bob never talked about his drinking, where he was living, or what had happened between him and Mimi. In those calls, he sounded like the same guy from Inman Square: plugging away, trying to make the best of things, sharing a joke. But word had circulated on the street that Bob had hit the bottle. Even Barbara and his sons heard the rumors, which made sense to Bobby after his father began approaching him for money. "I knew he was doing something he shouldn't have been doing, that he was going through a tough time," Bobby said. "So I just told him, 'If you ever need anything . . .'"

What Bob needed became apparent on the first morning of September, a Thursday, when he biked to the beach at 6:30 A.M. to begin a day like many others in that lost and lonely summer. Bob leafed through a day-old copy of the *Boston Herald*, the crime-sports-and-politics tabloid, and stopped at a column by Joe Fitzgerald, an old-school reporter who wrote about ordinary guys, overlooked neighborhoods, and everyday heroes in the blue-collar corners of a gentrified city.

Bob read of Chris Mulligan, a thirty-three-year-old alcoholic and marine veteran, who was found dead shortly after the *Herald* printed a letter in which he had asked forgiveness from his mother and two sisters. The letter had caused a stir because of its street-level humanity, which spoke directly to struggling, disappointed men just like Bob. "The disease of addiction can be a slowly painful death that begins by seducing your soul, slowly tearing it out, and holding it hostage along with the souls of the ones you love most," Mulligan wrote. "I am an addict in recovery, and only another addict can fully understand this. Not a day goes by that I don't crave something that can stop the pain," said Mulligan, a product of the city's Charlestown neighborhood.

"I had been living at home as a typical prodigal son the day my mother dropped me off at a hotel with all my worldly possessions. She says it was the worst day of her life. Well, Mom, I share that feeling with you. [But] what you did for me that day saved my life," Mulligan continued. "I am getting better.

One of the main reasons is my family. I feel their love every day. They give me a strength that's so ingrained in my heart and soul that there is nothing I cannot beat."

Two days later, Mulligan was found dead on the deck of his apartment. According to the *Herald*, neighbors reported that he had been drinking heavily during a heat wave. Bob, sitting alone on the beach, shook his head and laughed when he read of Mulligan's death. "Another rummy bites the dust," he chuckled, dismissing the story as just another news blip about a blame-dodging loser. He'd known guys like that his entire life.

Or so he thought. The more he read, the more Bob realized he was reading about himself. By the time he finished the column, he began to cry. "What the fuck am I laughing at?" Bob said. "I'm sitting over here with my thumb up my ass, no nothing going on here, and I'm laughing at this kid?" Bob put the paper down, gazed at the morning stillness of Dorchester Bay, and made the pledge of a frightened man who had just seen the path to a lonely, early grave. "What the fuck kind of a life is this?" he said. "I've got to pull out of this and get back on track. This is not me."

Bob walked slowly from the beach, steadied his bike, and began pedaling to Somerville, lost in thought as streams of early commuters began clogging the highways into Boston. Back in his room, Bob dug out his cell phone and called Mimi, who heard the familiar voice but did not answer. "I'm going to change, Mimi," Bob said, his voice both subdued and sincere. "I'm going to take care of things. Either I'm going to get help, or I'm gonna die."

Bob told Mimi he planned to contact a doctor at McLean Hospital in suburban Belmont, where, in the past, he had forced himself to sit through a few frustrating counseling sessions at one of the country's top psychiatric facilities. Mimi called ahead to tell the psychiatrist to expect a call. "I know you can't talk to me because of confidentiality reasons, but you can hear my message," she said. "Bob is going to see you, but he is probably not going to convey what happened between

us because I don't even know if he remembers." Mimi told the doctor about the incident, that police were summoned, and that she was extremely concerned about Bob's mental health and well-being.

Bob phoned the psychiatrist shortly afterward. "Hey, I need some help here," he said.

"Sure, come on over. We'll have a talk," the doctor answered.

The "talk" never materialized. When Bob walked into McLean, drawn and disheveled after months of steady drinking, the psychiatrist was startled.

"I gotta fuckin' straighten up here, brother," Bob said.

"Let's go," the doctor said sharply.

"Where we going? " Bob asked.

"You'll find out when we get there."

Bob was too tired to press for details. Instead, he followed dutifully as the psychiatrist escorted him to an in-patient facility at McLean, where Bob could sober up for three days while undergoing a battery of analysis and preliminary treatments.

The doctor pounded home how serious and damaging his problem had become. "You've got to stop this," he said.

"I am gonna stop," Bob answered.

"Stop drinking," the doctor repeated slowly.

"Okay." Bob nodded.

"Stop . . . drinking," the psychiatrist said again, pausing between the words for no-nonsense emphasis.

After three days at the hospital, Bob was released to a "sober house" of his choosing, where he could spend up to a month in a residential setting with supervision. Bob ran his finger down a list at McLean and selected a house in Quincy, just south of Boston and ten miles from Somerville. "Yeah, we have a place for you. Come on down," a staff member said.

The place Bob found was unlike anything he had ever experienced. Most of the residents were chronic alcoholics or drug addicts who had no intention, or will power, to change their ways. Some continued to shoot heroin at the "sober house,"

others popped Oxycontin, and more than a few residents placed calls on their cell phones for special drug deliveries to a supposed oasis of sobriety.

Without a home and nearly without hope, Bob wallowed in self-loathing and fearfully pondered the future from his new, small piece of hell. "It was awful," Bob said. "I was ashamed. I was embarrassed. How did my life get like this?" Bob fled, disgusted, after a week and returned to the attic in Arthur Downey's house. The experience had left him shaken but more determined to remain on the life-altering course he had promised himself.

Bob immediately enrolled in a three-week program that combined intense therapy for both substance abuse and trauma. He stayed clear of alcohol. He began attending Alcoholics Anonymous meetings. And he reached out to Mimi every so often to express his remorse. "I'm a different man," he'd say. "You'll see." Mimi was not convinced. "I was clear one hundred percent that it was over," she recalled. "I just didn't want to have anything to do with him. I couldn't trust him. And when the trust is broken, there's nothing left."

Over time, though, Mimi's resolve began to soften. She invited Bob to take some clothes from a batch her friend had just brought from Colombia. But when Bob arrived at the house, Mimi would not engage him, other than to point toward the coffeepot and silently indicate he could help himself. As he rummaged through the clothes, Mimi glanced quickly at his face. And there, in his eyes, she saw a genuine repentance that reminded her of the caring man who had touched her soul a decade before. "He looked so tormented by what he had done," she said. "And I didn't want to see him like that." Mimi's friend also noticed the sorrow. "You know, he really loves you," she said after Bob had left.

Through the autumn, Mimi kept her distance. But her friends would intercede for Bob, without his knowledge, and tell Mimi of his affection. Gradually, guided by their eyes, Mimi began to see a man who had suffered, endured, and now recognized all that he had lost. "Knowing Bob from before, I

knew him to be a good man," Mimi said. "And I knew, as upset as I was, that he would not have wanted this to happen to him. God, life had been horrible to this man."

By Christmas, four months after being banished, Bob returned to the house, a changed and sober man—just as he had promised. "I realized that it's just not yourself that you're hurting," Bob said later. "You think you're not bothering anybody, you're not hurting anybody, that people just need to leave you alone, you know? But you look around, and you see all the people that care about you, and how they're hurting because of you."

In retrospect, Bob knew he might never have changed if Mimi had not forced him to confront his demons. "She did what she had to do to help me out," he said. Bob was also grateful to a stranger named Chris Mulligan, a troubled man who became much more than just another "rummy" in a newspaper. "I think," Bob said, "he saved my life."

11

Into
the Light

WHEN THE "Monsignor" speaks at Alcoholics Anonymous meetings at a nineteenth-century church in downtown Boston, mixed among upscale shops and trendy restaurants in one of Boston's premier neighborhoods, the group pays close attention. Some are thieves who have served time in prison. Others are young professionals only a few years removed from college. And some are Beacon Hill socialites who just left the jewelry counter at Lord & Taylor. Most of the two-dozen people who sit here in a wide circle on metal folding chairs do not know the Monsignor by name. To them, he is just another recovering alcoholic, like themselves, trying to do the right thing and seeking reinforcement from others who struggle with the gnawing desire for another drink. And then another. And yet another until the mind loses track of the glasses or the bottles.

But a few know the identity of the Monsignor, a term of endearment given by one of the circle to Bob Curley, who checks more baggage outside these gatherings than anyone else and never discloses the full, staggering story of his long, personal walk with the devil. Instead, he brings to the meetings an unfiltered message that gets straight to the point and comes straight from the heart. In life as well as recovery, Bob has little time to waste anymore.

At one session, Bob leads the group in readings from Step 12 of the famed recovery program, focusing this night on the effects of alcohol on marriage. It's a subject he knows well, and Bob keeps his head down as he bends far forward and reads in a low monotone.

As the readings progress, Bob listens intently. At times, he sits with his arms folded and chin buried in his chest. At others, he clasps his hands behind his head and leans back in his chair. Dressed in khaki shorts, a T-shirt, and sandals, Bob appears the most at ease of anyone in the group, whose members mostly sit motionless as tales of desperation, crime, and ruin follow one another in harrowing, confessional succession.

"I failed miserably with life," says one former executive in his late sixties.

"I have no clue how to stay sober without you guys," says a younger man, who once slept on park benches but now wears a suit to work.

"I've been sober for thirty days," another man says to applause.

When Bob's turn arrives, he challenges a previous suggestion that alcoholism usually affects the well-to-do. "I don't see that," he offers, shaking his head slightly. Then, eyes trained on the parquet floor, he is characteristically blunt. "Things are going well," he says. "I'm glad to be here, glad to be sober, and grateful for another beautiful day. That's about it."

After an hour, Bob rises, grasps the hands of the people to either side of him, and leads the group forward into a tight circle. Together, they recite a familiar prayer: "God, grant me the serenity to accept the things I cannot change; courage to change the things I can; and wisdom to know the difference." Following a few, brief good-byes, Bob walks out the door, passes a window display of luxury fashions, and slips into his car for the quick ride home to Somerville.

Since he bottomed out on the beach, the meeting in the Back Bay has been only one of several AA groups that Bob frequents. There is another in Charlestown, hard by the tough Bunker Hill housing projects, where the Chris Mulligans of

the world can meet every day if they choose. There's also one in Somerville. "I got in touch with guys I know, regular jamokes like me, who just don't drink anymore," Bob says. "They'd tell me, 'You'll be all right. And even if it ain't all right, it's gonna be better than if you're drinking.' Now, someone can see a guy like me and everything that I've gone through and figure, If he can't drink for one day, maybe I can, too. You know what I mean?" Bob makes the AA rounds faithfully, not only because he likes the people but because he pledged he would never visit that South Boston beach again with even a single beer beside him. His marriage and his work for child safety are far too important.

Bob returned to the Fire Department in the summer of 2006, his back made healthy again through a tedious program at Spaulding Rehabilitation Hospital in suburban Woburn. "For once in my life, I paid attention to what I was supposed to be paying attention to, and I was kind of a little more receptive to being helped," Bob said. He even returned to South Boston as part of his recovery, walking at first and then running a little at the track at Columbus Park, only a short jog from the spot where he would mask his pain with daily drink. Eventually, as he became stronger, he entertained thoughts of one day entering the Boston Marathon.

During his dark period, Bob cut off communication with many of the organizations with which he had worked for better child protection and against the death penalty. But after he returned home, Bob reestablished himself as a passionate, articulate spokesman for those issues. To other advocates, Bob became a dependable friend who needed only to be asked to join a committee, speak to the public, or testify at the State House.

He also showed no hesitation when someone lost a child to a high-profile act of violence. Bob had reached out this way for years, both to comfort the parents of victims and to find solace for himself. Magi and John Bish, reeling from their daughter's disappearance, experienced that rare generosity of spirit soon after Molly was abducted from her lifeguard station in central Massachusetts in 2000. Bob telephoned them simply to offer his support and let them know they weren't alone.

Ever since, he has attended each annual vigil for Molly, whose body was discovered in 2003, and even organized a work party to build a ramp to the Bish home when John suffered a debilitating stroke in 2007. "Bob's help has been a gift," Magi Bish said. "He's showed us, from the earliest days, that you will survive and that the presence of evil, even in the worst of times, can bring out the best in people."

Bob has further contributed to the annual success of Missing Children's Day, an event promoted by the Bish family, in which family members and others gather at the Massachusetts State House every May to remember children who are missing and to comfort those who miss them. "Bob has always chosen to speak," Magi said. "He has such heart, but you can sense the sadness and the hurt. He's not afraid to show that, and I think that's good." She also knows Bob's work from a special task force formed by Governor Jane Swift in 2002, when the two of them joined the panel to help evaluate services available in Massachusetts to victims of sexual assault and abuse.

The task force included Richard Hoffman of Cambridge, an author and poet whose memoir about the sexual abuse he suffered as a ten-year-old led to the conviction of his former sports coach, a man who had assaulted more than four hundred children over four decades. Hoffman first met Bob as he moved through the receiving line at Jeffrey's wake. Hoffman disagreed with Bob's calls for the death penalty, but he had been impressed by Bob's efforts to calm the homophobic rage that erupted around the killing.

A year later, Hoffman formed an indelible impression of the man at a conference in Rhode Island for victims of sexual abuse. While Hoffman waited to deliver the keynote address, in which he planned to mention Jeffrey's murder, he noticed Bob walk into the room alone. Afterward, Hoffman introduced himself to Bob.

"I hope you didn't mind that," Hoffman said.

"No, no," Bob answered. "Not at all."

Hoffman, who had not met Bob since Jeffrey's wake, was stunned that he had attended the gathering. "Here's someone coming to a conference of adult survivors of sexual assault. Not as a speaker but just because he wanted to understand," Hoffman said. "This was not a sociologist going out to do a study. This was somebody who was out there with his heart still like a piece of raw meat. A lot of people would just close down, but he didn't. He wanted to learn what the hell the nature of this evil is all about. It just took tremendous courage."

Several years later, Bob reached out to Hoffman when the clergy sex-abuse crisis engulfed the Roman Catholic Archdiocese of Boston. Bob was furious about the unfolding allegations that priests had abused hundreds of youths in the archdiocese over decades, and that the church had failed to investigate or punish the predators adequately. "We've got to do something. We've got to shake this up," Bob told Hoffman. As a result, a hastily arranged news conference was held at the State House, where Bob and Hoffman, among others, demanded that an independent commission be convened to delve into the scandal. The Governor's Task Force on Sexual Assault and Abuse was formed a short time later.

Bob and Hoffman also lent their voices to the Enough Abuse Campaign, created in 2004 by the Massachusetts Child Sexual Abuse Prevention Partnership to increase awareness about the problem and develop innovative ways to combat what the American Medical Association had termed "a silent epidemic." The partnership, a statewide collaboration among twenty-three public and private entities, received seed money for its campaign from the U.S. Centers for Disease Control and Prevention, which ranked its proposal the best among applicants throughout the country. The campaign, according to its Web site (http://enoughabuse.org), seeks to energize "those who believe that we have had enough secrets, enough shame, enough hurt, enough confusion and enough denial that child sexual abuse is a serious epidemic." In an audio link, Bob underscores why more information and communication are indispensable

to the fight. "The only thing I ever taught Jeffrey about sexual abuse was all that I was ever taught, and that's, Don't talk to strangers."

Bob's willingness to spread the word also benefited Deborah Savoia, who worked hard to toughen the sex-offender registry in Massachusetts. "I don't know if there's one time that I've called him that he hasn't gone out. Bob has always stepped up to the plate, trying to make sure another parent doesn't go through what he's gone through," Savoia said. "You've got to remember that when he speaks in front of people, he's reliving everything that happened to him and his child. Yet, he does that, and he asks for nothing in return."

While Bob's work on child-safety issues expanded, the death penalty came to define him less and less in the public's eye. He attended the annual Sacco and Vanzetti memorial in Springfield, Massachusetts, on the anniversary of their notorious 1927 executions. He also testified several times at the State House against new attempts to reinstate the death penalty, an effort that faced longer and longer odds with each election cycle.

Although Bob Curley's work against the death penalty diminished gradually, his legacy on the issue endured for all those who worked against him in 1997 and later stood beside him following his watershed speech at Boston College. To Tom Lowenstein, whose father was murdered at the hands of a crazed gunman, Bob's role in the 1997 debate stands as a cautionary example of how victims' families can become movable pieces in the political chess game. "One of the important lessons about Bob is that the death penalty is not about the victim's family," Lowenstein argued. "If you're for the death penalty and they can trot you out, they'll do it. But if you turn around and say, 'I'm not sure how I feel about this,' they'll put you on ice as fast as they can." Bob said he experienced that dismissal firsthand when, after his public reversal on capital punishment, his telephone calls on child-safety issues no longer were welcome at the U.S. Department of Justice under Attorney General John Ashcroft, a staunch proponent of the death penalty.

To Renny Cushing, who for years had been supporting victims' families who opposed the death penalty for years, Bob stands as an empowering example of someone who, despite suffocating grief, came to that stance largely on his own. "For Bob to stand up and say, 'I've thought it over, and I've come to the conclusion that I don't support the death penalty anymore,' is incredibly powerful," Cushing said. "I find that people who spend so much time fixating on how their loved one died, end up forgetting how they lived. And that can consume your life, too. The murder claims more than one victim."

Bob understands that concept instinctively. Over the years, he has never lost the hatred in his eyes when he speaks of Jaynes and Sicari. But he has found a way to move beyond his rage and refocus on the potential of the positive. The man who has emerged can befriend people from opposite ends of the ideological spectrum, make his own decisions, and give an opinion that matters to those who take the time to listen.

The liberal pundit Jim Braude, who cohosted the television show that played a pivotal role in Bob's thinking, developed an abiding respect for a man who made, in Braude's view, a change of striking, singular courage. "It was a huge personal transformation at a huge political moment in Massachusetts," Braude said. "I'm an admirer of anybody who is big enough and honest enough to admit they were wrong, particularly when you know you're going to suffer some public ridicule."

The transformation was not limited to Bob's views on the death penalty. Margery Eagan, the other host of *Talk of New England*, was struck by the difference in Bob's appearance when she interviewed him some time later. "Before, he had looked very dark, just very gray," Eagan said. "And then you meet him again, sitting at his house, and everything is bright and colorful and cheerful. I remember thinking that day that he was just a very different guy."

To Mimi, Bob's impulse to help others was one more sign of healing. She credited Alcoholics Anonymous for much of the insight and support that helped Bob rechannel his energies. And the fellowship he found there, Mimi said, helped

provide a feeling of family that Bob had often seemed to be seeking. "He has found a sense of meaning there and connectedness, and I think that saved him," Mimi said. "At the latter stages of health, you sublimate what happened to you and look instead to help someone else. That's what he wants to do." Jimmy Tingle, a nationally known comedian from Cambridge, also became one of Bob's most important lifelines to recovery, faithfully calling his old friend from the neighborhood every day to keep him focused.

Despite her leap of faith, Mimi did not set unreachably high expectations when she gave Bob a second chance. "It was more like, let's wait and see," she said. "He had been very good to me, even in the midst of all the craziness, and part of me understood, when I put on my psychologist's hat, what he was going through. I don't think I could have done what he did, you know?" Mimi's ability to step back and evaluate the relationship, despite the hurt, helped persuade her to open the door. Maybe, she thought, Bob's long depression and ugly climax were sadly inevitable—possibly even necessary to force him to confront his grief. Maybe he will get better, she thought. He's admitted that he has a problem, he's doing something about it, and he's working. Together, they bought a condo in Florida near Mimi's half sister, visited Colombia, sampled ethnic restaurants in and around Boston, and continued to improve the home and garden where so much of their recovery from Jeffrey's murder had occurred.

The Fire Department, as always, provided a shelter where Bob could find comfort in the work, the easy banter, and the unspoken camaraderie of his coworkers. That bond, Bob knew, extended well beyond the firehouse doors, even ten years after the tragedy. Several firefighters, for example, answered Bob's call for volunteers to build the wheelchair ramp for John Bish.

Although Jeffrey's murder had long since disappeared from daily conversation, many firefighters still could glimpse its lingering effect. Bill McGovern, who has known Bob as long as anyone in the department, said his friend had reclaimed some of his old, upbeat personality—but only to a point. "He's

gotten better, but he's not the same Bob I knew ten years ago, twelve years ago, fourteen years ago," McGovern said a decade after the killing. "I don't think he ever will be, unfortunately." However, McGovern added, one important trait has remained. "If I ever got in trouble and asked Bob for a favor, without a doubt he'd be right there," McGovern said, nodding his head slowly in the firehouse. "He's just a great guy."

To Mimi, the friendship of firefighters like McGovern and a busy schedule have helped Bob avoid the psychological triggers that can spark angry, self-destructive behavior.

"He can't be without lots of empty spaces in his life. He has to be engaged," Mimi said. "But he created a structure, and he created enough support around him, and that is going to help." Bob, for his part, agreed to see a therapist. "He had lost everything and finally realized he needed it," Mimi said of the counseling. "It came to a point where he knew he had to have help, or he would just sink."

Bob readily admits he is radically changed, and he credits Mimi for the love she showed during Jeffrey's disappearance and its aftermath, for her patience during his manic bloodlust for revenge, and for her willingness to hope for a better day between them. "She was determined that she was going to straighten me out, she was going to help me, and she was going to stick with me through the whole thing," Bob said. "And she did."

Bob also credits Mimi's no-excuses approach and her decisive move to end the relationship in the wake of violence. If Mimi had not forced him from the house, Bob said, "maybe I would have hit that beach in South Boston and not bounced back." In retrospect, he said, "it might have been easy for other people to sympathize with me and just not have the courage to try to set me back on track. Somebody else, somebody not as strong as she is, probably wouldn't have taken that course. It was hard for her to change the locks, but you've got to do what you've got to do."

Besides tough love, Mimi brought home a professional toolbox that seemed ideally suited to deal with Bob's profound

and complex troubles. First at Children's Hospital in Boston and then at the Cambridge Hospital clinic, Mimi's experience with victims of sexual and domestic trauma helped hone her skills and sensitivity to deal with Bob's personal crisis. "She always got me back to normal things as quick as she could, without me even realizing it," Bob said.

What he does realize is how lucky he is, despite the long litany of past and painful horrors. And for that good fortune, Bob is grateful. "She loves her cat, and she loves me, too," Bob said, smiling. "I scratch my head and wonder how I'm still here and how I'm not completely insane, you know?" he said. "I look around and see a lot of people I know who are sick, not doing good, they're struggling, and I count my blessings every day. It sounds corny, but it's true."

A few miles away in East Cambridge, life after Jeffrey held no such promise for Barbara Curley. Her world, instead, became a dark place of dire ailments and incessant heartache, where the memory of her child remained fresh and ever-present in the small home where they had lived. From the beginning, Barbara's family helped care for an inconsolable woman who had lost the will and hope to continue living. She often had trouble dressing herself. She continued to be heavily medicated. And she took a year off from work by necessity, before returning for a time to a part-time job as a secretary for the Cambridge schools. Barbara also was battered by a cruel succession of debilitating physical problems. Breast and ovarian cancer, treated by chemotherapy and radiation, ravaged her already frail body. She developed diabetes.

As a result, Barbara became a grieving recluse in her own home, which she rarely left and where she often imagined she heard Jeffrey. "Everywhere I look, Jeffrey is there. I hear his voice calling, 'Mommy, Mommy, Mommy,'" Barbara said a decade after the murder. "I think about what they did to him, and what he must have gone through, and that he must have been crying for me."

After that first year following Jeffrey's murder, Barbara moved in with her mother, who had become seriously ill and needed intensive dialysis. What helped give Barbara the strength to face each day, she said, was her concern for Bobby and Shaun, who she feared would spiral downward. "My whole world is my two boys," she said. "I did not want them to turn their feelings into hate and revenge. That's all that went through my head. That's the only thing that I could think about."

Together, the three participated in therapy, but only for a short time as a family. The sessions helped purge some of Shaun's anger, but Bobby never opened up in counseling and regarded the sessions as a waste of time. His roiling anger was a problem he would analyze and conquer alone, Bobby said, and not something that any therapist would medicate away, even temporarily. "When it all happened, the doctors wanted to put me on this, that, and the other fucking thing," said Bobby, who belongs to the pipe fitters union. "I truly believe the medication only makes you worse, and that's why I've never taken anything."

Instead, Bobby said, he has tried to stay strong for his mother's sake and to focus on the positive, as difficult as that seems. The manner of Jeffrey's death, together with the insidious trap laid by its architects, have infected his life with a profound mistrust that continues to color his relationships with all but his closest friends. "Now, when something bad happens, you sort of look at people a little more," Bobby said. "Let me put it like this: If someone goes missing, I don't think it's a complete stranger that had something to do with it." He said he will not read the state's sex-offender registry because if someone on the list lives nearby, he might not be able to control his rage.

The world he knew before Jeffrey's murder no longer exists, Bobby said. "It just fucks with your head, some things that words can't even describe," he explained while looking at the beach from his condo in Revere, just north of Boston. "Psychologically, it does things to you that you don't even realize.

That day changed me forever." Still, despite the shadows, Bobby believes he has a divine patron. "I just think that God's on my side, you know? He knows I make a lot of right decisions, and he helps me."

Like his brother, Shaun lives with dark, persistent suspicion. "I can't trust no one no more. It's just real sad," he said. "There's all this anger, and all these memories, and all these thoughts that weigh on my shoulders every day." A licensed carpenter, Shaun continued to live at the Hampshire Street condo with his mother, wife, and two small children. For him, the tragedy reinforced the importance of family and the need to protect the most vulnerable within that circle.

In many ways, his primary responsibility became Barbara, who moved back to the condo after her mother died in the summer of 2007. Without a job, with little money, and still in fragile health, Barbara spent days at a time in the condo basement, which Shaun painstakingly renovated into an apartment for her. "She comes up, and I cook her dinner," Shaun said. "But she still can't go upstairs to the second floor because of Jeffrey, the nightmares, the visuals. I don't think she'll ever work again. I think she's too shattered. I tell her, 'I'll pay everything. I'll feed you. I'll pay the water, the gas, lights, cable, everything.' I can't leave my mother, you know?"

In addition to her daunting physical problems, Barbara remains plagued by guilt and second-guessing. "In the end, the fact is that this was done by Charles Jaynes and Sal Sicari," Barbara said at her kitchen table. "But even today, you blame yourself, you know? You say, maybe there was something I could have done."

Not a day passes that she doesn't think of Jeffrey. Often, the thoughts are happy ones. "I talk to him every day in my mind," Barbara said. "I know he watches out for us." She thinks fondly of Jeffrey's bold declaration that he wanted to live in Disney World, where Barbara once dispatched him with an uncle, aunt, and cousin. "I had to work, and we had to pay for the house, so I came up with the money so my brother could take him," Barbara recalled. "I wanted to take him my-

self at some point." Instead, she was rewarded by the vicarious pleasure of Jeffrey's awestruck memories of a children's paradise, where a city kid from East Cambridge could lose himself in an all-day fantasy of castles, thrill rides, and candy, and where the goblins and pirates were all make-believe.

Barbara reflects on how close they had become, and the memory of that bond is both heartening and heartbreaking. "His world just shined when he saw me, and mine shined when I saw him," Barbara said, dissolving into tears. "He absolutely adored me, and I adored him."

Barbara takes comfort in knowing that she and Bob fulfilled the promises they made to each other in that awful moment when she heard Sicari had confessed. "We both did what we promised each other we would do," she said. Bobby and Shaun overcame much of their anger. Barbara exposed them to counseling. And Bob kept his word by raising awareness about the dangers facing children.

That awareness extended to NAMBLA, which most New Englanders did not know existed before the Curley murder seared its name into the region's consciousness. In April 2008, Bob and Barbara dropped their $200 million federal lawsuit against the organization after a judge declared that the key witness for the family was mentally incompetent to testify.

Nevertheless, Bob and Barbara insisted that the effort had been worthwhile, if only for illumination. "Maybe this is going to prevent some kid from being kidnapped. Maybe it's going to prevent some kid from being raped," Bob said. "Maybe reading the Eight Rules of Safety means that some eight- or nine-year-old boy or girl comes in contact with somebody, the kid does the right thing, and the guy goes on his way."

The frustrating part of this work, Bob said, is not knowing when or whether it makes a difference. But the effort is worth that frustration, he continued, because any effort is better than inaction. For Bob, that maxim also applies to capital punishment. "Maybe a guy like me, talking about the death penalty and being able to look at it the way I have, maybe that's going to prevent some innocent guy from being put to death," he said.

When Bob thinks back to his rants for capital punishment, he shakes his head in bemused disbelief. From unknown
fire mechanic, to media magnet, to icon of a death-penalty
crusade he never sought to lead, Bob sometimes must remind
himself he has not lived a dream. "I look back and say, How
did this happen? Why did this happen?" Bob said. "I still can't
believe that all this happened to me. I still can't."

Bob is not an overtly spiritual man. But Jeffrey's murder,
he senses, happened for a reason, and it happened to a family
whose public sorrow would touch countless others. From the
earliest days after the murder, Bob began to believe that Jeffrey's death greatly superseded its gruesome details and shock
value. "It seemed to be something bigger than me and bigger
than life," he recalled. The legacy of Jeffrey's killing might
never be one, singular, towering accomplishment, Bob mused,
but possibly "a lot of little, good things along the way." And if
that's the case, he can live with the result.

Like Barbara, Bob thinks constantly of Jeffrey. He thinks
of him when he sees Jeffrey's friends in the neighborhood,
driving their cars and walking with girlfriends. He sees Jeffrey
when he passes Donnelly Field, where the sound of Little
League chatter fills a summer night, and the Gore Street ice
rink, where he changed Jeffrey's diapers while Bobby and
Shaun skated during hockey games. He sees Jeffrey when he
runs along the Charles River on a beautiful day and recalls the
priceless joys of a simple game of catch.

And when he sees his sons, Bob imagines how Jeffrey
would have grown from boy to man. "Maybe he'd be playing
hockey at Fitchburg State College or Salem State," Bob says.
"Maybe he would have been in the navy. Maybe he would have
been hammering nails with his brothers. Who knows?" Bob
looks around his house, where so much of Mimi's influence is
present, and envisions Jeffrey there on weekends, helping
with small renovations or getting his hands dirty in the garden.

Bob still dreams about Jeffrey, but most of those dreams
are pleasant. The nightmares return only occasionally, when
he confronts Jaynes and Sicari in the same kind of violent,

thrashing fantasies that tormented him during the trials. Now, when Bob sees Jeffrey in his dreams, his son is always in a safe place. He's laughing and joking, and in constant motion as the ten-year-old child he will always remain.

Bob sees Jeffrey riding his bike, doing wheelies, and flexing his muscles as he yells to his father, "Dad, I'm doing my push-ups and my pull-ups. I'm getting strong."

And in his dreams, just as he did in life, Bob will answer with a laugh, "You sure are. I can smell you over here!"

In East Cambridge, Jeffrey's legacy is preserved in neighbors' memories of a precocious kid with a perpetual smile and in a tragic reminder that community vigilance is a constant, unfortunate necessity. There, residents will always remember where they were, and what they thought, when the news of Jeffrey's murder spread like fire from house to house. Those neighbors, more than they know, helped Bob and his family endure, however imperfectly, an excruciating ordeal and its agonizing aftermath. The pain will never disappear for the Curleys, but neither will their gratitude. "There were a lot of good people out there who helped us, just by a kind word," Bob said. "That's the thing that really sticks out from those days, the simple kindness toward us."

In ways that constantly evolve, Bob has tried to return that goodness—to the friends who cried with him, to the strangers who reached out, and to the people who need a lift today. "A big focus has been just trying to do decent things, just trying to do the right things, just trying to help people the best I can," Bob said.

For many people, Bob will always be the kid from Inman Square, the kid from the corner who loved his friends, looked up to the veterans, laughed with the characters, and never felt compelled to explore beyond his crowded but colorful neighborhood. He's still an average guy, unremarkable to the casual observer, except for a wrenching journey that began in utter darkness and followed a twisting, torturous path to light.

And because of that experience, because of one horrible, transforming event, Bob Curley made a difference. Through a

rejection of vengeance and through Mimi's heroic patience, he discovered within himself the emotional means to move on— without Jeffrey, but with the knowledge that, despite incredible suffering, he had triumphed over his darkest impulses. He has made a difference in the lives of recovering alcoholics and of families crippled by tragedy through the humble, understated example of his mere survival.

And on the death penalty, the signature cause that catapulted him from obscurity to unwanted fame, Bob's opposition will never be quantified, its effect never translated into numbers. But his voice, that of the man who pushed Massachusetts to the brink, remains profound, powerful, and resonant. More than a decade after the awful day that changed his life forever, Bob lives simply and by a simple maxim.

"I'm gonna do the best I can," he vows.

For Jeffrey's sake.

Epilogue

On November 7, 2007, dozens of witnesses jockeyed for seats in a State House hearing room. The subject was the death penalty, and the Joint Judiciary Committee had convened to consider testimony on the latest effort to reinstate capital punishment in Massachusetts. Tellingly, the public hearing on what Governor Deval Patrick derided as an unfortunate "annual ritual" would no longer be held in the sumptuous, spacious confines of Gardner Auditorium. Instead, a large, boxy room served as an antiseptic setting to rehash the old arguments.

Bob Curley spoke first. Dressed in jeans and a blue shirt, his weathered face furrowed by deep lines, Bob addressed the panel without notes. "My name's Robert Curley. I'm from Somerville, and on October 1 of 1997, my ten-year-old son was kidnapped, and he was murdered," Bob said.

The committee members knew his story well, particularly Eugene O'Flaherty, who had risen since his tumultuous freshman year in 1997 to become House chairman of the panel. Bob reminded the lawmakers that he had led the charge for capital punishment after Jeffrey's death. But over time, he said, he met relatives of murder victims who saw the discussion differently and helped to change his mind.

Everyone in the room, legislators and the public, listened with rapt attention. "It took me a long time to get to the point where I did change my opinion on the death penalty," Bob continued. "It took me a long time, and it just didn't happen to

me overnight. But that's just the way I see it and pretty much all I have to say."

Bob was followed to the witness table by other relatives of the slain, by academics, politicians, clergy, and activists. The committee heard from Carol Steiker, a Harvard law professor, who told the legislators that in 2006, for the first time in its history, the Gallup Poll showed more Americans in favor of life without parole than the death penalty. "The citizens of Massachusetts know there are better alternatives to the death penalty, and they are right," Steiker said. "The death penalty will not make us safer, and it can only brutalize all of us—not only the dangerous offenders but also those of us who believe, with the great jurist Benjamin Cardozo, that the death penalty is 'an anachronism too discordant to be suffered.' Looking all around us, we continue to see that the tide has turned on this issue."

After two rancor-free hours of testimony, Robert Creedon Jr. of Brockton, the Senate chairman of the panel, scanned the room and invited supporters of the death penalty to take the microphone.

No one stepped forward. Creedon waited several seconds, looked left, then right, and finally grasped the gavel. "There being no further business before this committee," he said, "this hearing is closed."

The bill was resoundingly defeated.

NOTES

The sourcing for this book came almost exclusively from personal interviews by the author, his coverage of the murder as a reporter for the *Boston Globe*, and his review of police and legal documents related to the murder of Jeffrey Curley. Archival newspaper stories of important events in the book, particularly concerning the Massachusetts legislature's debate on capital punishment in 1997, were also referenced. The following notes, for the most part, denote where the author used quotes obtained by other reporters and newspaper columnists. Subjective descriptions of characters in this book, their emotions, and their motivations were offered by sources close to the characters described. In nearly all cases and wherever possible, multiple sources corroborated these assessments.

4. THE LONG JOURNEY HOME

86   "Why are you protecting . . ." Judy Rakowsky, *Boston Globe*, October 4, 1997.

90   Timothy Dugan, Cambridge Hospital child psychiatrist. "It's beyond our comprehension . . ." Mac Daniel, *Boston Globe*, October 8, 1997.

90   Drucilla Whiting. "I think what kills us . . ." Mac Daniel, *Boston Globe*, October 8, 1997.

96   Marilyn Abramofsky. "If they don't do something . . ." Jon Keller, *Boston Globe*, opinion piece, October 9, 1997.

97   Massachusetts State Police Sergeant Greg Foley. "We are looking at this . . ." Caroline Louise Cole, *Boston Globe*, October 7, 1997.

5. Storm at the State House

103 "When the brutal killers . . ." Don Feder, *Boston Herald*, October 13, 1997.

105 "Daddy shot Mommy." Daniel Vasquez, *Boston Globe*, October 23, 1997.

112 State Representative Timothy Toomey. "This whole thing . . ." Adrian Walker and Frank Phillips, *Boston Globe*, October 9, 1997.

115 State Senator Robert Antonioni. "What about the killers . . ." Doris Sue Wong, *Boston Globe*, October 22, 1997.

122 Marilyn Abramofsky. "They had no problem . . ." Scot Lehigh, *Boston Globe*, October 29, 1997.

123 State Representative William McManus. "Shame on you people . . ." Doris Sue Wong and Adrian Walker, *Boston Globe*, October 29, 1997.

124 John Curley. "Thank you for saving . . ." Doris Sue Wong and Adrian Walker, *Boston Globe*, October 29, 1997.

125 Governor Paul Cellucci. "This is a victory for justice . . ." Doris Sue Wong and Adrian Walker, *Boston Globe*, October 29, 1997.

125 State Representative Donna Cuomo. "I really did not want to disappoint . . ." Doris Sue Wong and Adrian Walker, *Boston Globe*, October 29, 1997.

125 Speaker of the House Thomas Finneran. "We live in a time . . ." Doris Sue Wong and Adrian Walker, *Boston Globe*, October 29, 1997.

125 Robert Curley. "I guess it's a step . . ." Doris Sue Wong and Adrian Walker, *Boston Globe*, October 29, 1997.

132 Robert Curley. "It's up to the people . . ." Tina Cassidy, *Boston Globe*, November 7, 1997.

132 Paul Cellucci. "We saw a phony vote . . ." Scot Lehigh and Frank Phillips, *Boston Globe*, November 8, 1997.

133 Rob Gray. "He's a profile in cowardice . . ." Carolyn Ryan, *Boston Herald*, November 7, 1997.

6. Uncharted Ground

136 Cellucci. "This battle is not over . . ." Frank Phillips and Scot Lehigh, *Boston Globe*, November 8, 1997.

136 Eleanor LeCain. "Running for state executioner . . ." Patricia Smith, *Boston Globe*, December 5, 1997.

136 State Representative Brian Joyce. "On such a personal matter . . ." Adrian Walker, *Boston Globe*, December 4, 1997.

144   Cellucci. "We need to do everything we can . . ." Jill Zuckman, *Boston Globe*, October 2, 1998.

145   Ed Cafasso. "I think it's clear . . ." Jill Zuckman, *Boston Globe*, October 2, 1998.

8. QUESTIONS AND BEGINNINGS

169   Cellucci. "Monsters who do not deserve hope . . ." Scot Lehigh and Frank Phillips, *Boston Globe*, February 17, 1999.

171   Cardinal Bernard Law. "The teachings of the church . . ." Diego Ribadeneira, *Boston Globe*, March 20, 1999.

9. RESURRECTION

198   "Let's hope those Massachusetts authorities . . ." Jeff Jacoby, columnist, *Boston Globe*, October 7, 1997.

202   Robert Curley. "What am I going to get . . ." Matthew Falconer, *Boston Globe*, March 30, 1999.

202   Lawrence Frisoli, Curley family attorney. "This is a measuring stick . . ." Ralph Ranalli, *Boston Globe*, August 24, 2000.

202   Charles Jaynes. "I will trust in the jury . . ." Ralph Ranalli, *Boston Globe*, August 22, 2000.

203   John Roberts, executive director, Massachusetts chapter of ACLU. "For us, it's a fundamental . . . " Ralph Ranalli, *Boston Globe*, August 31, 2000.

10. THE ROAD HOME

219   "We are an integral part . . ." Jennifer Bishop, Murder Victims' Families for Reconciliation, newsletter, December 3, 2002.

ACKNOWLEDGMENTS

In a nonfiction work with so many moving parts, the list of people who contributed their time, insight, passion, and suggestions is a lengthy one. But any acknowledgment of these contributions must start with the Curley family and with Bob's wife, Mimi, whose courage to tell their story had a profound effect on me. I will be forever grateful to them for their patience, their recollections, and their simple willingness to sit across a kitchen table and express, as well as relive, the sorrow that they have experienced.

To Bob Curley and Mimi, Barbara Curley, Bobby Curley Jr., Shaun Curley, the late Francine Downey, John Curley, and the late Muriel Francis, my heartfelt thanks for the many hours in which you educated and enriched me.

My thanks, as well, to the many fine members of the Cambridge fire and police departments who, without exception, were generous with their time and thoughts. To Bill McGovern, Fran Judd, and the crew of Engine 5, I'll never forget the hospitality of "The Nickel." And to John Fulkerson, Pat Nagle, Lester Sullivan, and Frank Pasquarello, whose police work was critical after Jeffrey's disappearance, thank you for your painstaking reconstruction of the investigation.

Likewise, I am grateful to John Geary of the Newton police for his vivid recollection of the fracas involving Charles Jaynes at Honda Village, and to Bill Freeman and Arthur Huntley, who searched for Jeffrey's body with the Massachusetts State Police dive team.

My research benefited immeasurably from the cooperation of the attorneys in this case. Thank you to David Yannetti, the prosecutor, who first sat down with me several years ago when the outlines of this book had only begun to take shape. In follow-up interviews over the years, his help and advice continued to prove invaluable. My gratitude also extends to the defense attorneys, Arthur Kelly and Robert Jubinville, who never

failed to respond to requests for an interview or an accuracy check. And I owe a debt to Corey Welford, the press liaison for the Middlesex District Attorney's Office, whom I bombarded with call after call for information and contacts.

The death-penalty debate in the legislature is a central part of this story, and I was fortunate to glean some of the background and context of those tumultuous times from many current and former Massachusetts politicians. I thank John Slattery, Bill Nagle, Paul Cellucci, Tim Toomey, Tom Finneran, Sal DiMasi, Marian Walsh, Paul Haley, Eugene O'Flaherty, Tom McGee, Maura Hennigan, Paul Demakis, and Bradley Jones for their interest and accessibility. Each of them was a pleasure to interview.

A debt is also owed to the passionate activists who joined that discussion. Norma Shapiro and Ann Lambert of the ACLU honored me with their time and buoyed me with their good humor. Renny Cushing, Tom Lowenstein, and Susannah Sheffer of Murder Victims' Families for Human Rights were inspirational in their dedication to the fight against capital punishment. And Martina Jackson, executive director of Massachusetts Citizens Against the Death Penalty, is the embodiment of commitment.

Magi Bish, who lost a daughter to murder, showed that the human spirit truly can be indomitable. Dan Moniz, who led the crusade to promulgate the "Eight Rules of Safety," was a marvel of energy. And Richard Hoffman, an author who suffered sexual abuse as a child, moved me with his admiration of his friend Bob Curley.

Marilyn Abramofsky showed me the power of plain speaking and the possibilities of believing in a cause. And Sister Helen Prejean showed me a down-to-earth godliness.

Giving voice to emotion played a critical role in understanding the depths of feeling of this book's main characters. Outside of the Curleys, no one did this better than Bud Welch, Bill Babbitt, and David Kaczynski. Welch welcomed me into his Oklahoma City home for two compelling interviews about the loss of his daughter Julie in the 1995 bombing of the federal building there. Babbitt and Kaczynski turned a long lunch in Schenectady, New York, into an unforgettable seminar on the impact of the death penalty and the factors that led to their wrenching decisions to turn over their brothers to the authorities.

The people who knew Charles Jaynes and Salvatore Sicari also provided invaluable insights. I particularly wish to thank Charlene Letourneau for helping me understand the relationship between the killers. I wish her peace. Her friend Michelle Ward also provided useful background and helped Charlene find the courage to speak about her troubled past. Input from Kris McGovern and Wayne Garber about Sicari and his family, their onetime neighbors, is appreciated. Rebecca Moffitt, who once taught Jaynes, provided a chilling example of his depravity.

My contacts in the news media were unfailingly helpful. A special thanks goes to Jim Braude, who painted a dramatic picture of Bob Curley's important appearance on *Talk of New England*. Likewise, to Margery Eagan, his cohost, and to Doreen Iudica Vigue, a former colleague at the *Boston Globe*, who is communications director for New England Cable News. Doreen's work in compiling video from the station's coverage of the murder investigation and the death-penalty debate provided me with an irreplaceable visual record.

No mention of the media, however, would be complete without mentioning *Globe* editor Martin Baron, who approved a leave of absence to write the book, granted an extension, and was supportive throughout.

Toby Leith and Joel Swanson of the *Globe* helped me find my way through a thicket of technical issues.

Thanks, too, to Karen Miranda, a psychologist and professor whose insights into human behavior were enlightening. Professor Alan Rogers of Boston College helped me navigate the history of the death penalty in Massachusetts. And the late Larry Frisoli, the Curley family lawyer, allowed me access to all his police and legal files on the case.

Writing this book became an all-consuming job of long, intense days in which a heinous crime was the harrowing and inescapable focus of my work. To Judy McClellan, who welcomed me into her beautiful home on the Fire Island Inlet as an oasis for writing and reflection, your bottomless generosity can never be repaid. Your integrity, heart, patience, and support became inspiring life lessons. A nod of the cap, too, to Chloe, a warm but feisty Chesapeake Bay retriever, whose undemanding companionship was a comfort and a revelation at the many times I needed that.

And to Steve Kurkjian, who allowed me the run of his house near a stunning perch on Cape Cod Bay, a special remembrance for Manomet.

Bringing this book from idea to reality would not have been possible without the encouragement and expert direction of Todd Shuster, my literary agent, and Rachel Sussman, who worked patiently with me on developing the proposal. A special thanks, as well, to my editor at Da Capo Press, Bob Pigeon, who saw the possibilities of a story in Bob Curley's saga and took a chance. And a well-done to Katy Brunault, who offered incisive critiques and cheerful commentary throughout the project.

Finally, I wish to thank my family—especially my mother, Rita; father, Jim; and sister, Lesley—for their unfailing belief that this was possible. And to my daughter, Fiona, the light of my life, who was born four months after Jeffrey Curley and remains for me a vibrant, loving reminder of why we must always cherish our children.

INDEX